The
School Counselor's
BOOK OF LISTS

Dorothy J. Blum, Ed.D.

JOSSEY-BASS
A Wiley Imprint
www.josseybass.com

Published by Jossey-Bass
A Wiley Imprint
989 Market Street, San Francisco, CA 94103-1741   www.josseybass.com

Jossey-Bass books and products are available through most bookstores. To contact Jossey-Bass directly call our Customer Care Department within the U.S. at 800-956-7739, outside the U.S. at 317-572-3986 or fax 317-572-4002.

Jossey-Bass also publishes its books in a variety of electronic formats. Some content that appears in print may not be available in electronic books.

Library of Congress Cataloging-in-Publication Data

Blum, Dorothy
    The school counselor's book of lists / Dorothy J. Blum
      p. cm.
    Includes bibliographical references and index.
    ISBN 0-87628-129-3
    ISBN 0-7879-6640-1 (layflat)
    1. Educational counseling—United States—Miscellanea.
    2. Educational counseling—United States—Handbooks, manual, etc.
    I. Title.
    LB1027.5.B56   1998
    371.4—dc21   97-31496

FIRST EDITION
HB Printing 10 9 8 7 6 5 4

DEDICATION

This book is dedicated to my parents, the late Forrest J. Scrivner and Eugenia Krause Scrivner, who were my role models and encouraged me to pursue lifelong learning and service to others.

ACKNOWLEDGEMENTS

School counselors, parents, teachers, counselor educators, and other professionals have provided information and encouragement in the development of this resource for school counselors. Professionals who have read and edited particular lists in this book include:

➤ Dr. Pat Schwallie-Giddis, Assistant Executive Director of the American Vocational Association (AVA)

➤ Nancy Perry, Executive Director of the American School Counselor Association (ASCA)

➤ Dr. Carol Dahir, Professional Research Chair, ASCA

➤ Dr. Robert Davison-Aviles, Associate Professor at George Mason University, Fairfax, VA

➤ Dr. Cheryl Bartholomew, Associate Professor at George Mason University, Fairfax, VA

➤ Ruth Perlstein, Consultant, author, and retired counselor at Potomac High School, Alexandria, VA

➤ Margaret Lunter, Counselor at Thomas Jefferson High School for Science and Technology, Alexandria, VA

➤ Marilyn Anderson, Supervisor of Student Services, Falls Church City Schools, VA

➤ Dr. Janice Christopher, Supervisor of Guidance at Loudoun County Public Schools, VA

➤ Manny Bartolotta, Counselor at Stuart High School, Falls Church, VA

➤ Sharon DeBragga, Guidance Director at Irving Middle School, Springfield, VA

➤ Sally Murphy, Doctoral Candidate at George Mason University, and previous counselor at Oak View Elementary School, Fairfax, VA

➤ Andrew Schaffer, Counselor at Brookfield Elementary School, Herndon, VA

➤ Gwen Jacobsen, Teacher of English at Grants Pass High School, Grants Pass, OR

➤ Mary Durgala, Counselor at Pine Springs Elementary School, Falls Church, VA

➤ Barbara Grimes, Counselor at Cardinal Forest Elementary School, Springfield, VA

➤ Veronique Lillianthall, Counselor at Westlawn Elementary School, Falls Church, VA and Rolling Valley, Springfield, VA

➤ Susan Lawrence, Counselor at Westlawn Elementary School, Falls Church, VA

➤ Ruthann Pisaretz, Counselor at Fairfax Villa Elementary School, Fairfax, VA

Professionals who have assisted in providing information for this book include:

- ➣ JoAnne Bloomingdale, Supervisor of Video Procurement, Fairfax County Public Schools (FCPS), VA

- ➣ Ginny Broadbent, Counselor at Sangster Elementary School, West Springfield, VA

- ➣ Bryan D. Carr, Director of Guidance, Meadowbrook High School, Richmond, VA

- ➣ Laurie Gouchet, Coordinator of Career Education, FCPS, VA

- ➣ Sylvia Nicenoff, Librarian at American Counseling Association (ACA)

- ➣ Sue Rexford, Career Specialist at West Springfield High School, Springfield, VA

- ➣ Sarah Rosenthall, Secretary, Chapel Square, FCPS, VA

- ➣ Dee Taylor, Retired Teacher of English and High School Administrator, Grants Pass, OR

- ➣ Dr. Al Verville, Coordinator of Central Student Registration, Fairfax County Public Schools (FCPS), VA

A special thank you to the school counselors and parents who were members of the FCPS Materials Advisory Committee from 1988 through 1996, and to the Office of Student Services, FCPS, for permission to use the information and critiques from the monthly meetings.

- ➣ Douglas C. Holmes, Director of the Office of Student Services, FCPS, VA

- ➣ Elsie Kirton, Coordinator of Elementary School Counseling and Guidance, FCPS, VA

- ➣ Nadine Maxwell, Coordinator of Secondary School Counseling and Guidance, FCPS, VA

- ➣ Jane Bowman, Secretary, Materials Advisory Committee, FCPS, VA

Another special thank you to Connie Kallback, the editor of this book, who was a constant inspiration and sounding board, as well as a professional with infinite patience.

ABOUT THE AUTHOR

Dorothy J. Scrivner Blum, Ed.D., is an experienced school counselor, high school guidance director, administrator of school counseling, and counselor educator with a doctorate degree in Counselor Education from the University of Virginia, and other degrees from the University of Nebraska (M.M.) and Midland College (A.B.). She is a Licensed Professional Counselor (LPC) in the Commonwealth of Virginia, a National Certified Counselor (NCC), and a National Certified School Counselor (NCSC). Currently she is the Development Relations Coordinator for the American School Counselor Association (ASCA).

Dr. Blum has recently retired as the Coordinator of the Elementary School Counseling and Guidance Program of Fairfax County Public Schools (FCPS) in Virginia. In this position she was the counseling supervisor for 176 elementary school counselors in 132 elementary schools. Previous to this position she was the Guidance Director at George C. Marshall High School, FCPS, for ten years.

This author has received the 1995 Virginia Career Service Award from the Virginia Counselors Association, the 1994 Post-Secondary Counselor of the Year Award from the Virginia School Counselor Association, the 1993 Distinguished Group Work Award from the Virginia Association for Specialists of Group Work, the 1988 Counselor of the Year Award from the Virginia Counselor Association, the 1985 Chapter Member of the Year Award from the Northern Virginia Counselor Association, and the 1984 Secondary School Counselor of the Year Award from the Virginia School Counselor Association.

Dr. Blum has taught graduate courses in school counseling for the University of Virginia, Virginia Tech, Western Maryland College, and currently is teaching as an adjunct faculty member at George Mason University. She is the author of the book, *Group Counseling for Secondary Schools* (1990, Charles Thomas) and has written chapters included in the books: *Quality Leadership and the Professional School Counselor* (1994, American Counselor Association), and *Contemporary Counseling* (1987, Accelerated Development). She has also written numerous articles published in professional journals.

Dorothy Blum has presented workshops for school counselors at conferences of the American Counselors Association (ACA), the American School Counselor Association (ASCA), state and university conferences, and has been a consultant for school counselors in the American Schools of Central America, Mexico, Colombia, and the Caribbean.

ABOUT THIS RESOURCE

This practical, well-organized, and comprehensive reference resource is a time saver for the busy school counselor who must retrieve a breadth of information upon a moment's notice. It includes accurate and up-to-date information about a broad range of topics that can be easily located in the index.

School counselors have described this reference book as a crystallized, practical compilation and handy reference for information that is comprehensive, yet succinct, and easy to read. It contains lists of activities, materials, and ideas for academic, career, and personal/social counseling, classroom guidance lessons, parenting education courses, and staff development for teachers. It includes lists of recommended books and periodicals, tips to assist in daily routines, lists of hotlines, addresses and phone numbers, and topics with Uniform Resource Locators (URLs) for easy access on the internet. Experienced school counselors have said that they are anxious to have this book as a ready-reference.

Counselor educators have confirmed that this *School Counselor's Book of Lists* will be an invaluable resource for new school counselors and graduate students studying to be school counselors. Many of the lists contain crucial and practical information that is not included in graduate school programs.

School administrators, teachers, school social workers and psychologists, and parents will find information in this book very useful and pertinent for daily activities conducted in the school. The guidelines, suggestions, and materials can help administrators, teachers, and parents work with the school counselor and student services team to help students succeed in school.

The annotated materials lists for students in all grade levels, K through 12, teachers, parents, and the school counselor are organized by topics. These annotated lists include descriptions of commercially produced materials that were reviewed by school counselors and parents. Most of the counseling materials listed in this book were rated as "Excellent" or "Very Good" by the Materials Advisory Committee (MAC) that reviewed counseling materials for the Fairfax County Public Schools (FCPS) in Virginia. Secondary school counselors and career resource specialists in FCPS reviewed the secondary school guidance materials.

Sections 6 through 12, the annotated materials sections, contain only materials that are recommended to meet the specific needs of the identified group in each section. (e.g., Section 6: Materials for Students K-3; Section 11: Materials for Teachers). The topics are alphabetical within each section but do not always have the same list number as the same topics in other sections (e.g., Communication is 6-2, 7-2, but 10-3, 11-3, and 12-3). All sections do not have all sequential numbers (e.g., 8-5 Decision Making, no 8-6 or 8-7; the next list in section 8 is 8-8, Emotions). See the Table of Contents for the specific lists within each materials section.

The grade levels overlap, K-3, 3-6, 6-9, and 9-12 because the grade levels are not mutually exclusive. The school counselor should preview materials, if at all possible, before using them with students to be certain that the materials are appropriate and meet the needs of the particular individual or group of students.

The reproducible lists, alphabetized both by title and topic, can be used as a quick reference for the counselor or copied and given to parents or teachers.

Approximate prices are included in sections 6–12 to help the counselor make initial decisions. The asterisks indicate the following prices:

       * $1 to $25
       ** $26 to $55
       *** $56 to $105
       **** $106 to $205
       ***** $206 to $505
       ****** $506 up

Because we want this to be the most accurate and useful resource book available to school counselors, we invite you to send comments and suggestions for further editions to the author at the following e-mail address: dblum@erols.com or positive comments are definitely welcome on the International Counselors Network (ICN) at: ICN@UTKVM1.UTK.EDU

Dorothy J. Scrivner Blum, Ed.D.

CONTENTS

Section 1

THE SCHOOL COUNSELING AND GUIDANCE PROGRAM K–12

Section 2

THE SCHOOL COUNSELOR

Section 3

ACADEMIC/EDUCATIONAL COUNSELING AND GUIDANCE K–12

Academic Counseling K–12   130

Section 4

CAREER COUNSELING AND GUIDANCE K–12

Career Development Theories and Assessment   149

National Career Competencies and Skills for Students   153

Career Goals for All Students   154

Career Guidance for All Students   155

Career Counseling K–12   *176*

Section 5
PERSONAL/SOCIAL COUNSELING AND GUIDANCE K-12

Personal/Social Goals   183

Information About Students   183

Personal/Social Guidance: Life Skills for All Students   199

Personal/Social Guidance: Programs for Prevention   236

Personal/Social Guidance: Dealing With a Crisis   278

Personal/Social Counseling K–12   282

Section 6

MATERIALS TO USE WITH GRADES K–3

Annotated List of Materials to Use with Students   321

Section 7

MATERIALS TO USE WITH GRADES 3–6

Annotated List of Materials to Use with Students   341

Section 8

MATERIALS TO USE WITH GRADES 6–9

Annotated List of Materials to Use with Students   359

Section 9

MATERIALS TO USE WITH GRADES 9–12

Annotated List of Materials to Use with Students   375

Section 10

MATERIALS TO USE WITH PARENTS

Annotated List of Materials   397

Section 11

MATERIALS TO USE WITH TEACHERS

Annotated List of Materials   417

Section 12

MATERIALS FOR THE COUNSELOR

Annotated List of Materials   429

Reproducible List of Materials 460

Reproducible List of Internet Resources 488

Section 13

POSITION STATEMENTS FOR THE COUNSELOR
(American School Counselor Association (ASCA))

Section 14

ACRONYMS AND GLOSSARY

Section 15

DISTRIBUTORS AND PUBLISHERS OF COUNSELING MATERIALS

Index   519

Section 1

THE SCHOOL COUNSELING AND GUIDANCE PROGRAM, K–12

THE SCHOOL COUNSELING AND GUIDANCE PROGRAM
1-1 NATIONAL STANDARDS

Purpose of the National Standards for School Counseling Programs
(AMERICAN SCHOOL COUNSELOR ASSOCIATION [ASCA], 1995)

➤ Create a framework for a national model for school counseling programs.

➤ Identify the key components of a school counseling model program.

➤ Identify the knowledge and skills that all students should acquire as a result of the K–12 school counseling program.

➤ Ensure that school counseling programs are comprehensive in design and delivered in a systematic fashion to all students.

➤ Establish school counseling as a integral component of the academic mission of the educational system.

➤ Encourage equitable access to school counseling services for all students, provided by a credentialed school counselor.

Components of National Standards for Counseling Programs
(AMERICAN SCHOOL COUNSELOR ASSOCIATION [ASCA], 1997)

I. Academic Development

STANDARD A: Students will acquire the attitudes, knowledge, and skills that contribute to effective learning in school and across the life span.

STANDARD B: Students will employ strategies to achieve success in school.

STANDARD C: Students will understand the relationship of academics to the world of work, and to life at home and in the community.

II. Career Development

STANDARD A: Students will acquire the skills to investigate the world of work in relation to knowledge of self and to make appropriate career decisions.

STANDARD B: Students will employ strategies to achieve future career success and satisfaction.

1

STANDARD C: Students will understand the relationship between personal qualities, education and training, and the world of work.

III. Personal/Social Development

STANDARD A: Students will acquire the attitudes, knowledge, and interpersonal skills to help them understand and respect self and others.

STANDARD B: Students will make decisions, set goals, and take appropriate action to achieve goals.

STANDARD C: Students will understand safety and survival skills.

Emphasis is on academic success for *all students*. Each standard is followed by a list of student competencies that enumerate desired student learning outcomes.

ADDITIONAL INFORMATION

ASCA [On-line] Available: http://www.edge.net/asca/

1-2   THE COMPREHENSIVE SCHOOL COUNSELING AND GUIDANCE CURRICULUM

The school counseling and guidance curriculum is focused on communication of information and prevention as well as crisis intervention and remediation. The purpose of the program is to facilitate academic, career, personal, and social development for all students.

Characteristics of the School Counseling and Guidance Curriculum

➤ Educational

➤ Organized, planned, and structured

➤ Designed for overall school population

➤ Integrated part of the total educational program

➤ Schoolwide involvement, cooperation, and collaboration of all school personnel *(List 2-47)*

➤ Inclusive involvement, collaboration, and support of the community

➤ Sequential K–12, based on the needs of students

➤ Preventative

➤ Proactive

➤ Present and future oriented:
  – Preparation for adulthood
  – Development of plans for postsecondary education and careers
  – Orientation and transition
  – Exploration of school responsibilities and opportunities
  – Exploration of work responsibilities and opportunities

➤ Comprehensive:
  – Assessment
  – Information
  – Consultation
  – Coordination
  – Counseling *(List 1-5)*
  – Referral
  – Placement
  – Follow-up

➤ Focused on skill development:
- Communication
- Conflict resolution
- Decision making/problem solving
- Peer-pressure resistance

– Respect
– Responsibility
– Safety
– Substance abuse prevention

ADDITIONAL INFORMATION

See *List 1-3, The School Counseling Program.*

See *List 2-47, Guidance, A Total School Responsibility Coordinated by the School Counselor.*

See *Lists 2-29 through 2-32, Presenter of Guidance Lessons.*

See *List 13-7, The School Counselor and Comprehensive Counseling.*

See *List 13-13, The School Counselor and Dropout Prevention/Students at-Risk.*

Gysbers, N. C. & Henderson, P. (1994). *Developing and managing your school guidance program. (List 12-3)*

Myrick, R. D. (1993). *Developmental guidance and counseling: A practical approach.* (2nd ed.). *(List 12-3)*

Paisley, P. O. & Hubbard, G. T. (1994). *Developmental school counseling programs: From theory to practice. (List 12-3)*

Wittmer, J. (Ed.). (1993). *Managing your school counseling program: K–12 developmental strategies. (List 12-3)*

1-3   THE SCHOOL COUNSELING PROGRAM

School counseling is focused on helping students resolve academic, social, personal, or emotional concerns that interrupt the educational process. The purpose of school counseling is to facilitate normal growth and development of students.

Types of School Counseling

➤ Individual

➤ Group

➤ Remedial or preventative

➤ Crisis intervention

➤ Referrals from self, teacher, parent, or other

Student Needs Appropriate for School Counseling

➤ Particular students:
- Desire specific skills.
- Desire specific learning opportunities.
- Have specific needs or concerns.
- May address sensitive issues.

Characteristics of School Counseling

➤ Confidential

➤ Situation oriented

➤ Brief resolution of immediate concern

➤ School-related

➤ Structured or nonstructured

➤ Written parental permission recommended for ongoing counseling

ADDITIONAL INFORMATION

See *Lists 2-19 through 2-24, Counselor of Individual Students.*

See *List 2-21, Confidentiality.*

See *Lists 2-8 through 2-18, Application of Counseling Theories.*

See *Lists 2-25 through 2-28, Leader of Small Groups.*

See *Lists 3-14 through 3-28, Academic Counseling K–12.*

See *Lists 4-24 through 4-28, Career Counseling With Students.*

See *Lists 5-73 through 5-98, Personal/Social Counseling K–12.*

Thompson, C. L. & Rudolph, L. B. (1996). *Counseling Children. (List 12-3)*

1-4   NEEDS ASSESSMENT

Purpose of a Needs Assessment

➤ Identify guidance priorities and expectations of students, teachers, and parents.

➤ Provide input for designing or restructuring the program.

➤ Assist in organizing the program:
  – Set priorities.
  – Establish program goals and objectives.
  – Select guidance activities.
  – Schedule counselor's time.

Method of Conducting a Needs Assessment or Survey

➤ Evaluate practicality of a sample of all students, teachers, and parents.

➤ Design objective multiple-choice items.

➤ Include open-ended items about the overall school climate for learning.

➤ Write the items using positive language.

➤ Assess a few specific areas and services.

➤ Limit the number of questions to one page.

➤ Plan to adapt the survey for young children and students with reading difficulties.

➤ Administer the survey to a "test-group" to identify unclear or misunderstood items.

➤ Involve the Guidance Advisory Committee in assisting *(List 1-7):*
  – Designing
  – Administering
  – Collecting

- Summarizing
- Reporting the results

➤ Distribute the results to all interested and involved persons.

➤ Prioritize the needs identified.

➤ Determine how and when to address the needs in the guidance program.

➤ Communicate results of all surveys and actions taken.

ADDITIONAL INFORMATION

See *List 1-19, Evaluation of the School Counseling and Guidance Program.*

Marino, T. W. (1996). Polling the population of your school. *Counseling Today, 39,* (5), 1, 8.

Morganett, R. S. (1990). Sample faculty group counseling needs assessment (p. 203). Sample student group counseling needs assessment (p. 204). *Skills for living: Group counseling activities for young adolescents. (List 12-17)*

Schmidt, J. J. (1991). Primary Student Needs Assessment, Middle School Parent Needs Assessment, Teacher Needs Assessment, and School Climate Survey. Chapter 2: Getting off the ground, and staying afloat. In *A survival guide for the elementary/middle school counselor. (List 12-3)*

1-5 GUIDANCE ADVISORY COMMITTEE (GAC)

The Guidance Advisory Committee (GAC) can provide input from students, parents, teachers, administrators, and others to ensure that the counseling and guidance program addresses the guidance needs of all students in the school. The GAC meets regularly to assist in planning, implementing, and evaluating the school counseling and guidance program.

Purpose of a GAC

➤ Assess student needs.

➤ Develop, administer, and analyze needs surveys of students, teachers, and parents to identify the guidance needs in the school.

➤ Report, distribute, and publicize the results of the surveys as appropriate.

➤ Recommend content of the philosophy or mission statement for the counseling and guidance program.

➤ Write a rationale statement for the counseling and guidance program.

➤ Develop the by-laws for the GAC.

➤ Assess the counseling and guidance program.

➤ Communicate needs for staff development.

➤ Help determine priorities for the counseling and guidance program.

➤ Develop an implementation calendar.

➤ Assist in designing a comprehensive counseling and guidance program.

➤ Inform students, staff, and community about the counseling and guidance program goals, procedures, objectives, and evaluation.

➤ Articulate the value and range of guidance services at PTA, school board, and community meetings in support of the counseling and guidance program.

➤ Make presentations to various citizen groups and the school board.

➤ Enlist parents to volunteer in the guidance department. *(List 2-54)*

➤ Establish and maintain a parent information center and parent resource library.

➤ Plan and conduct events and activities to focus on schoolwide guidance, parent involvement, student development, and school climate.

➤ Plan and conduct special schoolwide guidance events, e.g., career fair.

➤ Examine and recommend ways to cut down paperwork for counselors and teachers.

➤ Publicize and write reports to distribute information about the counseling and guidance program to the community.

➤ Assist in conducting an evaluation of the counseling and guidance program.

➤ Recommend revisions to the counseling and guidance program.

Selection of GAC Members

➤ Represent all grade levels and all social groups, cultural, ethnic, and socio-economic groups of students.

➤ Represent all grade levels or departments of faculty.

➤ Represent all geographical areas and socio-economic levels of parents and the community.

➤ Represent business/industry.

➤ Serve as an advocate for a strong counseling and guidance program.

➤ Be available to attend monthly meetings.

Mission or Philosophy Statement for the GAC

➤ Compatible with the mission statement of the school, district, and state.

➤ Clear rationale for guidance as an integral part of the instructional program.

➤ Reflection of entire school community.

➤ Specific goals and objectives for the counseling and guidance program.

Suggested By-Laws for the GAC

➤ Designate purpose of the GAC.

➤ Designate make-up of the GAC to represent all students in the school, the faculty, and administration.

➤ Indicate frequency of the meetings (usually monthly during the school year).

➤ Specify term of office of members.

➤ Specify criteria for appointment of members for representation of all.

➤ Indicate officers and their responsibilities.

➤ Specify procedure for drawing up the agendas.

➤ Specify report of each meeting to be in writing and given to school administrator.

ADDITIONAL INFORMATION

See **List 1-20,** *Communicating the Counseling and Guidance Program.*

Rye, D. R. & Sparks, R. (1991). *Strengthening K–12 school counseling programs: A support system approach.* Muncie, IN: Accelerated Development. Reproducible written school philosophy statements and needs surveys.

Schmidt, J. J. (1991). *A survival guide for the elementary/middle school counselor. (List 12-3)* Sample needs assessment surveys, assignment sheets for volunteer activities, and sample time/balance worksheets.

Tennessee University (1992). Process guide for developing a comprehensive career development program. *A guide for school counselors.* (Report No. CG02348) Knoxville, TN: Tennessee University (ERIC Document Reproduction Service No. ED 352570). Student, teacher, parent, and community survey forms, counselor calendar, and time and task analysis log.

Wittmer, J. (1993). *Managing your school counseling program: K–12 developmental strategies. (List 12-3)* Sample needs surveys and philosophy statement for GACs.

1-6 THE CRISIS PLAN, CRISIS TEAM, AND CRISIS INTERVENTION

A crisis may be any natural disaster or personal tragedy that causes human suffering.

The School Crisis Plan

➤ Updated annually

➤ Staff roles delineated

➤ Adaptable to fit the crisis

➤ Copy distributed to every staff member

➤ Evaluated periodically

The School Crisis Team

➤ Members designated annually by administrator

➤ Responsibilities clear and understood

Common Feelings of Students When in Crisis

➤ Fear

➤ Helplessness

➤ Loss

➤ Sadness

➤ Shock

➤ Worry about self

Possible Behaviors of Students When in Crisis

➤ Irritability

➤ Restlessness

➤ Moodiness

➤ Agitation

➤ Difficulty concentrating, eating, and/or sleeping

➤ Nausea

➤ Diarrhea

Needs of Students When in Crisis

➤ Safety:
  – Physical

  – Psychological
  – Emotional

Crisis Counseling

➤ Short term

➤ Classroom announcement and activities when necessary

➤ Small groups of students

➤ Small groups of parents and staff when appropriate

➤ Individual students as needed

➤ Follow-up

➤ Referrals

Process of Crisis Counseling

1. Learn the facts about the situation.
2. Assess severity objectively and subjectively.
3. Learn how each student is feeling.
4. Assess each student's ability to cope.
5. Learn each student's symptoms:
   - Health, insomnia, nightmares
   - Irritability, worrying, grades
6. Teach common reactions to crises.
7. Discuss how responses are helpful or not.
8. Summarize.
9. Develop action plans.
10. Encourage support for each other.
11. Ensure physical, emotional, and psychological safety.
12. Plan and conduct a follow-up 3 to 5 days later.
13. Arrange for individual counseling as needed.
14. Make referrals as needed.

ADDITIONAL INFORMATION

Petersen, S. & Straub, R. (1992). *School crisis survival guide.* *(List 12-6)*

Thompson, C. L. & Rudolph, L. B. (1996). *Counseling children* (4th ed.). *(List 12-3)*

1-7   PREVENTION OF VIOLENCE

Violence

This is behavior that intentionally harms or injures a person.

➤ Aggressive act to hurt another person:
   - Assault
   - Fight
   - Murder/homicide
   - Rape
   - Robbery
   - Verbal insults
➤ Suicide
➤ Possession of a weapon in school

Entertainment Associated With Violence

➤ Some media:
   - Television
   - VCR and feature films
   - Rock lyrics
   - News (disasters, accidents, violence)
➤ Some toys and games

Pro-Violent Values on Television

➤ Violence as a satisfactory answer to conflict
➤ Aggression as a solution to conflict

➤ Physical assault as acceptable

➤ Destruction of property as acceptable

Problems of Frequent Viewing of Violence
(APA, 1993)

➤ Correlates with increased acceptability of aggressive attitudes and behavior

➤ Increases fear of being a victim of violence

➤ Increases apathetic behavior

➤ Increases children's desensitization to violence

➤ Increases likelihood of harmful consequences to young children

Social Factors That Lead to Violence

➤ Poverty and unemployment

➤ Easy access to drugs and weapons

➤ Transient population and isolation of individuals

➤ Violence in home or community (accidents, robberies, homicides)

➤ Pro-violent values

Issues That Lead to Violence

➤ Desire for power and a sense of powerlessness

➤ Lack of anger control

➤ Fear of diversity

➤ Retribution for perceived disrespect

➤ Desire to gain or maintain social status

➤ Incompetence and frustration

➤ Alienation

➤ Belief that an aggressive act is the only recourse available

➤ Failure to consider long-term consequences

➤ Desire to continue conflict for excitement

Actions Preceding Violence

➤ Bullying or victimization

➤ Name-calling, put-downs

➤ Harassment

➤ Pressure or coercion

➤ Verbal insults

➤ Taking money

➤ Verbal or physical abuse, pushing around

➤ Disrespect

➤ Lack of social status

Positive Administrative Response to Violence

➤ Immediate action to learn facts and then discipline the perpetrator

➤ Identification and response to existing problems leading to violence

➤ Identification and action to address the underlying causes of violence

➤ Implementation of programs to deal with issues that lead to violence

Counselor's Actions to Prevent Violence

➤ Identify students who experience failure and alienation.

➤ Identify students who are vulnerable to victimization.

➤ Invite identified students to participate in group counseling *(Lists 2-25 through 2-28):*

  – Address and validate feelings.

  – Generate options other than aggressive retaliation.

  – Teach social skills to socially isolated and unpopular students. *(List 5-37)*

  – Teach interpersonal skills and concepts: personal values, interpersonal boundaries, and respect for others. *(List 5-16)*

  – Teach danger of retaliation and consequences of physical aggression.

  – Involve participants in developing or coming up with a peaceful solution.

  – Teach coping skills and brainstorm alternatives for dealing with stressful situations. *(List 5-35)*

  – Teach ways to relieve stress and frustration. *(List 5-38)*

  – Teach anger management. *(List 5-33)*

➤ Encourage identified students to become actively involved in school activities.

➤ Counsel victims about fear of attack and non-violent actions they can take for protection.

➤ Consult with teachers who can teach students how to avoid fights and deal with accusations and provocations.

➤ Consult with parents to suggest positive ways to deal with situations instead of physical retaliation.

➤ Consult with administrators:

  – Monitor dark hallways and hidden corners.

  – Provide healthy physical release of tension.

  – Discourage loitering.

➤ Institute conflict-resolution/peer-mediation training that teaches students how to negotiate and mediate, and teachers how to arbitrate. *(Lists 1-8; 5-34)*

➤ Collaborate with teachers to teach critical assessment of media.

ADDITIONAL INFORMATION

See *List 13-23, The School Counselor and the Promotion of Safe Schools.*

Fatum, W. R. & Hoyle, J. C. (1996). Is it violence? School violence from the student perspective: Trends and interventions. *School Counselor, 44,* 28–34.

Goldstein, A. P. (1996). *Violence in America: Lessons on understanding the aggression in our lives.* Palo Alto, CA: Publishing Consulting Psychologists Press, Inc.

Johnson, D. W. & Johnson, R. T. (1995). *Reducing school violence through conflict resolution. (List 12-4)*

McLaughlin, M. S. & Hazouri, S. P. *The race for safe schools: A staff development curriculum. (List 11-15)*

Peterson, S. & Straub, R. L. (1992). *School crisis survival guide. (List 12-6)*

1-8   CONFLICT-RESOLUTION/PEER-MEDIATION PROGRAMS

Three Models of Conflict-Resolution Training

1. Total school
2. Elective course
3. Student club

Initiating a Conflict-Resolution or Peer-Mediation Program

➤ Read research on school violence, aggression, and conflict resolution.

➤ Acquire specific training in conflict mediation, if needed.

➤ Get administrative support to initiate the program.

➤ Organize an advisory committee to include administrator, teachers, parents, and students.

➤ Get consensus of members of the advisory committee about practical decisions:
  - Goals for the program and school population to be served
  - Model to implement
  - Time and schedule to implement the program
  - Coordinator and supervisor of the program
  - Selection procedures of mediators
  - Training of mediators
  - Training of teachers
  - Communication of information about program
  - Resources and materials to be used for training
  - Evaluation of program

Developing the Conflict-Resolution or Peer-Mediation Program

➤ Inform teachers, students, and parents about program.

➤ Interview applicants and select peer mediators:
  - Represent cross-section of the student body.
  - Include diversity among the mediators.
  - Select students who have respect of other students.
  - Require a minimum level of academic performance.
  - Select students who are trustworthy and have good attendance.

➤ Train mediators between 10 to 20 contact hours:
  - Discuss purpose of the program.
  - Teach communication skills.
  - Teach problem-solving skills.
  - Describe mediation model to be used and steps to follow in mediation.
  - Provide time to practice communication skills.
  - Provide time to role play mediations.
  - Provide time for questions and answers.

➤ Solve practical problems:
  – Ongoing training
  – Matching disputants with mediators
  – Arranging for time for mediations
  – Scheduling mediations
  – Follow-ups with disputants

Conflict-Mediation Process

1. Introduce mediators, process, and set ground rules.

2. Listen and paraphrase disputants' definitions of problem (wants and needs).

3. Find common interests, brainstorm solutions, problem solve.

4. Choose one solution.

5. Conclude with written contract.

Conflict-Resolution Skills for Disputants

➤ Listen objectively to other person without blaming or interrupting.

➤ Identify the problem.

➤ Brainstorm alternatives.

➤ Agree to find a win-win solution.

➤ Attack the problem, not the person.

➤ Treat other person with respect.

➤ Accept responsibility for own behavior.

ADDITIONAL INFORMATION.

See *Lists 6-3, 7-3, 8-3, 9-4, 10-5, 11-4, 12-4* for Conflict-Resolution Materials.

Community Board. (1986). *Training middle school conflict managers.* San Francisco, CA.

Craig, M. & Carruthers, W. L. (1995). *The peer mediator's guidebook: A guide to successful mediations in schools.* (Available from Dispute Resolution Services of Raleigh, Inc., 5 West Hargett Street, Suite 208, Raleigh, NC 27601.)

Johnson, D. W. & Johnson, R. (1991). *Teaching students to be peacemakers.* **(List 12-4)**

Johnson, D. W. & Johnson, R. T. (1995). *Reducing school violence through conflict resolution.* **(List 12-4)**

National Association for Mediation in Education (NAME), 205 Hampshire House, Box 33635, University of Massachusetts, Amherst, MA 01003; (413) 545–2462.

Perlstein, R. & Thrall, G. (1996). *Ready-to-use conflict resolution activities for secondary students.* **(List 12-4)**

Sorenson, D. L. (1992). *Conflict resolution and mediation for peer helpers.* Minneapolis, MN: Education Media Corp.

Wampler, F. W. & Hess, S. (1992). *Conflict mediation for a new generation.* **(List 12-4)**

1-9   REGISTRATION, ORIENTATION, AND TRANSITION OF STUDENTS

Registration of New Students

➤ Know residency requirements and documentation requirements:
  - House contract, lease agreement, or temporary address
  - Parent/guardian who lives with the student

➤ Know admission requirements and documentation requirements:
  - Proof of birth or citizenship
  - Social security number
  - Health documentation
  - Previous education program documentation

➤ Know state compulsory attendance requirements.

Orientation of Students New to the School During the School Year

➤ Meet with new students in a group.

➤ Invite a student leader to share information at each meeting.

➤ Assign a peer facilitator or student host to each new student:
  - Someone with whom to eat lunch
  - Someone to introduce students to staff and other students
  - Someone to take the new student on a tour of school building

Topics for New Student Seminars

➤ Information about and expectations at the school:
  - Manners on the bus and at the bus stop
  - Assignment notebook and plans to complete homework
  - Excused absences and make-up work
  - Teachers and counselors to consult when help is needed
  - Expectations of students in new school
  - Activities and clubs

➤ Skills for new students:
  - Maintaining friendships long distance
  - Introducing self to others
  - Asking a teacher for help
  - Stopping someone from picking on you
  - Coping with a teacher who doesn't like you
  - Making new friends
  - Dealing with problems with friends
  - Learning to stop comparing present with the past

Transition from One School to Another School

➤ Group orientation for students and parents

➤ Opportunity to meet administrators, counselors, and respective teachers

➤ Information about school plant, location of classes and offices

➤ Information about program, classes, activities, rules:
  – Map of the school
  – Student handbook
  – Course guide
  – Course selection form

➤ Opportunity to meet current student leaders and peer facilitators

1-10   STUDENT APPRAISAL/ASSESSMENT

Process of Student Appraisal for Students Referred for Counseling

➤ Gather information about referred student, instructional approaches, and other factors that may affect the student's learning:
  – Observe student's behavior and attitude during counseling.
  – Observe student in location of behavioral difficulty, class, or recess to verify reported behavior.
  – Interview student, teacher, and if appropriate, parent.
  – Review cumulative record.
  – Examine test results, noting possible cultural bias of the test.
  – Note attendance and tardiness record.
  – Note pattern of grades and changes of the pattern.
  – Note recent stress-related experiences.

➤ Identify symptoms indicating possible need for special services.

➤ Refer student to child study team or local screening committee when appropriate *(List 2-56)*.

➤ Determine services needed by the student.

➤ Determine services needed by teacher and/or parent.

➤ Refer student to school or community resources for services or further diagnosis *(List 1-11)*.

➤ Assess progress while receiving identified services.

➤ Consult with student, teacher, and parent to review student progress.

Non-Traditional Methods of Student Appraisal/Assessment

➤ Performance test (e.g., Physical Fitness or GATB test)

➤ Portfolio/project *(List 4-14)*

➤ Self-report

➤ Individual student interviews

➤ Observations by professionals

➤ Anecdotal records

➤ Review of cumulative record

ADDITIONAL INFORMATION

Loesch, L. C. & Goodman, W. J. (1993). The K–12 developmental school counselor and appraisal. In Wittmer, J. (ed.), *Managing your school counseling program: K–12 developmental strategies,* (pp. 151–157). *(List 12-3)*

Schmidt, J. J. (1991). *A survival guide for the elementary/middle school counselor. (List 12-3)*

1-11   REFERRALS TO APPROPRIATE SCHOOL AND/OR COMMUNITY RESOURCES

Preparation and Process for Making Referrals

➤ Become acquainted with professionals at community mental health center.
➤ Become acquainted with professional resources in community.
➤ Consult with school psychologist, school social worker, and Student Services Team.
➤ Visit offices of professionals within the community.
➤ Assess the student *(List 1-12)*.
➤ Refer student to Child Study Team for further assessment *(List 2-56)*.
➤ Discuss reason for referral with parents (not child abuse cases).
➤ Provide information about at least three professional resources to parent:
  – Community mental health center
  – Two other resources
  – Names, addresses, phone numbers
  – Directions to offices
  – Fees for initial visit, if known

1-12   Standardized Testing and Testing Terms

The school counselor frequently interprets the results of standardized tests and consults with teachers, students, and parents about test results. The coordination of the standardized testing program, other than college-entrance tests (e.g., SAT, PSAT, ACT, and AP exams), is not considered a counselor's responsibility.

Interpretation of Standardized Tests

➣ Analyze test results by grade, class, or individual student.

➣ Schedule interpretation of test results to administrators, teachers, students, and parents.

➣ Consult with administrators, teachers, students, and parents about what the test results mean, and the appropriate use of the test results.

➣ Review schoolwide results with faculty.

Use of Test Results

➣ Facilitate student understanding of strengths and needs.

➣ Improve curriculum.

➣ Identify students who have difficulty learning.

➣ Redirect instruction to help students learn.

➣ Reaffirm activities and instruction in areas of student strength.

Kinds of Tests

➣ *Achievement Test:* Measures how much students know about a subject; results are often reported in percentiles.

➣ *Aptitude Test:* Predicts how well students may perform.

➣ *Criterion-Referenced Test:* Evaluates student's performance according to a set of criteria and not in comparison with others. Criterion-referenced tests are often used as placement or promotion tests.

➣ *Diagnostic Test:* Determines a student's strengths and weaknesses in a subject. Diagnostic test results answer the question, "Which of these skills or understandings does the student possess?"

➣ *Norm Referenced Test:* Compares a student's performance with the performance of similar students who have previously taken the test. (See **Norming Population** later in list.)

➣ *Performance Test:* Provides evidence demonstrating ability, skills, and/or knowledge in a specific area.

➣ *Proficiency Test:* Compares performance of the student with a standard or criterion used to describe a condition of proficiency or competence. (See **Criterion-Referenced Test** mentioned earlier in list.)

➣ *Projective Test:* Requires special training to administer such a psychological test to an individual student. Projective tests, such as the Rorschach Test, are usually administered by the school psychologist.

➣ *Standardized Test:* Has established norms or standards using a select population of students under set conditions.

➣ *Teacher-made Test:* Measures what the students know or have learned in a particular class.

Terms Used to Describe Tests

➤ *Grade Equivalent Score:* A statistically estimated grade level for which a test score is the presumed average score. *Example:* A student achieving a grade equivalent of 4.5 performed as well on the test as the average student midway through the fourth grade would have performed on that test.

➤ *Local Norms:* Performance standards established using school or district results on a test or other performance indicator.

➤ *Mean:* Arithmetic average of a group of scores.

➤ *Median:* Middle score in a group of scores.

➤ *Mode:* Score most frequently earned by the students.

➤ *National Norms:* Performance standards established by administering the test to a group of students representative of the national population.

➤ *Norm-Referenced Test:* A test that compares the performance of the student to the performance of similar individuals who have previously taken the test. (See **Norming Population.**)

➤ *Normal Distribution:* A statistical distribution of performance scores in which the mean, mode, and median scores are the same and the proportion of performance scores declines as performance moves away from the mean (Bell Curve).

➤ *Norming Population:* The group of students used to establish performance standards for age or grade levels on a test. The composition of the norming population must be similar to that of the student population for a standardized test to be appropriate.

➤ *Percentile Rank:* The comparison of the student's score with the scores of others and reported as the percentage of all students who scored equal to or below the particular student's test score. *Example:* A percentile rank of 89 means the student's score was equal to or above the score of 89 percent of the total group of students in the norming population.

➤ *Raw Score:* The number of items a student gets correct on a test. Raw scores have little meaning without a point of reference. *Example:* A raw score of 25 is very good if the highest possible score is 26; it is poor if the highest possible score is 100.

➤ *Reliability:* The extent to which a test would yield consistent results if given under the same circumstances an unlimited number of times. The higher the reliability coefficient of a test, the more likely the scores of the students are reasonable indicators of their performance on that test.

➤ *Score Choice:* The SAT II Score Choice provides the option to hold the scores from *all* of the SAT II examinations taken at a single administration. The student can select which of these individual scores to have sent to colleges. The timeline can present problems to seniors.

➤ *Standard Deviation:* A measure of the variability of the scores from the mean score.

➤ *Stanine Score:* A score from 1 to 9 assigned to a raw score for performance on a test or other performance indicator. Stanine scores have a mean of 5 and a standard deviation of 2.

➤ *Validity:* The measure of the extent to which a test measures what it purports to measure.

Standardized Tests Administered Frequently

➤ Advanced Placement Tests (AP Tests)

➤ American College Test (ACT)

➤ Armed Service Vocational Aptitude Battery (ASVAB)

- Cognitive Achievement Test (COGAT)
- Comprehensive English Language Test for Speakers of English as a Second Language (CELT)
- Comprehensive Test of Basic Skills (CTBS)
- Degrees of Reading Power (DRP)
- Differential Aptitude Tests (DAT)
- General Education Development Tests (GED)
- Iowa Test of Basic Skills (ITBS)
- Preliminary Scholastic Assessment Test (PSAT)
- Scholastic Assessment Test (SAT)
- Secondary Level English Proficiency Test (SLEP)
- Sequential Tests of Educational Progress (STEP)
- Test of English as a Second Language (TOEFL)
- Test of Spoken English (TSE)
- Test of Written English (TWE)
- Woodcock Language Proficiency Battery

ADDITIONAL INFORMATION

See **List 13-6**, *The School Counselor and College Entrance Test Preparation Programs.*

Buros Institute. [On-line] Available: http://www.unl.edu/buros/home.html

Frequently Asked Questions (FAQ) on Psychological Tests. [On-line] Available: http://www.apa.org/science/test.html

Hitchner, K. W. & Tifft-Hitchner, A. (1996). Admission testing (Chapter 28). In *Counseling today's secondary students.* **(List 12-3)**

1-13 AWARDING HIGH SCHOOL CREDITS IN SPECIAL CIRCUMSTANCES

Credit for Courses Completed in a Country Other Than the United States

➤ Evidence of completed courses:
   - Certified transcript translated by a person fluent in English and the respective language
   - Final examination or appropriate test for comparable course to verify knowledge of course content as well as grade awarded

➤ Suggestions for evaluation of a foreign language transcript:
   - Credits awarded and grade placement may be temporary based upon performance of the student in class
   - Discretion of school principal or designee
   - Letter grade or Pass/Fail deemed appropriate by the principal or designee
   - Foreign language teacher's assessment of student's learning of course content
   - Input from Education Specialist at respective embassy

Credit for Courses Taken in Home Schooling

➤ Evidence of completed courses:
   - Transcript from a correspondence school
   - List of courses taught at home with grades awarded

➤ Suggestions for evaluating a home instruction transcript:
   - Discretion of the school principal or designee
   - Letter grade or Pass/Fail deemed appropriate by the principal or designee
   - Statement attesting that information is true and correct with signature of parent
   - Documentation of course description, content, materials used, projects, papers, tests, etc.
   - Department chairs or subject area teachers' input in evaluation of course content
   - Final examination or appropriate test for comparable course to verify knowledge of course content as well as grade awarded
   - School transcript clearly indicating which courses were transferred from home instruction

1-14 PLACEMENT IN COURSES: GUIDELINES

Considerations in Course Placement of All Students

➤ Individual student's abilities, interests, values, and career aspirations compared with course content and actual demands of each course

➤ Learning styles, academic strengths and weaknesses of student and teacher

➤ Personal knowledge of student and teacher

➤ Language proficiency

➤ Student appraisal/assessment *(List 1-10)*

➤ Teacher recommendations

➤ Results on standardized tests

➤ Cumulative record

➤ Student relationships and group dynamics

➤ Course prerequisites

➤ Appropriate course sequence

➤ Information from meetings with subject area departments

Placement of Students With Special Needs

➤ Be familiar with federal, state, district, and local school laws, policies, procedures, and regulations regarding placement of students in exceptional programs.

➤ Know what constitutes the least restrictive environment.

➤ Be familiar with referral procedures to school child study team and local screening committee.

➤ Be familiar with development of Individual Education Plan (IEP).

➤ Help parents be aware of their rights, responsibilities, and involvement in evaluation and development of the IEP.

➤ Be sensitive to individual needs and feelings of students who are diagnosed as having special needs and are placed in a program for exceptional students.

➤ Encourage teachers to recognize students' strengths, to welcome exceptional students, and ensure that all students' worth and dignity are respected by their peers.

➤ Assist families of students with special needs to deal with their feelings and concerns when learning or when acknowledging that their child needs a program for exceptional children.

➤ Assist teachers to deal with their feelings and concerns when students with special needs are placed in their class.

➤ Provide teachers with resources, and consultation to learn strategies and techniques when teaching students with special needs.

➤ Provide teachers with a network for support when teaching students with special needs.

➤ Assist teachers of students with English as a Second Language (ESL) to assess aural, oral, reading, and writing skills to recommend appropriate placement.

➤ Assist administrators to understand individual needs of students and the need to be flexible.

➤ Assist parents and teachers to understand the system.

➤ Be aware of inclusion and needs of students and teachers for inclusion to be successful.

Placement of Students Who Are Gifted

➢ Know federal government definition of giftedness:
  – Intellectual capability
  – Creative capability
  – Visual and performing arts skills
  – Leadership skills
  – Psychomotor skills

➢ Recognize unique concerns and problems of some students who are gifted:
  – Perfectionism expected by self and others
  – Stress inflicted by self to excel academically
  – Poor self-esteem
  – Possible learning disability with giftedness
  – Insecurity
  – Depression and loneliness
  – Target of teasing
  – Indecisiveness in college and career planning
  – Rejection of advice of parents and others
  – Boredom and lack of enthusiasm for learning
  – Unreasonably high expectations of parents and/or self
  – Lack of physical or emotional maturity and/or social skills when compared to academic peers
  – Focused completely on academics
  – Better relationships with adults than with peers
  – Devastated when performance does not measure up to own unrealistic standards or expectations and thoughts of self-destruction
  – Inability to cope with failure
  – Consideration of suicide rather than face dishonor or possible failure at anything

Counselor's Actions

➢ Help parents and teachers develop insight and understanding of respective students.

➢ Encourage academically gifted students to take honors and advanced placement (AP) courses or an accelerated program for intellectual challenge and knowledge:
  – Monitor progress.
  – Encourage success.
  – Explore appropriateness of schedule change when failure is imminent.
  – Consider subsequent courses, prerequisites of corresponding subsequent courses, and chances for success in subsequent courses.

➢ Encourage artistically talented students to take art, music, and/or drama courses.

➢ Support unique students to accept and appreciate their differences and achieve their ultimate goals.

ADDITIONAL INFORMATION

See *List 3-25, Counseling Students Who Are Gifted.*

See *List 13-1, The School Counselor and Academic/Career Tracking.*

See **List 13-18,** *The School Counselor and Gifted Student Programs.*

Hitchner, K. W. & Tifft-Hitchner, A. (1996). Academic, long-range planning: Four- and six-year programs of study (Chapter 3). In *Counseling today's secondary students.* **(List 12-3)**

Kress, J. E. (1993). Assessment. In *The ESL teacher's book of lists.* West Nyack, NY: Center for Applied Research in Education.

Pierangelo, R. (1995). Evaluation and assessment procedures. In *The special education teacher's book of lists.* **(List 12-33)**

Snyder, B. & Offner, M. (1993). School counselors and special needs students. In J. Wittmer (Ed.), *Managing your school counseling program: K–12 developmental strategies.* **(List 12-3)**

1-15   PROGRAM CHANGES: DEPARTMENT GUIDELINES

Priorities for Making Program Changes

➤ Counselor or computer error

➤ Lack of prerequisite for course assigned

➤ Student's medical problem

➤ Wrong level of an academic course confirmed by teacher

➤ Request made during the specified time limit

➤ Request that helps balance classes

Recommendations for Program Changes

➤ Establish a policy for schedule changes and distribute to students and parents.

➤ Require signatures of teachers of both the present and desired courses prior to parent signature.

➤ Inform parent in writing and require parent signature when requested change affects graduation or college admission.

➤ Change course and subsequent courses on the student's four- or six-year educational plan.

➤ Require additional signatures of department chair and guidance director or assistant principal after deadline for schedule changes.

➤ Notify respective college of student schedule change.

Time Limits

➤ Time limit to change student programs agreed upon by administration, counseling department, and faculty.

➤ Time limit printed in the student handbook, course guide, and course selection form.

ADDITIONAL INFORMATION

Hitchner, K. W. & Tifft-Hitchner, A. (1987). Staying on top of today's curriculum (Chapter 7). In *A survival guide for the secondary school counselor.* **(List 12-3)**

1-16 CUMULATIVE OFFICIAL SCHOLASTIC RECORDS OF STUDENTS

Maintain Student Cumulative Official Scholastic Records

➤ Ensure safe location.

➤ Know and follow federal and state laws and regulations.

➤ Know and follow school district policies:
- Content and types of records to be included
- Procedure to amend or correct records
- Maintenance and storage
- Persons who have legal right to access
- Dates of review
- Record keeping of dates of review
- Fees for duplication of student scholastic record

Interpret Student Cumulative Records

➤ Be present when parents review records.

➤ Interpret content of cumulative record to parents upon request.

ADDITIONAL INFORMATION

United States Code, Title 20, Section 1232g.

United States Code, Section 20, Section 1400–1485.

1-17   COUNSELING AND GUIDANCE FOR POST-HIGH SCHOOL PLANNING

The school counselor must help students, parents, and teachers recognize the longitudinal planning necessary for success.

Post-High School Planning for Students

➤ Begin in elementary school:
- Explore personal interests and strengths.
- Develop breadth of information about careers.
- Begin personal/career portfolio.

➤ Continue in middle school:
- Gain experience with particular interests and strengths.
- Research careers of interest by interviewing and observing persons in those careers.
- Know educational/skill/personal/physical requirements to enter careers of interest.
- Consider a decision-making model. *(List 4-16)*
- Select appropriate courses/electives/experiences to develop knowledge and skill.
- Recognize how level of education enhances career opportunities.
- Begin four- or six-year career/educational plan.
- Continue development of the personal/career portfolio.

➤ Continue in high school:
- Set tentative college and career goals.
- Determine process necessary to achieve goals.
- Recognize progress as each step is accomplished.
- Update career/educational plan each year. *(List 4-13)*
- Develop academic strengths to enhance opportunities.
- Research careers and jobs in depth, recognizing the steps to success.
- Research colleges that offer strong programs for preparation.
- Interview and shadow persons successful in specific careers.
- Develop experience in specific career settings.
- Explore college experience as an opportunity to prepare for career.
- Recognize the continuum of education, skill, and personal growth necessary for success.

ADDITIONAL INFORMATION

See *List 3-7, Post-High School Educational Search.*

1-18   FOLLOW-UP OF HIGH SCHOOL STUDENTS

High School Graduates

➤ Join with high school alumni office to get information about graduates.

➤ Share database with alumni office.

➤ Send cards each year to update information:
  – Current work/career
  – Postsecondary education/training, dates, major
  – Transfer colleges, name of college, date
  – Graduation from college, name of college, date
  – Future plans
  – Satisfaction with high school, college, and work (Rank 1–5 [with 5 being highest])

Non-Graduates

➤ Keep name, address, phone, work on database.

➤ Call to keep in touch and suggest training or other opportunities:
  – Adult education
  – General Education Development (GED) tests
  – Possible return to school
  – Attendance at another school

➤ Update information

1-19   EVALUATION OF THE SCHOOL COUNSELING AND GUIDANCE PROGRAM

Purpose of Evaluation of the Program

> ➤ Assess current counseling and guidance program.

> ➤ Learn effects of the counseling and guidance program on students, teachers, and parents.

> ➤ Assess delivery of counseling and guidance services.

> ➤ Monitor use of time for counseling and guidance services.

> ➤ Determine priorities for counseling and guidance program in the future.

> ➤ Provide evidence of value of the counseling and guidance program.

> ➤ Build public relations and invite support for the program.

Guidelines to Evaluate the Program

> ➤ Clearly define goals and objectives of the counseling and guidance program:
>   - Academic achievement of students
>   - Career development of students
>   - Behavioral adjustment of students
>   - Personal development of students
>   - Social skills acquisition of students
>   - Provision of parent education seminars
>   - Provision of parenting library
>   - Provision of staff development seminars

> ➤ Design a brief, simple, clear, efficient survey that is easily read, responded to, summarized, and reported.

> ➤ Solicit survey answers from students, parents, and teachers about achievement of specified goals.

> ➤ Evaluate outcomes of activities continuously at the end of each activity.

Methods to Evaluate the Program

1. Begin with annual assessment of needs of students, parents, and teachers *(List 1-6)*.

2. Determine measurable program goals and learning objectives for students.

3. Plan what needs to be done to achieve the stated goals and learning objectives.

4. Conduct the program to achieve the stated goals.

5. Assess ongoing activities and monitor the progress toward achieving goals of the program:
   - Survey students, parents, or teachers at end of *each activity.* (Process data.)
   - Review existing records of students to determine if improvement occurred during counseling or after counseling.
   - Evaluate the worth of each activity and decide whether to do it again, revise it, or discontinue it.
   - Survey students, teachers, or parents about achievement of program goals, learning objectives, and specific services at the end of each school year.

6. Based upon results of the survey, make decisions about priorities of the program.

Reporting Results of Evaluation of the Program

➤ Present formal written report of results of achievement of the specified goals to supervisor and administrator(s).

➤ Report results of evaluation to all who completed surveys.

➤ Prepare and present a summary report with graphs to show results visually to the public:
  – Presentation to the school board or PTA/PTO board
  – Teacher bulletin
  – School newspaper
  – Parent newsletter
  – Local newspaper
  – Professional newsletter
  – Professional presentation

➤ Revise counseling and guidance program when indicated by survey results:
  – Changes in the program
  – Emphasis of the program

ADDITIONAL INFORMATION

See *List 1-4, Needs Assessment.*

See *List 1-5, Guidance Advisory Committee (GAC).*

See *List 2-6, Accountability and Performance Evaluation of the School Counselor.*

Hitchner, K. W. & Tifft-Hitchner, A. (1987). Accountability: Heading them off at the pass (Chapter 3). In *Survival guide for the secondary school counselor. (List 12-3)*

Schmidt, J. J. (1993). Counselor accountability: Justifying your time and measuring your worth, Chapter 22. In J. Wittmer (Ed.), *Managing your school counseling program: K–12 developmental strategies. (List 12-3)*

Schmidt, J. J. (1993). Elementary counselor's monthly report form, Student evaluation of group counseling, Student evaluation of a high school counseling program, Parent evaluation of a school counseling program, Teacher evaluation of a school counseling program, Counselor self-assessment form. Chapter 22: Counselor accountability: Justifying your time and measuring your worth. In J. Wittmer (Ed.), *Managing your school counseling program: K–12 developmental strategies. (List 12-3)*

1-20 COMMUNICATING THE COUNSELING AND GUIDANCE PROGRAM

Communicating Counseling and Guidance Services Within the School

➤ Enlist help from the Guidance Advisory Committee (GAC) or other parents.

➤ Speak to staff at inservices before school term, introducing plans for the year.

➤ Hold open-house for all departments to see guidance department.

➤ Offer to team-teach guidance lessons.

➤ Use bulletin boards throughout school when possible.

➤ Distribute flyers in school library.

➤ Speak at PTA and other parent meetings.

➤ Organize parent coffees to discuss guidance services.

➤ Enlist parents and staff members to become members of Guidance Advisory Committee or Materials Review Committee.

➤ Distribute results of evaluation of counseling and guidance program.

Communicating Counseling and Guidance Services in the Community

➤ Write a guidance newsletter to parents or a "guidance corner" of school newsletter.

➤ Serve on communitywide committees.

➤ Write a succinct description of school counseling and guidance program.

➤ Enlist the help of members of the Guidance Advisory Committee (GAC) *(List 1-7):*
  - Design a brochure.
  - Distribute brochure to public libraries, real estate offices, other community locations.
  - Design a home page for the guidance department.
  - Write articles for local newspaper describing counseling and guidance services.

➤ Be active in professional associations.

➤ Present programs in community describing counseling and guidance services.

➤ Get to know community leaders and news reporters.

➤ Hold open-house for community leaders.

➤ Speak at school and community meetings.

➤ Enlist volunteers for career center or guidance department.

➤ Enlist volunteers as mentors or tutors for students.

➤ Enlist volunteers as speakers at career day or career night.

➤ Distribute results of evaluation of counseling and guidance program.

➤ Communicate the role of the school counselor throughout neighborhoods and community.

➤ Advocate for school counseling at public and school board meetings.

ADDITIONAL INFORMATION

See *List 1-5, Guidance Advisory Committee (GAC).*

See *List 2-49, Materials Advisory Committee (MAC).*

Section 2

THE SCHOOL COUNSELOR

THE EFFECTIVE SCHOOL COUNSELOR
2-1 CHARACTERISTICS OF EFFECTIVENESS

Empathy

➤ Shows accurate and sensitive awareness of student's feelings, aspirations, values, beliefs, and perceptions

➤ Senses meaning of student's anger, fear, or joy; its antecedents and its consequences, without being overwhelmed

➤ Preserves student's self-respect and provides a trusting, safe atmosphere while student learns more about self

➤ Shows a sensitive understanding, not only of student's apparent feelings, but goes further to clarify and expand what is hinted by voice, posture, and content cues

Genuineness or Congruence

➤ Authentic in all encounters with students

➤ Does not hide behind a professional facade or role

➤ Provides an honest, nondefensive relationship that allows the counselor to point to unpleasant truths about the student rather than hiding behind a facade

Unconditional Positive Regard

➤ Provides a nonthreatening, safe, trusting, secure atmosphere through the counselor's acceptance, valuing, and nonpossessive warmth for the student

➤ Communicates warmth and respect, but confronts the student with his or her behavior and the consequences, not as socially undesirable traits, but as what the student is doing and what may happen as a consequence

➤ Stimulates the student to openly accept self, understand current behavior and its effect on others, accept pride or shame of past behavior, and share hopes and fears for the future, as well as plan future behavior

29

2-2   SCHOOL COUNSELOR COMPETENCIES

AMERICAN SCHOOL COUNSELOR ASSOCIATION (ASCA)

Knowledge Competencies

School counselors need to know:

➤ Human development theories and concepts

➤ Individual counseling theories

➤ Consultation theories and techniques

➤ Family counseling theories and techniques

➤ Group counseling theories and techniques

➤ Career decision-making theories and techniques

➤ Learning theories

➤ Motivation theories

➤ Effect of culture on individual development and behavior

➤ Evaluation theories and processes

➤ Ethical and legal issues related to counseling

➤ Program development models

Professional Competencies

School counselors should be able to:

➤ Conduct a self-evaluation to determine their strengths and areas needing improvement.

➤ Develop a plan of personal and professional growth to enable them to participate in lifelong learning.

➤ Advocate for appropriate state and national legislation.

➤ Adopt a set of professional ethics to guide their practice and interactions with students, staff, community, parents, and peers.

Skill Competencies

School counselors should be able to demonstrate skills in:

➤ Diagnosing student needs

➤ Individual counseling

➤ Group counseling

➤ Consultation with staff, students, and parents

➤ Coordination of programs, educational testing, career development, substance abuse

➤ Career counseling

➤ Educational counseling

➤ Identifying and making appropriate referrals

➤ Administering and interpreting achievement, interest, aptitude, and personality tests

- Cross-cultural counseling
- Ethical decision making
- Building supportive climates for students and staff
- Removing and/or decreasing race and gender bias in school policy and curriculum
- Explaining to the staff, community, and parents the scope of practice and functions of a school counselor
- Planning and conducting inservice for staff
- Identifying resources and information related to helping clients
- Evaluating the effectiveness of counseling programs

Personal Characteristics of Effective Counselors

- Have a genuine interest in the welfare of others
- Are able to understand the perspective of others
- Believe individuals are capable of solving problems
- Are open to learning
- Are willing to take risks
- Have a strong sense of self-worth
- Are not afraid of making mistakes and attempt to learn from them
- Value continued growth as a person
- Are caring and warm
- Possess a keen sense of humor

Training Standards for School Counselors
COUNCIL FOR THE ACCREDITATION OF COUNSELING AND RELATED EDUCATIONAL PROGRAMS (CACREP)

- Curricular experiences and demonstrated knowledge in common-core areas
- Supervised practicum experience for a total minimum of 100 clock hours
- Supervised internship of 600 clock hours after completion of practicum
- Specialized curricular experiences

ADDITIONAL INFORMATION

ACES (1989). *ACES standards for counseling supervisors*. Alexandria, VA: American Counseling Association.

AMCD (1995). *Multicultural counseling competencies*. Boston, MA: AMCD. *(List 12-23)*

CACREP (1993). *Accreditation procedures manual*. Alexandria, VA: CACREP.

ROLE DEFINITION OR JOB DESCRIPTION
2-3 ROLE DEFINITION

Foremost Responsibilities

➤ Individual counseling

➤ Small-group counseling

➤ Group guidance

➤ Consultation

➤ Coordination of counseling and guidance activities *(List 1-2)*

Significant Responsibilities

➤ Needs assessment

➤ Career education coordination

➤ Staff development

➤ Parent consultation

➤ Peer-facilitation or peer-mediation program

➤ Mentoring program

➤ Collaboration with student services team in defining school programs to serve all students

Student Advocate

➤ Ensure equity of program access for all students by providing input in school curriculum development.

➤ Develop student assistance programs.

➤ Meet regularly with administrator to inform about progress in establishing or maintaining student assistance programs and positive student actions.

➤ Meet regularly with administrator to assist in defining consequences for misbehavior.

➤ Be aware of community resources available for students.

➤ Consult with parents and staff on issues and trends relevant to students' welfare.

➤ Develop close ties with business and industry to increase opportunities for students.

➤ Teach conflict-resolution or peer-mediation skills to students and staff.

➤ Explore ways technology can extend guidance services, maintaining confidentiality.

➤ Continually sharpen career development skills and share them with students.

➤ Update all skills.

➤ Be clear about responsibilities.

Additional Proactive Activities

➤ Conduct discussion groups where parents can ask questions about the school and the counseling and guidance program.

➢ Conduct parent seminars on concerns about child rearing, discipline, and child development.

➢ Teach guidance lessons cooperatively with a teacher.

ADDITIONAL INFORMATION

See *List 1-5, Guidance Advisory Committee (GAC)*.

See *List 1-20, Communicating the Counseling and Guidance Program*.

ETHICAL STANDARDS AND LEGAL ASPECTS
2-4 ETHICAL STANDARDS

The counselor has ethical responsibilities to protect the safety, needs, confidentiality, and interests of students, parents, staff, colleagues, self, and the profession.

Ethical Standards

➢ Are personal, professional standards of moral duty and obligation

➢ Are self-imposed regulations

➢ Prevent internal disagreement

➢ Provide protection in case of litigation

Ethical Guidelines

➢ Act in the best interests of students and their parents at all times.

➢ Actively attempt to understand the diverse cultural backgrounds of students in the school, including own cultural/ethnic/racial identity and its impact on personal values and beliefs about counseling.

➢ Be aware of own personal values, attitudes, and beliefs and how they may hinder effectiveness when working with certain students.

➢ Only use procedures and techniques within the boundaries of personal training and competence.

➢ Be able to fully explain what you do and why you do it that way.

➢ Inform students at the beginning of individual and group counseling of the limitations of confidentiality in counseling.

➢ Inform or request written consent from parents when providing ongoing individual and group counseling to students.

➢ Encourage parent participation and involvement, particularly in areas that may be controversial.

➢ Follow written job description.

➢ Stay up-to-date with laws and current court rulings, particularly those pertaining to counseling with minors.

➤ Consult with other professionals (colleagues, supervisors, counselor educators, professional association ethics committee, etc.).

➤ Use caution when communicating on the Internet to protect the anonymity of any students and never provide specifics of any case.

➤ Realize that there is no certainty of the accountability, reliability, quality, and expertise of anyone offering counseling advice on the Internet. E-mail does not substitute for counseling supervision.

➤ Join appropriate professional associations.

➤ When a school counselor is also a licensed professional counselor, do not refer students or school employees who attend or work in the same school(s) as the school counselor, to a private practice in which the school counselor would benefit monetarily, or in which the school counselor is receiving supervision for licensure.

➤ When a school counselor is also a licensed professional counselor, do not conduct any private work in the school office or use any school facilities including telephones or courier service. Do not use any materials or information gained in the school for private business.

ADDITIONAL INFORMATION

ACA (1995). *ACA code of ethics and standards of practice.* **(List 12-13)**

ACA [On-line] Available: http://www.counseling.org/

ASCA (1996). Ethical standards. In *ASCA membership services guide.* **(List 12-13)**

ASCA [On-line] Available: http:www.edge.net/asca/

ASGW (1989). *ASGW ethical guidelines for group counselors.* **(List 12-13)**

ASGW [On-line] Available: http://www.uc.edu/~wilson/asgw/index.html

2-5   LEGAL STANDARDS AND RECOMMENDATIONS

Legal Standards

➤ Relate to federal, state, and municipal standards of practice as regulated by law

➤ Take precedence in a court of law over ethical standards

➤ Relate to "accepted professional practices" in the community

➤ Are minimum requirements

Recommendations for the Counselor

➤ Know current state laws relating to education and counseling:
  – Reporting suspected child abuse
  – Reporting to noncustodial parents
  – Privileged communication or lack of it
  – Reporting standardized test results
  – Dual relationships

➤ Know school district policies:
  – Cross-cultural counseling

- Using nonstandardized tests and inventories
- Conducting research of counseling and guidance
- Selecting school counseling materials
- Selecting and using school counseling techniques

Preparation and Suggestions for Court Appearances

➤ Notify administrator immediately when subpoena is served.

➤ Seek legal advice from school or private attorney prior to going to court.

➤ Listen to an entire question before answering.

➤ Take time before answering a question to answer thoughtfully.

➤ Only answer questions; do not volunteer information.

➤ Request clarification or repetition of a question when necessary.

➤ Stop immediately when the judge interrupts or an attorney objects.

➤ Stick to the facts; give no opinions.

➤ Give clear and concise answers.

➤ Do not say "That is all that happened." Say "That is all that I recall."

➤ Correct your answer or the interpretation when necessary.

➤ May ask judge if you *must* answer if the answer may jeopardize your relationship with the student.

➤ Never argue; do not show irritation or anger.

Additional Information

Brigman, G. & Moore, P. (1994). *School counselors and censorship: Facing the challenge. (List 12-3)*

Herlihy, B. & Corey, G. (1992). *Dual relationships in counseling.* Alexandria, VA: American Counseling Association.

Huey, W. C., & Remley, T. P., Jr. (Eds.) (1988). *Ethical and legal issues in school counseling.* Alexandria, VA: American Counseling Association.

Mitchell, R. W. (1991). *Documentation in counseling records.* Alexandria, VA: American Counseling Association.

Remley, T. P. (1991). *Preparing for court appearances.* Alexandria, VA: American Counseling Association.

Salo, M. M. & Shumate, S. G. (1993). Counseling minor clients. In T. Remley, Jr. (Ed.), *The ACA Legal Series, Vol. 4.* Alexandria, VA: American Counseling Association.

EVALUATION OF THE SCHOOL COUNSELOR

2-6   ACCOUNTABILITY AND PERFORMANCE EVALUATION

Accountability involves the systematic gathering of information relevant to the performance of the school counselor. It enables the counselor to: (1) make effective decisions regarding the counseling program and the counselor's role, (2) determine how well the counselor has met the specified goals, and (3) demonstrate the effectiveness of the counselor's services to students.

Types of Evaluations: Formative and Summative

➤ Formative evaluations are usually process evaluations conducted by persons within the school and are conducted to improve the services.

➤ Summative evaluations are usually outcome evaluations performed by a supervisor or person(s) from outside the school to determine and report the quality or worth of the service.

Types of Data Used for Evaluations

1. Enumerative data, usually tabulated and quantitative:
   ➤ Time devoted to various services (e.g., group counseling, group guidance, individual counseling)
   ➤ Frequency and length of counseling sessions
   ➤ Number of students or parents seen for counseling or consultation
2. Process data, information collected while the program is in process, and often qualitative:
   ➤ Effectiveness of the professional skills of the counselor:
     – Communication skills
     – Work habits
     – Time management
     – Follow-through
   ➤ Progress of members in a counseling activity or specified activities
3. Outcome data, collected after a particular activity is completed. Outcome data may be quantitative or qualitative or both:
   ➤ Student's grades improved
   ➤ Student's anger management skills improved
   ➤ Student's attendance improved
   ➤ Student's behavior in class improved
4. Follow-up data, collected several weeks or longer after the activity is completed, give additional information and may be qualitative or quantitative:
   ➤ Student maintained improved grades
   ➤ Student continued to control anger
   ➤ Student continued to attend regularly
   ➤ Student continued appropriate behavior in class

Data-Collection Methods

➤ Self-rating scale of counselor:
  – Tabulation of services delivered
  – Time analysis

- Questionnaires/rating scales completed by students, parents, or teachers after each activity
- Peer observation or review
- Survey to measure if counseling and guidance services were delivered and how well services were delivered throughout the school year
- Performance appraisal of counselor by supervisor and principal

Considerations When Selecting Evaluation Methods

- Easy to collect and compile and not require much time
- Relevant to the position and job description, and represent what the counselor does
- Reliable, error free, unbiased, and complete
- Comparable from year to year, within the school, and with the position in other schools

Report of the Results of the Evaluation of the Counselor

- Formal written report of supervisor or administrator(s)
- Accountability conference with supervisor and/or administrator(s)
- Written plan to improve the quality of services or service delivery
- Communicate the diversity of services provided
- Present an annual report of the program to the school board
- Assist in professional growth and development
- Demonstrate the need for the counselor position
- Verify the time spent in counseling activities

Counselor's Actions

1. Set measurable goals and responsibilities.
2. Plan what needs to be done to achieve the goals (procedures).
3. Do the work and monitor the progress.
4. Report the results.
5. Evaluate results, provide feedback.
6. Plan for improvement.

ADDITIONAL INFORMATION

See *List 1-19, Evaluation of the School Counseling and Guidance Program.*

See *List 13-15, The School Counselor and Evaluation.*

CERTIFICATION

2-7 ACCREDITATION, CERTIFICATION, AND LICENSURE

Accreditation, Certification, and Licensure

➢ Minimum standards

➢ State requirements vary

➢ National Certified Counselor (NCC)
- Professional certification issued by the National Board of Certified Counselors (NBCC)
- Voluntary

➢ National Certified School Counselor (NCSC)
- Specialty for school counselor
- Requires NCC first
- Voluntary

Certification of Counselor Education Programs

➢ Council for Accreditation of Counseling and Related Educational Programs (CACREP)
- Most rigorous regulating guidelines
- Voluntary

➢ National Council for Accreditation of Teacher Education (NCATE)

➢ State Departments of Education

➢ University Graduate Schools

State Certification of School Counselors

➢ Requirements determined by the respective state board of education

➢ Requirements administered by the respective state department of education

ADDITIONAL INFORMATION

See **List 13-10**, *The School Counselor and Credentialing and Licensure.*

APPLICATION OF COUNSELING THEORIES
2-8 COUNSELING THEORIES

Reason for Counseling Theories

Counseling theory attempts to explain and describe events and behavior, and predict future events and behavior. A school counselor's "core" theory provides a guide for:

1. Defining the counseling relationship
2. Conceptualizing students' presenting problems
3. Determining counseling goals and desired outcomes
4. Determining counseling responses and interventions

Interventions Based on Theory

The experienced school counselor may select, adapt, and integrate theories when working with different students who have differing needs. The counselor may identify a student's preferred learning style and use a theory that will help the student change or achieve a specified goal. There are three broad categories of theories and interventions. Change in any one of the categories is likely to produce change in the other two.

1. Interventions that produce *affective* change, used to help students express feelings, identify feelings, and alter or accept feelings
2. Interventions that produce *cognitive* change, used to help students alter or correct errors in thoughts, perceptions, and beliefs
3. Interventions that produce *behavioral* change, used to help students develop adaptive and supportive behaviors

In addition, there are interventions that produce *system* change, or change in the school environment.

ADDITIONAL INFORMATION

Corey, G. (1996). *Theory and practice of counseling and psychotherapy* (5th ed.). Pacific Grove, CA: Brooks/Cole.

Thompson, C. L. & Rudolph, L. B. (1996). *Counseling children* (4th ed.). *(List 12-3)*

2-9   ADLERIAN OR INDIVIDUAL COUNSELING

Counseling Method

➤ Establish a helping and mutually respectful relationship.

➤ Select and adapt techniques to the needs of the student.

➤ Analyze inferiority feelings or feelings of discouragement.

➤ Examine social adjustments.

➤ Identify the student's goal(s) of behavior or misbehavior.

➤ Help the student become aware of mistaken goal(s) of behavior.

➤ Help the student develop a more constructive goal.

➤ Help the student learn and use appropriate behavior.

➤ Administer logical consequences for irresponsible behavior.

ADDITIONAL INFORMATION

Classical Adlerian Psychology and Democracy. [On-line] Available:
   http:ourworld.compuserve.com/homepages.hstein/

Dinkmeyer, D. C., Dinkmeyer, D. C., Jr., & Sperry, L. (1987). *Adlerian counseling and psychotherapy* (2nd ed.). Columbus, OH: Merrill.

Dinkmeyer, D. C. & Eckstein, D. (1993). *Leadership by encouragement.* Dubuque, IA: Kendall/Hunt.

2-10   BEHAVIORAL COUNSELING

Counseling Method

➤ Establish a helping relationship.

➤ Define the problem precisely and identify the antecedents, observable behaviors, and consequences.

➤ Set behavioral goals or desired outcomes.

➤ Teach the problem-solving method.

➤ Teach self-direction and self-control.

➤ Collect and record data through counseling and a follow-up period.

➤ Evaluate the process.

➤ Match the reinforcement to the student's developmental level and personal preferences.

Optional Techniques

➤ Draw up contracts with clear goals, specific steps, and immediate reinforcement (children under age 12).

➤ Arrange a self-management program (students age 12 or older).

➤ Teach the student to rehearse and practice.

➤ Provide feedback.

➤ Role play a scenario for the student to observe his or her behavior, explore the consequences, and make a decision about changing the behavior.

➤ Instruct the student in role reversal.

➤ Provide counseling homework assignments to practice what was learned in counseling.

ADDITIONAL INFORMATION

Kazdin, A. E. (1994). *Behavior modification in applied settings* (5th ed.). Pacific Grove, CA: Brooks/Cole.

Spiegler, M. D. & Guevremont, D. C. (1993). *Contemporary behavior therapy* (2nd ed.). Pacific Grove, CA: Brooks/Cole.

Watson, D. L. & Tharp, R. G. (1993). *Self-directed behavior: Self-modification for personal adjustment* (6th ed.). Pacific Grove, CA: Brooks/Cole.

2-11   COGNITIVE-BEHAVIORAL COUNSELING

Counseling Method

➤ Establish a helping relationship.

➤ Teach cognitive restructuring by examining thoughts and self-talk.

➤ Teach how to change self-talk.

➤ Assign homework assignments to practice concepts learned in counseling.

➤ Teach problem-solving and self-management skills.

➤ Teach relaxation for anxiety-provoking situations.

➤ Teach self-control, assertiveness, self-evaluation, and social skills.

➤ Reinforce and encourage change.

ADDITIONAL INFORMATION

Cognitive & General Psychology Research. [On-line] Available: http://www.psych.stanford.edu/cogsci/

Kendall, P. (1993). Cognitive-behavior therapies with youth: Guiding theory, current status, and emerging developments. *Journal of Consulting and Clinical Psychology, 61,* 235–247.

Ronen, T. (1992). Cognitive therapy with children. *Child Psychiatry and Human Development, 23,* 19–30.

2-12 EXISTENTIAL COUNSELING

Counseling Method

- ➤ Establish a meaningful relationship with the student, being fully present and committed to listening and understanding the student.
- ➤ Model honesty, integrity, courage, and authenticity.
- ➤ Help student identify and examine assumptions and attitudes.
- ➤ Vary the method, depending upon the student and the situation.
- ➤ Actively listen.
- ➤ Help student become aware of him- or herself, responsibility, and ultimate concerns.
- ➤ Guide student to implement the examined and internalized values.

ADDITIONAL INFORMATION

May, R. & Yalom, I. D. (1995). Existential psychotherapy. In R. J. Corsini & D. Wedding (Eds.). *Current psychotherapies* (5th ed.), 262–292. Itasca, IL: F. E. Peacock.

Yalom, I. D. (1985). *The theory and practice of group psychotherapy* (3rd ed.). New York, NY: Basic Books.

2-13 GESTALT COUNSELING

Counseling Method

- ➤ Establish and maintain a person-to-person relationship.
- ➤ Create a climate in which the student will try new behaviors.
- ➤ Design experiments to increase student's self-awareness of what the student is doing and how he or she is doing it.
- ➤ Draw attention to nonverbal language of the student.
- ➤ Be a guide or catalyst, suggesting experiments.
- ➤ Share reactions and observations, particularly of language that does not indicate personal ownership—generalized use of "it" and "you," questions, qualifiers, and metaphors, the way the student expresses feelings and life experiences.
- ➤ Confront incongruities of behaviors, thoughts, and actions.
- ➤ Assist student to develop own awareness of the present, personal responsibility, and experiment with new, more appropriate behaviors.

ADDITIONAL INFORMATION

Association for the Advancement of Gestalt Therapy (AAGT). [on-line] Available: http://www.europa.com/~brownell/

Atkinson, D. R., Morten, G., & Sue, D. W. (1993). *Counseling American minorities: A cross-cultural perspective* (4th ed.). Madison, WI: Brown & Benchmark.

Jacobs, E. (1992). *Creative counseling techniques: An illustrated guide.* (List 12-3)

Sue, D. W. & Sue, D. (1990). *Counseling the culturally different: Theory and practice* (2nd ed.). (List 12-23)

2-14 MULTIMODAL COUNSELING

BASIC ID of Multimodal Counseling

BASIC ID is used to assess discrete, yet interactive functions (Thompson & Rudolph (1996)):

   B — *Behavior:* observable and measurable

   A — *Affect:* emotions, moods, strong feelings

   S — *Sensation:* touch, taste, smell, sight, hearing

   I — *Imagery:* memories, dreams, fantasies

   C — *Cognition:* insights, ideas, opinions, self-talk, judgments, fundamental values

   I — *Interpersonal relationships:* interactions with other students and teachers

   D — *Drugs/Diet:* nutritional habits, exercise, health

Counseling Method

➤ Identify the problem area, using the BASIC ID given above.

➤ Examine interactions among the functions in BASIC ID.

➤ Select or design interventions to address the problem before it becomes more serious.

➤ Adapt plan to meet the needs of the student and the particular situation.

➤ Use techniques that have been effective in dealing with the specific problem.

➤ Determine the interventions for various students and the reason specific procedures are selected to work with students with particular problems (technical eclecticism).

➤ Discuss concrete and measurable goals to address the problem with the student.

➤ Teach more appropriate behavior by using procedures such as role play, behavior rehearsal, data collection, and feedback to change behavior.

➤ Follow up as in behavioral counseling.

ADDITIONAL INFORMATION

Keat, D. (1990). *Child multimodal therapy.* Norwood, NJ: Ablex.

Lazarus, A. (1990). Multimodal applications and research: A brief overview and update. *Elementary School Guidance and Counseling, 24,* 243–247.

Thompson, C. & Poppen, W. (1992). *Guidance activities for counselors and teachers.* Knoxville, TN: Authors.

2-15 Person-Centered Counseling

Counseling Method

- ➤ Create a warm and accepting climate and a helping relationship.
- ➤ Actively listen to the student.
- ➤ Reflect the student's thoughts and feelings.
- ➤ Clarify the student's statements or request clarification.
- ➤ Summarize frequently what the student said.
- ➤ Confront contradictions of the student.
- ➤ Lead the student to self-exploration.

Additional Information

Knox, J. (1992). Bullying in schools: Communicating with the victim. *Support for Learning, 7(4),* 159–162.

Williams, W. & Lair, G. (1991). Using a person-centered approach with children who have a disability. *Elementary School Guidance and Counseling, 25,* 194–203.

2-16 Rational-Emotive-Behavior Counseling (REBC)

Counseling Method

- ➤ Identify the irrational belief the student is telling him- or herself.
- ➤ Dispute and challenge the identified irrational belief.
- ➤ Show the student how his or her irrational beliefs create undesirable consequences.
- ➤ Teach the student how to dispute specific irrational beliefs and replace them with rational beliefs using the A, B, C, D, E, and F Model:

  A — *Activating* event (something unpleasant happens)

  B — *Belief* or how the student evaluates the event, self-talk (student tells him- or her-self that it should not happen)

  C — *Consequence* or feelings resulting from belief (student feels upset)

  D — *Disputing* the irrational belief or self-talk (student questions why it is so awful)

  E — *Effect* of more helpful self-talk (student replaces the original self-talk with "It is too bad, but I can handle it")

  F —*Feeling* (new feeling that the student can take care of it)

- ➤ Persuade the student to replace irrational beliefs with rational beliefs.
- ➤ Assign counseling homework of reading, practicing, trying new self-talk.

Additional Information

Bernard, M. (1990). Rational-emotive therapy with children and adolescents: Treatment strategies. *School Psychology Review, 19,* 294–303.

Gossette, R. & O'Brien, R. (1993). Efficacy of rational-emotive therapy with children: A critical re-appraisal. *Journal of Behavior Therapy and Experimental Psychiatry, 24(1),* 15–25.

Institute for Rational-Emotive Therapy. [On-line] Available: http://www.IRET.org/

Joyce, M. R. (1990). Rational-emotive parent consultation. *School Psychology Review, 19,* 304–314.

2-17   REALITY COUNSELING OR CONTROL THEORY

Counseling Method

➤ Build a good relationship with the student, with trust and a climate in which the student feels free to express fears, anxieties, and concerns.

➤ Ask student to describe present behavior.

➤ Ask student to evaluate what is going on and how student is helping self with present behavior.

➤ Brainstorm and work with the student to look at possible alternatives to achieve more desirable results.

➤ Ask student to select an alternative to reach desirable goal, and make a commitment to try the alternative.

➤ Examine with the student the results of the commitment:
  – Do not accept excuses.
  – Change the alternative and the commitment.

➤ Use logical consequences.

➤ Engage the student in discussion.

➤ Show what is expected.

➤ Request student input.

➤ Encourage exploration.

➤ Assist student in evaluating work.

➤ Persevere.

ADDITIONAL INFORMATION

Glasser, W. (1990). *The quality school: Managing students without coercion.* New York, NY: Harper & Row.

Glasser, W. (1993). *The quality school teacher.* New York, NY: HarperCollins.

2-18 SOLUTION-FOCUSED BRIEF COUNSELING

Counseling Method

➤ Listen attentively to the student's description of the problem.

➤ Refocus toward solution of the problem and reframe with success terminology.

➤ Externalize the problem.

➤ Align with the student against the problem.

➤ Assist the student in setting the counseling goal.

➤ Focus on the visible and the specific.

➤ Ask student the "miracle question": "If the problem were solved overnight, how would the student know it was solved?" *"What would be different?"*

➤ Identify problem maintenance behaviors.

➤ Identify exceptions, times when the student had the problem under control.

➤ Encourage student to do the same thing(s) as he or she did during exceptions.

➤ Encourage adults in the school to see the student as competent and able to control the problem.

➤ Use a scale of 10 and ask student to place control of the problem on that scale.

➤ Caution students to go slowly and focus on tasks that lead to success.

➤ Notice time and place when examining successes.

➤ Recognize student as the expert and totally responsible for the success.

ADDITIONAL INFORMATION

Durrant, M. (1993). *Creative strategies for school problems.* Sydney, Australia: Eastwood Family Therapy Centre.

Eliason, G. T., Garner, N. E., & LaFountain, R. M. (1996). Solution-focused counseling groups: A key for school counselors. *School Counselor, 43(4),* 256–267.

Metcalf, L. (1995). *Counseling toward solutions: A practical solution-focused program for working with students, teachers, and parents. (List 12-3)*

Walter, J. & Peller, J. (1992). *Becoming solution-focused in brief therapy.* New York, NY: Brunner-Mazel.

COUNSELOR OF INDIVIDUAL STUDENTS
2-19 INDIVIDUAL COUNSELING

Purpose of Individual Counseling

The purpose of individual counseling is to help the student:

> ➤ Develop positive attitudes toward school, learning, and work.
> ➤ Make responsible choices.
> ➤ Respect self and others.
> ➤ Develop knowledge for further education and future employment.
> ➤ Develop appropriate behavior.
> ➤ Know and use conflict resolution skills.
> ➤ Resolve a problem.

Categories of Student Problems

> ➤ Interpersonal conflict, conflict with others
> ➤ Intrapersonal conflict, conflict with self (e.g., decision-making problem)
> ➤ Lack of information about self (e.g., abilities, interests, or values)
> ➤ Lack of information about the school (e.g., what it takes to succeed in school)
> ➤ Lack of skill (e.g., study, assertiveness, listening, how to make friends)

Counseling Versus Therapy

Counseling instead of therapy is conducted in schools.

> *Counseling*
> ➤ Addresses preventative and developmental concerns
> ➤ Addresses conscious concerns
> ➤ Assists with educational, career, and decision-making problems
> ➤ Uses teaching methods
> ➤ Makes referrals to parents for students with serious problems to receive help from professionals with clinical training

> *Therapy*
> ➤ Addresses serious disorders and personality problems
> ➤ Addresses unconscious concerns as well as conscious concerns
> ➤ Assists with personality reconstruction and other serious problems
> ➤ Uses healing methods
> ➤ Provides ongoing therapy to students referred by school counselor to parents

Individual Counseling Versus Group Counseling

Individual counseling instead of group counseling is conducted when:

➤ Problem is unique.

➤ Other students could not understand the problem.

➤ Crisis occurs that involves only that student.

➤ Confidentiality is essential.

➤ Interpretation of individual test results is needed.

➤ Student has anxiety and fear of talking in a group.

➤ Limited awareness and understanding of feelings, motivations, and patterns of behavior is shown.

➤ Behavior would be considered deviant by other group members.

➤ There is a need for individual attention and recognition.

Records of Individual Counseling Sessions

➤ Provide a summary of observations and content of sessions for the counselor

➤ Assist the counselor in recalling counseling sessions

➤ Include only facts, not perceptions or opinions

➤ Retained separately from academic record or cumulative folder

➤ Subject to review by parent of student under age 18

➤ Subject to review by student age 18 or over

➤ Can be subpoenaed by a court

Buckley Amendment (the Federal Family Rights and Privacy Act of 1974)

➤ Gives parents/guardians and young people of legal age the right to inspect records, letters, and recommendations about the student

➤ Requires that the counselor be knowledgeable about the national, state, district, and local guidelines regarding counseling records

Video and Audio Recording of Counseling Sessions

➤ Requires student and parent/guardian written permission before recording:
  – Purpose of recording
  – Persons who will hear or view the recording
  – When and how the recording will be destroyed

➤ Helps student view his or her behavior during counseling session

➤ Helps student understand how his or her behavior affects others

➤ Provides counselor with self-understanding, self-awareness, and professional growth

➤ Required for some graduate courses in counseling

➤ Provides a record of the interview

➤ Requires that the counselor be aware of state laws before deciding how to use, store, or destroy these records

ADDITIONAL INFORMATION

Hitchner, K. W. & Tifft-Hitchner, A. (1996). *Counseling today's secondary student.* *(List 12-3)*

Metcalf, L. (1995). *Counseling toward solutions.* *(List 12-3)*

Schmidt, J. J. (1991). *A survival guide for the elementary/middle school counselor.* *(List 12-3)*

Thompson, C. L. & Rudolph, L. B. (1996). *Counseling children* (4th ed.). *(List 12-3)*

Wittmer, J. (1993). *Managing your school counseling program: K–12 developmental strategies.* *(List 12-3)*

2-20 GUIDELINES

General Guidelines

➤ Be informed about all state and local guidelines that apply to counseling.

➤ Request parent/guardian and staff input for designing or revising the program.

➤ Develop or follow a clearly defined program that follows all state and district guidelines.

➤ Inform parents/guardians about the program in writing.

➤ Correlate local goals and objectives of the program to national, state, and regional guidance standards and research.

➤ Show counseling and guidance materials to parents/guardians.

➤ Work in coordination with other members of the student services team.

➤ Continually evaluate the program and get input from parents/guardians.

➤ Refer legal questions to administrator or supervisor.

The Hatch Amendment (the Protection to Pupil Rights Amendment)

➤ Requires parent or guardian permission before students involved in federally funded programs can be psychologically or psychiatrically tested or treated

➤ Requires that *all three* issues be present for the Hatch Amendment to apply to a curriculum challenge:

1. The materials or program must be fully supported by federal funds.
2. The materials or program must be experimental.
3. The materials or program's primary purpose of testing or treatment must be to reveal personal information about one or more of the following categories as they relate to the student or the student's family:

   – Political affiliations
   – Potentially embarrassing mental or psychological problems
   – Sexual behavior and attitudes
   – Illegal, antisocial, self-incriminating, and demeaning behavior
   – Income
   – Legally privileged relationships
   – Critical appraisals of family members

The First Amendment

➤ Ensures freedom of religion

➤ Protects students' rights to receive information at school

ADDITIONAL INFORMATION

ACA (1995). *ACA code of ethics and standards of practice.* *(List 12-13)*

ASCA (1992). Ethical standards for school counselors. In *ASCA Membership Services Guide.* *(List 12-13)*

Hubert, M. (1996). *Confidentiality and the minor student.* Alexandria, VA: ASCA. [On-line] Available: http://www.scsn.net/ASCA/conf_min.html

Kaplan, L. & Geoffrey, K. (1987). The Hatch Amendment: A primer for counselors, Part I. *The School Counselor, 34,* 9–16.

Kaplan, L. & Geoffrey, K. (1987). The Hatch Amendment: A primer for counselors, Part II. *The School Counselor, 35,* 88–95.

2-21   CONFIDENTIALITY

Information About Confidentiality of School Counseling

➤ Professional responsibility to respect and limit access to the student's personal information

➤ Parents/guardians of a student under age 18 retain many legal rights over their child:
- Granting permission for the student to receive a planned program of individual or group counseling
- Right of parent/guardian to know the goals of counseling sessions

Exceptions to Confidentiality

➤ Student is dangerous to self or others.

➤ Student and parent/guardian request the release of information. In the case of minors, written parental/guardian request is required.

➤ A court orders the release of information.

➤ Counselor is receiving systematic clinical supervision and the student and parent know that counseling information will be used during supervision.

➤ Clerical assistants need to process the information.

➤ Third party is present in the room in which case the student (and parent/guardian) waives his or her right to privacy.

➤ Confidentiality rights of a student who is under age 18 reside with the legal parent or guardian in most states.

Suggestions for the School Counselor

➤ Inform parents/guardians and staff about the role of the counselor.

➤ Assure parents/guardians of the counselor's best interest for the student.

➤ Keep school and district administrators informed concerning relevant program materials, curricula, and goals of the program.

➤ Know federal, state, and local school policy regarding confidentiality.

➤ Know ethical responsibility regarding confidentiality.

➤ Inform the student in counseling about the limits to confidentiality and what the counselor is obligated to report to authorities or parents/guardians.

➤ Establish and write a local school policy for confidentiality that specifies which counseling programs and services will require prior permission of parents/guardians if none exists.

➤ Present a written local school policy regarding confidentiality to the local Board of Education for adoption.

➤ Communicate the local school policy regarding disclosure and confidentiality to parents/guardians and staff.

➤ Obtain written proof of legal custody or natural parenthood before releasing any information.

➤ Consult with supervisor when there are questions of legality or confidentiality.

➤ Consult local, state, or national professional associations.

➤ Use best professional judgment.

Sharing Information in the School

1. Listen to student, parent/guardian, teacher, or other staff member.

2. Determine seriousness of the issue.

3. Report situation to administrator if there is reason to suspect abuse.

4. Prepare student to discuss the issue with the adult (teacher, other staff member, other) if no abuse is suspected:

    ➤ Demonstrate the statement and delivery:
    – "I feel uncomfortable when . . . ."
    – "I don't understand why . . . ."
    – "I am disappointed because . . . ."

    ➤ Have student practice delivery of the statement; rehearse behavior.

5. Follow up with student to learn the following:

    ➤ Does the problem still exist?
    ➤ Did student speak with the involved adult?
    ➤ Is student fearful of addressing the problem with the adult?

6. Determine if student still has a serious issue.

7. Determine further action:

    ➤ Approach the adult involved.
    ➤ Discuss the situation with the administrator.

ADDITIONAL INFORMATION

See *List 13-8, The School Counselor and Confidentiality.*

Brigman, G. & Moore, P. (1994). *School counselors and censorship: Facing the challenge. (List 12-3)*

Thompson, C. L. & Rudolph, L. B. (1996). *Counseling children* (4th ed.). *(List 12-3)*

2-22 PROCEDURES USED IN INDIVIDUAL AND GROUP COUNSELING

Overall Guidelines

➤ Select counseling procedures that are purposeful in assisting the student to define and work toward his or her specified goals.

➤ Be able to explain the reason for using the selected counseling procedure.

➤ Use only procedures within the training of the school counselor.

Procedures Used in Individual and Group Counseling

➤ Open-ended questions

➤ Goal setting *(List 3-2)*

➤ Application of selected counseling theory

➤ Problem solving *(List 2-23)*

➤ Decision making *(List 4-16)*

➤ Exploration of possible consequences

➤ Evaluation of counseling

ADDITIONAL INFORMATION

See *Lists 2-8 through 2-18*, *Application of Counseling Theories.*

See *Lists 3-14 through 3-28*, *Academic Counseling K–12.*

See *Lists 4-24 through 4-28*, *Career Counseling K–12.*

See *Lists 5-73 through 5-98*, *Personal/Social Counseling K–12.*

2-23 PROBLEM-SOLVING MODEL

Steps of the Problem-Solving Model

1. Define the problem specifically until all who are involved understand the problem.
2. Brainstorm or generate options or solutions to the problem.
3. Organize and delete duplications and unsatisfactory solutions.
4. Examine possible consequences of remaining solutions.
5. Select one best solution.
6. Agree to try out the selected solution.
7. Evaluate and revise as necessary at agreed-upon time.
8. Use the model for solving other problems.

Limitations to the Problem-Solving Model

➤ Requires a clear and specific definition of the problem

➤ Requires time

➤ Requires a willingness to try the process

➤ Requires commitment on both sides to arrive at a win–win solution

➤ Requires mutual respect

➤ Requires the following rules:
  – No blaming
  – No interrupting
  – Equal time to present each perspective of the problem
  – Equal time to present each person's needs and desires

2-24   USE OF PLAY IN COUNSELING

Information About Play in Counseling

➤ Play is a natural mode of communication for young children.

➤ Children express their thoughts, feelings, and behaviors in play.

Play Helps Children Deal With Concerns

➤ Loss and separation

➤ Behavior problems in the classroom

➤ Attention deficit disorder

➤ Anxieties and fears

➤ Anger and safe release

➤ Post-trauma

➤ Neighborhood violence

➤ Limits, rules, and adult expectations

➤ Pent-up emotions and need to release in an acceptable way

➤ Hopes and aspirations

Procedures for Play Counseling

➤ Determine and set the limits of time, space, and behaviors to safeguard the child, the counselor, and the property.

➤ Focus the sessions.

➤ Select or let the child select the play materials to be used.

➤ Observe play (and possibly become involved in the play).

➤ Listen, observe, and reflect feelings and thoughts as they occur during the play.

➤ Possibly interview the child during the play by asking open-ended questions.

Play Materials for Young Children

➤ Clay, crayons, fingerpaints

➤ Sand tray

➤ Safe toys and materials such as blocks, blunt scissors, newsprint, foam balls, puppets, and punching toys

ADDITIONAL INFORMATION

Play Therapy Association. [On-line] Available: www.playtherapy.org.

Kottman, T. (1995). *Partners in play: An Adlerian approach to play therapy.* *(List 12-3)*

Landreth, G. (1991). *Play therapy: The art of the relationship.* *(List 12-3)*

Oaklander, V. (1989). *Windows to our children.* Mansfield, OH: Gestalt Journal Press (1-800-247-6553).

Schaefer, C. E. & Cangelosi, D. M. (Eds.). (1993). *Play therapy techniques.* Northvale, NJ: Jason Aronson.

Thompson, C. L. & Rudolph, L. B. (1996). Play therapy (Chapter 12). *Counseling children* (4th ed.). *(List 12-3)*

LEADER OF SMALL GROUPS
2-25   VALUE OF COUNSELING GROUPS IN SCHOOLS

General Information About Group Counseling

➤ Natural setting for working with students

➤ Societal influences increase need for group counseling:
  – Increase in use of technology with little human contact
  – Absence of an extended family
  – Transient lifestyles
  – Decreased family stability
  – Natural/human need to discuss concerns and decisions
  – Economical concerns and lack of job security

Advantages of Group Counseling

➤ Counseling groups encourage members to:
  – Make commitments to improve behavior.
  – Achieve specific personal goals.
  – Take appropriate risks.
  – Accept responsibility for their growth and the growth of others.

➤ Group counseling is a safe atmosphere for students to:
  – Discuss their concerns.
  – Define goals.
  – Practice new appropriate behaviors.

Group Members Help Each Other

➤ Give their perceptions.

➤ Reveal similar problems.

➤ Suggest alternatives.

➤ Support each other in times of despair.

➤ Reflect what others say in relation to what they see them do.

➤ Confront inconsistencies.

➤ Learn to substitute appropriate behaviors for previous inappropriate behaviors.

➤ Learn how to relate more easily by interacting and receiving feedback.

➤ Share and interchange roles of helper and helpee.

➤ Verbalize concerns in a caring atmosphere.

➤ Set reasonable goals and learn to achieve positive behaviors.

Student Concerns Discussed in Group Counseling

➤ Entering a new school

➤ Experiencing divorce or remarriage of parents

➤ Returning from alcohol or other drug treatment program

➤ Needing study skills

➤ Having trouble making friends

➤ Having difficulty behaving in school

➤ Managing anger

➤ Considering, but fearing, gang activity

Factors That Help Counseling Group Participants

➤ Acceptance—by members and leader(s)

➤ Universality—not the only one with the problem

➤ Self-disclosure—trust leader and members, so reveal self honestly

➤ Insight—self-understanding

➤ Learning from interpersonal actions—learning from other members

➤ Catharsis—emotional release and feeling of relief afterwards

➤ Guidance—receiving and providing information and suggestions for improvement

➤ Vicarious learning—learning from observing and listening when others work

➤ Altruism— feeling of worthiness when helping others

➤ Hope—hope to improve because taking positive action

ADDITIONAL INFORMATION

See **List 13-19**, *The School Counselor and Group Counseling*.

Yalom, I. D. (1985). *The theory and practice of group psychotherapy* (3rd ed.). New York, NY: Basic Books.

2-26   PREPARATION BEFORE THE FIRST GROUP SESSION

Preparation for the First Session of Each Counseling Group

1. Meet with co-leader to determine logistics:
   - Number of members
   - Duration
   - Frequency
   - Location
   - Length of session
   - Other details

2. Get administrative support.

3. Publicize the groups to be offered.

4. Screen potential members individually, if possible:
   - Define group counseling.
   - Define member's role.
   - Indicate duration and frequency of meetings.
   - Determine reason student desires to be a member.
   - Discuss kinds of goals a group member may have.
   - Identify student's goal and help specify.
   - Discuss how group could help with meeting the goal.
   - Assess interest and ability student has to help others.
   - Determine other group experience student has had.
   - Determine counseling experience student has had.
   - Discuss confidentiality and recording, if this will be done.
   - Explain how video or audio tape will be used and erased.
   - Determine intensity of interest and desire for growth.
   - Obtain commitment to attend regularly and on time, if selected.
   - Obtain written parent/guardian permission, if required or advised.
   - Determine relationships with other members.

5. Select members:
   - Have voluntary members when possible.
   - Include at least one model when possible.
   - Formulate heterogeneous groups when possible.

6. Inform members of selection and give necessary forms and schedule.

7. Inform members and their teachers that leader will take attendance, and notify teachers of attendance.

8. Offer some alternative to candidates not selected.

9. Plan first session, "Get Acquainted and Ground Rules Session":
   - Purpose
   - Responsibility
   - Limits
   - Confidentiality

© 1998 by John Wiley & Sons, Inc.

10. Suggest ground rules:
    - ➤ Attend regularly, unless you have a test in class.
    - ➤ Be on time.
    - ➤ Be honest.
    - ➤ Listen to every member. Share your thoughts. Give helpful information, when appropriate.
    - ➤ Avoid put-downs.
    - ➤ Take turns talking.
    - ➤ Finish class assignments ahead of time and give them to the teacher before missing class for group.
    - ➤ Do not repeat or refer to anything said by another group member:
        - – Do not reveal who else is in the group.
        - – May repeat your goal and how you are working on it outside of group.
        - – May repeat what *you* said in the group.
    - ➤ Actively work to achieve the goal of the group and your individual goals.

ADDITIONAL INFORMATION

ASGW. *Ethical guidelines for group counselors (**List 12-13**).* [On-line] Available:
    http://www.uc.edu/~wilson/asgw/index.html

2-27   GROUP COUNSELING LEADERSHIP

Guidelines to Implement a Group Counseling Program

1. Assess needs:
    - ➤ Consider problems or concerns frequently mentioned by students.
    - ➤ Prepare a flyer and a newsletter article:
        - – List theme-centered groups that could be offered next quarter.
        - – Request student or parent/guardian to check counseling groups desired.
2. Discuss plan for group counseling with administrator.
3. Plan group meetings when most members do not have academic classes.
4. Inform members and teachers about group counseling:
    - ➤ Members can miss group when they have a test in class that they would miss.
    - ➤ Members have responsibility to hand in homework before missing class for group.
5. Include only volunteer members.
6. Include students of similar ages but heterogeneous in other ways.
7. Include one or two students as models in difficult groups:
    - ➤ Have experienced the problem.
    - ➤ Have made good choices and are doing better.
    - ➤ Can benefit from participation in group.
8. Plan groups for the quarter or semester schedule.

9. Design a plan for each group based upon the need:
   ➤ Determine and state specific goals that members will achieve in each group.
   ➤ Plan procedures to logically achieve the stated goals.
   ➤ Evaluate the achievement of the goals and procedures.
   ➤ Revise the design for a group next quarter.

Group Leadership Skills

➤ Plan each group session:
   - Set specific and stated goals.
   - Give precedence to members' expression of immediate problems or concerns.
   - Give precedence to members helping each other.

➤ Balance every group session addressing both maintenance and task functions:
   - Maintenance includes *how* the members are working together and helping each other.
   - Task is progress toward achievement of the group goal or purpose.

➤ Reinforce when the group members are helping each other.

➤ Teach good group membership skills.

➤ Help members transfer their learning to other areas of their lives.

➤ Use counseling skills:
   - Active listening
   - Reflection
   - Clarification
   - Summarization
   - Information giving
   - Encouragement
   - Use of open-ended questions
   - Use of voice
   - Empathy
   - Enthusiasm
   - Interpretation
   - Clear idea of how behavior change occurs
   - Clear idea about how to encourage positive behavior change in students

➤ Use leadership skills:
   - Tone setting
   - Use of eyes
   - Timing
   - Linking
   - Making content specific
   - Using first person or "I Statements"
   - Giving appropriate feedback
   - Making process statements
   - Blocking when necessary
   - Confronting sensitively
   - Teaching group membership skills

➤ Use goal-setting skills. *(List 3-2)*

ADDITIONAL INFORMATION

See *Lists 7-11, 8-11, 12-17, Materials for Group Counseling.*

Blum, D. J. (1990). *Group counseling for secondary schools. (List 12-17)*

Blum, D. J. (1994). A practical group counseling model. In D. G. Burgess & R. M. Dedmond (eds.), *Quality leadership and the professional school counselor* (Chapter 6, pp. 117–141). Alexandria, VA: American Counseling Association.

Corey, M. S. & Corey, G. (1997). *Groups process and practice* (5th ed.). *(List 12-17)*

Gladding, S. T. (1994, April). *Effective group counseling.* ED366856. ERIC Digest: Office of Educational Research and Improvement (OERI). [On-line] Available: http://www2.uncg.edu/~ericcas2/supervisory/dig02.html

Trotzer, J. P. (1989). *The counselor and the group: Integrating theory, training and practice. (List 12-17)*

2-28   EVALUATION OF A COUNSELING GROUP

Preparation of Group Members for Group Evaluations

➤ Inform students at the beginning of the group:
  – Limits of confidentiality
  – Need and method for evaluation of their progress toward achievement of goal

➤ Ask for group members' permission before consulting with teachers.

Pre- and Post-Objective Written Evaluations

➤ Grades

➤ Attendance

➤ Standardized test scores

Pre- and Post-Subjective Written Evaluations

➤ Teachers' written comments

➤ Students' ranking of achievement of goals on a Likert scale

➤ Parents'/guardians' written comments

Midway Evaluations

➤ Collect written information about process and progress of group.

➤ Unfinished sentences provide information to improve the group.

End-of-the-Group Evaluations

➤ Collect objective and anonymous information that can be tabulated and included in a written report.

➤ Collect outcome data.

Follow-Up Evaluations

See *List 2-6, Accountability and Performance Evaluation of the School Counselor.*

ADDITIONAL INFORMATION

ASGW. *Ethical guidelines for group counselors. (List 12-13)*

PRESENTER OF GUIDANCE LESSONS
2-29   GUIDANCE LESSONS OVERVIEW

Purpose of Guidance Lessons

➤ Meet students and have them know the school counselor.

➤ Teach students skills for success in school.

➤ Teach students how to prevent problems that occur at specific developmental level.

➤ Prevent or react to problems before they become acute.

➤ Teach students preparation for success at next grade, school, or developmental level.

➤ Describe counseling and guidance program.

Counselor's Skills in Presenting Guidance Lessons

➤ Teaching skills

➤ Scheduling skills

➤ Preparation of teaching plans

➤ Classroom control methods

➤ Skills for leading task groups

➤ Cooperative education

➤ Team-teaching skills

Counselor's Consideration of Others

➤ Knowledge of expectations and needs of teachers

➤ Consideration of teachers' time, schedules, requirements, and stress

➤ Preparation of a monthly calendar:
  – Schedule classroom guidance first
  – Schedule counseling groups second
  – Schedule individual counseling third

➤ Daily or weekly schedule posted on door

➤ Notification to parents and teachers of lessons, grade levels, and dates of guidance lessons

Well-Designed Guidance Units

➤ Clearly defined purpose or goal

➤ Age-appropriate activities (Lists of materials, Sections 6 through 9)

➤ Coordinated and sequential lessons

➤ Time for students to apply, reflect, and evaluate their learning

➤ Summary and evaluation of the unit

Guidance Lessons

➤ Address needs of students in the group.

➤ Designed to teach skills efficiently:

- Completion of college applications
- College-application essay
- College search process
- College selection process
- Interviewing skills
- Résumé writing
- Course selection for college preparation
- High school success
- Study skills, including note-taking and organization
- Test preparation
- Avoiding peer pressure
- Making wise decisions
- Choosing friends
- Being a good friend
- Overcoming fear of new situations, including a new school
- Preparing for middle school
- Dealing with a bully
- Getting attention in appropriate ways
- Communication skills, including listening
- Following directions of teachers and parents
- Following rules

ADDITIONAL INFORMATION

See Sections 6 through 12 for materials to use in guidance lessons.

Cuthbert, M. I. (1993). Large group developmental guidance (pp. 83–89). In J. Wittmer (Ed.), *Managing your school counseling program. (List 12-3)*

Gysbers, N. C. & Henderson, P. (1994). *Developing and managing your school guidance program* (2nd ed.). *(List 12-3)*

Hitchner, K. W. & Tifft-Hitchner, A. (1996). *Counseling today's secondary student.* **(List 12-3)**

Schmidt, J. J. (1991). *A survival guide for the elementary/middle school counselor.* **(List 12-3)**

2-30 CLASS MEETINGS

General Information About Class Meetings

They can be led by teachers after receiving training and observing the counselor leading a class meeting.

Advantages of Class Meetings

➤ Promote positive discipline in the classroom.

➤ Promote listening skills.

➤ Encourage students to give and receive compliments.

➤ Teach students to recognize and apply logical consequences.

➤ Provide opportunity for students to solve problems by brainstorming solutions.

Procedure for Leading Class Meetings

1. Form a circle.
2. Give compliments.
3. Review previous agenda or lesson.
4. Evaluate application of logical consequences for problems on the agenda last time.
5. Introduce agenda for this meeting.
6. Solve problem by brainstorming options or solutions.
7. Review logical consequences.
8. Provide chance for input by student who will be assigned a consequence.
9. Vote on one logical consequence for each problem behavior.
10. Schedule the logical consequence.

Agenda for Class Meetings

Agenda box or book contains a list of concerns or problems written by students when they occur throughout the week. These problems are the agenda for the next class meeting.

ADDITIONAL INFORMATION

Alexander, S. J. (1988). *Class meeting manual.* Los Angeles, CA: The California State University.

Cooper, J. (1989). *Class meetings—family meetings: creative consultant series. (List 10-3)*

Meder, F. J. (1992). Why class meetings? *Individual Psychology, 38 (2).* Austin, TX: University of Texas Press.

Nelsen, J., Lott, L., & Glenn, S. (1993). *Positive discipline in the classroom: How to effectively use class meetings and other positive discipline strategies. (List 11-13)*

Video: Meder, F. J. & Platt, J. (1992). *Class meetings.* A video program showing a class involved in a class meeting. Roseville, CA: Dynamic Training and Seminars, Inc.

2-31   CONSEQUENCES

Natural and Logical Consequences

➤ Natural consequences happen without anyone intervening.

➤ Logical consequences are planned and logical results of behavior:
  – Alternative to arbitrary punishment
  – Discussed with student before and after the misbehavior
  – Understood and accepted by the student as a logical result of his or her decision to misbehave

Four R's of Logical Consequences

1. *Related to the issue or event:* If a student hits another student, he or she is temporarily prevented from being with others.

2. *Reasonable but not too harsh:* Long enough for the student to learn his or her lesson, but not so long that the student resents the harshness of the consequence.

3. *Respectful of the student's dignity and self-worth:* Not humiliating; gives the guilty student a voice in determining the consequence and when it may be concluded.

4. *Responsible:* Demonstrates responsibility to all concerned and is possible to fulfill, given the circumstances.

Guidelines for Logical Consequences

➤ Do not use when there is a danger to person or property:
  – Immediate action or arbitration by authority is necessary.
  – Consequences take time.

➤ Do not use when in a power struggle.

➤ Expect performance and behavior appropriate for the developmental stage of student.

➤ Take time and thought to initiate the logical consequence of misbehavior.

➤ Express mild regret that student chose the action that results in the logical consequence.

➤ Discuss consequence and administer it calmly.

➤ Control tone of voice when administering consequence—firm but friendly.

➤ Help student maintain respect and dignity.

➤ Help student see relationship between his or her action and the resulting consequence.

➤ Give student an opportunity to make a better choice next time.

➤ Apply logical consequences consistently.

Pitfalls When Administering Logical Consequences

➤ Expect standards of behavior from student beyond the developmental level.

➤ Give student a second chance before he or she experiences the agreed upon consequence.

➤ Feel sorry for student and give in to his or her demands.

➤ Fear that the agreed upon consequence is too easy.

➤ Give consequences for more than one behavior at the same time.

➤ Be inconsistent or unable to follow through.

➤ Give way to expediency.

➤ Make consequences punitive or a show of superiority.

➤ Be impatient, ridicule, humiliate, shame, retaliate.

➤ Feel guilty or make the student feel guilty.

➤ Talk too much while specifying or administering consequence.

➤ Rub it in by saying, "I told you so."

➤ Demand immediate action.

ADDITIONAL INFORMATION

Alexander, S. J. (1988). *Class meeting manual.* Los Angeles, CA: The California State University.

2-32   PEER-FACILITATION PROGRAMS

Peer-facilitation programs should have a clear description of the particular type of program being offered, and the criteria for membership.

Some Examples of Peer-Facilitation Programs

➤ Tutoring children at lower grade levels

➤ Tutoring students in special education classes

➤ Informing and orienting students new to the school

➤ Providing information and modeling acceptable behavior for younger students

➤ Providing support when another student experiences frustrations, worries, or developmental concerns

➤ Providing assistance in recognizing and accepting responsibility

➤ Providing help and modeling acceptable academic and social skills

➤ Listening, and then providing empathy, understanding, and practical support to resolve various dilemmas

➤ Mediating conflicts between other students

➤ Educating other students about the dangers of tobacco, alcohol, and other drugs

➤ Educating others about the dangers of gangs and street violence

➤ Determining the need for referrals to professionals

➤ Referring students who need professional help to the school counselor

Application Process

➤ Recommendation forms from three teachers

➤ Application forms

➤ Self-evaluations including the reason the student believes he or she would be a good peer facilitator

➤ Parental or guardian letter with signature indicating approval

➤ Interview by at least three current peer facilitators

Selection Process

➤ Facilitators must be respected and trusted by their peers to have credibility.

➤ Be sure diversity of the student body is represented, not just students who do well academically, or who are a part of the majority culture.

➤ Tutors must excel in respective subject, and the teacher must confirm their cognitive skills in that subject.

Benefits to Peer Facilitators

➤ Develop leadership capabilities.

➤ Enhance self-esteem and personal growth.

➤ Develop altruism when helping others.

➤ Develop personal responsibility.

➤ Generate pride in the success of each member of the team.

➤ Improve communication skills.

➤ Increase mutual trust and cooperation.

➤ Promote positive peer influence.

➤ Develop self-confidence of peer facilitators as well as students assigned to peer facilitators.

➤ Develop good work habits of peer facilitators as well as students assigned to helpers.

Training of Peer Facilitators

➤ Specific, comprehensive, and thorough training

➤ Opportunity to practice skills

➤ Skills in communication, decision-making, problem-solving, conflict resolution, and leadership

➤ Ongoing regular training during the school year to assist peer facilitators:
  – Deal with the concerns of students.
  – Continue to learn, practice, and hone helping skills.
  – Make decisions about referrals to professional counselors.

Guidelines to Avoid Potential Problems

➤ Set time limits:
  – Activity period, homeroom period, or lunch time
  – Office assistant one period a day
  – Usually 2–3 hours per week in addition to training meetings

➤ Plan how to deal with peer facilitators and referred students who lose interest.

➤ Define the reason for possible dismissal from the program:
 – Student no longer shows commitment, time, or energy to devote to the program.
 – Helpee becomes dependent and does not work to improve.

➤ Specify referral procedure:
 – Helpees may refer themselves.
 – Teachers or parents/guardians may refer students to work with peer facilitators.

➤ Specify maximum number of helpees per peer facilitator:
 – One or two students at one time
 – One or two small groups

➤ Plan supervision by a teacher or counselor.

➤ Clarify coordination of the program:
 – Responsible for making certain that peer facilitators have parent/guardian permission
 – Responsible that helpees are not infringing upon their peer facilitator's time
 – Clarify if written permission of teachers, parents/guardians is required
 – Plan how to assure teachers and others that the time students spend together is used judiciously to help student, and not spent simply socializing

➤ Plan evaluation of the program to include specific data:
 – Pre- and post-grade point averages
 – School and class attendance and promptness
 – Disciplinary actions
 – Evaluations from teachers
 – Standardized test scores
 – Evaluations from parents/guardians
 – Self-reports about attitudes toward school

ADDITIONAL INFORMATION

See *List 13-22, The School Counselor and Peer Facilitation.*

Campbell, C. (1993). K–12 peer helper programs. In J. Wittmer (Ed.), *Managing your school counseling program: K–12 developmental strategies. (List 12-3).* This chapter includes a rationale for a peer-facilitator program, suggestions as to how to get started, peer-facilitator projects, cautions, and evaluation of the program. In addition there are forms for peer-facilitator applications, teacher recommendations, and parent notification.

Carr, R. *Peer helping.* http://www.islandnet.com/~rcarr/helping.html.

Perlstein, R. & Thrall, G. (1996). *Ready-to-use conflict resolution activities for secondary students. (List 12-4)*

Tindall, J. & Salmon-White, S. (1990). *Peers helping peers: Program for the preadolescent. (List 8-11)*

Tindall, J. (1995). *Peer programs: An in-depth look at peer helping: Planning, implementation and administration. (List 12-25)*

CONSULTANT TO PARENTS/GUARDIANS
2-33   CONSULTATION WITH GROUPS OF PARENTS/GUARDIANS

Effective Groups for Parents
➤ Comprehensive effort to reach out to all parents/guardians of students in the school
➤ Well-planned, with goals, objectives, tasks, and timelines
➤ Special effort to reach parents of "at-risk" students *(Lists 3-14 through 3-26)*
➤ Options through adult education courses
➤ Commitment to long-term efforts

Preparation for Large Groups
➤ Know the community.
➤ Know needs of families.
➤ Create partnerships with parents.
➤ Recognize parental barriers to school involvement:
  – Do not know how to become involved with the school
  – Fearful of going to the school because of past experiences
  – Have insufficient time because need to hold several jobs
  – Career commitments

Topics for Large Groups to Disseminate Information
➤ Transition from elementary to middle and from middle to high school
➤ Orientation to the school
➤ Information about the college search, application and selection process
➤ Information about financial aid for college
➤ Information about the counseling and guidance program of the school
➤ Other information

Topics for Small Groups to Interchange Ideas or Discussion
➤ Child-rearing concerns, setting limits, positive discipline, consistency
➤ Developmental stages of childhood, needs, skills, and expectations *(List 2-34)*
➤ Networking and organizing parent/guardian support groups
➤ Support and information for parents/guardians
➤ Empowerment of parents in their child-rearing roles
➤ Parent/guardian expectations and desires for the school
➤ Communication between the school and home
➤ The "defiant child"
➤ Stepparenting concerns

Some Parent Workshops

*Active Parenting (**List 10-4**)*

*How to Talk So Kids Will Listen and Listen So Kids Will Talk (**List 10-3**)*

*Parents on Board: Building Academic Success Through Parent Involvement (**List 10-26**)*

*Siblings Without Rivalry (**List 10-12**)*

*Strengthening Stepfamilies (**List 10-12**)*

*STEP Program (**List 10-4**)*

ADDITIONAL INFORMATION

See lists in Section 10 for Materials to Use With Parents.

See **List 13-16**, *The School Counselor and Family/Parenting Education.*

See *Reaching All Families: Creating Family-Friendly Schools.* [On-line] Available:
http://www.ed.gov/pubs/ReachFam/index.html

Falk, E. (1993). *Leading parent groups I, II, and III. (**List 10-4**)*

Johnson, C. D. & Johnson, S. (1995, April). *Families-And-Schools-Together (F-A-S-T).* Paper presented at the meeting of the American Counseling Association, Denver, CO. Information available from: Johnson & Johnson, 12 Toscany, Irvine, CA 92714; (714) 263-8965.

2-34 DEVELOPMENTAL STAGES OF CHILDHOOD AND ADOLESCENCE

Erikson's developmental tasks (1968) are a frame of reference to use when considering expectations, needs, and tasks during childhood and adolescence. Although the age for a student to complete specific developmental tasks is not absolute, most children will be able to complete most of the developmental tasks during the range of ages indicated.

Erikson's and Havighurst's Developmental Tasks
(ERIKSON 1963, 1968) AND (HAVIGHURST 1961). IN THOMPSON & Rudolph (1996).

Stages	Developmental Tasks
➤ Birth to Age 1-1/2 years	Basic Trust *versus* Basic Mistrust
➤ Ages 1-1/2 to 3 years	Autonomy *versus* Shame and Doubt
➤ Ages 3 to 5	Initiative *versus* Guilt
➤ Ages 6 to 11	Industry *versus* Inferiority
➤ Ages 12 to 18	Identity *versus* Role Confusion
➤ Adulthood	

Stages	Needs
➤ Birth to Age 1-1/2 years	Parents or caregivers who are affectionate, consistent, predictable, and help children trust and bond with family and friends
➤ Ages 1-1/2 to 3 years	Experiences in caring for themselves, e.g., feeding, toilet behaviors, dressing; parents who give children choices within limitations

➤ 3 to 5 years	Experiences in setting goals, carrying out projects, taking leadership; parents who let children participate in family work activities and projects; teachers and counselors who give children projects they can complete to gain a sense of achievement; parents, teachers, and counselors who correct children with logical consequences, love and care, as they teach them the correct way; sibling rivalry is frequent and children may feel guilty about contemplated aggressive goals
➤ 6 to 11 years	Experiences in building, creating, and accomplishing to gain a feeling of adequacy; encouragement and deserved praise to achieve competence; academic, physical, social, and work skills for healthy self-esteem; parents, teachers, and counselors who are nurturing to help children discover and develop special talents and abilities
➤ 12 to 18 years	Experiences in developing ego identity, including moral, social, and vocational identity; parents, teachers, and counselors who appreciate the adolescent as a unique and worthwhile individual; parents, teachers, and counselors who understand role confusion, and recognize the adolescent's learning style and adapt their interventions to his or her style: cognitive, affective, behavioral, physical, or eclectic

Basic Tasks for Children Ages 3–6

➤ Develop a sense of purpose and goal-directedness

➤ Need explicit examples, visual aids, and very clear directions

➤ Need adults who sit when they give directions, so they are eye-to-eye

➤ May need to repeat directions that they heard to understand them

Basic Tasks for Children Ages 6–12

➤ Become competent and see themselves as competent in achieving academic, physical, social, and work skills

➤ Need nurturance and help to discover and develop their special talents and abilities

Basic Tasks for Adolescents

See *List 2-35, Stress During Adolescence.*

ADDITIONAL INFORMATION

Erikson, E. (1968). *Identity, youth and crisis.* New York, NY: Norton.

Johnson, C. D. & Johnson, S. (1995, April). *Families-And-Schools-Together (F-A-S-T).* Paper presented at the meeting of the American Counseling Association, Denver, CO. Information available from: Johnson & Johnson, 12 Toscany, Irvine, CA 92714; (714) 263-8965.

Mussen, P., Conger, J., Kagan, J. & Huston, A. (1990). *Child development and personality* (7th ed.). New York, NY: HarperCollins.

Thompson, C. L. & Rudolph, L. B. (1996). Introduction to a child's world (Chapter 1). In *Counseling children* (4th ed.). *(List 12-3)*

2-35 STRESS DURING ADOLESCENCE

Basic Developmental Tasks for Adolescents—Second Most Critical Stage in Life

➤ Overcome confusion and frustration of dramatic physical changes.

➤ Develop personal identity:
  – Physical identity
  – Intellectual identity
  – Moral identity
  – Social identity
  – Career identity

➤ Develop a positive self-image.

➤ Recognize and identify things they do well.

➤ Learn about themselves by participating in group activities.

➤ Gain self-confidence and self-esteem.

➤ Develop the capacity for future orientation, think abstractly, and plan for the future:
  – Make educational decisions.
  – Make career decisions.
  – Make relationship decisions.

➤ Become emotionally independent of their parents.

➤ Continue to learn about self.

Some Adolescents at Risk—Not Likely to Receive Psychiatric Help When Needed

➤ Girls frequently experience greater drop of self-esteem in adolescence than boys.

➤ Some minority teenagers may experience difficulty when they must negotiate in two different cultures.

Characteristics Linked to Resilience of Adolescents

➤ Ability to absorb stress

➤ Resistance to antisocial peer pressure

➤ Ability to rebound from adversity

➤ Secure relationship with a caring, competent adult who rewards socially acceptable behavior

➤ Sense of belonging to a school

➤ Low levels of family stress as measured by the absence of poverty, unemployment, or domestic violence

➤ Willingness to seek help

Environmental Factors That Promote Resilience

➤ Reliable and stable care

➤ Problem-solving abilities

➤ Attractiveness to peers and adults

➤ Manifest competence and perceived efficacy

➤ Identification with at least one competent adult role model

➤ Goal-directed with aspirations

ADDITIONAL INFORMATION

Benard, B. (1995). Fostering resilience in children. ERIC Digest, August 1995. ericeece@uiuc.edu or 1-800-583-4135 http://ericps.ed.uiuc.edu/eece/pubs/digests/1995/benard95.html

Boodman, S. G. (1995, Monday, December 11). Stressed for success. *Washington Post.*

Haggerty, R. J., Sherrod, L. R., Gormezy, N. & Rutter, M. (1994). *Stress, risk, and resilience in children and adolescents.* New York, NY: Cambridge University.

Wang, M. C. (1996). Fostering resilience among children at risk of educational failure. [On-line] Available: http://ericae2.educ.cua.edu/db/riecije/ed401368.html

2-36 CONSULTATION WITH INDIVIDUAL PARENT/GUARDIAN

Consultation in this book refers to the collaboration between the counselor and the parent/guardian or group of parents. The purpose of consultation usually is to identify and apply methods to assist students to behave more effectively at home or at school. The tasks of the counselor-consultant are similar to the tasks listed in *List 2-23, Problem-Solving Model.*

Model of Consultation

➤ Collaborative relationship

➤ Involves parent/guardian training and development

➤ Reaches more students by teaching adults to respond or intervene in helpful ways to improve students' behavior at home or school

➤ Considers each student's unique needs:
  – Gather information about the problem.
  – Set goal of consultation.
  – Select responses or interventions.

Tasks of the Counselor-Consultant

1. Identify specific problem behavior of the student from the perspective of the parent/guardian.

2. Identify the goal of the consultation with the parent/guardian.

3. Identify the probable goal(s) of the child's misbehavior (attention, power, revenge, or withdrawal).

4. List everything parent/guardian has tried to achieve the goal.

5. Encourage parent/guardian to discontinue unsuccessful responses, or interventions.

6. Collect other information about the problem.

7. Encourage parent/guardian to teach student specifically what behaviors are acceptable and what behaviors are unacceptable using several learning styles: (1) visual, (2) auditory, and (3) kinesthetic.

8. Brainstorm responses, interventions, or procedures to be tried by parent/guardian to achieve the specified goal of consultation:

   ➢ Help student recognize logical consequences of behavior. *(List 2-31)*
   ➢ Focus on positive attributes and behavior of the student, and note the frequency of these behaviors.
   ➢ Use "I Messages" to express parent's/guardian's feelings about child's misbehavior and its effect on parent/guardian. *(List 5-29)*
   ➢ List and count the student's behaviors that irritate or frustrate the parent/guardian.
   ➢ Respond in an unexpected way to the student's behavior.
   ➢ Remove student from the group—without nagging, lecturing, or scolding—when his or her behavior is socially unacceptable (*logical consequence*).
   ➢ Remove self from situation when no physical harm or property damage is likely to occur.

9. Evaluate consultation by collecting concrete information from parent/guardian:

   ➢ Counselor's expertise:
      – Presenting content
      – Explaining procedure
      – Brainstorming alternative responses or interventions
   ➢ Counselor's skills:
      – Using time productively
      – Providing useful feedback
      – Assigning practical and useful work
   ➢ Counselor's interpersonal skill
   ➢ Extent to which goal was achieved
   ➢ Overall evaluation of the consultation

ADDITIONAL INFORMATION

See *List 2-31, Consequences.*

Johnson, C. D. & Johnson, S. (1995, April). *Families-And-Schools-Together (F-A-S-T).* Paper presented at the meeting of the American Counseling Association, Denver, CO. Information available from: Johnson & Johnson, 12 Toscany, Irvine, CA 92714; (714) 263-8965.

Kottman, T. & Wilborn, B. (1992). Parents helping parents: Multiplying the counselor's effectiveness. *School Counselor, 40,* 10–14.

Schmidt, J. J. (1991). *A survival guide for the elementary/middle school counselor. (List 12-3)*

Thompson, C. L. & Rudolph, L. B. (1996). *Counseling children* (4th ed.). *(List 12-3)*

2-37 INVOLVEMENT OF HARD-TO-REACH PARENTS/GUARDIANS

Possible Reasons

➤ Trust teachers to educate their children

➤ Ill-at-ease in a school

➤ Did not complete high school

➤ Bad experiences when attending school

➤ Fear they will embarrass their children

➤ Feel put down by school personnel

Suggestions to Enlist the Support of Hard-to-Reach Parents

➤ Meet individually, not in groups.

➤ Meet in a place other than the school.

➤ Enlist services of a parent liaison, minister, interpreter, neighbor, or another adult whom the parent trusts.

➤ Ask another parent of the same culture to notify parent of meeting.

➤ Do not ask a student to interpret for the parent.

➤ Present information in both a visual and auditory manner.

ADDITIONAL INFORMATION

Johnson, C. D. & Johnson, S. (1995, April). *Families-And-Schools-Together (F-A-S-T).* Paper presented at the meeting of the American Counseling Association, Denver, CO. Information available from: Johnson & Johnson, 12 Toscany, Irvine, CA 92714; (714) 263-8965.

Morrow, G. (1987). *Compassionate school: A practical guide to educating abused and traumatized children. (List 12-3)*

CONSULTANT TO TEACHERS

2-38 STAFF DEVELOPMENT OR TEACHER INSERVICES

Large Staff Meetings

➤ Presentation of information; examples:

- Classroom management strategies *(List 2-40)*
- Using standardized test results for instruction *(List 3-4)*
- Energizers for the classroom *(List 12-17)*
- Strategies for resistant learners *(Lists 3-14 through 3-28)*
- Conflict-resolution strategies *(Lists 6-3, 7-3, 8-3, 9-4)*
- Parent conference skills *(List 2-43)*
- Time management *(List 3-5)*
- Writing college recommendations *(List 3-10)*

Small Staff Meetings

➤ Collegial sharing of information by specific staff:

- Child study team or student assistance team
- Local screening committee for special services
- Grade-level team
- Department of study

➤ Collegial sharing of information with voluntary staff members:

- Case studies and successful techniques with certain students
- Teachers' expectations of students
- Students' organizational skills, study skills, and readiness to learn
- Homework assignments and test schedules
- Time management

Support Groups

➤ Opportunity to deal with teachers' professional and/or personal problems and concerns
➤ Led by a teacher who is well respected or by the school counselor
➤ Administrators attend only upon invitation

Successful Staff Development

➤ Seminars according to specific needs:

- Grade-level teams that work with the same students
- Departments that have similar objectives

➤ Voluntary attendance
➤ Scheduled at teachers' time preference
➤ Relevant topic
➤ Short
➤ Well-planned

➤ Active participation

➤ Collaborative problem solving

➤ Interpersonal communication:
  – Expectations, methods, and successes
  – Student-oriented discussions

➤ Expertise of teacher with credibility

➤ Confidentiality of support groups:
  – Safe place to express and listen to fears, stresses, anger, or despair
  – Free from administrative interruption or curiosity
  – Help teachers deal appropriately with their own concerns so they can devote their time and attention during the school day to students and students' concerns

➤ Opportunity to exercise, relax, or have fun together to vent frustration

➤ Opportunity for teachers to evaluate seminar or workshop anonymously

Positive Relationship With Staff

➤ Pass along positive comments.

➤ Act on teacher referrals promptly.

➤ Follow up teacher referrals of students with general statements.

ADDITIONAL INFORMATION

See *List 2-34, Developmental Stages of Childhood and Adolescence.*

See *List 3-15, Consulting With Teachers of Students With Academic Problems.*

See *List 3-20, Consulting With Teachers of Students With Learning or Physical Problems.*

See *List 3-27, Helping Students Learn From Failure.*

See *List 3-28, Helping Students Overcome Success-Inhibiting Factors.*

Borba, M. (1990). *Esteem builders for staff.* Rolling Hills Estates, CA: Jalmar Press.

Schultz, J. J. (1991). *A survival guide for the elementary/middle school counselor. (List 12-3).* This book has a teacher inservice survey form and a workshop evaluation form that can be adapted.

2-39 TEACHER-INITIATED INDIVIDUAL CONSULTATION

Student's Inappropriate Behavior

- ➤ Examples of student misbehavior:
  - – Cheating
  - – Temper tantrums
  - – Bullying
  - – Verbal abusiveness
  - – Swearing
  - – Lying
  - – Teasing
  - – Sexual harassment
  - – Stealing
- ➤ Problem-solving with the teacher:
  - – Goal of the student's misbehavior
  - – Procedures to try based upon the goal
  - – Behavioral contract for student
  - – Natural and logical consequences
- ➤ Provision of time for the teacher to try selected procedures
- ➤ Report of results after using selected procedures

Personal Problems

- ➤ Types of problems:
  - – With colleagues
  - – With administrator
  - – With spouse
  - – With own children
  - – Physical or emotional
  - – With finances
- ➤ Problem solving:
  - – Provide a chance to vent.
  - – Listen with empathy.
  - – Choose time to brainstorm.
  - – List alternatives.
  - – List probable consequences of each alternative.
- ➤ Time for teacher to make decision:
  - – Support decision.
  - – Encourage action.
  - – Encourage evaluation of decision.
- ➤ Follow up

2-40 CLASSROOM MANAGEMENT OR DISCIPLINE SKILLS

Prevention by the Teacher

- ➤ Prepare room to be student-centered, warm, and welcome.
- ➤ Manage routine clerical tasks to not take class time.
- ➤ Make lessons relevant and meaningful.
- ➤ Keep students involved and participating actively in their learning.
- ➤ Be familiar with the school's guidelines for student behavior.
- ➤ Present and clarify, at the beginning of each school term, the guidelines for behavior in the classroom.
- ➤ Ensure that the guidelines do not discriminate against individuals.
- ➤ Enforce consistently the guidelines for behavior.
- ➤ Establish positive relationships with students.
- ➤ Be aware of individual student needs and learning styles.
- ➤ Anticipate individual student's actions and reactions.
- ➤ Consider the needs of the entire class.
- ➤ Develop reinforcement procedures to recognize appropriate behavior.
- ➤ Communicate and use a procedure to warn students about approaching misbehavior.

Intervention by the Teacher

- ➤ Focus on the important issue.
- ➤ Don't be defensive with words or tone of voice.
- ➤ Know options and recognize the possible consequences of each option.
- ➤ Separate certain students.
- ➤ Remove one student from class for time-out, specifying where and who will supervise.
- ➤ Isolate student from rest of class and ask student to write about what happened and how he or she sees the problem.
- ➤ Recognize the need for the student to save face in class.
- ➤ Formulate a contract with specifics.
- ➤ Offer choices within clear limits, e.g., to change behavior or take time-out.
- ➤ Acknowledge anger and set a time and place without an audience to discuss the issue.
- ➤ Refer student to the counselor or administrator.
- ➤ Consult with the counselor.
- ➤ Call parents to inform and/or request a student–parent/guardian–teacher–counselor conference.

Prevention by the Counselor

- ➤ Help teachers, students, parents, and staff recognize and express appreciation for positive behavior.

➤ Encourage and work with administrators to ensure a positive environment for the entire school. *(List 2-45)*

➤ Remind staff of all students' desires:
  - To feel significant
  - To feel that their lives are important
  - To feel that they have some control over their lives
  - To feel capable
  - To feel connected with others
  - To feel that they are contributing to their school

➤ Help teachers look at their behavior and how it contributes to the way students behave.

Intervention by the Counselor

➤ Meet with student when referred by teacher.

➤ Assess situation, determine services needed, and consider options.

➤ Provide counseling or other services when needed.

Options for the Counselor

➤ Negotiate agreement with teacher and student about corrective action.

➤ Consider conference of teacher, parent, student, and counselor.

➤ Consider referral to appropriate administrator.

➤ Provide individual or group counseling.

➤ Consider other options.

Postvention by the Counselor

➤ Follow up with student and teacher separately.

➤ Evaluate procedure.

➤ Evaluate outcome.

Suggestions for Counselor and Teachers to Defuse Confrontations

➤ Focus on the behavior, not the person.

➤ Control own negative emotions.

➤ Avoid escalating the situation.

➤ Set a time to discuss misbehavior in private.

➤ Allow student to save face.

➤ Model nonaggressive behavior.

➤ Don't be led into a defensive position.

Private Discussions With Student

➤ Let student vent.

➤ Paraphrase the student's feelings.

➤ Clarify and reclarify the limits.

➤ Offer to work together to solve the problem.

➤ Explore solutions.

➤ Agree on a solution.

➤ Meet with counselor, as third party, if need other options/solutions.

➤ Evaluate the outcome.

ADDITIONAL INFORMATION

See *List 2-23*, *Problem-Solving Model.*

See *List 2-29*, *Guidance Lessons Overview.*

See *List 2-30*, *Class Meetings.*

See *List 2-31*, *Consequences.*

See *List 2-36*, *Consultation With Individual Parent/Guardian.*

See *List 2-41*, *Some Models of Discipline.*

See *List 2-46*, *A Positive Environment Throughout the School.*

2-41   SOME MODELS OF DISCIPLINE

➤ **Assertive Discipline:** Teacher training to encourage teachers to be proactive, anticipate certain problems, and be prepared to deal with them assertively. [Canter & Canter (1992). *Assertive discipline: Positive behavior management for today's classroom, New and revised;* Canter, L. (1993). *Succeeding with difficult students.* **List 11-7**, *Discipline.*]

➤ **Behavior Modification:** Analysis and control of the students' environment and its rewards. [Lundell, K. *Behavior contracting systems, Behavioral management in the classroom.* **List 11-7**, *Discipline.*]

➤ **Conflict Mediation:** Use the problem-solving model to resolve differences and find solutions to which all agree. [Kreidler, W. (1984). *Creative conflict resolution: More than 200 activities for keeping peace in the classroom.* **List 7-3**, *Conflict Mediation.* Perlstein & Thrall (1996). *Ready-to-use conflict resolution activities for secondary students.* See **List 12-4**, *Conflict Mediation.*]

➤ **Control Theory:** Acknowledge misbehavior and then confront the consequences and challenge the student to find a new and better way of behaving. [Glasser, W. (1977). Ten steps to good discipline. *Today's Education, 66,* 61–63.]

➤ **Cooperative Discipline:** Analysis of misbehavior and specific options to respond to change behavior and maintain student's self-esteem. [Albert, L. (1991). *A teacher's guide to cooperative discipline: How to manage your classroom and promote self-esteem.* **List 11-7**, *Discipline.*]

➤ **Invitational Education:** Invite students to use their best behavior and learn by including four elements: optimism, respect, trust, and intentionality. [Purkey, W. W. & Schmidt, J. J. (1996). *Invitational counseling: A self-concept approach to professional practice.* **List 12-3**, *Comprehensive Practice.*]

➤ **Logical Consequences:** Creative thinking by teacher and/or students to structure the consequence for the student to be logically connected to the misbehavior. [**List 2-31**, *Consequences.*]

➤ **Personal Influence:** Strong mutual relations and respect between teacher and student so the student respects what the teacher thinks and feels so the student does not misbehave, or feels reasonable remorse and resolves to not repeat mistake. [See Invitational Education above.]

➤ **Self-Awareness Training:** Teaching students how to recognize when they are angry, afraid, frustrated, or experiencing other feelings that lead to misbehavior. Then teach how to control their negative feelings and respond appropriately. [*Lists 6-8, 7-8, 8-8, Emotions, Feelings.*]

➤ **Skillful Teacher Training:** Teacher training to handle the many decisions, actions, and situations a teacher has to handle in the classroom to encourage students and promote a respectful environment. A program of workshops taught by certified trainers. [*List 11-12, Problem Solving.*]

➤ **Solution-Focused Short Term:** Creates mentorships between teacher and students, decreasing the power of being disruptive through compromising, and team-teacher meetings for new ideas, interventions, and strategies. [Metcalf, L. (1995). *Counseling toward solutions: A practical solution-focused program for working with students, teachers, and parents. List 12-3, Comprehensive Resource.*]

➤ **Teacher Effectiveness Training:** Clarify ownership of the problem, use specific skills to negotiate a win–win solution. [Gordon, T. (1984). *Teacher effectiveness training.* New York, NY: Wyden.]

➤ **Teacher Expectations and Student Achievement:** Teacher training in teacher-student interactions that promote equal opportunity in the classroom. A program of workshops taught by certified trainers. It includes teacher expectations, management of a teacher's time, how a teacher responds to students in the classroom, and evaluation of a teacher's classroom teaching by colleagues. [Kerman, S. & Martin, M. (1980). *Teacher expectations and student achievement.* Bloomington, IN: Phi Delta Kappa.]

2-42 LEARNING STYLES

Categories of Learning Styles

1. *Cognitive:* Way a person perceives, gets information, remembers, thinks, and solves problems

2. *Affective:* Way a person is persistent, shows locus of control, takes responsibility, is motivated, and interacts with peers

3. *Physiological:* Biologically based and related to nutrition and reaction to physical environment, such as different light, temperature, and room arrangement

Suggestions for Teachers to Address Multiple Learning Styles in the Classroom

➤ Encourage students to help each other learn and work together.

➤ Let students talk quietly with each other while working on individual assignments.

➤ Let students select their own seats in the classroom.

➤ Include both individual and group assignments.

➤ Make both short-term and long-term assignments.

➤ Provide step-by-step directions when these are necessary; otherwise, encourage students to use their own methods to get information.

➤ Give directions orally and in writing.

➤ Give at least one important oral assignment that will count for a grade.

➤ Give extra credit for some projects and recognize creativity.

➤ Provide both written and verbal comments on students' written work.

➤ Give chances for grades on assignments other than written tests.

➤ Encourage students frequently who have difficulty understanding or performing.

➤ Assign some work to be completed outside of class.

➤ Make certain instruction and homework is relevant to the students.

Some Inventories for Learning Style Assessment

➤ Myers–Briggs Type Indicator (MBTI), developed by I. B. Myers and Leslie Briggs, a personality profile based on Carl Jung's typology:
   – Introversion—Extroversion
   – Thinking—Feeling
   – Intuition—Sensing
   – Judging—Perceiving

➤ Learning Style Inventory (LSI), designed by Rita and Kenneth Dunn, based on the differences of student preferences when learning:
   – Environment: sound, light, temperature, design, or classroom arrangement
   – Emotional: motivation, persistence, responsibility, structure
   – Sociological: peers, self, pair, team, adult, varied
   – Physical: perception, intake, time, mobility

➤ Reading Style Inventory (RSI), based on the Learning Style Inventory

➤ Personal Style Inventory (PSI), designed by R. Craig Hogan and David W. Champagne, is based on the Myers–Briggs Inventory with the same categories

➤ Embedded Figures Test, designed by Witkin, examines how persons identify certain figures against a background in which they are embedded

➤ 4MAT System, developed by Berneice McCarthy, is based on Kolb's learning cycle, research on brain hemispheres, and other theories. This is an instruction model for teachers to use with any age level with content in all areas, and consists of four stages of a learning cycle instead of discrete mutually exclusive types:

- Concrete experience (feeling)
- Reflective observation (watching and listening)
- Abstract conceptualization (thinking)
- Active experimentation (doing)

ADDITIONAL INFORMATION

Bennett, C. I. (1990). *Comprehensive multicultural education: Theory and practice.* (2nd ed.). Boston, MA: Allyn and Bacon.

Gardner, H. (1995). Reflections on multiple intelligences. *Phi Delta Kappan, 77,* (3) 200–209. Pages 202 and 203 include Myth 3 about the difference between learning style and multiple intelligences.

Goleman, D. (1997). *Emotional intelligence* (2nd ed.). *(List 12-20)*

Learning modalities, styles and strategies (1996). [On-line] Available: http://www.fln.vcu.edu/Intensive/LearningStrategies.html

McCarthy, B. (1987). *The 4MAT system: Teaching to learning styles with right/left mode techniques.* Barrington, IL: Excel, Inc.

Myers, I. B. & McCauley, M. H. (1985). *A guide to the development and use of the Myers-Briggs type indicators.* Palo Alto, CA: Consulting Psychologists Press.

Reiff, J. C. (1992). *What research says to the teacher: Learning styles.* Washington, DC: National Education Association.

Sheldon, C. (1996). *E.Q. in school counseling: Promoting emotional intelligence.* Alexandria, VA: American School Counselor Association.

Sims, R. R. & Sims, S. J. (1995). *The importance of learning styles: Understanding the implications for learning, course design, and education.* Westport, CT: Greenwood Press.

2-43 PARENT/GUARDIAN–TEACHER–STUDENT–COUNSELOR CONFERENCES

Establishing Good Rapport

➤ Be thoughtful. There are three sides to every discussion: yours, mine, and the right one.

➤ Be willing to listen to other viewpoints, express yours, and try for compromise.

➤ Be enthusiastic; behave as if you believe in and love what you are doing.

➤ Be alert to ways to give service and reach compromise.

➤ Be respectful of values and feelings that differ from yours.

➤ Be considerate; remember the exceptions when the student did do the right thing.

➤ Be generous with genuine praise and be cautious about criticism.

➤ Be approachable and remember to speak, smile, and call people by name.

Tips for Successful Parent/Guardian Conferences

1. Consider seating arrangements and location of the meeting.
2. Use active listening to encourage parents/guardians to express their concerns.
3. Use nonverbal skills such as eye contact, relaxed body posture, etc.
4. Expect parents/guardians to be defensive initially and vent their personal feelings.
5. Listen! Ask them to summarize their main concerns about their child's learning.
6. Use words and terms that the parents/guardians will understand.
7. Do not get into a debate or argument.
8. Focus the conference on your desire to see the child happier and more successful.
9. Refocus the conference around these themes each time discussion strays.
10. Speak of the child's strengths and link these strengths with your suggestions to improve the child's behavior or learning.
11. Be deliberate; move at a slow, relaxed pace and don't talk too much or too fast.
12. Plan how to deal with angry, hostile persons.
13. Refuse to participate in a conference when someone is abusive, or is insulting an individual who is not in attendance.
14. Arrange for a "conference leader" to take notes, facilitate, and keep things moving.
15. Be responsible or assign responsibility for:
    - Reserving a conference room
    - Summarizing all items or concerns
    - Listing actions to be taken: who will do what and when
    - Adjourning the conference
    - Distributing notes to each participant after the conference
16. Summarize the concerns, and who agreed to do what and when at the end of the conference.
17. Note if, or when, another meeting will be held to review progress.
18. Follow up with a call or send a brief, positive note thanking the parents/guardians for their interest and concern.
19. Think of how you would wish a conference to be with your child's teacher.

Suggestions for Counselors When Mediating Parent/Guardian–Student–Teacher Conferences

1. Determine the need.

2. Invite both parents/guardians to the conference.

3. Inform each person about the conference and the things he or she may want to bring to the conference.

4. Suggest that the teacher read the "Tips for Successful Parent Conferences" and express desire that the conference end in a win–win situation that would help the student.

5. Plan and structure the conference.

6. Introduce the people and ensure that all are comfortable.

7. Express appreciation that all could get together and the desire that the conference result in understanding each other's perspective and a good outcome for all, especially the student.

8. Review the agenda for the conference.

9. Open with a positive statement about the student.

10. Ask the person who requested the conference to clarify the issue.

11. Use *List 2-23, Problem-Solving Model.* Set ground rules:
    – No blaming
    – No interrupting
    – Equal time to present each perspective of the problem
    – Equal time to present each person's needs and desires

12. Define the problem specifically until all understand and agree on the definition.

13. Ask for or give examples.

14. Focus on strengths of the student.

15. Invite each person to provide his or her perspective of the problem.

16. Ask for and respect parents' and student's opinions. Do not judge attitudes or behaviors.

17. Elicit from each person a statement of his or her needs to resolve the problem.

18. Stress collaboration for solving the problem.

19. Intervene appropriately.

20. Brainstorm or generate solutions to the problem.

21. Examine possible consequences of the solutions listed.

22. Focus on solutions rather than on the problem.

23. Use counseling skills: restate, reflect, clarify, and summarize.

24. Take consensus, when appropriate.

25. Select one solution.

26. Elicit a commitment from each person to implement the solution:
    – What will the student, parent, and teacher do?
    – When, where, and how will each person fulfill his or her commitment?

27. Clarify what each person will do, and when they will do it, to follow the solution.

28. If appropriate, ask the student or others to sign a contract or agreement to follow the solution for a specific length of time.

29. Summarize the solution and ask the student to summarize the conference and the solution.

30. Set a time to follow up with all involved to evaluate the solution.

31. End with a positive statement or encouraging comment.

32. Summarize soon after the conference:
    - Suggestions made
    - Agreements about best solution
    - Commitments agreed upon

33. Follow up one week after the conference.

ADDITIONAL INFORMATION

Blum, D. J. (1994). *Tips for parent conferences that work.* Fairfax County (Virginia) Public Schools. Unpublished manuscript.

Perlstein, R. & Thrall, G. (1996). *Ready-to-use conflict resolution activities for secondary students.* **(List 12-4).** The authors have provided a specific example of a very difficult parent-teacher-student conference. This example provides some tips for the teacher to begin the conference, find out what happened, find common interests, explore solutions, choose a solution, and conclude the conference.

2-44   PROFESSIONAL BURNOUT AND DISTRESS IN SCHOOLS

Professional Problems Associated With Burnout

➤ *Role Conflict:* Many responsibilities and no priorities, or priorities that are changed frequently

➤ *Role Ambiguity:* Unclear expectations and no acknowledgment of accomplishments or worth

➤ *Role Overload:* Too many responsibilities to experience achievement in any of them

➤ *Extreme Responsibility:* Feels solely responsible for others' safety, health, and welfare

Personal Risk Factors

➤ Perfectionist

➤ Unmarried, or unsatisfactory home life, recent separation, divorce, or death of a family member

➤ Serious illness

➤ Lack of self-confidence or patience

➤ Restricted social life

➤ Strong needs for approval and affection

➤ Financial worries

➤ High personal expectations and inability to accept reality or lower expectations

➤ High anxiety about own children

Professional Risk Factors

➤ Young and beginning a teaching career

➤ Teaching for over ten years

- Self-esteem and self-worth dependent upon success at work
- Lack of emotional support from family, co-workers, and friends
- Lack of assertiveness in interactions
- Difficulty with co-workers and supervisors
- Poor management skills
- Disrespectful or disruptive students and oversized classes
- Personal property damaged or stolen at school
- Unsafe conditions or violence in the school
- Recent involuntary transfer
- Excessive paperwork and workload
- Lack of specific rules for all students in the school
- Reorganization or major changes of instructions, policies, and/or procedures
- Lack of administrative support, unclear job description, unclear standards or expectations, and feedback only when performance is unsatisfactory
- Jeopardy of position because of budget cuts
- Disillusionment with profession
- Lack of recognition for work
- Inadequate rewards and incentives
- High staff turnover

Burnout Syndrome

- Emotional and physical exhaustion
- Depersonalization
- Feeling of personal inadequacy and depression

Signs of Emotional and Physical Exhaustion

- High absenteeism, tardiness, and excessive leave
- Increased negativism about the job and the students
- Boredom, sadness, and disillusionment
- Increased irritability and frustration, easily upset, temper tantrums
- Over- or under-identification with students
- Physical exhaustion
- Frequent headaches and backaches, minor aches and pains
- Cynicism, sarcasm
- Rigidity
- Paranoia
- High blood pressure
- Hypertension or a rapid pulse rate

➤ Inability to sit still

➤ Sleep disorders, insomnia, nightmares

➤ Eating disorders, loss of appetite

➤ Self-medication or prescription for tranquilizers

➤ Dread coming to work

Signs of Depersonalization

➤ Increased staff conflicts

➤ Emotional withdrawal and tuning out other people

➤ Increased impatience with self and others

➤ Detach psychologically from family and/or friends

➤ View students as problems or cases, instead of individuals

➤ Resentment of students and their problems

➤ Resentment of co-workers and everyone in the school

➤ Callousness toward others

➤ Loneliness and alienation at work

➤ Disorientation

Signs of Feeling Personally Inadequate

➤ Hopelessness, increasing inadequacy, and depression regarding work and the workload

➤ Powerlessness and emotional overload accompanied by continuous and unrewarded social interaction

➤ Overinvolved or overextended at work with overwhelming emotional demands and responsibilities

➤ Out of control, dissatisfied, and depressed about work

➤ Immobilized and ineffective

➤ Resentment of work

2-45   ACTIONS TO PREVENT OR DECREASE BURNOUT AND DISTRESS IN SCHOOLS

Administrative Actions to Reduce Stress at School

➤ Provide predictable schedules for teachers.

➤ Rotate after-school job duties.

➤ Arrange for weekly staff support groups or "rap sessions."

➤ Praise teachers for competent work.

➤ Provide time for teachers to participate in professional associations and attend conferences.

➤ Recognize teachers for professional competence and jobs well done.

➤ Notify teachers about individual exceptional students' needs prior to entering.

➤ Organize team-teaching opportunities.

➤ Encourage teachers to share successes.

Personal Actions to Reduce Stress at School

➤ Learn and practice time management skills.

➤ Learn and practice assertiveness skills.

➤ Manage work schedule and interact with colleagues.

➤ Set realistic goals for self.

➤ Check off tasks as they are accomplished.

➤ Prepare for future occasions and then realize limitations.

➤ Recognize and accept personal limits and extent of personal control.

➤ Cooperate and collaborate with others rather than confront them.

➤ Tune out worries about time productivity.

➤ Delegate responsibilities when possible.

➤ Share classroom experiences with supportive colleagues.

➤ Discuss fears and doubts with trusted colleagues.

➤ Recognize colleagues for personal attributes as well as professional competence.

➤ Arrange to team-teach when possible.

➤ Establish learning centers and individual projects.

➤ Share the responsibility of learning with the students.

➤ Leave the day's problems and frustrations at school.

Personal Actions to Reduce Stress at Home

➤ Exercise regularly for fun and to reduce stress.

➤ Enjoy a hobby unrelated to job.

➤ Laugh, regain a sense of humor.

➤ Listen to favorite music.

➤ Meet with friends.

➤ Volunteer to help others less fortunate.

➤ Talk to friends, family, or colleagues about feelings and concerns.

➤ Recognize irrational beliefs and confront them.

➤ Recognize signs of burnout and take action.

➤ Get sufficient rest.

➤ Follow good eating habits.

➤ Forgive self.

➤ Cry to reduce tension and experience relief.

➤ Visualize favorite scene and place.

➤ Read a good book.

➤ Avoid self-medication.

➤ Accept that it is not always essential to be right.

➤ Appreciate the present without striving for more.

➤ Enjoy activities that are not competitive.

➤ Set time each day for relaxation.

➤ Set limits and say "No."

➤ Realize that no person is indispensable.

➤ Plan new experiences, take appropriate risks.

➤ Use vacation for recreation for renewing self.

➤ Participate in interests and enjoy friends outside of work.

ADDITIONAL INFORMATION

Burnout (1996). [On-line] Available:
    http://www.fmi.uni-passau.de/worterklaerungen/burnout.html

Psychhosp2 (1996). Recognizing burnout. *Seeker Magazine*. [On-line] Available:
    http://www.brainiac.com/eodale/v0596/burnout.html

Maslach, C. (1982). *Burnout: The cost of caring*. New York, NY: Prentice-Hall.

COORDINATOR, COLLABORATOR, AND COMMITTEE CHAIR
2-46 A POSITIVE ENVIRONMENT THROUGHOUT THE SCHOOL

A Positive School Environment

- Respect shown to all who study or work in the school
- Respect shown to all who enter the school
- Establishment of clear procedures for student supervision throughout school day
- Written clear job descriptions for entire staff
- Procedures for handling student misbehavior communicated verbally and in writing to all students, parents, teachers, and staff
- Consistent expectations for positive student behavior
- Freedom, encouragement, and support to try new ideas or experiment without threat of making a mistake
- Alternative programs for students
- Recognition of students' strengths and their good behavior
- Policies and programs that don't discriminate against individuals or groups
- Group activities for teachers to focus on positive behaviors of students
- Positive relationships among all who work and learn in the school
- Respect for school and personal property
- Administrators, students, and parents who treat teachers as professionals
- Administrators, counselors, and teachers who use logical consequences
- Administrators and counselors who conduct parent education programs
- Administrators and counselors who conduct staff development programs that are relevant and meaningful to teachers
- Administrators and teachers who support peer-facilitation programs
- Teachers who are determined that all students will succeed and will learn
- Teachers who use the problem-solving model and conflict resolution and/or mediation
- Teachers who understand learning styles and teach to all styles
- Teachers who are cooperative, collaborative, and readily share ideas and materials
- Teachers who talk frequently about teaching, learning, strategies, and ideas
- Teachers who observe each other teaching without threat
- Teachers who plan and make instructional materials together
- Teachers who teach each other successful methods
- Teachers who implement and use class meetings
- Students who exhibit self-discipline and responsibility

2-47 GUIDANCE: A TOTAL SCHOOL RESPONSIBILITY COORDINATED BY THE SCHOOL COUNSELOR

Guidance in the school is a responsibility of the entire staff. The school counselor may initiate meaningful programs, coordinate or co-lead programs, or serve as consultant to staff members, parents, or other volunteers who lead programs. Coordination varies greatly among schools because the needs of each school are unique.

Programs/Committees Coordinated by the School Counselor

➤ Guidance department differentiated or diversified staffing responsibilities *(List 2-48)*

➤ Guidance advisory and/or materials advisory committee or guidance communication committee *(Lists 1-5, 2-49)*

➤ Classroom, grade level, team, or department guidance lessons *(List 2-29)*

➤ Volunteer program for guidance *(List 2-54)*

Programs/Committees That May Be Coordinated by the School Counselor

➤ Career fairs, career speaker days, career shadowing

➤ Class meetings *(List 2-30)*

➤ Teacher advisors program (TAP) or school mentoring program *(Lists 2-51, 2-53)*

➤ Parent–school partnership program *(List 2-52)*

➤ School-business or volunteer tutoring/mentoring program *(List 2-53)*

➤ Child study committee or school-based assistance team (SBAT) *(List 2-56)*

➤ School-to-work business partnership or program *(List 2-55)*

Guidelines for Making Guidance the Responsibility of the Entire School

1. Enlist staff to identify school guidance priorities.

2. Involve teachers in developing, implementing, following through, and evaluating guidance lessons.

3. Initiate and design, as a team, schoolwide programs that staff members and volunteers can lead or co-lead.

4. Share materials lists in Sections 6 through 12 with media coordinator to inventory materials already in the school:
   ➤ Mark available materials on reproducible materials lists.
   ➤ Share reproducible lists with staff.

5. Plan as a team materials that should be used and those that should be ordered to implement guidance lessons for the year.

6. Encourage and help staff plan and integrate guidance into the curriculum, e.g., career education in every classroom in the elementary school, team in the middle school, and every department in the high school; college application writing in English classes.

7. Encourage staff to use the counselor as a resource to prevent and solve problems together.

8. Evaluate counseling and guidance program together.

2-48 DIFFERENTIAL OR DIVERSIFIED STAFFING OF THE GUIDANCE PROGRAM

The staffing depends upon the needs of the individual school. The counselor who is designated for a differentiated staff assignment usually attends inservices and/or department meetings for that designation, communicates information about the topic to all counselors in the school, and serves as consultant to all counselors about that topic. In some schools the designation also determines the student caseload.

Possible Diversified Staffing

➤ Student registration, immunizations, boundaries

➤ Orientation to the school and to the counseling and guidance program

➤ Group counseling

➤ Financial aid and college recommendation writing

➤ Parent information center

➤ Peer-facilitation program

➤ Student mentoring or tutoring program

➤ Wellness and substance abuse prevention

➤ Standardized test interpretation

➤ Career/college center, military, college and career speakers

➤ Gifted and talented and selective colleges/universities

➤ Special services, special education

➤ High-risk students and stay-in-school program

➤ School-to-work program/military relations counselor

➤ Parent education and staff development

➤ Volunteer training and coordination

➤ Public relations and business partnership

➤ Follow-up of students after graduation, class reunions

➤ Personal/social counselor

➤ Academic support counselor

➤ Student records counselor

➤ Career counselor/jobs and benefits

➤ College counselor

➤ Financial aid counselor

➤ Counselor assigned to work with English as a second language (ESL/ESOL)

➤ Counselors assigned to work with specific departments, e.g., English department

➤ Counselors assigned to work with specific teams

2-49   MATERIALS ADVISORY COMMITTEE (MAC)

Importance of Careful Selection of Guidance Materials

➤ School budgets and funds for guidance are limited.

➤ Materials must reflect a pluralistic society with diverse cultures, ethnic backgrounds, religions, and values.

➤ Materials must meet all state and local guidelines.

➤ Materials must reflect the mission of the school.

➤ Materials must be educationally sound and age-appropriate.

➤ Materials must not reflect any racist, sexist, age, disability, religious, political, or other bias.

➤ Materials must reflect a wide range of levels of difficulty with diverse appeal and differing points of view.

➤ Materials must not promote any particular religion or political party.

➤ Challenges to the guidance program frequently are about materials.

Guidelines for Selection of Guidance Materials

1. Be familiar with the state guidelines for selection of instructional materials.

2. Be familiar with the district board of education policy on the selection of curriculum materials and for dealing with challenges to educational materials.

3. Inform the school Guidance Advisory Committee (GAC) or the school Materials Advisory Committee (MAC) of the state and local guidelines and the criteria for selection of materials, and request the help of the committee to review materials.

4. Assess needs of the particular school guidance program.

5. Develop a written review procedure to determine approved guidance materials and be familiar with the school procedure to deal with challenges of educational materials.

6. Inform school PTA, community service organizations, and school business partners of the needs for counseling and guidance materials.

7. Submit current materials for review and discard materials that are out-of-date, reflect bias, and/or are no longer useful.

8. Keep administrators informed of the guidance program, results of needs assessments or surveys, and procedures for selection and review of guidance materials.

9. Ensure administrators that the guidance materials are age-appropriate, safe, and nondiscriminatory.

10. Inform administrators of the level of community input in the selection of materials and support for the guidance program.

11. Consider pooling resources of several schools that are accessible.

12. Purchase materials for play counseling at garage sales.

13. Peruse materials in the exhibit area at professional conferences.

14. Talk with colleagues at professional conferences to get recommendations of current materials.

15. Make a list of materials used and recommended by presenters at professional conferences.

16. Visit exhibits at professional conferences to look at new materials and put your name on mailing lists for catalogs.

Challenges of Guidance Materials

➤ Notify administrators immediately if reconsideration of guidance materials is requested.

➤ Consider the request and put it on the MAC or GAC agenda.

➤ Review the materials, noting reason for the request.

➤ Provide the materials selection procedure in writing to the person(s) making the request.

➤ Know that courts have upheld the right of school officials to make choices regarding curriculum, textbooks, library books, and general subject matter (Brigman & Moore, 1994).

➤ Know that school boards have authority and responsibility for deciding what is taught in the classroom (Brigman & Moore, 1994).

Procedure to Determine Approved Materials

➤ Organize a Materials Advisory Committee (MAC) of parent, teacher, and counselor representatives to meet regularly to review all materials and make recommendations.

➤ Provide members of the MAC with state, district, and school guidelines for instructional materials.

➤ Provide members of the MAC with a guide and training to recognize bias in materials.

➤ Collect all current materials and distribute to members of MAC to review and make recommendations:
   – Approved or rejected
   – Rating of excellent, very good, or good

➤ Request materials to be sent on approval for MAC or GAC to review and make recommendations before purchase.

➤ Enter title, topic, media, grade levels, cost, rating, and date of meeting on a computer database.

➤ Inform parents and staff of the procedure used to review guidance materials.

➤ Inform parents and staff of time and location that materials are available for their review.

Additional Information

Brigman, G. & Moore, P. (1994). *School counselors and censorship: Facing the challenge.* *(List 12-3)*

2-50 A GUIDE TO RECOGNIZING BIAS IN MATERIALS

➤ Check all illustrations :
- Look for stereotypes—oversimplified generalization about a group, race, or sex that is demeaning.
- Look for tokenism—a lack of genuineness depicting a subtle hierarchy of white and/or male chauvinism.
- Notice the leadership and subservient roles depicted.

➤ Check the story line:
- Look for subtle white society standards for success.
- Look for passive acceptance of societal problems.
- Look for reasons females achieve success.

➤ Look at lifestyles:
- Look for implied negative value judgments.
- Look for inaccuracy and inappropriate depiction of any culture.

➤ Look at the relationships between people:
- Look at the people making decisions or people with power.
- Look at the way families are defined.
- Look at the way family relationships in different cultures are depicted.
- Look for realistic societal reasons for problems in relationships.

➤ Note the heroes:
- Look at whether the heroes reflect only the white male nondisabled societal values.
- Look for heroes with whom a minority student can identify.
- Look at whose interest the hero is serving.

➤ Consider the effects on a student's self-image:
- Look for limits on aspirations of any student.
- Look for white middle-class expectations.
- Look for one or more persons with whom a minority student can readily identify.

➤ Consider the author's or illustrator's cultural background:
- Look for the qualifications that the author possesses to address particular cultural themes.
- Look for the qualifications that the illustrator possesses to address particular cultural themes.

➤ Check out the author's perspective.

➤ Watch for loaded words:
- Look for words that have insulting overtones.
- Look for sexist language.

➤ Note the copyright date:
- Look for a reflection of multiracial society's values beginning in the 1970s.
- Look for nonsexist books beginning in the 1970s.

ADDITIONAL INFORMATION

Brigman, G. & Moore, P. (1994). *School counselors and censorship: Facing the challenge.* (**List 12-3**)

Council on Interracial Books for Children (1996). *Ten quick ways to analyze children's books for racism and sexism.* Council on Interracial Books for Children, 1841 Broadway, New York, NY 10023.

Fairfax County Public Schools of Virginia (1992, 1993). *Materials review procedure information for counselors (1993), Amendments B, and C (1992).* Unpublished manuscript.

Pedersen, P. & Carey, J. C. (1993). *Multicultural counseling in schools: A practical handbook.* *(List 12-23)*

2-51   TEACHER AS ADVISOR PROGRAM (TAP)

The purpose of the Teacher as Advisor Program (TAP) is to provide effective, continuous adult guidance for students in the school, especially students at risk.

Guidelines for Successful Teacher as Advisor Programs

1. Share the vision with staff of how the TAP could help students, especially students at risk.
2. Clarify to staff that teachers would use teaching skills.
3. Listen and incorporate input from interested staff members to make the program successful.
4. Appoint a committee to help design the program to meet the needs of the school.
5. Plan the program within the school day two or three days a week.
6. Prepare a written guide or handbook including lessons and reproducible lists of materials available.
7. Meet with interested staff to further explain and discuss the program.
8. Demonstrate teaching a guidance lesson using materials provided.
9. Train teachers to teach guidance lessons.
10. Assign 15–20 students to each volunteer staff member.
11. Coordinate the program and serve as consultant.

Aspects of Successful TAPs

➤ Advisors know and care about individual students and their learning:
   - Provide information about courses and scheduling.
   - Help students examine their abilities and interests as they pertain to plans.
   - Help students make wise curricular choices.
   - Discuss developmental issues.
   - Provide information about graduation requirements.
   - Provide information about college entrance requirements.
   - Help students with college and career planning.
   - Assist student in updating individual education and career plan.

➤ Advisors consult with the counselor and others in the school to help students.

➤ Advisors refer students to the counselor when uncomfortable or not sure how to handle a student's problem.

ADDITIONAL INFORMATION

See **List 13-25,** *The School Counselor and Student Assistant Programs.*

Gonzalez, G. M. & Myrick, R. D. (1993). The teachers as student advisors program (TAP): An effective approach for drug education and other developmental guidance activities. In J. Wittmer (Ed.), *Managing your school counseling program: K–12 developmental strategies.* (pp. 191–200). *(List 12-3)*

Myrick, R. D. & Myrick, L. (1990). *The teacher advisor program: An innovative approach to school guidance.* Ann Arbor, MI: ERIC Counseling and Personnel Services Clearinghouse.

Myrick, R. D. & Tobias, A. K. (1994). The teacher-advisor program. In D. G. Burgess & R. M. Dedmond (Eds.), *Quality leadership and the professional school counselor* (Chapter 10, pp. 217–241). Alexandria, VA: American Counseling Association.

2-52   PARENT/GUARDIAN–SCHOOL PARTNERSHIPS

Successful Parent/Guardian–School Partnerships

➤ Students are more apt to succeed in school when their parents/guardians are involved in their learning:
  - Monitor their children's schoolwork
  - Help their children learn
  - Motivate their children to learn

➤ Parents/guardians are more likely to be involved in their children's learning if they receive frequent and positive messages or information from the school:
  - Classroom activities
  - Strengths and progress of their children
  - Ways to help their children learn
  - Confidence that they can help their children learn

Parents/Guardians Help Students Learn

➤ Schedule daily homework time.

➤ Read together.

➤ Use television wisely.

➤ Keep in touch with the school.

➤ Offer praise and encouragement to the children.

➤ Talk with teenagers.

Teachers Establish Learning Partnerships

➤ Encourage teachers to define with parents/guardians:
  - Educational goals for students
  - Academic expectations for students
  - Responsibilities as partners for students' learning

➤ Train school staff to reach out to parents/guardians:
  - Assign homework that engages parents/guardians in the learning process.
  - Give parents/guardians a voice in decisions regarding their children.
  - Extend school hours to meet with parents.
  - Create parent/guardian resource centers.

Parenting Library

➤ Established by counselor

➤ Maintained and updated by guidance volunteer

➤ Materials for parents at different developmental stages of children

ADDITIONAL INFORMATION

See **Section 10**, *Materials for Parents.*

U.S. Department of Education Public Affairs (1996). *Connecting families and schools to help our children succeed.* [On-line] Available: //ericps.ed.uiuc.edu:70/00npin/res.pared/gen.resources/connect

2-53   SCHOOL TUTORING/MENTORING PROGRAM

Guidelines for a Successful Tutoring/Mentoring Program

1. Determine need for tutors/mentors from teachers, students, parents.
2. Obtain administrator support for tutoring/mentoring program.
3. Establish a planning committee that includes a member from the business community.
4. Establish purpose, objectives, and goals for program.
5. Specify criteria to select students for participation.
6. Specify characteristics and responsibilities of effective volunteer tutors/mentors.
7. Establish time parameters for tutors/mentors to meet with students weekly or monthly.
8. Specify how the tutor/mentor or the student can discontinue participation in the program.
9. Specify qualifications and screening procedures of tutors/mentors.
10. Design a tutoring/mentoring program manual specifying goals and objectives.
11. Inform local businesses and service organizations of the tutoring/mentoring program and characteristics of effective tutors/mentors.
12. Notify business/service organizations when the program is ready for them to recruit appropriate tutors/mentors.
13. Identify students who need and would benefit from a tutor/mentor relationship.
14. Involve parents/guardians and obtain their written permission.
15. Select tutors/mentors who model personal, professional, and ethical life skills, and build personal relationships with students.
16. Train tutors/mentors to demonstrate how they use their education in their careers.
17. Match tutors/mentors with groups or individual students.
18. Facilitate a get-acquainted meeting for tutors/mentors and students.
19. Hold tutor/mentor–student meetings.
20. Hold counselor–tutor/mentor debriefings.
21. Elicit feedback from respective students, teachers, and parents/guardians.
22. Provide feedback to tutors/mentors and planning committee from the counselor and teachers.
23. Evaluate program based on the objectives.
24. Thank and acknowledge publicly the participating planning committee, business/service organization, and tutors/mentors.

Advantages for Students of Tutoring/Mentoring Relationships

➤ Develop feelings of competence.

➤ Develop a sense of belonging.

➤ Learn the value of education and learning.

➤ Gain confidence about the future.

➤ Learn from a positive role model.

Characteristics of Effective Volunteer Tutors/Mentors

➤ Trustworthy

➤ Successful in their adult roles

➤ Believe in the value of education

➤ Have positive messages for young people

➤ Express caring for students and their efforts

➤ Able to commit to regular mentoring appointments

➤ Able to work within the boundaries of the program

➤ Communicate effectively including exhibit listening skills

➤ Communicate with students as friends who are respected and cared about

➤ Model personal, career, social, and educational responsibility

➤ Model healthy self-esteem, honesty, and integrity, adhering to their own values

➤ Recognize when to refer the student to the professional school counselor

Characteristics of Appropriate Students Seeking Mentors

➤ Understand the program and the advantages of participating

➤ Desire to participate in the program

➤ Have written permission from parents to participate in the program

➤ Agree to commit to a specific number of meetings with a tutor/mentor

➤ Understand that they can exit the program after attending a specific number of meetings

Training Components for Mentors

➤ Initial Training:
  – Developmental characteristics and how to deal with them *(List 2-34)*
  – Listening skills
  – Open-ended questions
  – Motivation

➤ Continuing training during tutoring/mentoring:
  – Encouragement
  – Making referrals to the counselor
  – Confidentiality *(List 2-21)*
  – Sharing appropriate information with parents
  – Resolving any problems as early as possible

- Sharing successes
- Sharing community resources
- Terminating the relationship

ADDITIONAL INFORMATION

Henderson, P. (1994). Mentoring programs. In D. G. Burgess & R. M. Dedmond (Eds.), *Quality leadership and the professional school counselor* (Chapter 12, pp. 259–278). Alexandria, VA: American Counseling Association.

2-54 COORDINATION OF GUIDANCE VOLUNTEERS

Possible Guidance Volunteer Responsibilities

➤ Parent information center assistant

➤ Career resource center; career materials assistant

➤ College materials assistant

➤ Tutoring/mentoring program assistant

➤ Part-time job placement for students assistant

➤ College and financial aid speakers assistant

➤ Career shadowing; career night assistant

➤ Local school, college field trip assistant

➤ Bulletin board designer

➤ Guidance newsletter/local newspaper reporter assistant

➤ Brochure and flyer designer

➤ Computer assistant to search, print, and distribute articles for students, parents, and staff

➤ Computer assistant to design a home page on the Internet

➤ Members of Guidance Advisory Committee to speak on behalf of guidance at community meetings, school board meetings, and other meetings

Limitations on Volunteer Responsibilities

➤ No confidential information

➤ No access to student records

ADDITIONAL INFORMATION

See **List 1-5**, *Guidance Advisory Committee (GAC).*

See **List 4-11**, *Career College Center.*

2-55   SCHOOL-TO-WORK PROGRAM

The School-to-Work Opportunities Act specifies career development activities for all students. These activities bridge experiences from school to the workplace. They include counseling and matching students with participating employers, and training job-site mentors and teachers.

School-to-Work Opportunities Act's Core Components

1. *School-based learning:* Classroom instruction based on high academic and occupational skill standards:
   - Career awareness, exploration, and counseling
   - Initial selection of a career by grade 11
   - Program of study to meet academic standards and to prepare for postsecondary education and a skills certificate
   - Program of instruction that integrates academic and vocational learning
   - Evaluations and problem solving with students and school dropouts to identify their strengths and needs

2. *Work-based learning:* Work experience structured training, and mentoring at job sites:
   - Work experience
   - Planned program of training and work experience
   - Workplace mentoring
   - Instruction in competencies in the workplace
   - Broad instruction in classroom and workplace that exposes students to all aspects of an industry

3. *Connecting activities:* Courses developed that integrate classroom and on-the-job instruction, match students with participating employers, train job-site mentors, and build and maintain bridges between the school and work for all students:
   - Matching students with the work-based learning opportunities of employers
   - School-site mentor serving as liaison among student, employer, teacher, administrator, and parent
   - Technical assistance and services to employers
   - Assistance to schools and employers to integrate school-based and work-based learning and to integrate academic and occupational learning into the program
   - Encouragement for active participation of employers with local education administrators in implementing activities
   - Assistance for students in finding jobs, continuing education, and training
   - Links between secondary education and postsecondary education
   - Analysis of information regarding post-program outcomes of participants on basis of demographics
   - Links between youth development achievement and industry strategies for upgrading skills of workers

Characteristics of Successful School-to-Work Programs
   - Business is a major participant; collaborative approach between the school and the employers
   - Community colleges have a pivotal role
   - High standards for all students
   - Incentives for students to meet high standards
   - Career guidance, exploration, and counseling for all students
   - Integrated academic and technical learning

> ➤ Integrated school-based learning with work-site learning
> ➤ Preparation of students for two futures: jobs requiring technical skills and further learning, either job-specific training or four-year college

Advantages to Students

> ➤ Can choose from a wider range of occupations and opportunities
> ➤ Have more opportunities for good jobs after graduation
> ➤ Obtain actual work experience while going to school
> ➤ Develop potential contacts that may broaden employment options
> ➤ Boost self-confidence and experience success at school and at work
> ➤ Get personal assistance in attaining educational and career goals
> ➤ Offers a wider variety of occupational and professional instruction
> ➤ Provides transitional programs such as tech-prep, cooperative education, and youth apprenticeships

Advantages for the Counselor and Teachers

> ➤ Increases college placement and employment rates of graduates
> ➤ Provides improved opportunities for professional development from recruitment to retirement
> ➤ Integrates school with actual work and life experiences
> ➤ Reduces dropout rates
> ➤ Improves attendance
> ➤ Increases enrollment
> ➤ Makes learning in school relevant
> ➤ Provides partnerships among educators, employers, parents, and community organizations to develop new learning opportunities
> ➤ Provides monitoring and instruction in the workplace

ADDITIONAL INFORMATION

See *List 4-5, Plan for Career Development Program K–12.*

National Library of Education (1995). *Bibliography on school-to-work.* [On-line] Available: http://www.ed.gov/NLE/work.html

National School-to-Work Opportunity Information Center, Room 3040, 400 Maryland Ave., S.W., Washington, DC 20202-3500; (202) 260-7278.

Packer, A. H. & Pines, M. W. (1996). *School-to-Work.* **(List 9-1)**

School-to-Work. [On-line] Available: http://www.ed.gov/Programs/stw.html

School-to-Work Transition: Resources for Counseling. Available from the American Vocational Association, 1410 King Street, Alexandria, VA 22314; (800) 826-9972; FAX: (703) 683-7424.

State Department of Education, School-to-Work or Vocational Liaison.

Vocational Curriculum Resource Center of Maine (1995). *Implementation guide of suggested school-to-work career guidance strategies for school personnel and students.* (Report No. CE070419.) Fairfield, ME: Vocational Curriculum Resource Center of Maine. (ERIC Document Reproduction Service No. ED389903.)

Winters, K. & Scoll, B. (1993). *Building bridges from school to work: A background paper for the Goals 2000.* Educate America Satellite Town Meeting. [On-line] Available: gopher://gopher.ed.gov:10001/00/OVAE/school2work/legsch/title1

2-56 CHILD STUDY TEAM, STUDENT ADVISORY TEAM, AND LOCAL SCREENING COMMITTEE

Child Study Team and Student Advisory Team

➤ Teachers identify students who are not progressing in school but are not in the special education program.

➤ Teachers refer identified student to the child study team to examine possible reasons the student is not succeeding.

➤ Members of the child study team enlist the help of the student's parent/guardian.

➤ Counselor invites parent/guardian to parent seminars or parent education.

Local Screening Committee for Special Services

➤ Members of the Local Screening Committee:
  - School psychologist
  - School social worker
  - Teacher of special education
  - Administrator or designee
  - May include grade-level teacher
  - May include school counselor

Local Screening Committee Procedures

➤ Meet with parent for permission to conduct assessments:
  - Psychological assessment
  - Social/cultural assessment, e.g., social case history
  - Behavioral assessment
  - Educational achievement assessment

➤ Meet with parent to discuss results of assessments and make decisions about placement.

➤ Develop Individual Educational Plan (IEP) with parents.

Counselor's Actions

➤ Know state law and district policies about special education placement.

➤ Serve as a member on the local screening committee.

ADDITIONAL INFORMATION

Kaplan, L. S. (1994). School-based assistance teams. In D. G. Burgess & R. M. Dedmond (Eds.), *Quality leadership and the professional school counselor* (Chapter 9, pp. 193–215). Alexandria, VA: American Counseling Association. Provides procedures, suggestions, and forms for the school-based assistance or child study team.

Pierangelo, R. (1995). *The special education teacher's book of lists.* **(List 12-33).** Includes guidelines, suggested interventions prior to evaluation, and options for the child study or pupil personnel team.

SUPERVISOR AND CHANGE AGENT

2-57 SUPERVISOR OF OTHER SCHOOL COUNSELORS, INTERNS, OR PRACTICUM STUDENTS

General Information About Counselor Supervision

➤ Continual assessment of the counselor's strengths and areas for improvement to enhance professional development

➤ Encourages greater self-awareness

➤ Fosters a professional identity as a school counselor

➤ Is in addition to evaluation

Administrative Supervision

➤ Conducted by the immediate supervisor, usually the building principal:
  – Attendance
  – Time management
  – Communication skills
  – Staff relationships
  – Adherence to institutional policies

Program Supervision

➤ Guides the counselor toward goals, objectives, and guidance services in the school and school system

➤ Conducted by on-site guidance director, lead counselor, central office supervisor, or peer counselor:
  – Guidance needs of the students and staff in the school
  – Guidance program in the school
  – Delivery of all counseling and guidance activities in the school
  – Delivery of all counseling and guidance activities to all students

Clinical Supervision

➤ Focuses on functions that are unique to counseling profession

➤ Conducted by trained professional counselor:
  – Counseling skills and counseling process
  – Consulting skills
  – Coordinating skills
  – Student appraisal knowledge and techniques
  – Professional practices and development

ADDITIONAL INFORMATION

See **List 2-48,** *Differential or Diversified Staffing of the Guidance Program.*

See **List 2-1,** *Characteristics of Effectiveness.*

See **List 2-6,** *Accountability and Performance Evaluation of the School Counselor.*

Association for Counselor Education and Supervision (ACES) (1993). *ACES standards for counseling supervisors.* Alexandria, VA: American Counseling Association. This list of ethical guidelines was adopted by ACES in March, 1993.

Borders, L. D. (1991). Supervision = \evaluation. *The School Counselor, 38,* (4), 253–255.

Borders, L. D., Bernard, J. M., Dye, H. A., Fong, M. L., Henderson, P. & Nance, D. W. (1991). Curriculum guide for training counseling supervisors: Rationale, development and implementation. *Counselor Education and Supervision, 31,* 58–80.

Dye, H. A. & Borders, L. D. (1990). Counseling supervisors: Standards for preparation and practice. *Journal of Counseling and Development, 69,* 27–32.

Henderson, P. (1994). *Supervision of school counselors.* (Report No. ED372353). Greensboro, NC: ERIC Clearinghouse on Counseling and Student Services. [On-line] Available: http://www.ed.gov/databases/ERIC_Digests/ed372353.html

Henderson, P. & Lampe, R. E. (1992). Clinical supervision of school counselors. *The School Counselor, 39,* (3), 151–157.

Schmidt, J. J. (1990). Critical issues for school counselor performance appraisal and supervision. *The School Counselor, 38,* (2), 86–94.

2-58   CHANGE AGENT OF THE SCHOOL ENVIRONMENT

Change affects students and staff, and may cause psychological stress. Counselors can help staff adjust to the changes brought about through the education reform movement. They can help the staff prepare for the great increase in school enrollment to the year 2006. Otherwise, the change and influx may have a negative effect on students as indicated by United States Secretary of Education, R. W. Riley (1996).

Readiness for Change in Schools

➤ Prepare for greatest growth of school enrollment in the suburbs.

➤ Prepare for increased diversity, particularly Hispanic Americans, African Americans, and Asian Americans.

➤ Prepare to provide increased attention to students and their needs individually and in groups.

➤ Prepare to provide parent liaisons for students of color.

➤ Prepare teachers to increasingly involve parents in the learning process.

➤ Prepare students for university admission:
   – Identify necessary courses in middle school and high school.
   – Communicate the need for course completion.
   – Help parents understand the necessity of six- and eight-year educational plans.

➤ Help parents plan for financing college education.

➤ Help staff maintain high expectations for educational achievement of students in poverty.

➤ Collaborate with other school and community members to facilitate change and design, construct, and coordinate school reform for students' success.

➤ Demonstrate initiative and imagination to create programs of prevention and intervention, integrating services for all students.

School Counselor, a Catalyst for a Positive School Climate Conducive to Learning

➤ Identify any condition that prevents the school from being a safe and comfortable environment in which students can learn.

➤ Bring the problem to the attention of the administrator.

➢ Determine the desired change or outcome for the student(s).

➢ Work on strategies/interventions to effect change.

➢ Provide staff inservices on topics related to school climate (e.g., multicultural and diverse school community). *(Lists 5-5 through 5-9)*

➢ Teach basic values so that students become independent, self-sufficient, and responsible citizens. *(List 5-17)*

➢ Inform students and parents of the opportunities for higher education and financial aid. (See *Section 3* and *List 9-2*)

ADDITIONAL INFORMATION

See *List 2-46*, *A Positive Environment Throughout the School.*

See *Lists 5-4 through 5-6*, *Fears or Stressors of Students and Ethnic Diversity of Students.*

See *Lists 5-16 and 5-17*, *Teaching Students to Respect Others and Teaching Responsibility and Educational Values.*

See *List 5-39*, *Program to Promote Student Safety.*

See *Lists 5-53 through 5-55*, lists about student harassment.

Allen, J. M. (1994). *School counselors collaborating for student success.* (Report No. ED377414). Greensboro, NC: ERIC Clearinghouse on Counseling and Student Services. ERIC Digest. [On-line] Available: http://www.ed.gov/databases/ERIC_Digests/ed377414.html

American School Counselor Association (1990). *The professional school counselor's role in educational reform.* Alexandria, VA: ASCA.

Atkinson, D. R. & Juntunen, C. R. (1993). School counselors and school psychologists as school-home-community liaisons in ethnically diverse schools (Chapter 6). In P. Pederson & J. C. Carey (Eds.), *Multicultural counseling in schools: A practical handbook.* *(List 12-23)*

Cummins, J. (1986). Empower minority students. *Harvard Educational Review, 56*, 18–36.

Thompson, R. (1992). *School counseling renewal: Strategies for the twenty-first century.* Muncie, IN: Accelerated Development.

U.S. Department of Education (1996, August). *A back-to-school special report: The baby boom echo.* [On-line] Available: http://www.ed.gov/NCES/bbecho/

USER OF RESEARCH

2-59 AMERICAN COUNSELING ASSOCIATION (ACA)

AMERICAN COUNSELING ASSOCIATION (ACA)
5999 Stevenson Avenue
Alexandria, VA 22304
(703) 212-8680
FAX: (703) 823-0252
1-800-823-9800
Home Page for ACA: http://www.counseling.org/

Publications of ACA

1. *Journal of Counseling & Development*
   http://www.counseling.org/jcd.htm

2. *Counseling Today*
   http://www.counseling.org/ctonline/ct.htm

Code of Ethics and Standards of ACA

   http://www.counseling.org/ethics.htm

Publications of Divisions of ACA

1. *Counseling and Values,* publication of Association for Spiritual, Ethical, and Religious Value Issues in Counseling (ASERVIC)

2. *Counselor Education and Supervision,* publication of Association for Counselor Education and Supervision (ACES)

3. *Journal for Specialists in Group Work,* publication of Association for Specialists in Group Work (ASGW)

4. *Journal of Addictions and Offender Counseling,* publication of International Association of Addictions and Offender Counselors (IAAOC)

5. *Journal of Employment Counseling,* publication of National Employment Counseling Association (NECA)

6. *Journal of Humanistic Education and Development,* publication of Association for Humanistic Education and Development (AHEAD)

7. *Journal of Mental Health Counseling,* publication of American Mental Health Counselors Association (AMHCA)

8. *Journal of Multicultural Counseling and Development,* publication of Association for Multicultural Counseling and Development (AMCD)

9. *Measurement and Evaluation in Counseling and Development,* publication of Association for Assessment in Counseling (AAC)

10. *Rehabilitation Counseling Bulletin,* publication of American Rehabilitation Counselors Association (ARCA)

11. *The Career Development Quarterly,* publication of National Career Development Association (NCDA)

12. *The Family Journal Counseling and Therapy for Families and Couples,* publication of International Association of Marriage and Family Counselors (IAMFC)

2-60 AMERICAN SCHOOL COUNSELOR ASSOCIATION (ASCA)

AMERICAN SCHOOL COUNSELOR ASSOCIATION (ASCA)
801 North Fairfax Street, Suite 310
Alexandria, VA 22314
(703) 683-2722
FAX: (703) 683-1619
1-800-306-4722
Home Page for ASCA: http://www.edge.net/asca/

Ethical Standards for School Counselors

http://www.edge.net/asca/ethicsld.html

Publications of ASCA

1. *Professional School Counseling,* journal published in September, November, January, March, and May. All ASCA members receive this journal.

2. *The ASCA Counselor,* newsletter published in October, December, February, April, and June.

3. *Elementary School Guidance and Counseling,* journal published in October, December, February, and April. All members of ASCA receive this journal.

2-61 OTHER ASSOCIATIONS THAT ARE RESOURCES

AMERICAN PSYCHOLOGIST ASSOCIATION (APA)
1400 N. Uhle Street
Arlington, VA 22201-2910
(202) 955-7600

AMERICAN VOCATIONAL ASSOCIATION (AVA)
1410 King Street
Alexandria, VA 22314
(800) 826-9972
FAX: (703) 683-7424

ORGANIZATION FOR EDUCATIONAL RESEARCH, (OERI)
http:www.ed.gov/offices/OERI/oeribro.html

NATIONAL ASSOCIATION OF SECONDARY SCHOOL PRINCIPALS (NASSP)
http://www.nassp.org

National Educational Service
www:nes.org/~nes/

National Service Learning Cooperation Clearinghouse
http://www.nicsl.coled.umn.edu

New England Comprehensive Assistance Center
http://www.edc.org/NECAC

U.S. DEPARTMENT OF EDUCATION (USDOE)
http://www.ed.gov

NATIONAL EDUCATION ASSOCIATION (NEA)
http://www.nea.org

ASSOCIATION FOR SUPERVISION AND CURRICULUM DEVELOPMENT (ASCD)
http://www.ascd.org/

INTERNATIONAL SOCIETY FOR TECHNOLOGY IN EDUCATION (ISTE)
http://isteonline.uoregon.edu/

Library Reference
http://www.nwrel.org/school_house/Library/Reference_and_Periodicals/Associations

List of Current Periodicals in Education
http://www.bloomu.edu/library/pages/educatio/html

List of Education Journals with Annotations
http://www.soemadison.wisc.edu/IMC/journals/anno_cd.html

List of Psychological Journals
http://www.gasou.edu/psychweb/resource/journals.html

USER OF TECHNOLOGY
2-62   THE INTERNET

The Internet is an immense library consisting of bibliographies, journal articles, research projects, abstracts, and all types of current information for counselors, teachers, and students.

Useful Terms

➤ *Home Page:* The web page that your browser is set to use when it starts up. Also refers to the main web page for a school, organization, person, or the main page of a collection of web pages, links to other home pages.

➤ *HTML (HyperText Markup Language):* Code used to create Hypertext documents for use on the World Wide Web. In HTML you can specify that a block of text, or a word, is linked to another file on the Internet. HTML files are viewed using a World Wide Web Client Program, such as Netscape or Mosaic.

➤ *Internet:* Vast collection of interconnected networks that all use the TCP/IP protocols. Connects thousands of independent networks into a vast global internet.

➤ *TCP/IP (Transmission Control Protocol/Internet Protocol):* Suite of protocols that defines the Internet. Your computer must have TCP/IP software to be on the Internet.

➤ *URL (Uniform Resource Locator):* Standard way to give the address of any resource on the Internet that is part of the World Wide Web (WWW). The most common way to use a URL is to enter into a WWW browser program, such as Netscape or Lynx.

➤ *WWW (World Wide Web):* A whole constellation of resources that can be accessed using Gopher, FTP, HTTP, telnet, USENET, WAIS, or some other tools. Also the universe of hypertext servers (HTTP servers) which are the servers that allow text, graphics, sound files, etc., to be mixed together.

Services Available on the Internet

1. *Electronic mail (e-mail)* is for sending and receiving mail from other users or from members on mailing lists:

- ➤ Messages may be addressed to one particular member or a small group of members
- ➤ *Mailing list:* Discussion group that communicates by e-mail; professional discussions, receiving on-line journals or recent public announcement, job seeking
- ➤ Mailing lists require a subscription by sending a message to the "listserv" computer host
- ➤ *Listserv:* Program that handles the group or list
- ➤ *Listname address:* Messages are sent to everyone who has subscribed to that list

2. *World Wide Web (WWW):*
   - ➤ Access to information for research, jobs, counseling courses
   - ➤ URLs of several varieties:
     - *.org:* nonprofit organization (e.g., www.counseling.org)
     - *.edu:* U.S. educational (e.g., www.gmu.edu/)
     - *.com:* U.S. commercial (e.g., www.microsoft.com)
     - *.gov:* U.S. government (e.g., www.ed.gov)
     - *.mil:* U.S. military (e.g., www.pentagon.mil)
   - ➤ URLs may change, but usually new URLs are available at the old sites
   - ➤ **List 12-43,** *Reproducible List of URLs for Counselors, Alphabetical by Topic*

3. *FTP (file transfers protocols)* enables users to download information, graphics, and software files.

4. *USENET and other interest-based discussion groups:* Newsgroups for online (delayed, not live) conversations with other users, and enables downloading of free software.

5. *Gopher* and *Archie* are information and file retrieval and transfer systems when searching for information.

6. *Internet Relay Chat (IRC)* is used for conversations with other users in "real time."

7. *Telnet* is a log to other computers used by many library catalogs. This is also a vehicle to go from one network to another.

Search Engines and Directories

These are WWW sites that enable users to search for information according to a specified process. Examples:

- ➤ Search engines:
  - Yahoo (http://www.yahoo.com)
  - Excite (http://www.excite.com)
  - Open Text Index (http://www.opentext.com/omw/f-omw.html)
- ➤ URLs of some professional associations:
  - American Academy of Child and Adolescent Psychiatry (AACAP)
    http://www.aacap.org/web/aacap/
  - College Board
    http://www.collegeboard.org/
  - National Association of College Admission Counselors (NACAC)
    http://www.nacac.com/
- ➤ Some professional mailing lists:
  - AERA-E (American Educational Research Association, Division E): Counseling and Human Development Forum. To sign on, send the message:
    "subscribe AERA-E (first name) (last name)" to
    listserv@asuvm.inre.asu.edu

- CESNET-L (Counselor Education and Supervision Network): To sign on, send the message: "subscribe CESNET-L (first name) (last name)" to listserv@univcsvm.csd.scarolina.edu
- ICN (International Counselor Network): To sign on, send the message: "subscribe ICN (first name) (last name)" to listserv@utkvm1.utk.edu

➤ Some newsgroups:
  - Attention Deficit Disorder (ADD)
    alt.support.attn-deficit
  - Cult Members—Former Cult Members Family and Friends Support
    alt.support.ex-cult
  - Depression, Family Support
    soc.support.depression.family
  - Grief
    alt.support.grief
  - Learning Disabled
    alt.support.learning-disab
  - Oppositional Defiant Disorder
    alt.support.opp-defiant
  - Parenting Help
    alt.parenting.solutions

➤ Chatting on the Internet
  - *Chatting:* Talking by writing text, in real time, to one person or a whole class or room of people:
    1) support groups, self-help groups
    2) professional conferences
  - *Kid Care:* Resource for parents of children under age 18:
    1) provides information, answers to questions
    2) scheduled discussion times with professionals and other parents to chat
    3) topics include growth and development, ADD, talking with teens about sex, and other topics

ADDITIONAL INFORMATION

Reproducible List of Internet Resources for the School Counselor (List 12-43)

Bartolotta, M. (1997). Personal communication.

Brady, V. M. Listservs for Counselors
http:plaid.hawk.plattsburgh.edu/cnet/Listservs%20test%20page/listserv.html

Davidson, C. T. & Jackson, M. L. (1996, September). The web we weave: Using the Internet for counseling research—Part II. *Counseling Today, 39*(3), 22–24.

Internet Literacy Consultants (1994–97). *Glossary of Internet Terms.*

Jackson, M. L. & Davidson, C. T. (1996, August). The web we weave: Using the Internet for counseling research—Part I. *Counseling Today, 39*(2), 20–22.

McCane, W. (1996, August). Internet resources for school counselors. [On-line] Available:
http://www.indep.k12.mo.us/WC/wmccane.html

Section 3

ACADEMIC/EDUCATIONAL COUNSELING AND GUIDANCE K–12

ACADEMIC/EDUCATIONAL GOALS

3-1 ACADEMIC/EDUCATIONAL GOALS FOR ALL STUDENTS

Goals for Students

➤ Achieve goals commensurate with individual potential:
  – Plan and pursue a balanced educational program.
  – Be prepared for postsecondary education or a full-time job.

➤ Become an independent learner:
  – Maintain a positive attitude toward learning.
  – Become aware of own abilities, interests, and educational needs.
  – Acquire knowledge of educational opportunities.
  – Prepare for next level of education.

➤ Apply effective skills for life-long learning:
  – Develop goal-setting skills. *(List 3-2)*
  – Develop study skills. *(List 3-3)*
  – Develop test-taking skills. *(List 3-4)*
  – Develop time-management skills. *(List 3-5)*
  – Develop problem-solving skills. *(List 2-23)*

➤ Accept personal responsibility for self-direction.

Counselor's Actions

➤ Provide academic guidance lessons to students:
  – Teach effective skills for learning.
  – Inform students of educational opportunities.

➤ Consult with parents/guardians:
  – Inform parents of higher education opportunities for students.
  – Inform parents about financial aid.
  – Assist parents with child-rearing concerns.
  – Assist parents to obtain necessary services for students with identified learning problems.

➤ Consult with teachers:
  – Identify learning problems early.
  – Identify successful procedures to help students learn.

➤ Provide individual and group academic counseling:
  – Review student progress through report cards.
  – Assist students to improve academically.

➤ Collaborate with parents/guardians, teachers, administrators, and other school personnel to provide services:
  – Ensure school is positive environment for learning of all students. *(List 2-46)*
  – Promote positive school-home relationships. *(List 2-52)*
  – Coordinate parent/teacher conferences. *(List 2-43)*

ADDITIONAL INFORMATION

See Lists 2-33 through 2-37, *Consultant to Parents/Guardians.*

See Lists 2-38 through 2-45, *Consultant to Teachers.*

ACADEMIC GUIDANCE FOR ALL STUDENTS
3-2 GOAL-SETTING SKILLS

Goal-Setting Criteria for Students

➤ Specify the goal or desired result:
  – Set a specific time frame to achieve it.
  – Make it concrete enough to plan and take action.
  – Make it specific enough to observe and recognize progress.
  – Make it realistic and achievable, given past experience.
  – Make it independent of another person's actions.

➤ Confirm that it is desirable and positive for all concerned.

➤ Confirm that it is considerate of others.

Goal-Setting Process for Students

➤ Identify and write a goal that meets all criteria.

➤ Identify possible barriers to achievement of the goal.

➤ Specify ways to overcome barriers to achievement.

➤ Specify resources to help achieve the goal.

➤ Commit to another person to work toward achievement of the goal.

➤ Itemize the steps required to achieve the goal.

➤ Note progress of achievement of each step.

➤ Use the problem-solving model. *(List 2-23)*

Example of Academic Goal-Setting

➤ *Goal:* Academic success in high school course(s), e.g., specific grade in course or grade point average (GPA).

➤ Steps to achieve goal:
  – Complete daily assignments. *(List 3-3)*
  – Study for tests, quizzes, labs. *(List 3-4)*
  – Participate in class.
  – Demonstrate attentive behavior.
  – Respond positively to criticism.
  – Work well with others.
  – Work well independently.

ADDITIONAL INFORMATION

Hitchner, K. W. & Tifft-Hitchner, A. (1996). Student performance report. In *Counseling today's secondary students* (p. 45). *(List 12-3)*

Lunter, M. (1990). Improve academic performance. In D. J. Blum (Ed.), *Group counseling for secondary schools* (pp. 3–21). *(List 12-17)*

3-3 STUDY SKILLS

Listening Skills for Students

➤ Learn teachers' expectations for students in all courses.

➤ Understand teachers' grading policies.

➤ Listen for main ideas and ways that teachers stress them.

Organizing Skills for Students

➤ Set aside a specific time and place to complete homework.

➤ Prepare to study by having all materials easily accessible.

➤ Preview the textbook.

➤ Read the textbook on schedule or before the lesson to be discussed.

➤ Write questions when reading the text:
  – Find answers by reading.
  – Find answers by asking these questions in class.
  – Find answers by asking the teachers after class.

➤ Summarize ideas from reading and notes.

Study Aids for Students

➤ Create visual images to aid memory.

➤ Use keywords, images in sequence, jingles, acronyms.

Note-Taking Skills for Students

➣ Underline or highlight the main ideas the teachers stressed.

➣ Write the main ideas the teachers stressed.

➣ Write explanations of problems.

➣ Write summaries of class discussions.

Reviewing Skills for Students

➣ Review first the main ideas that the teachers stressed.

➣ Review class notes before studying next assignment.

➣ Review notes and textbook before a test.

ADDITIONAL INFORMATION

See *List 3-5, Time-Management Skills.*

Perlstein, R. (1996). Family algebra night. *The Mathematics Teacher, 89*(1), 28.

3-4 TEST-TAKING SKILLS

Student Skills for All Tests

1. Listen to directions:
   – Listen to test administrator before starting to answer questions.
   – Keep directions in mind while completing the test.

2. Ask questions:
   – Know time limit.
   – Know advisability of guessing answers on particular test.

3. Work all examples and take examples seriously.

4. Scan the test:
   – Look over entire test before answering any questions.
   – Work all easy items first.
   – Leave blank any items that need computing and items to which answers are not known.

5. Read each item carefully.

6. Answer the precise question, paying particular attention to key terms.

7. Work as rapidly as possible with reasonable assurance of accuracy.

8. Work carefully on items that yield the most points.

9. Return to beginning, and answer all items left blank after completing all known items.

10. Guess between two answers if all but two answers of a multiple-choice item can be deleted.

11. Attempt to answer every question.

12. Analyze difficult questions, breaking them into sequential steps.

13. Translate material in a difficult question into a different form.

14. Re-read all questions and check all answers.

Student Preparation for Teacher-Made Tests

➤ Prepare in advance *(List 3-3):*
 – Complete assignments on time.
 – Review notes and textbook.

➤ Ask what the test will cover:
 – Highlight these things in notes and textbook before test.
 – Formulate and write sample test questions and write answers.
 – Review carefully and purposefully for test.

Student Preparation for the Preliminary Scholastic Assessment Test (PSAT) and the Scholastic Assessment Test (SAT)

➤ Practice taking tests, particularly standardized tests.

➤ Practice by taking previously administered PSATs and SATs.

➤ Read constantly: newspapers, plays, fiction, mysteries, and other literature.

➤ Make flash cards of new words.

➤ Review geometry.

➤ Use books and computer software for practice.

➤ Use SAT Question and Answer Service.

ADDITIONAL INFORMATION

See *List 9-2, College.*

8 Real SAT tests—Complete SATs with test-taking tips. *(List 9-25)*

Algebra smart—CD-ROM to prepare for the SAT I and SAT II.

Computer preparation for the SAT (Harcourt, Brace, Jovanovich), grades 9–12.

H.S. Vocabulary—SAT, vocabulary, and reading speed help (Public Brand Software).

SAT I Scholastic Assessment Test I: Reasoning Test. (List 9-25)

SAT II Scholastic Assessment Test II: Subject Tests—Albegra Smart, Science Smart, and Word Smart. *(List 9-25)*

Science Smart—CD-ROM to prepare for the SAT II. *(List 9-25)*

Test skills: A test preparation program for the PSAT/NMSQT. (List 9-2)

Testwise—Preparing for the SAT (College Board), grades 9–12.

Verbal Assault—Vocabulary help for SAT (Public Brand Software).

Vocabulary Helper—Vocabulary testing game (Sizzle Shareware Library).

Vocabulary Help Grades 6–12—SAT and vocabulary help (Software Excitement).

Word Smart—CD-ROM to prepare for SAT I and SAT II. *(List 9-25)*

Carris, J. D. *SAT success. (List 9-2)*

3-5 TIME-MANAGEMENT SKILLS

Time-Management Skills for Students

➤ Establish goals and priorities:
- – Set long-term and short-term goals.
- – Work consistently on long-term projects.
- – Estimate time required for each priority task.
- – Divide long-term assignment into parts or steps.
- – Estimate time required for each step.
- – Write steps and dates for completion of each step.
- – Plan backwards from due date.
- – Reassess priorities when necessary.

➤ Study actively:
- – Keep purpose of the assignment in mind.
- – Construct and use cue cards.
- – Discuss topics with a classmate.
- – Focus on content that teacher stressed as important.
- – Define next step before leaving each activity.
- – Do important work during best time of day.
- – Eliminate interruptions during study time.
- – Summarize frequently.

➤ Establish regular patterns of study:
- – Set a routine.
- – Complete all reading assignments on time.

➤ Keep a written schedule:
- – Enter all dates for tests, term papers, assignments.
- – Construct to-do lists for all projects daily.
- – Cross off completed tasks daily.
- – Include time for enjoyment, exercise, relaxation, eating, socializing.
- – Review and acknowledge progress weekly.

➤ Review frequently:
- – Assignments including reading assignments
- – Teacher's directions to complete assignments
- – Notes before class
- – Notes after class
- – Study aids

ADDITIONAL INFORMATION

See *List 3-3, Study Skills.*

3-6   COURSE SELECTION FOR FUTURE OPPORTUNITIES

Content of a Six-Year Educational/Career Plan for Students

➤ Credits earned

➤ Courses required for a technical high school program (Regular Diploma)

➤ Courses required for a technical high school program with college requirements (Advanced Diploma)

➤ Courses recommended for admission to a selective college/university

➤ Individual plan for courses each school year:
   – Complete in pencil so it can be revised easily.
   – Design for flexibility.
   – Review and update each semester.

Course Selection: Elementary School Preparation

➤ Help students identify their interests, strengths, values, experiences, and career aspirations.

➤ Encourage students to think about their career and educational future and keep their options open by beginning a six-year educational/career plan.

➤ Encourage students to have positive attitudes and develop strength in mathematics and science.

➤ Engage students and parents in long-range educational planning.

➤ Encourage students, particularly students of color and female students, to acknowledge their abilities, set high goals, and envision themselves as leaders.

Course Selection: Middle School

➤ Encourage students and parents to plan their postsecondary education and take the most challenging courses in which they can succeed.

➤ Assist students of color and female students to overcome any barriers to selecting the most challenging courses.

➤ Encourage all students, particularly students of color and female students, to try the more challenging courses and monitor their progress.

➤ Inform students, teachers, and parents of the need for specific mathematics, science, and foreign language credits for some postsecondary opportunities.

Course Selection: Middle School and High School

➤ Recommend that students consider their abilities, interests, values, and career aspirations when completing and updating the six-year plan of courses.

➤ Inform teachers of the academic course credits needed for graduation and admission to the most selective universities.

➤ Review the course guide and the course selection form with groups of students, parents, and teachers.

➤ Recommend that students indicate alternative courses.

➤ Encourage students and parents to heed advice of teachers about sequential courses.

➤ Be sensitive to ethnicity, gender, and social class of students and parents, making them aware of their opportunities.

➤ Encourage all students, particularly students of color and female students, to set high academic goals and make concrete plans, specifying high school courses needed to achieve the goals identified.

➤ Encourage female students to consider nontraditional careers, if desired.

➤ Inform students, teachers, and parents of various career opportunities and their course requirements.

➤ Update information and advise students and parents about course content, sequence of courses, prerequisites, number of credits, college admission requirements, teacher expectations, and actual demands of courses.

➤ Suggest curricular programs and/or classes to assist students of color and female students to succeed in mathematics, science, and foreign language courses, when appropriate.

➤ Confirm student requests for advanced placement (AP) courses as intellectual challenge or increased knowledge of the subject.

➤ Inform students that AP test scores are interpreted differently by different universities.

➤ Inform students, teachers, and parents that the strength of curriculum is important for college admission.

➤ Inform students, teachers, and parents that the mastery of higher mathematics and foreign language is necessary for admission to selective colleges.

➤ Encourage parents of students of color and female students to motivate their children to explore, experiment, and envision futures of leadership.

ADDITIONAL INFORMATION

See *College Admissions: Octameron.* *(List 9-2)*

Destination college: Planning with the PSAT/NMSQT. *(List 9-25)*

Hitchner, K. W. & Tifft-Hitchner, A. (1987). Staying on top of today's curriculum. In *A survival guide for the secondary school counselor* (pp. 87–102). *(List 12-3)*

Hitchner, K. W. & Tifft-Hitchner, A. (1996). Academic, long-range planning: Four- and six-year programs of study. In *Counseling today's secondary students* (pp. 19–22). *(List 12-3)*

3-7 POST-HIGH SCHOOL EDUCATIONAL SEARCH

Inform students and parents about the following.

Postsecondary Alternatives

➤ Public four- or five-year university

➤ Private four- or five-year university

➤ Public four- or five-year college

➤ Private four- or five-year college

➤ Military

➤ Private junior college

➤ Two-year community college

➤ Technical/business school

➤ Private career school

➤ Apprenticeship

➤ On-the-job training

➤ Volunteer service

Institutional Factors

➤ Enrollment

➤ Selectivity

➤ Teaching quality

➤ Competitiveness of students

➤ Work experience or cooperative education availability

➤ Social opportunities

➤ Cultural opportunities

➤ Retention of students

➤ Sports program

➤ Student support services

➤ Success of students with similar personal factors

➤ Transfer possibility

➤ Employability after graduation

➤ Rate of graduation in four or five years

➤ Special programs (tutoring, specific cultural, learning disabled, physically disabled, academic probation)

➤ Diversity or dominance of racial, ethnic, religious, and social cultures

➤ Flexibility about college major (uncertainty, creativity, double, changing)

➤ Acceptance of AP or CLEP for credit

➤ Remediation opportunities

Personal Factors

- ➤ Finances and economic responsibility
- ➤ Number of years available for college education
- ➤ Desirability of competition
- ➤ Academic ability
- ➤ Academic preparation
- ➤ Desired major
- ➤ Desired career or field of interest
- ➤ Family expectations
- ➤ Readiness to live away from home
- ➤ Proximity to home
- ➤ Desired social life
- ➤ Desired size of institution
- ➤ Locale in city, suburb, or rural area
- ➤ Determination, persistence, and effort
- ➤ Flexibility
- ➤ Need for employment
- ➤ Dependence/independence
- ➤ Attrition possibility
- ➤ Graduate school possibility

ADDITIONAL INFORMATION

See: http://www.[name of college].edu

List 9-2, *College Search: College Board Publications.*

Hitchner, K. W. & Tifft-Hitchner, A. (1996). To go or not to go. In *Counseling today's secondary students* (pp. 163–168). **(List 12-3)**

Peterson's Guides. **(List 9-2)**

3-8 COLLEGE APPLICATIONS

➤ Acquire personal knowledge about colleges to which many students apply:
  – Become personally acquainted with college admissions directors.
  – Shadow a college admissions director.
  – Call college admissions office when appropriate.
  – Explain grading policy when high school grades may not be understood in college admissions.

➤ Train volunteers to meet with college representatives, maintain, and update information to share with students and parents.

➤ Conduct workshops for teachers on how to write college recommendations.

➤ Encourage teachers to assist students in college search, applications, and essay writing.

➤ Exchange application information with counselors in other schools.

➤ Evaluate how the high school presents students for admissions:
  – Examine content and format of transcripts.
  – Evaluate the high school profile.
  – Compile profiles from other high schools.
  – Consult with staff, faculty, administrators, and parents to revise the high school profile.

➤ Inform administrators of the importance for easily understood grading system.

➤ Conduct follow-up of graduates during college years. *(List 9-2)*

➤ Compile, update, and share objective information about anonymous previous applicants and the admissions outcome. *(List 9-2)*
  – Range of SAT scores
  – Grade point average (GPA)

➤ Make information about previous applicants available to seniors, parents, and teachers.

➤ Provide opportunities for graduates to give information and support to applicants.

➤ Prepare students realistically for application process, including rejections.

➤ Encourage students to role-play college admissions committee and make decisions.

➤ Invite parents to observe the role-play of college admissions committee.

➤ Provide workshops for students and parents about college admissions.

➤ Assist students and parents to make informed decisions about colleges.

Special Applications Suggestions to Students

➤ Read directions on application carefully.

➤ Early action:
  – Apply early
  – No early commitment required
  – May be rejected and not deferred for regular consideration
  – Fewer colleges offer early action than early decision

➤ Early decision:
- Apply to only one participating college by mid-November
- When admitted in December, applicant *must* accept the offer
- Score Choice on SAT II not recommended for seniors
- If rejected as early decision, usually application is deferred for regular consideration

➤ Common application

Suggestions to Students and Parents

➤ Prepare personal portfolio early.

➤ Take challenging academic courses throughout high school.

➤ Take PSAT as a junior; strong students may take it additionally as a sophomore.

➤ Take the SAT I during junior year.

➤ Waive the right to read recommendations.

➤ Consider appropriate disclosure on application form.

➤ Consider writing the application form by hand.

➤ Complete all optional questions.

➤ Select samples of supporting materials judiciously.

➤ Select writers of recommendations carefully:
- Person who knows student well
- Person who will heed the deadline
- Person who is a good writer

➤ Stress a unique strength, experience, interest.

➤ Visit the college and have a personal interview, if possible.

➤ Consider taking the SAT I more than once.

➤ Determine desirability of submitting application technologically, on diskette or on-line.

ADDITIONAL INFORMATION

See *List 9-2*, *College*.

National Association of College Admissions Counselors. Alexandria, VA: Author.

Statement of principles of good practice

Statement on pre-college guidance and counseling/Role of the school counselor

Statement on recruitment and admission of student athletes

Guidelines for the traditionally underrepresented in higher education

Guidelines for admission decision options in higher education

Perlstein, R. (1990). Write for self-understanding: Write a college application essay. In D. J. Blum (Ed.), *Group counseling for secondary schools* (pp. 79–93). *(List 12-17)*

Swanson, S. (Annual). *The college counselor computer program database.* Washington, DC: The College Counselor. *(List 9-2)*

3-9   COLLEGE APPLICATION ESSAYS

Counselor Presentation in Classes

➢ Motivate students to plan ahead.

➢ Help students get started and not procrastinate.

➢ Assist students to affirm their experiences as worthwhile.

➢ Help students gain self-knowledge.

➢ Stimulate students to feel self-confident.

➢ Encourage students to brainstorm.

Writing Workshops With Parents/Guardians

➢ Co-lead with teacher of English 12.

➢ Invite parents to participate as a family group, or with other families.

➢ Assist parents to understand student's stress about college applications.

➢ Inform parents about the writing process and expectations of colleges.

➢ Encourage parents to read their child's college applications.

➢ Encourage parents to read and listen to their child's essay.

Suggestions to Students: Successful College Essays

➢ Maintain a personal tone:
  - Show how personal experiences have influenced you.
  - Reveal your character, cooperation, perseverance, self-discipline.
  - Examine your personal aspirations, interests, values, experiences.
  - Be open and honest.

➢ Practice writing, reading aloud, and receiving constructive criticism.

ADDITIONAL INFORMATION

Curry, B. & Kasbar, B. (1986). *Essays that worked.* *(List 9-2)*

Nourse, K. A. (1995). *How to write your college application essay.* *(List 9-2)*

Perlstein, R. (1990). Write for self-understanding: Write a college application essay. In D. J. Blum (Ed.), *Group counseling for secondary schools* (pp. 79–93). *(List 12-17)*

See *College Admissions: Octameron.* *(List 9-2)*

See *College Applications/Essays.* *(List 9-2)*

See *Peterson's Guides.* *(List 9-2)*

3-10 COLLEGE RECOMMENDATIONS

➤ Teacher recommendations:
  – Inform teachers and students of the procedures.
  – Give students and teachers written guidelines.
  – Inform teachers that recommendations may be seen by the student, even when confidential rights are waived.

➤ Suggestions to teachers for writing recommendations:
  – Be creative.
  – Contribute substantive content.
  – Describe the applicant vividly.
  – Describe the applicant's participation in specific class.
  – Provide specific examples.

➤ Suggestions for writing counselor recommendations:
  – Consult applicants' personal portfolios.
  – Request parental input each year.
  – Update students' written educational/career plans each year.
  – Request that students and parents specify in writing the strengths, interests, achievements, and experiences influencing the student when a senior.
  – Interview the student applicants.
  – Use applicants, teachers, and parents as resources.
  – Consult with previous counselors of the applicants.
  – Be succinct, objective, and honest.
  – Present the uniqueness of each applicant.
  – Address any discrepancies or probable questions of the applicant's record.
  – Write specific strengths of applicants and their mastery of the curriculum.

ADDITIONAL INFORMATION

Fields, T. (1993). The role of teacher and college recommendations in admission selection to highly competitive universities. *The Journal of College Admission,* Spring 1993, No. 139. *(List 9-2)*

3-11   FINAL COLLEGE SELECTION

Decision-Making Process for Students

Help students and family members apply the decision-making process by encouraging them to do the following:

1. Begin early.
   - ➤ Begin in Junior year.
   - ➤ Follow the calendar provided by guidance.
   - ➤ Attend meetings provided by guidance.

2. Determine the goal.
   See *List 3-2, Goal-Setting Skills for Students.*

3. Acquire information.
   - ➤ Assess self (Personal Factors in *List 3-7*):
     - – Interests
     - – Strengths
     - – Experiences
     - – Weaknesses
     - – Aspirations
     - – Goals
   - ➤ Assess college alternatives (Institutional Factors in *List 3-7).*
   - ➤ Research eight to ten colleges of interest:
     - – Consider college acceptance of graduates from respective high school.
     - – Consider academic credentials:
       1) High school courses completed
       2) Grade Point Average (GPA)
       3) Rank in Class (RIC)
       4) Standardized test scores (SAT/ACT)
       5) Extracurricular activities
       6) Other academic factors
     - – Consider personal factors.
   - ➤ Attend meetings with college representatives.
   - ➤ Visit colleges and attend college classes when possible.
   - ➤ Generate options.
   - ➤ List colleges that meet preferences.
   - ➤ List colleges that meet qualifications.

4. Examine probable consequences of each option.
   - ➤ Determine probability of acceptance at each college:
     - – One or two that are sure acceptances
     - – One or two that are reaches
     - – One or two that are probable acceptances

5. Select best option.
   - ➤ Select three to six colleges most likely to attend.

6. Take action.
   - ➤ Apply to three to six colleges selected.
7. Re-evaluate.
   - ➤ Re-evaluate and repeat process when accepted at more than one college.

ADDITIONAL INFORMATION

Hitchner, K. W. & Tifft-Hitchner, A. (1996). *Counseling today's secondary students.* *(List 12-3)*

Journal of College Admission. *(List 9-2)*

Pope, L. (1995). *Looking beyond the ivy league: Finding the college that's right for you.* *(List 9-2)*

Wilson, E. B. (1993). *100 best colleges for African-American students.* *(List 9-2)*

3-12   FINANCIAL AID SEARCH

Counselor's Actions

- ➤ Plan and conduct financial aid meetings for parents of students grades 7–12.
- ➤ Arrange for college/career center to be open one evening a week upon request.
- ➤ Teach students and parents how to find financial aid information.
- ➤ Encourage students and parents to research financial aid opportunities:
  - – Learn the average amount of financial aid awarded each year by college.
  - – Consider a community college or a private junior college when finances are limited.
  - – Request interview at college to discuss financial aid after admission, if aid is critical.
  - – Determine necessity of completing the Profile, computerized or paper version.
  - – Complete the Free Application for Federal Student Aid (FAFSA) accurately to be considered for any federal aid program.
- ➤ Advise students and parents that request for financial aid is not always withheld from college admissions office.
- ➤ Recommend to parents that they calculate expected family contribution (Practice FAFSA) on Internet.
- ➤ Advise students and parents to file the computerized version of the FAFSA (FAFSA Express) when possible.
- ➤ Update financial aid information.

ADDITIONAL INFORMATION

See *List 12-44. Reproducible List of Internet Resources.*

See *http://www.finaid.org* (this is the estimated family contribution).

See *http://www.ed.gov/prog-info/SFA/StudentGuide/Department of Education.*

See *http://www.ed.gov/offices/OPE/express.html* (to download FAFSA Express).

American College Testing Program (ACT). *Applying for financial aid.* Iowa City, IA: Author.

Bellantoni, P. (1996). *College financial aid made easy.* *(List 9-2)*

Cassidy, D. J. (1996). *The scholarship book,* (4th ed.) *(List 9-2)*

College Board. (1997). *College costs and financial aids handbook.* New York, NY: Author.

Heath Resource Center. (1996). *Heath resource directory.* A directory of financial resources for college. *(List 9-2)*

Leider, A. & Leider, R. (1996). *Don't miss out!* The ambitious student's guide to financial aid, (21st ed.), Alexandria, VA: Octameron. **(List 9-2)**

Office of Education Research. (1992). *Education, career, and financial aid guide.* Washington, DC: Author.

3-13   READINESS FOR COLLEGE

➤ Encourage, plan, and conduct interchange of college students and high school seniors.

➤ Encourage students to visit with college representatives.

➤ Encourage students to visit colleges:
  – Visit college classes.
  – Talk with college students.
  – Stay in residence hall with a friend.
  – Attend a college activity.

➤ Conduct group counseling for seniors:
  – Discuss living away from home.
  – Discuss difficulties of sharing a room.
  – Discuss time management.
  – Discuss study skills.

ADDITIONAL INFORMATION

College freshman survival guide. (1992). *(List 9-26)*

ACADEMIC COUNSELING K–12

3-14 COUNSELING STUDENTS WITH ACADEMIC PROBLEMS

Counselor's Actions

➤ Maintain a helpful relationship.

➤ Use counseling skills:
  - Listen empathetically and nonjudgmentally. *(List 2-1)*
  - Acknowledge and validate student's experience.
  - Reflect, clarify, summarize.
  - Use the problem-solving model. *(List 2-23)*
  - Promote change with selected counseling theory. *(Lists 2-8 through 2-18)*
  - Assist in prioritizing desired results.
  - Assist in visualizing the desired result.
  - Assist in specifying steps to achieve desired result.
  - Assist in recognizing strengths and resources to achieve steps toward success.
  - Assist in recognizing the success of each step.
  - Show how above procedure can be used to meet other goals.

➤ Follow up and evaluate.

ADDITIONAL INFORMATION

See *Lists 2-19 through 2-28, Counselor of the Individual* and *Leader of Small Group Counseling.*

Mandell, H. P. (1995). *Could do better: Why children underachieve and what to do about it.* New York, NY: John Wiley and Sons.

3-15 CONSULTING WITH TEACHERS OF STUDENTS WITH ACADEMIC PROBLEMS

Counselor's Actions

➤ Encourage teachers to do the following:
  - Maintain high standards and expectations.
  - Require effort and hard work from *all* students.
  - Notice and acknowledge effort.
  - Insist that students work to their full potential.
  - Clearly explain expectations, how to study, and grading procedures.
  - Give feedback on quizzes, homework, and tests.
  - Assign meaningful homework.
  - Give credit for successfully completing homework.
  - Provide opportunities for students to learn from their mistakes.

ADDITIONAL INFORMATION

Office of Educational Research and Improvement. (1992). Hard work and high expectations: Motivating students to learn. In *Issues in Education,* June 1992. Washington DC: U.S. Department of Education.

3-16 COUNSELING STUDENTS WITH LEARNING OR PHYSICAL PROBLEMS

Categories of Some Learning Problems

➤ Attention deficit disorder (ADD)

➤ Attention deficit disorder with hyperactivity (ADHD)

➤ Autism

➤ Behavior disorder (BD)

➤ Brain injury (BI)

➤ Emotional disturbance (ED)

➤ Learning disability (LD)

➤ Mental retardation (MR)

➤ Noncategorical

➤ Mildly handicapped

➤ Physically handicapped (PH)

Categories of Some Physical Problems

➤ Adolescent pregnancy

➤ Amputations

➤ Brain injury

➤ Cystic fibrosis

➤ Diabetes

➤ Drug addiction

➤ Eating disorders

➤ Epilepsy

➤ Hearing impairment

➤ Language delay

➤ Muscular distrophy

➤ Nicotine addiction

➤ Obsessive-compulsive disorder (OCD)

➤ Sickle cell anemia

➤ Somatic disorders

➤ Spina bifida

➤ Substance abuse

➤ Tourette's syndrome (TS)

➤ Visual impairment

Characteristics of Students With Learning or Physical Problems

Students may show the following characteristics:

- ➤ Inability to learn as other students
- ➤ Inability to form satisfactory personal relationships
- ➤ Inappropriate behavior
- ➤ Physical symptoms
- ➤ Pervasive despair or depression
- ➤ Frequent fights
- ➤ Auditory or visual misperceptions
- ➤ Temper tantrums
- ➤ Disobedience
- ➤ Hyperactivity
- ➤ Impulsivity
- ➤ Aggressive behaviors
- ➤ Social maladjustment and/or immaturity
- ➤ Anxiety and fearfulness
- ➤ Low self-confidence
- ➤ Low academic performance
- ➤ Withdrawal
- ➤ Problems with peers and adults
- ➤ Frequent distractibility
- ➤ Suicidal ideation
- ➤ Short attention span
- ➤ Anxiety
- ➤ Shame

Counselor's Actions

- ➤ Provide accepting relationship and unconditional positive regard.
- ➤ Obtain a basic knowledge of the problem:
    - General characteristics
    - Symptoms
    - Needs specific to exceptional condition
    - Assessment instruments
    - Prognosis
- ➤ Learn the student's particular strengths and potential.
- ➤ Help student and parent adjust to and cope with handicapping condition.
- ➤ Help student deal with feelings of rejection.
- ➤ Help student gain feelings of self-worth.

➤ Help student deal with repeated failures.

➤ Listen, accept, and reflect student's fears, anxieties, doubts, and insecurities.

➤ Reframe student's expressions into appropriate statements.

➤ Consider using behavioral modification techniques. *(List 2-10)*

➤ Teach personal and social skills in a group when possible.

➤ Help strengthen self-confidence.

➤ Provide outlets for student's release of tension.

➤ Introduce play therapy for student to ventilate or express emotions safely.

➤ Provide group counseling to observe and work with other students.

➤ Provide security and stability.

➤ Discuss appropriate behavior.

➤ Coordinate services for the student.

➤ Assist in making career plans.

➤ Help student become independent and in control of own life.

➤ Observe effects of medication and report to parents.

➤ Assist parents in setting realistic expectations for their child.

➤ Encourage parents to view their child as a unique individual.

➤ Coordinate meeting of teacher and parents for consistency of rules.

➤ Understand parents' feelings of stress, guilt, fear, and frustration.

➤ Consult and collaborate with parents, agencies, other professionals.

➤ Recommend services for the family.

ADDITIONAL INFORMATION

See *List 3-14, Counseling Students With Academic Problems.*

American Psychiatric Association. (1994). DSM IV *Diagnostic and statistical manual of mental disorders* (4th ed.). *(List 12-33)*

Lerner, J. (1989). *Learning disabilities, theories, diagnosis and teaching strategies* (5th ed.). Boston, MA: Houghton Mifflin.

Pierangelo, R. (1995). *The special education teacher's book of lists. (List 12-33)*

Thompson, C. L. & Rudolph, L. B. (1996). *Counseling children* (4th ed.). *(List 12-3)*

3-17 COUNSELING STUDENTS WITH ATTENTION DEFICIT DISORDER (ADD)

Characteristics of Students With ADD (Easily Confused With Other Problems)

Students exhibit the following characteristics frequently, intensively, and for some duration before age 7:

- ➤ Aggressive behavior
- ➤ Acting before thinking
- ➤ Careless, disorganized work
- ➤ Difficulty listening, focusing, and concentrating
- ➤ Difficulty paying attention
- ➤ Difficulty remaining in seat
- ➤ Difficulty staying on task or on play activity
- ➤ Difficulty with delayed gratification
- ➤ Difficulty waiting their turn
- ➤ Distractibility
- ➤ Failure in finishing things started
- ➤ Fidgeting excessively
- ➤ Hyperactivity (ADHD)
- ➤ Impulsivity
- ➤ Inappropriate risk-taking
- ➤ Interrupting class and others frequently
- ➤ Low self-esteem
- ➤ Requiring close supervision
- ➤ Running or climbing excessively
- ➤ Short temper
- ➤ Shy, withdrawn behavior
- ➤ Unpredictable mood swings

Problems That Can Mask, Coexist, or Be Confused With ADD

- ➤ Learning disabilities
- ➤ Depression
- ➤ Anxiety
- ➤ Hearing loss
- ➤ Sleep disorders
- ➤ Epilepsy

Needs of Students With ADD

➤ Room with limited stimuli

➤ Consistent schedule

➤ Structured environment

➤ Consistent rules at home and at school

Counselor's Actions

➤ Observe child in variety of school settings.

➤ Refer to school psychologist for observation and Child Study Team.

➤ Recommend to parents a physical examination and a comprehensive assessment to include:
  - Behavioral assessment
  - Educational assessment
  - Psychological assessment
  - Personal interview with child
  - Personal interview with parent

➤ Be aware of seriousness of misdiagnosis.

➤ Observe effects of medication and report to parents/guardians:
  - Stomach aches
  - Sleepiness
  - Slow response
  - Headaches
  - Loss of appetite
  - Weight loss
  - Dizziness
  - Nausea
  - Insomnia

Counseling Focus

➤ Consider behavioral techniques. *(List 2-10)*

➤ Plan a behavior management program with teacher, psychologist, and parents:
  - Apply and maintain consistent rules and structure.
  - Inform student of rules and consequences for breaking rules.
  - Teach student how to self-monitor behavior.
  - Reinforce attainment of short-term goals.

➤ Provide group counseling for effective social skills. *(Lists 2-25 through 2-28)*

➤ Teach problem-solving model. *(List 2-23)*

➤ Provide guidance for managing frustration.

➤ Provide reinforcement for managing frustration.

ADDITIONAL INFORMATION

See *List 3-14, Counseling Students With Academic Problems.*

See *List 3-16, Counseling Students With Learning or Physical Problems.*

See *List 9-2*, *College, Special Students.*

See *List 12-10*, *Disability Awareness.*

American Psychiatric Association. (1994). DSM IV *Diagnostic and statistical manual of mental disorders* (4th ed.). *(List 12-33)*

C.H.A.D.D., an organization with support groups. (812) 332-6155.

Goldstein, S. & Goldstein, M. (1990). *Managing attention disorders in children: A guide for practitioners.* New York: John Wiley & Sons.

McCarney, S. B. (1994). *Attention deficit disorders intervention manual (School version).* *(List 12-10)*

National Institute of Mental Health. *Attention deficit hyperactivity disorder.* Rockville, MD: Author.

Pierangelo, R. (1995). *The special education teacher's book of lists.* *(List 12-33)*

Quinn, P. O. & Stern, J. M. (1993). *The "putting on the brakes" activity book for young people with ADHD.* *(List 7-6)*

Thompson, C. L. & Rudolph, L. B. (1996). *Counseling children* (4th ed.). *(List 12-3)*

3-18 COUNSELING STUDENTS WITH OBSESSIVE-COMPULSIVE DISORDER (OCD)

Characteristics of Students With OCD

➤ Time-consuming recurrent thoughts *(obsessions)*

➤ Repetitive actions in response to thoughts *(compulsions)*

➤ May be accompanied by ADD, phobias, eating disorders, panic attacks, depression, or schizophrenia

➤ Increased incidence with Tourette's syndrome

➤ Symptoms usually appear during adolescence

➤ Males and females equally affected

➤ Insight insufficient to change behavior

➤ Experience shame and secrecy

➤ May include gifted students

Counselor's Actions

➤ Refer to child study committee or local screening committee *(List 2-56).*

➤ Recommend to parents that student be referred for diagnosis.

➤ May request parents' permission to confer with psychologist treating the student.

➤ Observe effects of medication and report to parents.

➤ See Counselor's Actions in *List 3-16*, *Counseling Students With Learning or Physical Problems.*

ADDITIONAL INFORMATION

See *List 3-14*, *Counseling Students With Academic Problems.*

See Counselor Connection.
    http://www.pris.bc.ca/joliver/dis.html

Johnston, H. F. (1993). *Obsessive compulsive disorder in children and adolescents: A guide.* *(List 12-10)*

Rapoport, J. (1989). *The boy who couldn't stop washing: The experience and treatment of obsessive compulsive disorder.* *(List 7-6)*

3-19   COUNSELING STUDENTS WITH TOURETTE'S SYNDROME (TS)

Characteristics of Students With TS

➤ Tics, motor:
- Grimaces, eye blinking
- Head jerking, shrugging
- Spitting, nose rubbing

➤ Tics, verbal:
- Uncontrollable outbursts of profanity or obscenity
- Compulsive repetition of words

➤ Symptoms typically occur during childhood

➤ May be accompanied by ADD/ADHD

➤ May be retarded socially

➤ May possess high intelligence

➤ Frequently confused with delinquency and misbehavior

➤ Males affected more commonly than females

Counselor's Actions

➤ See Counselor's Actions in **List 3-16,** *Counseling Students With Learning or Physical Problems.*

ADDITIONAL INFORMATION

See **List 3-14,** *Counseling Students With Academic Problems.*

Frith, U. (Ed.). (1991). *Autism and Asperger Syndrome.* New York, NY: Cambridge.

Haerle, T. (1992). *Children with Tourette Syndrome: A parent's guide.* University Press. *(List 10-8)*

3-20 CONSULTING WITH TEACHERS OF STUDENTS WITH LEARNING OR PHYSICAL PROBLEMS

Counselor's Actions

Alleviate teachers' anxieties and help teachers do the following:

- ➤ Set realistic, short-term goals for individual students.
- ➤ Look for student's strengths and potential.
- ➤ Provide structured environment.
- ➤ Provide limited stimuli.
- ➤ Provide consistency.
- ➤ Set reasonable limits and consistently enforce them.
- ➤ Design, explain, and follow behavioral contracts.
- ➤ Teach and require respectful and acceptable behavior.
- ➤ Require student to be responsible for own behavior.
- ➤ Determine consequences and be consistent in administering them.
- ➤ Provide a consistent schedule.
- ➤ Provide clear instructions and repeat frequently.
- ➤ Remain calm, patient, and consistent.

ADDITIONAL INFORMATION

Rief, S. F. (1993). *How to reach and teach ADD/ADHD children.* *(List 11-6)*

3-21 COUNSELING STUDENTS WHO ARE POTENTIAL DROPOUTS

Characteristics of Potential Dropouts

➢ Concerned about saving face and being embarrassed in class

➢ Cut class ten or more times

➢ Disruptive in classroom and school

➢ Don't participate in school activities

➢ Easily bored

➢ Feel alienated from school

➢ Show little interest in class work

➢ Have low or failing grades in two or more academic courses

➢ Missed ten or more days of school during semester before dropping out

➢ Moved shortly before dropping out

➢ Have poor or unrealistic self-concept

➢ Have poor peer relationships

➢ Have record of truancy or excessive absence from class

➢ Retained in elementary grades

➢ Suspended several times

➢ Unable to sit for long periods of time

Populations at Risk of Dropping Out of School

➢ Students who are African American, Hispanic American, or Native American

➢ Students who care for sick or elderly family member

➢ Students who changed schools two or more times since grade 8

➢ Students in families of migrant workers

➢ Students from a dysfunctional or abusive family

➢ Students whose families are not involved with the school

➢ Students who have kinesthetic, tactile, or auditory learning styles instead of visual learning style

➢ Students who are from low socio-economic class

➢ Students whose parents dropped out of school

➢ Students who have poor communication and language skills

➢ Students who view current job more important than school

Reasons Dropouts Give for Quitting School

➢ Disciplinary problems and suspensions

➢ Dislike of school

➢ Low academic achievement

➤ Need for money

➤ Pregnancy, parenting, or marriage

➤ Poor relationships with teachers and peers

➤ Problem with alcohol or other drugs

Counselor's Actions

➤ Identify students with poor attendance, grade retention, poor relationships, and failing grades.

➤ Inform administrators and teachers about characteristics of potential dropouts.

➤ Consult with parents of elementary students absent ten or more days.

➤ Refer identified students to child study team or local screening committee.

➤ Counsel identified students:
  – Learn about interests.
  – Learn about academic problems.
  – Learn about family and social influences.
  – Learn about aspirations.
  – Teach positive social behavior.
  – Help students develop a support system.
  – Guide students to set goals.
  – Identify procedures to meet goals.
  – Empower students to make some decisions in their school lives.
  – Help students connect what goes on in school to their present and future lives.
  – Encourage students to see career and job opportunities beyond high school.
  – Help students feel involved in school beyond the classroom.
  – Assist students to recognize opportunities for career and academic success.

➤ Conduct a group conference including student, parent, teachers, and counselor.

➤ Help students, teachers, and staff accept differences of social classes and ethnicity.

➤ Involve parents in the school.

➤ Encourage flexible educational environment to include all learning styles.

➤ Encourage administration to set realistic disciplinary policies and to be flexible.

➤ Encourage teachers to give short assignments and immediate feedback.

➤ Encourage teachers to provide individualized instruction and cooperative learning.

➤ Encourage teachers to maintain high standards and expectations.

➤ Encourage other adults to find something they like about these students.

➤ Monitor class attendance, punctuality, preparedness, and participation.

➤ Begin a mentoring program for at-risk students: *(List 2-52).*
  – Start small.
  – Recruit mentors early.
  – Provide orientation and support to mentors.
  – Provide time for mentors to discuss successes.
  – Set a mentoring schedule of activities.
  – Reward mentors with an award ceremony or other recognition.
  – Don't get discouraged.

➤ Recognize small steps of progress.

➤ Help parents, students, and teachers see progress as fewer F's and D's.

➤ Determine advisability of alternative learning program.

ADDITIONAL INFORMATION

See *List 1-18, Follow-Up of High School Students.*

See *List 3-14, Counseling Students With Academic Problems.*

See *List 3-16, Counseling Students With Learning or Physical Problems.*

Blum, D. J. & Jones, L. A. (1993, January). Academic growth group and mentoring program for potential dropouts. *The School Counselor, 40*(3), 207–217.

Calbert, T. N. (1990). Prevent dropouts. In D. Blum (Ed.), *Group counseling for secondary schools. (List 12-17)*

Doebler, M. K. & Baker, S. B. (1992, March). *Student assistance programs and school counselors: An opportunity to help at-risk students.* Baltimore, MD: American Association for Counseling and Development.

Kronick, R. & Hargis, C. (1990). *Dropouts: Who drops out and why—and the recommended action.* Springfield, IL: Charles C. Thomas.

Kushman, J. & Heariold-Kinney, P. (1996). Understanding and preventing school dropouts. In D. Capuzzi & D. Gross *Youth at risk* (2nd ed.). *(List 12-34)*

Richardson, V., Casanova, U., Placier, P. & Guilfoyle, K. (1989). *School children at-risk.* New York, NY: The Falmer Press.

3-22 COUNSELING STUDENTS WHO FEAR FAILURE

Characteristics of Students Who Fear Failure

➤ Do not try because they may fail.

➤ Consider a single event a catastrophe.

➤ May desire perfection. *(List 3-24)*

➤ Are unable to concentrate on a task. *(List 3-16)*

➤ Procrastinate taking action. *(List 3-26)*

➤ Become tense, immobilized with fear.

Steps for Progress

➤ Help students relax.

➤ Stress the value of effort regardless of success.

➤ Identify strengths and past successes.

➤ Stress the importance of taking action.

➤ Use counseling skills. *(List 3-14)*

➤ Assist students to gain a realistic perspective.

➤ Focus on solutions, not the problem.

➤ Provide information about effective study skills. *(List 3-3)*

➤ Provide information about effective test-taking skills. *(List 3-4)*

➤ Provide opportunities to learn study skills through media. *(Lists 6-20, 7-20, 8-20, 9-25)*

> Become familiar with various opportunities for students with varied interests.
> Consider Solution-Focused Brief Counseling. *(List 2-18)*
> Consider Rational-Emotive-Behavior Counseling. *(List 2-16)*

3-23 COUNSELING STUDENTS WHO FEAR SUCCESS

Characteristics of Students Who Fear Success

> Do not perform near their potential
> Do not study or complete homework
> Spend time socializing with friends
> Appear overly concerned with others' opinions
> Seem overly concerned about their acceptance by peers

Possible Reasons

> Desire acceptance of nonachieving friends *(friendship implications)*
> Desire acceptance by dominant male(s) *(gender implications)*

Steps for Progress

> Be aware of peer motives and peer pressure.
> Influence peer pressure for positive outcomes when possible. *(List 2-25)*
> Assist students to do the following:
> - Determine concrete future goals. *(List 3-2)*
> - Specify current options and future options.
> - Acknowledge advantage of maintaining a variety of options.
> - Commit to putting forth effort on a specific project or course.
> - Recognize the value of academic success.
> - Recognize time limits of options and opportunities.
> - Specify steps indicating progress.
> - Reward progress of each step.
> - Expect some backsliding.

3-24 COUNSELING STUDENTS WHO DESIRE PERFECTION

Characteristics of Students Who Desire Perfection

➢ Fear that they will make a mistake

➢ Become angry or hurt when criticized

➢ Are compulsive about perfect performance

➢ Believe their achievements are never adequate

➢ Fail to enjoy activities, hobbies, sports, leisure, rewards

➢ Feel driven to excel

➢ Dwell on past mistakes

➢ Compare selves with highest achievers

➢ Equate their self-worth with performance

➢ Procrastinate frequently

➢ Worry incessantly about performance

➢ Set rigid expectations

➢ Consider many expectations as catastrophes

➢ Feel compelled to understand every facet of every topic mentioned in class

Steps for Progress

Assist students to do the following:

➢ Set reasonable goals.

➢ Accept that perfection is an illusion.

➢ Acknowledge strengths and achievements.

➢ Value the process of working toward a goal.

➢ View mistakes as learning experiences.

➢ Encourage a hobby or noncompetitive sport.

➢ Encourage appreciation of people with their mistakes.

➢ Understand difference between being desirable and being necessary.

➢ Accept self as worthy after making mistakes.

➢ Acknowledge value of effort regardless of outcome.

➢ Acknowledge that self-worth is not dependent upon performance.

ADDITIONAL INFORMATION

Barrow, J. (1995). *Emotional health perfectionism.*
　　　http://www.mc.duke.edu/h-devil/emotion/perfect.html

Counseling Center, University of Illinois. *Brochures for problem solving, Perfectionism brochure.* **(List 9-15)**

Faull, J. (1996). *Angry young man.*
　　　http://family.starwave.com/experts/faull/archive/fa041296.html

3-25 Counseling Students Who Are Gifted

Characteristics of Students Who Are Gifted

➤ Show evidence of exceptional ability:
  - Intellectual pursuits
  - Creativity
  - Leadership
  - Performing or visual arts
  - Specific academic area

➤ May show any of the following characteristics:
  - Are impatient
  - Are independent and headstrong
  - Are insensitive to the feelings of others
  - Are perceptive
  - Are persistent
  - Are self-centered and sensitive of own feelings
  - Are self-critical and critical of others
  - Avoid routine tasks
  - Conceptualize, reason abstractly, and learn quickly
  - Compensate for any deficiency
  - Disguise concerns
  - Exhibit a mature sense of humor
  - Experience stigma and rejection from peers
  - Feel isolated and alienated
  - Have difficulty prioritizing interests and time
  - Have multiple and broad interests
  - Lack social relationships
  - Need to be challenged
  - Read avidly
  - Recognize inconsistencies quickly
  - Resist conforming
  - Show high verbal ability
  - Show intellectual curiosity
  - Solve cognitive problems well
  - Take inappropriate risks
  - Underachieve

Counselor's Actions

Also see *List 3-24.*

➤ Accept feelings of inadequacy as genuine.

➤ Assist in acceptance of abilities, interests, and limitations.

➤ Assist in accepting others' abilities and limitations.

➤ Assist in development of abilities.

➤ Assist in exploring opportunities.

➤ Assist in personal decision making.

➤ Help set realistic goals.

➤ Help acquire appropriate social skills.

➤ Help deal with stress.

➤ Help recognize career options.

➤ Realize students may experience poor social relationships.

➤ Recognize possibility of underachievement.

➤ Recommend problem-solving model. *(List 2-23)*

➤ Suggest appropriate books:
   – Recommend appropriate book.
   – Discuss content and personal significance.

➤ Understand possible low self-esteem.

➤ Help parents find appropriate services and resources.

ADDITIONAL INFORMATION

See *List 1-14, Placement in Courses: Guidelines.*

Thompson, C. L. & Rudolph, L. B. (1996). *Counseling children* (4th ed.). *(List 12-3)*

Webb, J. T., Meckstroth, E. A. & Tolou, S. (1982). *Guiding the gifted child. (List 10-7)*

3-26 COUNSELING STUDENTS WHO PROCRASTINATE

Characteristics of Students Who Procrastinate

Students who procrastinate may show the following characteristics:

➤ Avoid starting an activity

➤ Convince selves of need to complete preliminaries before taking action

➤ Desire to change past before moving forward

➤ Desire to complete the task perfectly

➤ Doubt ability to achieve the task

➤ Dwell on past mistakes or inabilities

➤ Fear change

➤ Put off until tomorrow

➤ Set lofty, unrealistic goals and standards

➤ Substitute low priority activities for important tasks

➤ Wait for inspiration

➤ Wait for perfect time

Steps for Progress

Assist students to do the following:

➤ Recognize and admit procrastination in past.

➤ Visualize results of accomplished task.

➤ Remember exceptions when task was achieved without procrastination. *(List 2-18)*

➤ Set clear, achievable, and measurable goals. *(List 3-2)*

➤ Believe in ability to control events.

➤ Realize that relapses may occur but can be controlled.

➤ Divide goals into action steps that can be accomplished in short time.

➤ Designate a short time period to complete first action step.

➤ Plan completion of the next action step.

➤ Check off action steps when completed.

➤ Do priority tasks first, reward when completed.

➤ Accept that motivation often follows action.

➤ Substitute positive self-talk for negative self-talk. *(List 2-16)*

➤ Commit to working toward achievable goals.

ADDITIONAL INFORMATION

See *Lists 2-8 through 2-18, Application of Counseling Theories.*

See *List 3-24, Counseling Students Who Desire Perfection.*

Counseling Center, University of Illinois. *Brochures for problem solving, Overcoming procrastination brochure. (List 9-15)*

Knaus, W. J. (1995). *Overcoming procrastination.*
    http://www.iret.org/essays/procrst2.html

Knaus, W. J. (1997). *Do it now: How to stop procrastinating* (revised edition). New York, NY: John Wiley & Sons.

Knaus, W. J. (1983). Children and low frustration tolerance. In A. Ellis & M. Bernard (Eds.), *Rational-emotive approaches to the problems of childhood.* New York, NY: Plenum.

3-27   HELPING STUDENTS LEARN FROM FAILURE

Concrete Failures

➤ Failing grade

➤ Grade-level retention

➤ College rejection

Steps for Progress

Assist students to do the following:

➤ Acknowledge and accept the decision.

➤ Separate worth of self from evaluation of performance.

➤ Value self and specify other strengths.

➤ Recall other successes.

➤ Focus on next chance.

➤ Identify new realistic goals.

➤ Visualize success.

➤ Specify steps to accomplish new goals.

➤ Divide into small steps to indicate progress.

➤ Acknowledge progress of each step.

➤ Identify what can be learned from the experience.

3-28   HELPING STUDENTS OVERCOME SUCCESS-INHIBITING FACTORS

Some Success-Inhibiting Factors

➤ Stress

➤ Limited time

➤ Unrealistic expectations

➤ Difficult personalities

➤ Unfair evaluation

➤ Boring classes

Steps Toward Progress

➤ Acknowledge that factors may actually exist.

➤ Help students acknowledge that the factors are undesirable, but not catastrophic.

➤ Use counseling skills. See Counselor's Actions in *List 3-16.*

➤ Help students design a plan of action.

➤ Help students specify steps toward success.

➤ Encourage students to take action to accomplish first step.

➤ Acknowledge success of each step.

➤ Continue to follow up.

Section 4

CAREER COUNSELING AND GUIDANCE K–12

CAREER DEVELOPMENT THEORIES AND ASSESSMENT

4-1 CAREER DEVELOPMENT THEORIES

Theories of career development and choice attempt to explain, describe, and predict career-related values and behavior. Theories are not clearly independent of each other.

Career Decision Theories

TRAIT-FACTOR AND PERSONALITY-BASED THEORIES—J. HOLLAND

➤ Matches individual's abilities and interests with career opportunities

➤ Personalities and work environments are classified according to six types:
1. Realistic
2. Investigative
3. Artistic
4. Social
5. Enterprising
6. Conventional

➤ Key variables:
– Interests
– Information about self and careers
– Environment
– Personal traits
– Aptitudes
– Needs

Family, Needs, and Personality-Based Theories—A. Roe

➤ Workers select their jobs because they see potential for meeting their needs.

➤ Personal orientations are related to familial patterns, particularly to parents' behaviors, beliefs, ambitions, and the goals they have for their children.

➤ Key variables:
– Family
– Early childhood experiences
– Desire to work with people, data, or things

Life Development Theories—D. Super, Ginzberg and Associates, D. Tiedemann, L. R. O'Hara, and Gottfredson

➤ Humanistic and developmental

➤ Vocational self-concepts develop on basis of children's observations and identification with adults involved in work.

➤ Career behavior follows regular and predictable patterns which result from psychological, physical, situational, and societal factors.

➤ Five life stages and career development:
   1. Growth
   2. Exploration
   3. Establishment
   4. Maintenance
   5. Disengagement

➤ Key variables:
   – Self-concept and self-awareness
   – Developmental stages and developmental tasks
   – Social variables
   – Aspirations and compromise
   – Lifelong process

Social Systems Theories—P. Blau and D. Duncan, L. Lipsett, V. Shah

➤ Societal circumstances beyond control of the individual contribute significantly to career choice.

➤ Principal task is to develop techniques to help individual cope with environment.

➤ Factors influencing level of aspiration assume importance.

➤ Parental occupation, family income, and parental educational background translate into social class.

➤ Education is the main element in individual choice and the primary agent of occupational mobility.

➤ Key variables:
   – Social class
   – Situational conditions
   – Family
   – Sex
   – Age
   – Race
   – Culture

Behavioral Theories—J. Krumboltz, H. Gelatt, M. Katz

➤ Social-learning model based on three goals:
   – Change maladaptive behavior.
   – Teach decision-making.
   – Teach problem-solving skills to be prepared for future.

➤ Lifelong process

➤ Key variables:

- Person, heredity, and special abilities
- Environmental conditions and events
- Learning experiences
- Reinforcers
- Task-approach skills:

    1) Problem-solving skills

    2) Work habits

    3) Mental sets

    4) Emotional responses

    5) Cognitive responses

ADDITIONAL INFORMATION

Brown, D. (1990). Summary, comparison, and critique of the major theories. In D. Brown, L. Brooks & Associates (Eds.), *Career choice and development: Applying contemporary theories to practice* (pp. 338–363). San Francisco, CA: Jossey-Bass.

Kapes, J. T., Mastie, M. M. & Whitfield, E. A. (1994). *A counselor's guide to career assessment instruments.* Alexandria, VA: National Career Development Association.

Osipow, S. H. & Fitzgerald, L. F. (1996). *Theories of career development* (4th ed.). Needham Heights, MA: Allyn & Bacon.

Seligman, L. (1994). *Developmental career counseling and assessment* (2nd ed.). *(List 12-1)*

Sharf, R. S. (1997). *Applying career development theory to counseling. (List 12-1)*

4-2 CAREER ASSESSMENT

Annotated Lists of Materials for Career Education *(Lists 7-1, 8-1, 9-1)* include descriptions of some career assessment instruments for elementary, middle, and high school students. Results of inventories are not absolute and should not limit a student's aspirations, but rather compliment them.

Some Career Interest and Aptitude Inventories

➤ ACT Explore—middle school *(List 8-1)*

➤ Armed Service Vocational Aptitude Battery (ASVAB)—grades 11 and 12 *(List 9-1)*

➤ Career Ability Placement Survey (CAPS)—grades 8–12 *(List 9-1)*

➤ Career Assessment Survey Exploration (CASE)—grades 6–9 *(List 8-1)*

➤ Career Futures—middle school *(List 8-1)*

➤ Career Occupational Preference Survey (COPS)—grades 10–12 *(List 9-1)*

➤ Career Occupational Preference Survey II (COPS II)—grades 7–9 *(List 8–1)*

➤ Career Occupational Preference Survey R (COPS-R)—grades 6–9 *(List 8-1)*

➤ Career Orientation and Planning Profile (COPP)—grades 7–9 *(List 8-1)*

➤ Career Orientation Placement Evaluation Survey (COPES)—grades 7–9 *(List 8-1)*

➤ Career Planning Program, Level I (CPP I)—grades 6–9 *(List 8-1)*

➤ CHOICES—high school *(List 9-1)*

➤ CHOICES JR., Planning My Future—elementary school *(List 7-1)*

➤ Differential Aptitude Tests (DAT)—grades 9 and 10 *(List 9-1)*

➤ DISCOVER—high school *(List 9-1)*

➤ ExPAN College and Occupation Search—high school *(List 9-2)*

➤ Explore the World of Work (E-WOW)—elementary school *(List 7-1)*

➤ Harrington–O'Shea Career Decision-Making System—high school *(List 9-1)*

➤ High School Career Course Planner—grades 8 and 9 *(List 8-23)*

➤ Interest, Determination, Exploration, and Assessment System (IDEAS)—middle school *(List 8-1)*

➤ Job-O Interest Inventory—middle school *(List 8-1)*

➤ Major–Minor Finder—grades 11 and 12 *(List 9-2)*

➤ Self-Directed Search (SDS)—high school *(List 9-1)*

➤ SIGI PLUS—high school *(List 9-1)*

➤ Strong–Campbell Interest Inventory (SCII)—high school *(List 9-1)*

➤ (VIP) Jr. Vocational Implications of Personality—high school *(List 9-1)*

NATIONAL CAREER COMPETENCIES AND SKILLS FOR STUDENTS

4-3 NATIONAL CAREER COMPETENCIES AND SKILLS

Career Development Competencies

(National Occupational Information Coordinating Committee [NOICC])

➤ Educational and occupational exploration:
- Knowledge of benefits of educational achievement to career opportunities
- Understanding the relationship between learning and work
- Skills to locate, understand, evaluate, and use career information
- Understanding the need for positive attitudes toward learning and work
- Skills to seek, obtain, maintain, and change jobs
- Understanding how societal needs and functions influence the nature and structure of work

➤ Career planning:
- Skills to make decisions
- Skills to interact positively with others
- Understanding the relationship of life roles
- Understanding the continuous changes in occupational roles

Secretary's Commission on Achieving Necessary Skills

(SCANS Report, Department of Labor)

➤ Competent individuals in the high-performance workplace need foundation skills:
- Basic skills
- Thinking skills
- Personal qualities

➤ Effective individuals can productively use workplace competencies:
- *Resources*—know how to allocate resources
- *Interpersonal skills*—communicate effectively
- *Information*—process information
- *Systems*—understand and use systems
- *Technology*—use correct technique to get specific jobs done

ADDITIONAL INFORMATION

Executive report. *What work requires*. [On-line] Available:
      http:www.cabrillo.cc.ca.us/Connect/docs/whatwork.html

NOICC [On-line] Available:
      http:www.profiles.iastate.edu/ided/ncdc/noice/htm

U.S. Department of Labor (1991). *SCANS report*. Washington, DC: Author.

Career Goals for All Students

4-4 Career Goals

Goals for Students

- ➤ Develop knowledge of careers:
  - – Preparation required
  - – Responsibility required
  - – Rewards of job
  - – Opportunities in job
  - – Independent work activities in job
  - – Teamwork activities in job
  - – Location of opportunities for job
  - – Stability of the job
- ➤ Develop an understanding of self:
  - – Abilities
  - – Skills
  - – Talents
  - – Experiences
  - – Limitations
  - – Values
  - – Aptitudes
  - – Interests
  - – Aspirations
  - – Opportunities
  - – Desired life style
- ➤ Maintain a positive attitude toward work.
- ➤ Acquire work-related skills.
- ➤ Acquire positive interpersonal skills.
- ➤ Develop career-planning and decision-making skills.
- ➤ Explore and progress toward educational and career goals.
- ➤ Continue to learn about careers and opportunities throughout lifetime.

CAREER GUIDANCE FOR ALL STUDENTS
4-5   PLAN FOR A CAREER DEVELOPMENT PROGRAM K–12

Career Development

- ➤ Sequential
- ➤ Systematic
- ➤ Comprehensive
- ➤ Collaborative
- ➤ Evaluative:
  - – Ongoing evaluation
  - – Continual improvement

Plan for a Career Development Program

- ➤ Collaborate with parents, administrators, counselors, and teachers (at elementary, middle, and high school), business, industry, labor, government, and service organizations:
  - – Involve local employers and community members.
  - – Involve parent volunteers.
- ➤ Organize steering or advisory committee or Guidance Advisory Committee (GAC): *(List 1-5)*
  - – Identify benefits of a sequential, systematic, comprehensive career development program K–12.
  - – Assess current career development programs at all levels.
  - – Conduct a career development needs assessment. *(List 1-6)*
  - – Elicit input from community.
  - – Elicit commitments of time and resources for the career development program.
- ➤ Plan staff development and involvement:
  - – Write role descriptions for staff.
  - – Plan opportunities for counselors and teachers to visit local businesses.
  - – Coordinate efforts and materials.
- ➤ Make decisions for development of the program:
  - – Plan to continually assess and acquire up-to-date resources for Career College Centers. *(List 4-11)*
  - – Coordinate work experience opportunities for high school students.
- ➤ Keep all contributors and participants informed.
- ➤ Design evaluation of the program: *(List 4-9)*
  - – Ongoing evaluation
  - – Plan for continual improvement

ADDITIONAL INFORMATION

NOICC. (1989). *National career development guidelines local handbook for elementary, middle, and high schools.* *(List 12-1)*

Schwallie-Giddis, P. & Kobylarz, L. (1993). Career development: The counselor's role in preparing K–12 students for the 21st century (Chapter 16). In J. Wittmer (Ed.), *Managing your school counseling program: K–12 developmental strategies.* *(List 12-3)*

4-6 CAREER DEVELOPMENT FOR ELEMENTARY SCHOOL STUDENTS

Help students do the following.

Develop Personal and Career Attributes

- Develop the desire to learn.
- Learn how to learn by listening, reading, discussing, and writing.
- Learn to follow directions from teachers.
- Learn to follow rules.
- Learn decision-making skills.
- Learn goal-setting skills and take action to achieve goals. *(List 3-2)*
- Learn about technology.
- Learn the value of work.
- Work with others in groups and on teams.

Relate Educational and Career Learning

- Relate experiences in school to experiences at work:
  - Relate good work habits in school to good work habits at work.
  - Relate personal responsibility in school to responsibility at work.
  - Relate behavior and consequences in school to behavior and consequences at work.
- Relate required education to different careers.
- Relate the importance of ability, effort, and achievement for success in school and at work.

Attain Career Information

- Learn about careers and jobs and the difference.
- Learn about workers in the community:
  - Attend a career day or career evening at school.
  - Shadow a parent or other adult at work.
- Learn from career presentations.

Understand Self

- Recognize personal strengths, interests, and abilities and relate them to careers.
- Learn about a career portfolio. *(List 4-14)*
- Prepare a six-year education plan for grades 7 through 12. *(List 4-13)*

4-7   CAREER DEVELOPMENT FOR MIDDLE SCHOOL STUDENTS

Help students do the following.

Develop Personal and Career Attributes

➤ Develop a zeal for learning.

➤ Express positive attitudes toward academic work and learning.

➤ Become increasingly self-directed.

➤ Accept responsibility for own behavior.

➤ Develop appreciation for quality of academic work.

➤ Develop positive interpersonal and social skills.

➤ Develop cooperative work skills.

➤ Grow in ability to make good decisions.

➤ Grow in self-confidence.

Relate Education and Career Learning

➤ Recognize relationship of educational achievement and career opportunities.

➤ Locate and use information in educational and career planning.

➤ Select electives related to desired career clusters.

Attain Educational and Career Information

➤ Develop a career vocabulary.

➤ Learn about workers in the community:
  – Participate in career day or career evening.
  – Shadow a parent or other adult at work.

➤ Learn from career speakers.

➤ Interview adults about their careers. *(List 4-21)*

➤ Become aware of the variety of careers available.

➤ Research careers of interest and make a presentation or write a report.

➤ Explore technical opportunities.

➤ Learn about job search, application completion, and interview skills.

➤ Apply technology to access current career information.

Understand Self

➤ Become more aware of and realistic about abilities and interests:
  – Understand results of achievement tests and relationship to educational and career goals.
  – Understand interpretation of results of appropriate interest inventories and aptitude assessments.
  – Begin to understand personal values and how they relate to work.

➤ Participate in activities to identify and prioritize interests.

➤ Learn decision-making model.

Plan for the Future

➤ Set career-oriented goals.

➤ Develop a six-year education plan for study in grades 7–12 that supports career goals. *(List 4-13)*

➤ Develop an educational/career portfolio to gather and maintain information to assist in formulating a career plan. *(List 4-14)*

ADDITIONAL INFORMATION

Kimeldorf, M. (1994). *Creating portfolios. (List 12-1)*

4-8 CAREER DEVELOPMENT FOR HIGH SCHOOL STUDENTS

Teachers and the counselor help students do the following.

Develop Personal and Career Attributes

➤ Develop an intense desire to continue to learn.

➤ Take responsibility and act with integrity.

➤ Develop ability to work both independently and interdependently.

➤ Develop and use interpersonal skills.

➤ Identify and work to eliminate biases at school and in the workplace:
  – Age bias
  – Ethnic background bias
  – Gender bias

➤ Recognize and reject career stereotypes:
  – Age stereotypes
  – Ethnic background stereotypes
  – Gender stereotypes

➤ Maintain positive attitudes toward work.

➤ Deal positively with change and be flexible.

➤ Use decision-making skills.

➤ Learn a marketable skill.

➤ Volunteer, work, or provide public service part-time when feasible.

➤ Learn skills to seek, assess, obtain, maintain, and change occupations or careers.

Relate Education and Career Learning

➤ Understand relevance of courses to future career opportunities.

➤ Relate current education to competency at work.

➤ Relate personal attitudes, aptitudes, and values to career search.

➤ Relate desired lifestyle to career goal.

Attain Educational and Career Information

➤ Participate in appropriate career presentations.

➤ Participate in appropriate college presentations including college fairs and financial aid meetings.

➤ Participate in appropriate military presentations.

➤ Participate in appropriate vocational or college tours.

➤ Manage and organize educational and career information.

➤ Research current full-time jobs:
   – Locate career information.
   – Evaluate career information.
   – Interpret career information.

➤ Develop skills to locate, obtain, maintain, and change jobs.

➤ Participate in a structured career experience.

➤ Explore postsecondary educational opportunities. *(List 3-7)*

➤ Use technology to learn about career and educational opportunities.

➤ Develop a breadth and depth of knowledge about occupations, and how these relate to themselves.

➤ Share information with parents.

Understand Self

➤ Complete an occupational interest inventory.

➤ Clarify realistic options after considering results of achievement tests.

➤ Clarify individual interests after considering results of interest inventories.

➤ Recognize individual needs and desires.

➤ Understand personal strengths and skills.

➤ Expect change, permit self to change, and deal with change.

Plan for the Future

➤ Relate personal values and priorities to career plans.

➤ Use goal-setting and decision-making skills when making high school and post-high school plans. *(Lists 3-2, 3-7, and 4-16)*

➤ Select a program of study in high school providing higher education and career opportunities.

➤ Use all data about education, careers, and self to formulate realistic options.

➤ Select a career of interest that is a realistic option.

➤ Conduct computer searches for post-high school education and career options.

➤ Plan secondary and/or postsecondary educational program to culminate in marketable employment.

➤ Plan how to advance within selected career.

➤ Understand the interrelationship of life and career roles and the importance of maintaining a balanced and productive life.

➤ Update six-year educational and career plan. *(List 4-13)*

➤ Update personal educational and career portfolio. *(List 4-14)*

ADDITIONAL INFORMATION

See *List 1-17*, *Counseling and Guidance for Post-High School Planning.*

See *List 3-1*, *Academic/Educational Goals for All Students.*

See *Lists 3-2 through 3-13*, *Academic Guidance for Students.*

Dictionary of occupational titles. (List 9-1)

Military career paths. (List 9-1)

Occupational outlook handbook. (List 9-1) [On-line] Available:
    http://www.bls.gov/ocohome.htm

Occupational outlook handbook quarterly. (List 9-1)

Kimeldorf, M. (1994). *Creating portfolios. (List 12-1)*

4-9 IMPLEMENTATION OF A CAREER DEVELOPMENT PROGRAM K–12

➤ Conduct staff development for teachers:
  – Encourage teachers to infuse career information throughout curriculum.
  – Include both academic and career development objectives.
  – Integrate career concepts with academics to make learning relevant.

➤ Conduct staff development for counselors:
  – Use computer programs to conduct career, education, and financial aid searches.
  – Relate career guidance activities to classroom instruction.
  – Team-teach career information in classrooms.
  – Assist in placement:
    1) post-high school education *(Lists 3-7 through 3-13)*
    2) post-high school job training
    3) employment
    4) military service
    5) other options

➤ Conduct training for staff of Career College Center:
  – Use computer programs to conduct career, education, and financial aid searches.
  – Organize accurate, current, and unbiased career information: *(List 2-50)*
    1) educational programs
    2) military employment and programs
    3) post-high school training programs
    4) employment opportunities

➤ Provide parent information:
  – Inform how to interpret results of achievement tests.
  – Inform how to interpret results of interest inventories.
  – Inform about current occupations and labor trends.

    – Teach how to research educational, career, and financial aid information.
- Notify staff, students, and parents of the career education services available:
  - Stress importance of involvement of *all* students.
- Provide career counseling to students. *(Lists 4-24 through 4-28)*
- Continue to consult with teachers and parents. *(Lists 2-33 through 2-44)*
- Continue to evaluate implementation of the program:
  - Conduct follow-up of students' progress in career development. *(List 1-18)*
  - Collect ongoing data and evaluation.
  - Revise and continually improve the program.

ADDITIONAL INFORMATION

See *List 2-55, School to Work.*

Florida blueprint for career preparation. (List 12-1)

Schwallie-Giddis, P. & Kobylarz, L. (1993). Career development: The counselor's role in preparing K–12 students for the 21st century (Chapter 16). In J. Wittmer (Ed.), *Managing your school counseling program: K–12 developmental strategies. (List 12-3)*

4-10 CAREER DEVELOPMENT FOR FEMALE AND MINORITY STUDENTS

Factors That Control Career Success of Female and Minority Students

- Self-Confidence:
  - Personal and academic confidence
  - Confidence to persist and overcome obstacles
- Role models:
  - Presence of role models
  - Desire to be role models
  - Availability of mentors
  - Examples of compatibility of family with career
- Social class
- Information about options that is accurate and specific:
  - Potential
  - Cost
  - Benefits
  - Knowledge of career and lifestyle options
- Cultural expectations:
  - Parental influence
  - Peer influence
- Gender-fair instruction
- Gender-fair counseling
- Strong support system in and out of school

➤ Rigorous and varied curriculum

➤ Opportunities for higher education

➤ Opportunities for work-site experience

➤ Critical events:
  – Experience with discrimination
  – Death or illness in family
  – Drug addiction of family member or friend

ADDITIONAL INFORMATION

See *List 13-11, The School Counselor and Cross/Multicultural Counseling.*

See *List 13-17, The School Counselor and Gender Equity.*

See *List 13-24, The School Counselor and Sexual Minority Youth.*

4-11   CAREER COLLEGE CENTER

Successful Career College Center

➤ Available to students, parents, and teachers

➤ Available to community

➤ Accurate, current, and unbiased multimedia materials: *(Lists 2-49, 2-50, 6-1, 6-2, 7-1, 7-2, 8-1, 8-2, 9-1, 9-2, 12-1)*
  – Career references *(Lists 9-1, 12-1)*
  – Military career and training information *(List 9-1)*
  – Occupational information *(List 9-1)*
  – Training and apprenticeship information
  – Vocational and technical information
  – Information about attaining and maintaining a job
  – College and university information *(List 9-2)*
  – Financial aid information *(List 9-2)*

➤ Accessible location for students, counselors, and teachers

➤ Accessible hours for students, counselors, and teachers

➤ Knowledgeable staff

➤ Multimedia *(List 9-1)*
  – Printed reference materials:
    1) Books
    2) Journals
    3) Magazines
    4) Posters
    5) Brochures
    6) College applications
    7) College catalogs

    8) Financial aid forms

    9) Test information

   10) Interest inventories

– Computer programs:

    1) Education

    2) Career

    3) Occupations

    4) Apprenticeships

    5) Military

– Microfiche

– Videotapes

– CD-ROMs and other electronic media

– Films, filmstrips

➤ Speakers bureau

➤ Visits by military representatives

➤ Job listings

➤ Summer opportunities

➤ Foreign exchange programs

➤ Volunteer programs

➤ Part-time job opportunities

4-12   SELECTING A COMPUTERIZED GUIDANCE DELIVERY SYSTEM

Components of Most Computerized Guidance Systems

Direct and intuitive search capability for:

- ➤ Interest inventories
- ➤ Occupational information
- ➤ Armed service information
- ➤ College and university information
- ➤ Technical and specialized schools
- ➤ Financial aid information
- ➤ Decision-making skills

Determine College and Career Counseling Needs for Guidance Delivery System

- ➤ Obtain input from the staff.
- ➤ Obtain objective information about computerized programs under consideration:
    - – Evaluate each component of the program.
    - – Compare the recommended user population to the student population.
    - – Consider cost of the software desired.
    - – Consider cost of the hardware required.
- ➤ Determine how frequently information is updated.
- ➤ Consider possibility of "network" version for minimizing cost.
- ➤ Obtain demonstration of all programs being considered:
    - – Preview personally.
    - – Buy "potential user" package to preview.
- ➤ Obtain sample printouts.
- ➤ Obtain estimated cost per student:
    - – Calculate maximum number of users.
    - – Calculate minimum number of users.
- ➤ Obtain ongoing charges for five years.

ADDITIONAL INFORMATION

Bartolotta, M. (1997). Personal communication.

4-13   SIX-YEAR EDUCATIONAL PLAN (GRADES 7–12)

This plan should be completed in pencil so it can be revised. It can be entered on the computer. The counselor should have a copy for each student.

➤ Name and date completed or updated

➤ Graduation requirements

➤ Grade-level requirements for each grade level

➤ Higher-education aspiration

➤ High school courses required for higher-education aspiration

➤ Preferred diploma if options exist

➤ Courses selected for each grade level 7 through 12

➤ Activity record for each grade level:
  – Career and education activities
  – School, community, employment, summer activities

➤ Awards, honors, and offices held

➤ Preferred career cluster or other more specific career plan

4-14   EDUCATIONAL/CAREER PORTFOLIO

This portfolio is a purposeful collection of student work documenting the student's efforts, progress, and achievement leading toward selection of a career.

Student's Involvement and Career Development

➤ Evidence of educational and career exploration

➤ Evidence of career decision-making based on self-knowledge and career exploration

➤ Evidence of a career goal

➤ Selection of portfolio content

➤ Evidence of self-assessment

Parent Involvement

➤ Parent serves as consultant to student

➤ Parent attends student-led parent conference explaining portfolio content

Suggested Content of Portfolio

➤ Copy of student's six-year educational plan *(List 4-13)*

➤ Copies of report cards

➤ Results of learning styles inventories *(List 2-42)*

➤ Results of interest inventories *(List 4-2)*

➤ Evidence of career research including samples of student work:
  – Oral reports presented
  – Written analyses

➤ Record of work experience

➤ Evidence of marketable skill *(List 4-18)*

➤ Evidence of decision-making process *(List 4-16)*

➤ Selection of personal career goal:
  – Accurate inference about abilities
  – Consistent with information presented

➤ Logical plan to pursue personal career goal

Purposes of Educational/Career Portfolio

➤ Promote student self-assessment and learning

➤ Support student-led parent conferences

➤ Certify student competence

➤ Build student self-confidence

➤ Demonstrate student's skills and abilities to employers

ADDITIONAL INFORMATION

ASCA (1996). *Get a life: Your personal planning portfolio. (List 12-1)*

Kimeldorf, M. (1994). *Creating portfolios. (List 12-1)*

Lester, J. N. & Perry, N. S. (1995). Assessing career development with portfolios. EDO-CG-95-22. [On-line] Available: http://www2.uncg.edu/~ericcas2/assessment/diga22.html

4-15   CAREER VALUES

Values Fulfilled in a Career

➤ Security	➤ Self-expression	➤ Variety
➤ Personal integrity	➤ Helping others	➤ Creativity
➤ Recognition	➤ Relationships	➤ Routine
➤ Adventure	➤ Leadership	➤ Time off
➤ Economic reward	➤ Autonomy	

Life Values of Students

1. Successful job or career	4. Lots of money	7. Help community
2. Close-knit family	5. Be a good citizen	
3. Good time	6. Religious standards	

4-16   DECISION-MAKING SKILLS

Steps to Making Decisions

1. Identify goal or decision to be made.

2. Gather information.

3. List possible choices or alternatives.

4. Specify the probable consequences of each choice.

5. Evaluate each choice by its consequences:
   - Will it help meet the specified goal?
   - What are the advantages?
   - What are the disadvantages?
   - What are the risks?
   - How will it effect others?
   - How will I feel about this choice?
   - How will my parents feel about this choice?
   - How will I feel about this choice a year from now?
   - How will I feel about this choice five years from now?

6. Rank choices by priority.

7. Make a decision by selecting one choice.

8. Plan to put the decision in effect.

9. Follow through with the plan.

10. Evaluate the decision.

11. Repeat the decision-making process when necessary.

4-17   JOB INTERVIEWING SKILLS

Before Interview

- ➤ Prepare answers for anticipated questions:
  - – Elaborate on "yes" or "no" answers.
  - – Keep to the point.
- ➤ Practice responses to anticipated questions with adult or friend.
- ➤ Research the hiring firm or agency.
- ➤ Prepare specific job-related questions to ask:
  - – Date of decision
  - – Date to begin work
- ➤ Practice interview on video or with tape recorder if possible.
- ➤ Plan personal appearance to make a good first impression.

During Interview

- ➤ Arrive early.
- ➤ Do not bring a friend.
- ➤ Do not chew gum.
- ➤ Relax.
- ➤ Shake hands upon arrival and departure.
- ➤ Bring pen and paper to take notes.
- ➤ Sit erect and look interviewer in the eye.
- ➤ Answer questions completely; elaborate when information is important.
- ➤ Provide a list of references.

After Interview

- ➤ Take notes on questions asked.
- ➤ Write thank-you letter.
- ➤ Don't give up.

4-18 MARKETABLE SKILLS

Job Skills

➤ Initiative

➤ Enthusiasm

➤ Honesty

➤ Courtesy

➤ Dependability

➤ Adaptability

➤ Sociability

➤ Resilience

Top Ten Skills Needed by Employees

(Hitchner & Tifft-Hitchner, 1996)

1. Self-analysis
2. Cooperative learning
3. Global thought
4. Conflict resolution
5. Passion for performing well
6. Willingness to change and accept change
7. Networking acumen
8. Optimism in the face of uncertainty
9. Facility with oral and written communication
10. Openness to criticism

Skills Employers Look For

(Hitchner & Tifft-Hitchner, 1996)

➤ Positive attitude

➤ Enthusiasm

➤ Ability to communicate

➤ Integrity

➤ Computer literacy

Skills for Advancement

➤ Interpersonal skills

➤ Sense of responsibility

➤ Dedication to quality

Reasons Applicants Are Rejected

➤ Poor personal appearance

➤ Lack of enthusiasm or interest in interview

➤ Poor eye contact with interviewer

➤ Late for interview

➤ Failure to raise questions about potential position

➤ "Know-it-all" attitude

➤ Inability to express self clearly

➤ Voice quality, diction, grammar

➤ Exhibit little, if any, goal setting and/or career planning

Characteristics Employers Seek

(670 employers, *Mid-Atlantic Guide to Information on Careers,* 1994)

1. Dependability
2. Honesty
3. Neatness
4. Punctuality
5. Reliability
6. Ability to communicate effectively
7. Ability to work in teams or groups
8. Commitment to the company (loyalty)
9. Willingness to work hard (work ethic) and learn new things
10. Adaptability/flexibility; able to change quickly and often

Employee Traits That Cause On-the-Job Difficulties

(*Job Choices in Business,* 1995)

1. Dishonesty and lying
2. Irresponsibility, goofing off, and attending to personal business on company time
3. Arrogance, egotism, and excessive aggressiveness
4. Absenteeism and tardiness
5. Not following instructions or ignoring company policies
6. Whining or complaining
7. Absence of commitment, concern, or dedication
8. Laziness and lack of motivation and enthusiasm

ADDITIONAL INFORMATION

Hitchner, K. W. & Tifft-Hitchner, A. (1996). *Counseling today's secondary students. (List 12-3)*

4-19   CAREER STEREOTYPES, BIASES, AND DISCRIMINATION

Job discrimination is lack of consideration or selection for a job.

Results of Job Discrimination

- Fewer opportunities:
  - Economic success
  - Organizational success:
    1) Promotions
    2) Positions of autonomy and power
    3) Positions of leadership
- Exclusion from activities of co-workers
- Lack of mentors
- Harassment:
  - Social rejection
  - Ridicule
  - Intimidation
  - Propositions
- Lack self-perception of success

Differential treatment is unfair treatment based on membership in a group categorized by age, disability, gender, ethnic, social-class, or other group rather than on work-related characteristics or performance.

Groups Sometimes Given Differential Treatment

- Age:
  - Too young
  - Too old
- Disability:
  - Physical appearance
  - Physical agility when not necessary on job
- Gender:
  - Marital status
  - Dependents
  - Possibility of pregnancy
  - Attractiveness
  - Preference
- Ethnicity:
  - African American
  - Asian American
  - Hispanic American
  - Other

➤ Social-Class:
  – Suspicion of applicants from lower social class
  – Suspicion of applicants from higher social class

ADDITIONAL INFORMATION

See **List 13-11,** *The School Counselor and Cross/Multicultural Counseling.*

See **List 13-17,** *The School Counselor and Gender Equity.*

See **List 13-24,** *The School Counselor and Sexual Minority Youth.*

American Association of University Women. (1992). *How schools shortchange girls.* **(List 12-16)**

Osipow, S. H. & Fitzgerald, L. F. (1996). *Theories of career development* (4th ed.). Needham Heights, MA: Allyn & Bacon.

4-20   STRUCTURED WORK EXPERIENCE

Goals for Structured Work Experience

➤ Ensure that students make connection between learning in school and work.

➤ Prepare students for the transition between school and work.

Types of Structured Work Experience

➤ Internships including paid and unpaid opportunities linked to specific course

➤ Technical course requiring work components in which students provide goods or services to the community

➤ Apprenticeships of paid and supervised job training

➤ Courses for Certificate of Mastery certifying job-entry competencies

Administration of Structured Work Experience

➤ Interdisciplinary collaboration

➤ Integration of academic and career curricula

➤ Business community involvement

➤ Joint responsibility of students, parents, counselors, teachers, and community

4-21 CAREER INFORMATION INTERVIEW

Suggestions to Obtain Information

➤ Prepare questions before the interview.

➤ Examples of questions:
  – When in life did you make your career decision?
  – What influenced your career decision?
  – How did you prepare for your career?
  – What characteristics or aptitudes are helpful in your career?
  – What education and training are necessary to succeed in your career?
  – What high school courses provide information helpful to succeed in your career?
  – What are the required skills?
  – What responsibilities do you have in your current job?
  – How did you get your current job?
  – What are the working conditions like?
  – What hours do you work?
  – What hours does a person at entry-level work?
  – What are the desirable elements in your career?
  – What are your greatest job satisfactions?
  – What are the future opportunities?
  – What geographical location provides the most opportunity in this career?
  – What are your biggest problems on the job?
  – What advice would you give to someone entering your career?

➤ Write answers to questions.

➤ Discuss interview and perception of the interview with parents.

➤ Evaluate desirability of the career and the job.

4-22   CAREER EXPLORATION AND LIFE PLANNING

Impact of Career Decisions

Teachers and the counselor help students:

➤ Recognize impact of career decision on lifestyle.

➤ Develop skills to plan, monitor, and manage personal, career, and lifestyle.

➤ Accept responsibility for own choices.

➤ Manage resources.

➤ Balance educational responsibility with work responsibility and personal responsibility:

- Balance working with school extracurricular activities, relationships, and other commitments.

- Recognize benefits and risks of working while attending school.

- Heed the warning signs when work is consuming too much time or energy.

Search and Plan for Career Opportunities Throughout Life

➤ Develop flexibility.

➤ Develop transferable job skills.

➤ Expect change.

➤ Develop avocations and hobbies.

➤ Visualize future possibilities.

➤ Continue education and life-long learning.

➤ Continue to develop skills for seeking, obtaining, keeping, and advancing in a job.

ADDITIONAL INFORMATION

FutureScan, Career exploration and planning site for teens. [On-line] Available: http://www.FutureScan.com

ASCA (1996). *Get a life: Your personal planning portfolio.* **(List 12-1)**

4-23 FUTURE CAREER OPPORTUNITIES

Fast-Growing Sectors

➤ Communications

➤ Mathematics

➤ Information processing

➤ Computer literacy

Future Trends

➤ Requirement for advanced technology skills

➤ Decline in traditional blue-collar jobs

➤ Telecommuting

➤ Frequent job/career changes

➤ Requirement for retraining

➤ Skill-based contract work

Required Skills

➤ Computer literacy

➤ Ability to prioritize large volumes of information

➤ Persuasive communication skills:
  – Write well
  – Speak well
  – Use multimedia

➤ Work well with others in groups

➤ Logic and reasoning

➤ Continual learning of new skills

➤ Specialized information

ADDITIONAL INFORMATION

FutureScan, Career exploration and planning site for teens. [On-line] Available:
    http://www.FutureScan.com

Career Counseling K–12

4-24 Career Counseling

Student Factors of Career Counseling

➤ Parental experience and expectations

➤ Experience of careers in family of origin

➤ Extent of knowledge of career opportunities

➤ Social status and desired style of living

➤ Results of career assessment *(List 4-2)*

➤ Career values *(List 4-15)*

➤ Personal career goals *(List 4-4)*

➤ Career-development maturity *(List 4-6, 4-7, 4-8)*

➤ Self-confidence

➤ Aptitude for risk-taking

➤ Flexibility

➤ Desire to learn cognitively and experientially

Suggested Procedure for Career Counseling

➤ Meet individually with all students and their parents:
  - Interpret and review standardized test results:
    1) Focus on what student does well
    2) Explore combinations of high scores
  - Review interest inventories. *(List 4-2)*
  - Review individual six-year education plan: *(List 4-13)*
    1) Acknowledge long-term goals, usually including college degree
    2) Recommend specification of short-term goals including a well-paying job while pursuing college degree
    3) Suggest an educational plan to include both a technical component and a university component
  - Review student's Personal Educational/Career Portfolio. *(List 4-14)*
  - Involve parents in all educational and career decisions. *(List 4-16)*

➤ Counsel high-risk students individually or in small groups. *(List 3-21)*

➤ Counsel students who have low quarter grades: *(List 3-14)*
  - Arrange and conduct student/teacher/parent/counselor conferences. *(List 2-43)*
  - Identify needed improvement.
  - Assist student and teacher in resolving relationship problems.
  - Write academic or behavioral contract for the student and ask student and parent to sign.

➤ Consult with teachers of high-risk students. *(Lists 3-15, 3-20)*

➤ Identify workable solutions for high-risk students. *(Lists 5-10, 5-11, 5-12)*

Additional Information

See *List 3-21, Counseling Students Who Are Potential Dropouts.*

See *Lists 3-14 through 3-28, Academic Counseling K–12.*

4-25   CAREER COUNSELING OF FEMALE AND MINORITY STUDENTS

➤ Examine own attitude toward the roles of women and minorities.

➤ Avoid sexist assumptions and stereotypes.

➤ Attend and then conduct gender- and minority-fair language and behavior workshops for the school staff.

➤ Evaluate career interest inventories in terms of gender- and minority-fairness. *(List 2-50)*

➤ Encourage students to explore cultural expectations of females and minorities in particular careers such as the military and business before making a commitment.

➤ Invite experts in gender-equity and minority-fairness, women and men role models, including those in nontraditional careers, to conduct staff development and speak to students.

➤ Help female and minority students locate support systems, role models, and mentors.

➤ Show videotapes of workers in nontraditional roles, particularly using mathematics and science.

➤ Use career resource materials that reflect gender- and minority-fair language and portray workers in nontraditional professions.

➤ Provide career counseling of female students in groups.

➤ Consider providing career counseling to students of the same cultural heritage in groups.

➤ Stress the importance of advanced math and science in higher education and career success.

➤ Encourage female and minority students to select advanced math and science courses.

➤ Validate female students for their intelligence and talents rather than for their physical appearance.

➤ Conduct activities to encourage self-confidence, risk-taking, and perseverance.

➤ Encourage female students to participate in sports.

➤ Encourage female and minority students to explore and pursue broad career options.

➤ Encourage female and minority students to examine possible existing unfair limitations in particular careers before deciding on a career.

➤ Help female and minority students deal with realistic issues and fears. *(Lists 4-27, 4-28)*

➤ Help female and minority students deal with discrimination and sexual harassment appropriately.

➤ Encourage female and minority students to define their values and goals, and then choose relationships that are compatible with their values and goals.

➤ Help female students become aware of the increasing necessity for women to be financially independent.

➤ Discuss how female students can overcome obstacles in nontraditional careers.

➤ Provide female and minority students with biographies of persons like themselves for role models in risk taking and career development. *(Lists 6-12, 7-12, 8-12)*

➤ Ask female and minority students to discuss current articles about accomplishments of females and minorities in different careers.

➤ Discuss gender-limiting stereotypes and effects of the messages portrayed in commercials, movies, greeting cards, language, toys, games, and clothing.

➤ Help parents become aware of how female and minority students are influenced by cultural stereotypes when considering career options.

ADDITIONAL INFORMATION

See *List 4-19*, *Career Stereotypes, Biases, and Discrimination.*

See *List 13-11*, *The School Counselor and Cross/Multicultural Counseling.*

See *List 13-17*, *The School Counselor and Gender Equity.*

See *List 13-20*, *The School Counselor and Military Recruitment.*

See *List 13-24*, *The School Counselor and Sexual Minority Youth.*

American Association of University Women. (1991). *How schools shortchange girls. (List 12-16)*

Bartholomew, C. G. (1993). *Horizons 2000: Career and life planning curriculum for girls. (List 12-16)*

4-26 CAREER COUNSELING OF STUDENTS WITH DISABILITIES

Counselor's Actions

➤ Acknowledge the impact the disability has on the student in everyday life.

➤ Help student explore feelings about disability.

➤ Help student gain self-awareness:

- Accept his or her condition as unfortunate, but realistic.
- Realize limitations produced by disability.
- Recognize capabilities and possibilities.

➤ Support student's plans and positive efforts to be self-sufficient.

➤ Inform student and parents of local assistance programs.

➤ Teach student assertiveness skills to request needed services.

ADDITIONAL INFORMATION

See *List 3-16*, *Counseling Students With Learning or Physical Problems.*

4-27 ISSUES OF FEMALE STUDENTS RELATED TO CAREERS

Possible Issues of Female Students Related to Career Search

➤ Fear social rejection when succeed academically *(List 3-23)*

➤ Anxious about planning a successful career

➤ Lack knowledge about nontraditional occupations

➤ Lack a professional network

➤ Lack a mathematical or scientific background necessary for some careers

➤ Lack understanding of importance of salary, benefits, and promotions

➤ Set goals beneath ability; underestimate self-worth

➤ Desire marriage and family *and* a successful career

Possible Issues Related to Integration of Marriage and Career

➤ Partner's encouragement or acceptance

➤ Partner's willingness to share responsibilities for home (cooking, shopping, cleaning, pet care)

➤ Agreement about responsibility for financial record keeping

➤ Career choice

➤ Career importance to both spouses

➤ Independence and interdependence

➤ Career permanence

➤ Opportunity for advancement

➤ Geographical location

➤ Responsibility for child care

➤ Effect on children

➤ Elder care

Coping Mechanisms of Women in Dual-Career Families

➤ Determine responsibilities with partner:
  – Care of the home, pets, automobile
  – Food purchase and preparation
  – Domestic help
  – Child care
  – Elder care

➤ Delegate when possible:
  – Tasks at work
  – Tasks at home

➤ Plan activities for stress reduction and leisure.

➤ Select and limit social relationships.

➤ Reduce social obligations.

➤ Limit number of personal contacts:
  – Family
  – Friends

➤ Plan time to be with spouse to develop relationship.

➤ Manipulate career and family schedules:
  – Flexible hours
  – Home-office employment

➤ Plan time for self.

➤ Reduce or eliminate overlap of career and home schedules.

➤ Increase observability of role at work.

➤ Avoid unnecessary debt.

➤ Lower career aspirations while children are young.

➤ Modify work involvement of both partners' careers.

ADDITIONAL INFORMATION

See *List 4-28*, *Issues of Minority Students Related to Careers*.

4-28   ISSUES OF MINORITY STUDENTS RELATED TO CAREERS

Issues of Minority Students Related to Career Search

➢ Anxiety when planning a successful career

➢ Extent of encouragement of family, teachers, and mentors to explore variety of careers

➢ Adequate educational preparation for post-high school opportunities

➢ Access to systems that provide career opportunities

➢ Opportunity for career exploration and entrance

➢ Opportunity for leadership

➢ Realistic career choice

Issues of Minorities Related to Career Success

➢ Career aspirations

➢ Career permanence

➢ Opportunities for advancement

➢ Geographical location

➢ Flexibility to move toward opportunity

➢ Collegial work relationships

➢ Equal recognition and status for equal work

➢ Access to computers and technology

Coping Mechanisms of Minorities for Success

➢ Persistence in overcoming obstacles

➢ Ability to deal with covert acts of discrimination:
  – Easily confused with unintentional acts
  – Difficult to detect
  – Impossible to prove
  – Learn from each situation

➢ Treat unintentional act of discrimination as a mistake:
  – If in doubt, overlook it
  – Inform about the unwitting act if important
  – Teach a more appropriate response for use in the future
  – Relax and realize unintentional mistakes do happen

➢ Develop a good sense of humor.

➢ Develop a unique, sought-after specialty.

Section 5

PERSONAL/SOCIAL COUNSELING AND GUIDANCE K–12

PERSONAL/SOCIAL GOALS

5-1   PERSONAL/SOCIAL GOALS FOR ALL STUDENTS

- ➤ Make safe and healthy choices.
- ➤ Develop meaningful relationships.
- ➤ Gain self-awareness and understanding.
- ➤ Develop resilience to cope with problems.
- ➤ Develop positive attitudes.
- ➤ Respect others.
- ➤ Take personal responsibility.
- ➤ Resolve conflicts peacefully.
- ➤ Make effective decisions.

INFORMATION ABOUT STUDENTS

5-2   NEEDS OF ALL STUDENTS

- ➤ Good physical health
- ➤ Safety from harm
- ➤ Caring, functional family
- ➤ Mutually caring friendships
- ➤ Freedom from stress
- ➤ Comfortable home
- ➤ Sufficient food
- ➤ Positive role models
- ➤ Respect
- ➤ Academic success that is relevant

➤ Positive relations within school

➤ Supportive conditions beyond school

➤ Sensitive staff

➤ Life skills *(List 5-13)*

5-3 PROBLEMS OF SOME STUDENTS K–12

➤ Poverty:
  - Homelessness
  - No medical insurance
  - Hunger

➤ Abuse or neglect: *(Lists 5-40 through 5-44):*
  - Physical or sexual abuse
  - Emotional abuse
    1) devaluation of student's talents and potential
    2) labeled as "problem child"

➤ Dysfunctional families

➤ Emotional problems

➤ Eating disorders

➤ High mobility from school to school and home to home

➤ Inadequate supervision

➤ Learning problems

➤ Low social-economic status

➤ Need to function in two cultures—one at home and one at school

➤ Poor language skills

➤ Physical disabilities

➤ Poor physical health

➤ School dropout

➤ Somatic disorders

➤ Substance abuse

➤ Suicide ideation

➤ Violence:
  - Bullying and harassment
  - Weapons in school
  - Death or injury of relative or friend by weapons

➤ Loss of parent(s) through death or divorce

➤ Few resources for learning at home:
  - No incentive to achieve from home
  - No "push" to excel from home

5-4 FEARS OR STRESSORS OF STUDENTS

➤ Death at an early age:
  – Being in a car accident
  – Storms, tornadoes, floods, hurricanes

➤ Economic problems

➤ Health of parents

➤ Loss of a parent:
  – Death
  – Remarriage of parent
  – Separation or divorce of parents

➤ Loss of a relationship:
  – Death of a family member, friend, relative
  – Loss of best friend—elementary and middle school
  – Loss of boyfriend or girlfriend—high school

➤ Loss of safety:
  – Fear of coercion
  – Fear of stealing at school
  – Fear of violence
  – Fear of water and air pollution

➤ Lack of social acceptance:
  – Peer group acceptance—middle and high school:
    1) People talking and gossiping about me—middle school
    2) Not having nice clothes—middle school
  – Relationships—high school

➤ Post-high school plans:
  – Acceptance to college—middle and high school
  – Financing college—high school
  – Job after high school, during college, after college—high school
  – Not living up to parents' expectations—middle school
  – Thwarted expectations for positive future—high school

➤ Relationship with parents:
  – Acceptance of parents
  – Expectations of parents (school, sports, activities, friendships)
  – Conflict with parents
  – Physical, emotional, or sexual abuse

➤ Schoolwork:
  – Changing schools
  – Competitiveness in school
  – Good grades

   – Humiliation in front of the class:
      1) Speaking or reading in front of the class—middle school
      2) Being teased and laughed at by classmates—middle school
   – Taking tests
➢ Sexual issues:
   – Getting AIDS—middle and high school
   – Getting pregnant—middle and high school
   – Not being attractive—middle school
   – Not having a boyfriend or girlfriend—middle and high school
   – Sex identity
   – Other issues of sexuality
➢ Substance abuse
➢ Violence:
   – Fear of bullies
   – Fear of drugs
   – Fear of gangs
   – Fear of guns
   – Fear of harassment

ADDITIONAL INFORMATION

University of Michigan's Institute for Social Research (1995). National household survey on drug abuse. In *Washington Post,* August 1995.

5-5 CULTURAL DIVERSITY OF STUDENTS

Culture is the patterns of learned perception, behavior, attitudes, and beliefs shared by a group of individuals. Culture provides individuals with a set of expectations, largely unconscious, to be used in a social context. (Shapiro, Sewell, et al. (1995)).

Cultural Diversity of Students

- ➤ Social class—similar incomes, lifestyles, values, educational backgrounds
- ➤ Gender—male and female learned roles
- ➤ Ethnicity—similar social and cultural heritage, customs, and traditions
- ➤ Race—easily classified by appearance (African, Asian, Caucasian)
- ➤ Exceptionality or disability *(List 5-10)*
- ➤ Sexual orientation—sexual identity
- ➤ Religion
- ➤ Language
- ➤ Age
- ➤ Affiliations

Concerns of Some Students of Cultures Different From Majority in the School

- ➤ Lack of acceptance
- ➤ Unfair treatment
- ➤ Powerlessness in communicating
- ➤ Coercion
- ➤ Ridicule or humiliation
- ➤ Violence
- ➤ Failure

Social Class Determinants

- ➤ Activities of parents and student
- ➤ Friends of parents and student
- ➤ Level of education of parents
- ➤ Lifestyle of parents and student
- ➤ Occupational aspirations of student
- ➤ Social environment of parents
- ➤ Social roles of parents

ADDITIONAL INFORMATION

Pederson, P. & Carey, J. C. (Eds.). (1993). *Multicultural counseling in schools: A practical handbook.* (**List 12-23**)

Shapiro, J. P., Sewell, T. E. & DuCelle, J. P. (1995). *Reframing diversity in education: Educational leadership for the 21st century.* Lancaster, PA: Technomic.

5-6   ETHNIC DIVERSITY OF STUDENTS

Ethnicity describes people who share a unique social/cultural heritage passed from generation to generation. (Gibbs, Huang & Associates (1989)).

Ethnic Diversity of Students

➤ Constitutes a framework for perceiving and responding to the world

➤ Shapes student's personal and social identity

➤ Establishes values, norms, and expectations for appropriate behavior

➤ Defines parameters for choices and opportunities:
  – Social
  – Educational
  – Occupational

➤ Impacts on how the student is perceived and treated in school

Possible Stressors in School Experienced by Students From Ethnic Groups

➤ Clashes of roles and values of specific culture with those of the dominant white culture

➤ High risk during adolescence:
  – Acculturation usually faster than parents
  – Struggles with identity issues; "Who am I?" "Where do I fit?"
  – May experience prejudice and social isolation
  – May be referred to by labels (e.g., That Chicano, Latino, Hispanic)
  – May experience heightened stress
  – Deals with four interrelated clashes:
    1) *Cultural clash*—difference between culture at home and dominant culture
    2) *Generational clash*—difference in moral standards expected in culture at home
    3) *Socio-economic clash*—difference between opportunities of minorities and dominant culture
    4) *Developmental clash*—difference between expectations of adolescents in dominant culture and adult role expected at home

➤ Minority status

➤ Realization that race may determine advantage and privilege

➤ Social isolation depending on ethnic, racial, and socio-economic composition of the school

➤ Vulnerable to three levels of rejection:
  – Verbal rejection
  – Discrimination
  – Physical attack

➤ Own perception of prejudice

Influence of Ethnicity on the Way Student Is Perceived in School

➤ Physical appearance

➤ Affect or way student shows emotions and responds to others

➤ Self-concept and self-esteem in school

➤ Attitudes toward dependence and independence

➤ Management of aggression and impulse control

➤ Coping and defense mechanisms:
  – Anger
  – Anxiety
  – Depression
  – Fear
  – Guilt

➤ Academic achievement

➤ Behavioral adjustment

➤ Psychological adjustment

➤ Relationship with peers

ADDITIONAL INFORMATION

Gibbs, J. T., Huang, L. N. & Associates (1989). *Children of color: Psychological interventions with minority youth.* (**List 12-23**)

Herring, R. D. (1996). *Multicultural counseling in schools: A synergetic approach.* Alexandria, VA: American Counseling Association.

5-7   ETHNIC BACKGROUNDS OF STUDENTS

African American Students

➤ Largest minority group nationally, varies from school to school

➤ Individuals very different depending upon unique family background

➤ Interrelationship of economic status, education, health care, stage of cultural acceptance, and other factors that effect student

➤ Gap between middle class and poor

➤ May reflect parents' fear of racism and unfair treatment

➤ Very capable of interpreting nonverbal

➤ Frequently mislabeled, perform lower than ability

➤ Frequently religion is very important

African American Adolescents

➤ May be reluctant to seek counseling because it may be perceived as punishment

➤ Adaptive behavior to survive discrimination and poverty

➤ Frequently vulnerable to others' actions:
  – Poverty, no good male role model
  – Limited opportunities for legitimate income
  – Mistreated frequently

- Victimized frequently
- May lack educational and employment opportunities
- More likely to be arrested, convicted, and incarcerated than white adolescents

➤ May be vulnerable to own poor decisions:
- Delinquency
- Substance abuse
- Teen pregnancy

➤ May be vulnerable to depression and dropping out of school

➤ Peers very influential

Asian American Students

➤ Most rapidly growing minority

➤ Diversity of cultures and languages within this ethnic group

➤ Needs and rates of acculturation differ

➤ Young persons may adopt American values and behaviors more quickly than their parents

➤ Shame or loss of face is shared by family

➤ Frequently value self-control, stoicism, and avoidance of expression of emotions

➤ Frequently value self-discipline, patience, humility, honor, and respect

➤ May avoid direct eye contact with teachers and authorities

➤ May believe that problems should be kept and solved within the family

➤ May show quiet, obedient behavior that is expected in the home

➤ National and international socio-political climate may influence acceptance of the child by peers

Asian Refugee Students

The political opinions of others may have resulted in unfair treatment of these students because of their race, religion, nationality, or social class (Huang 1989). Southeast Asian refugee children and adolescents. In J. T. Gibbs, and L. N. Huang, & Associates (1989).

➤ May need opportunity to express intense grief:
- Violent conditions, torture, witnessed atrocities
- Serious loss, discontinued schooling

➤ May experience identity issues

➤ May not be accepted by peers of same nationality or ethnic group

➤ Unaccompanied minors particularly at risk

➤ Possible post-traumatic syndrome

➤ Possible disdain for authority

➤ Possible ambivalence toward family, culture, native country, and new country

Amerasian Students

➤ Ostracized and discriminated against in native country

➤ High risk:
  – Homeless street children in native country
  – May be targets of hostility
  – May have difficulty with ethnic racial identity

Bi-Racial Students

➤ Usually identify with the minority culture

➤ Vulnerable to negative experiences:
  – Identity conflicts about racial/ethnic identity
  – Prejudice and discrimination
  – Alienation, isolation

➤ Frequently adopt coping strategies and defense mechanisms:
  – All or nothing behavior, not moderate
  – Oversocialize or undersocialize
  – Fear social rejection
  – May need chance to express confusion and anger

➤ Frequently develop nonachieving, negative attitudes toward school and unclear or unrealistic career aspirations

Hispanic American Students

➤ Second fastest growing minority group

➤ Diversity of cultures within this ethnic group

➤ Emphasize family, extended family, warmth, and dignity

➤ Parents may have difficulty with English language

➤ Distinctly different expectations for males and females

➤ Respect authority of male over female and age over youth

➤ Prefer high physical contact and close space in social situations

➤ Frequently held values:
  – Affiliation over confrontation
  – Cooperation over competition
  – Personal relationships over achievement
  – Present time frame over the future

➤ Frequent problems:
  – Poverty
  – Parental use of corporal punishment
  – Teen parenthood
  – High rate of dropouts
  – High rate of substance abuse, especially early inhalant use
  – Clashes between adolescents and parents

➤ May have fears about immigration status

Native American Students

➤ Strong cultural and tribe-specific beliefs and practices

➤ Deep respect for elders; committed to tribe and extended family

➤ Frequently pressured by white culture for acculturation

➤ Strongly held values:
  - Being more than doing
  - Cooperation, harmony, generosity, sharing, peace, and politeness
  - Harmony with nature, noninterference
  - Legends and cultural traditions
  - Present, not the future

➤ Common problems:
  - Academic apathy
  - Depression
  - Anxiety and adjustment
  - Substance abuse
  - Dependence
  - Self-destruction
  - Poverty
  - Unemployment

Additional Information

Gibbs, J. T., Huang, L. N. & Associates. (1989). *Children of color: Psychological interventions with minority youth.* (**List 12-23**)

Lee, C. & Richardson, B. (Eds.). (1991). *Multicultural issues in counseling: New approaches to diversity.* (**List 12-23**)

Sue, D. & Sue, D. W. (1990). *Counseling the culturally different: Theory and practice* (2nd ed.). (**List 12-23**)

5-8 VALUES OF THE DOMINANT CULTURE

Values That Are Expected in the United States

➤ Personal control valued more than fate and nature

➤ Change valued more than tradition

➤ Time and its control valued more than human interaction

➤ Equality valued more than hierarchy, rank, or status

➤ Individualism and privacy valued more than the group's welfare

➤ Self-help valued more than birthright inheritance

➤ Competition valued more than cooperation

➤ Future orientation valued more than past orientation

➤ Action and work orientation valued more than "being" orientation

➤ Informality valued more than formality

➤ Directness, openness, and honesty valued more than indirectness and ritual

➤ Practicality and efficiency valued more than idealism

➤ Materialism and acquisitiveness valued more than spiritualism and detachment

➤ Domination and aggression valued more than noninterference

➤ Nuclear family valued more than the extended family

➤ Mastery over nature valued more than harmony with nature

➤ Scientific explanations valued more than acceptance of reality

Most School Cultures

➤ Emphasize middle-class values

➤ Expect and reward ethnocentric or provincial beliefs

➤ Emphasize cognitive learning style

➤ Assume cultural universality versus cultural variability:
  – Fear of stereotyping
  – Believe congruent with egalitarian ideal

ADDITIONAL INFORMATION

Kohls, L. R. (1984). *The values Americans live by*. Washington, DC: Washington International Center.

5-9   VALUES OF SOME OTHER CULTURES

Cultural Values Different From Dominant Culture in the United States

➤ Acceptance of what happens as unavoidable or fate

➤ Avoidance of eye contact

➤ Celebration of different holidays

➤ Desire and expectation for direct advice

➤ Desire for varying amounts of personal space

➤ Expectation of cooperating on homework

➤ Expectation of formality in different situations

➤ Expectation of helping each other in class

➤ Restriction against dating, or required chaperone

➤ Immediate, short-range goals

➤ Importance of nonverbal behavior

➤ Indirect approach to problems

➤ Indirect ways to solve problems

➤ Issues for negotiation

➤ One-way communication from authority to other persons

➤ Respect of elders

➤ Respect of teachers and other authority figures

➤ Restraint from showing feelings outside the family

➤ Restraint of acknowledgment of strangers

➤ Restriction of decision-making to males

➤ Silence to show respect

➤ Strict religious values

➤ Strict religious fasting

➤ Value of the past and historical tradition

➤ Value of the privilege of rank and status

➤ Volume of speech

Cultural Stumbling Blocks

➤ Assume that I know all about my own culture.

➤ Assume that learning about other cultures is not necessary.

➤ Assume that my way is the only way or the right way.

➤ Assume that the person from the other culture should be the one to change.

➤ Be reluctant to ask questions about cultural differences.

➤ Believe that I do not have cultural biases.

ADDITIONAL INFORMATION

Sue, D. W. & Sue, D. (1990). *Counseling the culturally different.* **(List 12-23)**

5-10　EXCEPTIONAL STUDENTS

Types of Exceptionality

➤ Emotionally disturbed

➤ Gifted and talented

➤ Hard of hearing and deaf

➤ Learning disabled

➤ Mentally retarded

➤ Multihandicapped

➤ Orthopedically impaired

➤ Other health impaired

➤ Speech impaired

➤ Visually handicapped

Concerns of Exceptional Students

➤ Inability to perform as expected

➤ Ridicule or humiliation

➤ Failure

➤ Special fears depending on exceptionality

Students Covered Under Section 504

➤ Physical or mental impairment substantially limiting one or more major life activity, but not severe enough to warrant classification under the Individual Disability Education Act (IDEA)

➤ Entitled to regular or special education and related services

Students Covered Under Section 504 but Not Covered Under IDEA

➤ Do not have one of the 13 disabilities listed under IDEA

➤ Do not need special education but need related services or accommodations to benefit from an education

ADDITIONAL INFORMATION

See **List 1-14**, *Placement in Courses: Guidelines.*

See **Lists 3-14 through 3-28**, *Academic Counseling K–12.*

Pierangelo, R. (1995). *The special education teacher's book of lists.* **(List 12-33)**

5-11 STUDENTS AT RISK

All youth have the potential to develop at-risk behaviors. Students at risk are students in danger of a negative future event.

At-Risk Factors

➤ Individual factors:
  – Physiological factors
  – Early and persistent conduct problems
  – Alienation and rebelliousness
  – Early onset of drug use and crime

➤ Family factors:
  – Poor and inconsistent family management practices
  – Family discord and conflict
  – Drug behaviors and substance abuse by family members
  – Parental criminality
  – Low bonding to family

➤ Peer and social interactions:
  – Peer rejection in elementary school
  – Association with drug-using or delinquent peers

➤ School experiences:
  – Academic failure
  – Low degree of commitment to school
  – Low expectations for performance by school staff

➤ Community factors:
  – Laws and norms inattentive toward problem behavior
  – Availability of substances
  – Extreme neighborhood deprivation
  – Neighborhood disorganization

Characteristics of Students At Risk

➤ Impulsive

➤ Angry

➤ Disregard for sanctity of life

➤ Disregard for and unaware of others

➤ Involved in delinquent or criminal behavior

➤ Experienced harassment because of cultural identification

➤ Lack social skills

➤ Do not desire help

➤ Concerned about peer approval

➤ Easily bored

Counselor's Actions

➢ Collaborate with entire staff and community agencies to plan prevention and intervention programs.

➢ Consult with entire staff to determine needs of students at risk.

➢ Identify environmental factors in school that may attribute to lack of success.

➢ Conduct violence-prevention programs and mentoring services in elementary and middle schools. *(Lists 1-7, 2-53, 5-40 through 5-69)*

➢ Teach staff to recognize characteristics and identify students who need intervention services.

➢ Involve students in group counseling for positive peer pressure:
  – Provide structure.
  – Provide active and direct leadership.
  – Provide trust in their ability to change.
  – Do not give up, even though there will be recidivism.

➢ Teach cognitive–behavioral skills with role plays. *(Lists 5-21 through 5-38)*

➢ Obtain additional assistance as needed.

➢ Continue or revise as needed.

➢ Reinforce progress when justified.

➢ Involve all who participated to evaluate services conducted for students at risk.

ADDITIONAL INFORMATION

See *List 5-90, Counseling Students Engaged in High-Risk Behavior.*

Bernstein, N. (1996). *Treating the unmanageable adolescent: A guide to oppositional defiant and conduct disorders. (List 12-34)*

Capuzzi, D. & Gross, D. R. (1996). *Youth at risk: A prevention resource for counselors, teachers, and parents.* (2nd ed.). *(List 12-34)*

Consortium on the School-Based Promotion of Social Competence. (1994). The school-based promotion of social competence: Theory, research, practice, and policy (Chapter 8). In R. J. Haggerty, L. R. Sherrod, N. Garmezy, & M. Rutter, (Eds.). *Stress, risk, and resilience in children and adolescents.* New York, NY: Cambridge University Press.

5-12 STUDENTS WITH DIFFICULT FAMILY RELATIONSHIPS

Students may have increasing behavior problems that interfere with learning. Counselors do not judge, assess, or provide family counseling, but respond to the needs of students so that optimal learning can occur.

Problems That May Cause a Family to Be Temporarily Dysfunctional

➤ Diagnosis of a parent's major mental illness

➤ Hospitalization of a parent

➤ Substance abuse by a parent or sibling

➤ Numerous moves to live with parental boyfriends or girlfriends or a series of stepparents

➤ Physical, emotional, or sexual abuse of the student, a sibling, or parent

➤ Suicide or suicide attempts of a parent or sibling

➤ Assumption of parental roles by the child

➤ Homelessness

Students With Difficult Family Relationships

➤ Experience physical abuse from an angry parent

➤ Live with alcoholic parents

➤ Live with drug-addicted parents

➤ Meet a biological parent for the first time

➤ Need to understand a restraining order

➤ Need to adjust to a disliked stepparent, girlfriend, or boyfriend of parent

➤ Adjust to boyfriend or girlfriend moving in and bringing his or her own children and pets

➤ Being embarrassed by parental behavior

➤ Multiple parental marriages or affairs

➤ Absent parents

➤ Parents who ask children to take sides or criticize the other parent

➤ Required visitation of a parent the child fears

➤ Adjust to living in a series of shelters or foster homes

Children of Divorce

➤ Effects frequently do not dissipate over time without intervention

➤ Frequently have increased behavior problems that interfere with learning

➤ Often lack money and stability

➤ May move from one household to the other with different rules and expectations

➤ May experience a series of changes

➤ May have parents who are concerned about own problems and earning a living

➤ May have parents who have less time and energy to devote to children

➤ May listen to parent's problems and take on a parental role

➤ May look to peers for support

Children Living With Stepparents

➤ More likely to have developmental, emotional, and behavioral problems

➤ More likely to be victims of child abuse, especially sexual abuse

➤ More likely to be successful if stepparent assumes role gradually, earning the right to be a parent

ADDITIONAL INFORMATION

Evans, S. (1995). Two homes for the holidays: Families split by divorce create new traditions. *Washington Post*. Friday, December 22, 1995.

Stepp, L. S. (1995). Torn between two parents. *Washington Post*. Thursday, December 14, 1995.

PERSONAL/SOCIAL GUIDANCE: LIFE SKILLS FOR ALL STUDENTS
5-13 LIFE SKILLS

➤ Communication skills:
- Listening
- Verbal
- Nonverbal
- Assertiveness:
  1) Expressing needs and desires
  2) Peer-pressure refusal skills
  3) Victimization prevention skills

➤ Cognitive skills:
- Cognitive-behavioral
- Decision-making
- Problem-solving
- Self-control

➤ Conflict-resolution skills:
- Anger-management
- Conflict-mediation

➤ Healthy lifestyle skills:
- Nutrition
- Activity and exercise
- Coping
- Refrain from nicotine, alcohol, and other illegal substances
- Stress management

➤ Social skills:
- Making and keeping meaningful relationships
- Developing long-term friendships
- Relating to adults

Counselor's Actions

➤ Teach skills to others:
- Peer facilitators *(List 2-32)*
- Peer mediators *(List 1-8)*
- Parents *(List 2-33)*
- Teachers *(List 2-38)*

5-14   PROGRAMS TO TEACH LIFE SKILLS

Prevention Programs for All Students to Prevent Future Problems

➤ Conducted to reduce incidence of problems in the future *(List 5-11)*

➤ Necessary in elementary and middle school

➤ Include cumulative and transferable skills *(List 5-13)*

➤ Promote students helping each other

➤ Can be taught in guidance groups, counseling groups, or individual counseling

➤ Can be designed to meet needs of diverse populations

➤ Can be taught collaboratively

➤ Applicable in more than one context

➤ Empower students

Intervention Programs to Reduce Impact of Problem or Crisis

➤ Conducted to prevent escalation of a problem

➤ Include focused, theme-centered counseling groups in elementary, middle, and high school

➤ Include individual counseling when necessary

➤ Provide resources to resolve problem

➤ Provide support to students to control behavior

➤ Help students resolve some specific problems

Postvention Programs to Help Student Re-Enter After a Problem Is Resolved

➤ Conducted to reduce harm of crisis or problem

➤ Include focused, theme-centered counseling groups in elementary, middle, or high school

➤ Include individual counseling

➤ Assist in re-entry

➤ Help rebuild self-esteem

Counselor's Actions

➤ Teach skills from simple to complex:
   – Address needs of the students.
   – Modify to meet the developmental level of students.

➤ Teach cognitive–behavioral skills to students. *(List 5-21)*

5-15   HELPING STUDENTS UNDERSTAND THEIR OWN AND OTHERS' FEELINGS

Suggestions for Students to Recognize Their Own Feelings

➣ Recognize body signals when fearful or angry:
  - Heart beats faster
  - Out of breath
  - Breathe faster
  - Feel hot or cold
  - Feel stomach tighten up
  - Feel back tighten up
  - Face feels hot
  - Hands tighten up

➣ Identify what happened to make you feel that way.

➣ Decide what action you should take.

Suggestions for Students to Express Personal Feelings

➣ Select a word to label your feeling. *(List 5-24)*

➣ Decide if this feeling is important enough to take action or tell someone.

➣ Decide on the time and place to describe your feeling.

➣ Use an "I Message" to describe your feeling. *(List 5-29)*

➣ Listen to the other person's response. *(List 5-23)*

Suggestions for Students to Deal With Their Own Feelings

➣ Dealing with fear:
  - Recognize body signals.
  - Identify what you might be afraid of.
  - Decide if the fear is realistic.
  - Think of and take steps to reduce your fear:
    1) Get out of the location quickly
    2) Find friends to be with you
    3) Tell an understanding adult about your fear
    4) Avoid that location in the future

➣ Dealing with anger:
  - Recognize body signals.
  - Identify the event that happened prior to feeling angry.
  - Think about ways to control anger before reacting:
    1) Repeat positive self-talk *(Lists 2-16, 5-19, 5-33)*
    2) Think about something else
    3) Go for a walk
    4) Make a list and then talk about it with an understanding person
    5) Use a punching bag or a pillow
    6) Play a game and forget about it for the time being

       7) Resolve to not do anything now, but do something about it later

       8) Make yourself relax

       9) Close your eyes and imagine you are in your favorite place

      10) Count to 20

      11) Take three deep breaths

      12) Get a drink of water

   – Choose the best way to control your anger and do it.

   – Determine action to take to prevent anger about the same thing in the future when completely relaxed.

   – Talk with an understanding adult about your anger.

   – Use an "I Message" to express feelings to the person whose behavior irritates you. *(List 5-29)*

   – Consider conflict-management skills. *(List 5-34)*

   – Reward yourself when you have controlled your anger well. *(List 5-33)*

➤ Dealing with embarrassment:

   – Recognize when you are feeling embarrassed.

   – Identify the event that happened right before embarrassment.

   – Decide how to control embarrassment.

   – Practice ways of responding to teasing *(List 5-35).*

   – Select the best way to respond to embarrassing situations and practice it.

➤ Dealing with failure:

   – Decide if you have failed at something that matters to you.

   – Think about the possible reason you failed this time:

      1) Didn't study or prepare

      2) Didn't allow enough time

      3) Didn't put in sufficient effort

      4) Didn't really care

   – Consider what you could do to succeed the next time a similar event happens.

   – Decide if you want to try again.

   – Try using your idea to succeed.

   – Reward yourself if you overcome failure.

Suggestions for Students to Understand and Accept Others' Feelings

➤ Actively listen to others. *(List 5-23)*

➤ Observe others' behaviors. *(List 5-25)*

➤ Note nonverbal messages of others. *(List 5-26)*

➤ Listen for invitations or put-downs. *(List 5-28)*

➤ Listen as others describe people. *(List 5-30)*

➤ Observe others' body signals indicating their feelings.

➤ Don't expect others to always feel as you do.

➤ Learn to respect the rights of others to feel differently from the way you do.

ADDITIONAL INFORMATION

See *List 5-36, Relationship Skills.*

See *List 5-37, Social Skills.*

5-16 TEACHING STUDENTS TO RESPECT OTHERS

Teaching Students to Get Along Peacefully

➤ Encourage behaviors that influence positive communication. *(Lists 5-23 through 5-28)*

➤ Encourage verbal invitations. *(List 5-27)*

➤ Teach recognition and resistance to put-downs. *(List 5-28)*

➤ Encourage reframing to describe people. *(List 5-30)*

➤ Teach assertiveness skills and conflict-management skills when observing unfair treatment. *(Lists 5-31, 5-34)*

➤ Encourage respect of people with disabilities. *(List 5-20)*

➤ Encourage respect of all students, regardless of race, gender, and culture. *(Lists 5-5 through 5-9)*

➤ Teach students to refrain from saying anything negative about a person's appearance or performance. *(List 5-30)*

➤ Teach students to refrain from saying anything negative about a person's background, parents, or race.

➤ Teach students to refrain from saying anything negative about a person's holidays or religion.

➤ Teach students not to assume that their way is the only way or the right way.

➤ Teach students not to assume that the other person should be the one to change.

➤ Teach students not to assume that the other person doesn't like you.

➤ Teach students not to assume that the other person wants to hurt you or your feelings.

Counselor's Actions to Teach Respectful Behavior

➤ Teach staff to recognize biased statements and actions of students and teachers.

➤ Teach staff how to recognize and confront name-calling and unfair treatment.

➤ Teach staff how to counter stereotyping of racial and cultural groups, females, social classes, disabled, and others.

➤ Teach guidance lessons to peer facilitators and other students on the topic of respect.

ADDITIONAL INFORMATION

See Materials in *Lists 6-14, 7-14, 8-14, 11-13, 12-27.*

Many voices. Videos. *(List 12-23)*

5-17   TEACHING RESPONSIBILITY AND EDUCATIONAL VALUES

Educational Values

1. Appropriate and Courteous Behavior
   - Clearly articulated to all students
   - Consistently modeled by all adults
   - Consistently enforced by all adults
   - Expected of all students

2. Respect for Others and the Property of Others
   - Being courteous and polite to others
   - Showing tolerance and appreciation of others
   - Accepting individual differences
   - Defending rights of others
   - Protecting the property of others

3. Responsibility for Own Behavior
   - Thinking before acting
   - Considering consequences on all people affected by decisions
   - Being reliable
   - Being accountable
   - Accepting consequences for own choices
   - Disciplining self

4. Honesty
   - Being truthful
   - Being sincere

5. Fairness
   - Listening to others
   - Trying to understand others' thoughts and feelings
   - Making decisions that affect others only after considering their viewpoint
   - Discerning fair treatment
   - Treating all people fairly

6. Caring
   - Showing kindness
   - Sharing opportunities and privileges
   - Being compassionate
   - Helping others

7. Integrity
   - Keeping promises
   - Being trustworthy

8. Self-Discipline
   - Doing fair share
   - Considering others before acting on own behalf
   - Considering consequences before acting

9. Citizenship
   - Obeying all laws
   - Following rules of the school
   - Respecting authority
   - Helping in the community
   - Protecting the environment
   - Conserving natural resources

ADDITIONAL INFORMATION

Hitchner, K. W. & Tifft-Hitchner, A. (1996). Commitment, responsibility, and reality therapy (Chapter 13). In *Counseling today's secondary students. (List 12-3)*

5-18 RECOGNIZING IMPORTANCE OF SELF-ESTEEM

Self-esteem or **self-confidence** is a positive sense of self-worth and competence; a view of self as a responsible and successful person.

Clarification of Self-Esteem

- High levels of achievement and responsibility are associated with high self-confidence or high self-esteem.

- Cultural opinions differ about whether human existance is sufficient, or satisfactory performance is necessary, for self-esteem.

- American culture reinforces gender differences:
   - Females often gain self-esteem from physical appearance.
   - Males often gain self-esteem from what they do.

- Many emotional problems and high-risk behaviors are associated with lack of self-confidence or low self-esteem.

- Self-confidence and self-esteem are related to self-respect and self-worth.

Students With High Self-Esteem or Self-Confidence

- Have internal locus of control
- Assume responsibility for own choices and behavior
- Feel capable to achieve academic success when attempted
- Feel capable to influence environment
- Feel capable to make good decisions
- Feel competent to approach new and difficult tasks
- Are persistent in overcoming obstacles
- Feel confident to admit honest mistakes or errors and continue trying
- Accept and learn from criticism without being devastated
- Respond to peer pressure with confidence
- Stand up for their rights and beliefs without casting blame
- Tolerate frustration

Positive Influences on Students' Self-Esteem

➤ Realistic expectations for students

➤ Reasonable limits and consistency of consequences

➤ Positive feedback when warranted

➤ Respectful listening

➤ Acceptance and positive attention

➤ Good role models

➤ Assistance in adaptation to new culture or new expectations

➤ Appreciation of uniqueness of each student

➤ Expectation of self-discipline and self-competence

ADDITIONAL INFORMATION

See *Lists 6-18, 7-18, 8-18, 10-23, 11-17, 12-30, Self-Esteem.*

See *List 5-19, Helping Students Develop Self-Confidence.*

Meggert, S. S. (1996). Who cares what I think: Problems of low self-esteem (Chapter 5). In P. Capuzzi, & D. R. Gross (Eds.), *Youth at risk.* *(List 12-34)*

National Council for Self-Esteem.

Wiggins, J. D., Schatz, E. L. & West, R. W. (1994). The relationship of self-esteem to grades, achievement scores, and other factors critical to school success. *School Counselor, 41*, (4), 239–244.

5-19 HELPING STUDENTS DEVELOP SELF-CONFIDENCE

Goals for Students to Develop Self-Confidence

➤ Recognize personal capabilities.

➤ Perceive personal significance in school, family, and community.

➤ Believe in ability to influence own life.

➤ Develop intrapersonal skills:
 – Identify and express own feelings. *(List 5-24)*
 – Exercise self-control and self-discipline. *(List 5-33)*

➤ Develop interpersonal skills:
 – Develop communication skills. *(Lists 5-22 through 5-30)*
 – Develop relationship skills. *(List 5-36)*

➤ Set attainable and realistic goals for self. *(List 3-2)*

➤ Relate personal decisions and actions to consequences and results. *(Lists 2-31 and 4-16)*

Methods to Help Students Develop Self-Confidence

➤ Listen to student:
 – Without judgment
 – Respectful of thoughts and feelings

➤ Encourage expression of ideas and perceptions.

➤ Identify student's assumptions.

➤ Celebrate success:
 – Decision-making before action
 – Personal control and self-discipline

Counselor's Actions

➤ Teach life skills to students: *(Lists 5-13, 5-14, 5-21 through 5-38)*
 – Provide classroom guidance. *(Lists 2-29 through 2-32)*
 – Provide counseling groups for students. *(Lists 2-25 through 2-28)*
 – Provide school tutoring/mentoring program. *(List 2-53)*
 – Provide peer-facilitation programs. *(List 2-32)*

➤ Inform students about self-esteem. *(List 5-18)*

➤ Provide positive reinforcement when students make decisions in favor of good health and safety.

➤ Provide positive reinforcement when students solve own problems:
 – Resolve conflicts peacefully.
 – Express anger appropriately.
 – Ask teacher or others for help appropriately.

➤ Teach and engage students in decision-making. *(List 4-16)*

➤ Teach and engage students in meaningful problem-solving. *(List 2-23)*

➤ Teach students positive "self-talk":
  – "I am a worthwhile person."
  – "I am worthy of respect."
  – "I can solve problems."
  – "I can make good decisions."

➤ Teach students to reward themselves:
  – Identify the situation.
  – Identify the action taken.
  – Tell a trusted adult about the situation and action.
  – Receive the compliment from the adult graciously.

ADDITIONAL INFORMATION

Ford, M. E. (1992). *Motivating humans: Goals, emotions, and personal agency beliefs*. Phoenix, AZ: Sage Press.

Reasoner, R. (1982). *Building self-esteem: A comprehensive program. (List 11-17)*

Sunburst Seminar (1991). *Self-esteem curriculum module.* (Grades 5–9). *(List 8-18)*

5-20 PROMOTING SUCCESS OF STUDENTS WITH DISABILITIES

Attitudes and behaviors of the teacher, counselor, and other students profoundly influence the success of disabled students in school.

Attitude is a tendency to react to another person positively or negatively. Attitude is usually accompanied by beliefs that motivate one to behave in certain ways toward that person.

Attitudes

➤ Are learned and can be changed

➤ Are inferred by behavior

➤ Are assumed by observation of behavior

Information About Students With Disabilities

➤ Restriction on daily lives and tasks

➤ Significant psychological ramifications of dealing with disability

➤ Negative attitudes and corresponding behaviors of others can be more debilitating and damaging to disabled students than their disability

➤ Frequently experience negative behaviors from peers:
  – Fear
  – Ignore
  – Resent
  – Reject
  – Ridicule
  – Lack understanding and empathy

➤ Positive, accepting attitudes and behaviors help disabled students:
  – Achieve self-respect and self-confidence
  – Develop good interpersonal skills
  – Move toward independent, productive lives

Counselor's Actions

➤ Examine own anxieties, beliefs, and biases concerning disabilities.

➤ Serve as a role model, showing understanding, acceptance, and empathy.

➤ Become informed about students with disabilities:
  – Learn problems experienced by all students with disabilities.
  – Learn characteristics of students with specific disabilities.
  – Offer information about disabilities.

➤ Provide information to teachers about specific disability.

➤ Encourage teachers to examine own sensitivity, reluctance, and competence in working with students with disabilities:
  – Lack of experience with disabled people is the primary contributor to fears and prejudices.
  – Attitudes of teachers have significant impact on intellectual, social, and emotional development of students with disabilities.

➤ Act as student advocate, preventing discrimination through school policies, textbooks, or classroom activities that may isolate students with disabilities.

➤ Develop and implement programs to foster positive attitudes toward students with disabilities:
  – Classroom guidance lessons for sensitivity:
    1) Stories, puppets *(Lists 6-6, 12-10)*
    2) Videos *(List 12-10)*
    3) Speakers
    4) Honest discussions
  – Group counseling
    1) Together, students with and without disabilities
    2) Social skills
    3) Role plays
    4) Simulations
  – Consultation with teachers
  – Consultation with parents

➤ Foster positive interactions among all students:
  – Help students see ways in which students with disabilities are more like them than different.
  – Help students identify feelings and difficulties some peers have as they attempt to do school work.

Programs Combining Information and Experiential Learning About Disabilities

➤ Information about people with disabilities:
  – Books and videos *(Lists of Materials)*
  – Discussion about feelings of characters and reactions to those feelings

➤ Contact with people who know about disabilities:
  - Classroom visits by students or adults with disabilities
  - Classroom visits by parents of disabled students or professionals working with disabled students

➤ Experiential learning to experience some problems of disabled students:
  - Simulation activities
  - Role playing scenes that present problems to students with disabilities

ADDITIONAL INFORMATION

Bruce, A. B., Shade, R. A. & Cossairt, A. (1996). Classroom-tested guidance activities for promoting inclusion. *School Counselor, 43*, (3), 224–230.

Hal's Pals Dolls. (Puppets With Disabilities). *(List 12-10)*

Horne, M. D. (1985). *Attitudes toward handicapped students: Professional, peer, and parent reactions.* Hillsdale, NJ: Erlbaum.

Lombana, J. H. (1992). *Guidance for students with disabilities.* (2nd ed.). *(List 12-10)*

5-21   COGNITIVE-BEHAVIORAL SKILLS

Steps in Cognitive-Behavioral Skills Training

This is especially effective when student leaders of the same age or older help provide training to students.

1. Inform—Instruct students about the skill and when to use it.
2. Show—Model the skill for students or have peer model the skill.
3. Provide opportunity to practice—Have students rehearse or role play the skill.
4. Provide feedback—Reinforce students when their rehearsal warrants.
5. Coach—Show how to improve skills.
6. Encourage continued practice.
7. Encourage application in regular environment outside of counseling.
8. Encourage discussion of success or need for further practice.
9. Transfer skills to use when appropriate.

ADDITIONAL INFORMATION

See *List 2-11*, *Cognitive-Behavioral Counseling.*

5-22 COMMUNICATION SKILLS

➤ Active listening *(List 5-23)*

➤ Student behaviors that influence communication *(List 5-25)*

➤ Nonverbal communication *(List 5-26)*

➤ Feeling vocabulary *(List 5-24)*

➤ Verbal invitations or communication facilitators *(List 5-27)*

➤ Verbal put downs or communication blockers to recognize and avoid using *(List 5-28)*

➤ "I Messages" *(List 5-29)*

➤ Reframing descriptions of people *(List 5-30)*

➤ Assertive communication *(List 5-31)*

5-23 ACTIVE LISTENING

Active Listening Skills for Students

➤ Encouraging

➤ Clarifying

➤ Restating

➤ Reflecting

➤ Summarizing

➤ Validating

➤ Showing interest and attention:
  – Maintain eye contact with person who is talking.
  – Tune out distractions.
  – Concentrate on what is being said.
  – Wait your turn to talk.
  – Ask about ideas and opinions.
  – Ask open-ended questions.

➤ Encouraging talking

➤ Listening patiently:
  – Listen for the speaker's main ideas.
  – Do not interrupt.
  – Do not share your opinion until the speaker is finished.
  – Do not correct the speaker until finished.
  – Withhold judgment until speaker is finished.
  – Try not to be critical.

➤ Sharing thoughts and opinions when speaker has finished

➤ Reflecting feelings:
  – Restate feeling.
  – Rephrase feeling.
➤ Trying to understand how the speaker is feeling:
  – Note how the speaker is talking.
  – Attempt to see things from the speaker's point of view.

ADDITIONAL INFORMATION

Maxwell, M. J. (1981). *Listening games for elementary grades.* Washington, DC: Acropolis Books, Ltd.

Sunburst Video (1996). *Be a better listener. (List 6-2)*

Sunburst Video (1990). *Between you and me: Learning to communicate. (List 7-2)*

5-24 FEELING VOCABULARY

Words for Students to Express Feelings

GLAD

accepted	fortunate	pleasant
admired	free	pleased
alive	friendly	proud
amused	generous	relaxed
appreciated	grateful	relieved
blissful	happy	respectful
calm	honored	rewarded
cheerful	hopeful	satisfied
comfortable	impressed	secure
competent	joyful	supported
confident	jubilant	surprised
contented	likable	terrific
delighted	lively	thankful
eager	loved	thrilled
ecstatic	loving	trusted
elated	optimistic	valued
excited	overjoyed	welcomed
fantastic	patient	wonderful
fascinated	peaceful	

MAD

aggravated	frustrated	repelled
angry	furious	repulsive
annoyed	hateful	resentful
bitter	horrible	shattered
bothered	hostile	shocked
bugged	impatient	sore
burned up	imposed upon	stubborn
cheated	infuriated	suspicious
consumed	irritated	threatened
cornered	jealous	two-faced
defensive	lied to	ugly
disgusted	livid	unappreciated
disillusioned	mean	used
disturbed	manipulated	vengeful
dominated	offended	victimized
enraged	outraged	vindictive
envious	peeved	violent
exasperated	perturbed	
fed up	rejected	

SAD

bad	distressed	left out
betrayed	distraught	lonely
burdened	disturbed	low
concerned	down	melancholy
crushed	downcast	miserable
defeated	envious	misunderstood
dejected	friendless	needy
depressed	gloomy	overlooked
deprived	grouchy	pained
desolate	grumpy	persecuted
despondent	homesick	pessimistic
devastated	hopeless	remorseful
disappointed	hurt	serious
discouraged	inconsolable	slighted
dissatisfied	isolated	sorrowful

sorry	turned off	unpleasant
terrible	unhappy	weary
troubled	unloved	weepy

POWERFUL

alert	genuine	righteous
bold	helpful	safe
brave	important	secure
capable	in control	self-reliant
challenged	inspired	solid
committed	intense	steadfast
concerned	interested	strong
confident	involved	successful
curious	loyal	supportive
determined	needed	sure
devoted	open	tolerant
energetic	positive	tough
enthusiastic	powerful	vigorous
exhilarated	protective	vital
firm	psyched	
forceful	responsible	

WEAK

appalled	frail	lazy
apathetic	guilty	lifeless
ashamed	gutless	lost
awkward	helpless	numb
beaten	hopeless	phony
bored	ignored	powerless
chicken	impotent	quiet
cowardly	inadequate	run down
defenseless	incompetent	shaky
desperate	inferior	shallow
embarrassed	inhibited	shy
empty	insecure	strengthless
exhausted	insincere	timid

tired
thwarted

useless
vulnerable

wishy-washy
worn out

AFRAID

alarmed
anxious
apprehensive
awed
edgy
fearful
frantic
frightened

horrified
immobilized
intimidated
jittery
jumpy
panicked
panicky
petrified

scared
startled
stunned
tense
terrified
threatened

CONFUSED

ambivalent
baffled
bewildered
boxed in
clueless
cramped
crazy
curious
dazed
disorganized
disoriented
distracted
doubtful

evasive
fidgety
flustered
fragmented
guarded
indecisive
interested
mixed-up
paralyzed
perplexed
pressured
puzzled
restless

shook up
stuck
surprised
torn
trapped
troubled
uncertain
uncomfortable
uneasy
unresponsive
unsettled
unsure

WORRIED

bothered
freaked
impatient

irritable
nervous
overwhelmed

preoccupied
stressed
uptight

5-25 STUDENT BEHAVIORS THAT INFLUENCE COMMUNICATION

Student Behaviors That Inhibit Communication

➤ Arguing

➤ Blaming

➤ Ignoring

➤ Criticizing

➤ Insulting

➤ Name-calling

➤ Interrupting

➤ Judging

➤ Making fun of

➤ Persuading

➤ Ridiculing

➤ Using sarcasm

➤ Stating opinion as fact

Student Behaviors That Facilitate Communication

➤ Eye contact

➤ Facing the person

➤ Active listening

➤ Not doing anything else

➤ Not interrupting

➤ Using "I Messages"

➤ Leaning toward the person

➤ Keeping an open posture

➤ Encouraging the person

➤ Asking questions to clarify what the speaker said

➤ Repeating words the speaker has used

➤ Reflecting in your own words what the speaker said

➤ Summarizing what the speaker said

5-26   NONVERBAL COMMUNICATION

Nonverbal Messages for Students

➤ Tone of voice

➤ Facial expressions

➤ Energy level

➤ Posture

➤ Pace or speed of talking

➤ Changes in behavior patterns:
- Gestures with the hands
- Head nodding
- Foot tapping
- Yawning

➤ Crossed arms—closed posture

➤ Lowered head and eyes

➤ Hurried, empty laughter

➤ Change in pace of breathing

➤ Tensing of posture

Nonverbal Invitations for Students

Being courteous	Loaning a book
Being honest	Offering refreshments
Being on time	Offering someone a chair
Bringing a gift	Opening a door for someone
Congratulating someone	Remembering special occasions
Extending a hand	Sending a thoughtful note
Extending an apology	Shaking a hand
Establishing eye contact	Sharing a poem
Facing the person	Sending a valentine
Giving "wait-time"	Sharing an experience
Having a relaxed posture	Sharing laughter
Holding a door	Sharing lunch together
Leaning forward	Smiling
Letting others praise you	Taking turns
Listening carefully	Waiting

5-27 RECOGNIZING VERBAL INVITATIONS

Verbal Invitations

Come back soon!

Congratulations!

Fine.

Get well soon.

Good morning.

Good suggestion.

Happy Birthday!

Happy Holiday!

How are things going?

How are you?

How may I help you?

I acknowledge that.

I appreciate your help.

I can tell you're pleased.

I care about you.

I enjoy our time together.

I enjoyed having you here.

I like what you did.

I'll try.

I think I can do it.

I understand.

I want to help.

I'd like your opinion.

I'm glad you came by.

I'm impressed.

I've been thinking about you.

Let's do it together.

Let's get together.

Let's talk.

Let's talk it over.

Looking good!

May I help you?

Please come in.

Tell me about it.

Thanks.

That's a good suggestion.

That's even better.

That's O.K.

We missed you.

Welcome.

What a neat idea.

What can I do to help?

What do you think?

Yes!

You make me feel good.

You're special.

➤ Brainstorm more invitations

ADDITIONAL INFORMATION

Hughes, R. S. & Kloeppel, P. C. (1994). *S.A.I.L. Self-Awareness in language arts.* (**List 12-3**)

5-28   RECOGNIZING VERBAL PUT DOWNS

Verbal Put Downs for Students to Recognize and Avoid Using

Act your age!

Anybody can do that.

Because I said so, that's why.

Do as I say.

Don't question me!

Don't be so stupid!

Forget it.

Get lost!

Get out of my way!

Go sit down!

Hey, you!

How could you?

Keep out!

I couldn't care less!

I was here first!

I don't care what you do.

I don't have time.

I wasn't listening.

It won't work.

It's about time.

Not bad for a girl.

Shape up or ship out!

Shut up!

Sit down and shut up!

So what?

Stupid!

That is dead wrong.

That's a childish viewpoint.

That's mine!

That's not your idea, is it?

That's stupid!

This means you!

Use your head.

We don't want you on our side!

What's your excuse this time?

When you're older you'll laugh.

Who do you think you are?

Who's the broad?

Why didn't you stay home?

Why do you bother coming?

Woman driver!

You can't be *that* dumb!

You can't do that.

You can't have it!

You can't play with us!

You goofed again.

You have an attitude.

You shouldn't feel that way.

You'll have to call back.

You'll never make it.

You're last!

You're not trying.

You're wrong!

You better shape up!

You ought to know better.

You'll get over it.

➤ Brainstorm more put downs

ADDITIONAL INFORMATION

Hughes, R. S. & Kloeppel, P. C. (1994). *S.A.I.L. Self-Awareness in language arts.* **(List 12-3)**

5-29   "I MESSAGES"

Communication Using "I Message"

➤ Permits speaker to express own feeling

➤ Permits speaker to describe behavior of other person that effects the speaker

➤ Does not blame

➤ Permits speaker to describe desired behavior of other person in the future

Components of "I Message"

➤ Description of event or behavior: "When . . . ."

➤ Speaker's feelings at time of event: "I felt . . . ."

➤ Reason speaker felt that way: "Because . . . ."

➤ Specific desired actions in the future: "In the future, I would like . . . ."

Necessary Follow-Up

➤ Actively listen to other person's response. *(List 5-9)*

➤ Consider feelings of the other person.

➤ Agree on future actions.

Examples of "I Messages"

➤ "I feel . . . when you . . . because. . . . In the future I would appreciate . . . ."

➤ "I believe . . . ."

➤ "I think . . . ."

➤ "I like it when you . . . ."

➤ "I want to . . . ."

➤ "I don't agree with you when . . . because . . . ."

➤ "I have a different opinion; I think that . . . ."

➤ "I don't agree with you when . . . because . . . ."

5-30 REFRAMING DESCRIPTIONS OF PEOPLE

CRITICAL DESCRIPTION	MORE POSITIVE DESCRIPTION (REFRAMED)
➤ Afraid to open up	➤ Precise, objective
➤ Arrogant	➤ Usually right
➤ Autocratic	➤ Goal-oriented
➤ Bleeding heart	➤ Compassionate
➤ Bossy, controlling	➤ Independent
➤ Controlling	➤ Providing security
➤ Cool, aloof, unfeeling	➤ Calm, not easily rattled
➤ Critical, fault-finding	➤ Able to find flaws
➤ Disobeys rules	➤ Loves freedom
➤ Doesn't care about people	➤ Task-oriented
➤ Dull, boring	➤ Traditional, stable
➤ Easily duped	➤ Trusting
➤ Eccentric, weird	➤ Different, unique
➤ Emotionally controlled	➤ Objective
➤ Fawning	➤ Likes to please people
➤ Flaky	➤ Spontaneous
➤ Goofs off too much	➤ Carefree
➤ Heartless	➤ Strong
➤ Indecisive	➤ Sees shades of gray
➤ Intellectual snob	➤ Superior intellect
➤ Irresponsible	➤ Fun-loving
➤ Judgmental	➤ Decisive
➤ Lacking mercy, unfair	➤ Impartial
➤ Liar	➤ Imaginative
➤ Manipulative	➤ Manages well
➤ Mushy	➤ Romantic
➤ Not a team player	➤ Independent
➤ Not able to stay on task	➤ Has multiple interests
➤ Not to be trusted	➤ Flexible
➤ Opinionated	➤ Assertive

CRITICAL DESCRIPTION	MORE POSITIVE DESCRIPTION (REFRAMED)
➤ Overly emotional	➤ Sensitive, caring
➤ Pushover	➤ Wants harmony
➤ Resists closure or decisions	➤ Can deal with chaos
➤ Rigid	➤ Stable
➤ Doesn't face reality	➤ Visionary
➤ Scatterbrained	➤ Does many things simultaneously
➤ Smothering	➤ Caretaker
➤ Soft	➤ Sympathetic
➤ Stingy with praise	➤ Hesitant to comment
➤ Stubborn	➤ Persistent
➤ System-bound	➤ Realistic
➤ Talks too much	➤ Communicator
➤ Too nice	➤ Empathetic
➤ Too tenderhearted	➤ Willing to work tirelessly
➤ Too touchy-feely	➤ Emotional, affectionate
➤ Too trusting	➤ Believing
➤ Unappreciative of others	➤ Firm-minded
➤ Uncontrollable	➤ Free spirit
➤ Unimaginative	➤ Resolute
➤ Unrealistic	➤ Idealistic
➤ Uptight	➤ Concerned

5-31 ASSERTIVENESS SKILLS

Assertiveness is expressing thoughts, feelings, opinions, perceptions, and beliefs in direct, honest, and appropriate ways, and standing up for one's own rights without violating the rights of others. It is open and honest communication, respectful of the needs and rights of self, and the needs and rights of others.

Take Initiative for Self

➢ Act for own best interests:
- – Set and work toward meaningful goals.
- – Make life style decisions.
- – Trust own judgment for own welfare.
- – Ask for help when desired.
- – Participate socially as desired.
- – Start conversations.

➢ Stand up for self:
- – Say "No" to participating in undesirable behaviors. *(List 5-29)*
- – Prioritize activities and set limits on time and activities.
- – Respond appropriately to others' criticism and put downs .
- – Defend personal opinions without using put downs.

➢ Express feelings effectively: *(List 5-24)*
- – Show agreement and support honestly.
- – Disagree with others and remain friends.
- – Show anger appropriately and when warranted.
- – Show friendship and affection appropriately.
- – Admit fear or anxiety honestly.
- – Act spontaneously but with control.

Respect the Rights of Others

➢ Take initiative for self without hurting others.

➢ Refrain from calling others names, using labels or put downs.

➢ Refrain from intimidating others.

➢ Refrain from manipulating others.

➢ Refrain from controlling others.

➢ Refrain from using sarcasm.

➢ Refrain from bringing up situations in the past.

➢ Refrain from making sweeping, general judgments.

➢ Avoid overloading other person with own grievances.

Counselor's Actions

➤ Define aggressiveness, assertiveness, and nonassertiveness, showing distinct differences.

➤ Give examples of aggressive behavior and responses:
  – Glaring eyes; leaning forward; pointing a finger; loud, haughty tone of voice; snickering
  – Threats such as: "You'd better"; "If you don't watch out"; "Come on"; "You must be kidding"; "Should"; "Bad"; sexist or racist terms
  – Demanding behavior of others, dominating others
  – Sarcastic remarks to or about anyone who disagrees
  – Goal is to get everybody to do what they want, forcing others to "lose"; "Win–Lose"

➤ Give examples of assertive behavior and responses:
  – Eye contact, standing comfortably on two feet, hands loosely at sides, talking in a strong, steady tone of voice
  – "I Messages" such as: "I think"; "I feel"; "I want to"; "I like it when . . . ." *(List 5-26)*
  – Eliciting others' ideas: "How can we resolve this?"; "What do you think?"; "What do you see as the problem?"
  – Goal is to respect self and others; "Win–Win"

➤ Give examples of nonassertive behavior and responses:
  – Downcast eyes; shifting weight; slumped body; wringing hands; whining, hesitant, soft, or giggly tone of voice
  – Words such as: "Maybe"; "I guess"; "I wonder"; "I can't"; "Don't you think?"; "Well, uh"; "You know"; "It's not really important"; "Don't bother"
  – Fail to express own feelings, thoughts, beliefs
  – Permit others to "walk all over" them
  – Expressing self in apologetic and self-degrading manner
  – Goal is to please others and avoid conflict; "Lose–Win" or "Lose–Lose"

➤ Teach specific techniques for assertive behavior:
  – Be as specific and clear as possible about what you want, think, and feel.
  – Explain exactly what you mean and what you don't mean.
  – Do not demand that others agree with you or do what you want or desire.
  – Talk about a problem directly with the person involved, not a third party.
  – Acknowledge that your statements are your beliefs, perceptions, opinions, feelings, or desires.
  – Acknowledge that others have a right to their beliefs, perceptions, opinions, feelings, and desires even though you disagree.
  – Ask others to express their beliefs and opinions clearly and directly as feedback.
  – Listen to feedback even though you may disagree. *(List 5-23)*
  – Do not interrupt person giving feedback.

➤ Provide opportunities for students to practice assertive responses in realistic role-play situations.

➤ Elicit constructive ways to improve assertive responses.

➤ Coach students to continually improve their assertive responses.

➤ Encourage students to transfer assertive skills in realistic situations outside of the class or group.

➤ Encourage students to continually help each other to improve assertive skills.

➤ Teach students to recognize situations in which to use assertive behavior:
  – Responding to peer pressure or undue persuasion. *(List 5-29)*
  – Responding to aggressive behavior by another person
  – Standing up for one's rights and dignity
  – Standing up for the rights and dignity of a friend or other person
  – Responding to criticism
  – Handling anger of another person
  – Expressing a complaint and requesting a change
  – Making and refusing requests
  – Protecting own time
  – Negotiating for a desired compromise
  – Giving or receiving praise and compliments
  – Persuading others of a more fair decision

ADDITIONAL INFORMATION

See *List 5-36, Relationship Skills.*

See *List 5-37, Social Skills.*

Alberte, R. & Emmons, M. (1970). *Your perfect right.* San Luis Obispo, CA: Impact.

5-32 PEER-PRESSURE REFUSAL SKILLS

Ways Peer Pressure Is Applied

➤ Call names *(Chicken-Caller)*

➤ Bully by making physical threats *(Bully)*

➤ Coerce with bribes or threats *(Coercer)*

➤ Ridicule *(Ridiculer)*

➤ Reassure that it will be O.K. *(Reassurer)*

Examples of Peer Pressure to Do Something Wrong

➤ To cheat on tests or share homework

➤ To do something "off limits"

➤ To do something parents or teachers have told you not to do

➤ To "go along" with misbehavior of others

➤ To go somewhere "off limits"

➤ To ignore, tease, put down another student

➤ To laugh at something that isn't really funny

➤ To skip school

➤ To use alcohol and other drugs

Peer-Pressure Refusal Skills

➢ Know your feelings. *(List 5-15)*

➢ Express your feelings. *(Lists 5-24 through 5-27, 5-29)*

➢ Stand up for your own and others' rights. *(List 5-31)*

➢ Keep out of fights. *(List 5-34)*

➢ Leave the situation if it is in your best interest and safe to do so.

➢ Convince others of an alternate plan.

➢ Deal with accusations. *(Lists 5-28, 5-31)*

➢ Deal with group pressure. *(List 5-34)*

➢ Deal with someone else's anger. *(List 5-34)*

➢ Deal with fear. *(List 5-15)*

➢ Deal with teasing. *(List 5-38)*

➢ Deal with embarrassment. *(List 5-15)*

➢ Deal with feeling left out. *(Lists 5-15, 5-36)*

➢ Resolve a problem. *(List 2-23)*

➢ Ask for help. *(List 5-38)*

➢ Make a complaint. *(List 5-31)*

Use and Evaluation of Peer-Refusal Skills

➢ Use of assertive skills. *(List 5-31)*

➢ Ability to get out of situation safely

➢ Ability to maintain own values and dignity

➢ Ability to withstand peer pressure

➢ Ability to avoid repercussions

➢ Ability to terminate discussion or situation

Additional Information

See **List 5-21**, *Cognitive-Behavioral Skills.*

Alberte, R. & Emmons, M. (1970). *Your perfect right.* San Luis Obispo, CA: Impact.

5-33 ANGER-MANAGEMENT SKILLS

Expressions of Anger

- ➤ Low impulse control:
    - – Temper tantrum
    - – Physical abuse of others
    - – Physical abuse of self
    - – Threats to others

- ➤ Anger denial:
    - – Attempt to repress it
    - – Express in inappropriate ways

- ➤ Appropriate anger management or anger control

Methods to Control Anger

- ➤ Identify personal signs of anger:
    - – Body signals. *(List 5-15)*
    - – Thoughts
    - – Behaviors

- ➤ Rate intensity of anger to specific situations on scale of one to ten.

- ➤ Analyze anger: *(List 2-16)*
    - – Examine situation provoking anger—activating event.
    - – Examine thoughts or beliefs about activating event.
    - – Examine feelings accompanied with the anger.
    - – Identify "self-talk" accompanied with the anger.
    - – Examine actions when angry.
    - – Examine consequences to expression of anger.

- ➤ Describe "self-talk" accompanied with anger:
    - – "She can't say that about me"; "How dare she"; "He's dissing me"
    - – "I'm no good"

- ➤ Take responsibility for own anger and the consequences.

- ➤ Make a commitment to change.

- ➤ Distinguish between beliefs and feelings.

- ➤ Refine assertiveness skills. *(List 5-31)*

- ➤ Refine communication skills. *(Lists 5-22 through 5-30)*

- ➤ Identify alternative behaviors to blowing off or showing poor impulse control.

- ➤ Practice alternative behaviors.

- ➤ Practice healthy expression of anger.

- ➤ Practice new "self-talk":
    - – "She shouldn't say that about me, but it doesn't make me that way."
    - – "He shouldn't show disrespect to me, but I still have my dignity."
    - – "She shouldn't do that to me, but I can only be responsible for me."
    - – "I am a worthwhile person who deserves respect."

➤ Accept constructive criticism to improve anger control.

➤ Try new methods to control when really angry.

➤ Continue to improve controlling anger.

➤ Heal relationships damaged because of poor anger control.

➤ Establish healthy outlets for anger:
  – Make a list of resentments or things apt to promote anger.
  – Identify and distinguish feelings.
  – Take responsibility for controlling behavior when angry.

➤ Learn alternatives to fighting.

➤ Learn how to fight fairly.

Guidelines to Fight Fairly

➤ Limit remarks when angry to the specific behavior that bothers you now.

➤ Do not attack the parentage, appearance, or beliefs of the person.

➤ Do not tell the other person what you think of him or her.

➤ Do not bring up other problems with the person or past history.

➤ Do not blame the other person for the problem.

➤ Limit your comments to express your own feelings.

➤ Use "I Messages." *(List 5-29)*

➤ Do not use words: "Always"; "Never."

➤ Do not use put downs. *(List 5-28)*

➤ Be specific in describing the behavior that bothers you.

➤ Do not physically attack.

➤ Do not threaten.

➤ Use assertiveness skills. *(List 5-31)*

➤ Try to listen to the other person even though you disagree. *(List 5-23)*

➤ Do not interrupt while the other person describes his or her feelings.

➤ If possible, practice verbal message of anger.

Alternatives to Fighting

1. Think about why you are angry.

2. Think of ways to vent your anger without fighting or making threats.

3. Decide the best way to vent your anger without undesirable consequences.

4. Decide what you want to happen in the long run.

5. Take the action to avoid the fight.

ADDITIONAL INFORMATION

See *List 5-21, Cognitive-Behavioral Skills.*

See *Lists 6-3, 7-3, 8-3, 9-4, 10-5, 11-4, 12-4.*

See *Lists 6-8, 7-8, 8-8, 10-11, 12-12.*

5-34 CONFLICT-MANAGEMENT OR CONFLICT-RESOLUTION SKILLS

Conflict-Management Skills for Students

➤ Dealing with someone else's anger:
- Listen to and observe the person who is angry.
- Try to understand what the angry person is feeling.
- Show that you understand how the angry person is feeling:
  1) Paraphrase what you hear the person say.
  2) Clarify what you believe the person is feeling.
  3) Summarize how the person is feeling and why they feel that way.
- Decide on a time and place to try to help the person resolve the problem.
- Help the person use anger-management skills. *(List 5-33)*
- Help the person use the problem-solving model. *(List 2-23)*

➤ Solving a problem that you have with another person:
- Tell the other person your opinion.
- Listen with an open mind to the other person's perceptions. *(List 5-23)*
- Consider why the other person feels the way he or she described.
- Think of ways to resolve the problem. *(List 2-23)*
- Suggest a compromise or a way to resolve the problem.

➤ Responding to a complaint about your behavior:
- Listen to the complaint. *(List 5-23)*
- Ask the person to explain anything you don't understand.
- State your ideas about what happened.
- Accept the blame when appropriate.
- Offer ways to resolve the problem.
- If person refuses to resolve the problem, offer to take problem to conflict mediation or to a caring adult.

➤ Dealing with an accusation:
- Listen to the accusation.
- Consider ways to respond to the accusation.
- Consider apologizing if the accusation is true.
- Make certain to not make the same mistake again.
- If accusation is not true, offer to take situation to mediation or a caring adult for resolution.

➤ Preparing for a difficult conversation:
- Think about how you can talk about the topic without blaming anyone.
- Think about how you will feel during the conversation.
- Consider how the other person will feel.
- Think about what the other person may say in response.
- Think about other things that might happen during the conversation:
  1) Interruptions
  2) Person blaming you for what happened
  3) Person not believing you
  4) Person blaming someone else for what happened
  5) Person becoming very angry over the situation

- Practice saying what you need to say with a caring adult.
- Listen to suggestions the adult may have.
- Choose the best way to tell the person.
- Select the right time and place for the conversation.
- Tell the person you would appreciate their listening to your talking about a difficult situation.
- Reassure the person that if you made a mistake you will not make the same mistake again.
- Reward yourself for facing up to a difficult situation.

➤ Complaining about a situation:
- Decide if the complaint is important enough to discuss with the person involved or an adult.
- Decide to whom to complain.
- Tell the person your complaint describing your feelings. *(Lists 5-24)*
- Listen to the advice of the person to whom you complained. *(List 5-23)*

ADDITIONAL INFORMATION

See **List 1-8**, *Conflict-Resolution/Peer-Mediation Programs.*

See **Lists 5-36, 5-37, 5-31**, *Relationship Skills, Social Skills, and Assertiveness Skills.*

See **Lists 6-3, 7-3, 8-3, 9-4, 10-5, 12-4**, *Materials for Conflict Resolution.*

Perlstein, R. & Thrall, G. (1996). *Ready-to-use conflict resolution activities for secondary students. (List 12-4)*

5-35 COPING AND RESILIENCE SKILLS

Characteristics of Resilience

➤ Stable care

➤ Problem-solving abilities

➤ Attractiveness to peers and adults

➤ Manifest confidence and perceived efficacy

➤ Identification with competent role models

➤ Planfulness and aspirations

Coping With Loss

Loss of a person through separation or death, or loss of health or body part.

➤ Seek support from family and friends.

➤ Talk about what creates sadness or stress.

➤ Describe feelings to a caring adult.

➤ Try to accept the reality of things you cannot change.

➤ Take care of self.

➤ Continue normal activities as much as possible.

➤ Accept that some friends may not know what to say.

➤ Share memories of person or health.

➤ Seek help from a professional if feeling sadness or stress persists.

Coping With Discrimination

➤ Report to a caring adult.

➤ Maintain self-confidence and self-esteem, knowing that the person who is discriminating is wrong.

➤ Accept that you are the only person in control of your dignity.

➤ Maintain self-respect.

➤ Maintain self-control over thoughts, feelings, and behaviors.

➤ Try not to personalize biased statements, knowing it is a reflection of the person who makes such statements.

➤ Do not try to get even because this perpetuates the conflict.

➤ Develop friends who share your values.

➤ Develop a sense of humor.

Coping With Harassment and Bullying

➤ Follow all suggestions above.

➤ Avoid locations and situations where harassment has taken place.

➤ Do not maintain eye contact with the harasser.

➤ Be with friends when possible, not alone.

➤ Think and talk about something else to change the subject.

➤ If hurt, get to a well-lit, safe place immediately.

➤ Ask for help from an adult.

➤ Do not accept a dare or respond to a threat.

Coping With Disappointment

➤ Discuss unexpected low grade with teacher.

➤ Realize and accept that winning is not always possible when losing an important contest.

➤ Realize that a decision may result in the rejection of an opportunity.

➤ Realize when personally rejected that trust involves risk.

Counselor's Actions

➤ Take action and deal with harasser or change the environment if incidents involve discrimination. *(List 2-58)*

➤ Collaborate with entire staff to plan projects to help students deal with loss and disappointment in a positive way. *(List 1-6)*

➤ Encourage long-term planning instead of impulsive decision making.

➤ Teach staff to recognize signs of student stress.

➤ Train peer facilitators to help students deal with loss and disappointment. *(List 2-32)*

➤ Plan and lead ongoing counseling groups to deal with loss and disappointment. *(Lists 2-25 through 2-28)*

➤ Encourage students to use communication, assertiveness, and conflict-management skills. *(Lists 5-22 through 5-35)*

➤ Teach students to adjust to delayed gratification and long-term benefits instead of expecting immediate rewards.

➤ Encourage staff to plan cooperative learning experiences instead of entirely competitive projects.

➤ Help students approach life's problems in an active way, determining what they can change and accepting the things they cannot change.

➤ Take into consideration the coping pattern encouraged by the family.

➤ Encourage students who are grieving to seek help from their family and their religious leader.

➤ Help students and staff constructively perceive frustration, negative experiences, and pain.

➤ Help students believe life is positive and meaningful, even though there are difficult situations to deal with along the way.

➤ Help students in pain to gain positive attention from others.

➤ Help students see the need to continue to be competent in school.

➤ Invite community agencies to provide information to students about loss and disappointment.

ADDITIONAL INFORMATION

See *List 2-35, Stress During Adolescence.*

See *List 5-16, Teaching Students to Respect Others.*

See *Lists 5-70, 5-71, Dealing with Grief* and *Debriefing After a Tragedy or Natural Disaster.*

See *Lists 6-7, 7-7, 9-15, 10-12, Materials dealing with divorce of parents.*

See *Lists 6-4, 7-4, 9-15, 10-6, 11-5, 12-7, Materials dealing with grief.*

Haggerty, R. J., Sherrod, L. R., Garmezy, N. & Rutter, M. (1994). *Stress, risk, and resilience in children and adolescents.* New York, NY: University of Cambridge.

5-36   RELATIONSHIP SKILLS

Students in Small Groups *(Lists 2-25 through 2-28)*

Practice cognitive-behavioral skills: *(List 5-21)*

➤ Observe desired behavior performed by leader or model.

➤ Practice the behavior in the group.

➤ Receive feedback from the group about performance of behavior.

➤ Try behavior outside the group.

➤ Report results to the group.

➤ Continue to practice or add new behavior to behavioral repertoire.

Relationship Skills for Students

➤ Initiating conversation with desired friends

➤ Joining others in an activity

➤ Maintaining conversations

➤ Introducing people

➤ Understanding feelings of others *(Lists 5-15, 5-16)*

➤ Expressing friendship *(List 5-27)*

➤ Helping others

➤ Dealing with feeling left out

➤ Dealing with contradictory messages

➤ Responding to teasing

➤ Ending conversations

➤ Requesting desired action when appropriate

➤ Using "I Messages" when appropriate *(List 5-29)*

➤ Setting limits when appropriate

Relationship Skills With Adults

➤ Requesting help

➤ Requesting permission

➤ Demonstrating responsibility *(List 5-17)*

➤ Negotiating privileges *(Lists 5-21 through 5-26)*

➤ Requesting reconsideration *(Lists 5-22 through 5-27)*

Personal Qualities for Student Friendships

considerate	helpful	sensitive
dedicated	honest	serious
dependable	humble	strong
fair	kind	thoughtful
funny	good listener	truthful
fun to be with	loyal	understanding
gentle	patient	witty
generous	polite	
happy	popular	

Additional Information

See *List 5-30, Reframing Descriptions of People.*

See *List 5-37, Social Skills.*

See *Lists 6-10, 7-10, 8-10, 9-15, for materials about friendships.*

Gibbs, J. C., et al. (1995). *Equip program: Teaching youth to think and act responsibly through a peer-helping approach.* *(List 12-25)*

Goldstein, A. P., Reagles, K. W. & Amann, L. L. (1990). *Refusal skills: Preventing drug use in adolescents.* *(List 12-38)*

5-37 SOCIAL SKILLS

Social Skills for Students

➤ Listening actively *(List 5-23)*

➤ Introducing yourself

➤ Starting a conversation

➤ Maintaining a conversation

➤ Showing courtesy to others

➤ Asking a question

➤ Giving instructions

➤ Giving a compliment

➤ Accepting a compliment

➤ Following instructions

➤ Sharing something

➤ Apologizing

➤ Accepting an apology

Additional Information

See *List 5-21, Cognitive-Behavioral Skills.*

See *List 5-31, Assertiveness Skills.*

See *List 5-36, Relationship Skills.*

Gibbs, J. C., et al. (1995). *Equip program: Teaching youth to think and act responsibly through a peer-helping approach. (List 12-25)*

Goldstein, A. P., Reagles, K. W. & Amann, L. L. (1990). *Refusal skills: Preventing drug use in adolescents. (List 12-38)*

5-38   STRESS-MANAGEMENT SKILLS

Helping Students Cope With Stress

➤ Attempt to resolve problem rather than ignoring it.

➤ Change ways of thinking about problem.

➤ Use problem-solving skills: *(List 2-23)*

   1. Identify the problem.

   2. Generate alternatives.

   3. Consider consequence of each alternative.

   4. Choose one alternative or solution.

   5. Implement the solution.

   6. Evaluate the effectiveness of the solution.

➤ Use decision-making skills. *(List 4-16)*

➤ Seek adult help and support.

➤ Discuss the problem with a caring adult.

Counselor's Actions

➤ Collaborate with school staff to ensure the safety of all and minimize vulnerability of students when possible. *(List 2-45)*

➤ Teach staff to recognize student stress and reduce needless stressors.

➤ Teach staff to incorporate stress reduction and coping in all classes.

➤ Teach and encourage long-term planning to reduce the stress of reacting to unforeseen short deadlines and emergencies.

➤ Teach coping skills for resilience. *(List 5-35)*

➤ Teach peer facilitators to be aware of stress and to provide necessary support and understanding when students are stressed.

➤ Encourage cooperative learning instead of constant competitiveness in the classroom.

➤ Inform staff of student stress caused by time pressure and humiliation in classes.

➤ Encourage staff to look for competence of students instead of weaknesses.

➤ Recommend good health habits:

   – Nutrition

   – Exercise

   – Body and mind relaxation

➤ Encourage attempts to resolve the problem or change the way of thinking about the problem.

➤ Encourage students to evaluate physical and emotional safety of the situation.

➤ Encourage students to approach rather than flee from problems in which safety is not an issue. *(List 2-23)*

➤ Teach students positive "self-talk" and how to use it for positive thinking.

➤ Refer for intense stress reduction when needed:
  – Muscle relaxation
  – Visual imagery
  – Biofeedback

Additional Information

See *List 2-23, Problem-Solving Model.*

See *List 2-35, Stress During Adolescence.*

See *List 2-44, Professional Burnout and Distress in Schools.*

Capuzzi, D. & Gross, D. R. (1996). *Youth at risk: A prevention resource for counselors, teachers, and parents.* (2nd ed). *(List 12-34)*

Personal/Social Guidance: Programs for Prevention
5-39　Program to Promote Student Safety

Recommend a Committee of Parents and Staff

➤ Assess student protection from harassment and abuse.

➤ Assess need for students to be informed, have confidence, and feel safe..

➤ Plan a prevention program for safety.

➤ Include information for staff, students, and parents.

➤ Continue to examine school environment to ensure safety. *(List 5-54)*

Inform Entire Staff About Need for Student Safety

➤ Provide preservice and inservices to inform school personnel:
  – State law and school district procedures
  – Characteristics of abused and neglected children *(Lists 5-40 through 5-44)*
  – Guidelines for parental supervision of children *(List 5-45)*
  – Overall information about child and adolescent abuse and neglect *(List 5-51)*
  – Characteristics of abusive caretakers *(List 5-47)*

➤ Inform teachers of procedures for teachers, counselor, and administrator when abuse or neglect are suspected. *(Lists 5-48 through 5-49)*

➤ Inform staff about harassment and sexual harassment. *(Lists 5-53, 5-58)*

Inform Students of Their Right to Safety

➤ Safety at school:
  – Information to young students *(List 5-52)*

    – Information about abuse to adolescents and preadolescents *(Lists 5-40 through 5-43, 5-51)*

    – Information about harassment to adolescents and preadolescents *(Lists 5-53 through 5-57)*

➢ Safety between home and school *(List 5-52)*

➢ Safety at home and in the community:

    – Information for latchkey students *(List 5-46)*

    – Information about abuse *(Lists 5-40 through 5-42)*

    – Information about date rape and sexual harassment *(Lists 5-43, 5-57)*

Inform Parents About Student Safety

➢ Actions taken at school to ensure student safety *(List 5-55)*

➢ Information about abuse and harassment *(Lists 5-51, 5-53 through 5-58)*

➢ Guidelines for supervision of children *(List 5-45)*

➢ Information provided to young children *(List 5-52)*

➢ Information provided to adolescents and preadolescents *(Lists 5-43, 5-51, 5-53 through 5-58)*

➢ Parent training and counseling groups to assist parents: *(Lists 2-33, 2-34, 2-35):*

    – Information about child development *(List 2-34)*

    – Information about preadolescence and adolescence and parenting skills *(Lists 2-34, 2-35)*

    – Information about reasonable discipline and consequences *(Lists 2-31, 2-41)*

➢ Parent support groups:

    – Establishment of parenting networks *(List 2-33)*

    – Discussion of difficulties and joys of parenting

    – Sharing expectations and limits of children

    – Sharing appropriate methods of discipline

➢ Available resources for parents *(Section 10, Materials to use with Parents)*

➢ Suggestions for parents *(Lists 5-39 through 5-69)*

➢ Follow up on parent suggestions for the student safety committee

ADDITIONAL INFORMATION

Sabella, R. A. & Myrick, R. D. (1995). *Confronting sexual harassment: Learning activities for teens. (List 12-28)*

5-40 EMOTIONAL ABUSE

Emotional abuse is a systematic attempt to destroy a person's self-worth through words or actions. Continual harassment is emotional abuse.

➢ Examples of emotional abuse:
  - Chronic belittling
  - Humiliating
  - Rejecting
  - Ridiculing
  - Denying emotional needs
  - Ignoring
  - Isolating
  - Terrorizing

➢ Physical indicators:
  - Speech disorders
  - Delayed physical development
  - Poor appetite
  - Substance abuse
  - Ulcers, asthma, severe allergies

➢ Behavioral indicators:
  - Habit disorders (biting, sucking, rocking, thumb sucking)
  - Antisocial or destructive behaviors
  - Neurotic traits (sleep disorders, inhibition of play)
  - Behavioral extremes (compliant, passive, undemanding or aggressive, demanding, rageful)
  - Inappropriate developmental behavior (acting like a parent or inappropriately infantile)
  - Lying and/or stealing
  - Depression

➢ Possible effects:
  - Serious emotional problems
  - Behavioral disorders

ADDITIONAL INFORMATION

See *Lists 5-43, 5-53, Acquaintance/Date Rape* and *Information About Student Harassment.*

Hitchner, K.W. & Tifft-Hitchner, A. (1996). Child abuse and neglect (Chapter 15). In *Counseling today's secondary students.* *(List 12-3)*

Thompson, C. L. & Rudolph, L. B. (1996). *Counseling children.* (4th ed.). *(List 12-3)*

5-41 PHYSICAL ABUSE

Physical abuse is any act or behavior that inflicts or intends to inflict bodily harm. There are about equal proportions of male and female victims.

➤ Examples of physical abuse:
- Threat of injury to a child or adolescent
- Physical injury
- Unexplained bruises or patterns of bruises
- Patterned injuries (belt buckle, wire, coat hanger, burn patterns)
- Unexplained burns (cigarette, electric iron, immersion, spattering by hot liquids)
- Unexplained fractures, lacerations, or abrasions
- Injuries inconsistent with information offered

➤ Physical indicators (combinations of injuries may indicate physical abuse):
- Burns, cuts, fractures
- Bruises or black eyes
- Welts, abrasions
- Shaking, causing internal injuries
- Bald spots

➤ Behavioral indicators:
- Behavioral extreme of withdrawal or aggressiveness
- Uncomfortable with physical contact
- Complains of soreness or moves uncomfortably
- Arrives at school early or stays late as if afraid to be at home
- Appears afraid of caregiver and does not want to go home
- Chronic runaway
- Shrinks when approached by adults
- Wears clothing inappropriate for the weather to conceal injuries
- Avoids changing clothes in gym class
- Sudden change of behavior and/or grades
- Unexplained rage
- Signs of depression

➤ Possible effects:
- Increased number of classroom behavior problems
- Lower educational aspirations
- Grade repetition
- Lowered self-esteem
- Antisocial behavior
- Drop out of school
- Substance abuse
- Teen pregnancy
- Aggressive tendencies toward others
- Generalized anxiety
- Chronic anxiety and depression

- Extreme adolescent problems
- Emotional-thought disturbances
- Psychiatric problems
- Delinquency
- Helplessness, dependency
- Continue cycle of abuse by abusing own children when a parent
- Suicidal tendencies

ADDITIONAL INFORMATION

Capuzzi, D. & Gross, D. R. (1996). *Youth at risk: A prevention resource for counselors, teachers, and parents.* (2nd ed.). *(List 12-34)*

Hitchner, K. W. & Tifft-Hitchner, A. (1996). Child abuse and neglect (Chapter 15). In *Counseling today's secondary students.* *(List 12-3)*

Thompson, C. L. & Rudolph, L. B. (1996). *Counseling children.* (4th ed.). *(List 12-3)*

5-42   SEXUAL ABUSE

Sexual abuse is any sexual activity forced upon a person without his or her consent. This includes acquaintance/date rape. Girls are more frequent sexual abuse victims and the offender of girls is more often a male relative or friend of the family. Boys are more likely to be approached by strangers.

➤ Examples of sexual abuse:
- Any act of sexual assault
- Any sexual exploitation of minors
- Words, gestures, or touch
- Fondling
- Exhibitionism
- Sexual exploitation
- Act of power and control, not sexuality
- Not usually a single incident
- Frequently continues until victim reports or leaves home
- Accompanied with threats if revealed

➤ Physical indicators:
- Difficulty walking or sitting
- Torn or stained underclothing
- Pain or itching in genital area
- Bruises or bleeding in genital area
- Venereal disease
- Frequent urinary or yeast infections
- Pregnancy under age 13

➤ Behavioral indicators:
- Withdrawal, chronic depression, or infantile behavior
- Excessive seductiveness

- Role reversal, overly concerned for siblings
- Poor self-esteem, self-devaluation, lack of confidence
- Peer problems, lack of involvement
- Reluctance to change clothes in gym class
- Massive weight change
- Has unexplained money or "gifts"
- Hysteria, lack of emotional control
- Sudden school difficulties, behavior, performance, or attendance
- Inappropriate sexual behavior or premature understanding of sex
- Threatened by physical contact, closeness
- Regression or pseudo-mature behavior
- Restricted social life
- Phobic avoidance of a certain place or a particular person
- Suicide attempts

➤ Possible effects:
- Extreme guilt
- Extreme fear of consequences
- Excessive forgetting, fantasizing, and daydreaming
- Extreme ambivalence
- Multiple personality disorder or disassociative identity disorder
- Low self-esteem
- Depression
- Long-term psychiatric and behavioral problems
- Extreme anger, self-blame, self-doubts
- Long-term denial, repression, withdrawal, apathy
- Somatic symptoms, nightmares, phobias, insomnia
- No trust of adults
- Belief that all people are unpredictable and hostile
- Runaway
- Delinquent
- Eating disorders, binge eating
- Prostitution
- Anxiety disorders
- At risk for early sexual behavior, pregnancy, and sexually transmitted diseases
- Conduct disorders, lying, stealing, vandalism, or assaults on other children
- Sudden dependency

ADDITIONAL INFORMATION

Capuzzi, D. & Gross, D. R. (1996). *Youth at risk: A prevention resource for counselors, teachers, and parents.* (2nd ed.). **(List 12-34)**

Hitchner, K. W. & Tifft-Hitchner, A. (1996). Child abuse and neglect (Chapter 15). In *Counseling today's secondary students.* **(List 12-3)**

Thompson, C. L. & Rudolph, L. B. (1996). *Counseling children.* (4th ed.). **(List 12-3)**

5-43   ACQUAINTANCE/DATE RAPE

Date rape is sexual abuse and a crime of violence with serious consequences.

Inform Students of Behavior That May Lessen Likelihood of Date Rape Prevention

➤ Socialize with people who share your values.

➤ Select people near your own age to date.

➤ Double date or meet in public place with own transportation.

➤ Only go places where you feel safe.

➤ Do not enter anyone's home where there is no parent or other responsible adult.

➤ Set sexual limits.

➤ Do not send mixed messages; be clear.

➤ Make verbal and nonverbal messages consistent.

➤ Be forceful and firm.

➤ Be independent and aware.

➤ Do not do anything you do not want to just to avoid a scene.

➤ Be aware of any situation in which you do not feel in control.

➤ Trust gut-level feelings.

➤ Avoid being pressured.

➤ Be aware that alcohol and other drugs are often related to rape.

Actions When There Is Reason to Be Fearful

➤ Stay calm, think.

➤ Say *no* strongly and do not smile.

➤ Consider if it is safe to resist.

➤ Figure out how to escape.

➤ Act quickly.

➤ Protest loudly, leave, and get help when necessary.

Actions, if Necessary

➤ Flee, get help.

➤ Get medical attention.

➤ Report attack to police.

➤ Consider filing charges.

➤ Get support including counseling.

➤ Do not blame self.

Possible Effects of Date Rape

➤ Trauma
  – Fear of men
  – Fear of being alone
  – Sexual problems
  – Fear of retaliation
  – Afraid to trust
  – Feelings of anger, helplessness, or pain

➤ Depression

ADDITIONAL INFORMATION

Information about acquaintance/date rape: [On-line] Available:

  http://www.-scf.usc.edu/%7Eshore/paper.html

  http://www.cs.utk.edu/%7Ebartley/acquaint/acquaintRape.html#avoid

Atwell, C. (1987). "Friends" raping friends: Could it happen to you? In *Project on the status and education of women. (List 9-18)*

5-44   PHYSICAL NEGLECT

Physical neglect is failure or refusal to provide children with adequate care and supervision that they need to be healthy and safe.

➤ Physical indicators:
  – Abandonment or expelled from home
  – Unattended medical needs
  – Consistent lack of supervision
  – Consistent hunger, inappropriate dress, poor hygiene
  – Lice, distended stomach, emaciated
  – Malnourished, dirty, without proper shelter
  – Not allowed to return home after running away
  – Mentally ill parents
  – Not enrolled in school
  – Chronic truancy excused by parent
  – Substance abuse condoned by parent

➤ Behavioral indicators:
  – Regular fatigue or listlessness, falls asleep in class
  – Steals food, begs from classmates
  – Reports that no caretaker is at home
  – Frequently absent or tardy
  – Self-destructive
  – Exploited, overworked
  – Stays away from home for extended periods of time
  – Acts out aggressively or extremely affectionate
  – Shy, unable to make friends
  – Accident-prone, burns, poisoning, falls

➤ Possible effects:
   – Academic failure, school dropout
   – Runaway
   – Truant

ADDITIONAL INFORMATION

Thompson, C. L. & Rudolph, L. B. (1996). *Counseling children.* (4th ed.). *(List 12-3)*

5-45   GUIDELINES FOR SUPERVISION OF CHILDREN

All children should have emergency telephone numbers and a number to locate a parent or designated responsible adult.

AGE	SUPERVISION
0–6	A child may not be left unsupervised for any length of time.
7–9	A child may not be left alone for extended periods of time, no longer than one and a half hours.
10–11	A child may not be left alone for extended periods of time on a regular basis, no longer than three hours.
12–18	A child may be left alone if there are no emotional or medical problems, and if the child is comfortable with the situation.
12+	Children of this age may baby-sit for children who are at least four years old, for periods of time not to exceed four hours.
14+	Teenagers of this age and up may baby-sit for infants.
16+	Teenagers of this age may be left alone for several days at a time provided a trusted adult is near and can be contacted to intervene immediately. Teenagers should never be allowed to have parties in the home unsupervised by an adult.

5-46   LATCHKEY CHILDREN

Characteristics of Latchkey Children

➤ No difference from nonlatchkey children:
  – Level of anxiety
  – Level of social ability

➤ No more frequency of behavior problems

Procedures to Teach Precautions

➤ Stress the importance of following parent's directions when the parent is not at home.

➤ Discuss precautions for being safe from fire, falling, electricity, stoves, etc.

➤ Role-play to practice directions of parent:
  – Taking responsibility of house key
  – Answering phone and door bell
  – Reacting to emergency or other situation
  – Telling friends they are not to come into the house without supervision
  – Coping with boredom
  – Dealing with other problems

ADDITIONAL INFORMATION

See *Lists 6-16, 7-16,* Safety materials.

Bundy, M. & Boser, J. (1987). Helping latchkey children: A group guidance approach. *School Counselor, 35,* 58–66.

5-47   CHARACTERISTICS OF ABUSIVE CARETAKERS

- ➤ Equally represented among all socio-economic, racial, religious, and ethnic groups
- ➤ Can possess average or above-average intelligence
- ➤ Blame or belittle the child
- ➤ Ignore or reject the child
- ➤ Withhold love from the child
- ➤ Treat siblings unequally, jealousy, or favoritism shown toward child
- ➤ Refuse treatment for the child's problems
- ➤ Seem unconcerned about the child's problems
- ➤ Place unreasonable demands upon the child
- ➤ Give different, unbelievable reasons or no reason for how the child was hurt
- ➤ Talk about the child as being bad, stupid, or different
- ➤ Use harsh physical discipline
- ➤ Extremely protective or jealous of the child
- ➤ Frequent absence of nonabusing caretaker/spouse
- ➤ Socially isolated and few social skills
- ➤ Abusers of alcohol or other drugs
- ➤ Poor emotional adjustment
- ➤ Impulsive
- ➤ Untrusting
- ➤ Lack warmth, humor, and sensitivity
- ➤ Lack ability to care for or protect the child
- ➤ Maintain unrealistic expectations for the child
- ➤ Look to the child to fulfill own emotional needs
- ➤ Unable to nurture the child
- ➤ Maintain a chaotic home
- ➤ Mentally ill or diminished intelligence
- ➤ Consistent failure to keep appointments
- ➤ Rationalize behavior
- ➤ Low frustration tolerance
- ➤ Power–authoritarianism problem
- ➤ Lack coping skills
- ➤ Depressed

ADDITIONAL INFORMATION

Capuzzi, D. & Gross, D. R. (1996). *Youth at risk: A prevention resource for counselors, teachers, and parents.* (2nd ed.). *(List 12-34)*

5-48 PROCEDURES FOR TEACHERS WHEN ABUSE OR NEGLECT IS SUSPECTED

1. Listen to the student carefully.

2. Be certain you understand meaning of student's words and statements.

3. Ask for clarification of words or nonverbal expressions if you do not understand.

4. Do *not* suggest words or statements to the student; use student's own words.

5. Do *not* jump to conclusions.

6. Do *not* ask leading questions.

7. Discuss importance of telling someone about incidents that make student uncomfortable.

8. Reassure student that telling is not wrong and he or she will not be blamed.

9. Inform student that you must by law tell a counselor or administrator.

10. Report any suspicion of abuse or neglect to the counselor or administrator as soon as suspected.

11. Provide name, address, and phone number of the student, parent, or guardian.

12. Provide work phone numbers of parent or guardian.

13. Provide any additional information known about the student and parent.

14. Do not question or interrogate the student.

15. Do not promise the student confidentiality or make other promises.

16. Principal (designee) determines if a report should be made to protective agency and who will report it.

17. Administrator, counselor, or teacher requests agency social worker to meet with the student before school is out that day.

18. Written report is filed within two days.

19. If agency does not respond, refile report.

20. Follow up with counselor or administrator to protect future safety of student.

5-49   PROCEDURES FOR COUNSELOR WHEN ABUSE OR NEGLECT IS SUSPECTED

➤ Be familiar with specifics:
 – Respective state child abuse and neglect law
 – School district procedures for reporting suspected cases
 – Community services for helping families in trouble

➤ Know characteristics of abused and neglected children and their caretakers. *(Lists 5-40 through 5-44, 5-47)*

➤ Know appropriate techniques for working with abused and neglected children and their families.

➤ Establish close working relationships with agencies working with abused and neglected children and their families.

➤ Report incident when child may be in danger: *(List 5-50)*
 – If in doubt, resolve in favor of the child.
 – If not reported, reinjury may occur.

➤ Be an advocate for the child who may have been abused.

➤ Recognize your own feelings but do not be judgmental.

➤ Remain firm:
 – Can understand family's distress
 – Cannot condone or excuse abuse
 – Stress school's legal obligation to report any suspected incident
 – Be respectful and polite
 – Do not argue about the school's involvement
 – Listen attentively and acknowledge that you have heard

➤ Do not hesitate to seek administrative support.

➤ Be aware these people have serious problems for which they need help.

➤ Assure confidentiality within prescribed limits.

➤ Focus on future and caretakers' potential for change.

➤ Do not respond in anger at a perceived attack.

➤ Have information on hand about current programs:
 – Hotlines
 – Mental health centers
 – Parenting programs
 – Parent groups
 – Resources within the school and community

➤ Recognize that all situations will not be resolved pleasantly.

5-50   REPORTING SUSPECTED ABUSE

Procedures for Reporting

1. Inform the principal (designee) immediately when there is reason to suspect abuse or negligence.

2. Principal reviews the case and determines if report with reasonable cause should be made to appropriate referral agency.

3. Principal calls and reports the alleged abuse, or determines who will call and file the report.

4. Confidential written report must be sent within two working days.

5. Report may be sent registered mail.

6. If the appropriate agency does not respond within a reasonable time, the report is to be refiled.

Information in the Report

➤ Name and address of the student, parent, or guardian

➤ Home and work phone number of the parent or caretaker

➤ Student's sex

➤ Nature and extent of the student's injuries, abuse, or neglect

➤ Any evidence of prior injuries, abuse, or neglect

➤ Action, if any, taken to treat, shelter, or assist the student

➤ Name of the person or persons making the report

➤ Other pertinent information

5-51   OVERALL INFORMATION ABOUT CHILD AND ADOLESCENT ABUSE

Child and adolescent abuse occurs in all social, ethnic, economic, and educational levels of society.

Characteristics of Students Who May Be Abused or Neglected

➤ Sad, fearful, depressed, anxious

➤ Aggressively defiant or passively compliant

➤ Isolated or withdrawn, shy, unable to make friends

➤ Appear to have poor impulse control

➤ Frequently ill and absent from school

➤ Feel powerless

➤ Have low self-esteem

➤ Tend to take parental roles

➤ Fear abandonment

➤ Are at risk for substance abuse, sexual acting out, or running away

➤ Equate love with anger or acting out behavior

➤ Talk less than other students

➤ Have lost trust, security, and childhood

➤ Ambivalence and conflict of feelings

➤ Create defenses:
  – Denial
  – Repression
  – Disassociation
  – Eating disorders
  – Fighting
  – Substance abuse
  – Depression
  – Self-abuse
  – Escape from family, society, reality
  – Suicide

ADDITIONAL INFORMATION

Capuzzi, D. & Gross, D. R. (1996). *Youth at risk: A prevention resource for counselors, teachers, and parents.* (2nd ed.). *(List 12-34)*

Hitchner, K. W. & Tifft-Hitchner, A. (1996). Child abuse and neglect (Chapter 15). In *Counseling today's secondary students.* *(List 12-3)*

Thompson, C. L. & Rudolph, L. B. (1996). *Counseling children.* (4th ed.). *(List 12-3)*

5-52   INFORMATION TO YOUNG STUDENTS ABOUT THEIR RIGHT TO SAFETY

The **purpose of providing information to young students** is to give children information and confidence to handle situations to protect their safety.

Safety at School

➤ List all that is done to ensure their safety at school. *(Lists 5-39, 5-51 through 5-58)*

➤ Stress the difference between harmless teasing and harassment.

➤ Stress the need to respect others. *(List 5-16)*

➤ List the procedures to follow when they or others are being harassed:
  – Ignore at first.
  – Tell the person to stop.
  – Walk away from the situation.
  – Report to parent, teacher, counselor, or any school personnel.

Safety Between Home and School

➤ Inform about bus stops, walking pathways, and dangerous intersections.

➤ Recommend young children walk with other children or a trusted adult.

➤ Brainstorm with students the precautions they should take when walking or riding the bus to and from school.

Safety at Home

➤ Provide information to latchkey children. *(List 5-46)*

➤ Talk about child's rights regarding his or her body or touching someone else's body.

➤ Discuss examples of "good" and "bad" touching.

➤ Explain that "bad" touches can come from people we care about.

➤ Teach child how to say "No" to inappropriate touching.

➤ Discuss importance of telling parent, teacher, or counselor about anything that makes the child uncomfortable.

➤ Reassure child that he or she will not be blamed.

➤ Block any revelation or discussion in class by informing the children to speak privately to the teacher or counselor later.

➤ Offer counseling to any students suspected of being victims of harassment or abuse.

➤ Stress that they must follow the directions of their parents when they are playing in the community.

➤ Continue to stress the need for safety throughout the school year.

ADDITIONAL INFORMATION

Capuzzi, D. & Gross, D. R. (1996). *Youth at risk: A prevention resource for counselors, teachers, and parents.* (2nd ed.). *(List 12-34)*

Thompson, C. L. & Rudolph, L. B. (1996). *Counseling children.* (4th ed.). *(List 12-3)*

5-53 INFORMATION ABOUT STUDENT HARASSMENT

Harassment is physical, verbal, social, or emotional teasing, intimidation, or bullying that occurs over a period of time. Harassment is emotional abuse and includes verbal or physical threats, physical assaults, bullying, and theft of property.

Characteristics of Harassed Students

➤ Characteristics:
- Boys who are not good at sports
- Boys who are physically weaker
- Overprotected in the family
- Have a negative view of self; feel they are failures
- Feel stupid, ashamed, or unattractive
- Unsure of self
- Often loners
- More anxious and insecure than other students
- May be overweight
- Are not aggressive toward others; appear that they won't retaliate
- Fearful of reporting for fear of reprisal with consequent revictimization
- Lonely and unpopular
- Feel little personal control
- Unsure of sexual identity or orientation
- Sexual orientation different from mainstream
- Are of a minority culture
- Are of a different social class than majority of the students

➤ Frequent reactions of victims:
- React by crying
- React by showing anger
- React by withdrawing

Characteristics of Students Who Harass Others
- Want attention
- Want power
- Want revenge
- Believe violence is necessary or productive
- May be taught at home that "might makes right"
- May observe poor role models
- See victims in other areas of their lives
- Believe it is acceptable to push people around
- Observe that their aggressive behavior is condoned

Possible Effects of Harassment on the Victims
- Hate school
- Physical symptoms such as stomachaches, headaches, vomiting
- Become class clown

- Fearful of others
- Chronic absenteeism
- Reduced academic performance
- Lowered self-esteem
- Increased apprehension
- Loneliness and abandonment by peers
- Recurrent and distressful dreams
- Persistent avoidance of activities
- Diminished interest in significant activities
- Difficulty in concentrating
- Refuse to come to school
- Depression
- Suicide

ADDITIONAL INFORMATION

Hitchner, K. W. & Tifft-Hitchner, A. (1996). Harassment (Chapter 14). In *Counseling today's secondary students*. *(List 12-3)*

Murphy, C. S. (1997). *Resources dealing with bullying behavior.* Unpublished dissertation, George Mason University at Fairfax, Virginia. *(List 12-4)*

5-54 SCHOOL ENVIRONMENT AND STUDENT HARASSMENT

Locations Where Harassment May Occur in School

➤ Hallways, cafeteria, bathrooms

➤ Recess, break, gym class

➤ Bus stops, walks to school

➤ Classrooms

➤ School parking lots

Curriculum That May Promote Harassment

➤ Neglect prevention and social development activities

➤ Limit ways for students to achieve positive success and recognition

➤ Limit ways of showing value of cultural diversity

➤ Limit ways of providing gender equity

➤ Limit ways for student to provide input

➤ Disregard student input

➤ Limit ways of student expression of individual problems

➤ Disregard student problems

Teacher Behaviors That May Promote Harassment

➤ Disparaging remarks to or about students

➤ Threatening harsh punishments

➤ Taking no action to prevent or stop harassment

➤ Giving up on some students

➤ Maintaining inflexible, unrealistic discipline policies

➤ Teaching to fit only one learning style

➤ Paying attention only to misbehaving students and academically successful students

➤ Failing to notice the quiet, obedient but not outstanding student

➤ Demanding unrealistic expectations

➤ Discriminating against certain students

➤ Acting with cultural bias or prejudice

➤ Ridiculing students in front of others

5-55 TEACHER ACTIONS TO PREVENT AND STOP STUDENT HARASSMENT

Teacher Actions

➤ Survey students about their feelings of safety when coming to and being at school.

➤ Discuss with students the prevalence, places, and times that bullying takes place.

➤ Be present in areas of school where students feel unsafe or fearful.

➤ Know the state law defining criminal acts within the school.

➤ Know the district policy as it relates to gender and racial harassment.

➤ Be aware of own actions that may seem discriminatory or put students down.

➤ Develop, clarify, and implement class rules against bullying.

➤ Do not condone or give the appearance of condoning student harassment.

➤ Respond immediately to report of harassment.

➤ Reprimand quietly but firmly a student who verbally or physically abuses another.

➤ Define and discuss acceptable and unacceptable behaviors and consequences.

➤ Use stories or videos to show appropriate behavior.

➤ Conduct regular class meetings. *(List 2-30)*

➤ Praise and reinforce cooperative and friendly behavior.

➤ Assign responsible and desirable tasks for possible victim to get positive peer attention.

➤ Encourage possible harasser to participate in positive school activities for attention.

➤ Teach those being harassed how to respond to and not provoke further harassment.

➤ Isolate bully and assign time-out from social activities.

➤ Contract with bully to decrease harassing behaviors.

➤ Refer bully to administrator or counselor.

➤ Refer victim of harassment to counselor.

ADDITIONAL INFORMATION

See *List 12-23*, Series of videos: *Many Voices.*

See *List 1-9*, *Prevention of Violence.*

Gibbs J. T., Huang L. N., & Associates. (1989). *Children of color: Psychological interventions with minority youth. (List 12-23)*

Herring, R. D. (1997). *Counseling diverse ethnic youth: Synergetic strategies and interventions for school counselors.* New York, NY: Harcourt Brace College Publisher.

5-56 COUNSELOR ACTIONS TO PREVENT AND STOP HARASSMENT

➤ Recommend school policy statements against general and sexual harassment:
  – Clear written statements
  – Communicated to every student

➤ Be well-informed about legislation regarding abuse, neglect, and harassment.

➤ Collaborate with committee and staff to assess locations and frequency of teasing, bullying, and harassment at school, and to and from school.

➤ Help develop school procedures dealing with investigation and follow through of allegations of harassment.

➤ Teach staff to recognize that ridicule, physical intimidation, and social ostracism are serious offenses.

➤ Conduct staff development, guidance activities, group counseling, and individual counseling to prevent and counteract harassment.

➤ Encourage staff to enforce school rules, and not tolerate bullying or teasing.

➤ Teach entire staff, including custodians, cafeteria workers, and bus drivers, to recognize any incident of an intimidating nature.

➤ Teach entire staff how to intervene appropriately, quickly, directly, effectively, and respectfully: preserving the dignity and confidence of the victims.

➤ Teach entire staff how to respond to harassment:
  – Report incident immediately to administrator.
  – Get help for the victim.
  – Notify parent if serious.
  – Follow up to know what action was taken.
  – Follow up with victim to ensure condition and future safety.

➤ Teach guidance lessons to students:
  – Self-awareness *(List 5-15)*
  – Making healthy and safe choices *(Lists 5-32 through 5-34)*
  – Respecting others *(List 5-16)*
  – Developing relationship skills *(List 5-36)*
  – Resolving conflicts *(List 5-34)*
  – Making effective decisions *(Lists 2-23, 4-16)*
  – Responsible behavior *(List 5-17)*

➤ Train peer mediators to recognize harassment. *(Lists 1-8, 5-53 through 5-58)*

➤ Train peer facilitators to recognize harassment. *(Lists 2-32, 5-53 through 5-58)*

➤ Identify students who are victims or likely victims.

➤ Teach identified students assertiveness and conflict-resolution skills. *(Lists 5-31, 5-54, 5-78)*

➤ Teach identified students anger control. *(List 5-33)*

➤ Counsel harassers. *(List 5-78)*

ADDITIONAL INFORMATION

Roberts, W. B., Jr. & Coursol, D. H. (1996). Strategies for intervention with childhood and adolescent victims of bullying, teasing, and intimidation in school settings. *Elementary School Guidance & Counseling, 30* (2), 204–212.

Rowell, L. L., McBride, M. C. & Nelson-Leaf, J. (1996). The role of the school counselor in confronting peer sexual harassment. *The School Counselor, 43* (3), 196–207.

Strauss, S. & Espeland, P. (1992). *Sexual harassment and teens: A program for positive change. (List 12-28)*

5-57   INFORMATION FOR STUDENTS ABOUT SEXUAL HARASSMENT

Sexual harassment is unwelcome sexual advances, comments, gestures, and/or physical contact. It includes verbal or physical conduct of a sexual nature, and is closely associated with gender bias.

Inform All Students About Sexual Harassment

➤ Make known that examples include verbal comments, gestures, written comments, drawings, or offensive looks.

➤ Confirm that there will be no tolerance for sexual harassment.

➤ Notify that consequences for harassment are serious.

Inform Students of Their Rights

➤ Right to be treated with respect

➤ Right not to be teased about their bodies

➤ Right to say stop the teasing, and have their desires respected

➤ Right to complain and be taken seriously

➤ Right to report and have situation investigated

➤ Right to expect support from school authority

Possible Effects on Victims

➤ Embarrassed, self-conscious, ashamed

➤ Negative about themselves

➤ Loss of joy and freedom of young adolescence

➤ Alone and abandoned

➤ Lowered self-esteem and self-confidence

➤ Lowered career aspirations

➤ Similar to effects of sexual assault and rape

➤ Powerless and victimized

➤ Anger and confusion

➤ Deep emotional pain

➤ Sudden drop in grades and interest in school

➤ Distrustful of adults if victim reports and there is no consequence

➤ Repeatedly called names and targeted for violence

➤ Repeatedly exploited and devalued

➤ Face frightful situation daily

➤ Hate school and are afraid to attend

➤ Truant

➤ Drop out of school

➤ Depressed

➤ Suicidal ideation

ADDITIONAL INFORMATION

Sabella, R. & Myrick, R. (1996). *Confronting sexual harassment: Learning activities for teens.* **(List 12-28)**

Strauss, S. & Espeland, P. (1992). *Sexual harassment and teens: A program for positive change.* **(List 12-28)**

5-58 INFORMATION FOR TEACHERS ABOUT SEXUAL HARASSMENT

➤ Research confirms that sexual harassment is prevalent in most schools.

➤ Girls of all races experience more sexual harassment than boys.

➤ Sexual harassment is closely associated with gender bias.

➤ Students are harassed by both boys and girls.

➤ Sexual harassment takes a greater toll on girls than boys.

➤ Girls who speak out risk being labeled as troublemakers.

➤ Sexual harassment begins in elementary and middle school.

➤ Students who have sexual-identity issues or sexual orientation different from the mainstream may be harassed by other students.

➤ Homoprejudice begins at an early age, elementary and middle school.

➤ Teachers must intervene when any student is discriminated against or harassed.

➤ Sexual harassment must not be ignored, discounted, or tolerated.

➤ A school that condones harassment is not a safe environment for students.

➤ Students can sue for damages resulting from sexual harassment.

ADDITIONAL INFORMATION

See *List 5-57, Information for Students About Sexual Harassment.*

Harris, L. & Associates. (1993). *Hostile hallways: The AAUW survey on sexual harassment in America's schools.* **(List 11-15)**

5-59 GENDER EQUITY

Learning Style Preferences of Many Girls

➤ Cooperative activities

➤ Applied learning, especially in math and science courses

➤ Team teaching

➤ All-girl classes

➤ Access to computers for hands-on activities

➤ Fewer competitive activities

Teaching Strategies for Equity

➤ Examine own attitudes and behaviors toward ability of women.

➤ Be aware of traditional gender-biased practices.

➤ Model nonbiased behavior and nonbiased language.

➤ Model equitable power through arrangements and agreements.

➤ Use inclusive, parallel, or gender-sensitive language:

  – Use female pronoun before male pronoun half the time (she/he).
  – Avoid use of popular term "guys" for both female and male students.

➤ Teach students to recognize and eliminate biases and inequalities they observe in school.

➤ Encourage girls to take advanced mathematics and science courses.

➤ Use a variety of instructional strategies:
  – Cooperative as well as competitive activities
  – Small-group activities as well as lectures
  – Hands-on work as well as verbal
  – Opportunities for safe risk taking
  – Opportunities to integrate knowledge and skills

➤ Design lessons to explore many perspectives:
  – Use different sources of information.
  – Refer to female as well as male experts.

➤ Do not assume that all students have your cultural values:
  – May represent many races, religions, cultural backgrounds
  – May be from a different social status
  – May not be heterosexual

➤ Help and question male and female students equally:
  – Same frequency
  – Same specificity
  – Same depth
  – Same time to answer questions

➤ Make material relevant to interests and life experiences:
  – Consider both boys and girls.
  – Stress social aspects of the material.
  – Stress usefulness of activities, skills, and knowledge.
  – Refer to career opportunities in the field.

➤ Provide opportunity for female leadership.

➤ Encourage and reward integrative thinking as well as analysis:
  – Context as well as facts
  – Social, moral, and environmental impacts of decisions or events

ADDITIONAL INFORMATION

AAUW (1992). *The AAUW report: How schools shortchange girls.* **(List 11-8)**

Hansen, S., Walker, J., et al. (1995). *Growing smart: What's working for girls in school.* **(List 11-8)**

Ministry of Education of British Columbia (1995). *Gender equity.*
    http://www.est.gov.bc.ca/curriculum/irps/visart810/apcgen.htm

Orenstein, P. (1994). *SchoolGirls: Young women, self-esteem, and the confidence gap.* **(List 8-19)**

5-60 EATING DISORDERS

Risk Factors

➤ Adolescents between ages 14 and 18

➤ Girls more at risk than boys:
  - Have traditional gender expectations
  - Have low self-esteem
  - Are perfectionists

➤ Boys at risk:
  - Active in particular sports activities
  - Have had history of obesity
  - Have sex orientation different from the mainstream

➤ Students from different socio-economic classes at risk:
  - Middle- to upper-middle class more at risk for anorexia and bulimia
  - Lower socio-economic class more at risk for obesity

➤ Family problems frequently associated with students at-risk:
  - Chaotic and conflicted families, student may exhibit bulimic behavior.
  - Rigid and over-controlling families, student may exhibit anorexic behavior.

➤ Some athletes especially at risk:
  - Cheerleaders
  - Drill team members
  - Wrestlers—boys
  - Track team members—girls and boys
  - Gymnasts—girls and boys
  - Performing artists—girls and boys

Prevention

➤ Assist girls in maintaining self-esteem through adolescence.

➤ Place little emphasis on dieting and weight control.

➤ Place little emphasis on food as comfort or reward.

➤ Encourage physical education teachers to be alert to exaggerated physical fitness or strength.

➤ Keep family communication open:
  - Accept normal developmental desire for increased autonomy.
  - Expect growing independence and responsibility.
  - Give preadolescent freedom to grow.
  - Model tolerance for mistakes by self and child.
  - Model tolerance for imperfections in appearances.
  - Discuss expression of anger, deep feelings.
  - Admit family problems such as depression or alcoholism.

Counselor's Actions

➢ Know risk factors for eating disorders.

➢ Inform teachers of risk factors.

➢ Recognize symptoms.

➢ Provide educational and prevention programs:

– Stress need for good nutrition and moderation.

– Stress dangers of extreme dieting.

➢ Provide caring intervention:

– Individual counseling

– Group counseling

➢ Refer student and parents:

– Physician for assessment

– Specialist in eating disorders

– Family counseling

ADDITIONAL INFORMATION

Hitchner, K. W. & Tifft-Hitchner, A. (1996). Anorexia nervosa and bulimia (Chapter 18). In *Counseling today's secondary students. (List 12-3)*

Wright, K. S. (1996). The secret and all-consuming obsessions: Anorexia and bulimia. In D. Capuzzi, & D. R. Gross, (Eds.). *Youth at risk. (List 12-34)*

5-61 IRRESPONSIBLE SEXUAL RELATIONS

Dangers or Vulnerability of Students

➢ HIV/AIDS

➢ Sexually transmitted diseases

➢ Infection of others

➢ Unwanted pregnancies

➢ Teenage parenthood

➢ Babies born and reared by young adolescents

➢ Continued cycle of poor parenting

➢ Continued cycle of poverty

Characteristics of Adolescents Most At Risk

➢ Victims of neglect, rejection, or abuse

➢ Students who lack support and encouragement from parents

➢ Substance abusers

➢ Dropouts from school

➢ Students who are disabled

➤ Students who live in poverty

➤ Students with no career or educational aspirations

➤ Students who seek immediate gratification

➤ Students who feel powerless over their own lives

Successful Prevention Programs

➤ Start early, provide a sequential K–12 program.

➤ Incorporate multiple systems in planning and teaching:
  – Family
  – Community
  – School

➤ Include life skills for students:
  – Respect
  – Responsibility
  – Assertiveness
  – Decision making

ADDITIONAL INFORMATION

See *List 5-66, Preventing HIV/AIDS.*

Sherwood-Hawes, A. & Thompson, R. A. (1996). Adolescent pregnancy and childbearing: A focus on prevention. In D. Capuzzi, & D. R. Gross (Eds.). *Youth at risk (List 12-34)*

5-62   INFORMATION ABOUT GANGS

Gangs are groups of people who form an allegiance for a common purpose and engage in unlawful or criminal activity.

Reasons for Gang Involvement

➤ Identity, acceptance

➤ Excitement, recognition

➤ Freedom, loss of adult constraints

➤ Power, control

➤ Protection, security

➤ Sense of family, belonging, companionship

➤ Economics, material possessions

➤ Ethnic identity

Problems With Gang Involvement

➤ Endanger lives of members

➤ Endanger lives of family members

➤ Endanger lives of innocent bystanders

➤ Serious criminal and violent acts

➤ Provoke interracial tension

➤ Constant recruitment to expand members and territory

Gang Identification or Alliance

➤ Gang clothing and/or colors

➤ Gang graffiti

➤ Gang hand signals

➤ Gang tattoos, especially around neck

➤ Haircuts with symbols or asymmetrical

➤ Photographs showing gang insignia

➤ Peculiar vocabulary with code words

➤ Disclosure of gang membership by self or others

Characteristics of Gangs

➤ Predominantly male

➤ Distinctive dress and colors

➤ Loyalty to neighborhood and territory

➤ Drugs and weapon trafficking

➤ Frequently developed along racial and ethnic lines

- Extreme loyalty
- Specifics of different gangs vary and change

Characteristics of Schools With Gangs

- Increased school violence
- Increased student fear of violence and victimization
- Availability of drugs on campus
- Suspended students show up at school
- School dropouts show up at school

Characteristics of Gang Members

- Decline of grades
- Substance abuse
- Truancy
- Change of friends
- Late hours
- Sleep during day
- Money and expensive items with no explanation
- Defiance toward authority figures at home and at school
- Any race, ethnicity, social group, religion, socio-economic group
- Recruitment of children as young as 7 or 8
- Predominantly ages 12–18
- Announce and instigate fights
- Paint cans and paint on tips of fingers
- Permanent-marker stains on hands
- Graffiti displays on binders, back packs, clothing
- Deceit about activities
- Associates or friends with characteristics of gang members

ADDITIONAL INFORMATION

Boulder County Sheriff's Department. (1996). *Gangs? Not my kid! A tip sheet for parents.* Chicago, IL: National PTA. [On-line] Available: http://www.boco.co.gov/sheriff/gangs.htm

City of San Jose, CA Parks Recreation & Neighborhood Services. (1997). Profile of a tagger. In *The Walls of San Jose Newsletter,* Issue 9, Winter 1997. [On-line] Available: http://www.ccnet.com/~dougs/gangs.html

Gang Graffiti. [On-line] Available: http://www.courses.edu/graffiti.html

Gang Hand Signals. [On-line] Available: http://www.xmission.com/~gastown/Up-011/gang-signs.html

Goldstein, A. P. & Huff, C. R. (Eds.). (1992). *Gang intervention handbook. (List 12-4)*

5-63 PREVENTING GANG INVOLVEMENT

School's Actions

➤ Collaborate with community and religious organizations to offer alternatives for young people:
  – Develop strategies to offer viable alternatives to gang membership.
  – Address students' feelings of powerlessness.

➤ Educate entire school staff, including support staff, about how gangs develop and how to respond.

➤ Offer educational programs for students about gangs and how to avoid being drawn into membership.

➤ Offer programs for parents about gangs and how to deal with them as parents:
  – Reflect diversity of community.
  – Provide in a variety of languages.
  – Provide a special speaker on gang involvement.
  – Inform of characteristics of gang members, graffiti, and hand signals.

➤ Monitor nonstudents who "hang out" on or near the school.

➤ Read, report, and remove graffiti immediately.

➤ Establish conflict-resolution skills throughout curriculum and school.

➤ Establish school climate in which students feel valued.

➤ Consider stricter dress codes.

Counselor's Actions

➤ Identify students vulnerable to gang involvement.

➤ Provide special assistance to identified students:
  – Peer facilitators
  – Mentoring/tutoring
  – Conflict-resolution programs
  – Assertiveness management
  – Group counseling
  – Special program with police specialist

➤ Discuss consequences of being in a gang.

➤ Encourage participation in school activities.

➤ Encourage teachers to show interest in individual students at risk.

➤ Show interest in student at risk and her or his academic progress.

ADDITIONAL INFORMATION

Burnett, G. (1994). *Gangs in schools.* ERIC Digest No. 99, EDO-UD-94-5, ISSN 0889 8049. July 1994. [On-line] Available: http://eric-web.tc.columbia.edu/digests/dig99.html

Gaustad, J. (1991). *Schools respond to gangs and violence.* (ERIC Abstract) Eugene, OR: Oregon School Study Council.

Goldstein, A. P. & Huff, C. R. (Eds.). (1992). *Gang intervention handbook. (List 12-4)*

Trump, K. S. (1993). *Youth gangs and schools: The need for intervention and prevention strategies.* Cleveland, OH: Urban Child Research Center.

5-64   INFORMATION ABOUT COMMONLY ABUSED DRUGS

Commonly Abused Drugs

➤ Alcohol (most frequently abused drug):
  – Depressant
  – Available in many homes
  – Major drug used by students ages 13–18
  – Media presents as no problem
  – Addictive
  – Driving under influence causes injuries and fatalities
  – Relationship to homicides and suicide attempts
  – Fetal alcohol syndrome may result in growth and mental retardation of babies

➤ Nicotine:
  – Stimulant
  – Chewed, sniffed, smoked
  – Addiction resistant to intervention
  – Cognitive-behavioral programs appear most successful interventions
  – High incidence of serious health problems

➤ Marijuana:
  – Mind- or mood-altering substance
  – Referred to as "pot," "dope," "grass," "joint," "hash"
  – Addictive
  – Differing amounts are uncontrolled
  – Decreased performance

➤ Cocaine:
  – Central nervous system stimulant
  – Smoked, snorted, injected, inhaled
  – "Freebase," "crack"
  – Easily hidden
  – Addictive
  – Infection with needle use (AIDS, meningitis)
  – Potential for overdose
  – Very low cure rate
  – Cocaine babies addicted to cocaine

➤ Inhalants:
  – Commonly used items containing volatile solvents:
    1) Airplane glue
    2) Paint thinner
    3) Gasoline
    4) Dry cleaning solution
  – Commonly used items containing aerosols:
    1) Hairspray
    2) Whipped cream

3) Oil-based cooking sprays
- Used by younger adolescents
- Can cause permanent damage to central nervous system and organs
- Can cause sudden fatalities
- Psychologically addictive

➤ Hallucinogens such as LSD and PCP and designer drugs such as MPPP, AMF, or "China White":
- Taken orally
- Create distortions and hallucinations
- Inconsistent in effects
- May cause extreme mood disorders
- Highly addictive psychologically
- Many serious side effects

➤ Steroids:
- Taken orally or injected
- Prevalent in some sports
- Multitude of side effects
- May cause extreme aggressive behavior and depression
- Cessation of drug use leads to regression of secondary sex characteristics

➤ Heroin:
- Smoked or injected
- Very addictive
- Extremely difficult to treat
- High incidence of overdose
- Myriad of health problems
- Shared needles can result in AIDS
- Premature, stillborn, or addicted infants

Vulnerability and Predictions of Substance Abuse

➤ Ages 9–12:
- Begin by using tobacco and beer at age 11 or younger
- Older siblings encourage use
- Peer groups encourage use
- Fear is major deterrent at this age

➤ Ages 13-17:
- Marijuana and cocaine use established by age 13
- Age of first use of alcohol or other drug predicts current frequency and likelihood of addiction
- Friends who use alcohol or other drugs
- Party-use of alcohol or other drugs

ADDITIONAL INFORMATION

Gloria, A. M., Trainer, C. M., Beasley, J. F. & Robinson-Kurpius, S. E. (1996). In D. Capuzzi, & D. R. Gross. (Eds.). *Youth at risk: A prevention resource for counselors, teachers, and parents.* (2nd ed.). *(List 12-34)*

5-65 PREVENTING SUBSTANCE ABUSE

Substance abuse is the continued use of any substance despite adverse consequences to health, family, or parenting relationships, or to legal, financial, social, educational, or vocational dimensions of one's life. (Goldstein, Reagles, et al. [1990]).

Characteristics of Students Who Use Alcohol and Other Substances

➤ Nonparticipant in school activities

➤ Sometimes defiant

➤ Easily influenced by peers

➤ Skip school (six times the truancy rate of nonusers)

➤ Rebellious

➤ May cause trouble in school

➤ Poor grades

➤ Abrupt changes:
  – Mood
  – Attitude
  – Grades
  – Peer group
  – Extracurricular activities
  – Interactions with teachers and parents

➤ Exceptionally strong desires:
  – Independence from adults
  – Popularity and peer approval
  – Inclusion in social life
  – Excitement and experiments

➤ Feeling of immortality and invulnerability

Successful Substance Abuse Prevention Programs

➤ Conducted for students in elementary and middle school

➤ School-based peer-pressure refusal skills training programs

➤ Skills to resist peer pressure to use drugs while maintaining friendships

➤ Correct students' misperceptions that "everybody's doing drugs" when that is not the case

➤ Specific refusal-skills training by peer leaders same age or older:
  – Good role models respected by at risk students
  – Include minority student leaders
  – Good communication skills

➤ Training by counselors and peer leaders

➤ Training by teachers and peer leaders

➤ Training by trained parents and peer leaders

➤ Student-assistance programs

➤ Group and family counseling

Effective Prevention Strategies

➤ Emphasis on *how* to resist direct acquisition:
  – Teach to overlearn specific assertiveness skills.
  – Provide opportunity to practice specific skills to resist peer pressure.

➤ Provide alternative social activities:
  – Build social competence to have self-confidence.
  – Help broaden social experience.

➤ Provide accurate information about the percentage of students in the school who *are not* using drugs.

➤ Increase awareness of the actual number of students who *are not* resorting to drug use.

➤ Provide specific peer-pressure refusal training: *(List 5-32)*
  – Discuss methods to resist peer pressure.
  – Teach how to recognize, handle, and avoid situations.
  – Help to deal effectively with anxiety. *(List 5-15)*
  – Teach specific responses to being called "Chicken."
  – Teach content of refusal message.
  – Teach how to deliver refusal message.
  – Role play or show video of refusal message.
  – Provide opportunities to practice specific skills.
  – Encourage peer coaching and peer feedback by same-age or older peer leaders.

➤ Train to use cognitive-behavioral skills: *(List 5-21)*
  – Personal and social skills for self-confidence *(Lists 5-21 through 5-24, 5-37)*
  – Communication skills *(Lists 5-22 through 5-32)*
  – Decision-making skills *(List 4-16)*
  – Problem-solving skills *(List 2-23)*
  – Goal-setting skills *(List 3-2)*
  – Coping skills *(List 5-35)*
  – Assertiveness skills *(List 5-31)*

➤ Teach skills until overlearned to use comfortably in environment.

➤ Teach to use in a variety of realistic situations.

➤ Teach to generalize skills and use in many situations.

Effective Intervention Strategies

➤ Required attendance at substance abuse educational classes

➤ Required community service at drug treatment centers

➤ Individual and group counseling

➤ Program of reinforcement with demonstrated responsible behavior:
  – Detection and enforcement difficult
  – Assigned tasks with accomplishment resulting in desired privileges

➤ Alternative schools for changing behavior patterns

Effective Prevention and Intervention Strategies

➤ Cognitive and affective strategies:
- Accurate information about reasons of use and reasons to stop using
- Accurate information about health
- Honest concern for health and safety of adolescent

Ineffective Prevention or Intervention Strategies

➤ Scare tactics

➤ Punishment

➤ Suspension

➤ Generic approach:
- Too little emphasis on direct acquisition
- Too little emphasis on skills to resist peer pressure

➤ Inconsistent detection and enforcement

➤ Information only (Cognitive)

➤ Emotion only (Affective)

➤ Simplistic approach "Just Say No"

Additional Information

Dusenbury, L. (1994). *Recent findings in drug abuse prevention: A review from 1989 to 1994.* [On-line] Available: ...nform.umd.edu:8080/EdRes/Colleges/BSOS/Depts/Cesar/drugs/KSPREV

Gibbs, J. C., et al. (1995). *Equip program: Teaching youth to think and act responsibly through a peer-helping approach. (List 12-25)*

Goldstein, A. P., Reagles, K. W. & Amann, L. L. (1990). *Refusal skills: Preventing drug use in adolescents. (List 12-38)*

Schinke, S. P., Botvin, G. J. & Orlandi, M. A. (1991). *Substance abuse in children and adolescents: Evaluation and intervention. (List 12-38)*

U. S. Department of Education. *Drug prevention curricula: A guide to selection and implementation.* Provides general guidelines and kinds of questions to ask when selecting a curriculum. Available upon request.

5-66 PREVENTING HIV/AIDS

Community and Schoolwide Effort

➤ Collaborate with administrators, parents, teachers, and community members about ways to provide information about health issues to parents, teachers, and students:
  - Provide accurate and honest information.
  - Focus on health and safety.

➤ Solicit parental input at all stages of the program, including planning and providing information to students.

➤ Brainstorm ways to inform students about the cause, acquisition, treatment, and prevention of AIDS:
  - Invite a local physician or other expert to inform parents, teachers, and students about health and risk.
  - Invite expert to dialogue with young people providing honest answers to their questions.
  - Request expert to provide access to students to answer individual questions privately.
  - Provide hotline numbers to students who have questions.
  - Provide access to further resources when requested by students and parents.

➤ Encourage school district to develop a clear written policy and specific procedures dealing with students who have AIDS:
  - School attendance
  - Confidentiality of cases
  - Safety for all students
  - Mandatory testing
  - Other guidelines

➤ Brainstorm ways to inform students, parents, and teachers about casual contact with a student who has AIDS:
  - Safe and unsafe contact with the student
  - Harm in ostracizing such a student

Resources for Information

National School Board Association
HIV/AIDS Education Project
1680 Duke Street
Alexandria, VA 22314
(703) 838-6722

Helps school board members, superintendents, and other school officials deal effectively with issues of HIV and AIDS in schools.

CDC National AIDS Clearinghouse
P.O. Box 6003
Rockville, MD 20849-6003
(800) 458-5231

National references, referral, and publication distribution service for AIDS and HIV information. Helps locate publications about HIV infection and AIDS for school personnel.

CDC National AIDS Hotline
P.O. Box 13827
Research Triangle Park, NC 27709
(800) 342-AIDS

Provides current and accurate information about HIV infection and AIDS to general public. Access available at any time, day or night.

ADDITIONAL INFORMATION

See *List 5-61, Irresponsible Sexual Relations.*

Gray, L. A. & House, R. M. (1996). Adolescents and AIDS: Education, compassion, and reason (Chapter 10). In D. Capuzzi, & D. R. Gross, (Eds.). *Youth at risk. (List 12-34)*

HIV/AIDS Ministries Network Focus Paper #16. [On-line] Available: http://198.139.157.2/programs/hiv/focus/focus016.html

Thompson, C. L. & Rudolph, L. B. (1996). Counseling children with special concerns. In *Counseling children. (List 12-3)*

5-67 PREVENTING AND RECOGNIZING CHILDHOOD AND ADOLESCENT DEPRESSION

Characteristics (usually a combination)

➤ Experienced a recent major loss *(List 5-70)*

➤ Feeling unloved and lonely

➤ Feeling helpless, inadequate, and inferior

➤ Feeling frustrated

➤ Feeling that he or she failed to meet internalized expectations of others

➤ Resentful of dependency

➤ Anger of others turned inward

➤ Lethargy

➤ Slow physical response

➤ Decreased attention span

➤ May have ADD (Attention Deficit Disorder)

➤ Frequent crying

➤ Unkempt appearance

➤ Disinterest in school or activities

➤ Suicidal thoughts *(List 5-68)*

➤ Social withdrawal, isolated

➤ Self-blame

➤ Little or no concern for others

➤ Irritable mood

➤ Disruptive behavior

➤ Self-destructive behavior

➤ Anxiety disorder

➤ Alcohol or other drug use

➤ Eating disorder:
  – Overeating, or
  – Loss of appetite
➤ Oversleeping or inability to sleep

Masks of Depression

➤ Consistent restlessness
➤ Involvement in high-risk behaviors
➤ Sexual promiscuity
➤ Adoption of "I don't care" attitude
➤ Consistent inappropriate joking

Problems of Detection

➤ Parental denial
➤ Insufficient knowledge of symptoms by parents and teachers

Counselor's Actions

➤ Teach staff the characteristics and frequent causes.
➤ Provide parent workshops. *(Lists 2-33 through 2-36)*
➤ Develop a positive relationship with student.
➤ Explore the student's complaints, relationships, and expectations.
➤ Suggest possibility of depression when suspected.
➤ Notify parents when reason to suspect depression:
  – Recommend referral to outside specialist.
  – Provide list of three referral sources.
  – Help parents deal with their own feelings.
  – Ask parents to sign a release form for communication with referral source.
➤ Consider cognitive-behavioral counseling. *(List 2-11)*
➤ Be alert to student's anger toward self and others.
➤ Be prepared for anger to be directed at counselor because it is safe.
➤ Use any hope or positive feelings of the student, particularly for the future.
➤ Help student gain self-esteem.
➤ Teach coping skills to deal with future problems. *(List 5-35)*
➤ Teach relationship and social skills to make friends. *(Lists 5-36, 5-37)*

ADDITIONAL INFORMATION

Hitchner, K. W. & Tifft-Hitchner, A. (1996). Depression and suicide (Chapter 16). In *Counseling today's secondary students*. *(List 12-3)*

5-68 INFORMATION ABOUT SUICIDE

Prevention is a schoolwide program to reduce the probability of a student choosing suicide instead of learning to cope with a problem.

Intervention is an effective counseling and referral system to help students at risk.

Postvention is a plan of action to reduce the possibility of a suicide cluster after a suicide has occurred.

Personal Risk Factors for Suicide (usually a combination of several factors)

➤ A sense of isolation and not belonging in a school

➤ A sense of having a restricted future because of doing poorly in school

➤ A sense of hopelessness and/or helplessness

➤ Desire to live but incapable of seeing alternatives for their problems

➤ Intense need to achieve

➤ Low self-esteem

➤ A tendency to be alone

➤ High stress

➤ Poor communication skills

➤ Chemical dependency

➤ A sense of guilt

➤ Experienced a recent major disaster from the view of the student

➤ Intense desire for attention

➤ Confusion over sex identity

➤ Learning disabled and/or emotionally disturbed

Environmental Risk Factors for Suicide

➤ Alienation and rejection from peer group

➤ Social climate with strong cliques and factions

➤ Recent transitions in life, or imposed by the system

➤ Know someone who recently committed suicide

➤ Recent loss of a parent through death or separation

➤ Recent loss of a friend

➤ Alienation from family

➤ Low level of family support

➤ Parental suicidal attempt

➤ Family violence or abuse

➤ High incidence among Native American students

➤ Lack of specialized programs to help students in the school

➤ Undue attention given to previous suicide threats or attempts

Suicide-Prevention Program

➤ Training for staff and parents:
  - Awareness of risk
  - Importance of communication with adults
  - Identification and referral of high risk youth
  - Provision for positive emotional development of students
  - Ways to communicate with student at risk:
    1) Direct questions do not increase suicidal risk
    2) Lecturing or minimizing the student's problem is not helpful
  - Provision of suicide-prevention program *(List 5-69)*
  - Readiness of a crisis plan, crisis team, and crisis intervention *(List 1-6)*
  - Intense help for suicidal student is imperative:
    1) Not out of danger immediately (frequently suicide three months after first attempt)
    2) Questions and answers

➤ Guidance program for all students at all levels *(List 1-2)*

➤ Continual evaluation of troubled youth

➤ Counseling suicidal students *(Lists 5-67, 5-83)*

➤ Follow-up of referrals and contacts

➤ Evaluation of program

ADDITIONAL INFORMATION

Dempsey, R. A. *The trauma of adolescent suicide.* *(List 12-28)*

Petersen, S. & Straub, R. (1992). *School crisis survival guide.* *(List 12-6)*

5-69 SUICIDE-PREVENTION PROGRAM FOR STUDENTS AND PARENTS

Introduction—Purpose for This Lesson

➤ Help students to help each other.

➤ Discuss reaction of the subject with class.

➤ Explain reason for guidance lesson topic:

  – Students are the first to know and recognize trouble.

  – Students who seek help for friends are the real friends.

  – Suicidal student does not really want to commit the act, but sees no alternative at particular time when problem seems overwhelming.

Content of Lesson About Suicide Prevention

➤ Describe students who are most at risk:

  – Recent problem that seems insurmountable

  – Depressed about a recent severe loss

  – Desire to "get even" with someone they feel has "done them wrong"

  – Depressed about some particular area in life

  – Desperate to get someone to help them or get help for them

  – Previous suicide attempt

  – Preoccupation with death and dying

➤ Teach warning signs of depression and suicide (usually a combination of actions):

  – Giving away prized possessions

  – Telling friends they probably won't see them in the future

  – Hinting that they are going away without any plans

  – Desire to see others suffer

  – Desire to be important to others and cause them to be remorseful

  – Steep decline in grades and achievement

  – Discussing death as peaceful and desirable

  – Depressive writing or artwork

  – Trouble eating or sleeping

  – Withdrawing from friends and activities

  – Losing interest in hobbies, school, and work

  – Making a will or final arrangements

  – Taking unnecessary risks

  – Losing interest in personal appearance

  – Increasing use of alcohol or other drugs

  – Desire to escape punishment

  – Rapid change of mood, interests, involvements, and lifestyle

  – Major disappointment seen as a catastrophe

➤ Suggested actions:

  – Listen.

  – Always consider seriously a student's threat to take his or her life.

  – Notify parent, counselor, teacher, or administrator immediately.

- Get adult help for the student who has mentioned suicide.
- Build trust, but don't lie or make false assurances.
- Never assure the suicidal student that you won't tell anyone.
- Avoid philosophical discussions about the "right to die."
- Point out value of trying to resolve situation.
- Point out that suicide is irreversible, no chance to change mind.
- Point out that others left will resent student's act to make them miserable.
- Never challenge the student to commit suicide.
- Get a commitment to not take any action until the student gets help from a responsible adult.
- Offer to go with the student to talk with an adult the student trusts.

➤ Coping skills: *(List 5-35)*
- Identification of feelings of depression
- Problem-solving skills *(List 2-23)*
- Decision-making strategies *(List 4-16)*
- Stress management *(List 5-38)*

➤ Resources:
- Hotline numbers: National Adolescent Suicide Hotline, (800) 621-4000
- Community agencies and churches

ADDITIONAL INFORMATION

See *List 5-68, Information About Suicide.*

Capuzzi, D. & Gross, D. R. (1996). "I don't want to live": The adolescent at risk for suicidal behavior (Chapter 11). In *Youth at risk.* Guidelines for middle and high school settings. *(List 12-34)*

PERSONAL/SOCIAL GUIDANCE: DEALING WITH A CRISIS

5-70 DEALING WITH GRIEF

Stages of Grief

1. Denial/Shock
   - Feeling of numbness
   - Belief or feeling that deceased will return
   - Insomnia/sleeplessness
   - Loss of appetite
   - Inconsistent behavior
   - Bargaining with God
   - Persistent dreams or nightmares
   - Inability to concentrate
   - Preoccupation without being able to identify source
   - Confusion

2. Fear
   - Nightmares
   - Sleeplessness
   - Easily startled
   - Anxiety and restlessness
   - Verbal expressions of false bravado
   - Phobias

3. Anger
   - Irritability
   - Provocative in fights
   - Sarcastic remarks
   - Anti-social behavior
   - Vandalism
   - Refusal to comply with rules

4. Guilt
   - Often masked by anger
   - Self-destructive behavior
   - Apologetic attitude
   - Acting out in response to praise or compliments

5. Depression/Sadness *(List 5-67)*

6. Acceptance
   - Accepts reality
   - Resumes normal self-care
   - Resumes normal activities
   - Temporary recurrence of anger and sadness

Help Student Recover From Grief

➤ Be proactive in providing help.

➤ Encourage student to get support from family and friends.

➤ Encourage self-care:
  – Get exercise.
  – Get rest.
  – Drink fluids.

➤ Listen without judging.

➤ Encourage talking about loss.

➤ Invite sharing of memories.

➤ Encourage resumption of normal activities.

➤ See Counselor's Actions in. *List 5-86*

5-71 DEBRIEFING AFTER TRAGEDY OR NATURAL DISASTER

Tragedies or natural disasters are situations that cause human suffering or create human needs that the victims cannot alleviate without assistance.

Debriefing Procedure

A counselor should be at the door to ensure that anyone who leaves debriefing early is all right.

1. *Facts:* Request names and how they were affected by the tragedy.
2. *Thoughts:* Ask about their thoughts now about the tragedy.
3. *Reactions:* Ask them to share the worst thing about the tragedy to them.
4. *Symptoms:* Review symptoms of stress such as irritability, insomnia, and nightmares.
5. *Re-entry:* Elicit statements of anything positive as a result of the tragedy:
  – Provide a list of general stress reactions that are typical.
  – Provide a list of resources for help later if needed.

Natural Disasters

➤ Hurricane

➤ Tornado

➤ Storm

➤ Flood

➤ High water

➤ Wind-driven water

➤ Tidal wave

➤ Earthquake

➤ Volcanic eruption

- Drought
- Blizzard
- Pestilence
- Famine
- Fire

Personal Tragedies

- Explosion
- Building collapse
- Transportation accident
- Murder
- Rape
- Suicide
- Other situation that causes human suffering

Counselor's Goals

- Resolution of the crisis
- Change the perception of danger
- Restoration of social functioning to precrisis level

Counselor's Actions

- Intervene with little or no information available.
- Ascertain the meaning of the catastrophic event to the student(s).
- Provide names and phone numbers of resources that are available after school hours.
- Determine which students are at risk of pathological reaction to the incident.
- Provide debriefing to all students and their parents, teachers, and school staff affected.

ADDITIONAL INFORMATION

See **List 1-6,** *The Crisis Plan, Crisis Team, and Crisis Intervention.*

5-72   PROCEDURES AFTER A SUICIDE

Use the crisis plan and crisis team. *(List 1-6)*

➤ Inform staff and students of the fact and the family's wishes.

➤ Hold meetings with teachers:
  – Prepare them to talk with their students.
  – Offer to speak with students in classes of the deceased.
  – Help teachers deal with own issues.

➤ Invite friends of deceased to meet at specific location and time:
  – Have crisis team and several counselors available.
  – Could use community mental health center.

➤ Conduct meeting with friends of the deceased:
  – Give friends the facts about what is known.
  – Inform friends of the family's wishes.
  – Help friends plan an appropriate memorial:
    1) Donation of blood to Red Cross
    2) Poems, art, or other expressions of grief
    3) Scholarship
    4) Dedication of yearbook
    5) Not a show of veneration
  – Do *not* glorify the deceased.
  – Point out the needless pain that the deceased's actions caused.
  – Debrief with group. *(List 5-71)*
  – Give the message that life is precious and precarious.

➤ Debrief with involved students and staff. *(List 5-71)*

➤ Identify students most at risk:
  – Meet in a small group.
  – Counsel with these students.
  – Note students in need of additional help.
  – Notify parents of students who need referral services.

➤ Debrief with counselors at end of day and plan next day according to identified needs.

➤ Plan parent meeting within next few days:
  – Give facts about situation and family's wishes.
  – Give facts about actions taken at school.
  – Explain debriefing process.
  – Open to questions and answers.

➤ Plan staff meeting within next few days:
  – Reinforce guidelines about discussions with students.
  – Help them identify students who need help dealing with crisis.
  – Review guidelines for referrals to guidance.
  – Dispel inaccurate information or rumors.
  – Stress need for teachers to be calm, serious, and undramatic.

➤ Plan a way for counselors to relax and discuss something pleasant.

PERSONAL/SOCIAL COUNSELING K–12

5-73 COUNSELING STUDENTS WITH DISABILITIES

Focus of Counseling Students With Disabilities

➤ Focus on self-esteem and self-concept: *(List 5-19)*
- Provide emotional support.
- Accept desire to be understood as other students of the same age.

➤ Assist in dealing with special needs:
- Adjustment to disability
- Societal expectations and self-awareness
- Relationship building
- Dealing with opinions and reactions of others

➤ Assist with adolescent issues:
- Desire for psychological independence although physically dependent
- Sexuality
- Future education and career

➤ Assist with educational and/or career placement.

Methods When Counseling a Student With a Disability

➤ Direct counseling

➤ Structured approach:
- Routine
- Regularity
- Repetition

➤ Concrete, activity-oriented counseling:
- Role plays
- Art counseling
- Play counseling

➤ Structured group counseling:
- Interact and gain acceptance from peers
- Practice relationship skills

➤ Bibliocounseling:
- Suggest appropriate book.
- Discuss the book and feelings inspired by the book.

➤ Opportunity to succeed:
- Tutor younger children
- Library or media assistant

ADDITIONAL INFORMATION

See *List 3-16, Counseling Students With Learning or Physical Problems.*

See *List 5-20, Promoting Success of Students With Disabilities.*

See *List 13-14, The School Counselor and the Education of the Handicapped Act.*

See *Lists 6-6, 7-6, 10-8, 11-6, 12-10* for materials for disability awareness.

Lombana, J. H. (1992). *Guidance for students with disabilities.* (2nd ed.). *(List 12-10)*

5-74 CROSS-CULTURAL COUNSELING COMPETENCIES

Counselor Awareness of Own Assumptions, Values, and Biases

➤ Be aware and sensitive to own cultural heritage and values, and respect differences.

➤ Be aware of own values and biases and how they may affect minority students.

➤ Be comfortable with differences that exist between self and students in terms of race and beliefs.

➤ Be sensitive to circumstances (personal biases, stage of ethnic identity, socio-political influences, etc.) that may dictate referral of minority student to a counselor of his or her own race or culture.

➤ Acknowledge and be aware of own racist attitudes, beliefs, and feelings.

Counselor Understanding of the World View of the Culturally Different Student

➤ Possess specific knowledge and information about the minority student group in student caseload.

➤ Understand the socio-political system's operation in the United States with respect to treatment of minorities.

➤ Have a clear and explicit knowledge and understanding of the generic characteristics of counseling.

➤ Be aware of institutional barriers that prevent minorities from using mental health services.

Counselor Development of Appropriate Intervention Strategies and Techniques

➤ Be able to generate a wide variety of verbal and nonverbal responses.

➤ Be able to send and receive both verbal and nonverbal messages accurately and appropriately.

➤ Be able to exercise institutional intervention skills on behalf of minority student when appropriate.

➤ Be aware of own helping style, recognize the limitations possessed, and anticipate the impact upon the culturally different student.

ADDITIONAL INFORMATION

Arredondo, P., Toporek, R., Brown, S. P., Jones, J., Locke, D. C., Sanchez, J. & Stadler, H. (1996). Operationalization of the multicultural counseling competencies. *Journal of Multicultural Counseling and Development, (24)*, 42–78.

Association for Multicultural Counseling and Development (1995). *Multicultural counseling competencies.* **(List 12-23)**

5-75 BARRIERS TO CROSS-CULTURAL COUNSELING

Cross-cultural counseling is any counseling relationship in which two or more of the participants differ with respect to cultural background, values, and lifestyle.

Cultural encapsulation of the counselor is the lacking of cultural awareness, whereby the school counselor may impose his or her own cultural values or rigid beliefs on all students, reflecting insensitivity to students' values that differ from the counselor.

Barriers That Hinder Cross-Cultural Counseling

Culture-Bound Barriers

- Individual *or* group orientation
- Competition *or* cooperation
- Expressiveness *or* restraint
- Assertiveness *or* subtlety
- Insight *or* lack of self-centeredness
- Self-disclosure *or* privacy
- Cause and effect *or* holistic orientation
- Exploration of alternatives *or* advice and immediate solutions
- Ambiguity *or* clarity and structure
- Client-centered *or* direct authority

Class-Bound Barriers

- Self-direction *or* survival
- Low energy *or* hunger, lack or sleep
- Passivity *or* poverty
- Truancy *or* work for family
- Exploration of desires *or* immediate solutions
- Punctuality *or* indefinite time frame
- Insight *or* tangible suggestions
- Student initiative *or* immediate and concrete advice
- Long-range planning *or* immediate relief
- Resistance *or* reluctance
- Individual power *or* societal, environmental power

Language Barriers

- Direct and confrontive *or* subtle and respectful
- Issue-oriented *or* impassioned and interpersonal
- Standard English vocabulary *or* vernacular
- Upright posture and body language *or* relaxed posture and body language

➤ Middle class gestures and inflections *or* relaxed gestures and inflections

➤ Reliance on verbal *or* reliance on nonverbal

➤ Grammatically correct English *or* simple words for complex thoughts and feelings

➤ Clear precise English *or* imagery, analogies

➤ Verbal interaction to build rapport *or* nuances to build rapport

➤ Expression of self using English *or* inability to express self verbally

➤ Reserved communication style *or* animated communication style

ADDITIONAL INFORMATION

See *Lists 5-5 through 5-9*, Cultural and Ethnic Diversity and Cultural Values.

See *List 12-23, Multicultural Counseling Competencies.*

See *Lists 6-12, 7-12, 8-12, 10-15, 11-10, 12-23* for lists of materials for multicultural awareness.

See Videos, *Many voices. (List 12-23)*

Arredondo, P., Toporek, R., Brown, S. P., Jones, J., Locke, D. C., Sanchez, J. & Stadler, H. (1995). *Multicultural counseling competencies. (List 12-23)*

Sue, D. W. & Sue, D. (1990). *Counseling the culturally different: Theory and practice.* (2nd ed.). *(List 12-23)*

5-76 SENSITIVE CROSS-CULTURAL COUNSELING

Stereotypes are the rigid preconceptions held about *all* people who are members of a particular group. Stereotypes may become impervious to logic or experience.

Preferences of Many Minority Students

➤ Directive counseling

➤ Active counselor

➤ Structured counseling

➤ Immediate, concrete information, suggestions, and advice

➤ Outside the counselor's office

➤ Vocational, educational, and career goal-oriented

➤ Differential approaches consistent with life experiences of student

➤ Less verbally-oriented approaches

➤ Solution-focused brief counseling

➤ Self-disclosure of counselor prior to expected self-disclosure of student

➤ Willingness of counselor to consider system and societal responsibility as well as individual student responsibility

➤ Alternative counseling approaches:
  – Group counseling with several members of the same minority group
  – Training of minority peer facilitators

Culturally Sensitive Counselor

➤ Does not expect immediate trust or acceptance

➤ Establishes credibility by being trustworthy and well-informed

➤ Gives clear information about expectations in counseling

➤ Gives clear information about school expectations such as punctuality, attendance, work habits, and individual responsibility

➤ Uses techniques consistent with lifestyle, experiences, and cultural values of student

➤ Recognizes student as a unique individual as well as a member of a group

➤ Acknowledges possible social injustices

➤ Helps student establish strong self-concept and positive self-esteem

➤ Acknowledges limitations in helping style and impact they may have on student

➤ Encourages student to develop positive ways to function and succeed in the dominant society

➤ Encourages student to use existing support system

➤ Respects cultural and religious holidays and learns about particular customs

➤ Works to create or continue a positive school environment inviting and comfortable for all students

➤ Works to ensure that school policies and decisions are fair for all students

➤ Works with teachers, administrators, parents, influential citizens, and students to bring about any needed positive changes in school policies or decisions

➤ Ensures that all students have equal opportunities for higher education

➤ Refers, when necessary, to agency familiar with and supportive of particular ethnic minority

Considerations When Counseling African American Students

➤ Usually desire close conversational distance

➤ Collaborate with family

➤ Group counseling and peer counseling are often effective

➤ Usually prefer practical advice, directions, and interpretations

Considerations When Counseling African American Adolescents

➤ Avoid power struggles

➤ Establish working alliance

➤ Group and peer counseling are frequently effective

Considerations When Counseling Asian American Students

➤ May feel counseling is shameful, embarrassing, and a sign of failure

➤ May seek advice, consolation, and suggestions

➤ Usually prefer logical, rational, goal-oriented, and structured approach

Considerations When Counseling Bi-Racial Students

➤ Presenting problem may cover an ethnic-identity concern

➤ Help student to integrate two racial identities

➤ Assist student to develop strong self-esteem

➤ Involve entire family when possible

Considerations When Counseling Hispanic American Students

➤ Respond to anecdotes, humor, and proverbs

➤ Respond to personal warmth and acceptance

➤ Avoid interpretations and confrontations at beginning

➤ When possible, involve the family, particularly as a support system

➤ Realize desire for close distance when conversing

➤ May outwardly agree to something to be cooperative, but not follow up

➤ Parents may feel humiliated if children are asked to translate for them

➤ Group counseling is frequently effective

Considerations When Counseling Native American Students

➤ May avoid counseling as a sign of weakness

➤ Respond to self-esteem enhancement

➤ Respond when collaboration with traditional healers

➤ Need life skills to succeed

➤ Respond to social cognitive or combination of client-centered and behavioral interventions

ADDITIONAL INFORMATION

See *Lists 5-6, 5-7, Ethnic Diversity of Students* and *Ethnic Backgrounds of Students.*

See *List 13-11, The School Counselor and Cross/Multicultural Counseling.*

See Videos, *Many Voices.* **(List 12-23)**

Arredondo, P., Toporek, R., Brown, S. P., Jones, J., Locke, D. C., Sanchez, J. & Stadler, H. (1995). *Multicultural counseling competencies.* **(List 12-23)**

Gibbs, J. T., Huang, L. N. & Associates. (1989). *Children of color: Psychological interventions with minority youth.* **(List 12-23)**

Herring, R. D. (1996). *Multicultural counseling in schools: A synergetic approach.* Alexandria, VA: American Counseling Association.

Sue, D. & Sue, D. W. (1990). *Counseling the culturally different: Theory and practice.* (2nd ed.). **(List 12-23)**

5-77 COUNSELING STUDENTS WITH LOW SELF-ESTEEM

Counseling a Student Who Is Withdrawn

➢ Use active listening skills.

➢ Use art, music, talk about pets.

➢ Involve student in projects with other students.

➢ Give student responsibilities that are easy for him or her.

➢ Suggest to the teacher that the student be a teacher helper.

➢ Ask student to list things he or she would like to be able to do.

➢ Ask student to choose one realistic goal to work on from the list.

➢ Help the student achieve the goal.

Counseling Student Who Has a Poor Self-Concept

➢ Learn how the student sees family relationships and parental expectations.

➢ Establish a trusting relationship with the student and his or her parents.

➢ Offer effective parenting skills to parents:
  – Recognize the positive attributes of their children.
  – Listen for and respond to their children's feelings.
  – Show acceptance and pride in their children.
  – Help their children work on projects of interest.

➢ Encourage student to become involved in group activities.

➢ Encourage student to express what he or she finds uncomfortable or difficult.

➢ Continue to respond empathically to the student's thoughts and feelings.

➢ Enlist help of teacher to model and note positive student behaviors.

➢ Help student set realistic goals.

➢ Help student rehearse new behaviors and use them outside of counseling.

➢ Encourage positive thinking and rational coping skills.

➢ Encourage teachers to provide genuine praise when justified.

➢ Encourage teachers to use student as mentor when warranted.

ADDITIONAL INFORMATION

See **List 5-19**, *Helping Students Develop Self-Confidence.*

Hitchner, K. W. & Tifft-Hitchner, A. (1996). Self-concept, self-assessment, and valuing (Chapter 12). In *Counseling today's secondary students.* **(List 12-3)**

5-78 COUNSELING STUDENTS WHO HAVE BEEN HARASSED OR ABUSED

Counseling Victim of Harassment

➤ Support students who have been harassed or abused.

➤ Review feeling vocabulary. *(List 5-24)*

➤ Teach conflict-resolution skills. *(List 5-34)*

➤ Teach anger control. *(List 5-33)*

➤ Procedures:
- Stories or books (Materials lists)
- Simulations
- Puppets with young children
- Discussions
- Role play
- Practice new responding behaviors
- Teach new "self-talk" *(Lists 5-19, 5-33)*

➤ Involve in peer group to learn assertiveness skills *(List 5-31)*

Counseling Victim of Abuse

➤ Give hotline numbers to students.

➤ Give examples of places in community to find help during weekends.

➤ Use role play, puppets, videos, sand box, play counseling with younger student alone.

➤ Tell the student when a report suspecting abuse must be filed.

➤ Support the student who has been abused:
- Reassure that student has done right thing to report abuse.
- Accept student's fear, anger, guilt, ambivalence, and confusion.
- Be advocate for student without offender-bashing.
- Assess suicidal risk of student, particularly adolescent.

Counseling Harasser

➤ Provide appropriate books and bibliocounseling (Materials lists).

➤ Teach acceptable conflict-resolution skills. *(List 5-34)*

➤ Discuss acceptable behavior toward others.

➤ Involve in a peer group:
- Include well-liked, well-behaved students.
- Role play particular situations.
- Reverse role play to show how behavior effects others.
- Practice and use new acceptable behavior.

➤ Evaluate student's change of behavior toward others.

ADDITIONAL INFORMATION

Gibbs, J. C., et al. (1995). *Equip program: Teaching youth to think and act responsibly through a peer-helping approach.* *(List 12-25)*

Thompson, C. L. & Rudolph, L. B. (1996). *Counseling children.* *(List 12-3)*

5-79   COUNSELOR'S ACTIONS WHEN ABUSE IS SUSPECTED

Actions When Abuse Is Reported or Suspected

➤ Be calm.

➤ Believe the student.

➤ Get the important facts, but don't interrogate.

➤ Reassure that it was right to have the courage to tell a responsible adult.

➤ Get help for the student.

➤ Report to supervisor or administrator.

➤ Report any new allegation that is revealed.

Important Points to Cover With an Abused Student

➤ It is *always* right for the student to report abuse to a responsible adult.

➤ It is *never* the student's fault when abuse occurs.

➤ The abuser is *wrong*.

➤ Individuals who abuse students need help.

➤ Promise that you will assist the student in getting help by telling others who know what to do.

Supportive Responses

➤ "It must have been really hard for you to keep that a secret."

➤ "I bet this has made you really sad."

➤ "It must have been hard to tell me."

➤ "I'm really glad that you could tell me."

➤ "I'm so sorry this happened to you."

ADDITIONAL INFORMATION

See *List 12-28* for Associations that can help when there is suspected abuse.

See *List 13-5, The School Counselor and Child Abuse/Neglect Prevention.*

Clarke, J. I. (1986*). A family affair.* San Francisco, CA: Harper & Row.

Morrow, G. (1987). *Compassionate school: A practical guide to educating abused and traumatized children. (List 12-3)*

Petersen, S. & Straub, R. (1992). *School crisis survival guide: Management techniques and materials for counselors and administrators. (List 12-6)*

5-80 COUNSELING STUDENTS WITH SEXUAL-IDENTITY ISSUES

Characteristics of Students With Sexual-Identity Issues

➤ Extremely vulnerable

➤ Confused

➤ May be depressed

Goals of Counseling

➤ Respect dignity of student.

➤ Help student face major life issues:
  – Possibility of rejection and becoming ostracized by family
  – Possibility of isolation and rejection by peers
  – Possibility of contacting life-threatening illness

➤ Promote welfare of student to succeed academically.

Counselor's Actions

➤ Listen nonjudgmentally and empathically to student.

➤ Inform student that counselor does not have privileged communication.

➤ Inform student of the extent of confidentiality that counselor can keep.

➤ Provide unconditional positive regard.

➤ Recognize vulnerability and importance of trust.

➤ Provide bibliocounseling.

➤ Understand intense feelings:
  – Loss
  – Betrayal
  – Fear and anxiety

➤ Help student clarify problem:
  – Explore thoughts, feelings.
  – Discuss wounds.
  – Discuss aspirations.

➤ Help student use problem-solving model: *(List 2-23)*
  – Identify alternatives.
  – Identify consequences.

➤ Help student use decision-making skills. *(List 4-16)*

➤ Suggest student tell his or her parents.

➤ Help student maintain self-esteem and self-worth.

➤ Recognize the student may become depressed.

➤ Recognize the student may become suicidal.

➤ Recommend that student report any harassment immediately.

➤ Refer student to a counselor who specializes in sexual-identity issues.

ADDITIONAL INFORMATION

See *List 13-24*, *The School Counselor and Sexual Minority Youth.*

Hitchner, K. W. & Tifft-Hitchner, A. (1996). Counseling youth with different sexual preferences (Chapter 19). In *Counseling today's secondary students.* *(List 12-3)*

Slaby, A. (1994). *No one saw my pain: Why teens kill themselves.* New York, NY: W. W. Norton.

5-81   COUNSELING STUDENTS WITH EATING DISORDERS

Types of Eating Disorders

- Anorexia
- Bulimia
- Obesity

Counselor's Actions

- Establish trusting and supportive relationship.
- Help student communicate feeling about self.
- Help student learn to tolerate ambiguity.
- Help student recognize that it is all right to be imperfect.
- Consider cognitive-behavioral approach: *(Lists 2-11, 5-21)*
  - Challenge irrational beliefs.
  - Address self-esteem and body image.
  - Teach "self-talk." *(Lists 5-19, 5-33)*
- Refer to specialist in eating-disorder counseling.
- Refer for family counseling.
- Refer for group counseling:
  - Screen to assess extent of disorder.
  - Screen to learn extent of rigidity.
  - Screen to avoid weight competitiveness in group.

ADDITIONAL INFORMATION

See *List 5-60*, *Eating Disorders.*

5-82   COUNSELING STUDENTS WITH SELF-DESTRUCTIVE BEHAVIORS

Counseling Students Who Show Agitated Anxiety

➤ Use physical exercise, play counseling, puppets, or safe objects to help release anger.

➤ Help students verbalize their feelings. *(List 5-24)*

➤ Suggest time-outs, contracts to the teacher.

➤ Suggest appropriate books (Materials lists).

➤ Teach coping skills. *(List 5-35)*

➤ Invite student to join an anger-management group.

Counseling Students With Self-Destructive Behavior

➤ Be alert to loss of loved ones, pets, feelings of failure, shame, grief, or other traumatic issue.

➤ Do not judge or deny the student's feelings.

➤ Be alert to threats or hints of hurting self.

➤ Follow threats with questions about the event that triggered the threat.

➤ If reason for concern, tell the student the reason for the concern.

➤ Explore self-destructive thoughts, fantasies, dreams, or plans.

➤ Ask student to write thoughts or draw a picture.

➤ Inform student when you must contact the parent.

➤ Inform parents of your concern.

Providing Help to Parents

➤ Listening skills *(List 5-23)*

➤ Recognizing danger signals and being prepared to handle crises

➤ Realizing student's inability to comprehend the finality and irreversibility of death

➤ Realizing the need for student to talk with responsible adult outside of school hours

➤ Realizing the importance of careful supervision of a suicidal student

➤ Realizing the importance of continuing help after the initial threat is over

ADDITIONAL INFORMATION

See **List 5-83**, *Counseling Suicidal Students*.

5-83   COUNSELING SUICIDAL STUDENTS

Counselor's Actions

➤ Listen, assess, direct, monitor, guide.

➤ Always take seriously a student's threat to take his or her life.

➤ Notify parent immediately.

➤ Notify administrator.

➤ Assess suicidal risk using all resources available:
  – Assess student's statement subjectively, from the student's point of view.
  – Assess student's statement objectively.
  – Consider all that you know about the student.

➤ Remain calm.

➤ Assess the student's ability to cope:
  – Current emotional state
  – Emotional history

➤ Encourage student disclosure.

➤ Ask direct questions:
  – "Are you thinking about taking your own life?"
  – "How?" "When?" "Where?"

➤ Assess the student's plan:
  – Amount of detail
  – Likeliness to happen

➤ Be directive but nonjudgmental.

➤ Broaden student's perspective of past and present situation:
  – Point out that the problem may be temporary.
  – Point out that it is difficult in the present to see all aspects.
  – Elicit positive aspects of student's past and present that can be regained.

➤ Be positive in your outlook of future:
  – Build trust, don't give false assurances.
  – Hook student on idea that you know something about a positive future.
  – Student's predictions about hopelessness are only guesses.
  – Contrast finality of death with uncertainty of the future.
  – Speculate how student's life would be different with just one or two changes.

➤ Help student to increase perception of alternatives to suicide:
  – Consider what student hopes to accomplish by suicide.
  – Generate alternative ways of reaching student's goal.
  – Suicidal students frequently rule out viable options.
  – Try to elicit possible deterrents to committing suicide.
  – Point out survivors may be angry with person for causing their sorrow.
  – Point out possiblity of being paralyzed or brain-damaged for life.

➤ Act specifically:
  – Help student begin to make concrete plans to resolve problem.
  – Identify small steps to be taken.
  – Give student something definite to plan for.
  – Convey firmness and self-assurance.
  – Assure student that whatever is necessary and appropriate will be done.
  – Set a time to meet very soon.
  – Do *not* leave student alone or unobserved for any length of time.

➤ Evaluate resources of student:
  – Help student identify resources of support.
  – Assure student that you will help and others can help.

➤ Make a referral and ask for assistance:
  – Do *not* handle case alone.
  – Do *not* believe the problem is solved in one session.

➤ Follow up:
  – Follow up with referral source.
  – Follow up with student.
  – Consider cognitive-behavioral counseling. *(List 2-11)*
  – Teach positive self-statements.
  – Teach problem-solving skills. *(List 2-23)*

ADDITIONAL INFORMATION

Hitchner, K. W. & Tifft-Hitchner, A. (1996). Depression and suicide (Chapter 16). In *Counseling today's secondary students.* *(List 12-3)*

Thompson, C. L. & Rudolph, L. B. (1996). *Counseling children.* *(List 12-3)*

5-84   COUNSELING STUDENTS WHO ARE TRUANT FROM SCHOOL

Truancy is the deliberate absence from school without a valid reason.

Problems of Truancy

➤ Often leads to dropping out of school

➤ Often linked to daytime criminal activity

➤ Predictor of delinquent behavior

Characteristics of Truants

➤ Discouraged academically, often poor students

➤ Feel little or no guilt about school absences

➤ Perceive learning as lacking relevance

➤ Perceive social activities outside of school as more attractive than school

➤ Often experience inconsistent discipline at home

➤ Parents are often unaware of absences or do not encourage students to attend school

➤ May have family responsibilities

Counselor's Actions

➤ Identify students with three or more unexcused absences.

➤ Listen for real reasons of absence versus excuses.

➤ Take personal interest in student and attendance.

➤ Involve parent in efforts to improve school attendance.

➤ Enlist teacher's cooperation.

➤ Make a plan or contract with student:
   – Contract for attendance one day.
   – Renegotiate contract, increasing days of attendance.
   – Include responsibility for all work missed because of absence.
   – Include rewards and penalties.

➤ Enlist teacher's help in involving student in enjoyable school activities.

➤ Enlist teacher's help in involving student in responsibility for desired project.

➤ Enlist help from peer facilitator.

➤ Discourage administrator from suspending student for absence.

➤ Encourage attendance reporting every period in high school.

➤ Use cognitive-behavioral techniques: *(List 5-21)*
   – Visualize and describe desired future career.
   – List requirements to obtain such a career.
   – List reasons to attend school and reasons not to attend.
   – Rehearse behaviors to cope with expected problems.
   – Draw up a behavioral contract with logical consequences. *(List 2-31)*

➢ Arrange for academic help for student:
  – Tutoring or mentoring *(List 2-53)*
  – Listening skills *(List 5-23)*
  – Study skills *(List 3-3)*
  – Assertiveness skills *(List 5-31)*

➢ Inform parents of their legal responsibility for student's attendance.

ADDITIONAL INFORMATION

Thompson, C. L. & Rudolph, L. B. (1996). Children's conflicts with self: Alternatives for intervention, Appendix B. In *Counseling children.* (4th ed.). *(List 12-3)*

U.S. Department of Education in cooperation with U.S. Department of Justice (1996). *Manual to combat truancy.* Washington DC: U.S. Department of Education. For copy: 1-800-624-0100.

5-85 COUNSELING STUDENTS WHO HAVE SCHOOL PHOBIA

School phobia is the extreme and irrational fear of attending school.

Characteristics

➢ Often 6–10 years of age or at transition points of schooling

➢ Fear abandonment or separation from parents

➢ Prefer to be home rather than at school

➢ Experience parent ambivalence or no encouragement to attend school

➢ Over-dependency on parents

➢ Experience intense emotional anxiety

➢ Fear the unknown

➢ Fear failure or humiliation

➢ Often socially rejected by peers

➢ Associate traumatic, unpleasant, or embarrassing situation with attending school

Counselor's Actions

➢ Coordinate treatment team. *(List 2-56)*

➢ Enlist help of parent to designate parental hopes and desires for student.

➢ Collaborate with parent and teacher to develop a daily routine.

➢ Collaborate with parent, teacher, administrator, and student to write a contract specifying tangible reward for school attendance.

➢ Renegotiate contract, increasing length of time in school.

➢ Establish trust and security.

➢ Actively listen for feelings.

➢ Enlist young child in play activities, puppets, or stories.

➤ Discover student's irrational ideas and replace with rational ideas.

➤ Discover student's defeating "self-talk" and replace with successful "self-talk." *(Lists 5-19, 5-33)*

➤ Prepare student for any new situations at school.

➤ Encourage student to practice new ways of handling anxiety-provoking situations.

➤ Arrange for academic help for student when needed.

➤ Enlist teacher's help to make appropriate accommodations:
  – Provide enjoyable activities at school.
  – Let student sit near door.
  – Let student attend for short periods of time at first.

➤ Enlist help of peer facilitator.

➤ Recommend to administrator that student be allowed to participate in school activities.

➤ Expect relapses after vacations.

➤ Request written permission from parents to use systematic desensitization or get help outside the school system for student's extreme anxiety. *(List 2-10)*

Suggestions for Parents

➤ Do not convey or project own anxiety to student about going to school.

➤ Do not expect student to be anxious about attending school.

➤ Suggest relaxation exercises for student.

➤ Avoid tearful farewells or overemphasis on separating.

➤ Avoid overemphasizing tests or requiring success.

➤ Set realistic goals for school performance, not perfection.

➤ Persist in getting student to school every day.

➤ Have young child visit classes and playground prior to attending school.

➤ Enlist help of pediatrician if psychosomatic ailments persist.

➤ Seek family counseling if student continues to show extreme anxiety about school attendance.

ADDITIONAL INFORMATION

Jenni, C. B. (1995). *A model for home-school collaboration in the resolution of school phobia.* Unpublished manuscript, University of Montana at Missoula.

Paige, L. Z. (1993). ERIC NO. ED 366863. *The identification and treatment of school phobia.* Publication No. 6503. Silver Spring, MD: National Association of School Psychologists.

Thompson, C. L. & Rudolph, L. B. (1996). Children's conflicts with self: Alternatives for intervention, Appendix B. In *Counseling children.* (4th ed.). *(List 12-3)*

5-86   COUNSELING STUDENTS EXPERIENCING SEPARATION OF PARENTS

Effects of Divorce on Some Children

➤ Less stability

➤ Less parental involvement

➤ Less money

Children Who Recover Well

➤ Have excellent role models

➤ Have parents not traumatized by their own problems

➤ Are assured of continual love and care of both parents

➤ Are not forced to choose between parents

➤ Do not hear blame of a natural parent

➤ Do not sense competition for their love

➤ Do not "tattle" on absent natural parent

Frequent Feelings of Children Experiencing Divorce

➤ Feel torn apart

➤ Sometimes feel abandoned

➤ Worry about life, current and future

➤ Feel uncertain with series of changes

➤ Feel in constant turmoil or transition

➤ Feel tension between parents

➤ Feel responsible for parents' divorce

➤ Feel responsible for relationship between both parents

➤ Feel responsible for parents' happiness

➤ Fear losing both parents

Counselor's Actions

➤ Establish trusting relationship with student.

➤ Actively listen to student's feelings.

➤ Suggest student join theme-centered counseling group with other students.

➤ Request written parental permission for joining counseling group about divorce.

Group for Students Experiencing Divorce

➤ Organize opportunity for students to express similar concerns.

➤ Include students at different stages of separation, divorce, and remarriage of parents.

➤ Encourage students to learn from each other and support each other:
  – How to relate well to both parents

 – How to live in two homes with different rules
 – How to prepare for holidays
 – How to establish new family traditions
 – How to prepare for next stage—divorce or remarriage

Group for Parents Experiencing Divorce

➤ Provide opportunity for parents to meet other parents in a support group.

➤ Provide information to parents:
 – How to help child recover well from loss
 – Guidelines for parents considering or involved in divorce
 – Guidelines for stepparents

Guidelines for Parents Considering or Involved in Divorce

➤ Assure children that you will always be their mother or father; you will always love them and be available when they need you.

➤ Continue to serve as role model for children.

➤ Do not force children to choose between parents.

➤ Expect the first year to be the hardest for all concerned.

➤ Do not compete with ex-spouse for the love, appreciation, and affection of children.

➤ Always show respect for ex-spouse in front of children.

➤ Always be honest with children but do not criticize ex-spouse in children's presence.

➤ Listen to children to learn about their anxieties and fears.

➤ Do not ask children to serve as messengers between parents.

➤ Do not expect children to adapt readily to boyfriend, girlfriend, or future spouse.

➤ Discuss plans for remarriage with children prior to serious marriage plans.

➤ Respect and be considerate of children's feelings, but maintain the right to make the decision about relationships and remarriage.

➤ Set clear rules for the household.

➤ Specify who will discipline the children, when, how, and why.

➤ Insist on respect, consideration, and cooperation of children with parents and stepparents.

➤ Encourage children to discuss feelings and needs and respect their feelings with confidentiality.

➤ Try to never show partiality toward one child over another.

➤ Plan ahead for new holiday traditions.

Guidelines for Stepparents

➤ Assume role of parent gradually.
 – Start as a friend.
 – Earn the right to parent.

➤ Encourage children to maintain relationship or memory of absent parent.

ADDITIONAL INFORMATION

See *List 5-12, Students With Difficult Family Relationships*.

See *Lists 6-7, 7-7, 8-9, 9-15* for materials for students experiencing divorce.

See *List 10-12*, for materials for parents experiencing divorce.

Costa, L. & Stiltner, B. (1994). Why do the good things always end and the bad things go on forever: A family change counseling group. *The School Counselor, 41* (4), 300–304.

5-87   COUNSELING STUDENTS EXPERIENCING THE DEATH OF A LOVED ONE

Possible Characteristics of Students Experiencing Death (each case is unique)

➤ Confused or shocked

➤ Angry that person was taken from them

➤ Fearful of own death

➤ Feel guilty, remembering previous anger at person who died

➤ Sad, quiet, decreased activity

➤ Isolated in grief, less support than public disaster

➤ Introverted

➤ Lack concentration

➤ Withdrawn

➤ Lack commitment to work

➤ Less cooperative than usual

➤ Less conforming than usual

➤ Find relief in cognitive concentration

➤ React in unique, individual ways and times

➤ May have temporary eating disorders

➤ May have temporary sleeping disorders

Counselor's Actions

➤ Listen to student:
  - Assess the meaning of death to the individual student.
  - Feel with the student.
  - Respect the personal nature of each student's grief.

➤ Avoid probing when student doesn't want to talk about subject.

➤ Be available for nurturing and caring when student desires.

➤ Answer questions honestly and clearly.

➤ Be prepared to repeat details many times.

➤ Understand student's need to reprocess information about the life and death at different times and repeatedly.

➤ Reassure that the student did not cause the death.

➤ Emphasize that death does not mean that someone else will die soon.

➤ Emphasize that death does not mean that the person did something wrong.

➤ Encourage student to share positive memories and recollections about loved one.

➤ Provide names of appropriate books about death at respective developmental level.

➤ Encourage student to ask questions of parents.

➤ Give the message of the preciousness and precariousness of life.

➤ Expect student to take time to get over the shock, don't rush.

➤ Educate staff about grieving students and helpful responses.

Signs Indicating Need for Additional Professional Help

➤ Stating desire to join the dead person

➤ Excessively imitating the dead person

➤ Extended period of mourning beyond six months

➤ Long-term denial of death of the person

➤ Long-term loss of interest in daily activities

➤ Long-term acting much younger than developmental level

➤ Withdrawal from friends

➤ Sharp drop in school performance

➤ Refusal to attend school

ADDITIONAL INFORMATION

See *List 5-70, Dealing With Grief.*

Cassini, K. K. & Rogers, J. L. (1990). *Death and the classroom: A teacher's guide to help grieving students. (List 11-5)*

Kramer, K. (1988). *The sacred art of dying: How world religions understand death. (List 12-7)*

5-88   COUNSELING YOUNG CHILDREN AND THEIR PARENTS EXPERIENCING THE DEATH OF A LOVED ONE

Possible Characteristics of a Young Child Dealing With Grief (each case is unique)

➤ Confused

➤ Angry at being left alone

➤ Fearful about who will care for him or her

➤ Fearful other parent will die

➤ Guilty, believing he or she may have caused the death

➤ Guilty, feeling that had she or he acted differently, the death may have been prevented

➤ Regress to previous developmental behaviors

➤ May lack parental attention because parent may be overcome with own grief

➤ May find school and cognitive learning a relief from intense emotion

➤ Additional characteristics *(List 5-87)*

Patterns of a Young Child's Understanding of Death

➤ Age dependent

➤ Denial at first

➤ Misunderstanding of finality

➤ Sadness on and off at unexpected times

➤ Crying at various unexpected times

➤ Anger expressed in various ways

➤ May feel deserted by dead parent or grandparent

➤ May interpret literally what he or she is told:
  – If told the person is asleep, then expects that person to wake up
  – If told the person went to the hospital, may think of hospital as location where people die

➤ May lack concepts to understand about death:
  – Irreversibility
  – Universality
  – Nonfunctionality
  – Causality

➤ Usually returns to normal routine in about six months

Frequent Questions of a Young Child About Death

➤ "Why did they leave?"

➤ "Was I to blame?"

➤ "If I get angry at someone, will they die?"

➤ "Will my parents die?"

➤ "Will I die?"

- "When you die, do you live somewhere else?"
- "Where does your body go when you die?"
- "Why does death happen?"
- "What is death?"

Preparation of a Young Child for Death of a Loved One

- Discuss stories and television programs that include death.
- Discuss news and deaths of public figures when they happen.
- Discuss deaths of friends of the family.
- Grieve together:
  - Share feelings.
  - Talk about feelings.
  - Explore religious convictions.
- Discuss death of a pet:
  - Treat seriously because it is devastating to the child.
  - Encourage venting of grief and anger.
  - Encourage conducting a ritual.
  - Discourage getting another pet soon.
  - One life cannot be replaced with another.

Counselor's Actions

- Encourage student to ask questions of parents.
- Consult with parents:
  - Respect their desires when meeting with the student.
  - Ask how they see their child's understanding, feeling, and reactions to the event.
  - Give parent resources if desired.
- Listen to student:
  - Feel with the student.
  - Assess the meaning and concepts of death to the individual student.
- Expect the child to take time to get over the shock, don't rush the child.
- Educate staff about grieving students and helpful responses.
- See counselor's actions when counseling students experiencing the death of a loved one. *(List 5-87)*

Additional Information

See *List 5-70, Dealing With Grief.*

Fitzgerald, H. (1992). *The grieving child. (List 10-6)*

Perry, B. D. (1994). The child's loss: Death, grief and mourning. Houston, TX: CIVITAS Child Trauma Programs. [On-line] Available: http://www.bcm.tmc.edu/civitas/publicat/death_pr.html

5-89 COUNSELING STUDENTS EXPERIENCING THE DEATH OF A CLASSMATE

Suggestions for Teachers When a Student Dies

➤ Speak with bereaved parents:
  - Do not say that you know how they feel unless you have lost a child.
  - Give suggestions only when questioned or requested.
  - Share with parents patterns of young children's understanding of death if asked. *(List 5-88)*

➤ Prepare how to tell classmates:
  - Do not hesitate mentioning student's name.
  - Do not try to find something positive about student's death.
  - Reassure students that all medical resources were used.
  - Let students talk about endearment and relationship to the student.

➤ Give the message that life is precious and precarious.

➤ Listen.

➤ Let students cry in counselor's office.

➤ Be loving.

➤ Be truthful and honest.

➤ Be accepting.

➤ Be consistent.

➤ Match information with student's ability to understand.

Suggestions for Parents When Their Child Dies

➤ Let children see you grieve, no reason to hide.

➤ Give special attention to other children in family:
  - Tell child honestly about death and your beliefs in language child can understand.
  - Reassure child that medical care was best possible.
  - Repeatedly assure that child is not to blame for death.
  - Share religious beliefs with child.
  - Include child in family and religious rituals if child desires.
  - Do not force child to do anything within the ritual that results in discomfort.
  - Prepare child for family and religious rituals.
  - Have supportive adult with child during family and religious rituals.

➤ Realize that child may feel vulnerable to own death and to parents' death.

➤ Listen to child, encourage expression through stories and play.

Suggestions for Parents When a Child Is Terminally Ill

➤ Encourage sibling to visit child in hospital if sibling desires.

➤ Actively involve sibling in the care of the sick child:
  - Comfort the sick child
  - Well child will be more able to accept inevitable loss of sick child

➤ Encourage sibling to draw pictures or write about own feelings followed by discussion with parent.

➤ Encourage sibling to write letters to sick child.

➤ Encourage sibling to do community service in honor of sick sibling.

➤ Encourage sibling to share memories of fun times with sick sibling.

Counselor's Actions When a Student Dies

➤ Coordinate with teacher or administrator:
  – Implement crisis plan. *(List 1-6)*
  – Determine who will do what and when.

➤ Inform staff in the way parents desire.

➤ Pay special attention to siblings and special friends:
  – Listen to their explanations and expressions of grief.
  – Let them cry in office.
  – Let them use puppets, sandbox, stories, or play when they need to express feelings.

➤ See Counselor's Actions. *(Lists 5-87, 5-88)*

➤ When parents are ready, recommend support group such as Compassionate Friends.

ADDITIONAL INFORMATION

See *List 1-6*, *The Crisis Plan, Crisis Team, and Crisis Intervention.*

See *List 5-71*, *Debriefing After a Tragedy or Natural Disaster.*

See *List 5-72*, *Procedures After a Suicide.*

See *List 5-87*, *Counseling Students Experiencing the Death of a Loved One.*

See *List 5-88*, *Counseling Young Children and Their Parents Experiencing the Death of a Loved One.*

5-90 COUNSELING STUDENTS ENGAGED IN HIGH-RISK BEHAVIOR

High-risk behavior is behavior that is potentially lethal to self or others.

Leading Causes of Death During Adolescence

➤ Accidents

➤ Homicide

➤ Suicide

Some Risk-Taking Behaviors

➤ Reckless driving

➤ Inhalant use

➤ Alcohol and other drug abuse

➤ Playing with weapons

➤ Criminal behavior:
  – Gang involvement
  – Burglary
  – Robbery

➤ Irresponsible sexual behavior

➤ Running away from home

➤ Fighting

➤ Smoking

Influences on Attitudes of Youth Toward Risk

➤ *Social class*—risk is a social concept

➤ *Age*—risk accompanies adolescent's feeling of invulnerability

➤ Way risk is regarded at home and in school

➤ Individual decides the acceptability of risk taking:
  – Consider dangers and own vulnerability
  – Denial of long-term adverse consequences
  – Behave in dangerous ways despite knowledge of consequences

Factors That Put Youth At Risk

➤ Poverty

➤ Abuse during childhood

➤ Violence in popular culture

➤ Violence in environment

➤ Unstable family life

➤ Lack of positive role models

➤ Alcohol and other drug abuse

➤ Failure in school

➤ Involvement in antisocial groups

➤ Peer influences

➤ Media influences

➤ Access to weapons

Clash of School Values and Student Values

➤ School values:
  - Hard work
  - Long-term goals
  - Future orientation
  - Averse to risk as undesirable and unnecessary
  - Sanctity of life
  - Dignity and worth of each person
  - Tolerance toward others
  - Peaceful coexistence

➤ Values of some students:
  - Excitement
  - Fun
  - Short-term goals
  - Present-orientation
  - Enjoyment of the thrill of danger
  - Risk-taking as regular and respectable
  - Invulnerability
  - Competitiveness, self-interest, self-centeredness

➤ Views of some students:
  - Risk as inevitable
  - Survival of risk as victory over death
  - Temptation of fate as defiance of reality

Frequent Reaction to Teacher's Values

➤ Respect but don't identify with teachers

➤ Resist and reject teacher's arguments

➤ Deny physical results and finality of suicide

➤ May listen and later reflect on teacher's statements

Counselor's Actions

➤ Collaborate with teachers and administrators to develop a team approach.

➤ Lead groups to develop positive peer pressure.

➤ Listen respectfully to students' reasons for risk-taking.

➤ Understand the world from point-of-view of student.

➤ Treat students' reasons as worthy for consideration, but worthy to challenge.

➤ Challenge how students reconcile their opinion with their other views.

➤ Present own ideas about risk and back them up with facts.

➤ Relate facts to students' own lives.

➤ Arrange for speakers to discuss the dangers of risk-taking:
  - Learn how some adults turned their lives around.
  - Learn how some adults have limited freedom and limited futures.

➤ Arrange for field trips and discuss students' futures:
  - Talk with college students and teachers.
  - Talk with successful employees.
  - Talk with prison inmates and law officers.

➤ Provide local 24-hour hotline numbers.

➤ Assist students to consider all implications of their actions:
  - Effect on others
  - Probable consequences
  - Desired future
  - Reasons they take risks such as peer or media influence
  - Effect of negative consequences on themselves and others

➤ Discuss what happens when people are hurt, maimed, or killed:
  - Help students picture how consequences would be for them personally.
  - Help students develop a clear idea of what it is like to suffer long-term consequences.
  - Link decisions to inhibiting their future.
  - Help students picture people being affected as real people with only one life.

➤ Present own view as an alternative.

➤ Encourage reflection on how they can lead the life they want.

➤ Help students consider rationally what they are doing and why.

➤ Encourage reflection on how they can control their lives.

➤ Encourage rational decision-making.

➤ Don't ever give up on any student.

ADDITIONAL INFORMATION

Fulton, R. (1995). AIDS and our children (Chapter 8). In *Beyond the innocence of childhood: Factors influencing children and adolescents' perceptions and attitudes toward death*. D. W. Adams & E. J. Deveau, (Eds.). *(List 11-5)*

Leaman, O. (1995). Talking to children about risk (Chapter 5). In *Death and loss: Compassionate approaches in the classroom*. *(List 11-5)*

Wass, H. (1995). Appetite for destruction: Children and violent death in popular culture (Chapter 6). In D. W. Adams & E. J. Deveau, (Eds.). *Beyond the innocence of childhood: Factors influencing children and adolescents' perceptions and attitudes toward death*. *(List 11-5)*

5-91 COUNSELING STUDENTS WITH HIV/AIDS

Preparation for Dealing With AIDS Cases in the School

➤ Be familiar with school district policy and procedures dealing with AIDS cases.

➤ Inform parents and students of the policy and procedures.

Possible Characteristics of Students With AIDS

➤ Vulnerable emotionally

➤ Fearful of the future

➤ Regretful and embarrassed

➤ Feelings of guilt

➤ Angry:
   - Angry at what happened to them
   - Angry at being isolated and ostracized
   - Angry about loss of strength
   - Angry about present dependence on others
   - Angry about causing family problems

➤ Denial of future problems

➤ Physical pain and loss of strength

➤ Isolated socially

Counselor's Actions

➤ Examine own feeling about student with AIDS:
   - Facing life-threatening illness
   - Facing probable death
   - Facing probable stigmatism
   - Regretful of mistakes

➤ Listen empathically.

➤ View the world from student's viewpoint.

➤ Be supportive, honest, and caring.

➤ Confront denial about diagnosis of HIV/AIDS.

➤ Help deal with specific and current concerns:
   - Stigma and rejection
   - Loss and grieving

➤ Teach stress reduction.

➤ Encourage student to join a support group for people with AIDS.

➤ Refer student and parents for additional professional counseling.

➤ Bridge communication with friends and family.

➤ Help siblings deal with their feelings:

    – Stigmatism and ostracism because of sibling

    – Fear for their own health

    – Remorse for brother's or sister's declining health

    – Guilt because of concern for self

➤ Help friends of the student with AIDS:

    – Face realistic health issues.

    – Deal with feelings of relief and guilt.

    – Encourage safe contact.

➤ Provide friends of the student with resources.

ADDITIONAL INFORMATION

See *List 5-66, Preventing HIV/AIDS.*

Gray, L. A. & House, R. M. (1996). Adolescents and AIDS: Education, compassion, and reason (Chapter 10). In D. Capuzzi & D. R. Gross, (Eds.). *Youth at risk. (List 12-34)*

HIV/AIDS Ministries Network Focus Paper #16. [On-line] Available: http://198.139.157.2/programs/hiv/focus/focus016.html

Thompson, C. L. & Rudolph, L. B. (1996). Counseling children with special concerns. In *Counseling children. (List 12-3)*

5-92 COUNSELING STUDENTS INVOLVED IN SUBSTANCE ABUSE

Characteristics of Possible Substance Abuse

➤ Physical characteristics:

    – Dilated pupils, red eyes

    – Extreme sluggishness

    – Drastic weight loss

    – Abnormal hunger or thirst; brings munchies to class

    – Easily agitated, giggles inappropriately

    – Sleeps or seems abnormally sleepy in class

    – Slow, slurred, sometimes incoherent speech

    – Lack of coordination, unsteady walk

    – Responds inappropriately to easy questions

    – Smells of alcohol or other chemicals

    – Change in facial color, flushed face

    – Change in alertness from hour to hour or day to day

➤ Academic performance:

    – Lower grades, lower achievement

    – Decreased interest in school

    – Impairment of vision, memory, ability to think clearly

    – Loss of communication skills

➤ Attendance:

    – Excessive absences

    – Chronic tardiness

- Leaves class early, with or without excuse
- Arrives at school late in the morning
- Spends time in the bathroom or in the halls
- Is absent from school with other students

➤ Attitude:
- Low motivation and loss of interest in school
- Often hostile when criticized
- Argumentative, involved in arguments and fights
- Extreme negativism
- Stereotyped thinking
- Denial of any problem, appears fearful of detection
- Low self-esteem
- Remorse, promises to change
- Complacent or "laid-back" attitude
- Paranoia, restlessness, anxiety, irritability
- Volatile mood changes
- Withdrawal of active interest in school sports, activities
- Loss of curiosity
- Secretive
- Assumption of "Don't hassle me" attitude

➤ Contact with others:
- Avoidance of contact with concerned persons
- Change of friends, new friends suspected of drug use
- Goes to parties frequently
- Spends less time at home, and then alone in room
- Makes appointments but does not show up
- Avoids talking about or minimizes drug use
- May brag about partying with peers
- Overheard talking about parties and drug involvement

Successful Substance-Abuse Intervention Programs

➤ Required attendance at substance-abuse educational classes

➤ Required community service at drug treatment centers

➤ Alternative social activities:
- Build social competence to acquire self-confidence
- Broaden appropriate social experience

➤ Reinforcement program dependent upon demonstrated responsible behavior:
- Detection and enforcement difficult
- Assigned tasks with accomplishment resulting in desired privileges

➤ Alternative schools may be influential in changing behavior patterns

➤ Individual and group counseling

Counselor's Actions

> Listen.

> Identify students who are suspected drug users and counsel about high risk. *(List 5-90)*

> Be supportive and accepting of students with a problem.

> Use cognitive and affective strategies:
  - Accurate information about reasons to stop using
  - Accurate information and concern about health
  - Accurate information and concern for safety

> Describe specific behavior of the student and cite specific incidents.

> Respond to alcohol and tobacco use the same as any other substance abuse.

> Stress that alcohol and other drugs are dangerous and illegal.

> Give facts; do not use scare tactics.

> Encourage participation in Alcoholics Anonymous or Narcotics Anonymous.

> Stress that alcohol is illegal, regardless of whether the user is driving.

> Keep up-to-date with information about substances and slang terms.

> Inform parents to never serve alcohol at teenage parties.

> Encourage parent support groups to share rules and expectations.

> Inform parents who suspect their child is using drugs about enabling behavior.

> Encourage family members of suspected drug users to attend Al-Anon.

> Encourage family members of suspected drug users to get additional professional assistance.

ADDITIONAL INFORMATION

See *List 5-65, Preventing Substance Abuse.*

Center for Substance Abuse Prevention. *Keeping youth drug-free.* Free book: 1-800-729-6686.

Center for Substance Abuse Treatment, National Drug Information and Treatment Referral Hotline. 1-800-662-HELP or 1-800-66-AYUDA (Spanish).

Gibbs, J. C. et al. (1995). *Equip program: Teaching youth to think and act responsibly through a peer-helping approach.* *(List 12-25)*

Goldstein, A. P., Reagles, K. W. & Amann, L. L. (1990). *Refusal skills: Preventing drug use in adolescents.* *(List 12-38)*

Schinke, S. P., Botvin, G. J. & Orlandi, M. A. (1991). *Substance abuse in children and adolescents: Evaluation and intervention.* *(List 12-38)*

5-93   COUNSELING CHILDREN OF ALCOHOLICS (COAs)

COAs Are Students At Risk

➤ More likely to become alcoholics than children of nonalcoholics

➤ More likely to have oppositional or conduct disorders

➤ More likely to marry before they reach 16 years of age

➤ More likely to be delinquent

➤ More likely to develop mental illness

➤ More likely to commit suicide

➤ More likely to begin drinking alcohol by age 13

Possible Characteristics of COAs

➤ May be isolated and fearful

➤ May seek approval, be overly responsible, extremely self-critical

➤ May be overly nurturing, assume adult role prematurely

➤ May hide feelings

➤ May fear abandonment

➤ May show neglect or possible abuse

➤ May be angry or hostile toward parents

➤ May lack internal locus of control

➤ May have learning disabilities

➤ May exhibit antisocial behaviors

➤ May deny reality

Some Frequent Problems of COAs

➤ Lack of money

➤ Lack of parental attention

➤ Lack of security

➤ Lack of consistent rules

➤ Lack of consistent parental behaviors and discipline

➤ Lack of predictable environment

➤ Lack of consistent family rituals or happy holidays

➤ Distress due to family quarreling, possible neglect or abuse

➤ Shame or embarrassment of family or home

Counselor's Actions

➤ Get written permission from nonalcoholic parent to counsel student.

➤ Provide a safe environment for expression of feelings.

➤ Determine degree of neglect or abuse occurring in the family.

➤ Educate student about drinking and life in an alcoholic family.

➤ Help student understand that he or she can love parents without liking their behavior.

➤ Help student feel worthwhile as an individual.

➤ Recommend books or videos to help student understand the parent's problem.

➤ Encourage student to practice new ways of responding without enabling.

➤ Teach assertiveness skills to express needs and rights, and to refuse using drugs. *(Lists 5-31, 5-32)*

➤ Teach positive "self-talk" and relaxation to reduce stress. *(Lists 5-19, 5-33, 5-38)*

➤ Provide activities to improve self-esteem. *(List 5-18)*

➤ Teach problem-solving and decision-making skills. *(Lists 2-23 and 4-16)*

➤ Encourage the nonalcoholic parent:
  – To seek help for self
  – To learn about codependency
  – To learn and use consistent parenting skills
  – To teach children about alcoholism and communication skills

ADDITIONAL INFORMATION

Thompson, C. L. & Rudolph, L. B. (1996). *Counseling children.* (4th ed.). *(List 12-3)*

Wilson, J. & Blocher, L. (1990). The counselor's role in assisting children of alcoholics. *Elementary School Guidance and Counseling, 25,* (2) 98–106.

5-94   COUNSELING PREGNANT STUDENTS AND TEENAGE PARENTS

Characteristics of Most Adolescent Parents

- ➤ Unintended pregnancy
- ➤ Grew up in single-parent family
- ➤ May have suffered from parental neglect, rejection, or abuse
- ➤ Few educational and career aspirations
- ➤ Frequently desire autonomy without responsibility
- ➤ Have babies that are more prone to physical and mental problems

Counselor's Actions

- ➤ Listen nonjudgmentally.
- ➤ Stress importance of future for self and baby.
- ➤ Encourage responsibility by both parents.
- ➤ Stress the need for safe child care and proper nutrition.
- ➤ Stress the need for career goals to provide for themselves and baby.
- ➤ Work out a realistic plan step-by-step to lead toward high school graduation.
- ➤ Help student plan for realistic career with work training.
- ➤ Arrange for mentoring if possible.
- ➤ Include in support group with available child care.
- ➤ Offer a group for teenage fathers:
    - Provide knowledge, resources, care, and support.
    - Encourage caring involvement with their child.

5-95   COUNSELING STUDENTS WHO MAY RUN AWAY

Characteristics of Students Who Run Away from Home

➤ Frequently not running toward anything

➤ May be running from abusive situation

➤ Desire to be independent, not a burden to family

➤ May desire increased parental attention

➤ May feel abandoned, rejected, or unloved

➤ Frequently feel denial, shame, and pain

➤ May desire to explore the world

➤ Need parental understanding, compassion, love, and respect

Counselor's Actions

➤ Listen nonjudgmentally.

➤ Learn if this is a recent or long-term problem.

➤ Offer to meet with parents along with student to explain seriousness.

➤ Caution student about danger of not returning home:
  – Cannot continue to stay with friend's family without host family getting into trouble
  – Will be reported as missing
  – Will be contacted by law enforcement
  – Will be in further danger if student leaves the area

➤ Determine further action in particular situation for safety of student.

➤ Warn of possible dangers if student leaves area:
  – Hunger
  – Incarceration
  – Disease
  – Child molesters
  – Dispair, shame
  – Prostitution

➤ Provide with number for runaway hotline.

➤ Recommend that student read book, *Runaway Me: A Survivor's Story* before making decision.

ADDITIONAL INFORMATION

Cutler, E. K. (1994). *Runaway me: A survivor's story.* **(List 12-28)**

National Runaway Switchboard: 1-800-621-4000.

Strouf, J. L. H. (1993). *The literature teacher's book of lists*, p. 291. **(List 12-3)**

5-96 COUNSELING STUDENTS WHO ARE HOMELESS

Reasons for Homelessness

- Poverty
- Escape from abusive home
- Escape from other abusive situation
- Unaccompanied immigrants

Counselor's Actions

- Enable registration in school, even without permanent address.
- Help find social services to meet needs.
- Treat with respect.
- Collaborate with social service agencies within community.
- Help develop skills for employment, positive relationships, and good parenting.
- Help adolescent feel worthwhile even though he or she made mistakes.
- Support efforts to return home.
- Support efforts to become legally employed and self-sufficient.

5-97 BIBLIOCOUNSELING

Bibliocounseling is the use of books to help students solve problems.

Reasons for Bibliocounseling

- Introduce a problem for discussion.
- Assist students to understand that others have had the same or a similar problem.
- Help students broaden interests and knowledge.
- Help students develop self-concept.
- Assist students to understand others' behavior and motivations.
- Invite students to appraise own attitudes and behavior.
- Assist students to relieve emotional pressure.
- Encourage students to consider alternatives for a solution.
- Help students plan a constructive course of action to solve a problem.

Selection of Books

- Well-written
- Easily read by the student
- Deals with the problem in a caring, sympathetic way

➤ Meets goal for bibliocounseling with the student.

Counselor's Actions

➤ Be familiar with books appropriate for the age level and reading level of students.

➤ Select particularly good books dealing with topics frequently brought to counselor.

➤ Select particularly good books for students to read even though they may be hesitant to approach the counselor about the topic.

➤ Have these books available to loan to students at the precise time when they need them.

➤ Do not recommend a book that you have not read.

➤ Motivate the student to read the book.

➤ Provide time for the student to read and reflect.

➤ Set a time to talk with the student about the book:
   – His or her feelings about the characters in the book
   – What he or she particularly liked or didn't like about the book
   – If there was anything in the book that he or she could relate to

➤ Continue counseling.

ADDITIONAL INFORMATION

Aiex, N. K. (1982). Bibliotherapy. [On-line] Available: http://www.indiana.edu/~eric_rec/eo/digests/d82.html

Donavin, D., (Ed.). (1982). *Best of the best for children.* New York, NY: Random House.

Dreyer, S. (1985). *The bookfinder: When kids need books.* Circle Pines, MN: American Guidance Service.

Gillespie, J. & Naden, C. (1990). *Best books for children preschool through grade 6.* (4th ed.). New Providence, NJ: R. R. Bowker.

Strouf, J. L. H. (1993). *The literature teacher's book of lists.* *(List 12-3)*

Thompson, C. L. & Rudolph, L. B. (1996). *Counseling children.* (4th ed.). *(List 12-3)*

5-98   SELF-CARE FOR THE CAREGIVER

Counselor's Actions

➤ Give yourself the same care as you give to others.

➤ Do not take school problems home with you.

➤ Eat well.

➤ Exercise.

➤ Relax.

➤ Follow suggestions to prevent burnout. *(List 2-45)*

➤ Take time to be with people you love.

➤ Receive love graciously.

➤ Recognize that your life is precious.

Section 6

MATERIALS TO USE WITH GRADES K–3

ANNOTATED LIST OF MATERIALS TO USE WITH STUDENTS

(PERMISSION OF FAIRFAX COUNTY PUBLIC SCHOOLS OF VIRGINIA)

Cost Guide: * ($1-$25) ** ($26-$55) *** ($56-$105) **** ($106-205) ***** ($206-$505) ****** ($506-$1,000)

6-1 CAREER EDUCATION

TITLE:	**Early Occupational Awareness Program**
MEDIA/COST:	Set & Guide Student Activity Set * Guide and Activities * 10 Activity Sets **
GRADES/LENGTH:	K–2/Student Set, 60 pages; Guide, 47 pages
AUTHORS:	Parramore & Hopke
PUBLISHER/ COPYRIGHT:	Garrett Park Press/1994

NOTES: Helps students expand awareness of jobs. Their attention is directed to focus on key questions about jobs such as: "What does this worker do?" "Where and when is the work done?" "What tools or equipment are used?" "What training or education is needed?"

TITLE:	**E-WOW (Explore the World of Work)**
MEDIA/COST:	Packet
GRADES/LENGTH:	1–3
PUBLISHER/ COPYRIGHT:	CFKR Career Materials, Inc./1988

NOTES: Career awareness and exploration learning activity with a game-like format. Helps students learn about and compare careers, and become aware of job activities and job titles.

TITLE:	**Working Moms Books**
MEDIA/COST:	Books
GRADES/LENGTH:	2–4
PUBLISHER/ COPYRIGHT:	Twenty-First Century Books/1991

NOTES: Series that introduces young readers to real women with careers and families. Careers represented: engineering, drafting, law, pediatrics, music teaching, park service, theater production, and veterinary medicine.

6-2 COMMUNICATION

TITLE:	**Be a Better Listener**
MEDIA/COST:	Video/Guide ***
GRADES/LENGTH:	2–4/15 minutes
PUBLISHER/ COPYRIGHT:	Sunburst Communications, Inc./ 1996

NOTES: Several strategies to develop good listening: (1) Focus on the speaker, (2) Sit up straight, (3) Concentrate on what is being said, (4) Don't daydream, and (5) Ask questions when you don't understand. Activity book includes a letter to parents in both English and Spanish, nine activity sheets, suggested activities, and a list of resources.

6-2 COMMUNICATION (*CONTINUED*)

TITLE: **Communication**

MEDIA/COST: Book

GRADES/LENGTH: K–5

AUTHOR: Aliki

PUBLISHER/
      COPYRIGHT: Scholastic/1993

NOTES: A series of cartoon strips showing different ways that people communicate (i.e., listening, speaking, reading, writing, and sign language). In both the front and back of this book, the alphabet (upper and lower case) is presented, including both the Sign Language and Braille alphabets. Emphasizes the importance of communication for getting information, solving problems, and resolving conflicts. Illustrations are very appealing.

6-3   CONFLICT RESOLUTION

TITLE: **Helping Kids Handle Conflict**

MEDIA/COST: Book/Worksheets *

GRADES/LENGTH: K–5/101 pages

PUBLISHER/
      COPYRIGHT: National Crime Prevention Council
                             Fulfillment Center/1995

NOTES: Good strategies with specific steps for managing conflict. Communication skills and mediation techniques are clearly described and examples are given. Activities are for levels K-1, 2-3, and 4-5. Informative letters to parents give tips on teaching children to respect diversity, deal with violence in the media, and recognize the danger of weapons.

TITLE: **How I Learned Not to Be Bullied**

MEDIA/COST: Video/Guide/Worksheets ***

GRADES/LENGTH: 2–3/14 minutes

PUBLISHER/
      COPYRIGHT: Sunburst Communications, Inc./
                             1996

NOTES: Hosted by two children who tell how they have dealt with and overcome bullying. They analyze the motives of bullies, give tips for handling bullies, and discuss how being bullied makes a person feel. Worksheets available in Spanish.

TITLE: **It's Not Fair**

MEDIA/COST: Video/Guide/Worksheets ***

GRADES/LENGTH: 2–4/14 minutes

PUBLISHER/
      COPYRIGHT: Sunburst Communications, Inc./
                             1994

NOTES: Helps students learn to resolve their own conflicts. This lively video presents three scenarios and a "You Solve It" section in which problems or disagreements are presented but not resolved. Students are encouraged to use their new skills and brainstorm ways to make the situations fair.

TITLE: **My Name Is Not Dummy**

MEDIA/COST: Book *

GRADES/LENGTH: K–4/30 pages

AUTHOR: Crary

PUBLISHER/
      COPYRIGHT: Parenting Press, Inc./1983

NOTES: Can be read straight through or used as an "alternative book" in which the student decides what the characters will do. Student participates in solving a social problem by choosing behaviors for the characters. Eduardo calls his friend Jenny "a dummy." The reader is asked, "What should Jenny do so Eduardo won't call her a dummy?" Possible solutions are listed and the reader continues the story with the chosen solution, learning the possible consequence of the chosen behavior.

TITLE: **No More Teasing**

MEDIA/COST: Video/Guide/Worksheets ***

GRADES/LENGTH: 2–4/14 minutes

PUBLISHER/
      COPYRIGHT: Sunburst Communications, Inc./
                             1994

NOTES: Scenarios and follow-up discussions help viewers understand the reasons people tease and the impact on the victims. Other topics include: (1) individual traits that attract teasing, (2) the importance of confidence and self-respect in dealing with teasing, and (3) three techniques that can be used to handle teasing. *Caution:* Viewers should be told that a physical confrontation may develop even though the suggested techniques are used, and sometimes the only way to stop teasing is to seek help from an adult.

6-3 CONFLICT RESOLUTION (CONTINUED)

TITLE: **Playground Push-Around**

MEDIA/COST: Book/Workbook *

GRADES/LENGTH: K–2/16 pages

AUTHORS: Boulden & Boulden

PUBLISHER/
  COPYRIGHT: Boulden Publishing/1994

NOTES: Feelings are acknowledged about being bullied and ways to handle bullies are presented. Explains why some children assume the role of bullies and what they can do to give up that role. Interest level of primary children is high with the format of this short activity book.

TITLE: **Push & Shove**

MEDIA/COST: Booklet/Worksheets *

GRADES/LENGTH: 2–5/32 pages

AUTHORS: Boulden & Boulden

PUBLISHER/
  COPYRIGHT: Boulden Publishing/1994

NOTES: Basic information about bullies, victims, and how each one behaves and why. The authors point out that girls are bullies as well as boys. A list of things to do when being picked on is given. Counselor talks to Butch "the bully" about other ways of getting attention, making new friends, and being a peace maker. Counselor also talks to Luis "the victim" about being a victim, and how a victim often walks and talks.

TITLE: **Student Workshop: Solving
                   Conflicts**

MEDIA/COST: Video/Program/Binder ****

GRADES/LENGTH: 2–4/26 minutes

PUBLISHER/
  COPYRIGHT: Sunburst Communications, Inc./
                   1994

NOTES: Introduces students to the conflict-resolution process. Objective is to teach the skills of conflict resolution step-by-step. Each skill is taught, demonstrated, and then applied as students do the activities that accompany the video.

TITLE: **Teaching Conflict Resolution
                   Through Children's Literature**

MEDIA/COST: Activity Book *

GRADES/LENGTH: K–2/112 pages

AUTHOR: Kreidler

PUBLISHER/
  COPYRIGHT: Scholastic Professional Books/1994

NOTES: Helps students become more effective and independent in handling conflicts. Follows the peaceable classroom model. Each chapter features the following: (1) introduction to the conflict-resolution concept, (2) introduction activities and extension activities, (3) book titles that reinforce and extend the topic, and (4) follow-up activities. There are five themes emphasized: (1) communication, (2) cooperation, (3) emotional expression, (4) appreciation for diversity, and (5) conflict resolution.

TITLE: **Ten Things to Do Instead of
                   Hitting**

MEDIA/COST: Video ****

GRADES/LENGTH: K–2/21 minutes

PUBLISHER/
  COPYRIGHT: Sunburst Communications, Inc./
                   1996

NOTES: Outstanding video. Students learn that angry feelings are normal. Ten strategies are given to use instead of hitting, stamping feet, yelling, pushing, breaking things, or saying unkind words. For each of the ten strategies, a scenario is presented. Topics are current and pertinent to children: a sibling playing with a favorite toy, bedtime, cutting in line, a parent unable to provide something promised, not being able to find a toy, and being blamed for something the child did not do.

TITLE: TITLE: **We Can Work It Out!
                           Conflict Resolution**

MEDIA/COST: Video/Audio Cassette/Guide ****

GRADES/LENGTH: K–2/Video, 11 minutes

PUBLISHER/
  COPYRIGHT: Sunburst Communications, Inc./
                   1994

NOTES: Realistic vignettes introduce young children to nonviolent techniques for resolving conflicts. Three sections: (1) Ask questions and listen, (2) Use your own words, and (3) Try different ideas. Each section is followed by lively music and a video sequence. Guide includes suggested activities.

6-4   DEATH AND GRIEF

TITLE: **Buford Listens**

MEDIA/COST: Book *

GRADES/LENGTH: PreK–3/30 pages

AUTHOR: Sneed

PUBLISHER/
   COPYRIGHT: Mar*Co Products, Inc./1992

NOTES: Mice characters explain in a simple way the feelings children may experience as they work through a significant loss like death. Buford, the mouse, is a good nonjudgmental listener, who helps children work through their sad feelings and gives them hope of feeling happy again.

TITLE: **Everett Anderson's Good-bye**

MEDIA/COST: Book

GRADES/LENGTH: K–4

AUTHOR: Clifton

PUBLISHER/
   COPYRIGHT: Holt, Rinehart, & Winston

NOTES: A story of a young African American boy who mourns the loss of his father.

TITLE: **Fall of Freddie the Leaf: A Story of Life for All Ages**

MEDIA/COST: Book */Video ***

GRADES/LENGTH: K–5

AUTHORS: Buscaglia & Slack

PUBLISHER/
   COPYRIGHT: Holt, Rinehart, & Winston/1982

NOTES: Beautiful book explaining cycles of life and death. Video presents the life of Freddie as a lovely metaphor.

TITLE: **Good-Bye Forever**

MEDIA/COST: Booklet/Workbook *

GRADES/LENGTH: K–2/16 pages

AUTHORS: Boulden & Boulden

PUBLISHER/
   COPYRIGHT: Boulden Publishing/1994

NOTES: Explains the meaning of death to the primary-age child. The rituals surrounding death are described and feelings are explored. It can be used for individual as well as small-group counseling. Reproducible workbook.

TITLE: **Sad Hug, Mad Hug, Happy Hug**

MEDIA/COST: Booklet

GRADES/LENGTH: PreK–3/19 pages

PUBLISHER/
   COPYRIGHT: Channing L. Bete Company/1994

NOTES: A warm, sensitive children's story about a teddy bear that feels extremely sad feelings when his grandma dies and he receives a sad hug from his mother. The author gives a simple, easy-to-understand explanation for young children about the funeral service and cemetery. At the end, the teddy bear shares that, although it took a while, the happy feelings did return as noted in his dad's happy hug.

TITLE: **Saying Good-Bye (Book)**

MEDIA/COST: Book/Workbook *

GRADES/LENGTH: 2–5

AUTHORS: Boulden & Boulden

PUBLISHER/
   COPYRIGHT: Boulden Publishing/1989

NOTES: Appropriate for all faiths and religions. Book awarded first prize by National Hospice. Available in Spanish.

TITLE: **Saying Good-Bye (Video)**

MEDIA/COST: Video/Guide/Activity Sheets ***

GRADES/LENGTH: 2–4/Video, 12 minutes

PUBLISHER/
   COPYRIGHT: Sunburst Communications, Inc./
   1993

NOTES: Introduces students to death and loss in a positive, reassuring way. Beginning with a low-key classroom scene in which the pet rabbit has died, children's common questions about death are answered. Students learn that it is normal to experience many different emotions when a pet or person dies.

6-4 DEATH AND GRIEF (CONTINUED)

TITLE:	**Someone Special Died: Student's Book** **Helping Children Cope With Death: Teacher's Book**
MEDIA/COST:	Book *
GRADES/LENGTH:	K–3/Student's Book, 32 pages Teacher's Book, 63 pages
AUTHOR:	Prestine
PUBLISHER/ COPYRIGHT:	Fearon Teacher Aids/1993

NOTES: Excellent book that helps children understand their feelings and identify and deal with the five stages of grief. Discussion questions are included on the last page of the book. In this beautifully illustrated book, concepts are presented in such a clear, warm, gentle, and simple manner that very young children find comfort and reassurance in reading the book with parents or teachers. Guide includes activities to help young children cope with feelings of grief, anger, fear, confusion, and loss. Annotated bibliography lists appropriate resources.

6-5 DECISION MAKING

TITLE:	**Choices, Choices: On the Playground**
MEDIA/COST:	Education Software (Macintosh or Apple)/Guide, Lesson Plans, Activity Sheets, and Picture Cards ***
GRADES/LENGTH:	K–4/15 to 20 minutes per session
AUTHORS:	Snyder & Dockterman
PUBLISHER/ COPYRIGHT:	Tom Snyder Productions/1994

NOTES: Offers students the opportunity to make choices and face the consequences of those choices. Students select goals and behaviors and then rate themselves (numerically) on whether the goals were met.

TITLE:	**Deciding: From Dilemmas to Decisions** (*Making Choices—Growing Stronger* Series)
MEDIA/COST:	Guidance Units *
GRADES/LENGTH:	2–3/30 pages
AUTHOR:	Falk
PUBLISHER/ COPYRIGHT:	Elizabeth Falk, M.A., LPC/1992

NOTES: These materials teach students about making decisions and feeling confident when making decisions. Handouts, poems, mobiles, and role plays—presented with humor—appeal to students and they become involved. Appropriate with large groups, small groups, or individuals.

TITLE:	**Free the Horses**
MEDIA/COST:	Kit: Puppets/Video *****
GRADES/LENGTH:	1–3
PUBLISHER/ COPYRIGHT:	Active Parenting/1991

NOTES: Kit—with posters, activity sheets, stickers, and a puppet—presents a medieval adventure that assists children in learning about belonging, contributing, cooperating, being responsible, and having courage.

TITLE:	**I Can Make Good Choices**
MEDIA/COST:	Video/Guide/Worksheets ***
GRADES/LENGTH:	2–4/Video, 17 minutes
PUBLISHER/ COPYRIGHT:	Sunburst Communications, Inc./1995

NOTES: Three easy steps for students to follow when faced with difficult decisions. Through several short scenarios, students are encouraged to: (1) get all the information needed before making a decision, (2) look at all the options, and (3) consider how they will feel in the future about the decision. Video is stopped after each scenario for students to discuss the process and reach a decision. An easy-to-follow guide and eight reproducible worksheets accompany this video. Recommended by *Booklist* and *School Library Journal*.

6-5 DECISION MAKING (CONTINUED)

TITLE: **My Friend Sneezy**

MEDIA/COST: Book

GRADES/LENGTH: K–3/42 pages

AUTHOR: Walker

PUBLISHER/
COPYRIGHT: Mar*Co Products, Inc./1990

NOTES: Sneezy, a mouse, is confronted with four situations that require a choice. Girls and boys are asked to come to Sneezy's rescue when he makes poor choices. A delightful way that invites children to reflect on past experiences while learning and using decision-making skills. Situations involve friendship, stealing, lying, and good grooming.

TITLE: **Responsible Rascal**

MEDIA/COST: Book *

GRADES/LENGTH: K–1/32 pages

AUTHOR: Schwartz

PUBLISHER/
COPYRIGHT: The Learning Works, Inc./1991

NOTES: Rascal does not follow through with his responsibilities at home or at school. His dad tells him to clean out the hamster cage. Before he finishes, he leaves to go play with a friend. When Rascal gets back, the hamster has gotten out of the cage. He is very upset but eventually finds his hamster. This teaches him a lesson to be more responsible. Great follow-up activities.

TITLE: **Tonia the Tree**

MEDIA/COST: Kit: Video/Book/Guide/Complete Kit ***/ Story Book */ Guide *

GRADES/LENGTH: 1–4/Video, 12 minutes; Book, 33 pages

AUTHOR: Stryker

PUBLISHER/
COPYRIGHT: Marsh Media/1988

NOTES: Deals with the concept of change. When Tonia stops growing, changes need to be made so that she can continue to grow. This story addresses change as an integral part of life. In this story, change is presented as a normal, inescapable source of adventure.

TITLE: **Too Smart for Trouble**

MEDIA/COST: Book *

GRADES/LENGTH: K–3/97 pages

AUTHOR: Scott

PUBLISHER/
COPYRIGHT: Human Resource Development Press, Inc./1990

NOTES: A read-along guide to teach students how to say "No" to trouble, yet still be liked by their friends. Can be read along with the counselor, parent, or teacher. Skills are taught partially through the eyes of a dog named Nicholas.

TITLE: **You Can Choose: Saying No (to Smoking)**

MEDIA/COST: Video/Guide ***

GRADES/LENGTH: 2–4/28 minutes

PUBLISHER/
COPYRIGHT: Live Wire Video Publishers/1991

NOTES: An imaginative skit in which one character makes a tough choice with the help of an elementary teacher. Missie Mouse has to choose whether to say no to a friend or do something she knows is wrong.

6-6 DISABILITIES

TITLE: **Alex Is My Friend**

MEDIA/COST: Book

GRADES/LENGTH: K–2

AUTHOR: Russo

PUBLISHER/
COPYRIGHT: Greenwillow Books/1992

NOTES: A boy tells about how he met his friend, Alex. When he turns five and Alex is six he notices that Alex is shorter than he is. Alex has a physical problem and will always be small. The boy sees his friend go through back surgery and recovery. He realizes that Alex will never run fast like he can, but they can still be friends. They can find many fun activities to do together. A great book for children to understand disabilities.

6-7   DIVORCE

TITLE:	**Dinosaurs Divorce: A Guide for Changing Families**
MEDIA/COST:	Book *
GRADES/LENGTH:	K–3/32 pages
AUTHORS:	Brown & Brown
DISTRIBUTOR/ COPYRIGHT:	Paperbacks for Educators/1986

NOTES: A charming book for young children that addresses their feelings and thoughts related to the divorce of their parents. Childhood reactions are shown in a way that makes feelings and reactions to divorce acceptable and helps children understand their feelings and responses.

TITLE:	**Divorce Happens**
MEDIA/COST:	Booklet/Workbook *
GRADES/LENGTH:	K–2/16 pages
AUTHORS:	Boulden & Boulden
PUBLISHER/ COPYRIGHT:	Boulden Publishing/1994

NOTES: An excellent and easy-to-read activity book that includes many important concepts about divorce. "Buddy" helps students understand their feelings and explains causes of divorce and changes to expect. Students learn that their parents will always be their parents, divorce is an adult decision, it is not their fault, and they are not alone. A positive and encouraging approach to a difficult change in a child's life. Reproducible workbook.

TITLE:	**Let's Talk: Early Separation and Divorce Activity Book**
MEDIA/COST:	Activity Book/Workbook *
GRADES/LENGTH:	K–3/31 pages
AUTHORS:	Boulden & Boulden
PUBLISHER/ COPYRIGHT:	Boulden Publishing/1991

NOTES: Activities in this book motivate children to draw, discuss, and write their feelings about the divorce of their parents. Can be used with individuals or with groups. Reproducible workbook.

TITLE:	**When Mom and Dad Separate: Children Can Learn to Cope With Grief From Divorce (Drawing Out Feelings Series)**
MEDIA/COST:	Book *
GRADES/LENGTH:	K–3/32 pages
AUTHOR:	Heegaard
PUBLISHER/ COPYRIGHT:	Woodland Press/1991

NOTES: Teaches children the concepts about divorce and helps them recognize and express feelings of grief as a result of family change. Encourages open communication and allows adults to recognize any unhealthy misconceptions children may have. Author emphasizes art as a way for students to express their ideas and feelings that they may otherwise be unable to express.

TITLE:	**When Your Mom and Dad Get Divorced**
MEDIA/COST:	Video/Guide/Worksheets ***
GRADES/LENGTH:	2–4/Video, 20 minutes
PUBLISHER/ COPYRIGHT:	Sunburst Communications, Inc./ 1992

NOTES: Excellent program to help children understand that divorce is not the end of their world, but a *change* in their world. Divorce is a problem between grown-ups; it is never the children's fault. Michelle's parents have just gone through a divorce that has caused many changes in her life, including a new home and a new school. On her first day at the new school, Michelle develops a stomachache. Michelle and her teacher discuss divorce and the teacher invites Michelle to take part in a discussion group with other kids from divorced families.

6-8   EMOTIONS

TITLE: **All Feelings Are OK**
MEDIA/COST: Activity Book/Materials
GRADES/LENGTH: K–3 or 4
AUTHOR: Shapiro
PUBLISHER/
   COPYRIGHT: Center for Applied Psychology, Inc.

NOTES: A consumable workbook to help students identify and discuss a variety of feelings. Contains 100 comical cartoons depicting various situations students may encounter in and out of school. One character in each cartoon is faceless. Students may draw in the face or use the face stamps included to express their feelings. On the page opposite the cartoon are two suggestions. The first suggestion is for the student to express feelings about the situation illustrated in the cartoon. The follow-up suggestion helps the student discuss the feeling and look at the events that led to the feeling. Four different feeling face stamps, one stamp pad, a small box of crayons, and a card showing 34 alternate feeling faces are included.

TITLE: **Bright Beginnings**
MEDIA/COST: Kit *****
GRADES/LENGTH: K–1
PUBLISHER/
   COPYRIGHT: Timberline Press, Inc./1990

NOTES: Kit includes stories, poems, songs, and puppets to help students build and maintain a positive self-image. It is a skill-based five-week program that teaches children to control their feelings, cope with loss, and overcome unnecessary fears. Topics include feeling capable, feeling special, and controlling anger, as well as other topics.

TITLE: **Dealing With Feelings Series**
                    I'm Frustrated!
                    I'm Mad!
                    I'm Proud!
MEDIA/COST: Books *
GRADES/LENGTH: K–4/32 pages each
AUTHOR: Crary
PUBLISHER/
   COPYRIGHT: Parenting Press, Inc./1992

NOTES: *I'm Frustrated:* Helps children accept their feelings and decide how to respond. Shows a parent and child discussing feelings openly. Offers specific options for children and verbal, physical, and creative ways to express feelings. Good resource for the parenting library to help parents who wish to change the way they respond to their children's feelings.

I'm Mad: Helps students accept and handle their anger. The author recommends that an adult and child read the book together in order to help the child verbalize his or her angry feelings and choose alternative ways to handle these strong emotions.

I'm Proud: Promotes appropriate self-esteem in children by providing choices children make when trying to achieve success, and discussing these choices.

TITLE: **Everyone Gets Scared Sometimes**
MEDIA/COST: Video/Audio Cassettes ***
GRADES/LENGTH: K–2/Video, 15 minutes
PUBLISHER/
   COPYRIGHT: Sunburst Communications, Inc./
                    1993

NOTES: Helps children understand that being afraid is natural and is experienced by everyone. Three short vignettes help children work through their fears by understanding them and learning strategies to overcome them. Discussion questions, role plays, activities, and worksheets are included to reinforce the concepts presented in the video.

6-8 EMOTIONS (*CONTINUED*)

TITLE: **Feelings: Glad, Mad, Sad**

MEDIA/COST: Video/Guide/Activity Sheets ***

GRADES/LENGTH: 2–4/Video, 18 minutes

PUBLISHER/
   COPYRIGHT: Sunburst Communications, Inc./
                  1993

NOTES: Excellent video using a lively game-show format. Students become active participants helping the video teams compete. There are three rounds of play: (1) Describe how you can tell how someone feels. Several feelings are acted out. Team members identify the feelings. (2) "Stop and Think Action Round": Teams act out conflictual situations. Points are awarded to the team that completes the role play with a positive resolution to the problem. (3) Different conflict situations: Teams generate alternative activities to work out feelings. Video stresses that students need to take responsibility for their behavior.

TITLE: **I Get So Mad!**

MEDIA/COST: Video/Audio Cassettes/Guide/
                  Worksheets ***

GRADES/LENGTH: K–2/Video, 13 minutes

PUBLISHER/
   COPYRIGHT: Sunburst Communications, Inc./
                  1993

NOTES: Excellent video that helps students recognize and accept their own feelings, especially their angry feelings. A storyteller introduces each video segment. She reappears after each segment, summarizes the story, and asks follow-up discussion questions. *Part I* helps students learn that "talking about angry feelings can help to make them feel better." *Part II* helps students think about and verbalize their angry feelings. They can then more easily choose nonaggressive or nondestructive behavior. *Part III* teaches students several techniques for redirecting the "angry" energy into positive alternative activities. Students learn "fun" activities to work out their angry feelings—screaming into pillow, marching, etc. Available in Spanish.

TITLE: **Mad, Sad, Glad Game**

MEDIA/COST: Board Game *

GRADES/LENGTH: K–3 (may be used with older children)

PUBLISHER/
   COPYRIGHT: Social Studies Service/1990

NOTES: Helps students identify and talk about their own feelings and develop empathy for the feelings of others while playing a fun-filled board game.

TITLE: **PALS: Playing and Learning
                  Successfully**

MEDIA/COST: Kit: Puppets/Games/Songs/
                  Binder Kit *****

GRADES/LENGTH: K–3/Kit for 20 students

PUBLISHER: PALS

NOTES: Lesson plans in binder with other media to teach 20 half-hour lessons to 20 students. Lessons include anger control, good behavior, preventing conflicts, and preventing student disruption in class.

TITLE: **When Someone Has a Very
                  Serious Illness: Children Can
                  Learn to Cope With Loss and
                  Change
                  (Drawing Out Feelings Series)**

MEDIA/COST: Book *

GRADES/LENGTH: K–3/36 pages

AUTHOR: Heegaard

PUBLISHER/
   COPYRIGHT: Woodland Press/1991

NOTES: Children learn basic concepts of serious illness and how to express related feelings through art. Helps children correct misconceptions, resolve conflicts, and increase self-esteem as well as develop coping skills.

6-9 FAMILY

TITLE: **All Together: Blended Family
                    Activity Book**
MEDIA/COST: Booklet *
GRADES/LENGTH: 1–4/31 pages
AUTHORS: Boulden & Boulden
PUBLISHER/
    COPYRIGHT: Boulden Publishing/1991

NOTES: Deals with blended families through parent's remarriage. Feelings of children in blended families are addressed and dealt with in a positive manner. Disposable booklet for students to record their own feelings about specific situations.

TITLE: **We're a Family**
MEDIA/COST: Video/Guide/Worksheets ***
GRADES/LENGTH: 2–4/Video, 15 minutes
PUBLISHER/
    COPYRIGHT: Sunburst Communications, Inc./
                    1992

NOTES: Four parts with each part depicting a different family constellation. Shows a child in the family coping in a constructive way with his or her feelings about the way his or her family is different from others, or the way the family has changed. Provides a nice introduction to the study of families or changing families.

6-10 FRIENDSHIPS

TITLE: **Best Friends**
MEDIA/COST: Book *
GRADES/LENGTH: PreK–1/25 pages
AUTHOR: Davis
DISTRIBUTOR/
    COPYRIGHT: Paperbacks for Educators/1992

NOTES: A story about friendship that uses the characters from Sesame Street to help children explore their feelings about being left out and being a part of a group.

TITLE: **Kid's Guide to Getting Along
                    With Your Classmates**
MEDIA/COST: Video ****
GRADES/LENGTH: K–3/4 parts; each part, 11 minutes
PUBLISHER/
    COPYRIGHT: Learning Tree Publishing, Inc./1992

NOTES: Excellent four-part video in cartoon style that helps students learn social skills to get along with classmates. *Part I* discusses what is meant by being "cool" and getting to know other individuals beneath the external surface. *Part II* explains how cooperation and compromise are helpful strategies to work out disagreements. *Part III* teaches students how to handle teasing and name-calling. *Part IV* describes strategies students can use to settle differences on their own.

TITLE: **My Friends and Me**
MEDIA/COST: Video ***
GRADES/LENGTH: 2–4/15 minutes
PUBLISHER/
    COPYRIGHT: Sunburst Communications, Inc./
                    1992

NOTES: Helps students explore issues and feelings concerning friendship, and develop skills for building and maintaining rewarding friendships. Key concepts include: (1) Taking the first step in making a friend can have positive results, (2) There is more than one style of friendship, (3) It's important to treat friends like you would want to be treated, and (4) A friend is someone who really cares.

6-12   MULTICULTURAL

TITLE: **The Land of Many Colors**
MEDIA/COST: Book
GRADES/LENGTH: K–2/27 pages
AUTHOR: Klamath County YMCA Family
                  Preschool
PUBLISHER/
   COPYRIGHT: Scholastic/1993

NOTES: Respect for differences is the theme of this book. People of different color get into a fight and are reminded that they can still get along despite differences. Counselor should be aware that the term "war" is on page 10 and a statement about animals being hurt is on page 12.

6-13   PROBLEM SOLVING

TITLE: **Do I Have to Go to School Today?**
MEDIA/COST: Booklet *
GRADES/LENGTH: K–3/53 pages
AUTHOR: Shles
PUBLISHER/
   COPYRIGHT: Jalmar Press/1989

NOTES: Students like this story and the illustrations, although it is entirely in black and white. A boy says he is afraid to go to school because he feels lost and confused. He does not feel that he can succeed, even in PE or music, and the lunchroom and food are not good. At the end, he thinks of positive things about school, his teacher, and how she accepts him just as he is. He agrees to go to school.

TITLE: **OOPS! I Messed Up!**
MEDIA/COST: Video/Guide ***
GRADES/LENGTH: 2–4/22 minutes
PUBLISHER/
   COPYRIGHT: Sunburst Communications, Inc./
                  1995

NOTES: Addresses making mistakes and how to overcome them. Professor Blunder, a bumbling inventor, is trying to develop a bubble gum machine. He has had a series of failures but does not become discouraged because he believes every mistake is just one more step on the road to success. He says that it's normal to feel mad and frustrated but it's important to accept that you made a mistake, look at what went wrong, figure out how to fix it, and try again. He introduces three children who go through this process and overcome their mistakes.

TITLE: **Problem Solving Series**
                  I Can't Wait
                  I Want It
                  I Want to Play
                  I'm Lost
                  Mommy, Don't Go
MEDIA/COST: Books *
GRADES/LENGTH: K–3/30 pages each
AUTHOR: Crary
PUBLISHER/
   COPYRIGHT: Parenting Press, Inc./1982

NOTES: These books help children in three ways: (1) show children how to think about a problem *before* they act, (2) offer children several different ways to handle each situation, and (3) show children how one person's behavior affects others. Excellent resources to help young children make decisions and relate feelings and actions.

I'm Lost: A character in the story is in a wheelchair which adds the dimension of disability awareness to the story.

6-13 PROBLEM SOLVING *(CONTINUED)*

TITLE:	**Stressbusters**
MEDIA/COST:	Video/Guide/Worksheets ***
GRADES/LENGTH:	2–4/15 minutes
PUBLISHER/ COPYRIGHT:	Sunburst Communications, Inc./ 1994

NOTES: Hosted and enacted by elementary children, this video has three parts with very up-beat rap music. The situations and comments by the children define stress and give positive ways in which to deal with it. The guide and worksheets provide a step-by-step program in recognizing stress and dealing with it. The plan includes three suggestions: (1) Talk about the stress with someone you trust, (2) Engage in a physical activity to release the stress, and (3) Make a list of stressful things, then make a plan.

TITLE:	**What Do You Think?**
MEDIA/COST:	Book
GRADES/LENGTH:	1–3/32 pages
AUTHORS:	Wassermann & Wassermann
PUBLISHER/ COPYRIGHT:	Walker Publishing Company, Inc./ 1990

NOTES: Several short stories, each involving a different problem. Children, representing various cultures, work together to solve each problem; however, the reader is brought into the stories by being asked to solve the problem and to think of the positive and negative consequences of each possible solution.

TITLE:	**What Might Happen Next?**
MEDIA:	Video/Guide/Audio Cassette ***
GRADES/LENGTH:	K–2/Video/15 minutes
PUBLISHER/ COPYRIGHT:	Sunburst Communications, Inc./ 1996

NOTES: Three short vignettes featuring children who use the "stop and think" strategy to make decisions regarding their actions. The vignettes are realistic situations that involve safety, friendship, and the effects of angry feelings. Children are taught cause and effect and the importance of thinking before they act.

6-14 RESPECT

TITLE:	**(DUSO I and DUSO II) Developing Understanding of Self and Others**
MEDIA/COST:	Kits
GRADES/LENGTH:	K–4
AUTHOR:	Dinkmeyer
PUBLISHER/ COPYRIGHT:	American Guidance Service, Inc. (AGS)/1983

NOTES: *DUSO I:* A diverse kit that helps children understand themselves and others. Includes excellent stories and topics that generate worthwhile discussion by students. Provides models and a rationale for socially acceptable behavior.

DUSO II: A comprehensive, well-structured program dealing with understanding self and others, getting along with others, and effective decision making. Forty-two goals are presented and each goal has a variety of activities including communication skills, role playing, and career awareness. Activities relate to curriculum areas such as art, language arts, math, health, music, physical education, science, and social studies.

6-14 RESPECT (*CONTINUED*)

TITLE:	**No Fair!**
MEDIA/COST:	Video ***
GRADES/LENGTH:	K–2/12 minutes
PUBLISHER/ COPYRIGHT:	Sunburst Communications, Inc./ 1995

NOTES: Three short stories about children who believe they are being treated unfairly. Students learn that unfair situations can be corrected and that fairness doesn't mean that an individual always gets his or her own way. Students also realize that rules help make situations fair for everyone.

TITLE:	**Not Better—Not Worse—Just Different**
MEDIA/COST:	Book *
GRADES/LENGTH:	K–4/118 pages
AUTHOR:	Scott
PUBLISHER/ COPYRIGHT:	Human Resource Development Press/1992

NOTES: Narrated by Nicholas, a cocker spaniel, this book is about being kind to each other. Animal friends teach children how to accept and respect all types of differences. Also deals with what to do when others tease you. A great discussion starter or for certain students to read independently.

TITLE:	**Peacemaking Skills for Little Kids**
MEDIA/COST:	Kit: Guide/Puppet/Audio Cassette Kit ***
GRADES/LENGTH:	K–2
PUBLISHER/ COPYRIGHT:	Grace Contrino Abrams Peace Foundation/1988

NOTES: Music activities teach lessons on friendship, cooperation, feelings, learning, etc. The handbook suggests reading materials that can be checked out from school libraries. Art activities are also suggested.

TITLE:	**Respect Yourself and Others, Too**
MEDIA:	Video/Guide/Worksheets ***
GRADES/LENGTH:	2–4/17 minutes
PUBLISHER/ COPYRIGHT:	Sunburst Communications, Inc./ 1996

NOTES: Allows children an opportunity to explore the concepts and applications of respect and how it applies to their own lives. Four parts: (1) Respect other people's things, (2) Respect the other person's way, (3) Respect other people's feelings, and (4) Respect other people's dreams.

TITLE:	**Second Step: A Violence Prevention Curriculum Grades Preschool-Kindergarten**
MEDIA/COST:	Kit: Guide/2 Puppets/Tape *****
GRADES/LENGTH:	PreK–K/28 lessons
AUTHOR:	Beland
PUBLISHER/ COPYRIGHT:	Committee for Children/1992

NOTES: Excellent series to teach: (1) empathy, (2) impulse control, and (3) anger management. A multisensory approach to teach young children how to identify problems and feelings, reduce their anger, solve problems, and get along with others. In addition, the 28 lessons build self-esteem and reduce impulsive and aggressive behavior in young children. Excellent lessons for teaching conflict resolution, problem solving, and decision making.

TITLE:	**Second Step: Grades 1–3**
MEDIA/COST:	Kit: Photos/Video/Binder *****
GRADES/LENGTH:	1–3/49 lessons
AUTHOR:	Beland
PUBLISHER/ COPYRIGHT:	Committee for Children/1988

NOTES: A well-organized violence-prevention series that helps students respect others and reduce their impulsive-aggressive behavior. Each of the 49 lessons consists of a large photograph of students from diverse populations. On the back of the big-book size photograph are objectives for the lesson, notes for the counselor, story with discussion, suggested role plays, and activities. A short video is included to review concepts learned at the end of each of the three units. Photos are large enough for classroom guidance lessons and are appropriate for individual or small-group sessions.

TITLE:	**Tator Tales**
MEDIA/COST:	Booklet *
GRADES/LENGTH:	K–3
PUBLISHER/ COPYRIGHT:	Mar*Co Products, Inc./1988

NOTES: Teaches younger children how to identify peer pressure, how to handle peer pressure, and how to promote positive peer pressure.

6-14 RESPECT (CONTINUED)

TITLE: **Time for Horatio**

MEDIA/COST: Kit: Video/Guide/Book/Kit, ***

GRADES/LENGTH: K–3/Video, 19 minutes; Book, 48
                    pages

AUTHOR: Paine

PUBLISHER/
    COPYRIGHT: Marsh Media/1990

NOTES: Charming book about a child and his kitten who decide it is time to turn away from violence and stand up for peace with respect for all living things. This story points out the need for harmony to achieve happiness and contentment. Guide includes numerous activities. The book can be used alone and may be purchased separately.

TITLE: **What's Respect?**

MEDIA/COST: Video/Guide/Audio Cassette ***

GRADES/LENGTH: K–2/15 minutes

PUBLISHER/
    COPYRIGHT: Sunburst Communications, Inc./
                    1995

NOTES: Characters analyze each of the five short, realistic situations and learn why respect is important. Respect for rules, personal property, individual differences, ideas, and the environment is explored. Activity book contains discussion questions and follow-up activities.

6-16   SAFETY

TITLE: **Inside/Out: A Whole-Person
                    Educational Approach to Health
                    and Safety**

MEDIA/COST: Video/Activities/Free

GRADES/LENGTH: K–6/Video, 22 minutes

AUTHOR: State Farm Insurance Companies

PUBLISHER/
    COPYRIGHT: State Farm Insurance Companies/
                    1993

NOTES: Units address health, safety, self-esteem, and good habits. Children learn about hazards and dangers, and develop knowledge for crisis situations. Twenty-one reproducible masters accompany the unit activities. Excellent introduction to a safety program. Free upon request on school letterhead stationery.

TITLE: **My Body Belongs to Me**

MEDIA/COST: Video/Guide/Storybook ***

GRADES/LENGTH: K–1/Video, 24 minutes

AUTHOR: Glickman

PUBLISHER/
    COPYRIGHT: Sunburst Communications, Inc./
                    (book) 1989, (video) 1992

NOTES: Video has two parts: (1) A conversation between a puppet and a male counselor with a live audience of children. They introduce the concept of privacy and explain that the parts of the body covered with a bathing suit are considered private. (2) A different puppet plays school with several children from the audience to review the previously taught lessons on good touch and bad touch. Follow-up questions and activities are provided.

Note: There are no African American children as participants in the audience.

6-17   SELF-DISCIPLINE

TITLE: **Playing the Game**

MEDIA/COST: Book *

GRADES/LENGTH: K–2

AUTHORS: Petty & Firmin

PUBLISHER/
    COPYRIGHT: Barron's Educational Series, Inc./
                    1991

NOTES: Joel is a poor sport because he doesn't play by the rules and gets along poorly with others. He often feels that others are not being fair to him and doesn't like having so many rules in games until it comes to his favorite game of soccer. He is often pointing out the rules and calling "Foul." He understands why there are rules in soccer and, with the help of the coach, he realizes the importance of rules for all games. Good suggestions in the back of the book for follow-up activities.

6-18 SELF-ESTEEM

TITLE: **Belief in Self: You Can If You Think You Can**

MEDIA/COST: Kit/Video/Audio Cassette ***

GRADES/LENGTH: K–3/4 separate segments

PUBLISHER/
COPYRIGHT: American Guidance Service, Inc. (AGS)/1992

NOTES: Full animation, catchy music, bright colors, and excellent puppetry make this a very entertaining and helpful video to boost student self-esteem. Many varied activities stress the important lessons of belief in self and working to make that belief come true. Each of four segments can be shown separately or all used as a unit.

TITLE: **Building Self-Esteem With Koala-Roo Can-Do**

MEDIA/COST: Workbook *

GRADES/LENGTH: K–3/228 pages

AUTHOR: Fendel

PUBLISHER/
COPYRIGHT: Good Year Books/1989

NOTES: Lessons and activities, involving an invented animal, Koala-Roo Can-Do, help students develop self-esteem. Many activities are interrelated and are cross-referenced within the text. All activities present the message: "You can do it if you try." Each lesson is complete or can be taught with reading, math, and language arts.

TITLE: **Feeling Good About Me**

MEDIA/COST: Video/Guide ***

GRADES/LENGTH: 2–4/16 minutes

PUBLISHER/
COPYRIGHT: Sunburst Communications, Inc./1991

NOTES: Complements the guidance curriculum on self-esteem. Stresses that students can improve their self-image by not allowing others to give them negative messages. The video uses real-life dramatization. Recommended by Quest International in the Skills for Growing Program.

TITLE: **Happy to Be Me**

MEDIA/COST: Booklet/Workbook *

GRADES/LENGTH: K–2/16 pages

AUTHORS: Boulden & Boulden

PUBLISHER/
COPYRIGHT: Boulden Publishing/1994

NOTES: Basic alternatives for students to consider. The main character, Luis, thinks everything is his fault and thinks people are saying only mean things about him. Authors show Luis how to look at the positive side and give suggestions about how to look for people who will be good friends. Reproducible workbook master.

TITLE: **A Kid's Guide to a Positive Attitude**

MEDIA/COST: Video/Guide

GRADES/LENGTH: 2–4/20 minutes

PUBLISHER/
COPYRIGHT: Learning Tree Publishing, Inc./1990

NOTES: Presents positive thinking and how positive thinking impacts on one's self-esteem. Video ends with questions for discussion.

TITLE: **Kylie's Song**

MEDIA/COST: Kit: Video/Book/Guide/Kit, ***

GRADES/LENGTH: 1–3/Video, 12 minutes; Book, 32 pages

AUTHOR: Sheehan

PUBLISHER/
COPYRIGHT: Marsh Media/1988

NOTES: A delightful story of a baby koala that loves to sing and continues to work at it while constantly being told that koalas aren't supposed to sing. This video and beautifully illustrated book are excellent materials to help children cherish the qualities that make them unique. The book alone can be very effective.

6-18 SELF-ESTEEM (CONTINUED)

TITLE:	**No One Quite Like Me . . . Or You**
MEDIA/COST:	Video ***
GRADES/LENGTH:	2–4/15 minutes
PUBLISHER/ COPYRIGHT:	Sunburst Communications, Inc./ 1992

NOTES: Focuses on individual uniqueness and emphasizes that differences are not only normal, but valuable. Scenarios help students explore what it means to be unique and how special qualities define who they are.

TITLE:	**Nobody Is PERFICK**
MEDIA/COST:	Book *
GRADES/LENGTH:	1–5/128 pages
AUTHOR:	Waber
PUBLISHER/ COPYRIGHT:	Houghton Mifflin Books/1971

NOTES: Eight "snippets" depicting life's trials and tribulations that are humorous and enjoyable. Sections deal with trust, gossip, teasing, and perfectionism to illustrate a point or to elicit discussion. The incorrect spelling of the word "perfect" (perfick) is humorous and illustrates a point.

TITLE:	**Self-Esteem Curriculum Module**
MEDIA/COST:	Kit: 6 Videos/Guide/ Worksheets ******
	VIDEOS IN THE KIT (Videos can be purchased separately) (1) *All About Anger* (2) *Feeling Good About Me* (3) *Getting Better at Getting Along* (4) *Home Alone: You in Charge* (5) *My Friends and Me* (6) *No One Quite Like Me*
GRADES/LENGTH:	2–4
PUBLISHER/ COPYRIGHT:	Sunburst Communications, Inc./ 1992

NOTES: Teaches students the skills and concepts needed to build and maintain their self-esteem. The videos and activities promote self-discovery and awareness that self-esteem can be developed by each person.

TITLE:	**Wonderful Me!**
MEDIA:	Video/Guide/Audio Cassettes/Activity Sheets ***
GRADES/LENGTH:	K–2/Video, 16 minutes
PUBLISHER/ COPYRIGHT:	Sunburst Communications, Inc./ 1993

NOTES: Three realistic vignettes help children develop a positive sense-of-self when facing new and challenging situations. Each segment is followed by questions that generate excellent discussions on ways to develop and maintain positive self-esteem.

6-18 SELF-ESTEEM *(CONTINUED)*

TITLE: **You Can Choose Series**
Appreciating Yourself
Asking for Help

MEDIA: Video/Guide/ ***

GRADES/LENGTH: K–3/28 minutes

PUBLISHER/
COPYRIGHT: Social Studies School Service/1992

NOTES: A ten-part video series designed to help children develop a range of important life skills and a healthy self-esteem.

Appreciating Yourself: Helps students learn to value others' as well as their own positive qualities. A discussion follows a skit that encourages students to discuss self-esteem and helps the character, Tuggy, make the right decision. The skit resumes with the other characters teaching Tuggy that they value him for his inner qualities, and not just what he has accomplished.

Asking for Help: Focuses on a student who must decide whether to continue hiding his reading deficiency or ask for help in overcoming it. Presented in a lively, entertaining format. Questions and discussions regarding feelings, being perfect, and decision making.

6-19 SOCIAL DEVELOPMENT

TITLE: **Communicate Junior**

MEDIA/COST: Game **

GRADES/LENGTH: 1–3

AUTHORS: Mayo, Gajewski, Hirn, & Kafka

PUBLISHER/
COPYRIGHT: Thinking Publications (Childswork/ Childsplay)/1991

NOTES: A fun board game that reinforces the appropriate use of basic social skills: rules, manners, listening, eye contact, conversations (starting, maintaining, and ending), sharing, and taking turns. Before playing the game, the counselor should teach students the targeted social skill(s).

TITLE: **Ready-to-Use Social Skills Lessons & Activities for Grades PreK-K**

MEDIA/COST: Activity Book *

GRADES/LENGTH: PreK–K/166 pages

AUTHOR: Begun (Editor)

PUBLISHER/
COPYRIGHT: Center for Applied Research in Education/1995

NOTES: One of four books in a "Social Skills Activities" series. Practical and helps counselor teach social skills lessons. Over 50 detailed lessons for developing specific social skills accompanied by reproducible activity sheets. Written for and by teachers. The last pages to parents *cannot* be reproduced.

TITLE: **Skillstreaming in Early Childhood**

MEDIA/COST: Book/Program Forms/Book, *; Forms, *

GRADES/LENGTH: PreK–K/Book, 200 pages; Forms, 76 pages

AUTHORS: McGinnis & Goldstein

PUBLISHER/
COPYRIGHT: Research Press Co., Inc./1990

NOTES: A step-by-step program to teach 40 specific social skills to young children. Provides ways to identify and evaluate children for skill streaming as well as how to begin, plan, and implement such a program. Excellent resource for helping young children learn appropriate ways to interact with others.

6-19 SOCIAL DEVELOPMENT *(CONTINUED)*

TITLE: **Social Skills Activities for Special Children**

MEDIA/COST: Activity Book **

GRADES/LENGTH: K–4/405 pages

AUTHOR: Mannix

PUBLISHER/
  COPYRIGHT: Center For Applied Research In Education/1993

NOTES: Outstanding collection of 142 lessons designed to help elementary children learn acceptable social behavior skills. Each lesson contains specific discussion questions and activity sheets. *Section I* teaches how to interact with teachers and other adults within the school, and classroom rules and responsibilities. Each rule is taught in an individual lesson. *Section II* provides 30 lessons on friendships. *Section III* helps students learn proper etiquette for various social situations.

TITLE: **Taking Part: Introducing Social Skills to Children**

MEDIA/COST: Kit: Puppets/Guide ****

GRADES/LENGTH: K–3/163 pages

PUBLISHER/
  COPYRIGHT: American Guidance Service, Inc. (AGS)/1992

NOTES: Puppets teach children verbal, aural, and visual skills necessary to fully participate in classroom and social activities. Teaches appropriate behavioral patterns through demonstration and discussion. Examples of social skills are featured with practice segments for children to reinforce newly-learned behaviors and maintain follow-up for continual reinforcement.

6-20 STUDY SKILLS

TITLE: **Bag Bingo**

MEDIA/COST: Book/Worksheets/Bingo Cards *

GRADES/LENGTH: 2–3

AUTHOR: Cooper

PUBLISHER/
  COPYRIGHT: Mar*Co Products, Inc./1994

NOTES: Includes nine study skills: (1) Work quietly; (2) Do your own work; (3) Listen to the teacher; (4) Stay in your seat; (5) Don't bother others; (6) Raise your hand; (7) Complete your work; (8) Think before you answer; and (9) Try your hardest. Bag Bingo includes directions, a leader's guide, activity sheets, thirty bingo cards, and calling cards for the game. After discussing study skills and completing a worksheet, the students play the game Study Skills Bingo.

TITLE: **A Kid's Guide to Getting Along in School**

MEDIA/COST: Video ****

GRADES/LENGTH: K–2/50–60 minutes

PUBLISHER/
  COPYRIGHT: Learning Tree Publishing, Inc.

NOTES: This series covers: (1) being quiet, (2) listening to directions, (3) punctuality, (4) independence, (5) responsibility, and (6) cooperation. Each topic is well organized, beginning with the explanation of the issue, followed by situations to further describe the concept, and ending with a summary and discussion questions. Cartoon characters and bright colors are visually appealing to young children.

6-20 STUDY SKILLS (CONTINUED)

TITLE: **Kid's Guide to Getting Organized**

MEDIA/COST: Filmstrip/Cassette ***

GRADES/LENGTH: K–3

PUBLISHER/
  COPYRIGHT: Learning Tree Publishing, Inc./1990

NOTES: Filmstrips in cartoon format demonstrate the reason for organization, and how to plan ahead and manage time. Excellent introduction to an essential attribute for success in school.

6-21 SUBSTANCE ABUSE PREVENTION

TITLE: **Drug Free Me**

MEDIA/COST: Board Game **

GRADES/LENGTH: 2–4

PUBLISHER/
  COPYRIGHT: Sunburst Communications, Inc./ 1992

NOTES: Teaches factual information about alcohol and other drugs, and appropriate concerns related to self-esteem, peer pressure, decision-making skills, influence of role models, and adversity. Blank cards are included to encourage students to write their own questions and these cards can be used with older students as well. Counselor may want to preview and delete certain questions.

TITLE: **McGruff's Elementary Drug Prevention Activity Book**

MEDIA/COST: Activity Book/Free upon request

GRADES/LENGTH: K–4

PUBLISHER: National Crime Prevention Council

NOTES: Reproducible activities lend themselves to further discussion. Complements other materials. Additional resources for teachers and/or parents are listed in the back. Following components are included: (1) explanation of drug prevention and what is appropriate at different grade levels, (2) tips for parents, (3) signs and symptoms of drug use, and (4) specific drug information.

TITLE: **Sooper Puppy Series**
Drink, Drank, Drunk
Flying High
Puff of Smoke

MEDIA/COST: Videos/Each Video ***

GRADES/LENGTH: K–4/Each, 17 minutes

PUBLISHER/
  COPYRIGHT: MTI Film and Video/1989

NOTES: *Drink, Drank, Drunk:* Puppets and animation teach how alcohol affects the body and why it can be dangerous to health and well-being. Illustrates saying "NO" to peer pressure and to drinking alcohol.

Flying High: Shows resisting peer pressure and understanding the difference between general enjoyment and "artificial fun." Discusses the effects of drugs on the body and encourages children to not take drugs.

Puff of Smoke: Puppets and animation teach what nicotine addiction and smoking can do to one's body. Emphasizes why it is better not to start smoking in the first place.

6-22 TEST-TAKING SKILLS

TITLE: **Try Test Bingo**

MEDIA/COST: Game *

GRADES/LENGTH: K–3/30 cards

AUTHOR: Jackson

PUBLISHER/
  COPYRIGHT: Mar*Co Products, Inc.

NOTES: Helps students learn and understand important elements associated with successful test-taking. Topics include: listening to directions, erasing wrong answers, trying to do the best you can, and thinking about answers.

6-23   TRANSITION

TITLE: **Maggie Doesn't Want to Move**

MEDIA/COST: Book *

GRADES/LENGTH: K–4/14 pages

AUTHOR: O'Donnell

PUBLISHER/
  COPYRIGHT: Aladdin Books/1987

NOTES: Fourteen pages of wonderfully presented information about a little boy, Simon. Simon, who does not want to move, explains that it is his sister who does not want to move. Simon tells his mom his plan for Maggie to stay with his friend's mom, and for Simon to stay so Maggie doesn't get scared. They move to the new house and Simon finds that he likes everything. At the end of the story, Simon's mom asks him if he still thinks that Maggie should stay with his friend's mother. Simon responds, "I don't think so, Mom, Maggie doesn't want to move."

TITLE: **Moving Gives Me a Stomachache**

MEDIA/COST: Book *

GRADES/LENGTH: K–3/22 pages

AUTHOR: McKend

PUBLISHER/
  COPYRIGHT: Black Moss Press/1988

NOTES: Discusses a family's moving day and the fact that one family member, the little boy, has a stomachache. The story shows the sadness felt by the little boy, the items he couldn't take with him, like the large tree outside his bedroom window and his friend Pinkie. The author also shows how the boy becomes involved in the move when his mom gives him a large box so he can pack anything he wants. The end shows the little boy in his new home, with a tree outside his window and a new friend next door. The stomachache goes away.

TITLE: **Where in the World Are You Going?**

MEDIA/COST: Activity Book

GRADES/LENGTH: 1–3/37 pages

PUBLISHER/
  COPYRIGHT: Overseas Briefing Center

NOTES: Excellent activity book for students moving overseas or within the country. Deals with all aspects of moving and gives children the opportunity to write and draw their feelings. Many helpful tips on how to learn more about the area or country to which the student is moving, and how to take along special memories.

Section 7

MATERIALS TO USE WITH GRADES 3–6

ANNOTATED LIST OF MATERIALS TO USE WITH STUDENTS

(PERMISSION OF FAIRFAX COUNTY PUBLIC SCHOOLS OF VIRGINIA)

Cost Guide:	* ($1-$25)	** ($26-$55)	*** ($56-$105)	**** ($106-205)	***** ($206-$505)	****** ($506-$1,000)

7-1   CAREER EDUCATION

TITLE: **ACK—American Careers for Kids**

MEDIA/COST: Activity Book/Guide

GRADES/LENGTH: 4

AUTHORS: Orwig & Dick

PUBLISHER/
   COPYRIGHT: Career Communications, Inc./1996

NOTES: Colorful, easy-to-read activity book includes activities under language arts, math, science, and other academic subjects. Also includes additional activities and parent letters.

TITLE: **Alphabet Careers**

MEDIA/COST: Game/Worksheets *

GRADES/LENGTH: 2–5/52 careers, 26 cards

AUTHOR: Sahlin

PUBLISHER/
   COPYRIGHT: Mar*Co Products, Inc./1993

NOTES: Alphabet cards include information about two careers on each card. Includes careers not usually discussed, such as quarry worker and quiz show hostess. Good ethnic and gender balance. Numerous career activities and worksheets that can be reproduced.

TITLE: **Career Education: CAREER Motivational Activities for the Teaching of Career Education**

MEDIA/COST: Book *

GRADES/LENGTH: 2–6/221 pages

AUTHORS: Eddy & Gierman

PUBLISHER/
   COPYRIGHT: Opportunities for Learning, Inc./ 1991

NOTES: A variety of interesting lessons for teaching career awareness. Many areas are covered in all career clusters. Activities are especially recommended for classroom guidance lessons or for teacher follow up. This is part of the "Spice Series" that may be used by classroom teachers.

TITLE: **Children's Dictionary of Occupational Titles**
Activities for Grades 3 and 4
Activities for Grades 5 and 6

MEDIA/COST: Dictionary, * Activity Sheets for Grades 3 & 4, * Activity Sheets for Grades 5 & 6, *

GRADES/LENGTH: 3–6/130 pages

AUTHORS: Hopke & Parramore

PUBLISHER/
   COPYRIGHT: Meridian Education Corporation/ 1992

NOTES: Excellent resource for children who are beginning career exploration. Organized in several ways: (1) alphabetically, (2) career areas, and (3) career families. A special section details early jobs for teenagers. Highly recommended for a career library in an elementary school.

341

7-1 CAREER EDUCATION (CONTINUED)

TITLE:	**Children's Occupational Outlook Handbook**
MEDIA/COST:	Book *
GRADES/LENGTH:	3–6 (depending on reading level)/219 pages
AUTHORS:	Schwartz & Wolfgang
PUBLISHER/ COPYRIGHT:	CFKR Career Materials/1994

NOTES: Excellent resource with timely information, that is well-organized and easy to use. Job information with needed education, job outlook, earnings, job description, working conditions, related jobs, subjects to study, places to observe, and where to find more information. A useful reference tool for the classroom library. Available in computer software.

TITLE:	**CHOICES JR.**
MEDIA/COST:	IBM or Macintosh Computer Program
	Site License, *****
GRADES/LENGTH:	3–6
AUTHOR:	Canada Employment and Immigration Commission
PUBLISHER/ COPYRIGHT:	Careerware/1992

NOTES: Excellent program for students to have available in the classroom. Starts with student's individual interests and proceeds to educational levels needed for job clusters that have been indicated through student choice. Good graphics and available printouts make this a desirable computer program. Students become interested in creating their list of career preferences and learning the educational background needed. Information can be saved and revised or followed up throughout the year. Printouts can be used in career portfolios.

TITLE:	**E-WOW**
MEDIA/COST:	Self-Test *
GRADES/LENGTH:	4–6
PUBLISHER/ COPYRIGHT:	CFKR Career Materials/1994

NOTES: Concise and easy to understand. Useful material for career education. Students color their responses and then count the colors indicating their career interests.

TITLE:	**JOB-O-E:** *Job-O-E Dictionary* *Job-O-E Folder/Booklet*
MEDIA/COST:	Booklet *
GRADES/LENGTH:	4–6/20 pages, 40–minute class period
AUTHORS:	Cutler, Ferry, Kauk, & Robinett
PUBLISHER/ COPYRIGHT:	CFKR Career Materials/1994

NOTES: *Dictionary:* Information about a vast number of jobs: high school preparation, job-entry requirements, and related jobs. Very fine print. Available on computer software.

Folder/Booklet: Representative jobs and job values within six major career groups. Students learn factual information about careers, and then use that information by doing activities that promote self-awareness.

TITLE:	**When I Grow Up**
MEDIA/COST:	Kit/Video
GRADES/LENGTH:	3–6/Video, 22 minutes
PUBLISHER/ COPYRIGHT:	McDonald's Corp. and CBS/1989

NOTES: Twenty-two vignettes of one minute each, which were shown on CBS. Real-life occupational role models inspire children and interest them in various work opportunities. Videos show how particular school subjects relate to future career choices.

7-1 CAREER EDUCATION (CONTINUED)

TITLE: **When I Grow Up (Professional Women)**

MEDIA/COST: Video *

GRADES/LENGTH: 3–6

PUBLISHER/
COPYRIGHT: Fairfax Network/1995-96

NOTES: Introduces women who are doctors, scientists, lawyers, television reporters, journalists, and business owners. Stresses that women can be anything they want to be if they prepare through study and dedication. Encourages both girls and boys to pursue aspirations and emphasizes that gender should not limit career options.

7-2 COMMUNICATION

TITLE: **Between You and Me: Learning to Communicate**

MEDIA/COST: Video ****

GRADES/LENGTH: 6

PUBLISHER/
COPYRIGHT: Sunburst Communications, Inc./1990

NOTES: Three-part video covers good communication, differences between fact and opinion, body language, active listening skills, and communication roadblocks. Presents a four-step negotiating technique.

TITLE: **RAPP! Resource of Activities for Peer Pragmatics**

MEDIA/COST: Workbook **

GRADES/LENGTH: 3–6/138 pages

AUTHORS: McConnell & Blagden

PUBLISHER/
COPYRIGHT: Lingui Systems, Inc./1986

NOTES: Activities include role plays for students to learn 14 interpersonal skills. Examples include: giving and requesting information, expressing feelings, disagreeing, and supporting others. Also includes interpersonal language skills with a checklist, a vocabulary log, and a glossary of terms for each section. Large illustrations throughout book demonstrate effective and ineffective communication skills. Reproducible workbook.

7-3 CONFLICT RESOLUTION

TITLE: **Be Cool: Coping With Bullying**

MEDIA/COST: 4 Videos/Guide

GRADES/LENGTH: 3–5/Each, 10 minutes

AUTHOR: Stanfield

PUBLISHER/
COPYRIGHT: James Stanfield Publishing Co./ 1995

NOTES: Strategies addressed: (1) Look the Look, (2) Talk the Talk, (3) Talk the Talk II, and (4) Stand Your Ground/Get Help. Guide with step-by-step directions and follow-up activities for each lesson.

TITLE: **Conflict Managers: Student Workshop**

MEDIA/COST: Kit/Video/Binder ****

GRADES/LENGTH: 3–6/27 minutes

PUBLISHER/
COPYRIGHT: Sunburst Communications, Inc./ 1996

NOTES: Comprehensive step-by-step plan and resources for problem solving and conflict mediation. Well-organized binder has the following sections: program summary, script, ground rules for mediation, brainstorming information for solutions, worksheets, and agreement making. Video keeps students' attention because the steps are presented by an athletic coach who uses terms used in sports. Throughout the video, a scoreboard flashes to introduce information and to review or summarize information. Received Silver Award from Questar Awards.

TITLE: **Conflict Resolution Curriculum**

MEDIA/COST: Kit: 8 Videos/Worksheets/ Binder ******

GRADES/LENGTH: 3–7/Guide, 125 pages with 10 information sheets; Worksheets, 24; Role-Play Cards, 24

PUBLISHER/
COPYRIGHT: Sunburst Communications, Inc.

NOTES: A very complete kit with 8 videos about conflict mediation, including a video for staff development. Many reproducible sheets, activities, role plays, and complete plans. Everything in the kit is usable and focused on resolving conflicts that students experience during these grade levels. Tremendous resource.

7-3 CONFLICT RESOLUTION (*CONTINUED*)

TITLE:	**Creative Conflict Resolution: More Than 200 Activities for Keeping Peace in the Classroom**
MEDIA/COST:	Activity Book
GRADES/LENGTH:	3–6
AUTHOR:	Kreidler, Jr.
PUBLISHER/ COPYRIGHT:	Scott Foresman/1984

NOTES: Excellent book with many activities to use in the classroom to help students respect each other and be responsible for their own actions.

TITLE:	**Creative Conflict Solving for Kids**
MEDIA/COST:	Book/Guide/Worksheets/Poster *
GRADES/LENGTH:	3–6/Book, 46 pages
AUTHORS:	Schmidt & Friedman
PUBLISHER/ COPYRIGHT:	Grace Contrino Abrams

NOTES: Excellent resource for conflict mediation. Activities help students build self-esteem, respect differences, develop interpersonal skills, and handle frustration and anger. Explains causes of conflict and gives suggestions to practice conflict-resolution strategies.

TITLE:	**Getting Along Program**
MEDIA:	Kit: Guide/Booklets/Audio Cassettes ***
GRADES/LENGTH:	4–6
PUBLISHER/ COPYRIGHT:	American Guidance Services (AGS)/1990

NOTES: A behavior-management and social-development program. Develops skills in cooperation, caring for others, critical thinking, and positive conflict resolution. Includes posters and activities.

TITLE:	**Getting Better at Getting Along**
MEDIA/COST:	Video/Guide/Worksheets ***
GRADES/LENGTH:	3–6/Video, 16 minutes
PUBLISHER/ COPYRIGHT:	Sunburst Communications, Inc./ 1992

NOTES: Introduction to conflict resolution in the classroom. Effective communication, cooperation, and compromise are introduced and defined. Mediation is introduced to help children understand that at times they may have to seek outside help. Opportunities to solve problems occur throughout the video to promote discussion.

TITLE:	**Mediation for Kids: Kids in Dispute Settlement**
MEDIA/COST:	Book
GRADES/LENGTH:	4–6
AUTHORS:	Schmidt, Friedman & Marvel
PUBLISHER/ COPYRIGHT:	Peace Education Foundation, Inc./ 1992

NOTES: Complete and organized book to teach students the mediation process. Lessons can be used in small groups and guidance lessons as well as for training student mediators.

7-4　DEATH AND GRIEF

TITLE:　**Helping Children Cope With Separation and Loss**

MEDIA/COST:　Book *

GRADES/LENGTH:　3–6

AUTHORS:　Jarratt & Doka (Ed.)

PUBLISHER/
　COPYRIGHT:　Harvard Common Press/1994

NOTES: Helps counselors and teachers assist children as they deal with difficult circumstances. Separation may be due to death of a loved one, divorce of parents, or loss of a pet.

TITLE:　**I Wish I Could Hold Your Hand: A Child's Guide to Grief and Loss**

MEDIA/COST:　Book *

GRADES/LENGTH:　3–6/27 pages

AUTHOR:　Palmer

PUBLISHER/
　COPYRIGHT:　Impact Publishers/1994

NOTES: Helps children understand and accept their feelings of anger, sadness, loneliness, and guilt. Loss includes divorce, travel of parent, moving, and loss of pets. Easily read, reassuring, and reaffirming.

7-5　DECISION MAKING

TITLE:　**Finders, Keepers**
　　　　(*Decision Is Yours* Series)

MEDIA/COST:　Book *

GRADES/LENGTH:　2–5/59 pages

AUTHOR:　Crary

PUBLISHER/
　COPYRIGHT:　Parenting Press, Inc./1987

NOTES: High-interest books in this series teach children to think about social problems. Students decide the action the character should take and then they see the consequences of each decision. In this book, two boys decide what to do when they find a wallet and are tempted to keep some of the contents.

TITLE:　**You Can Choose: Decision Making**
　　　　Dealing With Disappointment
　　　　Doing the Right Thing

MEDIA/COST:　Videos/Guides ***

GRADES/LENGTH:　3–6/28 minutes

AUTHORS:　Elkind & Sweet (producers)

PUBLISHER/
　COPYRIGHT:　Social Studies School Service/1992

NOTES: *Dealing With Disappointment:* Helps students learn how to handle disappointments. In an appealing skit, Missie must decide whether to let her frustration over losing a game cause her to quit her baseball team. Students explore the issue and help. Missie discovers the personal rewards that come from making good choices.

　Doing the Right Thing: The characters, Rhonda and Fiona, must decide what to do when they find a lost wallet on the playground. They must decide between doing what is right and doing what they can get away with.

7-6　DISABILITIES

TITLE:　**The Boy Who Couldn't Stop Washing: The Experience and Treatment of Obsessive-Compulsive Disorder**

MEDIA/COST:　Book

GRADES/LENGTH:　3–6

AUTHOR:　Rapoport

PUBLISHER/
　COPYRIGHT:　NAL-Dutton/1989

NOTES: Written so children can understand the behavior of a child with obsessive-compulsive disorder.

TITLE:　**Friends for Life: Kids on the Block**

MEDIA/COST:　Puppets Stage Show

GRADES/LENGTH:　2–6

AUTHORS:　Aiello & Shulman

PUBLISHER/
　COPYRIGHT:　Twenty-First Century Books/1989

NOTES: AIDS is the subject of this book, one lesson presented by the "Kids on the Block" puppets stage show. Children learn about AIDS in an appealing format with the puppets providing accurate information.

7-6 DISABILITIES (CONTINUED)

TITLE: **Friends Who Care**

MEDIA/COST: Kit: Video/Curriculum **

GRADES/LENGTH: 3–6/40 minutes

PUBLISHER/
    COPYRIGHT: National Easter Seal Society/1990

NOTES: Short video clips interviewing kids with various disabilities. Includes activities for students to experience for a short time how it feels to have each particular disability.

TITLE: **Hi, I'm Adam!**

MEDIA/COST: Book *

GRADES/LENGTH: 3–6/35 pages

AUTHOR: Buehrens

PUBLISHER/
    COPYRIGHT: Hope Press/1991

NOTES: A child's book about Tourette's Syndrome teaching children to understand this disorder and understand and accept a child who may experience behavioral difficulties due to this disorder.

TITLE: **Jumpin' Johnny Get Back to Work!**

MEDIA/COST: Book

GRADES/LENGTH: 3–5/24 pages

AUTHOR: Gordon

PUBLISHER/
    COPYRIGHT: GSI Publications/1991

NOTES: Excellent resource on Attention Deficit Hyperactivity Disorder (ADHD) which can be used with small groups or individuals.

TITLE: **Putting on the Brakes: Young People's Guide to Understanding Attention Deficit Hyperactivity Disorder (ADHD)**

MEDIA/COST: Book *

GRADES/LENGTH: 3–8

AUTHORS: Quinn & Stern

PUBLISHER/
    COPYRIGHT: Magination Press Book (Brunner/ Mazel, Inc.)/1991

NOTES: Excellent resource for children with ADHD and their families and teachers. Helps students learn about ADHD and ways to deal with this disability.

TITLE: **The Unforgettable Pen Pal: A Story About Prejudice and Discrimination**

MEDIA/COST: Video *

GRADES/LENGTH: 3–6/28 minutes

AUTHOR: Berry (video is from her book series)

PUBLISHER/
    COPYRIGHT: Social Studies School Service/1989

NOTES: A story about A. J. who loves basketball and is thrilled to learn that Joey, his new pen pal, also enjoys the sport. Even though they have never met, the boys become friends. Their friendship crumbles, however, when A. J. tells Joey that disabled people make him feel uncomfortable, only to find that Joey must use a wheelchair. Discrimination against older people (senior citizens) is also discussed. Concludes with five steps to avoid prejudice.

7-7   DIVORCE

TITLE: **My Two Homes**

MEDIA/COST: Game **

GRADES/LENGTH: 3–6/2–4 players

PUBLISHER/
    COPYRIGHT: Childswork/Childsplay/1992

NOTES: Teaches basic facts about divorce to help students communicate their feelings about their parents' divorce. Players move around the board by answering questions relating to Mom's House, Dad's House, or Me (the child's feelings). Chips are given to students who answer the factual cards or give any answer to the situational cards. Intended to be played with the counselor. Reading the board and some cards may be too difficult or inappropriate for younger children. Parents should be consulted before using this game with children.

7-7 DIVORCE *(CONTINUED)*

TITLE:	**When Your Parents Get a Divorce: A Kid's Journal**
MEDIA/COST:	Activity Book *
GRADES/LENGTH:	3–6/62 pages
AUTHOR:	Banks
PUBLISHER/ COPYRIGHT:	Penguin Books USA, Inc./1990

NOTES: Excellent combination journal and activity book. Includes many projects for kids starting from when they first learn about the separation of their parents until they've begun assimilating the experience. After going through the experience, they can help other children who are in a similar situation.

7-8   EMOTIONS

TITLE:	**Face Your Feelings**
MEDIA/COST:	Book *
GRADES/LENGTH:	3–6/52 pictures
PUBLISHER/ COPYRIGHT:	Childswork/Childsplay/1993

NOTES: Real photographs on game cards depict various ages and ethnic groups and teach children to recognize and share their feelings. Directions are given for ten separate games.

TITLE:	**Moms Don't Get Sick**
MEDIA/COST:	Book
GRADES/LENGTH:	3–7
AUTHORS:	Brack & Brack
PUBLISHER/ COPYRIGHT:	Melius and Peterson Publishing/ 1990

NOTES: A true story about the mother of a ten-year-old boy who found out she had breast cancer. The book relates the events and feelings experienced by ten-year-old Ben and his mother, struggling to adapt to this situation and salvage their close relationship. Together Ben and his mother dealt with cancer, surgery, and chemotherapy. Three years later Ben's mother had a new form of cancer which meant more treatment. The mother is a survivor, and Ben shares his emotions. Ben thought his experience could help other kids who have to go through similar experiences. Readers feel the emotion and learn how to cope with serious difficulties.

TITLE:	**The Stop, Relax and Think Game**
MEDIA/COST:	Game **
GRADES/LENGTH:	3–6
PUBLISHER/ COPYRIGHT:	Childswork/Childsplay/1992

NOTES: A board game that helps students become more aware of their feelings and actions. Stresses importance of thinking before expressing feelings and reacting. When a student lands on "Stop," she or he must do one of the things listed on the stop sign. When students land on "Relax," they must breathe deeply, tell or do something funny, count to 10 to calm down, etc. In the "Think" section, students must think of a useful plan to solve a problem. Helps players look carefully at their feelings and learn effective strategies to handle these feelings.

TITLE:	**Who Me? Mad? Nah!** *(Making Choices—Growing Stronger Series)*
MEDIA/COST:	Guidance Units *
GRADES/LENGTH:	4–6/23 pages
AUTHOR:	Falk
PUBLISHER/ COPYRIGHT:	Elizabeth Falk, M.A., LPC/1993

NOTES: Unit for small-group counseling that stresses how anger is a result of: (1) being fussy and irritable, (2) being disappointed and sad, or (3) being jealous and resentful. Students compile a list of things to do when mad and then practice these remedies in succeeding sessions. Recognition of normal anger in everyday life. Student activities include brainstorming, pantomiming, and role playing.

7-9   FAMILY

TITLE: **Kid's Guide to Getting Along With Others or Getting Along With Your Family**

MEDIA/COST: Video

GRADES/LENGTH: 3–5/10 minutes

PUBLISHER/
    COPYRIGHT: Learning Tree Publishing, Inc.

NOTES: Focuses on getting along with family members. Compromise, cooperation, sharing, and trust are explained with examples. The PTA/PTO may want to purchase this for the school.

7-10   FRIENDSHIPS

TITLE: **Feeling Good About Friends**
                (*Making Choices—Growing Stronger* Series)

MEDIA/COST: Guidance Units *

GRADES/LENGTH: 3–4/23 pages

AUTHOR: Falk

PUBLISHER/
    COPYRIGHT: Elizabeth Falk, M.A., LPC/1992

NOTES: Organized sessions for a counselor to use with small groups or classrooms to assist students in improving their friendships. Reproducible activity sheets may be copied and used with students.

TITLE: **"How Can I Fit In?"**
                (*The Guidance Club for Kids*)

MEDIA/COST: Video ***

GRADES/LENGTH: 3–6/20–26 minutes

PUBLISHER/
    COPYRIGHT: Ready Reference Press/1992

NOTES: Current questions and concerns that many students have regarding friends, include: "What is popularity?" "How can I make friends?" "Getting along in groups," "What if others don't like me?" "Look for one special friend," "Being popular," "Peer pressure," "Avoid negative people," "Being popular isn't everything," and a conclusion. Not animated, but made from still shots and pictures.

7-12   MULTICULTURAL

TITLE: **Black Is My Color: The African American Experience**

MEDIA/COST: Video/Guide ***

GRADES/LENGTH: 3–6/15 minutes

PUBLISHER/
   COPYRIGHT: Rainbow Educational Video/1992

NOTES: Broad coverage of the African American experience, beginning with the diverse cultural roots in Africa, moving on to slavery in America, the fight for civil rights, and ending with insights on contributions made by African Americans to society. Recommended for multicultural and self-esteem groups.

TITLE: **Earth Keepers Series**

Chico Mendes: Fight for the Forest—Susan DeStefano

Gaylord Nelson: Day for the Earth—Jeffrey Shulman

George Washington Carver: Nature's Trailblazer—Teresa Rogers

Henry David Thoreau: Neighbor to Nature—Catherine Reef

Jacques Cousteau: Champion of the Sea—Catherine Reef

Jane Goodall: Living With the Chimps—Julie Fromer

Marjory Stoneman Douglas: Voice of the Everglades—Jennifer Bryant

Rachel Carson: The Wonder of Nature—Catherine Reef

MEDIA/COST: Books *

GRADES/LENGTH: 3-6/Each, 68–75 pages

PUBLISHER/
   COPYRIGHT: Henry Holt & Co., Inc./1992

NOTES: ***Chico Mendes*** improved conditions for all rubber tappers, fought against deforestation, and helped educate the world to seek ways to live with the forest without harming its fragile ecosystem. ***Gaylord Nelson,*** governor and a U.S. senator, influenced environmental legislation because of his love of nature. ***George Washington Carver,*** African American scientist, is remembered for his agricultural research and innovations. He achieved many different things, including creating sweet potatoes. His contributions from 1898-1942 are listed. ***Henry David Thoreau*** was one of the first persons to write about ecology. ***Jacques Cousteau*** loved and researched the sea. ***Jane Goodall*** studied chimpanzees and her work became a model for wildlife observation. ***Marjory Stoneman Douglas*** became known as the "Grandmother of the Glades" because she fought to preserve the Florida Everglades against misuse and development. A glossary and index of her contributions are listed. ***Rachel Carson,*** a biologist and conservationist, is known for her writings on the environment. The book about her life also touches on such universal themes as hard work, commitment to a goal, caring for others, and facing death.

7-12 MULTICULTURAL (CONTINUED)

TITLE: **Pioneers in Health & Medicine Series**

The Life of Elizabeth Blackwell—Elizabeth Scheichert

The Life of Dorothea Dix—Elizabeth Scheichert

The Life of Charles Drew—K. S. Talmadge

The Life of Louis Pasteur—Marcia Newfield

MEDIA/COST: Books *

GRADES/LENGTH: 3–6/Each, 80 pages

PUBLISHER/
COPYRIGHT: Henry Holt & Co., Inc./1992

NOTES: *Elizabeth Blackwell* became the first female medical doctor in the United States and was placed on the British Medical Record. *Dorothea Dix* came to the aid of the mentally ill at a time when culture and the medical communities were not certain of treatment. *Charles Drew* is an African American surgeon noted for his research on blood plasma. *Louis Pasteur* had a love of learning and a motivation to work and study hard, which is an inspiration to all students.

7-13   PROBLEM SOLVING

TITLE: **Being Friends: You Can Choose!**

MEDIA/COST: Video/Guide ***

GRADES/LENGTH: 2–5/28 minutes

PUBLISHER/
COPYRIGHT: Social Studies School Service/1992

NOTES: Excellent presentation of social "in groups" and "out groups." Helps children brainstorm alternatives in their relationships with friends. A guide with helpful suggestions, an outline of the story, and additional activities. Particularly helpful to students struggling between "in groups" and "out groups."

TITLE: **Making Choices—Growing Stronger**

MEDIA/COST: Booklet *

GRADES/LENGTH: 5–7/23 pages

AUTHOR: Falk

PUBLISHER/
COPYRIGHT: Elizabeth Falk, M.A., LPC/1992

NOTES: Eight sessions in which students explore factors necessary to develop self–control and responsibility. Also focuses on learning how to solve problems and set goals.

7–14   RESPECT

TITLE: **Second Step: Grades 4–5**

MEDIA/COST: Kit: Large Picture Cards/Binder *****

GRADES/LENGTH: 4–5

PUBLISHER/
COPYRIGHT: Committee for Children/1992

NOTES: Complete and well-organized units dealing with empathy training, impulse control, and anger management. Each unit begins in fourth grade with review and continues in fifth grade. Excellent pictures with good representation of all cultures, large enough to be shown to a class. Suggestions for role plays and questions on the back of the picture cards. Parent letters describing the program can be duplicated. Wonderful resource!

7-14 RESPECT (CONTINUED)

TITLE: **Working Together**

MEDIA/COST: Kit ****

GRADES/LENGTH: 3–6/272 pages

AUTHORS: Cartledge & Kleefeld

PUBLISHER/
COPYRIGHT: American Guidance Service, Inc. (AGS)/1994

NOTES: Uses a folk-literature approach to teach social skills to children. Program is for grades 3-6 and for older students with special needs. Five units: (1) Making conversation and expressing feelings, (2) Co-operating with peers, (3) Playing with peers, (4) Responding to conflict and aggression, and (5) Performing in the classroom. Folk tales come from all over the world and students are encouraged to locate the country or region and explore the culture of that folk tale. Excellent program that integrates social skills into the language arts curriculum.

7-15 RESPONSIBILITY

TITLE: **I Can Do It: Taking Responsibility**

MEDIA/COST: Video/Guide/Worksheets ***

GRADES/LENGTH: 3–6/Video, 12 minutes

AUTHOR: Mazzarella

PUBLISHER/
COPYRIGHT: Sunburst Communications, Inc./ 1992

NOTES: Four scenarios dealing with students taking responsibility for their actions: (1) walking a neighbor's dog, (2) joining the school chorus, (3) not attending Cub Scout Weeblo meetings, although a member, and (4) discovering a favorite park has been trashed. Scenes are open-ended and encourage class discussion. Ideas for role plays are included and reproducible worksheets complement the video and lead to class discussion.

7-16 SAFETY

TITLE: **Alone at Home: A Kid's Guide to Being in Charge**

MEDIA/COST: Activity Book *

GRADES/LENGTH: 3–7/56 pages

AUTHOR: Banks

PUBLISHER/
COPYRIGHT: Penguin Books/1989

NOTES: Helps kids stay busy and safe when they are on their own. Three main groups of activities: (1) basic information, (2) safety rules, and (3) helpful hints on time management and the development of good work and study habits. Parents' section with excellent suggestions and tips.

TITLE: **Books About Safety from Abuse:**
Daisy—**E. Sandy Powell**
The Girl Who Lived on the Ferris Wheel—**Louise Moeri**
The Lottery Rose—**Irene Hunt**
Mary Jane Harper Cried Last Night—**Joanna Lee & T. S. Cook**
Maury, Wednesday's Child—**Maury Blair & Doug Brendel**
Things Are Seldom What They Seem—**Sandy Asher**

GRADES/LENGTH: 3–5

NOTES: Counselor is advised to read books before recommending them or reading them with students. Situations are unique and the counselor must ensure that the book she or he recommends is the right book at the right time for the particular student.

Daisy is a story about a young girl dealing with the emotional and physical problems of being a victim of child abuse. Powerful and thorough. Recommended that the counselor read the book *with* the student to provide immediate support, discussion, and interaction.

7-16 SAFETY (CONTINUED)

TITLE: **Get Real About Violence**

MEDIA/COST: Kit: 2 Videos/Audio Cassette

GRADES/LENGTH: 4–6/3 modules

PUBLISHER/
COPYRIGHT: CHEF (Comprehensive Health Education Foundation)/1995

NOTES: Three modules: (1) Vulnerability to Violence [video], (2) Contributors to Violence [audio cassette], and (3) Alternatives to Violence [video]. Goal is to make schools safer and more supportive. Modules explain some of the factors that contribute to violence and teach students ways to prevent violence. Introduction, lesson plans, follow–up plans, and additional resources are in the guide.

TITLE: **Home Alone: You're in Charge**

MEDIA/COST: Video/Guide/Worksheets ***

GRADES/LENGTH: 3–6/Video, 12 minutes

PUBLISHER/
COPYRIGHT: Sunburst Communications, Inc./ 1991

NOTES: Helps children understand the importance of adopting a home-alone plan that will keep them safe. Ideas for activities, hobbies, and other interests for children to use when at home. Colorful graphics and lively songs teach safety rules and activities. Recommended by Quest International: Skills for Growing.

7-17 SELF-DISCIPLINE

TITLE: **The Classroom Behavior Game**

MEDIA/COST: Game **

GRADES/LENGTH: K–6/Playing time, 30 minutes or less

PUBLISHER/
COPYRIGHT: Childswork/Childsplay

NOTES: Excellent way to teach and reinforce appropriate classroom behavior. Game is for students who are new to the school, who have difficulty following school rules, or who have special needs. A "report card" lists twelve appropriate classroom behaviors and days of the week for students to monitor their own behavior or for teachers to record the weekly improvement. Motivates students in a fun manner to learn and work on appropriate classroom behaviors such as: keeping your hands to yourself, waiting your turn, being positive, being quiet, working hard, following the rules, being polite, raising hand before speaking in class, and listening carefully.

TITLE: **The Good Behavior Game**

MEDIA/COST: Board Game **

GRADES/LENGTH: K–6

AUTHOR: Shapiro

PUBLISHER/
COPYRIGHT: Center for Applied Psychology

NOTES: Excellent board game that helps children learn the importance of good behavior in a fun format. Recommended for students ages 4-12 and has been adapted for different ages, learning abilities, and behavioral concerns. *Version I* is an easy, non-reader format. *Version II* uses open-ended questions related to home, school, community, and playground/play. Students respond to and discuss the importance of good behavior. Helps students distinguish between appropriate and inappropriate behavior.

7-17 SELF-DISCIPLINE (CONTINUED)

TITLE:	**The Self-Control Patrol**
MEDIA/COST:	Game *
GRADES/LENGTH:	4–8
PUBLISHER/ COPYRIGHT:	Mar*Co Products, Inc./1992

NOTES: Helps students increase their awareness of anger as a normal emotion, and learn constructive ways of handling their anger. A game board with cards to match color-coded squares. Colored cards present situations for making a decision, distinguishing between feelings and behaviors, and selecting ways to handle behavior. "Power Talk" cards help students respond with "I Messages." "Encounter" cards teach strategies for handling situations. "Self-Control Chart" helps students monitor their own behavior.

TITLE:	**The Self-Controlled Classroom**
MEDIA/COST:	Computer Software ****
GRADES/LENGTH:	3–6/10–15 minutes each day
AUTHORS:	Shapiro, Wagner, & Cullinan
PUBLISHER/ COPYRIGHT:	Center for Applied Psychology, Inc./1994

NOTES: Helps students monitor their own behavioral goals. Students work on up to five goals at one time. Counselors or teachers can add their own individualized goals for specific students. Each student needs five minutes of computer time in the morning to preview daily goals and five to ten minutes in the afternoon to check off the daily progress made on specified goals. Counselor or teacher must be available to open the program each morning and to reset it each afternoon. Students need to be able to read their goals or recognize certain words to work independently, and they must be able to type an explanation of why a goal was not met when it wasn't achieved.

Very effective for particular students who need to recognize and improve their behavior every day. Self-reporting on the computer leads toward self-discipline and self-improvement.

Can accommodate up to thirty students on one computer. Schools wishing to use the program on multiple computers must purchase a multisite license from the publisher.

TITLE:	**The Tough Kid Tool Box**
MEDIA/COST:	Book/Worksheets *
GRADES/LENGTH:	K–6/213 pages
AUTHORS:	Jenson, Rhode, & Reavis
PUBLISHER/ COPYRIGHT:	Sopris West/1995

NOTES: Ready-to-use materials designed to reduce disruptive behavior and increase student motivation. Supplements *The Tough Kid Book*, but can be used independently since each intervention lists step-by-step instructions. Reproducible worksheets; behavior observation forms; motivators; point cards; reinforcer lists; take-home behavior charts; self-monitoring forms and charts; behavior contracts for classroom, lunchroom, homework, and recess. Time-saving resource. Also available in Spanish.

7-18   SELF-ESTEEM

TITLE:	**The Building Blocks of Self-Esteem**
MEDIA/COST:	Activity Book *
GRADES/LENGTH:	3–6
AUTHOR:	Shapiro
PUBLISHER/ COPYRIGHT:	Center for Applied Psychology, Inc./1993

NOTES: Introduces self-esteem as a multidimensional concept derived from at least six major dimensions: affect, behavior, cognition, development, education, and social system. Children enjoy these interesting and thought-provoking activities.

TITLE:	**Kid Counselor Musicals and Songfest**
MEDIA/COST:	Books/Audio Cassettes *
GRADES/LENGTH:	3–6
PUBLISHER/ COPYRIGHT:	Mar*Co Products, Inc./1987

NOTES: *Kid Counselor Musicals:* Six short musical plays are presented on common guidance themes. Reinforce classroom guidance in a novel way.

Kid Counselor Songfest: Nine songs and worksheets cover self-esteem, decision-making, communication, responsibility, drugs, test anxiety, careers, and exercise. Reinforce guidance lessons.

7-18 SELF-ESTEEM (CONTINUED)

TITLE:	**Stick Up for Yourself!**
MEDIA/COST:	Book/Guide *
GRADES/LENGTH:	4–6/80 pages
AUTHORS:	Kaufman & Rephael
PUBLISHER/ COPYRIGHT:	Free Spirit Publishing, Inc./1990

NOTES: Teaches students how to stick up for themselves without putting others down and without getting into trouble. Also helps students develop positive self-esteem. Student's book may be used independently of guide. Resource for individual and group counseling, and for parents.

7-19   SOCIAL DEVELOPMENT

TITLE:	**Unsheltered Lives**
MEDIA/COST:	Activity Book
GRADES/LENGTH:	4–9/84 pages
AUTHOR:	Messinger
PUBLISHER/ COPYRIGHT:	Vermont Department of Education/ 1991

NOTES: Deals with the sensitive issue of homelessness and incorporates lessons in language arts, health, math, social studies, science, and art. About half of the activities are suitable for elementary students. Helps children understand and become knowledgeable about the societal issue of homelessness.

7-20   STUDY SKILLS

TITLE:	**Guidance Units: Study Skills**
	Developing Your Potential . . . At School, At Home, With Friends *
	Doing Your Best in School *
	How to Be a Better Student *
	Yes! I Can Achieve *
GRADES/LENGTH:	3–7/30–60 pages
AUTHOR:	Falk
PUBLISHER/ COPYRIGHT:	Elizabeth Falk, M.A., LPC/ 1990–1993

NOTES: ***Developing Your Potential:*** Eleven sessions for a classroom or small-group counseling. Each unit deals sequentially with major contributors to self-image: (1) personal feelings and attitudes, (2) friendships and peer pressure, (3) motivation for school achievement, and (4) roles within families. Interesting activities with many opportunities for student interaction.

Doing Your Best in School: Activities for a classroom or small group include role-playing situations, pantomime, and personal evaluations.

How to Be a Better Student: Wide range of topics to improve study habits. Goals and objectives are clearly stated with activities that are effective and practical. Fifteen units are included.

Yes! I Can Achieve: Focuses on traditional study skills, time management, and organization skills. Also deals with aspects of poor achievement such as poor attitudes and excuses. Techniques such as contests and role plays reinforce the topic.

7-20 STUDY SKILLS (CONTINUED)

TITLE: **How to Study**
MEDIA/COST: Booklet *
GRADES/LENGTH: 3–6/16 pages
PUBLISHER/
    COPYRIGHT: Channing L. Bete Co., Inc./1991

NOTES: Good information about study skills in a cartoon format. Study skills are well organized and presented in easy steps.

TITLE: **It's OK to Learn Differently**
MEDIA/COST: Book *
GRADES/LENGTH: K–5/16 pages
AUTHOR: Cody
PUBLISHER/
    COPYRIGHT: Mar*Co Products, Inc./1993

NOTES: Analogy of cars as a nonthreatening technique to assist students in understanding different learning styles. Activities are short and concise. Younger students may have difficulty understanding the symbolism of two cars representing two learning styles, and older students may find some of the activities too simplistic. Great resource for learning-disabled students.

TITLE: **Kid's Guide to Good Study Habits**
MEDIA/COST: 3 Filmstrips/3 Cassettes ***
GRADES/LENGTH: 4–6
PUBLISHER/
    COPYRIGHT: Learning Tree Publishing Inc.

NOTES: Introduces the relationship of school success and feeling good about self. Tips for getting school work done efficiently. Good resource when beginning a study-skills program.

TITLE: **Study Skills Matinee**
MEDIA/COST: Activity Book
GRADES/LENGTH: 3–4/75 pages
PUBLISHER/
    COPYRIGHT: Mar*Co Products, Inc./1989

NOTES: Contains 18 plays for improving study habits of elementary students. Each lesson has three parts: (1) a one-act play script, (2) discussion questions, and (3) a worksheet or classroom activity.

7-21   SUBSTANCE ABUSE PREVENTION

TITLE: **Brainstorm: Outreach Project: The Truth About Your Brain on Drugs**
MEDIA/COST: Video/Guide   (Free from U.S. Army)
GRADES/LENGTH: 4–6/60 minutes
AUTHOR: Outreach Project from Children's Television Workshop
PUBLISHER/
    COPYRIGHT: Community Education Services/1994

NOTES: Helps children learn about their brains and what happens when drugs enter their bodies. Excellent resource to use with at-risk students. Also helpful for teachers. Guide has follow-up activities to supplement each of the four 15-minute sections.

TITLE: **Kids Say Don't Smoke**
MEDIA/COST: Book *
GRADES/LENGTH: 3–6
AUTHOR: Tobias
PUBLISHER/
    COPYRIGHT: Workman Publishing Company/1991

NOTES: Excellent information about the consequences of smoking and breathing second-hand smoke. Important facts in an interesting and appealing format, using information from many sources. Emphasis on tobacco industry and how this industry has conveyed its message through the years.

7-21 SUBSTANCE ABUSE PREVENTION *(CONTINUED)*

TITLE:	**Let's Talk About Drugs**
MEDIA/COST:	Video/Skits/Worksheets ***
GRADES/LENGTH:	2–6/16 minutes
PUBLISHER/	
COPYRIGHT:	Sunburst Communications, Inc./ 1994

NOTES: Points out the dangers of drugs and tobacco. Seven activity sheets. Particularly good with small groups.

TITLE:	**My Dad Loves Me, My Dad Has a Disease**
MEDIA/COST:	Workbook *
GRADES/LENGTH:	3–6
AUTHOR:	Beach
PUBLISHER/	
COPYRIGHT:	MAC Publishing/1990

NOTES: Explains alcoholism from the viewpoint of the child. Drawings by children portray the disease concept, personality changes, blackouts, relapses, and recovery. Recommended that parents be consulted before using this workbook with children.

TITLE:	**My Dad's Definitely Not a Drunk**
MEDIA/COST:	Book *
GRADES/LENGTH:	4–6/100 pages
AUTHOR:	Carbone
PUBLISHER/	
COPYRIGHT:	Talman Company/1992

NOTES: Story about 12-year-old Corey, who lives with the pain of an alcoholic father. Initially, Corey believes that her dad just drinks too much, but later she realizes that he is an alcoholic. With the help of family members and a social worker, Corey's father is confronted about his alcoholism.

TITLE:	**The Power of No: The Wizard Returns**
MEDIA/COST:	Video ***
GRADES/LENGTH:	4–6/23 minutes
PUBLISHER/	
COPYRIGHT:	MTI Film & Video/1990

NOTES: Eleven-year-old Alice doesn't want to let her friends down. She told them that she would get liquor for a party. The "Wizard of No" helps Alice find the power and self-confidence within herself to say "No." Alice learns that her father suffers from alcoholism, a disease that affects the entire family.

Caution: The idea of a wizard talking to a child may be frightening and some parents may object.

TITLE:	**Say No and Mean It**
MEDIA/COST:	Video/Guide/Worksheets ***
GRADES/LENGTH:	2–5/Video, 17 minutes
PUBLISHER/	
COPYRIGHT:	Sunburst Communications, Inc./ 1991

NOTES: Helps students understand the importance of saying "No" and provides specific techniques that show students how to stand up for their rights, take charge of their lives, withstand peer pressure, and behave consistent with their own values. Four true-to-life scenarios hold students' interest and foster lively classroom discussions. "Questions to Think About" follow each segment. Also includes an upbeat musical number and reproducible worksheets.

TITLE:	**Stop, Think, and Go**
MEDIA/COST:	Game/Guide **
GRADES/LENGTH:	5–6
PUBLISHER/	
COPYRIGHT:	Sunburst Communications, Inc./ 1990

NOTES: Teaches students factual information about alcohol and other drugs, and encourages critical thinking about substance abuse. Questions for students to discuss with an adult.

TITLE:	**What Every Kid Should Know About Alcohol**
MEDIA/COST:	Booklet *
GRADES/LENGTH:	4–6
PUBLISHER/	
COPYRIGHT:	Channing L. Bete Co./1982

NOTES: Thorough booklet on alcohol and addiction. Excellent resource for counselors to have in their rooms for parents, students, and staff to borrow.

7-21 SUBSTANCE ABUSE PREVENTION *(CONTINUED)*

TITLE: **Why I Won't Do Drugs**
MEDIA/COST: Video/Guide/Musical Score/
                        Worksheets
GRADES/LENGTH: 3–6
PUBLISHER/
    COPYRIGHT: Sunburst Communications, Inc.

NOTES: Upbeat video that focuses on respecting one's body and learning facts about how the body works and how alcohol and other drugs affect one's body. Music reinforces the message in an appealing way.

TITLE: **The Wizard of No**
MEDIA/COST: Video ****
GRADES/LENGTH: 4–6/19 minutes
PUBLISHER/
    COPYRIGHT: MTI Film & Video/1990

NOTES: Twelve-year-old Billy is not pleased with himself for giving in to peer pressure to smoke. With the help of "Wizard of No," Billy discovers the amazing power within himself, the power of self-assertiveness—the power to say "No."

   Caution: The idea of a wizard talking to a child may be frightening and some parents may object.

7-22   TEST-TAKING SKILLS

TITLE: **Think Test Bingo Game**
MEDIA/COST: Game *
GRADES/LENGTH: 3–6/30 bingo boards
AUTHOR: Jackson
PUBLISHER/
    COPYRIGHT: Mar*Co Products, Inc.

NOTES: Addresses factors and strategies essential for successful test-taking. Areas include: working quietly, asking for clarification, concentrating, sleeping the night before, and checking work. Helpful to improve scores on standardized and teacher-made tests.

7-23   TRANSITION

TITLE: **First Day Blues**
                        (*The Decision Is Yours* Series)
MEDIA/COST: Book *
GRADES/LENGTH: 3–5/59 pages
AUTHOR: Anderson
PUBLISHER/
    COPYRIGHT: Parenting Press, Inc./1992

NOTES: Children decide what action the character should take and then see the consequences of each decision. Deals with a fifth-grade girl's first day in a new school. Reader experiences the anxieties of moving and starting in a new school. Opportunities for beginning new friendships are offered. Good book to read to students at the beginning of a new school year.

TITLE: **How to Succeed in Middle School**
MEDIA: Video/Guide ****
GRADES/LENGTH: 5–9/24 minutes
PUBLISHER/   Sunburst Communications, Inc./
    COPYRIGHT: 1994

NOTES: Helps students make the transition from elementary to middle school. Four eighth-grade students film a video to be shown to incoming students and their parents at the orientation meeting. Students interview current middle school sixth-grade students who share their anxieties and concerns about adjusting to middle school. Topics discussed are school work, lockers, schedules, time management, planning and organizational skills, interpersonal relationships, and extracurricular activities. Includes a guide with a self-management checklist, questions for discussion, role plays, and additional activities.

7-23 TRANSITION *(CONTINUED)*

TITLE:	**Moving On:**
	Moving On Video
	Moving On Workbook
MEDIA/COST:	Video/Lesson Plans/Workbook ***
GRADES/LENGTH:	5–7/Video, 15 minutes; Workbook, 28 pages
AUTHOR:	Greer (executive producer)
PUBLISHER/ COPYRIGHT:	Doulos Productions/1992

NOTES: Practical tips and strategies to alleviate the anxieties of middle school-bound students. Topics include: making friends, lockers, schedules, study tips, test-taking tips, showers, time management and goal setting, organization, studying at home, note-taking, getting to know teachers, and twelve keys to success. Lesson plans and activities. Seeking help and advice from school counselors is emphasized frequently.

Workbook reviews specific skills and strategies taught in the video. Workbook complements the video and allows students opportunity to discuss and record each topic in detail after seeing the video.

Counselors may want to coordinate meetings for parents with PTA/PTO presidents to alleviate parental anxiety as well as student anxiety.

Section 8

MATERIALS TO USE
WITH GRADES 6–9

ANNOTATED LIST OF MATERIALS TO USE WITH STUDENTS
(PERMISSION OF FAIRFAX COUNTY PUBLIC SCHOOLS OF VIRGINIA)

Cost Guide: * ($1-$25)   ** ($26-$55)   *** ($56-$105)   **** ($106-205)   ***** ($206-$505)   ****** ($506-$1,000)

8-1   CAREER EDUCATION

TITLE:	**ACT Explore**
MEDIA/COST:	Interest Inventory
GRADES/LENGTH:	7–9
PUBLISHER:	American College Testing (ACT)

NOTES: Excellent beginning to exploring and selecting careers. It can be used for a conference with student and parents to talk about possible career planning. Coordinated with DISCOVER. (List 9-1)

TITLE:	**Career Futures**
MEDIA/COST:	Computer Program ***** per site license
GRADES/LENGTH:	6–9
PUBLISHER:	Careerware

NOTES: Simplified version of CHOICES. Helpful in educational and life-career planning. Activities checklist to focus on clusters of occupations that relate to the students' interests. Students can then research occupations within respective career clusters. Information helps students select courses for high school, consider traditional and nontraditional jobs, and become aware of a variety of options.

TITLE:	**Career Game**
MEDIA/COST:	Booklet
GRADES/LENGTH:	6–9
PUBLISHER/ COPYRIGHT:	Rick Trow Productions/1996

NOTES: Excellent activities to help students clarify their interests and associate these with possible careers. As students choose a few careers in which they are interested, they can use the *Children's Occupational Outlook Handbook* and the *Job-O Dictionary* which are available both as printed materials and as computer software.

TITLE:	**Career Skills**
MEDIA/COST:	Book
GRADES/LENGTH:	6–9/256 pages
AUTHORS:	Kelly & Dolvolz-Patton
PUBLISHER/ COPYRIGHT:	Glencoe Publishing/1987

NOTES: Colorful and easy-to-read book. General information about careers. Appropriate for career center, library, or classroom.

8-1 CAREER EDUCATION *(CONTINUED)*

TITLE:	**Careers Tomorrow: The Outlook for Work in a Changing World**
MEDIA/COST:	Book *
GRADES/LENGTH:	7–12/159 pages
AUTHOR:	Cornish (Editor)
PUBLISHER/ COPYRIGHT:	World Future Society/1988

NOTES: Provides general information. Helpful for students learning about different careers. Particularly appropriate for students in middle school.

TITLE:	**CASE: Career Assessment Survey Exploration**
MEDIA/COST:	Interest Inventory
GRADES/LENGTH:	6–9/35 minutes
PUBLISHER/ COPYRIGHT:	Instructional Technology

NOTES: Interest inventory of 156 careers presented in a visual format in which reading is not required. Filmstrip projector and cassette player are needed. Provides information on 13 career clusters. Correlated with the *Dictionary of Occupational Titles* (DOT).

TITLE:	**CHOICES JR.: Planning My Future (for IBM)**
MEDIA/COST:	Computer Program *****
GRADES/LENGTH:	6–8
AUTHOR:	Canada Employment and Immigration Commission
PUBLISHER/ COPYRIGHT:	Careerware/1992

NOTES: Helpful in educational and life-career planning. Activities checklist to focus on clusters of occupations that relate to students' interests. Student can then research occupations within the particular career clusters. Helps students select courses for high school. Wide variety of jobs, but information is not in depth. Graphics are good, but could be more colorful.

TITLE:	**COPES: Career Orientation Placement and Evaluation Survey**
MEDIA/COST:	Interest Inventory
GRADES/LENGTH:	7–9/20–30 minutes
PUBLISHER/ COPYRIGHT:	Educational and Industrial Testing Service

NOTES: Comprehensive measurement of personal values that have been demonstrated to reflect the major dimensions in career selection. Scores provided: (1) Investigative vs. Accepting, (2) Practical vs. Carefree, (3) Independent vs. Conformity, (4) Leadership vs. Supportive, (5) Orderliness vs. Noncompulsive, (6) Recognition vs. Privacy, (7) Esthetic vs. Realistic, and (8) Social vs. Self-Concerned. Work values are related to the satisfactions derived from the work. Can be used in conjunction with COPS and CAPS (List 9-1) to create a sequential decision-making activity resulting in a five- or six-year plan.

TITLE:	**COPP: Career Orientation and Planning Profile**
MEDIA/COST:	School Starter Set ***
GRADES/LENGTH:	7–9
PUBLISHER/ COPYRIGHT:	Center on Education and Training for Employment

NOTES: Includes student career planning guides and career portfolios, counselor and teacher manuals, parent materials, etc., for a class of 30 students. Complete and helpful, but materials are disposable.

TITLE:	**COPS II: Career Occupational Preference Survey II** *(Intermediate Inventory)*
MEDIA/COST:	Personal Preferences Inventory and Planning Guide
GRADES/LENGTH:	7–9
AUTHOR:	Knapp & Knapp
PUBLISHER/ COPYRIGHT:	Educational and Industrial Testing Service/1981

NOTES: Helps develop an awareness of how personal preferences and attitudes influence career choices. Results enable students to understand themselves and choose activities, training, and school courses which help them in preparing for particular careers. Self scored. Helps students make meaningful decisions based on information.

8-1 CAREER EDUCATION *(CONTINUED)*

TITLE: **COPS-R: Career Occupational Preference Survey-R**

MEDIA/COST: Interest Inventory

GRADES/LENGTH: 6–9/Administration, 30–40 minutes; Scoring, 15–20 minutes

PUBLISHER/
COPYRIGHT: Educational and Industrial Testing Service

NOTES: Simplified form of the COPS. Provides scores in 14 clusters of occupations including professional and skilled levels. Scores are related to school courses and comprehensive occupational information in the *Occupational Outlook Handbook* (OOH) and the *Dictionary of Occupational Titles* (DOT). (List 9-1) Provides a structured decision-making process for students to compare their interests, abilities, and values to the major occupational information sources and to generate a five-year written educational plan.

———————

TITLE: **CPP: Career Planning Program, Level I**

MEDIA/COST: Interest Interview

GRADES/LENGTH: 6–9

PUBLISHER: American College Testing Program (ACT)

NOTES: Prepares students to select courses for high school. Fits well into an orientation program to help students begin to investigate groups of careers that have the characteristics of their own personal preferences.

———————

TITLE: **Dream Catchers: Developing Career & Educational Awareness in the Intermediate Grades**

MEDIA/COST: Workbook

GRADES/LENGTH: 6–9/58 pages

AUTHOR: Lindsay

PUBLISHER/
COPYRIGHT: JIST Works/1993

NOTES: Career clusters with activities to help students discover their skills. Indicates importance of ability, effort, and achievement. Basic information for career awareness.

TITLE: **IDEAS: Interest, Determination, Exploration, and Assessment System**

MEDIA/COST: Interest Inventory * (for 25)

GRADES/LENGTH: 6–9/40–50 minutes

PUBLISHER/
COPYRIGHT: Interpretive Scoring Systems

NOTES: Excellent short, simple, easy-to-administer, and self-scorable inventory for middle school students. Results can be used immediately. Good technical base with validity and reliability rooted in the Career Assessment Inventory (CAI). The CAI is particularly for students entering occupations requiring high school or a minimal degree of postsecondary training. Excellent to introduce students to well-organized career exploration and planning. Interest areas are: (1) mechanical/fixing, (2) electronics, (3) nature/outdoors, (4) science, (5) numbers, (6) writing, arts/crafts, (7) social service, (8) child care, (9) medical service, (10) business, (11) sales, office practices, and (12) food services. Refers to the *Dictionary of Occupational Titles* (DOT) and *Occupational Outlook Handbook* (OOH). (List 9-1)

8-1 CAREER EDUCATION *(CONTINUED)*

TITLE:	**JOB-O**
MEDIA/COST:	Interest Inventory ** (for 25 booklets)
GRADES/LENGTH:	6–9/40 minutes
AUTHOR:	Kauk
PUBLISHER/ COPYRIGHT:	CFKR Career Materials/1994

NOTES: Unique, game-like format to match educational aspirations and job interests with 120 major job titles. Reusable self-assessment booklets and consumable answer folders. Information about six major career groups includes: definition, representative jobs, and job values. Students learn factual information about careers and then can act on that information by doing activities that promote self-awareness. Leads to self-awareness, job exploration, and matching jobs with personal needs. Self-scoring format provides immediate feedback and is in simple language. Available on computer disk.

TITLE:	**Life Centered Career Education, Activity Books One and Two**
MEDIA/COST:	Activity Books
GRADES/LENGTH:	5–9/100 pages
AUTHORS:	Miller, Glascoe, & Kokaska
PUBLISHER/ COPYRIGHT:	Council for Exceptional Children/1986

NOTES: Lesson plans to infuse career education in the classroom with excellent activity books. Specific activities help students develop daily living skills, personal/social skills, and occupational skills. Teachers and counselors find these books helpful.

TITLE:	**Opportunities for a Lifetime: A Health Careers Reference Manual**
MEDIA/COST:	Booklet
GRADES/LENGTH:	7–12/124 pages
AUTHOR:	Howland (Editor)
PUBLISHER/ COPYRIGHT:	Virginia Health Council, Inc./ 1993–94

NOTES: Information about many health careers and addresses for more information. Descriptions are clearly written and helpful to students.

TITLE:	**OVIS: Ohio Vocational Interest Survey II**
MEDIA/COST:	Interest Inventory
GRADES/LENGTH:	6–9
PUBLISHER/ COPYRIGHT:	Psychological Corporation

NOTES: Combines a complete interest inventory with a career planning questionnaire and a local survey. Provides students with a starting point for career exploration and planning. OVIS II is correlated to the *Dictionary of Occupational Titles* (DOT) and the *Occupational Outlook Handbook* (OOH). Summary data assists counselor in planning guidance services and making decisions about high school courses. Filmstrips and other aids are available. Hand or computer scored.

TITLE:	**Pathfinder: Exploring Career & Educational Paths**
MEDIA/COST:	Workbook
GRADES/LENGTH:	7–12/101 pages
AUTHOR:	Lindsay
PUBLISHER/ COPYRIGHT:	JIST Works/1994

NOTES: Encourages students to discover their interests, research careers of interest and necessary education, and plan their future. Stresses the need for particular levels of education for specific careers.

TITLE:	**Pathfinders: Women in the Workforce**
MEDIA/COST:	Video *
GRADES/LENGTH:	7–12/4-part series
PUBLISHER/ COPYRIGHT:	Fairfax Network/1995–96

NOTES: Women who are veterinarians, acupuncturists, CEOs, stockbrokers, lawyers, and judges encourage students to set goals and work to achieve them. These professional women talk about selecting a course of study, deciding on a career, and following a path to success. Four parts: (1) Careers in Medical Professions, (2) Careers in Business, (3) Careers in Law and Government, and (4) Careers in Journalism.

8-1 CAREER EDUCATION *(CONTINUED)*

TITLE: **Working Today and Tomorrow: Teacher's Edition and Workbook**

MEDIA/COST: Workbook/Guide

GRADES/LENGTH: 7–12/405 pages

AUTHOR: Weisser (Editor)

PUBLISHER/
  COPYRIGHT: Council for Exceptional Children

NOTES: Business oriented. Can be used for a course on career preparation. Colorful pictures and hands-on activities help students explore future roles as workers and consumers. *Part One* helps students understand themselves and the nature of work. *Part Two* shows the work force. *Parts Three, Four,* and *Five* help students learn how to become effective workers and manage resources efficiently, making good financial decisions.

8-3 CONFLICT RESOLUTION

TITLE: **Alternatives to Violence: A Two-Part Program on Conflict Resolution, Negotiation & Mediation**

MEDIA/COST: 2 Videos/Guide

GRADES/LENGTH: 6–10/14 lessons, 77 pages

AUTHORS: Hitchcock & Compton

PUBLISHER/
  COPYRIGHT: United Learning/1994

NOTES: *Part 1* introduces concepts and skills of conflict resolution, negotiation, and mediation to students. *Part 2* is for staff development and focuses on alternatives to violence and how to implement a conflict-resolution and peer-mediation program in the school.

TITLE: **Creative Conflict Solving for Kids Grades 4-9**

MEDIA/COST: Book/Guide/Worksheets/Poster *

GRADES/LENGTH: 4–9/Book, 71 pages

AUTHORS: Schmidt & Friedman

PUBLISHER/
  COPYRIGHT: Grace Contrino Abrams

NOTES: Excellent resource for conflict mediation. Lessons can be easily incorporated into the curriculum. Helps students develop interpersonal skills, respect differences, understand causes of conflict, practice conflict resolution, and learn ways to handle frustration and anger.

TITLE: **Don't Pick on Me!**

MEDIA/COST: Video/Guide ****

GRADES/LENGTH: 6–9/21 minutes

PUBLISHER/
  COPYRIGHT: Sunburst Communications, Inc./ 1994

NOTES: Helps children develop an understanding of harassment and the ways it can be camouflaged. *Part I* explores the behavior of a bully. *Part II* shows how devastating ostracism can be. Students are taught three techniques: (1) ignore the teasing, (2) find allies and use them for support, and (3) leave the situation. Guide contains activities, summary, script, role plays, and bibliography.

TITLE: **Fighting Fair: For Kids Grades 4–9**

MEDIA: Video/Booklet/Guide/Poster ***

GRADES/LENGTH: 6–9

PUBLISHER/
  COPYRIGHT: Grace Contrino Abrams/1990

NOTES: Relevant concepts and ideas based on the teaching of Dr. Martin Luther King, Jr. Gives a perspective of Black History. Excellent resource for a conflict-mediation program. Video is powerful and shows scenes from the civil rights movement.

8-3 CONFLICT RESOLUTION *(CONTINUED)*

TITLE: **Getting Along: Conflict Resolution**

MEDIA/COST: Video/Guide ****

GRADES/LENGTH: 6–12/26 minutes

PUBLISHER/
COPYRIGHT: Sunburst Communications, Inc./ 1992

NOTES: Teaches students the essential skills of conflict resolution. Shows how to avoid conflict, resolve problems, and build better relationships. Three major components: "What's Your Conflict Style?," "The Key Is Communication," and "Peace at Last."

TITLE: **Silence the Violence: Skills for Prevention**

MEDIA/COST: Video/Guide ****

GRADES/LENGTH: 6–9/20 minutes

PUBLISHER/
COPYRIGHT: Sunburst Communications, Inc./ 1995

NOTES: Motivates students to learn and use skills to resolve conflicts, prevent violence, and gain greater control over conflicts in their lives. Guide has additional follow-up activities and worksheets that support the skills needed to resolve conflicts.

TITLE: **Student Workshop: Conflict Resolution Skills**

MEDIA/COST: Video/Guide ****

GRADES/LENGTH: 5–9/30 minutes

PUBLISHER/
COPYRIGHT: Sunburst Communications, Inc./ 1994

NOTES: Teaches six basic skills of conflict resolution: (1) Getting the facts, (2) Active listening, (3) Body language, (4) Tone of voice, (5) "I Messages," and (6) Brainstorming. Each segment contains excellent examples of the skill being taught. Role plays and activities motivate students to practice what they learn.

TITLE: **Working It Out: Conflict Resolution**

MEDIA/COST: Video/Guide ****

GRADES/LENGTH: 5–9/30 minutes

PUBLISHER/
COPYRIGHT: Sunburst Communications, Inc./ 1992

NOTES: Teaches effective communication skills and techniques for resolving conflicts. A teen call-in radio show hosted by Dr. Advice; the "rules of the road" for conflict resolution are introduced. Focuses on cooperation and compromise and helps students gain insight into their behavior while learning practical problem-solving strategies.

TITLE: **Working It Out . . . Solving Conflicts**

(Making Choices—Growing Stronger Series)

MEDIA/COST: Guidance Unit *

GRADES/LENGTH: 6–8/40 pages

AUTHOR: Falk

PUBLISHER/
COPYRIGHT: Elizabeth Falk, M.A., LPC/1992

NOTES: A nine-session guidance unit to help students: (1) identify problems and sources of conflicts, (2) review their own problem-solving methods, and (3) learn strategies for stressful situations. Includes techniques to introduce and reinforce concepts.

8-5   DECISION MAKING

TITLE:	**Change My Attitude? Yes!**
	(*Making Choices—Growing Stronger* Series)
MEDIA/COST:	Guidance Unit *
GRADES/LENGTH:	5–7/22 pages
AUTHOR:	Falk
PUBLISHER/	
COPYRIGHT:	Elizabeth Falk, M.A., LPC/1993

NOTES: A six-week program that addresses a student's desire: (1) to be liked and accepted, (2) to achieve, and (3) to develop life-long competencies. Activities address results of a good attitude versus a poor attitude. Activities also link present attitudes and goals for the future. Each weekly lesson is between 20 and 30 minutes.

TITLE:	**I Blew It! Learning From Failure**
MEDIA/COST:	Video ***
GRADES/LENGTH:	5–9/24 minutes
PUBLISHER/	
COPYRIGHT:	Sunburst Communications, Inc./ 1988

NOTES: Vignettes showing different results of different decisions, and how to learn even when one feels that he or she has failed. Honorable Mention, National Educational Film and Video Festival. Recommended by *Booklist,* and *School Library Journal.*

TITLE:	**Taking Chances: Teens and Risk**
MEDIA/COST:	Video/Guide ****
GRADES/LENGTH:	5–9/27 minutes
PUBLISHER/	
COPYRIGHT:	Sunburst Communications, Inc./ 1994

NOTES: The content (drinking, smoking, and risk taking) is appropriate for middle school students.

TITLE:	**You Can Say No: Here's How**
MEDIA/COST:	Video/Guide ****
GRADES/LENGTH:	5–9/23 minutes
PUBLISHER/	
COPYRIGHT:	Sunburst Communications, Inc./ 1990

NOTES: Excellent video of students in vignettes that require them to exercise good judgment, peer-refusal skills, and sound decision making. Radio disc jockey, "Dr. Advice," teaches teens and preteens appropriate ways to handle various situations such as refusing to go along with a friend's prank, discussing job requirements with an adult, returning defective merchandise to a store, and standing up for their rights, even with an adult. Appropriate social skills are stressed in each scenario.

8-8   EMOTIONS

TITLE:	**Feelings: Inside, Outside, Upside Down**
MEDIA/COST:	Video/Guide ****
GRADES/LENGTH:	6–9/19 minutes
PUBLISHER/	
COPYRIGHT:	Sunburst Communications, Inc./ 1994

NOTES: Teenagers and the physical, emotional, and social changes experienced during puberty: "What's happening to me?" "Is it normal?" "Should I be feeling this way?" Guide has several activities and questions. Script available so students can put on their own skit. Can be used with counseling groups and parents. *Caution:* The author refers to this information as sexual education, and suggests that parental permission be obtained before the child views this video.

8-8 EMOTIONS *(CONTINUED)*

TITLE:	**When Anger Turns to Rage**
MEDIA/COST:	Video/Guide ***
GRADES/LENGTH:	5–9/27 minutes
PUBLISHER/ COPYRIGHT:	Sunburst Communications, Inc./ 1995

NOTES: Excellent video for fifth- and sixth-grade students. Anger is presented as a natural, normal emotion that everyone experiences. Teaches students "triggers" that may cause angry feelings and ways to control their behavior when they have angry feelings. Anger can also motivate positive change. Gold Medal Questar Award. Recommended by *School Library Journal* and *Booklist.*

TITLE:	**When You're Mad, Mad, Mad—Dealing With Anger**
MEDIA/COST:	Video/Guide ***
GRADES/LENGTH:	5–9/27 minutes
PUBLISHER/ COPYRIGHT:	Sunburst Communications, Inc./ 1993

NOTES: Excellent video for Anger Management group or for classroom guidance. Golden Eagle Award from Council on International Non-Theatrical Events (INE). Recommended by *School Library Journal, Video Rating Guide for Librarians,* and *Emergency Librarian.*

8-9   FAMILY

TITLE:	**Me and My Parents: Working It Out**
MEDIA/COST:	Video ****
GRADES/LENGTH:	6–9/23 minutes
PUBLISHER/ COPYRIGHT:	Sunburst Communications, Inc./ 1994

NOTES: Examines communication between students and their parents. Students are given practical and helpful ways to communicate their concerns to their parents. Also offers insights and practical help to parents.

8-10   FRIENDSHIPS

TITLE:	**Being a Friend: What Does It Mean?**
MEDIA/COST:	Video/Guide ****
GRADES/LENGTH:	5–9/20 minutes
PUBLISHER/ COPYRIGHT:	Sunburst Communications, Inc./ 1995

NOTES: Explores issues that frequently arise when adolescents change their expectations for peers and peer groups. Scenarios show social concerns such as taking risks, making new friends, understanding the expectations of others, and learning to handle and evaluate the inevitable crises that arise in friendships. Recommended by *School Library Journal* and *Booklist.* Gold CINDY Award from Association of Visual Communication.

TITLE:	**When to Say Yes! and Make More Friends**
MEDIA/COST:	Book *
GRADES/LENGTH:	6–12/107 pages
AUTHOR:	Scott
PUBLISHER/ COPYRIGHT:	Human Resource Development Press, Inc./1988

NOTES: Follows Sharon Scott's previous book *How to Say No and Keep Your Friends.* Nine miniskills on feeling good, doing good, building self-esteem, and growing positively with friends. Can be read by an individual student or used by a counselor in a small or large group.

8-11   GROUP COUNSELING

TITLE:	**Peers Helping Peers: Program for the Preadolescent**
MEDIA/COST:	Book
GRADES/LENGTH:	6–9
AUTHOR:	Tindall
PUBLISHER/ COPYRIGHT:	Accelerated Development/1990

NOTES: Practical book for middle school students. Lessons for peer-counseling training.

8-11 GROUP COUNSELING (CONTINUED)

TITLE: **Teaching Helping Skills
                to Middle School Students:
                Program Leader's Guide**

MEDIA/COST: Book

GRADES/LENGTH: 6–9

AUTHORS: Myrick & Sorenson

PUBLISHER/
  COPYRIGHT: Educational Media/1992

NOTES: Particularly helpful in middle school. Guidelines for selection of peer facilitators and training for the selected facilitators. Good manual to follow when leading peer-facilitation groups.

8-12   MULTICULTURAL

TITLE: **Images**

MEDIA/COST: Book *

GRADES/LENGTH: 6–12/184 pages

AUTHOR: Circle Project, California State
                Dept. of Ed.

DISTRIBUTOR/
  COPYRIGHT: Paperbacks for Educators/1988

NOTES: A framework for girls to look at their past, present, and future. Motivation for researching the history of the African American race and culture as well as individual family history. Activities to help students examine their images, assess the need for change, and consider career goals. Excellent resource for girls who are at–risk of substance abuse, dropping out of school, or teen pregnancy.

TITLE: **Open Minds to Equality: A
                Sourcebook of Learning Activities
                to Promote Race, Sex, Class, and
                Age Equity**

MEDIA/COST: Book

GRADES/LENGTH: 6–9

AUTHORS: Schniedewind & Davidson

PUBLISHER/
  COPYRIGHT: Allyn & Bacon/1993

NOTES: Activity book for elementary and middle school. Equality, respect, and school climate are presented at developmental level of students.

TITLE: **Takeoff: African American Role
                Model Series—Programs 1, 2, 3, 4,
                5, and 6**

                1. *Fire Fighter*
                2. *Assembly Advisor*
                3. *Iron Worker*
                4. *Corporation Executive Officer*
                5. *Auto Dealership Owner*
                6. *Media Producer*

MEDIA/COST: Videos

GRADES/LENGTH: 7–12/20 minutes

PUBLISHER/
  COPYRIGHT: Producers Communication
                Services, Inc./1991

NOTES: Provides students with a realistic insight into careers of average Americans, not stereotypical. Positive African American role models discuss their jobs and experiences. Three different workers stress the importance of education, communication skills, and initiative. Well-written and well-produced. Upbeat message, encouraging, and informative. Supportive advice for educational goals and the work ethic.

8-12 MULTICULTURAL (CONTINUED)

TITLE: **Takeoff: Hispanic Experience—Opportunities in the 21st Century Workplace**

1. *News Photographer*
2. *Restaurant Owner*
3. *Interior Designer*
4. *FBI Agent*
5. *Home Health Care Attendant*

MEDIA/COST: Video

GRADES/LENGTH: 7–12/36 minutes

PUBLISHER/
COPYRIGHT: Producers Communication Services, Inc./1991

NOTES: Good role models discuss their jobs, how they got their jobs, and what they like about them. Informative, encouraging, and motivating.

8-14   RESPECT

TITLE: **Best Foot Forward: A Manners Video**

MEDIA/COST: Video/Guide ****

GRADES/LENGTH: 5–8/19 minutes

PUBLISHER/
COPYRIGHT: Sunburst Communications, Inc./1994

NOTES: Excellent video for preteens. Answers many questions young people may have and helps them become more aware of how good manners will increase their comfort level in social situations, allowing them to become more confident and have improved self-esteem.

TITLE: **Facing Up**

MEDIA/COST: Video/Guide *****

GRADES/LENGTH: 6–8/20 minutes

PUBLISHER/
COPYRIGHT: Committee for Children/1992

NOTES: Illustrates inner struggles of two boys as they gain the skills needed to face up to and interrupt the cycle of violence. Skills are modeled in a life-like situation. Demonstrates use of problem-solving strategies, assertive responses to bullying, anger management with self-talk, and viable alternatives to bullying. Helps students identify resource people for support. Suggestions for role plays and discussion situations are in the guide.

TITLE: **Second Step: Grades 6–8**

MEDIA/COST: Kit *****

GRADES/LENGTH: 7–9/15 lessons (5 weeks)

PUBLISHER/
COPYRIGHT: Committee for Children/1992

NOTES: Reduces impulsive and aggressive behavior while it increases respect for others through social-skill training and anger-management techniques. Great to use in classrooms and in small groups. Counselors are given questions for each lesson. Transparencies and role-play cards reinforce instructional techniques for all learning styles. Culturally balanced and contemporary. Excellent, practical program. Lessons do not need to be used in sequence, but can be selected as needed. Take-home letters are included in the binder. Wonderful resource to use with many groups.

8-15   RESPONSIBILITY

TITLE: **Trust Me! Learning to Be Responsible**

MEDIA/COST: Video/Guide ****

GRADES/LENGTH: 6–9/22 minutes

PUBLISHER/
COPYRIGHT: Sunburst Communications, Inc./1995

NOTES: Six typical scenarios of middle school experience. Thought-provoking discussion questions include responsibility as a student, family member, and friend. Bronze medal from International Film and TV Festival of New York, Bronze CINDY Award, Association of Visual Communications. Recommended by *School Library Journal*.

8-16   SAFETY

TITLE: **Books About Safety**

Are You in the House Alone?— Richard Peck

*Did You Hear What Happened to Andrea?—*Gloria D. Miklowitz

*The Voices of Rape—*Janet Bode

Why Me? The Story of Jenny— Patricia Dizenzo

MEDIA/COST: Books *

GRADES/LENGTH: 6–9

NOTES: Counselor is advised to read the book before recommending it to a student to read. Situations are very unique and the counselor must ensure that the book he or she recommends is the right book at the right time for that particular student.

TITLE: **Is It Love . . . Or Is It Gross? Is It Sexual Harassment?**

MEDIA/COST: Video ***

GRADES/LENGTH: 7–12/26 minutes

PUBLISHER/
   COPYRIGHT: National Center for Violence Prevention/1992

NOTES: A call-in radio show for teens discusses sexual harassment. Defines sexual harassment. Discusses several different situations and provides suggestions about how to cope with each situation.

TITLE: **Sexual Harassment**

MEDIA/COST: Video ***

GRADES/LENGTH: 7–12/30 minutes

PUBLISHER/
   COPYRIGHT: National Center for Violence Prevention/1994

NOTES: A discussion of harassment, date rape, and differences between honest affection and harassment.

TITLE: **Sexual Harassment: Crossing the Line**

MEDIA/COST: Video ***

GRADES/LENGTH: 7–12/30 minutes

PUBLISHER/
   COPYRIGHT: Karol Video/1993

NOTES: Explains different kinds of sexual harassment. Describes the factors that motivate harassers and provides specific techniques for dealing effectively with sexual harassment.

TITLE: **Sexual Harassment: It's Hurting People**

MEDIA/COST: Video *****

GRADES/LENGTH: 5–9/18 minutes

AUTHOR: National Middle School Association & Quality Work Environments

PUBLISHER/
   COPYRIGHT: Sunburst Communications, Inc.

NOTES: Excellent video to help the four out of five students who say they are sexually harassed often or occasionally. Makes clear that harassment is demeaning and wrong. Shows harassers how their behavior hurts other people. Details how schools can stop sexual harassment. Presented in a sensitive way and students pay attention.

TITLE: **Sexual Harassment: Minimize the Risk**

MEDIA/COST: Videos/Guide

GRADES/LENGTH: 6–11

AUTHOR: McGrath

PUBLISHER/
   COPYRIGHT: McGrath Systems/1993

NOTES: Comprehensive training program. Includes three multimedia training packages: Six videos with accompanying printed materials. Three-part section for educators and staff and two-part section for students. Package for students; *Sexual Harassment: Pay Attention!*, can be used without video. Includes definitions, examples, and how to avoid being victimized.

8-16 SAFETY *(CONTINUED)*

TITLE:	**Sexual Harassment: Pay Attention!**
MEDIA/COST:	Booklet
GRADES/LENGTH:	6–9
AUTHOR:	McGrath
PUBLISHER/ COPYRIGHT:	McGrath Systems/1993

NOTES: Excellent book with lesson plans that include student activities, vignettes, and reproducible activity sheets. Specifies procedures students can take to get immediate help in the school. A no-nonsense approach to harassment that is easily implemented in a school and provides comfort and relief to students who are harassed frequently. Package designed for classroom lessons. Includes definitions, examples, and how to avoid being victimized.

TITLE:	**What Is Sexual Harassment?**
MEDIA/COST:	Video ***
GRADES/LENGTH:	6–10/23 minutes
PUBLISHER/ COPYRIGHT:	KIDSRIGHTS/1994

NOTES: Clearly and concisely defines and delineates sexual harassment from flirting. Sexual harassment is explained, dealing with real issues at school and at work. Raises awareness of acceptable and unacceptable conduct.

TITLE:	**What Young People Should Know About AIDS**
MEDIA/COST:	Booklet
GRADES/LENGTH:	6–9
PUBLISHER/ COPYRIGHT:	Channing L. Bete

NOTES: Easy-to-read, informational booklet to inform students about AIDS. Also available in Spanish.

8-17   SELF-DISCIPLINE

TITLE:	**Go, Go, Goals!: How to Get There**
MEDIA/COST:	Video/Guide ****
GRADES/LENGTH:	5–9/26 minutes
PUBLISHER/ COPYRIGHT:	Sunburst Communications, Inc./ 1994

NOTES: Demonstrates that goals can be achieved by using a step-by-step process, beginning with selecting a goal. The characters are middle school students, extremely believable and likable. The Elizabeth Falk material on goal setting is a good follow up to this video.

TITLE:	**Trouble at School**
MEDIA/COST:	Video/Guide ****
GRADES/LENGTH:	5–9/21 minutes
PUBLISHER/ COPYRIGHT:	Sunburst Communications, Inc./ 1994

NOTES: A story of three students experiencing a crisis at school. Students work through their problems and obtain help from the school counselor and their classmates. The guide accompanying the video has a list of discussion questions and suggested activities that involve writing, art, and role plays.

8-18   SELF-ESTEEM

TITLE:	**Girls in the Middle: Working to Succeed in School**
MEDIA/COST:	Report/Video *
GRADES/LENGTH:	6–9/128 pages
AUTHORS:	Cohen, Blanc, Christman, Brown, & Sims
PUBLISHER/ COPYRIGHT:	AAUW Sales Office/1996

NOTES: Shows how adolescent girls—regardless of race, ethnicity, socioeconomic status, or area of the country—use a common set of behaviors to meet challenges of middle school. These behaviors have risks. Success in school by girls sometimes is linked to some school reforms such as team teaching and cooperative learning. Some reforms confronting real student concerns such as violence, pregnancy, and social norms benefit boys as well as girls.

8-18 SELF-ESTEEM (CONTINUED)

TITLE: **I Like Being Me: Self-Esteem**

MEDIA/COST: Video/Guide ***

GRADES/LENGTH: 5–9/26 minutes

PUBLISHER/
     COPYRIGHT: Sunburst Communications, Inc./
                 1990

NOTES: Three vignettes with two pauses for discussion. Worksheets to assist students with understanding the decision-making process and designed to be used during the pauses in the video. Throughout the program, a group of students—representing various levels of self-esteem—dramatize situations familiar to middle school students. Finalist in American Film and Video Festival. Received Honorable Mention in National Educational Film and Video Festival.

TITLE: **Only One Me . . . Only One You**

MEDIA/COST: Video/Guide ****

GRADES/LENGTH: 5–9/25 minutes

PUBLISHER/
     COPYRIGHT: Sunburst Communications, Inc./
                 1994

NOTES: Helps students understand and appreciate themselves as individuals and encourages students to accept and value differences that make each person special. Three scenarios are presented: *Part I—Do Your Own Thing*, *Part II—Sharing What Makes Us Different*, and *Part III—Not So Different After All*. The guide contains questions for discussion, activities, role plays, and worksheets.

TITLE: **Self-Confidence: Step-by-Step**

MEDIA/COST: Video/Guide ****

GRADES/LENGTH: 5–9/21 minutes

PUBLISHER/
     COPYRIGHT: Sunburst Communications, Inc./
                 1994

NOTES: Middle school students frequently struggle with issues of self-confidence, such as one's appearance, handling put downs, and taking on new skills. Jenni learns to risk being laughed at in order to gain the pleasure of participating in sports at school. Willie learns to allow himself to fail and try again at photography. Tony learns to handle put downs and turn negative "self-talk" into positive "self-talk." This program emphasizes the importance of starting small and not trying to change one's whole life all at once. Students learn to talk to someone else about a problem, to break a goal into small steps, and to take one step at a time to begin a process they will use for a lifetime.

TITLE: **Self-Esteem Curriculum Module**

MEDIA: Kit/Videos ******

GRADES/LENGTH: 5–9/8 Videos

PUBLISHER/
     COPYRIGHT: Sunburst Communications, Inc./
                 1991

NOTES: Uses cooperative learning to help students develop a sense of worth. Topics include liking yourself, friends and you, being assertive, making decisions, and success and failure. Includes videos, lesson plans, role-play cards, and other activities as well as staff-development plans and video to make this a schoolwide program.

8-19   SOCIAL DEVELOPMENT

TITLE: **Ready-to-Use Social Skills Lessons and Activities**

MEDIA/COST: Activity Book **

GRADES/LENGTH: 6–10/212 pages

AUTHOR: Begun (Editor)

PUBLISHER/
     COPYRIGHT: Center for Applied Research in
                 Education/1995

NOTES: Includes lesson plans and reproducible activity sheets that can be used in small-group counseling or the classroom. Helps students build self-esteem, improve communication skills, set goals, solve problems, use self-control, cope with anger, respect others, stop false rumors, and deal with prejudice. Activities are particularly appropriate for grades 6–9.

TITLE: **SchoolGirls: Young Women, Self-Esteem, and the Confidence Gap**

MEDIA/COST: Book

GRADES/LENGTH: 6–9

AUTHOR: Orenstein

PUBLISHER/
     COPYRIGHT: AAUW Sales Office/1993

NOTES: Adolescent girls at two middle schools are followed through the school year. One girl is from a predominantly white and middle class school, the other from a predominantly black and economically disadvantaged school. This book, written by a journalist, was inspired by the survey reported in *Shortchanging Girls, Shortchanging America*. (See List 11-8)

8-20   STUDY SKILLS

TITLE: **Crossroads: A Mentor's Guide, Parts I, II, III, and IV**

MEDIA/COST: Videos *

GRADES/LENGTH: 6–9/57 minutes

PUBLISHER/
    COPYRIGHT: Fairfax Network/1993-94

NOTES: Excellent videos explaining mentoring programs throughout the nation. *Part II* is a handbook for mentors of at-risk youth. Guests include a middle school counselor, a child psychologist, a Big Brother caseworker, a Big Brother who had been a Little Brother, and a mentor from Mentors, Inc. Overview of issues in setting up and running a mentoring program. Important information to have when implementing such a program.

TITLE: **Ellen Glasgow Mentor Program Components**

MEDIA/COST: Book *

GRADES/LENGTH: 6–9/66 pages

AUTHOR: Aiello

PUBLISHER/
    COPYRIGHT: Fairfax Network/1996

NOTES: Excellent resource and handbook for mentors. Includes warm-up and relation-building activities, ideas for structure and accountability, and formative and summative program evaluation instruments. A training model and reference for mentors. Describes a mentor, includes a contract, student questionnaire, study-skills self-assessment, teacher assessment of student performance, a program timeline, and many other helpful forms. Program is successful in a middle school where 75 percent of the population is minority.

TITLE: **Mentor Program for At-Risk Youth:**

                    (Developing a School-Based Mentor Program for At-Risk Youth)

                    Handbook for Mentors

MEDIA/COST: Books *

GRADES/LENGTH: 6–9/Book, 119 pages; Handbook, 63 pages

AUTHOR: Adams

PUBLISHER/
    COPYRIGHT: Chesterfield Communities in Schools/1995

NOTES: Excellent resources to develop a mentor program to prevent students from dropping out of school. Program can be implemented in a middle school. Handbook helps mentor understand the role of the mentor in the school.

TITLE: **Study Skills Plus Attitude: The Winning Combination**

MEDIA/COST: Video ****

GRADES/LENGTH: 6/32 minutes

PUBLISHER/
    COPYRIGHT: Sunburst Communications, Inc./ 1989

NOTES: Helps sixth-grade students recognize different study styles and introduces ideas on how to improve their grades.

8-21   SUBSTANCE ABUSE PREVENTION

TITLE: **Downfall: Sports and Drugs**

MEDIA/COST: Video

GRADES/LENGTH: 6–12/29 minutes

PUBLISHER/
    COPYRIGHT: NCADI (Order from PRIDE)/1988

NOTES: Shows sports figures who have jeopardized their futures and ruined their careers and their lives because of drugs.

8-21 SUBSTANCE ABUSE PREVENTION (CONTINUED)

TITLE: **Drugs, Your Friends, and You**

MEDIA/COST: Video ****

GRADES/LENGTH: 5–9/26 minutes

PUBLISHER/
    COPYRIGHT: Sunburst Communications, Inc./
                    1989

NOTES: Examines various ways that peer pressure may be exerted. Outlines techniques for dealing assertively with this pressure. Shows how to find new interests and new friends when uncomfortable or bored with friends who are using alcohol or other drugs.

TITLE: **Project Alert Training**

MEDIA: Training/Video ***

GRADES/LENGTH: 5–8/8- to 11-week program; Video,
                    35–50 minutes

PUBLISHER/
    COPYRIGHT: Project Alert/1985

NOTES: Program of 11 sessions to correct misperceptions about prevalence of use of drugs, and develop necessary skills and motivation to resist pressure to use drugs. Eight sessions in seventh grade and three sessions in eighth grade. Includes skills to resist peer pressure, and activities for students to practice resisting the use of drugs. Includes a workshop, curriculum, videos, and lesson plans for teachers. No turnaround training.

Project has been evaluated using a strong research design that included urban, suburban, and rural schools; low- and high-risk youth; as well as a diverse ethnic population. Significantly reduced use of cigarettes and marijuana in 15-month follow up.

TITLE: **STAR Midwestern Prevention Program, Project STAR**

MEDIA/COST: Curriculum

GRADES/LENGTH: 6–7

PUBLISHER/
    COPYRIGHT: Available from U. S. Department of
                    Education

NOTES: Practical step-by-step approach to teaching resistance skills to middle school students in ten sessions. A school-based curriculum that includes parents, media, and community-program components. Over 22,000 adolescents received the program that showed significant reduction in tobacco and marijuana use maintained for three years. Research shows success.

TITLE: **Straight at Ya**

MEDIA/COST: Video

GRADES/LENGTH: 6–9/50 minutes

PUBLISHER/
    COPYRIGHT: National Clearing House for
                    Alcohol & Drug Information/1988

NOTES: A class discussion on substance abuse prevention. During the discussion the teacher gives examples of how students are pressured into drug use and what to do to avoid it. The format and information is presented so that students pay attention and enjoy it. There is a mixture of class discussion, cartoons, and vignettes.

TITLE: **Substance Abuse Prevention Activities**
                    (*Just for the Health of It!* Series)

MEDIA/COST: Workbook *

GRADES/LENGTH: 6–9/160 pages

AUTHOR: Toner

PUBLISHER/
    COPYRIGHT: Center for Applied Research in
                    Education/1993

NOTES: Ready-to-use activities to inform students of the effects and dangers inherent in the use of tobacco, alcohol, marijuana, and other drugs. Includes games, puzzles, and other appealing activities. Worksheets are reproducible.

TITLE: **Tanya Talks About Chemical Dependence in the Family**

MEDIA/COST: Handbook ***

GRADES/LENGTH: 6–8/232 pages

AUTHORS: Schmidt & Spencer

PUBLISHER/
    COPYRIGHT: Johnson Institute

NOTES: Students learn the rules for maintaining good relationships. They also learn to make their anger work for them and develop skills that they need in order to cope when living with a chemically-dependent family member. *Note:* The counselor must be cautious in using this handbook.

8-23 TRANSITION

TITLE:	**High School Career Course Planner**
MEDIA/COST:	Interest Inventory
GRADES/LENGTH:	8–9
PUBLISHER:	CFKR Career Materials

NOTES: Comprehensive folder contains activities: (1) Self-assessment of job interests, (2) match of interests with 16 major occupational clusters (OOH), (3) occupational cluster of highest interest, (4) job titles and educational planning for jobs within occupational clusters, and (5) a high school plan (grades 8–12) based on self-assessed career interests and available high school courses.

Section 9

MATERIALS TO USE WITH GRADES 9–12

ANNOTATED LIST OF MATERIALS TO USE WITH STUDENTS

(PERMISSION OF FAIRFAX COUNTY PUBLIC SCHOOLS OF VIRGINIA)

Cost Guide: * ($1–$25)   ** ($26–$55)   *** ($56–$105)   **** ($106–205)   ***** ($206–$505)   ****** ($506–$1,000)

9-1   CAREER EDUCATION

TITLE:	**200 Letters for Job Hunters: How to Conduct a Successful Job Search**
MEDIA/COST:	Book *
GRADES/LENGTH:	9–12/345 pages
AUTHOR:	Frank
PUBLISHER/ COPYRIGHT:	Ten Speed Press/1990

NOTES: Actual letters and a section entitled "What to Do for a Quick Job-Search." May be helpful to certain students.

TITLE:	**90-Minute Resume: For Job Hunters Who Want Top-Notch Results—Fast!**
MEDIA/COST:	Booklet
GRADES/LENGTH:	9–12/86 pages
AUTHOR:	Schmidt
PUBLISHER/ COPYRIGHT:	Peterson's Guides/1990

NOTES: A "quick guide" to writing resumes. It provides some helpful hints about format.

TITLE:	**ASVAB: Armed Service Vocational Aptitude Battery**
MEDIA/COST:	Aptitude Test/Free
GRADES/LENGTH:	10–12/3 hours

NOTES: A multiple aptitude test battery administered and interpreted by the military. Provides workbooks to interpret results and includes the Self-Directed Search (SDS) free to every student who takes the ASVAB. Excellent tool. Three academic composites: (1) Academic Ability, (2) Verbal Ability, and (3) Math Ability. Four occupational composites: (1) Mechanical and Crafts; (2) Business and Clerical; (3) Electronics and Electrical; and (4) Health, Social and Technology. Scored by the Department of Defense. The scores are returned to participating schools within 30 days. Although the ASVAB includes an extensive list of occupations, it is limited to vocations for which the armed forces provide training. Some students may be identified as possible ROTC scholarship candidates. *Caution:* Students who score well will be contacted by recruiters.

9-1 CAREER EDUCATION *(CONTINUED)*

TITLE: **Books About Careers**

Life After High School *

Preparing Teens for the World of Work *

School-to-Work Transition *

Student's Guide to the Hottest Jobs for the 21st Century *

Successful Strategies: Building a School-to-Career System **

PUBLISHER: American Vocational Association (AVA)

NOTES: **Life After High School:** A short booklet explaining how vocational–technical education can be a stepping stone to college. Students explain how they went from technical education to college.

Preparing Teens for the World of Work: A guide for school-to-work transition for counselors, teachers, and career specialists. Reproducible activity sheets to use with students and workplace mentors. Each activity is marked for school or for work. Appeals to students.

School-to-Work Transition: Describes 20 jobs that are believed to offer a large number of openings and advancement opportunities in the 21st century. Pay expectations, educational needs, advancement, job outlook, and where to get more information. Students answer questions about themselves before each career description. Guide identifies jobs that match their personalities. Attractive and easy to read.

Successful Strategies: Information about successful school-to-work programs. Case studies of integrating academic and vocational education. Ready-to-use forms are included.

American Vocational Association (AVA) provides some free and inexpensive materials for the Career Resource Center.

TITLE: **Books About Interviews**

Dynamite Answers to Interview Questions *

Interview for Success *

Salary Success: Know What You're Worth and Get It *

PUBLISHER: Impact Publications

NOTES: **Dynamite Answers to Interview Questions:** Excellent suggestions to prepare applicant to interview successfully. Includes a chapter about nonverbal components and questions the interviewee should ask.

Interview for Success: Information about interviews—myths and realities. Specific information about how to: organize a job search, network for interviews, communicate nonverbally, prepare for the interview, manage the verbal interchange, negotiate salary, and conduct the follow-up to the interview.

Salary Success: Interesting chapters: (1) The Salary Game; (2) Myths, Mistakes, and Money in Your Future; (3) Future Salary and Benefit Trends; and (4) Communicate Your Value in Interviews. Good addition to the Career Resource Center.

TITLE: **Books About Jobs**

America's 50 Fastest Growing Jobs *

Revised Handbook for Analyzing Jobs *

Using the Internet in Your Job Search: An Easy Guide to Online Job Seeking and Career Information *

Your Career: Thinking About Jobs and Careers *

PUBLISHER: JIST Works, Inc.

NOTES: **America's 50 Fastest Growing Jobs:** Reference book that is accurate, easy-to-read, and contains information about trends in the economy and workplace.

Revised Handbook for Analyzing Jobs: Detailed information about physical and academic requirements of some jobs. Helpful when considering specific jobs.

Using the Internet in Your Job Search: Informative guide with information about using Internet classifieds, databases, and support groups as well as electronic resumes and job-hunting etiquette on the Internet.

Your Career: Emphasizes the difference between a job and a career, and having a job as a step along a career path. Helps students consider ways to achieve a meaningful career and is helpful for them to have as a background before making career decisions.

9-1 CAREER EDUCATION (CONTINUED)

TITLE: **CAM Report**

MEDIA/COST: Newsletter/Annual; published semi-monthly ***

GRADES/LENGTH: 9–12

AUTHOR: McKinley (Editor)

PUBLISHER: Priam Publications

NOTES: Informative and helpful newsletter that provides career information facts. Excellent to have in the Career Resource Center.

TITLE: **CAPS: Career Ability Placement Survey**

MEDIA/COST: Aptitude Test

GRADES/LENGTH: 9–10/Administration, 55 minutes; Scoring, 15–20 minutes

PUBLISHER: Educational and Industrial Testing Service

NOTES: The ability battery of the COPS system. Brief, time-efficient, multiability battery that may be used in conjunction with measures of interests and work values in the career clusters provided in the COPS System. Can be used in conjunction with COPS and COPES to create a sequential decision-making activity resulting in a five- or six-year educational plan.

TITLE: **Career Assessment: Where Do You Fit?**

MEDIA/COST: Video ***

GRADES/LENGTH: 9–12/25 minutes

PUBLISHER/
  COPYRIGHT: Learning Seed/1993

NOTES: Excellent video to introduce career assessment and use with groups of students to begin a career unit in high school.

TITLE: **Career Choices Curriculum**

MEDIA/COST: Set ***

GRADES/LENGTH: 9–12

AUTHORS: Bingham & Stryker

PUBLISHER/
  COPYRIGHT: American Vocational Association (AVA)

NOTES: The set includes a guide for students to understand how to develop their own abilities to build successful careers, a workbook and portfolio that is consumable, an instructor's guide and counselor's guide, and two other booklets on writing skills and algebra skills. Each component can be purchased separately.

TITLE: **Career Education: Preparing for the 21st Century**

MEDIA/COST: Book

GRADES/LENGTH: 9–12

AUTHOR: Hansen (Editor)

PUBLISHER/
  COPYRIGHT: ERIC Counseling and Personnel Services/1989

NOTES: Great book for students to learn about careers in the future.

TITLE: **Career Exploration Inventory**

MEDIA/COST: Interest Inventory

GRADES/LENGTH: 9–12

AUTHOR: Liptak

PUBLISHER: JIST Works, Inc.

NOTES: Easily used by students in grades 9–12. Includes a leisure activity component. This is a fold-out inventory in which the student graphs his or her own responses. There are follow-up activities to use the results.

TITLE: **Career Opportunities News**

MEDIA/COST: Newsletter/Annual; published 6 times a year **

GRADES/LENGTH: 9–12/16 pages

AUTHOR: Calvert, Jr. (Editor)

PUBLISHER: Garrett Park Press

NOTES: Informative newsletter providing practical information about career opportunities. In addition, there is a section on minority issues, women's issues, book reviews, and surfing the net. Excellent resource for the school counselor.

TITLE: **Career World**

MEDIA/COST: Magazine/Minimum 15 subscriptions; 7 times a year, September through May ****

GRADES/LENGTH: 9–12

PUBLISHER: Career World

NOTES: Up-to-date articles about careers and colleges. Recent issue included articles about high-tech careers, tips for first week on the job, double majors for the college bound, cover letters, scholarship search.

9-1 CAREER EDUCATION (CONTINUED)

TITLE: **CHOICES for Career and College Decisions, Education Search, Occupation Search, Financial Aid Search**
Career Area Interest Inventory, Personal Occupation Exploration

MEDIA/COST: Computer Program ****** (Site license)

GRADES/LENGTH: 9–12

PUBLISHER/
COPYRIGHT: Careerware/Updated periodically

NOTES: Interactive program that helps students learn about themselves, develop decision-making skills, set priorities, and explore colleges and careers. Stores and uses individual student results of interest inventories. Counselor can enter local scholarship information and local course offerings to enable students to consider courses in relation to their career area of interest. Students should enter criteria in order of importance with most important criteria first. Printout may be taken home.

Information about occupations is related to college programs and majors as well as to colleges offering the programs. Colorful graphs and charts. Interest surveys are linked to CHOICES occupations. Includes an occupational, educational, training, and financial aid database. Also includes interest surveys and a CHOICES Planner that connects with Career Portfolios.

TITLE: **Chronicle Occupational Briefs**

MEDIA/COST: CD-ROM, Briefs, Updates ******

GRADES/LENGTH: 9–12/Over 700 occupational briefs

PUBLISHER/
COPYRIGHT: Chronicle Guidance Publications, Inc./Updated every 4 years, all replaced every 5 years

NOTES: Very complete and cross-referenced with major references such as DOT, OOH, Holland's Codes, etc. Briefs include a description, work performed, working conditions, hours and earnings, education and training, licenses, personal qualifications, where employed, employment outlook, entry methods, advancements, related occupations, and further research. Well worth the investment.

TITLE: **CIP: A Classification of Instructional Programs**

MEDIA/COST: Book

GRADES/LENGTH: 10–12

PUBLISHER: U.S. Department of Labor

NOTES: Describes elementary through postsecondary programs in 31 areas, subdivided into 50 categories. Educational programs relate to preparation for jobs or careers. Includes coded classifications and definitions of program purpose.

TITLE: **COPS: Career Occupational Preference Survey**

MEDIA/COST: Interest Inventory

GRADES/LENGTH: 10–12/40–45 minutes

COPYRIGHT: 1995

PUBLISHER: Educational and Industrial Testing Service

NOTES: Job activity interest scores related to career clusters for use in educational- and career-decision making. Clusters of occupations include both professional and skilled levels. Measures include: science, technology, consumer economics, outdoor, business, communication, arts, and service. Scores are linked to related courses of study, sample occupations, and major occupational information systems including the *Occupational Outlook Handbook* (OOH) and the *Dictionary of Occupational Titles* (DOT). May be used in conjunction with Career Ability Placement Survey (CAPS) (List 9-1) and Career Orientation Placement and Evaluation Survey (COPES). (List 8-1)

TITLE: **Create Your Own School Career Information Centre: A Practical Guide**

MEDIA/COST: Book

GRADES/LENGTH: 9–12/125 pages

AUTHOR: Cox

PUBLISHER/
COPYRIGHT: North York Career Centre/1994

NOTES: Excellent resource to set up a school career information center. A list of recommended resources is included.

TITLE: **DAT: Differential Aptitude Test**

MEDIA/COST: Aptitude Test and Career Planning Questionnaire

GRADES/LENGTH: 9–10/Aptitude Test, 3 hours; Questionnaire, 30 minutes

PUBLISHER: The Psychological Corp./Updated periodically

NOTES: Usually administered to students in grade 9 or 10, this series of tests measures student ability in verbal reasoning, numerical ability, abstract reasoning, clerical speed and accuracy, mechanical reasoning, and language usage. Results are used to assist students in planning their educational and career programs.

Results of the career questionnaire along with the aptitude test determine the relationship between student interests and abilities. Scoring options include summary reports, individual narrative reports, and a thorough career planning program.

9-1 CAREER EDUCATION (*CONTINUED*)

TITLE: **Dictionary of Holland Occupational Codes (3rd ed.)**

MEDIA/COST: Book **

GRADES/LENGTH: 9–12/768 pages

AUTHORS: Gottfredson & Holland

PUBLISHER/
  COPYRIGHT: Psychological Assessment Resources/1989

NOTES: A reference book that classifies information in many different ways. It takes some time to understand how to use this directory which is used in conjunction with the *Dictionary of Occupational Titles* (DOT). Occupations are classified as (1) Realistic, (2) Investigative, (3) Artistic, (4) Social, (5) Enterprising, or (6) Conventional.

TITLE: **DISCOVER: Developmental Career Guidance Curriculum**

MEDIA/COST: Computer Program/****** per site

GRADES/LENGTH: 9–12

AUTHOR: Harris-Bowlsbey

PUBLISHER/
  COPYRIGHT: American College Testing (ACT)/Continually updated

NOTES: Excellent interactive system using auditory and visual learning styles for student self-assessment. Has multimedia CD-ROM disk with new technology, video with sound, that connects to television and does not require a computer. Based on the World-of-Work Map by ACT, it links education to work and ties together the student's interests, abilities, and experiences to help the student make appropriate decisions. DISCOVER has current data on almost every postsecondary option and career. Includes the UNI-ACT Interest Inventory and CDI Abilities Inventory. Produces a cover letter, resume, job-shadowing opportunities, student career research papers, and gives career activities for each grade level with handouts. Also has information about financial aid. Results from other ACT programs such as ACT Assessment, PLAN, CPP, and VIESA can be integrated with DISCOVER. One of the most well-organized and extensive approaches to career planning. Many nontraditional students love this program.

TITLE: **DOT: Dictionary of Occupational Titles, Vols. I and II (4th ed.)**

MEDIA/COST: Book **
  Computer Software *****

GRADES/LENGTH: 7–12/2 Volumes; 1,404 pages

AUTHOR: U. S. Department of Labor

DISTRIBUTOR/
  COPYRIGHT: Wintergreen Orchard House/1991

NOTES: A necessary reference for the Career Resource Center. Occupations are organized in many ways and include: the occupational code number, occupational title, typical industry, and alternate titles. Contains detailed definitions of tasks performed and related occupations. Also includes descriptions of the skills needed to perform the required work. Students should learn how to use this classic reference.

TITLE: **The Encyclopedia of Careers and Vocational Guidance (10th ed.)**

MEDIA/COST: Encyclopedia of 4 Volumes ****

GRADES/LENGTH: 7–12/Each volume, 550 pages

AUTHOR: Hopke (Editor)

DISTRIBUTOR/
  COPYRIGHT: Wintergreen Orchard House/1996

NOTES: Easy-to-use encyclopedia providing important information about careers. *Volume 1:* Industries and the broad development of different industries. *Volumes 2, 3, and 4:* Individual job descriptions. Five hundred forty jobs are divided into: (1) Professional, Administrative, and Managerial; (2) Clerical; (3) Sales; (4) Service; (5) Agriculture, Forestry, and Conservation; (6) Processing; (7) Machine Trades; (8) Bench Work; (9) Structural Work; (10) Emerging Technicians; (11) Engineering and Science Technicians; (12) Broadcast, Media, and Arts Technicians; (13) Medical and Health Technicians; and (14) Miscellaneous Occupations. *Volume 4:* DOT code for cross-reference.

TITLE: **ExPAN College Search and Occupational Search (List 9-2)**

9-1 CAREER EDUCATION *(CONTINUED)*

TITLE: **Ferguson's Guide to Apprenticeship Programs**

MEDIA/COST: Book

GRADES/LENGTH: 9–12/428 pages

AUTHORS: Summerfield & Cosgrove (Editors)

PUBLISHER/
    COPYRIGHT: J. G. Ferguson Publishing Company/1994

NOTES: *Volume 1:* Traditional apprenticeships, and *Volume 2:* Nontraditional apprenticeships. Companies are listed with requirements, application documents, addresses, phone numbers, and starting wages. Excellent resource for the career center and counselor's office.

TITLE: **Free Career Materials: A Resource Directory**

MEDIA/COST: Book/Free

GRADES/LENGTH: 9–12/821 sources

AUTHOR: Hecht (Editor)

PUBLISHER/
    COPYRIGHT: Garrett Park Press/1995

NOTES: Helpful resource for the counselor. Many company names, addresses, and phone numbers are provided.

TITLE: **Free Materials: Geographical Guide to Information on Careers**

MEDIA/COST: Printed Materials/Free

GRADES/LENGTH: 9–12

PUBLISHER/
    COPYRIGHT: State Labor Department and SOICC (State Occupational and Information Coordinating Committee)/Annual

NOTES: Career information available within each state. Computer-based information, microfiche, job hunter's guide, directory of apprenticeships, state employment outlook, training opportunities, and wage rates. Available with a phone call to the respective State Labor Department and/or SOICC.

TITLE: **Harrington O'Shea Career Decision-Making System**

MEDIA/COST: Interest Inventory

GRADES/LENGTH: 10–12

PUBLISHER: American Guidance Services (AGS)/ 1993

NOTES: Helps students understand themselves; select school courses, activities, and training to prepare them for occupations and a lifetime career. Includes information for determining the kinds of occupations that fit their interests. Students score their interest survey and complete a summary profile identifying the cluster that contains the most matches. From the cluster, they choose one or two occupations for further research. Compares vocational interests with five major elements in choosing a career: (1) abilities, (2) job values, (3) future plans, (4) school subjects, and (5) occupational preferences.

TITLE: **Job Skills for the 21st Century: A Guide for Students**

MEDIA/COST: Book

GRADES/LENGTH: 9–12

AUTHOR: Jones

PUBLISHER/
    COPYRIGHT: Oryx Press/1995

NOTES: Importance of marketable job skills and competition in the workplace written by people currently in the workforce. These 17 skills are derived from the Secretary's Commission on Achieving Necessary Skills (SCANS Report, U.S. Department of Labor).

TITLE: **Military Career Paths**

MEDIA/COST: Booklet

GRADES/LENGTH: 7–12/122 pages

PUBLISHER: U.S. Department of Defense

NOTES: Career descriptions of a sample of military careers. Promotes developing a career plan and provides information about enlisted and officer careers.

9-1 CAREER EDUCATION (CONTINUED)

TITLE: **OOH: Occupational Outlook Handbook**

MEDIA/COST: Reference Book/Internet *

GRADES/LENGTH: 7–12

AUTHOR: U.S. Department of Labor

DISTRIBUTOR/
   COPYRIGHT: Wintergreen Orchard House/ Updated every two years

NOTES: Necessary reference for the Career Resource Center. Well-written descriptions of various occupations that highlight: occupational descriptions; nature of the work; training and advancement possibilities; job outlook and employment projections; related jobs; and additional job information. Addresses for more information about specific occupations. Good source for free brochures. Index of job titles by DOT code.

TITLE: **OOH: Occupational Outlook Handbook Quarterly**

MEDIA/COST: Journal

GRADES/LENGTH: 9–12

PUBLISHER/
   COPYRIGHT: U.S. Department of Labor/Four times a year

NOTES: Current descriptions of careers and occupations with responsibilities, salaries, and other information. Certain occupations are featured in each issue. A great resource for the Career Resource Center.

TITLE: **Peterson's Career & College Quest**

MEDIA/COST: Computer Program (MAC or Windows)

GRADES/LENGTH: 9–12

PUBLISHER/
   COPYRIGHT: Peterson's Guides/Annual

NOTES: Integrated program for students to search careers to match their interests and skills; select a college, university, or vocational school based upon their career goals; and then find a financial package to provide them with the ability to pay. The financial aid component estimates financial need. Has 400 career fields and 6,000 vocational schools as well as colleges in the computer base.

TITLE: **Peterson's Internships**

MEDIA/COST: Book

GRADES/LENGTH: 7–12/537 pages

PUBLISHER/
   COPYRIGHT: Peterson's Guides/1995

NOTES: Explanations about internships in business and technology; communications; creative, performing, and fine arts; environmental organizations and parks; human services; international relations; public affairs; and research organizations. Comprehensive directory of internship opportunities in the U.S. and abroad.

TITLE: **School-to-Work**

MEDIA/COST: Book

GRADES/LENGTH: 9–12

AUTHORS: Packer & Pines

PUBLISHER/
   COPYRIGHT: Eye on Education/1996

NOTES: Good book by author who has practical knowledge and has served on many school-to-work committees.

TITLE: **SCII: Strong–Campbell Interest Inventory**

MEDIA/COST: Interest Inventory

GRADES/LENGTH: 10–12/30–40 minutes

PUBLISHER: Interpretive Scoring Systems

NOTES: Particularly strong decision-making aid for students considering careers requiring four or more years of college. Consists of like–dislike and yes–no items on an NCS form. Two computer score reports are available: (1) a single sheet profile report or (2) a 20- to 22-page narrative description. *Caution:* There may be some cultural bias.

9-1 CAREER EDUCATION *(CONTINUED)*

TITLE:	**SDS: Self-Directed Search**
MEDIA/COST:	Career Interest Inventory/Kit ****
GRADES/LENGTH:	9–12/35–45 minutes
AUTHOR:	Holland
PUBLISHER/ COPYRIGHT:	Psychological Assessment Resources, Inc./1994

NOTES: Simple directions. Self-administered, self-scored, and self-interpreted by students. Matches career with personality, interests, and skills. Includes over 1,300 occupational titles. Based on Holland's six personality types: realistic, investigative, artistic, social, enterprising, or conventional. Some criticism of limited career considerations for women.

Assessment workbook scored by the student and a reusable booklet, *The Occupations Finder.* Available on computer disk.

TITLE:	**SIGI PLUS: System of Interactive Guidance and Information**
MEDIA/COST:	Computer Software
GRADES/LENGTH:	9–12
PUBLISHER/ COPYRIGHT:	Educational Testing Services/ Periodical Updates

NOTES: Self-directed, interactive computer software program that includes a comprehensive self-assessment of values, skills, and interests. Includes up-to-date information about hundreds of occupations, college and graduate schools, and financial aid. Also includes local items such as occupations, financial assistance, and regulations for obtaining credit for knowledge and skills. Many nontraditional students like this program.

TITLE:	**Student's Guide to Bias-Free Career Planning: Opening All Options**
MEDIA/COST:	Booklet
GRADES/LENGTH:	9–12/30 pages
AUTHORS:	Stovall & Teddlie
PUBLISHER/ COPYRIGHT:	Career, Education, & Training Associates, Inc./1993

NOTES: Encourages students to be aware of sex bias or stereotyping when considering careers. Places responsibility on the student to not limit his or her choices, and to take control of personal decisions, not just let things happen. One chapter deals with traditional versus nontraditional careers.

TITLE:	**Sure-Hire Resumes**
MEDIA/COST:	Book
GRADES/LENGTH:	9–12/177 pages
AUTHOR:	Kaplan
PUBLISHER/ COPYRIGHT:	AMACOM/1990

NOTES: Recommendations about what should be included and not included in the job resume. In addition, it provides examples of resumes before they were "polished" and after the recommendations were implemented. Excellent resource for writing resumes.

TITLE:	**Surviving After High School: Overcoming Life's Hurdles**
MEDIA/COST:	Book *
GRADES/LENGTH:	9–12/242 pages
AUTHOR:	Heine
PUBLISHER/ COPYRIGHT:	J-Mart Press/1991

NOTES: Information about money: salary, benefits, taxes, forms, employee rights and responsibilities, budget, checking account, credit cards, and tax returns. Other practical aspects include transportation, shelter, food, clothing, health, and recreation. Helpful book for students who may not be realistic or understand the realities of living on their own.

TITLE:	**Sweaty Palms: The Neglected Art of Being Interviewed**
MEDIA/COST:	Booklet
GRADES/LENGTH:	9–12/254 pages
AUTHOR:	Medley
PUBLISHER/ COPYRIGHT:	Ten Speed Press/1993

NOTES: Essentials for a successful interview including enthusiasm, questions and answers, dress, and salary. Also information about assumptions, discrimination, and decisions.

9-1 CAREER EDUCATION (CONTINUED)

TITLE:	**Teenagers: Preparing for the Real World**
MEDIA/COST:	Book/Guide *
GRADES/LENGTH:	9–12/Book, 122 pages; Guide, 66 pages
AUTHOR:	Foster
PUBLISHER/ COPYRIGHT:	American Vocational Association (AVA)/1995

NOTES: Funny stories about Foster's life and the lives of celebrities such as Michael Jordan, Arnold Schwarzenegger, and Elton John. Foster encourages students to strive academically while staying open to career options and to developing a network and communication skills for success.

TITLE:	**VIP Jr.: Vocational Implications of Personality**
MEDIA/COST:	Interest Interview
GRADES/LENGTH:	9–12/Assessment, 30 minutes; Interpretation, 40 minutes
PUBLISHER:	Talent Assessment Inc.

NOTES: Helps students identify their learning style and personality type. Consists of 64 multiple-choice statements. Results produce a personality profile to better understand themselves. Personality profile coordinates results with the Guide for Occupational Exploration. Can be done entirely on computer. Additional assessments may be purchased.

TITLE:	**Whole Career Sourcebook**
MEDIA/COST:	Book
GRADES/LENGTH:	9–12/166 pages
AUTHOR:	Kaplan
PUBLISHER/ COPYRIGHT:	American Management Association/1991

NOTES: Includes making contacts, looking for leads, and interviews. Helpful book for students.

TITLE:	**Women in Aerospace, Parts I, and II**
MEDIA/COST:	Video *
GRADES/LENGTH:	7–12/Part I, 45 minutes; Part II, 45 minutes
AUTHOR:	Garcia and NASA
PUBLISHER/ COPYRIGHT:	Fairfax Network/1993

NOTES: *Part I* stresses opportunity for women as pilots, astronauts, aerospace engineers, mechanical engineers, aircraft maintenance chiefs, public affairs managers, and other careers in aerospace. Women in these careers show and describe what they do in their careers. *Part II* stresses the relationship of high school courses to careers, the need for confidence, determination, and ability to learn from mistakes. Job outlook, need for math and computer courses as well as communication skills are stressed. Opportunities for African American females and career changes are discussed. Excellent video to point out the need for young women to succeed in math and science courses and to keep their options open.

9-2 COLLEGE

TITLE:	**100 Best Colleges for African American Students**
MEDIA/COST:	Book *
GRADES/LENGTH:	9–12
AUTHOR:	Wilson
PUBLISHER/ COPYRIGHT:	Penguin/1993

NOTES: Subjective commentary about schools that meet the needs of African American students.

9-2 COLLEGE *(CONTINUED)*

TITLE: **The Best Guide to the Top Colleges: How to Get into the Ivys or Nearly Ivys**

MEDIA/COST: Booklet *

GRADES/LENGTH: 9–12/111 pages

AUTHOR: Mitchell

PUBLISHER/
  COPYRIGHT: Garrett Park Press/1990

NOTES: General information about researching colleges and the application process. Section for parents and section for school counselor. Articles about teacher recommendations, college essay, campus visits, and interviews. Also a glossary and a list of books about college admissions.

TITLE: **The Black Student's Guide to Colleges**

MEDIA/COST: Book

GRADES/LENGTH: 9–12/496 pages

AUTHOR: Beckham

PUBLISHER/
  COPYRIGHT: Beckham House Publishers, Inc./ 1992

NOTES: Excellent reference for students who are exploring different colleges. Table of contents includes a glossary, learning the system, how to size up a college, study skills, writing tips, and how to manage stress.

TITLE: **Black Students in Interracial Schools: A Guide for Students, Teachers, and Parents**

MEDIA/COST: Book *

GRADES/LENGTH: 9–12/126 pages

AUTHOR: Smith

PUBLISHER/
  COPYRIGHT: Garrett Park Press/1994

NOTES: Addresses the needs of African American students who attend interracial schools. Strategies for students to cope, survive, and succeed in colleges and universities where they are the minority.

TITLE: **Cass and Birnbaum's Guide to American Colleges**

MEDIA/COST: Book *

GRADES/LENGTH: 9–12

AUTHORS: Cass & Birnbaum

PUBLISHER/
  COPYRIGHT: HarperCollins/1994

NOTES: Excellent factual guide to colleges. Includes attrition rates and a religious index.

TITLE: **College Admissions**

Behind the Scenes: An Inside Look at the Selective College Admission Process *—Wall, E.B.

Do It Write: How to Prepare a Great College Application *— Ripple, G.G.

MEDIA/COST: Booklets

PUBLISHER: Octameron

NOTES: ***Behind the Scenes:*** Question-and-answer sections, case studies, and mini-biographies of students. Admission process is explained by a previous admissions director from Amherst. Importance of standardized test scores and course selection, how an admissions committee makes decisions, early decisions, value of a liberal arts education, and the relationship between financial aid and the admissions process.

Do It Write: Explains how to write winning essays that will stand out from others and make a favorable impression on the college admission committee.

TITLE: **College Admissions Data Handbook**

MEDIA/COST: Books: Geographical Volume **

National Edition w/o binders ****

CD-ROM ****

GRADES/LENGTH: 9–12/3,500 pages of 2-page profiles

PUBLISHER/
  COPYRIGHT: Orchard House/Revised annually

NOTES: Easy-to-use, detailed, factual guide organized in volumes by geographical region. Totally objective. Ranked by Carnegie Foundation as most accurate college guidebook. Students use these references when available.

9-2 COLLEGE (CONTINUED)

TITLE: **College Applications/Essays**
                 Writing Your College Application Essay *—McGinty, S.M.
                 Your College Application *

MEDIA/COST: Booklets

PUBLISHER: College Board Publications

NOTES: *Writing Your College Application Essay:* Helps students understand the focus and reason for the essay. A section deals with analyzing six college essays. Many good suggestions for writing the essay.

   Your College Application: Basic information about college application process. Good book for students in grades 9 and 10 to inform about the overall college application process.

TITLE: **College Connector**

MEDIA/COST: Computer Program

GRADES/LENGTH: 9–12

PUBLISHER: American College Testing (ACT)

NOTES: College planning and application service to assist students in selecting and applying to colleges. Includes a college search, inquiry service, application service, and financial aid need estimator. High school can purchase the package or families can purchase a modified package for home computers.

TITLE: **The College Counselor Computer Program Database**

MEDIA/COST: Computer Database/Set-Up ******
                 Annual Update ****

AUTHOR: Swanson

PUBLISHER/   The College Counselor/Updated
COPYRIGHT: Annually

NOTES: Can save a counselor hundreds of hours and provide motivation to students as early as grade 9. Organizes all college application decisions for every student entered. Information presented graphically on a scattergram using SAT or PSAT scores, and grade point averages. Shows the student's position in comparison to all other students from your school or district who have applied to that college. Gives the average grade point average (GPA) and SAT acceptance rating for the college. Students and parents love it because it is concrete and shows graphically the student's chances of acceptance to specific colleges. Also provides reports for school district, school, parents, or media with or without names, and the reports are available immediately.

   History of students from every graduating class can be tracked using graduation date, attendance in college, and graduate school. Tremendous resource for the counselor, students, parents, and school.

TITLE: **College Explorer PLUS**

MEDIA/COST: Computer Program
                 Single Computer ****
                 Multicomputer *****

PUBLISHER: College Board (computer)

NOTES: Interactive college search program. Database of college's curriculum, tuition and fees, majors, sports, and student body size. Students can search by using 800 options. Possible to renew computer disks annually and save 50 percent of the price.

TITLE: **College Freshman Survival Guide**

MEDIA/COST: Video/Workbook **

GRADES/LENGTH: 12/40 minutes

PUBLISHER/
COPYRIGHT: Octameron/1992

NOTES: College students offer incoming freshmen advice on how to cope with the transition from high school to college and from home to college. Tips on study habits, test anxiety, social life, homesickness, personal safety, and time management. Excellent video to alleviate anxiety of the college-bound students.

9-2 COLLEGE (CONTINUED)

TITLE: **College Search**

Campus Visits and College Interviews *

College Handbook (Annual) *

College Handbook, Foreign (Annual) *

College Handbook for Transfer Students *

Index of Majors and Graduate Degrees *

Summer on Campus *

MEDIA/COST: Booklets/Books

PUBLISHER: College Board Publications

NOTES: **Campus Visits:** Pointers to make the most of college visits and college interviews. Questions interviewers ask and questions the student may want to ask the interviewer. Appendix includes a list of college guides for specialized needs.

College Handbook: Complete college guide with information about all colleges in the U.S. Includes Internet addresses for electronic access to colleges. A must for every high school counseling office.

College Handbook for Transfer Students: Good reference book for the Career Center. Transfer policies and services at over 2,000 two- and four-year colleges.

Index of Majors and Graduate Degrees: Information about accelerated programs, cooperative education, double majors, semester at sea, study abroad, telecourses, and weekend college as well as information about majors in college. Reference book for the counselor's office or Career Resource Center.

Summer on Campus: Information about summer programs on college campuses for high school students. Descriptions of summer programs organized by state.

TITLE: **The Complete Guide to College Visits**

MEDIA/COST: Book

GRADES/LENGTH: 9–12/609 pages

AUTHORS: Spencer & Maleson

PUBLISHER/
COPYRIGHT: Carol Publishing Group/1993

NOTES: Organized by state. Certain colleges and universities are included with information about tours; on-campus interviews; class visits; overnight dorm stays; airport, train, and bus service; as well as directions to the campus. Helpful to have in the counselor's office.

TITLE: **Essays That Worked**

MEDIA/COST: Booklet

GRADES/LENGTH: 9–12/142 pages

AUTHORS: Curry & Kasbar

PUBLISHER/
COPYRIGHT: Mustang Publishing/1986

NOTES: Fifty essays written by students who were successful in being admitted to very selective colleges. Examples are helpful for some students.

TITLE: **ExPAN Comprehensive:**

College Search and Occupational Search

Personal Portfolio

Fund Finder

MEDIA/COST: ExPAN Comprehensive ****** (one school license)

Fund Finder ****

PUBLISHER: College Board (computer)

NOTES: **ExPAN College Search and Occupational Search:** Excellent program for college and career searches to identify appropriate higher education and career options. Annually updated information on 3,000 colleges to help student search and then apply to appropriate colleges. Includes two- and four-year colleges and universities, the cost, selectivity, and other statistics. Helps students explore occupations, make decisions, and plan for their lifetime careers.

ExPAN Personal Portfolio: Helps a student organize personal information into an updated personal portfolio. Stores and revises personal information, grades, extracurricular participation, activities, and correspondence throughout a student's high school career. A student is encouraged to compile and record this information in grade 9, updating each year. The common application or individual college applications can be printed or sent electronically. Counselor reports are also generated. When the school purchases the package, it is free to students.

Fund Finder contains a database of scholarships and grants.

TITLE: **How to Write Your College Application Essay**

MEDIA/COST: Booklet

GRADES/LENGTH: 9–12/95 pages

AUTHOR: Nourse

PUBLISHER/
COPYRIGHT: VGM Career Horizons/1995

NOTES: Basic information about the college application essay.

9-2 COLLEGE (CONTINUED)

TITLE: **Hunter's Guide to the College Guides**

MEDIA/COST: Directory

GRADES/LENGTH: 9–12

AUTHOR: Hunter

PUBLISHER/
  COPYRIGHT: Hunter's Guide to the College Guides/1995

NOTES: A review of 140 college guides and reference books currently on the market. Guides are listed by category. Includes a section for the student with a learning disability.

TITLE: **Insider's Guide to the Colleges**

MEDIA/COST: Book *

GRADES/LENGTH: 9–12

PUBLISHER/
  COPYRIGHT: St. Martin's Press/1997

NOTES: Compiled and edited by the staff of the *Yale Daily News*. Candid profile of a number of colleges and includes students' opinions about academics and campus life.

TITLE: **The Interactive Fiske Guide to Colleges**

MEDIA/COST: CD-ROM ***

GRADES/LENGTH: 11–12/2 hours

AUTHOR: Fiske (Editor)

PUBLISHER/
  COPYRIGHT: Times Books/1996

NOTES: Only college guide to receive highest rating from the American Bookseller. Interactive, thorough descriptions of hundreds of colleges and universities with pictures and sound.

TITLE: **The Internet Guide for College-Bound Students**

MEDIA/COST: Book *

GRADES/LENGTH: 10–12/160 pages

AUTHOR: Hartman

PUBLISHER/
  COPYRIGHT: College Board Publications/1996

NOTES: Standard areas for surfing the World Wide Web for college information to learn about the "real" life on campus. Covers how to interpret and analyze Internet information and how to find financial aid and scholarship opportunities.

TITLE: **Ivy League Programs at State School Prices**

MEDIA/COST: Book *

GRADES/LENGTH: 9–12

PUBLISHER/
  COPYRIGHT: Arco/1994

NOTES: Subjective list of recommendations of colleges with good programs that are bargains for state residents.

TITLE: **The Journal of College Admission**

MEDIA/COST: Journal **

GRADES/LENGTH: 9–12

PUBLISHER/
  COPYRIGHT: National Association for College Admissions (NACAC)/Quarterly, Winter, Spring, Summer, Fall

NOTES: Many excellent articles about college applications and college admissions.

TITLE: **Looking Beyond the Ivy League: Finding the College That's Right for You**

MEDIA/COST: Book *

GRADES/LENGTH: 9–12

AUTHOR: Pope

PUBLISHER/
  COPYRIGHT: Penguin/1995

NOTES: Addresses the application, interview, and selection. Describes more than 200 colleges with a checklist of specific questions to ask when visiting a college. Addresses myths that can lead student astray. Provides advice about what the student can do in high school to prepare for college and also includes financial aid information.

TITLE: **Lovejoy's College Guide**

MEDIA/COST: Book *

GRADES/LENGTH: 9–12

PUBLISHER/
  COPYRIGHT: Monarch Press/1995

NOTES: Worthwhile resource to conduct college and career planning simultaneously. Career section lists college majors and colleges with accredited programs for particular majors. Helpful for student wanting a program strong in a particular major.

9-2 COLLEGE (CONTINUED)

TITLE:	**Major-Minor Finder**
MEDIA/COST:	Interest Inventory *** (for 25)
GRADES/LENGTH:	11–12
PUBLISHER:	CFKR Career Materials

NOTES: Reusable assessment booklet with answer insert folders. Upon completion, student will have: (1) matched aptitudes and interests with nine college majors, (2) learned about jobs related to college majors, (3) learned about the different skills and interest required of 99 majors, and (4) listed the college majors most compatible with his or her educational goals and career interests. Students profit from this career-oriented approach to selecting a college major and career planning.

TITLE:	**Making a Difference in College Admission: A Step-by-Step Guide for the Secondary School Counselor**
MEDIA/COST:	Book **
GRADES/LENGTH:	9–12/276 pages
AUTHORS:	Hitchner & Tifft-Hitchner
PUBLISHER/ COPYRIGHT:	Center for Applied Research in Education/1989

NOTES: Three sections help the counselor work with students in college admissions: (1) Enhancing Your Skills, (2) Developing a Well-Designed Program, and (3) Counselee, Family, and You. Helpful guide for counselors to provide good college counseling. Information from over 200 college admission officers who responded to the authors' survey.

TITLE:	**Multicultural Student's Guide to Colleges**
MEDIA/COST:	Book *
GRADES/LENGTH:	9–12
PUBLISHER/ COPYRIGHT:	Noonday/1993

NOTES: Guide for students from a diverse population.

TITLE:	**Peterson's Guides**
	Colleges With Programs for Learning-Disabled Students
	Counseling for College: Professional's Guide
	Peterson's Guide to Four-Year Colleges
	Peterson's Guide to Two-Year Colleges
	Practically Painless Guide to Writing a Winning College Application Essay
MEDIA/COST:	Books/Booklets *
PUBLISHER:	Peterson's Guides

NOTES: *Colleges With Programs for LD Students:* Good reference list of two- and four-year colleges with programs and services for LD students. Parents appreciate this helpful reference.

Counseling for College: Encourages and gives good suggestions to students whose families are not familiar with the college process. Particularly helpful in a school with a diverse population.

Peterson's Guides to Two- and Four-Year Colleges: Easy-to-use for career preparation as well as for four-year college preparation.

Practically Painless Guide: Concise and easy-to-read handbook that makes writing the college essay manageable. Well worth the price of the book if the student reads it and carefully follows the suggestions.

TITLE:	**Rugg's Recommendations on the Colleges**
MEDIA/COST:	Book *
GRADES/LENGTH:	9–12/141 pages
AUTHOR:	Rugg
PUBLISHER/ COPYRIGHT:	Ruggs Recommendations/1997

NOTES: Subjective but helpful list of colleges. More helpful for the counselor than for the student. Supplementary reference, specifying strong programs in different areas. Ruggs also presents informative workshops for counselors.

TITLE:	**Surfing for a College**
MEDIA/COST:	WWW/Free
GRADES/LENGTH:	9–12
ADDRESS:	http://www.collegeview.com

NOTES: Detailed information for counselors, parents, and students on 3,500 two- and four-year colleges and universities. Degrees offered in each major, availability of services, and closest airport to campus. Direct on-line application forms are available to students. Students may complete the form via the Internet or by mail.

9-2 COLLEGE (CONTINUED)

TITLE:	**A Taste of College: On-Campus Summer Programs for High School Students**
MEDIA/COST:	Book *
GRADES/LENGTH:	9–12/188 pages
AUTHORS:	Nowitz & Nowitz
PUBLISHER/ COPYRIGHT:	College Bound Communications, Inc./1994

NOTES: Directory of summer programs organized by state, program name, minority and women's programs, and by subject. Good resource for the counselor's office.

9-2   COLLEGE, FINANCIAL AID

TITLE:	**College Financial Aid Made Easy**
MEDIA/COST:	Handbook *
GRADES/LENGTH:	9–12
AUTHOR:	Bellantoni
PUBLISHER/ COPYRIGHT:	Ten Speed Press/1996

NOTES: Comprehensive handbook providing guidance on completing all federal forms currently required for financial aid.

TITLE:	**Financial Aid: College Board**
	ABCs for Athletes (Video) **
	College Costs and Financial Aid (Annual) *
MEDIA/COST:	Video/Booklets
PUBLISHER:	College Board Publications

NOTES: *ABCs for Athletes:* Important information for students who want to play sports in college. Covers NCAA regulations, academic requirements, and recruiting pressures.

College Costs and Financial Aid: College costs, financial aid, and scholarships available at over 3,000 two- and four-year colleges.

TITLE:	**Financial Aid**
	A's and B's of Academic Scholarships (booklet) *
	Don't Miss Out (booklet) *
	How to Pay for College (video)**
MEDIA/COST:	Booklets/Video
PUBLISHER/ COPYRIGHT:	Octameron

NOTES: *A's and B's of Academic Scholarships:* Describes 100,000 academic awards offered by nearly 1,200 colleges. Many of these scholarships are not based on financial need.

Don't Miss Out: Popular consumer guide for learning about student aid. Covers scholarships, grants, loans, and personal finance strategies. Worksheets for IBM software to calculate estimated financial contribution. Worksheets found in *Don't Miss Out* can be used to calculate expected family contribution for college costs. Disk size, 3 1/2 or 5 1/4.

How to Pay for College: Fast-paced, interesting, and informative video. A lot of information is compressed with graphics and guidebook provides specific information. Ranges from basic to the sophisticated strategies to get more financial aid.

TITLE:	**Heath Resource Directory**
MEDIA/COST:	Directory/Free
GRADES/LENGTH:	9–12
PUBLISHER/ COPYRIGHT:	Heath Resource Center/1996 http://www.und.nodak.edu/dept/ dss/heath.htm

NOTES: A compiled list of financial aid resources.

TITLE:	**Scholarship Book**
MEDIA/COST:	Book *
GRADES/LENGTH:	9–12/450 pages
AUTHOR:	Cassidy
PUBLISHER/ COPYRIGHT:	Prentice Hall/1996

NOTES: A compilation of databases of financial aid information from private colleges and universities throughout the nation. Complete guide of scholarships, grants, loans, internships, and contest prizes for undergraduates.

9-2 COLLEGE *(CONTINUED)*

TITLE:	**The Student Guide (Annual)**
MEDIA/COST:	Book/Free
GRADES/LENGTH:	12
PUBLISHER:	U. S. Department of Education

NOTES: Information about financial aid from the U. S. Department of Education. The award year is from July 1 through June 30 each year.

9-2   COLLEGE, SPECIAL STUDENTS

TITLE:	**ADD and the College Student: A Guide for High School and College Students with Attention Deficit Disorder**
MEDIA/COST:	Directory
GRADES/LENGTH:	9–12
AUTHOR:	Quinn
PUBLISHER/ COPYRIGHT:	Magination Press/1993

NOTES: Excellent resource for students with ADD and their parents.

TITLE:	**College Guide for Students with Learning Disabilities**
MEDIA/COST:	Book *
GRADES/LENGTH:	9–12/372 pages
DISTRIBUTOR/ COPYRIGHT:	Wintergreen Orchard House/1996

NOTES: Five sections provide: (1) advice on how to choose a college, (2) information about colleges with specific programs for students with LD, (3) two-year colleges and technical schools with specific programs for LD students, (4) colleges that offer services for students with LD but do not have specific programs, and (5) information about summer programs.

TITLE:	**Guiding the Learning Disabled Student: A Directory of Programs and Services at NACAC Member Institutions**
MEDIA/COST:	Directory
GRADES/LENGTH:	9–12
PUBLISHER/ COPYRIGHT:	National Association for College Admission Counseling (NACAC)

NOTES: Directory of services and programs at colleges that belong to NACAC.

TITLE:	**K & W Guide to Colleges for the Learning Disabled: A Resource Book for Students, Parents, and Professionals**
MEDIA/COST:	Directory
GRADES/LENGTH:	9–12
AUTHORS:	Kravets & Wax
PUBLISHER/ COPYRIGHT:	HarperCollins/1993

NOTES: Excellent resource for students who are learning disabled and their parents.

9-4   CONFLICT RESOLUTION

TITLE:	**Conflict Resolution: A Secondary School Curriculum**
MEDIA/COST:	Binder of Activities
GRADES/LENGTH:	9–12
AUTHORS:	Sadalla, Henriquez, & Holmberg
PUBLISHER/ COPYRIGHT:	The Community Board Program, Inc./1987

NOTES: Activities that have been used with students in public and private schools. Addresses dynamics underlying prejudice—differences in values, assumptions, and perceptions between people. Conflicts in schools and in society frequently result from prejudice. Idea that conflict can be positive and can serve to enhance important relationships. Excellent program including skills for effective communication and activities for resolving conflicts.

9-14   PEER FACILITATION

TITLE:	**Peervention: Training Peer Facilitators for Prevention Education**
MEDIA/COST:	Book
GRADES/LENGTH:	9–12
AUTHORS:	Myrick & Folk
PUBLISHER/ COPYRIGHT:	Educational Media/1991

NOTES: Excellent book with training manuals to begin or continue a peer-facilitation program in secondary school.

9-15   PROBLEM SOLVING

TITLE:	**Brochures for Problem Solving**
	Adult Children of Alcoholics
	Addictive Relationships
	Assertiveness
	Coming Out
	Committed Relationships and School
	Eating Disorders
	Grief and Loss
	Loneliness
	Overcoming Procrastination
	Perfectionism
	Permanent Weight Control
	Self-Confidence
	Stress Management
	Suicide Prevention
	Surviving Child Sexual Abuse
	Test Anxiety
	Time Management
	Understanding Depression
	Your Parent's Divorce
MEDIA/COST:	Brochures * (sample packet)
GRADES/LENGTH:	9–12/Each brochure, 4–5 pages
PUBLISHER/ COPYRIGHT:	Counseling Center, University of Illinois/1984

NOTES: Excellent brochures to have available in counseling office for students to take and read. Students can then decide to speak with a counselor about a topic of concern. Content is very helpful.

9-18   SAFETY

TITLE:	**Books for Safety from Rape**
	Coping with Date Rape and Acquaintance—Andrea Parrot
	Everything You Need to Know About Date Rape—Frances Shuker-Haines
MEDIA/COST:	Books *
GRADES/LENGTH:	9–12
PUBLISHER:	Different publishers

NOTES: Counselor is advised to read the book before recommending it to a student to read. Situations are very unique and the counselor must ensure that the book he or she recommends is the right book at the right time for that particular student.

TITLE:	**"Friends" Raping Friends: Could It Happen to You? Project on the Status and Education of Women**
MEDIA/COST:	Monograph *
GRADES/LENGTH:	9–12
AUTHOR:	Atwell
PUBLISHER/ COPYRIGHT:	Association of American Colleges/1987

NOTES: Excellent information specifying causes, effects, danger signals, and how to avoid acquaintance/date rape. Also a list of resources.

TITLE:	**In Real Life: Sexual Harassment in Schools**
MEDIA/COST:	Video *****
GRADES/LENGTH:	7–12/25 minutes
PUBLISHER/ COPYRIGHT:	Atschul Group/1996

NOTES: Very good video explaining harassment and how it can be recognized by presenting actual behaviors that happen in schools.

9-24   SUBSTANCE ABUSE PREVENTION

TITLE:	**Counseling the Adolescent Substance Abuser: School-Based Intervention and Prevention**
MEDIA/COST:	Book *
GRADES/LENGTH:	
AUTHOR:	Gonet
PUBLISHER/ COPYRIGHT:	M.G.G. Enterprises (Sage)/1995

NOTES: Written by a substance abuse prevention counselor with Ann Arbor Public Schools. Includes prevention and intervention techniques, how to predict adolescent drug use, and effects of alcohol and other drugs on adolescent development.

TITLE:	**If You Change Your Mind**
MEDIA/COST:	Video *
GRADES/LENGTH:	9–12/31 minutes
PUBLISHER/ COPYRIGHT:	National Clearinghouse for Alcohol and Drug Abuse/1991

NOTES: Young adults who were previously addicted to drugs share their experiences. Shows how drugs are being used in animal research, the effects drugs have on unborn babies if the mothers are addicted during pregnancy, and ways drugs alter the human brain.

TITLE:	**Making the Grade: A Guide to School Drug Prevention Programs**
MEDIA/COST:	Book
GRADES/LENGTH:	9–12
PUBLISHER/ COPYRIGHT:	Drug Strategies

NOTES: Information to help teachers, counselors, and principals determine which programs can work best in their schools to prevent drug abuse in the school and community. It rates how well each program works. Information is available upon request.

9-25   TEST-TAKING SKILLS

TITLE: **ACT: American College Test**
MEDIA/COST: Test
GRADES/LENGTH: 11–12
PUBLISHER: American College Testing (ACT)

NOTES: Generally used for admission by colleges in the middle section of the country. Students should check the catalogs of colleges to which they are planning to apply to know which admission test the college accepts.

TITLE: **AP Tests: Advanced Placement Program and Tests**
MEDIA/COST: Test
GRADES/LENGTH: 11–12/3 hours
PUBLISHER/
  COPYRIGHT: College Entrance Examination Board (CEEB)/Annual

NOTES: Gives students the opportunity to pursue college-level studies in high school and usually receive both high school and college credit. Provides course descriptions and examinations on 29 introductory courses in 16 fields. Examinations are administered in May. Students are charged to take the exam. Participating colleges, upon receiving the grade, may grant placement and/or credit to students with qualifying grades.

TITLE: **Destination College: Planning With the PSAT/NMSQT**
MEDIA/COST: Video **
GRADES/LENGTH: 9–12/18 minutes
PUBLISHER/
  COPYRIGHT: College Board Publications/1995

NOTES: Explains to students the benefits of the PSAT/NMSQT score report. Interviews with high school and college students. Helps students evaluate career goals, consider course selection, and plan for college. Excellent preparation for the SAT.

TITLE: **Gruber's Complete Preparation for the New SAT**
MEDIA/COST: Book *
GRADES/LENGTH: 9–12/766 pages
AUTHOR: Gruber
PUBLISHER/
  COPYRIGHT: Harper & Row/1996

NOTES: Particularly good refresher for math with good explanations for the answers to questions on the practice tests.

TITLE: **Inside the SAT and ACT**
MEDIA/COST: CD-ROM **
GRADES/LENGTH: 10–12
PUBLISHER/
  COPYRIGHT: Princeton Review/1997

NOTES: Although these lessons are from the Princeton Review course, they can be done alone on the computer. Detailed lessons on every type of question, key vocabulary words, and practice tests with computer-analyzed results. Student can specify amount of time he or she can study, and an individualized study plan is created. Great test-preparation software.

TITLE: **Official Guide to SAT II: Subject Tests**
MEDIA/COST: Book *
GRADES/LENGTH: 9–12/380 pages
PUBLISHER/
  COPYRIGHT: College Board Publications/1994

NOTES: Actual practice subject tests in Writing, Literature, American History, World History, Math I, Math IIC, Biology, Chemistry, and Physics with answer sheets. Minitests in foreign languages, descriptions of the five SAT II: Language Tests With Listening, and samples of the Writing Test.

9-25 TEST-TAKING SKILLS *(CONTINUED)*

TITLE:	PSAT/NMSQT Preliminary Scholastic Assessment Test and the National Merit Scholarship Qualifying Test
MEDIA/COST:	Tests
GRADES/LENGTH:	10–11
PUBLISHER:	College Board Publications

NOTES: Interpretation of results are extremely helpful for student who will take the SAT. All students planning to apply to college should take the PSAT.

Only the test results from the junior year are considered in National Merit competition, the National Achievement Scholarship Program for Outstanding Negro Students, and the National Hispanic Scholar Awards Program.

TITLE:	SAT I Scholastic Assessment Test I
	Reasoning Test
	8 Real SATs
MEDIA/COST:	Tests * each
GRADES/LENGTH:	9–12
PUBLISHER:	College Board Publications

NOTES: The **Reasoning Test** is required for admission by many colleges on east and west coasts. Most colleges select the best math and verbal scores to use for admission criteria. Juniors are encouraged to take the SAT I in the spring. Seniors should take it in the fall. College Board sends test scores directly to four colleges of the student's choice. Special education students may request an untimed College Board test.

8 Real SATs is good preparation prior to taking the SATs. Actual SAT tests that were administered May 1996. Test-taking tips and two PSAT/NMSQT tests.

Title:	SAT II Subject Test Preparation on CD-ROM
	Algebra Smart
	Science Smart
	Word Smart
MEDIA/COST:	CD-ROMs ** each
GRADES/LENGTH:	11–12
PUBLISHER/ COPYRIGHT:	Princeton Review/1996

NOTES: *Algebra Smart:* Makes learning algebra fun for students. Twelve interactive lessons with 120 videos, drills, 500 practice problems, and games. Students who need to develop their math skills can do it in a fun way.

Science Smart: An interactive program with diagrams, animated graphics, practice problems, and plain-English explanations. Complex scientific operations are presented in such an interesting way that students improve their knowledge and their grades in classes as well as their scores on the SAT II-Achievement exams.

Word Smart: Makes learning and remembering words fun and easy. Students learn how interesting words can be and they improve their vocabulary skills by traveling through a Hollywood studio and making a movie. Can help student raise scores on the vocabulary portions of the SAT, as well as communicate effectively.

Award-winning interactive CD-ROM of SAT II Achievement Tests in science and tutoring for algebra, general vocabulary, and SAT I preparation.

9-25 TEST-TAKING SKILLS (CONTINUED)

TITLE:	**SAT Success**
	SAT Success
	Success With Words
MEDIA/COST:	Books *
GRADES/LENGTH:	9–12
AUTHOR:	Carris
PUBLISHER:	Peterson's Guides

NOTES: *SAT Success:* A practical, skill-building book to help with SAT I preparation. Verbal and math sections with basic word lists and math test-taking tips.

   Success With Words: A humorous book to build vocabulary. Deals with roots and vocabulary in and out of context.

TITLE:	**Score Builder for the SAT**
MEDIA/COST:	CD-ROM **
GRADES/LENGTH:	11–12
AUTHOR:	Gruber
PUBLISHER/	
COPYRIGHT:	Learning Co.,
	http://www.learningco.com/1997

NOTES: Tailors a course of study for the student based upon identified math and verbal skills. Two teachers coach the student and serve as tutors. Includes many directions for this personalized study plan for the SATs.

TITLE:	**Test Skills: A Test Preparation Program for the PSAT/NMSQT**
MEDIA/COST:	Book **
GRADES/LENGTH:	9–11
PUBLISHER/	
COPYRIGHT:	College Board Publications/1996

NOTES: A complete sample test plus 24 lesson plans to help all students prepare for the PSAT. Emphasizes strategies for critical reading passages, calculator use, student-produced response questions, and strategies that allow all students to be prepared for the PSAT/NMSQT.

TITLE:	**TOEFL: Test of English as a Foreign Language**
MEDIA/COST:	Test
GRADES/LENGTH:	11–12
PUBLISHER:	College Board Publications

NOTES: Should be taken by students whose second language is English. Most colleges require this test and have a minimum score. Check catalogs of colleges to which the student is planning to apply.

TITLE:	**Tooth and Nail: A Novel Approach to the New SAT**
MEDIA/COST:	Book **
GRADES/LENGTH:	9–12/366 pages
AUTHORS:	Elster & Elliot
PUBLISHER/	
COPYRIGHT:	Harcourt Brace/1994

NOTES: Students enjoy reading this book! Truly unique and interesting, as well as painless approach to supplement other SAT preparation books. Not a textbook or workbook, every boldfaced word in the novel or story is an SAT word. A glossary is given in the back for all of the boldfaced words. Students learn vocabulary in context of a novel. A few exercises in the back. Excellent resource for students.

Section 10

MATERIALS TO USE WITH PARENTS

ANNOTATED LIST OF MATERIALS

(PERMISSION OF FAIRFAX COUNTY PUBLIC SCHOOLS OF VIRGINIA)

Cost Guide: * ($1-$25)   ** ($26-$55)   *** ($56-$105)   **** ($106-205)   ***** ($206-$505)   ****** ($506-$1,000)

10-1 CAREER EDUCATION

TITLE:	**How to Help Your Teenager Find the Right Career**
MEDIA/COST:	Book/Interest Inventory
GRADES/LENGTH:	9–12/203 pages
AUTHOR:	Shields
PUBLISHER/ COPYRIGHT:	College Entrance Examination Board (CEEB)/1988

NOTES: Empowers and maintains interest of parents. Stresses the influence parents have on their child's curiosity and realizing the need for academic and professional preparation in career planning. Good information about how high school subjects relate to careers. Presents career clusters and provides difference between career and job. Stresses the importance of exploring careers versus choosing a career, and how important it is to learn about alternatives. Practical and self-scoring Shield's Interest Inventory is included.

TITLE:	**How to Prepare Your Teen for Work: 10 Tips for Parents**
Media/Cost:	Brochure ** per 100
GRADES/LENGTH:	9–12
PUBLISHER:	American Vocational Association (AVA)

NOTES: Helps parents understand their role in helping their child prepare for a productive career.

10-2 COLLEGE

TITLE:	**College Counsel: The Parent's College Advisor**
MEDIA/COST:	Booklet
GRADES/LENGTH:	9–12/42 pages
PUBLISHER/ COPYRIGHT:	College Counsel/1994

NOTES: General information, particularly about financing college. Parents will find it a helpful reference.

10-3 COMMUNICATION

TITLE:	**Books: Communication**
	Getting Closer—Ellen Rosenberg
	How to Talk to Children About Really Important Things— Charles E. Schaefer
	Listen to Your Child— David Crystal
	To Listen to a Child— Berry Brazelton
MEDIA/COST:	Books
GRADES:	K–7

NOTES: Great practical references when teaching about family communication in parenting education classes.

10-3   COMMUNICATION (CONTINUED)

TITLE:	**Class Meetings—Family Meetings** (*Creative Consultant* Series)
MEDIA/COST:	Book *
GRADES/LENGTH:	K–6/32 pages
AUTHOR:	Cooper
PUBLISHER/ COPYRIGHT:	Mar*Co Products, Inc./1989

NOTES: Outlines the purpose, procedure, benefits, and "trouble spots"of class meetings and family meetings. Leader's guides are included for either a staff or parent workshop.

TITLE:	**How Can Parents Model Good Listening Skills?**
MEDIA/COST:	Brochure/Free
PUBLISHER/ COPYRIGHT:	ACCESS ERIC/1982-83

NOTES: Informative. Points out the importance of good listening. Many suggestions and examples to demonstrate good listening skills.

TITLE:	**How to Talk So Kids Will Listen and Listen So Kids Will Talk**
MEDIA/COST:	Kit/Videos Video Series **** Separate Videos ** Books * Binders **
GRADES/LENGTH:	K–12
AUTHORS:	Faber & Mazlish
PUBLISHER/ COPYRIGHT:	Faber/Mazlish Workshops LLC/ 1996

NOTES: Structured workshop for parents using videos and workbooks. Workshop involves parents purchasing individual workbooks. Counselor may conduct classes using the reusable books. Leader's guide.

TITLE:	**Parent Involvement: The Relationship Between School-to-Home Communication and Parents' Perceptions and Beliefs, Report No. 15.**
MEDIA/COST:	Report *
GRADES/LENGTH:	K–12
PUBLISHER/ COPYRIGHT:	Center on Families, Communities, Schools, and Children's Learning/1994

NOTES: Shows that parents who receive information from the school become more involved in their children's learning, and these children become more successful in school. Positive communications are extremely important to share with parents.

TITLE:	**Successful Parenting—Part Two: Communication Is Crucial**
MEDIA/COST:	Video/Guide/Facilitator's Guide **
GRADES/LENGTH:	Video/19 minutes
AUTHORS:	Richards & Taylor
PUBLISHER/ COPYRIGHT:	Richards & Taylor Productions/ 1994

NOTES: Video, facilitator's guide, and user's guide are great for a parent workshop. Facilitator's guide includes suggested time frames for a one- or two-hour presentation as well as time for discussion questions. Video consists of vignettes exemplifying effective and ineffective communication. Following each vignette is a discussion with tips for the sender and receiver to avoid common pitfalls and communicate in a positive, effective way. Vignettes are relevant and interesting, representing a diverse population.

10-4   COMPREHENSIVE

TITLE:	**Active Parenting** *Active Parenting Today* (newly revised edition) ***** *Active Parenting of Teens* (grades 5–9) *****
MEDIA/COST:	Workshop Kit: Videos/Leader's guides and parents' guides
GRADES/LENGTH:	K–6 and 5–9/6 sessions; each session for each program, 2 hours
AUTHOR:	Popkin
PUBLISHER/ COPYRIGHT:	Active Parenting Publishers/ 1992/1989

NOTES: *Active Parenting Today:* Helps parents achieve concrete parenting skills and techniques that they can use immediately. Prevents problems from occurring and promotes positive communication and mutual respect between children and parents. Parents can teach their children how to make good decisions and discipline using natural and logical consequences. Leader's guide is easy to use with step-by-step process for each session. Videos with 50 vignettes deal with typical family situations.

Active Parenting of Teens: Video-based group discussion program helps parents deal with concerns of preteens and teens. Helps parents prevent problems during this important development stage of their children's lives.

Good balance between video and group discussion. Counselor needs to complete training to lead Active Parenting programs.

10-4 COMPREHENSIVE (CONTINUED)

TITLE: **Building Resilient Children**

MEDIA/COST: Book

GRADES/LENGTH: K–4/4 sessions; each, 2 hours

PUBLISHER:: Southeast Regional Center for Drug-Free Schools and Communities

NOTES: Use with parents whose children are enrolled in kindergarten through fourth grade; however, adaptable to other age groups. Sample agenda and detailed guide for each session. Parents participate in role plays, group discussions, and homework assignments.

_____

TITLE: **Facts for Families (Family and Parenting Series)**

No. 1—*Children and Divorce*

No. 8—*Children and Grief*

No. 14—*Children and Family Moves*

No. 15—*The Adopted Child*

No. 20—*Making Day Care a Good Experience*

No. 22—*Normality*

No. 27—*Stepfamily Problems*

No. 43—*Discipline*

MEDIA/COST: Brochures * (for set of 45 plus shipping)

GRADES/LENGTH: K–12/each, one page

PUBLISHER/
COPYRIGHT: American Academy of Child & Adolescent Psychiatry/1992

NOTES: Excellent ready reference to establish rapport and begin building a relationship with families in need of assistance. Great addition to the counselor's reference collection and parenting library.

_____

TITLE: **Growing Up: Grades 1–6**

MEDIA/COST: Weekly newsletter for parents *

GRADES/LENGTH: 1–6

PUBLISHER/
COPYRIGHT: Growing Up/Annual

NOTES: Although material is accurate, there is an assumption of age and developmental level according to grade level. Counselor should read and summarize before sending to parents. Some articles may not be appropriate for counselors to send to parents.

TITLE: **Guiding Children to Success: What Schools and Communities Can Do**

MEDIA/COST: Book

GRADES/LENGTH: Adults/24 pages

AUTHORS: Mendel & Lincoln

PUBLISHER/
COPYRIGHT: South Carolina ETV/1990

NOTES: Well-written and researched document on importance of counseling children through their entire school career. Statistical evidence as well as case studies show how good counseling can influence a student's success. Importance of parents and community involvement and support are stressed.

_____

TITLE: **How Can I Be Involved in My Child's Education?**

MEDIA/COST: Brochure/Free

GRADES/LENGTH: K–12

PUBLISHER/
COPYRIGHT: ACCESS ERIC/1982-83

NOTES: Easy-to-read pamphlet with main points highlighted. Suggestions for parent involvement are applicable to any school situation.

10-4 COMPREHENSIVE (CONTINUED)

TITLE: **Leading Parent Groups I, II, and III: Prescriptions and Possibilities** (*Making Choices—Growing Stronger* Series)

MEDIA/COST: Books *

GRADES/LENGTH: K-2, 3–4, 5–8/I and II, 32 pages; III, 46 pages

AUTHOR: Falk

PUBLISHER/
  COPYRIGHT: Elizabeth Falk, M.A., LPC/1993

NOTES: Excellent resources for counselors.

Leading Parent Groups I: Two-session program of one to two hours each. Theme of first session: Children and School Readiness. Parents select best responses to typical problems in an activity entitled: "What Would You Say?" Parents are invited to explore their own needs as well as those of other members in their families. Second session emphasizes developmental ages and stages and parental expectations for primary-age children.

Leading Parent Groups II: Focuses on parenting skills and parenting groups. Logistics and strategies for parents of students in grades three and four. Formats for parent discussions on family meetings and study skills as well as developmental stages for children ages eight and nine.

Leading Parent Groups III: Two-session program deals with parental concerns of the parents of ten- to twelve-year-olds. First session deals with developmental issues and communication skills. Second session deals with family meetings and the transition to middle school. Guide with concrete information about preadolescence.

TITLE: **Megaskills**

MEDIA/COST: Book *

GRADES/LENGTH: K-6/348 pages

AUTHOR: Rich

PUBLISHER/
  COPYRIGHT: Houghton Mifflin Co./1992

NOTES: Age-appropriate activities for parents to use with children that enhance confidence, motivation, effort, responsibility, initiative, perseverance, caring, teamwork, common sense, and problem solving. Fun activities that strengthen parent–child relationships.

TITLE: **Parent Connection**

MEDIA/COST: Video *

GRADES/LENGTH: K–12

PUBLISHER: Fairfax Network

NOTES: Promotes home–school relationship by suggesting activities and strategies for parents by discussion and demonstration. Topics include: (1) participating in parent–teacher meetings, (2) motivating the underachiever, (3) selecting educational toys for children, (4) preparing for kindergarten, (5) competing in the classroom, (6) financing college, and (7) taking educational family vacations.

TITLE: **Parent Information and Resource Centers**

MEDIA/COST: WWW/Free

GRADES/LENGTH: K–12

PUBLISHER: U.S. Department of Education
http://www.ed.gov/Family/ParentCtrs/index.html

NOTES: Provides examples of 28 schools in different states that have various kinds of parent information and resource centers. Excellent resource for counselors setting up parent resource centers.

TITLE: **Parenting Insights for Parents of 7-14 Year Olds**

MEDIA/COST: Newsletter *

GRADES/LENGTH: 3–9/15 pages

PUBLISHER/
  COPYRIGHT: Parenting Insights/1994, 6 issues per year

NOTES: Short articles on a variety of topics, often spiced with humor and real life examples. Many articles offer a recommended reading list or a synopsis of key points at the end. Available in Spanish. Great resource to refer to parents or to send home.

TITLE: **The Parenting Series:** *Self-Esteem, Read With Children Responsibility, Talk and Listen Motivation, Learn at Home*

MEDIA/COST: Booklets * (minimum of 25 must be ordered)

GRADES/LENGTH: K–6/13 pages

PUBLISHER/
  COPYRIGHT: The Parent Institute/1991

NOTES: Good strategies for parents that are basic and easy to read. Counselor may suggest that PTA/PTO purchase these booklets for members.

10-4 COMPREHENSIVE (CONTINUED)

TITLE: **Parents and Children Together (PACT)**

MEDIA/COST: 6-session Program

GRADES/LENGTH: K–12/150 pages

AUTHOR: Virginia Dept. of Education

PUBLISHER/
  COPYRIGHT: Commonwealth of Virginia/1993

NOTES: Provides skills and strategies for parents. Six sessions: (1) It's Tough Being a Parent, (2) Parenting Styles: Which Way Is Best?, (3) Practice Makes Perfect: Habits of Effective Parents, (4) Children at Risk: Parent in the Way, (5) STAT! Students Take a Turn, (6) For Fathers Only.

TITLE: **Parents and Teachers Take Action**

MEDIA/COST: 3 Videos *

GRADES/LENGTH: K–12/30 minutes

PUBLISHER:: Fairfax Network

NOTES: Three video programs focus on student behavior, cultural diversity, and the parent's role in supporting the mission of the school. Appropriate for parents, teachers, and counselors. Everyone wins when parents and teachers work together for students.

TITLE: **Parents Make the Difference: Practical Ideas for Parents to Help Their Children**

MEDIA/COST: Magazine

GRADES/LENGTH: K–12/4 pages

AUTHORS: Wherry & Amundson

PUBLISHER/
  COPYRIGHT: The Parent Institute/Monthly Sept. through May

NOTES: Good resource to share with parents to encourage positive, practical parenting skills. Great practical ideas for parents to help their children regarding school, social relationships, communication, homework, and a variety of other important topics. Includes topics of children with disabilities, study skills, and activities that can be completed at home. Nothing can be copied.

TITLE: **Raising Children in Troubled Times (Parenting Video Series)**

Arguing—20 minutes
Bedtimes—20 minutes
Chores—20 minutes
Curfews/Whereabouts—20 minutes
Drugs—20 minutes
Fighting—27 minutes
Homework—28 minutes
Lying—27 minutes
Parties and Concerts—20 minutes
Peers—20 minutes
School Behavior—20 minutes
Sex—28 minutes
Studying—27 minutes
Temper Tantrums—20 minutes
Togetherness—27 minutes

MEDIA/COST: Set of Videos/Manuals ***** (for the set of 15 videos)

GRADES/LENGTH: K–12

PUBLISHER/
  COPYRIGHT: American Guidance Service, Inc. (AGS)/1994

NOTES: Excellent set of videos to use with parents. Leader's guide provides pre- and post-viewing questions, follow-up activities, and a list of other related topics. Vignettes are realistic and show a diversity of cultures. Bases parental discipline on three elements: (1) clearly defined and stated rules, (2) follow-through and monitoring based on the child's needs, and (3) consistency. Preview questions encourage parents to examine their busy work schedules and parenting responsibilities. Tremendous resource for a parenting library or parenting workshops.

10-4 COMPREHENSIVE *(CONTINUED)*

TITLE: **STEP Program: Systematic Training for Effective Parenting**
STEP/Teen
Next STEP
Padres eficaces con entrenamiento sistematico (PECESO)

MEDIA/COST: Workshop Kit/Professional Training ****

GRADES/LENGTH: K–12

AUTHOR: Dinkmeyer & McKay

PUBLISHER/
COPYRIGHT: American Guidance Service (AGS)/ 1987

NOTES: Gives parents a practical method of parenting, emphasizing respect and cooperation among all family members. Skills are taught through reading, videos, discussions, and activities.

Specific professional training in the entire STEP program is offered to counselors with continuing education credit. Charge for the training. Includes training in: (1) *STEP*, (2) *Early Childhood STEP*, and (3) *STEP/Teen.*

STEP/Teen: Addresses the challenges of raising teens. Includes practical, workable principles for opening communication during the years when this is vital.

The Next STEP: Helps parents practice and refine skills they learned in STEP and STEP/Teen. Introduces the problem-solving group. Videos supplement sessions.

PECESO: Spanish-language version of STEP helps Spanish-speaking parents improve family relationships.

10-5 CONFLICT RESOLUTION

TITLE: **Fighting Fair for Families**

MEDIA/COST: Booklet *

GRADES/LENGTH: K–12

PUBLISHER/
COPYRIGHT: Peace Education Foundation/1995

NOTES: Easy-to-read booklet about identifying the problem, attacking the problem—not the person; listening, respecting others' feelings, and taking responsibility for own actions. Conflict is a normal, natural part of life. What is important is the way that we handle conflict. Suggestions for handling anger, choosing the appropriate time to discuss problems, and listening attentively. Excellent guide for families to refer to because it is easy for everyone in the family to understand. "Rules for fighting fair" poster in the back of the book could be posted on the refrigerator.

10-6 DEATH AND GRIEF

TITLE: **About Dying**

MEDIA/COST: Book

GRADES/LENGTH: K–8

AUTHOR: Stein

PUBLISHER/
COPYRIGHT: Walker and Company/1984

NOTES: Parents can use this book with young children to explain death. Has photos and well-written text.

TITLE: **The Grieving Child: A Parent's Guide**

MEDIA/COST: Book *

GRADES/LENGTH: K–9

AUTHOR: Fitzgerald

PUBLISHER/
COPYRIGHT: Simon & Schuster/1992

NOTES: Excellent resource for parents as they explain death to a child; for counselor as well as parents. Sensitively written, explains how children feel when someone close to them dies. Author presents practical and compassionate advice for parents as they explain such things as: visiting seriously ill or dying loved ones, using language understandable to a child, discussing topics such as suicide and murder, deciding whether a child should attend a funeral, dealing with the child experiencing the stages of grief. Author has led many groups for children and adults to help them through the grieving process.

TITLE: **How Do We Tell the Children? Helping Children Understand and Cope When Someone Dies**

MEDIA/COST: Book *

GRADES/LENGTH: PreK–8

AUTHORS: Schaefer & Lyons

PUBLISHER/
COPYRIGHT: Newmarket Press/1988

NOTES: A step-by-step guide of how to tell children about death. Explains what children of different ages think, understand, and feel. Provides ways adults can help children deal with their feelings. Includes examples of how parents can talk with their children about particular issues, including AIDS. Outline to find words to tell children about a personal tragedy. Excellent examples and concepts according to age level of the children.

10-7 DECISION MAKING

TITLE:	**Couch Potato Kids: Teaching Kids to Turn Off TV and Tune into Fun** (*Effective Parenting* Series) *Help! It's Homework Time: Improving Your Child's Homework Habits* *Managing the Morning Rush: Shaping Up Your Family's Morning Routine* *No More Bedtime Battles: Simple Solutions to Bedtime Problems* *Surviving Sibling Rivalry: Helping Brothers and Sisters Get Along* *Winning the Chores Wars: How to Get Your Child to Do Household Jobs*
MEDIA/COST:	Booklets *
GRADES/LENGTH:	K–6/48 pages
AUTHORS:	Canter & Canter
PUBLISHER/ COPYRIGHT:	Lee Canter & Associates/1993

NOTES: Practical solutions to everyday dilemmas of parents. Authors suggest that parents attack problems head on. Short, concise, and to the point. Easy-to-follow suggestions. Counselor can use with many parent groups.

TITLE:	**Guiding the Gifted Child: A Practical Source for Parents and Teachers**
MEDIA/COST:	Book
GRADES/LENGTH:	K–12/262 pages
AUTHORS:	Webb, Meckstroth, & Tolan
PUBLISHER/ COPYRIGHT:	Ohio Psychology Publishing Company/1982

NOTES: Information about motivating and disciplining the gifted student. Provides information about stress management, depression, and other problems, as well as opportunities for gifted students.

TITLE:	**The Hurried Child: Growing Up Too Fast Too Soon (Revised)**
MEDIA/COST:	Booklet *
GRADES/LENGTH:	Parents/217 pages
AUTHOR:	Elkind
PUBLISHER/ COPYRIGHT:	Addison-Wesley/1988

NOTES: Good advice to parents to help children enjoy age-appropriate activities, and not be pressured to grow up too fast. Pervasive and timely topic. Cautions about pressuring children to achieve in everything they do, thereby losing the precious gift of a happy, carefree childhood. Author provides insights into how to parent in an appropriate manner, meeting the special needs of children.

TITLE:	**Perfectionism: What's Bad About Being Too Good?**
MEDIA/COST:	Booklet
GRADES/LENGTH:	4–9/115 pages
AUTHORS:	Adderholdt-Elliott
PUBLISHER/ COPYRIGHT:	Free Spirit/1987

NOTES: Excellent resource to use with parents and students. Parents may not realize the pressure and stress of always demanding perfection. Points out how perfectionism can effect students physically, mentally, and emotionally. Suggestions about how to control life as well as to cope and ease up on demanding too much from self. Also suggestions about how the counselor can address such stress-related problems as eating disorders.

10-8 DISABILITIES

TITLE:	**After the Tears**
MEDIA/COST:	Book *
GRADES/LENGTH:	K–6/89 pages
AUTHOR:	Simions
PUBLISHER/ COPYRIGHT:	Harcourt Brace Jovanovich/1985

NOTES: A story of how parents of disabled children have struggled, learned, and grown while raising their children. Shared stories to give others the benefit of their experiences. Topics include guilt and anger, isolation, marital stress, relatives, siblings, strangers, and working with the school system.

10-8 DISABILITIES *(CONTINUED)*

TITLE:	**Attention Deficit Hyperactivity Disorder (ADHD)**
MEDIA/COST:	Booklet/Free
GRADES/LENGTH:	K–6/41 pages
PUBLISHER/ COPYRIGHT:	National Institute of Mental Health/1995 http://www.nimh.nih.gov

NOTES: Informative booklet available by writing or on NIMH Web site.

———————————

TITLE:	**Children and the AIDS Virus: A Book for Children, Parents, and Teachers**
MEDIA/COST:	Book
GRADES/LENGTH:	K–4
AUTHOR:	Hausherr
PUBLISHER/ COPYRIGHT:	Clarion/1989

NOTES: Two children who have AIDS are described. Within this context the author explains what a virus is, how the AIDS virus affects the body, and how it is contracted.

———————————

TITLE:	**Children With Tourettes Syndrome: A Parent's Guide**
MEDIA/COST:	Book
GRADES/LENGTH:	K–6
AUTHOR:	Haerle (Editor)
PUBLISHER/ COPYRIGHT:	Woodbine House/1992

NOTES: An introduction to Tourettes Syndrome (TS), its manifestations, its treatment, and other behavioral problems the disorder may cause. An overview with practical suggestions for family members, teachers, and others who will have to deal with a child with TS.

TITLE:	**Facts for Families (Problem Series)**
	No. 2—*Children with Eating Disorders*
	No. 3—*Teens: Alcohol and Other Drugs*
	No. 4—*The Depressed Child*
	No. 6—*Children Who Can't Pay Attention*
	No. 7—*Children Who Won't Go to School*
	No. 10—*Teen Suicide*
	No. 11—*The Autistic Child*
	No. 12—*Children Who Steal*
	No. 16—*Learning Disabilities*
	No. 18—*Bedwetting*
	No. 19—*The Child with a Long-Term Illness*
	No. 23—*Children Who Are Mentally Retarded*
	No. 29—*Children's Major Psychiatric Disorders*
	No. 33—*Conduct Disorders*
	No. 34—*Children's Sleep Problems*
	No. 35—*Tic Disorders*
	No. 38—*Manic-Depressive Illness in Teens*
	No. 40—*The Influence of Music and Rock Videos*
MEDIA/COST:	Pamphlets * (for set of 45 plus shipping)
GRADES/LENGTH:	K–12/one page
PUBLISHER/ COPYRIGHT:	American Academy of Child & Adolescent Psychiatry (AACAP)/1992

NOTES: Easy-to-read information on numerous topics. Each sheet provides concise information. Excellent resources and a worthy addition to a parent resource library.

10-8 DISABILITIES (CONTINUED)

TITLE: **Losing Uncle Tim**

MEDIA/COST: Book

GRADES/LENGTH: 2–4

AUTHOR: Jordan

PUBLISHER/
COPYRIGHT: Whitman/1989

NOTES: Parents may decide to share the story of Daniel and his concern and grief of his uncle. Daniel's mother told him when they learned that his Uncle Tim has AIDS. Daniel reacts as he sees his Uncle Tim's condition worsen because of the virus. Daniel grieves when his Uncle Tim dies of AIDS. However, he appreciates the joy and courage of his uncle, and has good memories of him.

TITLE: **My Book for Kids With Cansur**

MEDIA/COST: Book *

GRADES/LENGTH: 1–6/30 pages

AUTHOR: Gaes

PUBLISHER/
COPYRIGHT: Melius & Peterson Pub., Inc./1987

NOTES: Written in phonetic English by an eight-year-old cancer patient. This is an excellent reference book for counselors, parents of children with cancer, and students with the disease. Use with care for particular children. Discuss the book with parents before using it with their child. Be aware of particular religious overtones.

TITLE: **Power Parenting for Children with ADD/ADHD: A Practical Parent's Guide for Managing Difficult Behaviors**

MEDIA/COST: Book **

GRADES/LENGTH: K–6/256 pages

AUTHOR: Flick

PUBLISHER/
COPYRIGHT: Center for Applied Research in Education/1996

NOTES: A resource that counselors can use when working with parents of children with ADD/ADHD. Techniques for building children's self-esteem and activities that parents can use to help their children.

TITLE: **Siblings Information Network Newsletter**

MEDIA/COST: Newsletter

GRADES/LENGTH: K–12

PUBLISHER/
COPYRIGHT: Siblings Information/Annual Network Newsletter

NOTES: Organization for families with children with disabilities. Provides articles for parents and siblings.

TITLE: **The Sleep Book for Tired Parents: Help to Solving Children's Sleep Problems**

MEDIA/COST: Book

GRADES/LENGTH: K–6

AUTHOR: Huntley

PUBLISHER/
COPYRIGHT: Parenting Press, Inc./1991

NOTES: A helpful book for parents when children have sleep disorders, including sleep terror.

TITLE: **Talking With Your Child About Cancer**

MEDIA/COST: Booklet/Free

GRADES/LENGTH: K–12

AUTHOR: U.S. Department of Health and Human Services

PUBLISHER/
COPYRIGHT: National Cancer Institute/1989

NOTES: Illustrated booklet that helps parents talk with children about coping with a terminal illness.

TITLE: **Uncle Jerry Has AIDS: Attitudes & Emotions Activity Book**

MEDIA/COST: Book/Workbook *

GRADES/LENGTH: K–6 (individual student)/31 pages

AUTHORS: Boulden & Boulden

PUBLISHER/
COPYRIGHT: Boulden Publishing/1992

NOTES: Written parental permission should be received prior to showing this book to a child, and only with a child who is known to have a close relationship with someone who has AIDS. A story about a child who has an uncle with AIDS. Explores feelings and perceptions that people may have toward others who have AIDS. It is written for young children and helps give them more information about AIDS and how to deal with a relative or family member who has AIDS.

10-9   DISCIPLINE

TITLE: **Assertive Discipline: Parent Resource Guide**
MEDIA/COST: Book *
GRADES/LENGTH: K–12/110 pages
AUTHORS: Canter & Canter with Schadlow
PUBLISHER/
  COPYRIGHT: Lee Canter & Associates/1985

NOTES: Focuses on ten areas in which parents frequently have problems disciplining their children. Specific consequences and rewards are presented in a clear and concise manner. These practical ideas help parents develop a discipline plan to ensure more consistency. "Assertive Discipline" can help parents who are looking for answers and who are ready to take action.

TITLE: **Behavior Management in the Home**
MEDIA/COST: Kit ***
GRADES/LENGTH: K–12
AUTHOR: Lundell
PUBLISHER::   Behavioral Products

NOTES: The kit includes (1) overhead transparencies, (2) cassette tape recording, (3) instructions and text, and (4) duplication masters. Simulated problem situations to enable parents to work as a group in generating problem-solving strategies. Includes changing homework habits.

TITLE: **How to Help Improve Your Child's Behavior in School**
MEDIA/COST: Video/Guide/Workbook/
                    Video ***; Book *
GRADES/LENGTH: K–12/Video, 25 minutes;
                    Workbook, 24 pages
AUTHORS: Canter & Canter
PUBLISHER/
  COPYRIGHT: Lee Canter & Associates/1992

NOTES: Asset to a parenting library. Practical examples of problems that will probably be faced by most parents. All ethnic cultures portrayed. This video can be used with other books on the subject.

TITLE: **The Parents' Guide**
MEDIA/COST: Book
GRADES/LENGTH: Parents/247 pages
AUTHOR: McCarney
PUBLISHER/
  COPYRIGHT: Hawthorne Educational
                    Services/1989

NOTES: Provides possible solutions for 102 of the most common behavioral problems exhibited by children. These approaches are logical and demonstrate a common sense attitude for parents when dealing with their children. While other solutions/approaches may, and should be considered, this manual is an excellent starting point, especially for younger, inexperienced parents.

TITLE: **Successful Parenting—Part Three: Discipline Makes the Difference**
MEDIA/COST: Video/Guide/Facilitator's Guide **
GRADES/LENGTH: K–12/19 minutes
AUTHOR: Taylor
PUBLISHER/
  COPYRIGHT: Richards & Taylor Productions/
                    1994

NOTES: Can be a one- or two-hour workshop. Information is well-organized and promotes group interaction. Facilitator's guide has open-ended questions to use with the group. Main topics: (1) establishing clear expectations, (2) natural consequences, (3) logical consequences, (4) behavior modification, (5) time-out, (6) improving a specific behavior, (7) contracts, (8) family meetings, and (9) temper tantrums. Parenting styles also discussed and guide has a chart of the ten suggestions for disciplining children. Personal planner also included.

TITLE: **Winning at Parenting Without Beating Your Kids**
MEDIA/COST: Video/Book/Audiotape
GRADES/LENGTH: K–12/Video, 2 hours
AUTHOR: Coloroso
PUBLISHER/
  COPYRIGHT: Kids Are Worth It

NOTES: Video that is fun and practical for parent education. Reflects author's sense of humor.

10-11 EMOTIONS

TITLE:	**Books:**
	The Berenstain Bears and the Bad Dream—Stan & Jan Berenstain
	Can't You Sleep Little Bear?—Martin Waddell
	Ira Sleeps Over—Bernard Waber
	Sam's Worries—Maryann MacDonald
	Whatever I Do, the Monster Does Too—Tracey E. Dillis
	Where the Wild Things Are—Maurice Sendak
MEDIA/COST:	Books
GRADES/LENGTH:	K–6
COPYRIGHT:	1971–1995

NOTES: Helpful when children express fears, especially at going to bed at night.

TITLE:	**A Child's First Book About Play Therapy**
MEDIA/COST:	Book *
GRADES/LENGTH:	K–5
AUTHORS:	Nemiroff & Annunziata
PUBLISHER/ COPYRIGHT:	American Psychological Association (APA)/1991

NOTES: Recommended that this book be read by the parent to the child. Beautifully written and illustrated book for children to understand the reasons to visit a therapist. Helps ease a child's worries by explaining what happens when a child visits the office, the meaning of confidentiality, play therapy, the role of the therapist, and how the child will improve with therapy.

TITLE:	**Not So Scary Things**
MEDIA/COST:	Game *
GRADES/LENGTH:	K–2
PUBLISHER/ COPYRIGHT:	Mar*Co Products, Inc./1989

NOTES: Encourages children to master their fears in a positive way and inspires confidence in the process. Children and parents can play the game together.

10-12 FAMILY

TITLE:	**Alone Together: Single Parent Activity Book**
MEDIA/COST:	Activity Book *
GRADES/LENGTH:	K–3
AUTHORS:	Boulden & Boulden
PUBLISHER/ COPYRIGHT:	Boulden Publishing/1992

NOTES: Excellent format that draws children into topics or feelings that accompany single-parent families and sometimes cause children to feel uncomfortable. Characters are animals.

TITLE:	**Human Development and Family Life Bulletin**
MEDIA/COST:	Newsletter on WWW/Free
GRADES/LENGTH:	K–12
AUTHOR:	Ohio State University
PUBLISHER:	Ohio State University http://www.hec.ohio-state.edu/ famlife/index.html

NOTES: Quarterly newsletter that covers many subjects such as divorce, adolescent problem behavior, parenting programs for children experiencing difficulties, and other current issues related to helping children and families. Title is misleading. Helpful for counselors and parents and available in e-mail format. Send e-mail message to:

listserv@agvax2.ag.ohio-state.edu with the words "subscribe HDFL-Bulletin" in the body of the message.

10-12 FAMILY *(CONTINUED)*

TITLE: **Me and My Stepfamily: A Kid's Journal**

MEDIA/COST: Activity Book *

GRADES/LENGTH: 3–6/64 pages

AUTHOR: Banks

PUBLISHER/
  COPYRIGHT: Penguin Group/1990

NOTES: Combination journal and activity book that helps child express feelings through writing and drawing. Some activities can be completed by the child alone; others with the help of an adult family member. Sections of the book deal with the child's first (natural) family, mother's home, father's home, new stepfamily, and self. Child completes worksheets to help understand own feelings and fears when adjusting to a changing family situation. Excellent resource to recommend to parents.

TITLE: **Siblings Without Rivalry**

MEDIA/COST: Kit/Guide/Cassettes ***

GRADES/LENGTH: K–12/6 cassettes

AUTHORS: Faber & Mazlish

PUBLISHER: Faber/Mazlish Workshops LLC

NOTES: Parental actions that help siblings deal with their feelings about each other. Suggestions for parents when kids fight, and a ten-step approach to help children solve problems.

TITLE: **Strengthening Stepfamilies**

MEDIA/COST: Kit

GRADES/LENGTH: K–12

AUTHORS: Albert & Einstein

PUBLISHER/
  COPYRIGHT: American Guidance Service (AGS)/1986

NOTES: Provides stepparents with information to understand their new family and skills needed to improve troublesome situations. Stepfamily members learn how to communicate effectively, resolve conflicts, and structure their home life to improve relationships.

10-15 MULTICULTURAL

TITLE: **DIFFERENT and Wonderful: Raising Black Children in a Race-Conscious Society**

MEDIA/COST: Book *

GRADES/LENGTH: K–12/242 pages

AUTHORS: Hopson & Hopson

PUBLISHER:/
  COPYRIGHT: Prentice Hall Press/1990

NOTES: Excellent book for African American parents. Offers valuable suggestions for instilling positive values, productive lifestyles, and feelings of self-worth and self-respect. Specific suggestions on many topics, including helping the child deal with prejudicial remarks and actions. Highly recommended for parenting libraries.

TITLE: **Parents and Schools**

MEDIA/COST: Video/Guide

GRADES/LENGTH: K–12/15 minutes

PUBLISHER: Guidance/Career Development Services

NOTES: Stresses importance of school systems working with Hispanic parents to ensure that Hispanic children receive the best public education. Guide is available in Spanish and English.

10-17   PROBLEM SOLVING

TITLE: **Facts for Families (Treatment Series)**

No. 21—*Psychiatric Medication for Children*

No. 24—*Being Prepared (When to Seek Help)*

No. 25—*Being Prepared (Where to Find Help)*

No. 26—*Being Prepared (Know Your Health Insurance Benefits)*

No. 28—*Responding to Child Sexual Abuse*

No. 32—*11 Questions to Ask Before Psychiatric Treatment of Children and Adolescents*

No. 41—*Making Decisions About Substance Abuse Treatment*

No. 42—*The Continuum of Care*

No. 44—*Children and Lying*

No. 46—*Home Alone Children*

MEDIA/COST: Pamphlets * (for set of 45 plus shipping)

GRADES/LENGTH: K–12/One page

PUBLISHER/
   COPYRIGHT: American Academy of Child and Adolescent Psychiatry (AACAP)/ 1992

NOTES: Important information for parents with clear and concise treatment explanations, guidelines, descriptions, and questions. Excellent to have available when parents request such information.

TITLE: **Here's What You Need to Know About School Refusal**

MEDIA/COST: Brochure/Free

GRADES/LENGTH: K–12

PUBLISHER/
   COPYRIGHT: American Day Treatment Centers/ 1994

NOTES: Excellent resource for parents of students who have poor attendance. Describes behaviors that may indicate childhood depression when child complains of being bored in school and refuses to attend school.

TITLE: **A Parent's Guide to Children's Problems**

MEDIA/COST: Card/Brochure/Free

GRADES/LENGTH: K–12/One card

PUBLISHER: Laurel Oaks Hospital (800) 225-4930 or (407) 352-7000

NOTES: Provides information about puberty, sexual activity, smoking, stress, suicide, alcohol, discipline, drugs, eating disorders, and peer pressure. Stresses (1) common signs, (2) how to avoid problems, and (3) what to do if you have problems. Although the suggestions may seem simplistic, the pull-out format makes it very easy to use when parents are busy.

TITLE: **What Do Parents Need to Know About Children's Television Viewing?**

MEDIA/COST: Brochure/Free

GRADES/LENGTH: K–12

PUBLISHER/
   COPYRIGHT: ACCESS ERIC/1982-83

NOTES: Easy and quick to read. Practical guidelines for parents to monitor their children's television viewing. Especially good information about analyzing commercials.

10-20   RESPONSIBILITY

TITLE: **How Can We Help Children Learn to Be Responsible Citizens?**

MEDIA/COST: Brochure/Free

GRADES/LENGTH: K–12

PUBLISHER/
   COPYRIGHT: ACCESS ERIC/1982-83

NOTES: Suggestions to promote responsible citizenship. The more information parents have, the better able they are to make the best choices for their children.

10-21   SAFETY

TITLE: **Child Lures**

MEDIA/COST: 2 Videos/Guide *****

GRADES/LENGTH: K–6 and 7–12 (2 separate programs)/Student Video, 7 minutes; Training Video, 40 minutes

PUBLISHER/
   COPYRIGHT: Wooden Publishing House/1994

NOTES: Involve parents before presenting to students. Objectives and lesson plans for presentations to grades K–6. Handouts with tips for parents and a letter inviting parents to a presentation is included. Innovative, up-to-date information and a comprehensive approach to the dangers of child lures.

TITLE: **Facts for Families (Special Issue Series)**

   No. 5—*Child Abuse—The Hidden Bruises*

   No. 9—*Child Sexual Abuse*

   No. 13—*Children and TV Violence*

   No. 17—*Children of Alcoholics*

   No. 30—*Children, Adolescents and HIV/AIDS*

   No. 31—*When Children Have Children*

   No. 36—*Helping Children After a Disaster*

   No. 37—*Children and Firearms*

   No. 39—*Children of Parents with Mental Illness*

   No. 45—*Lead Exposure in Children Affects Brain and Behavior*

MEDIA/COST: Pamphlets * (for set of 45)

GRADES/LENGTH: K–12/One page

PUBLISHER/
   COPYRIGHT: American Academy of Child & Adolescent Psychiatry/1992

NOTES: Basic information on each topic. Important to have in the counselor's office to be given to parents when appropriate.

TITLE: **How to Talk to Your Children About AIDS**

MEDIA/COST: Brochure

GRADES/LENGTH: K–12/15 pages

PUBLISHER/
   COPYRIGHT: Sex Information and Education Council of the U.S./1989

NOTES: Provides parents with guidelines for discussing AIDS with children. Specific guidelines for all developmental stages of children. Also available in Spanish.

TITLE: **Strong Families, Competent Kids**

MEDIA/COST: Book

GRADES: K–12

PUBLISHER/
   COPYRIGHT: Virginia Extension Service

NOTES: Excellent guide for parents who must leave their children alone at home. School counselor should have this material available to give to parents or to children.

TITLE: **Violence Prevention Brochures**

MEDIA/COST: Brochures

GRADES: K–12

PUBLISHER/
   COPYRIGHT: National Crime Prevention Council/1995

NOTES: Topics, each on a separate page: (1) Managing conflict, (2) Talking with kids about drugs, (3) Preparing kids to be at home alone, (4) Raising streetwise kids, (5) Ensuring bike safety, (6) Alcohol, (7) Guns/violence, and (8) Gangs. Brief, includes addresses and phone numbers for additional information. Good points for discussions at parent meetings.

© 1998 by John Wiley & Sons, Inc.

10-22 SCHOOL-PARENT PARTNERSHIPS

TITLE:	Bibliography on Parental Involvement in Education
MEDIA/COST:	bibliography/ Free
GRADES/LENGTH:	K-12/1 page
AUTHOR:	National Library of Education
COPYRIGHT:	1999
PUBLISHER:	National Library of Education
ADDRESS:	

<http://oeri2.ed.gov/BASISDB/EDPUB/.ECT_DESC=
PARTNERSHIPS+IN+EDUCATION>

NOTES: A list of journals, reports, and books about parental involvement in schools.

TITLE:	Family Involvement in Education
MEDIA/COST:	Web Site/ Free
GRADES/LENGTH:	K-12/1 page
AUTHOR :	U. S. Department of Education
COPYRIGHT :	1999
PUBLISHER :	U. S. Department of Education
ADDRESS :	<http://pfie.ed.gov/>

NOTES: Ideas to increase opportunities for family involvement in their children's learning. Include: Building Partnerships, Partner Listing, Initiatives, Publications, What's Up in Education, and How to Join.

TITLE:	Partners for a Safer Community: Vol. 12, Winter 1999
MEDIA/COST:	Newsletter/ Free
GRADES/LENGTH:	K-12/4 pages
AUTHOR :	National Library of Education
COPYRIGHT :	1999
PUBLISHER :	National Library of Education
ADDRESS :	

<http://pfie.ed.gov/BASISDB/EDPUB/.26M%3D5%
26K%3D1282%26R%3DY%26U%3D1>

NOTES: Presents articles on safety issues in the community. This newsletter discusses danger on the farm, poison prevention resources, and strategies for securing project funding.

10-23 SELF-ESTEEM

TITLE:	Bound for Success: Guiding Your Child Toward Higher Self-Esteem
MEDIA/COST:	Booklet *
GRADES/LENGTH:	K-9/101 pages
AUTHORS:	Simmons & Simmons
PUBLISHER/ COPYRIGHT:	Lee Canter & Associates/1993

NOTES: Helpful and practical suggestions for parents about guiding child's achievement, goals, positive attitude, and responsibility.

TITLE:	Home Esteem Builders
MEDIA/COST:	Booklet **
GRADES/LENGTH:	K-8/304 pages
AUTHOR:	Borba
PUBLISHER/ COPYRIGHT:	Jalmar Press/1990

NOTES: Contains 40 activities that parents can use to build esteem of their children. Includes 15 parent newsletters, handouts, and complete script for a parent inservice.

TITLE:	MIRRORS—A Program About Self-Esteem
MEDIA/COST:	Video **
GRADES/LENGTH:	K-12/11 minutes
AUTHOR:	Produced by National PTA & Keebler Company
PUBLISHER/ COPYRIGHT:	Modern Sponsored Marketing Services/1989

NOTES: Excellent video that shows parents how to help children maintain high self-esteem. Ways of relating positively to their children are demonstrated.

TITLE:	Successful Parenting—Part One: Self-Esteem Is the Key
MEDIA/COST:	Video/Guide/Facilitator's Guide **
GRADES/LENGTH:	K-12/18 minutes
AUTHOR:	Taylor
PUBLISHER/ COPYRIGHT:	Richards & Taylor Productions/ 1994

NOTES: Helps parents improve their skills to boost their children's self-esteem. Facilitator's guide provides framework for a one- or two-hour workshop. Focus is on ten concrete suggestions to raise self-esteem, beginning with working on one's own self-esteem.

10-24   SPANISH (MATERIALS IN THE LANGUAGE)

TITLE: **Comunicacion Entre Nosotros**

MEDIA/COST: Video *

GRADES/LENGTH: 7–12

PUBLISHER: Fairfax Network

NOTES: Explores communication issues between parents and teens. Guests discuss topics: peer pressure, parental involvement at school, similarities and differences in Hispanic and American cultures, and transition from child to teen. (1) Immigration: Why Should I Care? (2) Culture Clash/Un Choque Cultural, (3) Are You My Family? Gangs in the Hispanic Community, and (4) No Mixed Signals: Strategies to Prevent Child Abuse.

10-25   SPECIAL EDUCATION

TITLE: **Parents' Complete Special Education Guide**

MEDIA/COST: Book **

GRADES/LENGTH: PreK–12/336 pages

AUTHORS: Pierangelo & Jacoby

PUBLISHER/
   COPYRIGHT: Center for Applied Research in Education/1996

NOTES: Information to parents about the special education processes; Individual Education Plans (IEPs), screening procedures, related school services, and practical parenting skills. Materials to help students with homework, schoolwork, discipline, and communication.

10-26   STUDY SKILLS

TITLE: **Homework Without Tears: A Parent's Guide for Motivating Children to Do Homework and to Succeed in School**

MEDIA/COST: Book *

GRADES/LENGTH: K–12/157 pages

AUTHORS: Canter & Hausner

PUBLISHER/
   COPYRIGHT: Lee Canter & Associates/1987

NOTES: Excellent help for developing motivation, communication skills, and responsibility. Humorous and entertaining with cartoon anecdotes for added interest. Specific examples of schedule planners and checklists. Concepts can be incorporated into parent education. Builds a positive relationship between parents and the school.

TITLE: **How Important Is Homework?**

MEDIA/COST: Brochure/Free

GRADES/LENGTH: K–12

PUBLISHER/
   COPYRIGHT: ACCESS ERIC/1982-83

NOTES: Informative with helpful ideas and free to parents.

10-26 STUDY SKILLS (CONTINUED)

TITLE:	**How to Help Your Child Succeed with Homework**
MEDIA/COST:	Video/Guide/Workbook/Video, ***; Book, *
GRADES/LENGTH:	K–6/Video, 25 minutes; Workbook, 24 pages
AUTHOR:	Canter
PUBLISHER/ COPYRIGHT:	Lee Canter & Associates/1992

NOTES: Good video for parent education. Teaches parents skills to help their children achieve in school. Six-step approach to homework success: (1) State that you expect homework to be completed; homework is important. (2) Set up daily homework time. (3) Check to see that your child is doing homework. (4) Provide positive support for your child's good homework efforts. (5) Back up your words with actions. (6) Work closely with the teacher when there is a problem. May be oversimplified for the resistant or unmotivated student. Some video scenes appear unrealistic.

TITLE:	**Parents on Board: Building Academic Success Through Parent Involvement**
MEDIA/COST:	Kit/2 Videos *****
GRADES/LENGTH:	K–9/3 hours
AUTHOR:	Popkin
PUBLISHER/ COPYRIGHT:	Active Parenting Publishers/1995

NOTES: Encourages parents to become involved with their children's learning. Kit includes two videos, leader's guide, two posters, 20 brochures, sample parent letter, one handbook, a parent's booklet, and a completion certificate. Excellent book that covers topics in depth, information, techniques, and skills that are not covered in the short videos. Excellent booklet that is short with an outline of helpful tips and activities for parents.

TITLE:	**Succeed in School**
MEDIA/COST:	Video/Guide/Parent Packet ***
GRADES/LENGTH:	Parents/Video, 60 minutes
AUTHOR:	Rosemond
PUBLISHER/ COPYRIGHT:	Doulos Productions/1993

NOTES: Discussion of three R's: (1) Respect, (2) Responsibility, and (3) Resourcefulness, and how these topics are associated with success in school. Guides for leader and parents are included.

TITLE:	**Successful Parenting—Part Four:** *School Success Takes Teamwork— The Basics* *Taming the Homework Monster*
MEDIA/COST:	2 Videos/2 Guides/**
GRADES/LENGTH:	K–12/Video, 17 minutes
AUTHOR:	Taylor
PUBLISHER/ COPYRIGHT:	Richards & Taylor Productions/ 1995

NOTES: Basic suggestions for parents of children kindergarten through high school. Facilitator's guide provides information about various problems. One segment on the video "Taming the Homework Monster" is especially helpful.

10-27   SUBSTANCE ABUSE PREVENTION

TITLE:	**Common Sense Strategies for Raising Alcohol- and Drug-Free Children**
MEDIA/COST:	Video/Guide/Handouts/Brochures
GRADES/LENGTH:	K–12/4 parent meetings
AUTHOR:	GTE Corporation/National PTA
PUBLISHER/ COPYRIGHT:	GTE Corporation/National PTA/ 1990

NOTES: (1) Statistics on alcohol and other drug use; (2) guidelines on prevention including setting limits, being a good role model, and building bonds with family and school. Practical, easy-to-use program requires little planning and is an excellent resource for the counselor.

TITLE:	**Drug-Proofing Your Children**
MEDIA/COST:	Audio Tape *
GRADES:/LENGTH:	K–12/90 minutes
PUBLISHER:	Western Public Radio

NOTES: Outstanding audio tape for parent/teacher education. Emphasizes the importance of preventing drug use. Can reinforce other prevention messages and/or be loaned to interested parents. Suggestions for talking with children *before* there is a problem. Context is accurate and messages presented in a palatable way.

10-27 SUBSTANCE ABUSE PREVENTION (*CONTINUED*)

TITLE: **Helping Your Pre-Teen Say "NO"**

MEDIA/COST: Booklet/Free

GRADES/LENGTH: 6–12/12 pages

AUTHOR: U.S. Department of Health & Human Services

PUBLISHER/
COPYRIGHT: National Clearinghouse for Alcohol Information/1986

NOTES: Excellent booklet for parents of preteens to help them with ways of saying "no."

TITLE: **My Mom Doesn't Look Like an Alcoholic**

MEDIA/COST: Book *

GRADES/LENGTH: K–3/36 pages

AUTHORS: Hammond & Chesnut

PUBLISHER/
COPYRIGHT: Health Communications/1984

NOTES: Written from a child's perspective. Excellent book for parent to read with the child. Counselor should have written parental permission before using this book with a child. Appropriate for a Children of Alcoholics (COA) group when all members have written parental permission. Story details an alcoholic mother's behaviors and how the child feels. Explains Alcoholics Anonymous, the recovery process, and the effect of the recovery process on the child.

TITLE: **Parenting for Prevention**

MEDIA/COST: Book/Overheads/Handouts/ Discussion Guides *

GRADES/LENGTH: K–12

PUBLISHER: Johnson Institute

NOTES: Gives parents facts about alcohol and other drugs. Presents risk factors and training in life skills that help children live drug-free.

TITLE: **Ten Steps to a Drug-Free Future**

MEDIA/COST: Booklet/Free

GRADES/LENGTH: K–12/3 pages

AUTHOR: U.S. Department of Health & Human Services

PUBLISHER/
COPYRIGHT: Public Health Department/1992

NOTES: Outstanding booklet for parents to help them talk with their children about drug prevention.

TITLE: **What Kids Should Know About Parents and Drinking**

MEDIA/COST: Booklet * (for 100-449 booklets)

GRADES/LENGTH: 3–6/15 pages

PUBLISHER/
COPYRIGHT: Channing L. Bete Co./1989

NOTES: Explains the treatable disease of alcoholism and ways in which the disease affects children. Effective booklet to use with children in a group for Children of Alcoholics (COAs) when they have prior written parental permission.

TITLE: **What's "Drunk," Mama?**

MEDIA/COST: Booklet *

GRADES/LENGTH: K–4/30 pages

PUBLISHER/
COPYRIGHT: Al-Anon Family Groups/1977

NOTES: Explains why the adult alcoholic behaves as he or she does, and offers hope for help for the whole family through Alcoholics Anonymous (AA).

10-29   TRANSITION

TITLE:	**Notes from a Traveling Childhood: Readings for Internationally Mobile Parents and Children**
MEDIA/COST:	Booklet
GRADES:	Parents/123 pages
AUTHOR:	McCluskey (Editor)
PUBLISHER/ COPYRIGHT:	Foreign Service Youth Foundation/ 1994

NOTES: Practical information to parents who move internationally. Helps children benefit from the opportunities and prevents problems with moving and living among different cultures. Cross-cultural adaptation, safety, and many other issues of living and going to school abroad.

TITLE:	**Ready, Set, Go! To Kindergarten**
MEDIA/COST:	Video ***
GRADES/LENGTH:	PreK–K/15 minutes
PUBLISHER/ COPYRIGHT:	Doulos Productions/1993

NOTES: Helps parents of children entering kindergarten. Emphasis on techniques parents can use to help their children make a smooth transition from home to school. Overview of kindergarten program, types of readiness tests given to students, and tips for having successful parent–teacher conferences.

Section 11

MATERIALS TO USE WITH TEACHERS

ANNOTATED LIST OF MATERIALS

(PERMISSION OF FAIRFAX COUNTY PUBLIC SCHOOLS OF VIRGINIA)

Cost Guide: * ($1-$25)   ** ($26-$55)   *** ($56-$105)   **** ($106-205)   ***** ($206-$505)   ****** ($506-$1,000)

11-1   CAREER EDUCATION

TITLE:	Career Information in the Classroom: Workshop Guide for Infusing the Occupational Outlook Handbook (OOH)
MEDIA/COST:	Book
GRADES/LENGTH:	9–12
AUTHORS:	Kimmel-Boyle & Wheldon
PUBLISHER/ COPYRIGHT:	Meridian Education Corporation/ 1986

NOTES: Instructor's manual and seven modules for teachers to understand the information in the OOH and infuse these concepts in their lessons. The modules cover: basic principles of career development, infusing career education activities, understanding the labor market and the economy, and exploring careers. Sample handouts and workshop outlines.

11-3   COMMUNICATION

TITLE:	Parents on Your Side: A Comprehensive Parent Involvement Program for Teachers
MEDIA/COST:	Book/Workbook
GRADES/LENGTH:	K–6/Book, 209 pages; Workbook, 128 pages
AUTHOR:	Canter
PUBLISHER/ COPYRIGHT:	Lee Canter & Associates/1991

NOTES: Helps parents communicate effectively to be a partner with the school in helping their child achieve. The workbook includes conference planning sheets, home–school contracts, and back-to-school night activities that teachers can use to win parental support.

11-4   CONFLICT RESOLUTION

TITLE: **Break It Up: A Teacher's Guide to Managing Student Aggression**

MEDIA/COST: Book *

GRADES/LENGTH: K–12/252 pages

AUTHOR: Goldstein, et al.

PUBLISHER/
   COPYRIGHT: Research Press/1995

NOTES: A great guide for teachers to take action when students misbehave and are aggressive in conflicts with other students.

TITLE: **Conflict Resolution: Staff Development**

MEDIA/COST: Video/Binder Notebook ****

GRADES/LENGTH: 5–12/24 minutes

PUBLISHER/
   COPYRIGHT: Sunburst Communications, Inc./ 1992

NOTES: Helps teachers, counselors, and administrators understand components of a successful conflict-resolution program. Plans and handouts for a staff training session. General overview of a conflict-resolution program.

TITLE: **The Disruptive Child: How-to Strategies for De-Escalating Elementary School Students**

MEDIA/COST: Video *****

GRADES/LENGTH: K–6

PUBLISHER/
   COPYRIGHT: National Crisis Prevention Institute, Inc./1994

NOTES: These techniques were condensed from a 12-hour training program. Helps educators use basic preventative techniques to defuse potentially violent situations.

TITLE: **Peace in the Classroom: Practical Lessons in Living for Elementary-Age Children**

MEDIA/COST: Book *

GRADES/LENGTH: K–6/130 pages

AUTHOR: Adams

PUBLISHER/
   COPYRIGHT: Peguis Publishers/1994

NOTES: Excellent compilation of activities incorporating many academic areas. Activities are quick and easy to plan and organize. Extends from basic knowledge to specifics for implementing conflict mediation in the school.

TITLE: **Preventing Violence and Intervening Safely**
                  Dealing with the Potentially Violent Student
                  Intervening Safely During Fights
                  Preventing Violence in Your Classroom
                  (#1, #3, and #4, Scared Scared or Prepared Series)

MEDIA/COST: Videos/Books/Manuals ****

GRADES/LENGTH: K–6/125 pages

AUTHOR: Canter & Garrison

PUBLISHER/
   COPYRIGHT: Lee Canter & Associates, Inc./1995

NOTES: ***Dealing with the Potentially Violent Student:*** A kit for staff training in dealing with potentially violent students. Content is divided into the three stages of student confrontation: (1) agitation, (2) confrontation, and (3) resolution. It can be presented in one or two sessions. Teachers can apply these skills for good classroom-management techniques.

Intervening Safely During Fights: Basic stages in student fights and techniques to use to intervene safely and effectively during each stage. An additional segment deals with student aggression involving weapons. Staff will be prepared to safely and confidently handle violent and life-threatening situations if or when they arise at school.

Preventing Violence in Your Classroom: Violence-prevention program to implement in the classroom. Shows violent situations and suggests practical and effective solutions. Counselor may help the teacher develop plans and help lead classroom discussions. Also covers guns and gangs.

11-4 CONFLICT RESOLUTION *(CONTINUED)*

TITLE:	"Teacher They Called Me a _____!"
MEDIA/COST:	Book
GRADES/LENGTH:	K–6/56 pages
AUTHOR:	Byrnes
PUBLISHER/ COPYRIGHT:	Anti-Defamation League of B'nai B'rith/1985

NOTES: Deals sensitively and effectively with topics: prejudice, discrimination, disabilities, race and ethnicity, appearance, religion, family and lifestyle, and gender. Encourages teacher to think about his or her own feelings, knowledge, and understanding about the topic at the beginning of each chapter. Bibliography of children's books is included.

TITLE:	**Teaching Students to Get Along**
MEDIA/COST:	3 Videos/Manual *****
GRADES/LENGTH:	K–6
AUTHORS:	Canter & Petersen
PUBLISHER/ COPYRIGHT:	Lee Canter & Associates, Inc./1995

NOTES: Two staff development videos and one video showing "classroom scenes." Strategies are acted out step-by-step for teachers of elementary grades. Teachers may want to watch the video several times to review concepts and strategies, and practice activities. Key points, discussion questions, group activities, classroom application activities, and summary.

TITLE:	**The Tough Kid Book**
MEDIA/COST:	Book *
GRADES/LENGTH:	K–12/120 pages
AUTHORS:	Rhode, Jenson, & Reavis
PUBLISHER/ COPYRIGHT:	Sopris West, Inc./1993

NOTES: Practical classroom–management strategies to deal with difficult students, "tough kids," and improve interactions with parents. Emphasizes anticipation of problem behaviors and preventive strategies. Distinguishes between bribes and reinforcers as procedures for effective positive reinforcement. Ready reference with emphasis on a positive classroom with research-based techniques appropriate for all regular and special education teachers.

11-5   DEATH AND GRIEF

TITLE:	**Beyond the Innocence of Childhood: Factors Influencing Children and Adolescents' Perceptions and Attitudes Toward Death (Volumes I, II, III)**
MEDIA/COST:	Books **
GRADES/LENGTH:	K–12/90 pages
AUTHORS:	Adams & Deveau (Editors)
PUBLISHER/ COPYRIGHT:	Baywood/1995

NOTES: Excellent resource for teachers and parents. Provide essential information about how children understand death and how to explain death to them. Also includes perceptions and attitudes toward risk, life-threatening illness, and death.

TITLE:	**Death and the Classroom: A Teacher's Guide to Assist Grieving Students**
MEDIA/COST:	Book *
GRADES/LENGTH:	K–12/108 pages
AUTHORS:	Cassini & Rogers
PUBLISHER/ COPYRIGHT:	Griefwork of Cincinnati, Inc./1990

NOTES: Excellent book for educators to know how to provide resources to students after the death of a peer, parent, sibling, or sibling of a peer.

TITLE:	**Death and Loss: Compassionate Approaches in the Classroom**
MEDIA/COST:	Book **
GRADES/LENGTH:	K–12/160 pages
AUTHOR:	Leaman
PUBLISHER/ COPYRIGHT:	Wellington House/1995

NOTES: Excellent resource about students' understanding of death and risk and the differences between social classes in their understanding.

11-6   DISABILITIES

TITLE: **Could Do Better: Why Children Underachieve and What to Do About It**

MEDIA/COST: Book

GRADES/LENGTH: K–12

AUTHORS: Mandell & Marcus

PUBLISHER/
   COPYRIGHT: John Wiley & Sons/1995

NOTES: Describes six different underachiever styles, how to identify them, and suggestions to help underachievers improve. Also addresses underachievers with learning disabilities, gifted underachievers, "combination" underachievers, and even those who don't seem to match any profile.

TITLE: **How to Reach & Teach ADD/ADHD Children**

MEDIA: Book **

GRADES/LENGTH: K–6

AUTHOR: Rief

PUBLISHER/
   COPYRIGHT: Center for Applied Research in Education/1996

NOTES: Information about the identification of ADD/ADHD and techniques to help these students in the classroom. Activities have been successfully used with students.

TITLE: **Last One Picked . . . First One Picked On (For Teacher and Parent)**

MEDIA/COST: Video/Guide **

GRADES/LENGTH: K-8/68 minutes

AUTHOR: Lavoie

PUBLISHER/
   COPYRIGHT: PBS Video/1994

NOTES: Addresses social problems that children face, especially children with learning disabilities. Practical solutions that are particularly helpful when shown to teachers at an inservice at the beginning of the school year.

11-7   DISCIPLINE

TITLE: **Active Teaching: Enhancing Discipline, Self-Esteem and Student Performance**

MEDIA/COST: 2 videos/Handbook/Guide *****

GRADES/LENGTH: K–6

PUBLISHER/
   COPYRIGHT: Active Parenting Publishers/1994

NOTES: A training program of six to 15 hours that empowers teachers to effectively handle behavior problems by engaging students in decision making, active communication, and cooperation. Six sessions with two parts each. Part I is video-based and Part II provides optional practice and discussion. Excellent training to assist teachers in implementing class meetings. Supports *Active Parenting* programs for families, encouraging parents, teachers, and students to have a positive attitude at home and at school.

TITLE: **Assertive Discipline: Positive Behavior Management for Today's Classroom, (New and Revised)**

MEDIA/COST: Books/Workbooks *

GRADES/LENGTH: K–5, 6–8, 9–12/Book, 263 pages; Workbook, 128 pages

AUTHORS: Canter & Canter

PUBLISHER/
   COPYRIGHT: Lee Canter & Associates/1992

NOTES: Empowers teachers to respond positively while taking action to correct misbehavior, and to teach students to choose responsible behavior. Classroom-discipline plan and classroom-management plan. Workbooks have sample lesson plans, awards, posters, discipline cue cards, planning sheets, and behavior-management checklists.

11-7 DISCIPLINE (CONTINUED)

TITLE: **Behavior Management in the Classroom**
Behavior Contracting Systems

MEDIA/COST: Kits ***

GRADES/LENGTH: K–12

AUTHOR: Lundell

PUBLISHER: Behavioral Products

NOTES: *Behavior Management in the Classroom:* Kit for staff development includes: (1) Introduction, (2) Principles of learning, (3) Specific techniques for strengthening desired behaviors, and (4) Specific techniques for weakening undesirable behaviors. Materials include: (1) overhead transparencies, (2) cassette tape, (3) instructions and text, and (4) duplication masters.

Behavior Contracting Systems: Kit includes: (1) overhead transparencies, (2) cassette tape, (3) instructions with text, and (4) duplication masters. Describes how contracts can help teachers and parents manage social and academic behavior problems. Contract forms and simulation exercises enable participants to develop contracts for problem situations.

TITLE: **Classroom Discipline & Control: 101 Practical Techniques**

MEDIA/COST: Book **

GRADES/LENGTH: K–12/204 pages

AUTHORS: Chernow & Chernow

PUBLISHER/
COPYRIGHT: Parker Publishing Co./1981

NOTES: Topics include: (1) Classroom control, (2) Prevention of problems, (3) Self-discipline for students, (4) Overcoming vandalism and violence, and (5) Working as a team member with staff and parents.

TITLE: **Collaborative Discipline for At-Risk Students**

MEDIA/COST: Book **

GRADES/LENGTH: 9–12/260 pages

AUTHOR: Byers

PUBLISHER/
COPYRIGHT: American Vocational Association/ 1994

NOTES: Many ready-to-use activities with very effective suggestions to help at-risk students remain in school. Includes worksheets, handouts, schedule for beginning of school year, and other very practical resources.

TITLE: **Cooperative Discipline: How to Manage Your Classroom and Promote Self-Esteem**

MEDIA/COST: Kit: Videos/Handbook/Book, **; Kit, ******

GRADES/LENGTH: K–12/Book, 165 pages

AUTHOR: Albert

PUBLISHER/
COPYRIGHT: American Guidance Service (AGS)/ 1989

NOTES: Based on Adlerian theory, the book helps teachers identify the goals of students' misbehavior, and then react in effective ways so the student does not continue to misbehave. Goals of misbehavior: (1) Attention-seeking, (2) Power, (3) Revenge, and (4) Avoidance of failure. The video promotes discussion, is practical, and presents strategies for avoiding and defusing confrontations. Excellent to use in seminars to help teachers recognize, practice, and use disciplinary methods that retain the self-respect of students. Book alone is an excellent resource for teachers.

TITLE: **Levels of Discipline**

MEDIA/COST: Kit ***

GRADES/LENGTH: K–12

AUTHOR: Lundell

PUBLISHER: Behavioral Products

NOTES: Kit includes: (1) overhead transparencies, (2) cassette tape, (3) instructions and text, and (4) duplication masters. Seven discipline techniques with step-by-step instructions. Simulation exercises and discipline record forms are included.

TITLE: **Praise-Criticism Ratio: Teacher (Behavior = Student Output)**

MEDIA/COST: Kit ***

GRADES/LENGTH: K–12

AUTHOR: Brown

PUBLISHER: Behavioral Products

NOTES: Helps teachers examine their current classroom management methods and compare them with new methods in a workshop. Segments of teacher interactions with tallies comparing the number of times teachers use praise versus criticism of students. Kit includes: (1) overhead transparencies, (2) cassette tape, (3) instructions and text, and (4) duplication masters.

11-7 DISCIPLINE (CONTINUED)

TITLE:	**Succeeding With Difficult Students**
	New Strategies for Reaching Your Most Challenging Students
MEDIA/COST:	Book, *; Workbook, *; 4 Videos, ******
GRADES/LENGTH:	K–12/Book, 255 pages; Workbook, 144 pages; Videos, 5 hours
AUTHORS:	Canter & Canter
PUBLISHER/ COPYRIGHT:	Lee Canter & Associates/1993

NOTES: Excellent resource to assist teachers as they work with students who are continually disruptive, persistently defiant, demanding of attention, or unmotivated. Detailed steps and charts help teachers teach appropriate behavior, classroom rules, and consequences to disruptive students. Theme focuses on building relationships with the very students professionals tend to keep at a distance. Workbook contains student interest inventories, behavior profiles, lesson plans, and home-school plans. Book and workbook are sufficient for staff development.

TITLE:	**The Teacher's Guide to Behavioral Interventions: Intervention Strategies for Behavior Problems in the Educational Environment**
MEDIA/COST:	Book
GRADES/LENGTH:	K–12/291 pages
AUTHOR:	Wunderlich
PUBLISHER/ COPYRIGHT:	Hawthorne/1988

NOTES: Numbers are assigned to specific student behaviors, and then specific steps for intervening appropriately and changing inappropriate behavior are clearly provided. Helpful to both new and experienced teachers who desire to help students improve their classroom behavior.

11-8   GENDER EQUITY

TITLE:	**The AAUW Report: How Schools Shortchange Girls**
MEDIA/COST:	Book *
GRADES/LENGTH:	K–12/240 pages
AUTHOR:	Wellesley College Center for Research on Women
PUBLISHER/ COPYRIGHT:	AAUW/1992

NOTES: Reveals that girls receive less attention in the classroom than boys; girls are not pursuing math-related careers in proportion to boys; although the gender gap in math is shrinking, the gender gap in science is increasing. African American girls are more likely than white girls to be rebuffed by teachers; curricula ignore or stereotype women. Reports of sexual harassment of girls are increasing; and many standardized tests contain elements of gender bias.

TITLE:	**Gender Bias: In the Classroom and Interaction in the Curriculum**
MEDIA/COST:	Kit/Video
GRADES/LENGTH:	K–12/Video, 23 minutes
AUTHORS:	Sadker, Sadker, & Lewit
PUBLISHER/ COPYRIGHT:	National Education Association/ 1995

NOTES: Makes teachers aware of the impact of treating one gender of students differently from the other. Four-hour training, but the curriculum and interaction can be taught in separate sessions.

11-8 GENDER EQUITY (CONTINUED)

TITLE: **Growing Smart: What's Working for Girls in School**

MEDIA/COST: Guide, *
Report/Guide, **

GRADES/LENGTH: K–12/Guide, 60 pages;
Report, 97 pages

AUTHORS: Hansen, Walker, & Flom

PUBLISHER/
COPYRIGHT: AAUW/1995

NOTES: Insights into strategies that foster girls' achievement and healthy development. A review of more than 500 reports and studies on girls in grades K-12. Innovative approaches such as team learning, all-girl classes, and hands-on access to computers benefit girls' ability to succeed in school. Strategies for schools and approaches that enhance school achievement and healthy development for boys as well as girls.

TITLE: **Shortchanging Girls, Shortchanging America**

MEDIA/COST: Video, ** Executive Summary *

GRADES/LENGTH: 4–10/Video, 15 minutes; Summary, 20 pages

AUTHOR: Greenberg-Lake: The Analysis Group

PUBLISHER/
COPYRIGHT: AAUW/1995

NOTES: Examines impact of gender on self-esteem, career aspirations, educational experiences, and interest in math and science. As girls reach adolescence, they experience a significantly greater drop in self-esteem than boys experience. Girls are systematically discouraged from a wide range of academic pursuits, particularly math and science. Video integrates poll results and the faces and voices of American girls with educational experts examining these questions.

TITLE: **Teacher's Guide to Student Bias-Free Career Planning: Influencing Option Building Through Instruction**

MEDIA: Booklet

GRADES/LENGTH: 7–12/30 pages

AUTHORS: Slater-Hill & Boyett

PUBLISHER/
COPYRIGHT: Career, Education, & Training Associates, Inc./1993

NOTES: Provides teachers with information about achieving sex equity in their classrooms. Methods to allow males and females to develop themselves without gender limitations.

TITLE: **Women in Math and Science: Four Programs**

MEDIA/COST: Video *

GRADES/LENGTH: 7–12/57 minutes

PUBLISHER/
COPYRIGHT: Fairfax Network/1995

NOTES: Four programs: (1) Women in Medicine, (2) Women in the Military and Police, (3) Women in Engineering, and (4) Women in Research. Emphasizes the need for female students to pursue math and science studies so they can consider careers involving these important skills in their futures.

11-9　LEARNING STYLES

TITLE:　**Learning Styles**
MEDIA/COST:　Booklet
GRADES/LENGTH:　K–12/40 pages
AUTHOR:　Reiff
PUBLISHER/
　COPYRIGHT:　National Education Association/ 1992

NOTES: Overview and some specifics of different learning styles and programs that address them. Extensive bibliography and some excellent lists.

TITLE:　**Multiple Intelligences in the Classroom**
MEDIA/COST:　Book *
GRADES/LENGTH:　K–12/185 pages
AUTHOR:　Armstrong
PUBLISHER/
　COPYRIGHT:　Association for Supervision and Curriculum Development (ASCD)/1994

NOTES: Translates the theory of multiple intelligences into practical teaching strategies that can be used in classroom management, assessment, special education, and other areas. Some teachers will be interested in the application of this theory.

TITLE:　**Research on Educational Innovations**
MEDIA/COST:　Book
GRADES/LENGTH:　K–12/203 pages
AUTHORS:　Ellis & Fouts
PUBLISHER/
　COPYRIGHT:　Eye On Education/1993

NOTES: General information about the research on learning styles, outcome-based education, cooperative learning, and a number of other subjects. Glossary of terms used in research in education.

11-10　MULTICULTURAL

TITLE:　**Holiday Facts & Fun: Martin Luther King Day**
MEDIA/COST:　Video/Guide ***
　　(1 video of a series of 11)
GRADES/LENGTH:　1–4/10 minutes
PUBLISHER/
　COPYRIGHT:　Rainbow Educational Video/1992

NOTES: Dr. Martin Luther King experienced discrimination as a child and it remained in his memory. He became painfully aware of segregation when he was growing up. His life is portrayed through school and the Montgomery Bus Boycott and the March on Washington. Video ends with the national holiday named in honor of Dr. Martin Luther King. Guide includes a lesson plan and learning activities to be conducted before and after viewing the video.

11-12　PROBLEM SOLVING

TITLE:　**The High-Performing Teacher: Avoiding Burnout and Increasing Your Motivation**
MEDIA/COST:　Book
GRADES/LENGTH:　Teachers of K–12/136 pages
AUTHOR:　Canter
PUBLISHER/
　COPYRIGHT:　Lee Canter and Associates/1994

NOTES: Problem-solving skills for overcoming challenges, taking risks, and getting results. Shows how to build positive relationships with students and parents. Also shows how to plan time to get more for effort.

11-12 PROBLEM SOLVING (CONTINUED)

TITLE: **The Skillful Teacher: Building Your Teaching Skills**

MEDIA/COST: Books and Training

GRADES/LENGTH: K–12

AUTHORS: Saphier & Gower

PUBLISHER/
  COPYRIGHT: Research for Better Teaching/1988

NOTES: Excellent resource for teachers. Comprehensive repertoire of teacher actions to promote a mutually respectful classroom with the teacher firmly in control. Presents a broad repertoire of ways in which teachers can be effective with very concrete suggestions. Practical suggestions for teachers to develop skills to motivate and maintain a classroom to help students succeed. Tremendous resource for teachers.

11-13 RESPECT

TITLE: **Class Meetings**

MEDIA/COST: Video/Guide **

GRADES/LENGTH: K–6/30 minutes

AUTHORS: Meder & Platt

PUBLISHER: Dynamic Training & Seminars, Inc.

NOTES: Outlines the steps and gives the specific structure for a class meeting. Points for developing a circle, giving compliments, developing the agenda, maintaining the agenda book, and brainstorming consequences. Explains these fundamentals first, and then shows an actual class meeting being held. Excellent introduction to class meetings for adults and students. A good training approach to use with teachers because it shows an example of a class in a class meeting; however, the quality of the video is very poor.

TITLE: **Positive Discipline in the Classroom: How to Effectively Use Class Meetings and Other Positive Discipline Strategies**

MEDIA/COST: Book

GRADES/LENGTH: K–12

AUTHORS: Nelsen, Lott, & Glenn

DISTRIBUTOR/
  COPYRIGHT: Dynamic Training & Seminars/1993

NOTES: Excellent book with directions for leading class meetings and using other methods to promote a positive, mutually caring environment. Particularly helpful for the teacher or counselor leading class meetings for the first time.

TITLE: **Teaching Tolerance**

MEDIA/COST: Magazine/Free

GRADES/LENGTH: K–12

PUBLISHER: Southern Poverty Law Center

NOTES: Mailed twice a year at no charge to educators upon request.

11-14 RESPONSIBILITY

TITLE: **Responsible Kids in School and at Home (6 videos)**

(1) I Have a Reason: The Basics of Behavior

(2) Look at Me! Attention-Seeking Behavior

(3) Let's Fight! Power Struggles

(4) I'll Get Even! Revenge Behavior

(5) Leave Me Alone! Avoidance of Failure Behavior

(6) You're the Greatest! Building Self-Esteem, Encouragement

MEDIA: 6 Videos/Guide *****

GRADES/LENGTH: 6–9/Video, 20 minutes

AUTHOR: Albert

PUBLISHER/
  COPYRIGHT: American Guidance Service (AGS)/ 1994

NOTES: Videos for staff development and parent meetings that focus on developing an understanding of why kids do what they do. Answers the questions: "Why do kids choose irresponsible behaviors?" and "Where do I start when I want to help turn kids around?" Information presented by two reporters interspersed with segments depicting real-life scenarios. Reporters discuss cooperative discipline and building self-esteem through encouragement. Encouragement is contrasted with using praise, which is not the same. Tips for parents on how to be encouraging to their children.

11-14 RESPONSIBILITY (CONTINUED)

TITLE: **Teach Responsibility? Yes!**

                    (*Making Choices—Growing Stronger
                    Series*)

MEDIA/COST: Units *

GRADES/LENGTH: 5–7/23 pages

AUTHOR: Falk

PUBLISHER/
   COPYRIGHT: Elizabeth Falk, M.A., LPC/1992

NOTES: Through sports and game analogies, connects with preadolescents. Activities invite discussion, and are fun and interesting. Positive focus. Examples relative to kids this age to help them recognize their behavior instead of just hearing about it. Excellent guides to facilitate group lessons on responsibility.

11-15   SAFETY

TITLE: **"Caring Connections": Helping
                    Young People from Troubled
                    Homes**

MEDIA/COST: Kit *

GRADES/LENGTH: K–12/64 pages

PUBLISHER/
   COPYRIGHT: "Caring Connections"/ 1994

NOTES: A handbook and four identical brochures for people who work with children. Basic information on how to help children from troubled homes. Many useful lists of indicators of different types of abuse. Information about different programs for children that can be conducted in schools. Useful resource for anyone working with children.

TITLE: **Does AIDS Hurt? Educating
                    Young Children About AIDS**

MEDIA/COST: Book

GRADES/LENGTH: K–5

AUTHORS: Quackenbush & Villarreal

PUBLISHER: Network Publications

NOTES: Suggestions for teachers, parents, and counselors of children. Gives suggestions about age-appropriate information for children and questions they ask. Also provides suggestions about how to talk to children about family members at risk of AIDS.

TITLE: **Hostile Hallways: The AAUW
                    Survey on Sexual Harassment in
                    America's Schools**

MEDIA/COST: Book *

GRADES/LENGTH: Teachers of K–12/28 pages

AUTHOR: Harris and Associates

PUBLISHER/
   COPYRIGHT: AAUW/1993

NOTES: Survey of sexual harassment in public schools based on experiences of 1,632 students in grades 8 through 11. This research found that 85 percent of the girls and 76 percent of the boys surveyed have experienced sexual harassment. Teachers and counselors should be aware of other very important information reported in this scientific study.

TITLE: **The Race for Safe Schools: A Staff
                    Development Curriculum**

MEDIA/COST: Binder **

GRADES/LENGTH: K–12/144 pages

AUTHORS: McLaughlin & Hazouri

PUBLISHER/
   COPYRIGHT: Educational Media

NOTES: Staff development curriculum to address school climate, diversity, and increasing security by addressing the causes of violence. Ideas for student and faculty participation in ensuring a safe school. Reproducible handouts and transparencies for each topic.

TITLE: **Victory Over Violence**

MEDIA/COST: Video *

GRADES/LENGTH: K–12/1 hour

PUBLISHER/
   COPYRIGHT: Fairfax Network/1996

NOTES: Shows how relationships among home, school, and community can overcome violence among today's youth. Focuses on ways to combat violence and highlights successful school–community programs. This program in the '97 Passport Collection is appropriate for parents, teachers, and counselors.

11-17   SELF-ESTEEM

TITLE: **100 Ways to Enhance Self-Concept in the Classroom: A Handbook for Teachers and Parents**

MEDIA/COST: Book *

GRADES/LENGTH: K–12/253 pages

AUTHORS: Canfield & Wells

PUBLISHER/
COPYRIGHT: Prentice Hall/1976

NOTES: A classic. One of the best books in the field of self-esteem. Activities can be adapted for every grade level.

TITLE: **Building Self-Esteem: A Comprehensive Program**

MEDIA/COST: Guide

GRADES/LENGTH: K–8

AUTHOR: Reasoner

PUBLISHER/
COPYRIGHT: Consulting Psychologists Press/1982

NOTES: Comprehensive curriculum materials for creating and sustaining a self-esteem program in schools. Written by a school superintendent. A five-component model for self-esteem in elementary and middle school.

TITLE: **Inviting School Success: A Self-Concept Approach to Teaching and Learning**

MEDIA/COST: Book

GRADES/LENGTH: K–12

AUTHORS: Purkey & Novak

PUBLISHER/
COPYRIGHT: Wadsworth Publishing Co./1984

NOTES: A manual for esteem building in all school settings. A school-based approach for enhancing self-esteem of all students.

TITLE: **Self-Esteem in the Classroom: A Curriculum Guide**

MEDIA/COST: Book

GRADES/LENGTH: K–12

AUTHOR: Canfield

PUBLISHER/
COPYRIGHT: National Council for Self-Esteem/1987

NOTES: Includes over 200 activities that can be adapted for all grade levels.

TITLE: **Staff Development: Self-Esteem, Elementary Grades**

MEDIA/COST: Video/Guide/Handouts ****

GRADES/LENGTH: K–6/26 minutes

PUBLISHER/
COPYRIGHT: Sunburst Communications, Inc./1992

NOTES: Encourages administrators and teachers to build self-esteem into their schools and classrooms. Features two schools with strong self-esteem programs. The teachers from these schools show activities and strategies that work, demonstrate ways to encourage parent and community involvement, and stress the importance of a schoolwide climate that nurtures self-esteem.

11-19   SPECIAL POPULATIONS

TITLE: **Florida's Challenge: Guide to Educating Substance-Exposed Children**

MEDIA/COST: Video/Workbook

GRADES/LENGTH: K–12/Video, 25 minutes; Booklet, 84 pages

AUTHOR: Florida Department of Education

PUBLISHER/
COPYRIGHT: U.S. Department of Education/1994

NOTES: Information and current research of effective strategies for working with substance-exposed children. Outstanding video and booklet with detailed risk factors and protective factors for substance-exposed children.

11-21 SUBSTANCE ABUSE PREVENTION

TITLE: **Children of Alcoholics**

MEDIA/COST: Booklet * (each for 100–499 booklets)

GRADES/LENGTH: K–12/15 pages

PUBLISHER/
  COPYRIGHT: Channing L. Bete Co./1992

NOTES: Excellent booklet for a counselor to use when presenting an inservice with staff members about Children of Alcoholics (COAs). Explains the reason for the concern, the roles within an alcoholic family, and how the experience can affect adulthood, and lists resources for help.

TITLE: **Children of Alcoholics: How School Can Help**

MEDIA/COST: Video/Guide ***

GRADES/LENGTH: 3–9

PUBLISHER: Instructional Media Institute (IMI)

NOTES: Excellent video for teacher seminars. Informative for teachers, counselors, and administrators. Includes the reason educators should be concerned about Children of Alcoholics (COAs), the risk factors, impact, and characteristic concerns of COAs. Provides warning signs of students who are at risk because of being COAs, and how to respond to these warning signs to help students.

TITLE: **Talking About Drugs & Alcohol**

MEDIA/COST: Video/Guide ****

GRADES/LENGTH: K–6/26 minutes

PUBLISHER/
  COPYRIGHT: Sunburst Communications, Inc./ 1990

NOTES: A panel discussion on alcohol and other drug issues. A discussion guide, handouts, and activities for role play. Good faculty presentation.

TITLE: **Teaching Children Affected by Substance Abuse**

MEDIA/COST: Video/Guide/Free

GRADES/LENGTH: K–3/Video, 30 minutes; Guide, 69 pages

PUBLISHER/
  COPYRIGHT: Drug Planning and Outreach Staff/ 1994

NOTES: Excellent resource with many practical interventions for working with high-risk children. The title is somewhat misleading. Guide describes a broader combination of risk factors such as family instability which contribute to developmental problems. Six suggestions to work with high-risk children in regular education settings: (1) Creating a safe/supportive classroom environment, (2) Encouraging cooperative learning, (3) Facilitating transitions, minimizing distractions, (4) Helping students manage their behavior, (5) Assessing for educational progress, and (6) Building home–school connections.

MATERIALS FOR
THE COUNSELOR

ANNOTATED LIST OF MATERIALS

(PERMISSION OF FAIRFAX COUNTY PUBLIC SCHOOLS OF VIRGINIA)

Cost Guide:	* ($1-$25)	** ($26-$55)	*** ($56-$105)	**** ($106-205)	***** ($206-$505)	****** ($506-$1,000)

12-1 CAREER EDUCATION

TITLE:	**Applying Career Development Theory to Counseling (2nd ed.)**
MEDIA/COST:	Book
GRADES/LENGTH:	K–12/450 pages
AUTHOR:	Sharf
PUBLISHER/ COPYRIGHT:	Brooks/Cole/1997

NOTES: Excellent resource that shows how to apply career development theory. Four theoretical areas are covered: (1) trait and type, (2) life span, (3) special focus theories, and (4) theoretical integration. Numerous case examples are presented with a practical perspective. Applications are given for women and for people of color.

TITLE:	**Career Tracks 2000**
MEDIA/COST:	4 Videos *
GRADES/LENGTH:	7–12/30 minutes
PUBLISHER/ COPYRIGHT:	Fairfax Network/1996-97

NOTES: Profiles successful professionals. Highlights particular career, offers advice on setting and achieving goals, and the impact that technology has had on particular careers. *Part one:* engineer, graphic artist, comptroller, and veterinarian. *Part two:* Fire and Rescue paramedic, architect, advertising director, and musician with U.S. Air Force. *Part three:* Broadcast journalist, mechanic, human resource manager, and physical therapist. *Part four:* Systems support engineer, web page designer, attorney, and executive chef.

TITLE:	**Careers 2000 (3-part series)**
MEDIA/COST:	3 Videos/3 Guides *****
GRADES/LENGTH:	6–12/25 minutes
AUTHORS:	Farr & Christophersen
PUBLISHER/ COPYRIGHT:	JIST Works/1997

NOTES: Videos: *(1) Where Do I Fit In?, (2) Exploring Career Options, (3) Preparing NOW for Success in the Future.* Workbooks: *(1) Knowing Yourself, (2) Your Career, and (3) Career Preparation.* Helpful to students in a class or a small group, but workbooks are disposable. Very good program.

12-1 CAREER EDUCATION *(CONTINUED)*

TITLE: **Counselor and Bias-Free Career Planning Programs: Preparing Students for Improved Decision Making**

MEDIA/COST: Booklet

GRADES/LENGTH: 7–12/17 pages

AUTHOR: Hinkle

PUBLISHER/
   COPYRIGHT: Career, Education, and Training Associates/1993

NOTES: Information about counseling women, men, and giving bias-free career planning. Suggestions for working with teachers and parents as well as with students.

TITLE: **Creating Portfolios**

MEDIA/COST: Guide/Workbook *

GRADES/LENGTH: 7–12/Guide, 64 pages; Workbook, 85 pages

AUTHOR: Kimeldorf

PUBLISHER/
   COPYRIGHT: American Vocational Association (AVA)/1994

NOTES: Great guides for making portfolios meaningful and manageable. The students will learn how to create their portfolios.

TITLE: **Developmental Career Counseling and Assessment (2nd ed.)**

MEDIA/COST: Book **

GRADES/LENGTH: K–12/571 pages

AUTHOR: Seligman

PUBLISHER/
   COPYRIGHT: Sage Science Press/1994

NOTES: Applies career development theories to career practices. Covers career issues that arise during childhood, early adolescence, and adolescence. Articulates the developmental milestones of each period and accompanies each with stage-appropriate career counseling interventions and resources.

TITLE: **Florida Blueprint for Career Preparation**

MEDIA/COST: Book

GRADES/LENGTH: K–12

PUBLISHER: Bureau of Career Development, Florida Department of Education

NOTES: A model of a complete K–12 program for effective career development. Provides a framework to prepare students to enter and remain in chosen fields of work.

TITLE: **Get a Life**

MEDIA/COST: Portfolios *

GRADES/LENGTH: 7–12

PUBLISHER/
   COPYRIGHT: American School Counselor Association (ASCA)/1996

NOTES: Portfolios for students to compile information about self. Includes tabs for: (1) self-knowledge, (2) life roles, (3) educational development, and (4) career exploration and planning. Explains the importance of career education and counseling. A great resource.

TITLE: **National Career Development Guidelines, K-Adult Handbook**

MEDIA/COST: Handbook

GRADES/LENGTH: K–12

PUBLISHER/
   COPYRIGHT: National Occupational Information Coordinating Committee (NOICC)/ 1996
                  http://www.profiles.iastate.edu/ided/ncdc/noice.htm

NOTES: Specific guidelines to strengthen career development programs in all schools at all levels. Suggested competencies and indicators for elementary school, middle/junior high school, and high school. Tips for getting started, examples of lesson plans and activities, and contact information for successful programs. Proven implementation for career development in new and existing programs.

12-3 COMPREHENSIVE

TITLE: **ASCA Student Competencies: A Guide for School Counselors**

MEDIA/COST: Booklet *

GRADES/LENGTH: K–12/22 pages

AUTHORS: Sears, Pregitzer, & Jackson

PUBLISHER/
COPYRIGHT: American School Counselor Association (ASCA)/1990

NOTES: Excellent resource for all school counselors. Provides personal/social goals, educational goals, and career goals for students from prekindergarten through postsecondary school. Designated by grade level and stated behaviorally in terms of what students will be able to do as a result of a comprehensive, developmental counseling and guidance program. A recommended resource.

TITLE: **Career Resource Center Materials**

MEDIA/COST: Handbook *

GRADES/LENGTH: 7–12/25 pages

PUBLISHER/
COPYRIGHT: Devonshire Administrative Center/ 1996

NOTES: Excellent resource with title, category, publisher, and copyright date for materials for: (1) job counseling, (2) career counseling, (3) college counseling, (4) social and psychological counseling, (5) special populations and group counseling, (6) classroom and school management, (7) academic counseling, (8) cassettes, (9) videos, and (10) software.

TITLE: **The Challenge of Counseling in Middle Schools**

MEDIA/COST: Book **

GRADES/LENGTH: 6–9

AUTHORS: Gerler, Hogan, & O'Rourke

PUBLISHER/
COPYRIGHT: American School Counselor Association (ASCA)/1996

NOTES: Practical suggestions and recommendations that middle school counselors have found to be successful with students and parents.

TITLE: **Compassionate School: A Practical Guide to Educating Abused and Traumatized Children**

MEDIA/COST: Book **

GRADES/LENGTH: K–12/240 pages

AUTHOR: Morrow

PUBLISHER/
COPYRIGHT: Prentice Hall/1987

NOTES: Excellent reference for counselors. Information about latchkey children, child abuse, divorce, remarriage, single-parent families, death, and establishing a staff support system. Straightforward, easy-to-understand explanations and suggestions for promoting social development that instills altruistic attitudes and respect for all students. Ways to ensure that students are helped as they react to traumas. Some forms are inappropriate for schools.

TITLE: **Conners' Rating Scales (CRS)**

MEDIA/COST: Scales/Manual ****

GRADES/LENGTH: K–12

AUTHOR: Conners

PUBLISHER: Psychological Assessment Resources (PAR)

NOTES: These scales identify behavior problems and can be administered individually or in a group. Teacher rating forms and parent feedback forms. Short version has 48 items.

TITLE: **Counseling and Human Development**

MEDIA/COST: Monthly Report ** (annual subscription)

GRADES: K–12

PUBLISHER: Love Publishing Company

NOTES: Up-to-date information for the counselor with such subjects as strategies, peer pressure, counselor stress, and techniques to use with certain students. Articles are usually practical for the school counselor.

12-3 COMPREHENSIVE (CONTINUED)

TITLE: **Counseling Children (4th ed.)**

MEDIA/COST: Book **

GRADES/LENGTH: K–12/633 pages

AUTHORS: Thompson & Rudolph

PUBLISHER/
  COPYRIGHT: Brooks/Cole/1996

NOTES: Excellent resource that provides details for counseling in schools that are not in other books. Information about counseling students from different cultures, students in satanic cults, and students in violent situations. Specifies application of specific counseling theories when counseling students. Special topics such as consultation, group counseling, and legal and ethical considerations. Suggested books for children with specific concerns are listed. Extremely valuable resource with practical suggestions for elementary and secondary school counselors, both new and experienced.

TITLE: **Counseling Today's Secondary Students**

MEDIA/COST: Book **

GRADES/LENGTH: 7–12/319 pages

AUTHORS: Hitchner & Tifft-Hitchner

PUBLISHER/
  COPYRIGHT: Prentice Hall/1996

NOTES: A practical and up-to-date guide in four sections: (1) Secondary educational development, (2) Personal and social development, (3) Postsecondary educational development, and (4) Career development. Many topics are included that are not found in other reference books for the counselor. Forms and letters that counselors can adapt or reproduce to save time. A great resource for counselors in middle and high schools.

TITLE: **Counseling Toward Solutions: A Practical Solution-Focused Program for Working with Students, Teachers, and Parents**

MEDIA/COST: Book **

GRADES/LENGTH: K–12/282 pages

AUTHOR: Metcalf

PUBLISHER/
  COPYRIGHT: Center for Applied Research in Education/1995

NOTES: Practical handbook for school counselors. Positive approach in which the focus is on the solution, not the problem. Encourages student to identify times when he or she was successful in coping with the presenting problem, called exceptions. Gives students clues to how to solve the problem, or do things successfully again. Applicable for individual and group counseling. Numerous worksheets to help identify the problem, develop goals, and search and identify exceptions. Suggestions, exercises, ideas, and case examples illustrate strategies in the school setting.

TITLE: **Counselor in the Classroom**

MEDIA/COST: Book

GRADES/LENGTH: 3-6 (Variation for 1–2)/167 pages

AUTHORS: Schwallie-Giddis, Cowan, & Schilling

PUBLISHER/
  COPYRIGHT: Innerchoice Publishing/1993

NOTES: Guidance lessons cover such topics as: self-esteem, cooperation, friendship, peer-pressure, critical thinking, problem solving, and safety. Each lesson states overall purpose, materials needed, directions, discussion questions, and suggestions for adapting the lesson for younger children. Games, writing, and art are integrated into many of the lessons.

TITLE: **Creative Counseling Techniques: An Illustrated Guide**

MEDIA/COST: Book *

GRADES/LENGTH: K–12/152 pages

AUTHOR: Jacobs

PUBLISHER/
  COPYRIGHT: Psychological Assessment Resources, Inc. (PAR)/1992

NOTES: Demonstrations of how counselors can use props, movement, chairs, writing, drawing, and analogies to make counseling concrete. Activities for children, adolescents, and groups.

12-3 COMPREHENSIVE (*CONTINUED*)

TITLE: **Developing and Managing Your
                  School Guidance Program
                  (2nd ed.)**
MEDIA/COST: Book **
GRADES/LENGTH: K–12/501 pages
AUTHORS: Gysbers & Henderson
PUBLISHER/
   COPYRIGHT: American Counseling Association
                  (ACA)/1994

NOTES: Information to establish, implement, and manage a new guidance program or improve an existing K–12 program. A theory-based framework to systematically organize and manage school counseling content, methods, and techniques.

TITLE: **Developmental Guidance and
                  Counseling: A Practical Approach**
MEDIA/COST: Book **
GRADES/LENGTH: K–12/390 pages
AUTHOR: Myrick
PUBLISHER/
   COPYRIGHT: Educational Media Corporation/
                  1993

NOTES: An up-to-date reference that addresses the many responsibilities of the elementary school counselor.

TITLE: **Developmental School
                  Counseling Programs: From
                  Theory to Practice**
MEDIA/COST: Book *
GRADES/LENGTH: K–12/221 pages
AUTHORS: Paisley & Hubbard
PUBLISHER/
   COPYRIGHT: American Counseling Association
                  (ACA)/1994

NOTES: Techniques for counseling individual students, groups, parents, and teachers. More than 50 lesson plans for K–12 developmental guidance with goals and competencies appropriate for group work at all stages of development.

TITLE: **Elementary School Counseling: A
                  Blueprint for Today and
                  Tomorrow**
MEDIA/COST: Book **
GRADES/LENGTH: K–6/436 pages
AUTHOR: Worzbyt
PUBLISHER/
   COPYRIGHT: CAPS Publications/1989

NOTES: Many counseling activities appropriate for children, parents, teachers, and others that are easy to lead and practical. Philosophy, how to plan for program effectiveness, counseling curriculum, and challenge of the future.

TITLE: **Guidance and Counseling
                  Programs for the Year 2000 and
                  Beyond: Strengthening Work-
                  Related Education & Training**
MEDIA/COST: Monograph *
GRADES/LENGTH: 7–12/12 pages
AUTHOR: Guidance Division, American
                  Vocational Association
PUBLISHER/
   COPYRIGHT: Center on Education and Training
                  for Employment/1993

NOTES: A monograph highlighting the importance of comprehensive, developmental school counseling programs from kindergarten through grade 12. Emphasizes need for structured guidance interventions for all students in a systematic, developmental program: (1) guidance is a program; (2) guidance and counseling programs are developmental and comprehensive; (3) guidance and counseling programs focus on individuals' competencies, not just their deficiencies; (4) guidance and counseling programs are built on a team approach; and (5) guidance and counseling programs mandate articulation.

12-3 COMPREHENSIVE (CONTINUED)

TITLE: **Invitational Counseling: A Self-Concept Approach to Professional Practice**

MEDIA/COST: Book **

GRADES/LENGTH: K–12/215 pages

AUTHORS: Purkey & Schmidt

PUBLISHER/
COPYRIGHT: Brooks/Cole/1996

NOTES: An overall view of invitational counseling that includes four elements: (1) optimism, (2) respect, (3) trust, and (4) intentionality. Five "P" factors must receive focus for invitational counseling to be effective. Particular attention must be given to: (1) people, (2) places, (3) policies, (4) programs, and (5) processes. Confrontation and interpretation are two skills that are essential in invitational counseling. Worthy reference to improve skills when counseling with students, parents, and teachers.

TITLE: **Kindness Is Contagious . . . Catch It!**

MEDIA/COST: Book/Guide

GRADES/LENGTH: K–6/30 pages

AUTHORS: Ziegenhorn & Unell

PUBLISHER/
COPYRIGHT: Stop Violence Coalition of Kansas City/1992

NOTES: Objective of this activity booklet is to teach children that when one person performs acts of kindness, both parties win. Activities can be easily adapted for the school, classroom, or individual student.

TITLE: **Literature Teacher's Book of Lists**

MEDIA/COST: Book **

GRADES/LENGTH: K–12/405 pages

AUTHOR: Strouf

PUBLISHER/
COPYRIGHT: Center for Applied Research in Education/1993

NOTES: Excellent resource for bibliocounseling. Lists books for children and adolescents under headings for bibliocounseling. Examples include: Adoption; Disability, Mental and Physical; Drugs and Alcohol; Ethnic and Multicultural Literature; Heroes and Heroines; African American; Native American Authors and Literature; and Women's Issues. Books listed under Young Adult Concerns include: Abuse and Rape; Courage; Disaster; Divorce; Eating Disorders; Ecology; Family Relationships; Pregnancy; Runaways; Search for Self; and Suicide and Death.

TITLE: **Managing Your School Counseling Program: K–12 Developmental Strategies**

MEDIA/COST: Book *

GRADES/LENGTH: K–12/276 pages

AUTHOR: Wittmer (Editor)

PUBLISHER/
COPYRIGHT: Educational Media Corporation/ 1993

NOTES: Accurate, up-to-date, and comprehensive reference book written by well-recognized authorities of school counseling. Useful forms are included.

TITLE: **Olympic Spirit: Building Resiliency in Youth**

MEDIA/COST: Video/Guide/Free

GRADES/LENGTH: K–12

AUTHOR: U.S. Department of Education's Safe and Drug-Free Schools Program

PUBLISHER/
COPYRIGHT: U.S. Department of Education/1995

NOTES: Project to foster students' resiliency and thus increase their resistance to drug use, violence, and other harmful behaviors. Definition of resiliency is ability to adapt to changes and transition, and deal with difficult problems and situations in a positive way. Video and activity guide provide counselors with a creative approach to supplementary classroom drug and violence prevention lessons.

TITLE: **Partners in Play: An Adlerian Approach to Play Therapy**

MEDIA/COST: Book **

GRADES/LENGTH: K–6/219 pages

AUTHOR: Kottman

PUBLISHER/
COPYRIGHT: American Counseling Association (ACA)/1995

NOTES: Adlerian counseling with step-by-step directions about how to integrate Adlerian theory into play counseling. This book includes limits in the playroom, consultation, and teaching healthy relationship skills.

12-3 COMPREHENSIVE (CONTINUED)

TITLE: **PIC: Practical Ideas for Counselors**

MEDIA/COST: Newsletter *

GRADES/LENGTH: K–6

PUBLISHER/
COPYRIGHT: Childswork/Childsplay/annual, 5 bimonthly issues

NOTES: Excellent resource for the elementary school counselor. May want to keep in a binder and copy some articles for parents or teachers.

TITLE: **Play Therapy: The Art of the Relationship**

MEDIA/COST: Book

GRADES/LENGTH: K–5

AUTHOR: Landreth

PUBLISHER/
COPYRIGHT: Accelerated Development/1991

NOTES: One of the best books about this topic. Recommended for any counselor who plans to incorporate play into counseling with young students.

TITLE: **The Prepare Curriculum: Teaching Prosocial Competencies**

MEDIA/COST: Book **

GRADES/LENGTH: 7–12/700 pages

AUTHOR: Goldstein

PUBLISHER/
COPYRIGHT: Community Intervention, Inc./ 1988

NOTES: Strategies to teach interpersonal skills to aggressive, antisocial young people, as well as those withdrawn and socially isolated. Plans are primarily for adolescents and present sequential lessons to provide training in: problem solving, interpersonal skill, situational perception, anger control, moral reasoning, stress management, empathy, and cooperation. Good activities that are focused and different.

TITLE: **S.A.I.L.: Self-Awareness in Language Arts**

MEDIA/COST: Book *

GRADES/LENGTH: K–5/224 pages

AUTHORS: Hughes & Kloeppel

PUBLISHER/
COPYRIGHT: Educational Media Corporation/ 1994

NOTES: Excellent resource for kindergarten through fifth grade. Three main sections with six lessons for each grade level. Main sections: Self-Esteem, Decision Making, and Peer Relationships. All lessons state objectives, needed materials, procedure for conducting the lesson, closure, and ideas for supplemental activities. Writing, reading, and speaking activities as well as poetry are incorporated into the lessons. Many of the lessons lead to activities for science and social studies.

TITLE: **School Counselors and Censorship: Facing the Challenge**

MEDIA/COST: Book **

GRADES/LENGTH: K–12/182 pages

AUTHORS: Brigman & Moore

PUBLISHER/
COPYRIGHT: American School Counselor Association (ASCA)/1994

NOTES: Excellent reference with practical suggestions for any school, school system, or state that is undergoing challenges as to the value of counseling in the schools. Research support for developmental counseling, what to expect from the challengers, how to prevent challenges, what to do during a challenge, developing and utilizing community support, and helpful organizations and resources are all in this superb reference book.

TITLE: **School Counselor's Letter Book**

MEDIA/COST: Book **

GRADES/LENGTH: 7–12/288 pages

AUTHORS: Hitchner, Tifft-Hitchner, & Apostol

PUBLISHER/
COPYRIGHT: Center for Applied Research in Education/1991

NOTES: A compilation of 220 model letters, memoranda, forms, policy statements, and information sheets designed to help save the counselor time and effort in four general areas. These models can easily be adapted to particular situations. Examples are provided for the following areas: (1) Counseling for Educational Development, (2) Personal Counseling, (3) Conseling for the Future, (4) Communication, and (5) Professional Development.

12-3 COMPREHENSIVE (CONTINUED)

TITLE: **Solution-Focused Counseling in High School and Middle School**

MEDIA/COST: Book *

GRADES/LENGTH: 7–12/260 pages

AUTHOR: Murphy

PUBLISHER/
  COPYRIGHT: American Counseling Association (ACA)/1997

NOTES: Techniques to use with the most difficult students in school. Students who have disruptive classroom behavior, failing grades, truancy, and violence require effective strategies.

TITLE: **Student Aggression: Prevention, Management, and Replacement Training**

MEDIA/COST: Book **

GRADES/LENGTH: 7–12/280 pages

AUTHOR: Goldstein

PUBLISHER/
  COPYRIGHT: Guilford Press/1994

NOTES: Practical book to replace ineffective responses to peer pressure with effective refusal skills for at-risk students. Includes notes and ways to model skills for the trainer. Excellent resource.

TITLE: **Substance Abuse Prevention: A Dramatic Approach**

MEDIA/COST: Book of plays ***

GRADES/LENGTH: K–12/146 pages

AUTHORS: Goldwasser & Perlman

PUBLISHER/
  COPYRIGHT: Sunburst Communications, Inc./ 1992

NOTES: Compilation of stories and plays that deal with many topics: (1) peer pressure, (2) problem solving, (3) transition to middle school, (4) impact of the media, (5) talking to parents, (6) sharing uncomfortable feelings, (7) deciding what to do when a friend uses drugs, (8) dealing with rejection, and (9) learning how to have a good time without substances. Strong no-use message about alcohol and other drugs is consistent throughout the plays and stories. Discussion questions follow each story and play.

TITLE: **Survival Guide for Elementary and Middle School Counselors**

MEDIA/COST: Book **

GRADES/LENGTH: K–9/304 pages

AUTHOR: Schmidt

PUBLISHER/
  COPYRIGHT: Center for Applied Research in Education/1991

NOTES: Guidelines to build a comprehensive counseling program and prioritize counseling activities in a school. Practical and ready-to-use ideas, techniques, procedures, materials, including reproducible forms, and time-saving tips. Needs assessment can be completed by children in lower elementary grades. Excellent resource for every elementary and middle school counselor.

TITLE: **Survival Guide for the Secondary School Counselor**

MEDIA/COST: Book **

GRADES/LENGTH: 9–12/245 pages

AUTHORS: Hitchner & Tifft-Hitchner

PUBLISHER/
  COPYRIGHT: Center for Applied Research in Education/1987

NOTES: Easy-to-read guide with practical suggestions for handling tasks of the school counselor, including tips for working with "typical kids" as well as exceptional students, college admissions, curriculum, and accountability. Many reproducible forms save counselors time.

TITLE: **Tales and Tails, Volumes 1, 2, 3**

MEDIA/COST: Book *

GRADES/LENGTH: K–6/57 pages

AUTHOR: Leonard

PUBLISHER/
  COPYRIGHT: Mar*Co Products, Inc./1989

NOTES: A collection of short stories with activity sheets for each story. Topics in first volume: divorce, adoption, conceit, obeying rules, lying, responsibility, accepting oneself, and abuse. Topics in second volume: sharing, being unkind, stealing, bullying, getting along with siblings, and playing practical jokes. Topics in third volume: fear, truancy, career, sleep, manners, commitment, weight, and procrastination. Stories are well written, and hold appeal for children. Characters are animals that have human-like feelings and characteristics. Helpful with individuals and groups.

12-3 COMPREHENSIVE (CONTINUED)

TITLE: **Total Quality Counseling**

MEDIA/COST: Handbook *

GRADES/LENGTH: K–8

AUTHOR: Burgess

PUBLISHER/
   COPYRIGHT: Mar*Co Products, Inc./1995

NOTES: Practical plans for individual counseling, group counseling, and group guidance. Reproducible forms, charts, and checklists make this book an excellent overall resource for both new and experienced counselors.

12-4 CONFLICT RESOLUTION

TITLE: **Bully-Proofing Your School**

MEDIA/COST: Book **

GRADES/LENGTH: K–6/367 pages

AUTHORS: Garrity, Jens, Porter, Sager, & Short-Camilli

PUBLISHER/
   COPYRIGHT: Sopris West/1994-95

NOTES: Promotes a physical and psychological safe and caring school environment. Staff members plan a schoolwide program to meet the needs of their own school population in preventing bully–victim problems. Classroom instruction provides interventions for all students to recognize and stop bullying behavior. Lessons stress healthy thinking styles, anger management, empathy, and social problem-solving skills. Strategies for working with parents of victims and bullies.

TITLE: **Childhood Bullying and Teasing: What School Personnel, Other Professionals, and Parents Can Do**

MEDIA/COST: Book *

GRADES/LENGTH: K–6/260 pages

AUTHOR: Ross

PUBLISHER/
   COPYRIGHT: American Counseling Association (ACA)/1996

NOTES: Procedures to intervene when there is bullying and teasing in the school. The interventions help the victim and the harasser. Also includes ways to get parents involved to prevent further occurrences.

TITLE: **Conflict Mediation for a New Generation**

MEDIA/COST: Handbook **

GRADES/LENGTH: 4–12/146 pages

AUTHORS: Wampler & Hess

PUBLISHER/
   COPYRIGHT: Community Mediation Center/ 1992

NOTES: A comprehensive guide for training student conflict mediators that is divided into three sections: Elementary, Middle, and High School. Each section provides step-by-step directions on how to set up and conduct a mediation program at a particular grade level. Also includes sample letters, calendars, and forms.

TITLE: **Conflict Resolution Complete Kit**

MEDIA/COST: Kit/Videos/Binder ******

GRADES/LENGTH: 3-7/8 videos

PUBLISHER: Sunburst Communications, Inc.

NOTES: Very complete kit. Includes a video for staff development, reproducible sheets, activities, role plays, and complete plans. Everything in the kit is usable and focused on resolving conflicts that students experience during elementary and middle school years. Excellent resource.

12-4 CONFLICT RESOLUTION (CONTINUED)

TITLE: **Conflict Resolution: An Elementary School Curriculum**

MEDIA/COST: Binder **

GRADES/LENGTH: K–6/337 pages

AUTHORS: Sadalla, Holmberg, & Halligan

PUBLISHER/
  COPYRIGHT: Community Board Program, Inc./ 1990

NOTES: Teaches children about conflict and how to deal with it appropriately. *Part I:* Activities dealing with (1) conflict in the lives of all children, (2) appreciation of others, (3) understanding feelings, (4) communication and listening skills, and (5) resolving conflicts. *Part II:* Application in the classroom of skills learned in Part I. Excellent resource for mediation training, classroom guidance, or small group.

TITLE: **Gang Intervention Handbook**

MEDIA/COST: Book **

GRADES/LENGTH: 7–12/532 pages

AUTHORS: Goldstein & Huff (Editors)

PUBLISHER/
  COPYRIGHT: Research Press/1992

NOTES: Great resource for counselor to understand and intervene effectively when students are considering or involved in gangs.

TITLE: **Kelso's Choice: Conflict Management for Children**

MEDIA/COST: Guide **/Kit ****/Puppets *

GRADES/LENGTH: K–6/65 pages

AUTHORS: O'Neill & Glass

PUBLISHER/
  COPYRIGHT: Rhinestone Press/1991

NOTES: Nine lessons that are well organized and easily implemented to teach *all* students to be peacemakers. Authors incorporate different learning styles and a variety of techniques to reinforce the concepts for conflict mediation.

TITLE: **Preventing Gang Activity in School**
(#5 Scared Scared or Prepared Series)

MEDIA/COST: Video/Guide/Book ****

GRADES/LENGTH: K–6

AUTHORS: Canter & Garrison

PUBLISHER/
  COPYRIGHT: Lee Canter & Associates, Inc./1995

NOTES: Helps all students and staff in the school to be astute to preventing gang activity.

TITLE: **Ready-to-Use Conflict Resolution Activities for Secondary Students**

MEDIA/COST: Book **

GRADES/LENGTH: 7–12/349 pages

AUTHORS: Perlstein & Thrall

PUBLISHER/
  COPYRIGHT: Center for Applied Research in Education/1996

NOTES: Practical activities for students to learn communication skills, collaborative problem solving, and mediating. A section on conflict in the counselor's office and conducting difficult parent–teacher–student conferences. Methods of resolution for win-win solutions included in every case. Additional information: conflict resolution in groups, in the classroom, and in extracurricular activities. Directions to begin a peer mediation program in the school and ideas to publicize the peer mediation program. Help for the teacher: (1) preventing conflict in the classroom, (2) resolving conflicts in the classroom, (3) dealing with undercurrents of dissension, and (4) teacher–student conflicts. Scenarios with examples and reproducible worksheets. Outstanding book of activities.

12-4 CONFLICT RESOLUTION (CONTINUED)

TITLE: **Reducing School Violence Through Conflict Resolution**

MEDIA/COST: Book

GRADES/LENGTH: K–12/119 pages

AUTHORS: Johnson & Johnson

PUBLISHER/
    COPYRIGHT: Association for Supervision and Curriculum Development (ASCD)/ 1995

NOTES: Specific programs and activities to reduce violence and stress, and a sequence of steps to implement violence prevention and conflict resolution programs. Practical and specific strategies for implementing violence-prevention programs in schools. Includes a chapter on teaching students to negotiate and mediate conflicts among students. Excellent resource.

TITLE: **Resources Dealing With Bullying Behavior**

MEDIA/COST: Bibliography *

GRADES/LENGTH: K–12/15 pages

AUTHOR: Murphy

PUBLISHER/
    COPYRIGHT: Available: cmurphy@gmu.edu/1997

NOTES: This complete and current bibliography provides resources for the following subjects: (1) Anger/Aggression, (2) Bullying Behavior, (3) Bully Behavior—Children's Books, (4) Conflict Resolution, (5) Counseling Theories, (6) Gangs, (7) Multicultural, (8) School and Youth Violence, and (9) Theories/ Models/Prevention. Very helpful resource for the school counselor.

TITLE: **Teaching Students to be Peacemakers**

MEDIA/COST: Book

GRADES/LENGTH: K–6

AUTHORS: Johnson & Johnson

PUBLISHER/
    COPYRIGHT: Interaction Book Company/1991

NOTES: Activities and strategies to teach conflict-resolution skills. Information about constructive conflicts, cooperative classroom environment, negotiating, managing anger, mediating conflicts among students, and managing developmental conflicts. Teaches students to respect other people and become cognizant of their own behavior.

12-6 CRISES

TITLE: **Children's Literature on Floods and Natural Disasters**

MEDIA/COST: WWW/Free

GRADES/LENGTH: K–12

AUTHOR: Pike

PUBLISHER/
    COPYRIGHT: University of Illinois/1995

NOTES: Excellent annotated list of books for grades K–3, 4–6, middle school, and high school. Counselors can print this list for future reference.

TITLE: **Death in the School Community: A Handbook for Counselors, Teachers, and Administrators**

MEDIA/COST: Book *

GRADES/LENGTH: K–12/129 pages

AUTHOR: Oates

PUBLISHER/
    COPYRIGHT: American Counseling Association (ACA)/1993

NOTES: Step-by-step plans for coping with post-traumatic stress disorder, facilitating healthy grief responses, and leading loss and grief groups. Includes case studies; announcements for students, staff, and parents; and sample forms and letters.

TITLE: **School Crisis Survival Guide: Management Techniques and Materials for Counselors and Administrators**

MEDIA/COST: Book

GRADES/LENGTH: K–12/195 pages

AUTHORS: Petersen & Straub

PUBLISHER/
    COPYRIGHT: Center for Applied Research in Education/1992

NOTES: Easy-to-use resource with steps for setting up a school crisis team and a checklist for a school crisis plan. Suggestions to educate staff and provide grief counseling to students and parents. Individual and group activities to help students resolve the trauma of grief. Authors focus on crisis as an opportunity to produce growth and bring about permanent, positive change.

12-7   DEATH AND GRIEF

TITLE:	**Bereavement Support Group for Children** ·
MEDIA/COST:	Guide/Workbook *
GRADES/LENGTH:	K–8/Guide, 87 pages; Workbook, 33 pages
AUTHORS:	Haasl & Marnocha
PUBLISHER/ COPYRIGHT:	Accelerated Development, Inc./1990

NOTES: Helps grieving children share their experiences with others who have lost a loved one. Information to gain understanding, express feelings, and recognize appropriate alternatives in expressing grief. In-depth description on how to set up a bereavement group, and points that counselors can keep in mind when leading this type of group.

TITLE:	**Drawing Out Feelings: Facilitator Guide for Leading Support Groups**
MEDIA/COST:	Book *
GRADES/LENGTH:	1–6/110 pages
AUTHOR:	Heegaard
DISTRIBUTOR/ COPYRIGHT:	Paperbacks for Educators/1992

NOTES: Suggestions for developing grief support groups and directions for using art to help students cope with loss and change. Four workbooks that can be purchased separately. Curriculum includes: (1) When someone very special dies, (2) When something terrible happens, (3) When someone has a serious illness, and (4) When Mom and Dad separate.

TITLE:	**The Mourning Handbook: A Complete Guide for the Bereaved**
MEDIA/COST:	Book *
GRADES/LENGTH:	K-12/306 pages
AUTHOR:	Fitzgerald
PUBLISHER/ COPYRIGHT:	Simon and Schuster/1994

NOTES: Information about how to extend sympathy when it is needed; how the counselor can reach out to grieving families; and how the counselor can represent the school in times of sadness.

TITLE:	**The Sacred Art of Dying: How World Religions Understand Death**
MEDIA/COST:	Book *
GRADES/LENGTH:	K-12
AUTHOR:	Kramer
PUBLISHER/ COPYRIGHT:	Paulist Press/1988

NOTES: Resource for counselors that focuses primarily on different religious attitudes toward death, dying, and after life. Each chapter focuses on a different tradition in three ways; through a story or stories central to the tradition, conceptual teachings, and death rituals. Eleven traditions covered: Hindu, Buddhist, Zen, Tibetan, Chinese, Egyptian, Greek, Hebraic, Christian, Islamic, and American Indian.

12-8   DECISION MAKING

TITLE:	**Laugh, Learn and Live with Mistakz**
MEDIA/COST:	Book *
GRADES/LENGTH:	K–8/60 pages
AUTHORS:	Kienzle & Simmons
PUBLISHER/ COPYRIGHT:	Mar*Co Products, Inc./1991

NOTES: Activities that show how one can learn from mistakes and feel comfortable after making mistakes. Helps a perfectionist put mistakes into proper perspective.

12-9   DIRECTORY

TITLE:	**Help for Children from Infancy to Adulthood (4th edition)**
MEDIA/COST:	Directory
GRADES/LENGTH:	K–12/207 pages
AUTHOR:	Wilson
PUBLISHER/ COPYRIGHT:	Rocky River Publishers/1989

NOTES: Includes short descriptions, phone numbers, and addresses of national hotlines, helplines, organizations, agencies, and other resources. Excellent compilation of resources to have readily available to help students and parents in need of services. Includes: (1) Child Safety, (2) Teens in Distress, (3) Abused and Missing Children, (4) Children's Health, (5) Children's Mental Health and Mental Retardation, (6) Children with Handicaps, (7) Maternal and Child Care, (8) Help for Parents, and (9) International Children's Organizations.

TITLE:	**A Network of Educational Opportunities**
MEDIA/COST:	Directory/Free
GRADES/LENGTH:	K–12/21 pages
AUTHOR:	NACAC
PUBLISHER/ COPYRIGHT:	National Association for College Admission Counselors (NACAC)/1996

NOTES: World Wide Web addresses and electronic mail lists compiled by NACAC. Available online: http://www.nacac.com

---

TITLE:	**Paperbacks for Educators: Catalog, School Counselor Edition, K-12**
MEDIA/COST:	Booklet/Free
GRADES/LENGTH:	K–12
DISTRIBUTOR/ COPYRIGHT:	Paperbacks for Educators/Annual

NOTES: Annual catalog that can be requested from Paperbacks for Educators. Annotated list of books dealing with topics such as addictions, at-risk students, career planning, conflict resolution, discipline, group activities, group counseling, learning problems, loss, peer pressure, social skills, suicide, time management, and values.

12-10   DISABILITIES

TITLE:	**Attention Deficit Disorders Intervention Manual (school version)**
MEDIA/COST:	Book
GRADES/LENGTH:	K–12/404 pages
AUTHOR:	McCarney
PUBLISHER/ COPYRIGHT:	Hawthorne/1994

NOTES: A manual to be used in conjunction with the *Attention Deficit Disorders Evaluation Scale*. Interventions are organized by Behavior Number, making it very easy to find respective interventions that are listed by steps. Excellent resource for the counselor to use when consulting with parents and teachers as they work with students with Attention Deficit Disorder. Very helpful reference book.

TITLE:	**Attention? ADD in School: Identification, Intervention, Strategies**
MEDIA/COST:	3 Videos/Guide/Set *****; Guide *; Video ****
GRADES/LENGTH:	K–12/Videos, 19 to 26 minutes
AUTHOR:	Fowler
PUBLISHER/ COPYRIGHT:	TS Media/1992

NOTES: Comprehensive information in eight sections: (1) The Disability Named ADD, (2) ADD Goes To School, (3) Factors That Compromise Learning, (4) Identification and Assessment, (5) Interventions: Principles and Practices, (6) Behavioral Interventions, (7) Parents and Schools Working Together, (8) ADD: A Brief Legal Summary. Appendix includes the U.S. Dept. of Education Policy Memorandum, CHADD Guide to Medical Management and Controversial Treatments for Children with ADHD. *Video #1:* Symptoms, behaviors and causes. *Video #2:* What can be done about ADD. *Video #3:* Strategies for the counselor/teacher to use in the classroom.

12-10 DISABILITIES (CONTINUED)

TITLE: **Autism and Asperger Syndrome**

MEDIA/COST: Book *

GRADES/LENGTH: K–12

AUTHOR: Frith (Editor)

PUBLISHER/
  COPYRIGHT: Cambridge University Press/1991

NOTES: Behavioral difficulties of children initially diagnosed as having "High-Functioning Autism" or "Pervasive Developmental Disorder of the Asperger Type" are ultimately diagnosed as having Tourette's Syndrome (TS). Excellent description of TS, important to school personnel because frequently the child is intelligent and the behavior is thought by school authorities to be controllable. Counselors need to know about the behaviors and TS to inform parents and other school personnel so an accurate diagnosis by a medical doctor can be made.

TITLE: **Chris Has an Ostomy**

MEDIA/COST: Book

GRADES/LENGTH: K–6/18 pages

AUTHORS: Held & Klostermann

PUBLISHER/
  COPYRIGHT: United Ostomy Ass'n., Inc./1983

NOTES: Excellent resource for a counselor when a student has had an ostomy. The counselor will want to introduce the book to the parents of the child first, and together decide about making the book accessible to classmates of the student.

TITLE: **Guidance for Students with Disabilities (2nd ed.)**

MEDIA/COST: Book

GRADES/LENGTH: K–12/186 pages

AUTHOR: Lombana

PUBLISHER/
  COPYRIGHT: Charles C. Thomas/1992

NOTES: Comprehensive information about classroom guidance, group counseling, teacher consultation, and parent consultation to help students with disabilities in schools. Excellent information about teacher consultation and burnout. Although a counselor cannot possibly do everything suggested, the author has excellent ideas and suggestions.

TITLE: **Hal's Pals Dolls**

MEDIA/COST: Dolls ***

GRADES/LENGTH: K–4

DISTRIBUTOR: Jesana

NOTES: Soft-sculptured, safety-tested 19-inch dolls. Hal is a ski instructor who skis on one leg; Kathy is in a pink party dress, with leg braces and canes; Bobby, in a sweatsuit, in a wheelchair; Suzie, in a sweatsuit, wears dark glasses because she is blind. Laura has a tutu and is wearing two hearing aids. These dolls are a great way to teach children about the ways children with disabilities are the same as other children, with one difference, their disability.

TITLE: **Obsessive Compulsive Disorder in Children and Adolescents: A Guide**

MEDIA/COST: Book

GRADES/LENGTH: 3–12

AUTHOR: Johnston

PUBLISHER/
  COPYRIGHT: Child Obsessive-Compulsive Information Center/1993

NOTES: Basic information for the counselor to share with teachers and other school personnel to help them deal with a child with this disorder.

12-12   EMOTIONS

TITLE: **Human Race Club: A Story About Handling Emotions**

MEDIA/COST: Videos *

GRADES/LENGTH: 1–6/30 minutes

PUBLISHER/
  COPYRIGHT: Social Studies School Service/1989

NOTES: Videos focus on handling emotions/feelings and are based on the Human Race Club featured in the books written by Joy Berry. Different videos deal with appropriate subjects in ways that hold children's attention.

12-12 EMOTIONS (CONTINUED)

TITLE:	**Windows to Our Children: A Gestalt Therapy Approach to Children and Adolescents**
MEDIA/COST:	Book *
GRADES/LENGTH:	K–8/352 pages
AUTHOR:	Oaklander
PUBLISHER/ COPYRIGHT:	Gestalt Journal/1989

NOTES: A beautiful book that gives a lot of information about children's emotional concerns and also what the counselor can do when children have these concerns, and the reason that the counselor can help in particular ways. Describes appropriate play counseling, drawing, working with clay, and other media.

12-13   ETHICS

TITLE:	**ACA Code of Ethics and Standards of Practice**
MEDIA/COST:	Booklet *
GRADES/LENGTH:	K–12/36 pages
AUTHOR:	Governing Council, American Counseling Association
PUBLISHER/ COPYRIGHT:	American Counseling Association (ACA)/1995

NOTES: Ethical requirements and standards of practice for counselors as revised by the ACA Governing Council, effective July 1, 1995. Standards for: (1) the counseling relationship; (2) confidentiality; (3) professional responsibility; (4) relationships with other professionals; (5) evaluation, assessment, and interpretation; (6) teaching, training, and supervision; (7) research and publication; and (8) resolving ethical issues.

TITLE:	**ACES Standards for Counseling Supervisors**
MEDIA/COST:	Booklet
GRADES/LENGTH:	K–12
AUTHOR:	Association for Counselor Education and Supervision (ACES)
PUBLISHER:	American Counseling Association (ACA)

NOTES: Resource for the counselor who supervises other counselors. Ethical standards for administrative, program, and clinical supervision.

TITLE:	**ASCA Membership Services Guide**
MEDIA/COST:	Booklet *
GRADES/LENGTH:	K–12/46 pages
AUTHOR:	American School Counselor Association
PUBLISHER/ COPYRIGHT:	American School Counselor Association (ASCA)/1993

NOTES: Excellent resource for the school counselor. Includes ASCA Ethical Standards, ASCA Role Statement for the School Counselor, ASCA Bylaws, and ASCA Position Statements with rationales.

TITLE:	**ASGW Ethical Guidelines for Group Counselors**
MEDIA/COST:	Booklet
GRADES/LENGTH:	K–12
AUTHOR:	Association for Specialists in Group Work (ASGW)
PUBLISHER/ COPYRIGHT:	American Counseling Association (ACA)/1989

NOTES: Ethical guidelines for the group counselor to know and follow when leading groups. Covers: (1) Providing information and orientation, (2) Screening of members, (3) Confidentiality, (4) Voluntary/Involuntary participation, (5) Leaving a group, (6) Coercion and pressure, (7) Imposing counselor values, (8) Equitable treatment, (9) Dual relationships, (10) Use of techniques, (11) Goal development, (12) Consultation, (13) Termination from group, (14) Evaluation and follow up, (15) Referrals, and (16) Professional development.

12-14   FAMILY

TITLE:	**Every Kid's Guide to Understanding Parents**
MEDIA/COST:	Book *
GRADES/LENGTH:	K–6/48 pages
AUTHOR:	Berry
PUBLISHER/ COPYRIGHT:	Living Skills Press/1987

NOTES: Helps children cope with everyday family situations. Emphasis is on helping children understand why parents need to supervise and discipline their children. Also explains biological parents, adoptive parents, and stepparents.

12-16   GENDER EQUITY

TITLE:	**Horizons 2000: Career and Life Planning for Girls and Boys**
MEDIA/COST:	2 Videos/Handbook/Workbook
GRADES/LENGTH:	5–6; 7–8; 10–11; 12 through Adult
AUTHOR:	Bartholomew
PUBLISHER/ COPYRIGHT:	Salzberger and Graham/1993, 1995, 1997

NOTES: A weekly developmental program for career-and-life planning for boys in grades 5 and 6, and girls in grades 5 through 12. Helps students improve self-esteem, look at the roles of women and men in our society, discuss gender stereotypes, and explore a variety of career and lifestyle options. Eighteen-week course, one lesson per week, with a detailed teacher's manual. Each lesson is from 45-50 minutes. All three books are well-written and easy to use.

TITLE:	**How Schools Shortchange Girls**
MEDIA/COST:	Book
GRADES/LENGTH:	K–12
AUTHOR:	American Association of University Women (AAUW)
PUBLISHER/ COPYRIGHT:	National Education Association (NEA)/1992

NOTES: Helps school personnel recognize differences in curriculum and treatment of females that may be unrecognized or unconscious until pointed out.

TITLE:	**Meeting Guidance and Counseling Needs of Boys**
MEDIA/COST:	Book *
GRADES/LENGTH:	K–12/108 pages
AUTHOR:	Beymer
PUBLISHER/ COPYRIGHT:	American Counseling Association (ACA)/1995

NOTES: Constructive techniques to meet the special needs of boys. Includes: gender roles, family dynamics, sexuality, identity formation, self-esteem, and career planning issues of boys at all developmental levels.

12-17   GROUP COUNSELING

TITLE:	**Anger Management and Violence Prevention: A Group Activities Manual for Middle and High School Students**
MEDIA/COST:	Book
GRADES/LENGTH:	7–12
AUTHOR:	Schmidt
PUBLISHER/ COPYRIGHT:	Johnson Institute

NOTES: Activities for students who have difficulty controlling their anger which can become abusive. Appropriate for individuals or small groups.

TITLE:	**Complete Group Counseling Program for Children of Divorce**
MEDIA/COST:	Book
GRADES/LENGTH:	1–6/226 pages
AUTHOR:	Margolin
PUBLISHER/ COPYRIGHT:	Center for Applied Research in Education/1996

NOTES: Excellent compilation of activities for a group helping children cope at different stages of the divorce of their parents. Issues addressed include: (1) Why parents marry and divorce; (2) Changes; (3) Two houses; (4) Feeling angry, feeling guilty, and grieving; (5) Legal issues; (6) Step-parenting; and (7) Achieving closure.

TITLE:	**The Counselor and the Group**
MEDIA/COST:	Book **
GRADES/LENGTH:	K–12/490 pages
AUTHOR:	Trotzer
PUBLISHER/ COPYRIGHT:	Accelerated Development/1989

NOTES: Practical information for beginning or continuing a group counseling program in the school. Activities for each stage of group process.

12-17 GROUP COUNSELING (CONTINUED)

TITLE: **Effective Group Counseling: Leading Groups Successfully in Different Settings**

MEDIA/COST: Book *

GRADES/LENGTH: K–12/165 pages

AUTHOR: Gladding

PUBLISHER/
  COPYRIGHT: American Counseling Association (ACA)/1995

NOTES: Excellent resources and practical ideas for the group leader. Author is experienced elementary school counselor and group leader.

TITLE: **Elements of Group Counseling: Back to the Basics**

MEDIA/COST: Book

GRADES/LENGTH: K–12

AUTHORS: Carroll & Wiggins

PUBLISHER/
  COPYRIGHT: Love Publishing Company/1990

NOTES: Resource for peer support groups and other school groups.

TITLE: **Energizers and Icebreakers**

MEDIA/COST: Book *

GRADES/LENGTH: K–12/158 pages

AUTHOR: Foster

PUBLISHER/
  COPYRIGHT: Educational Media Corporation/1989

NOTES: Icebreakers that are appropriate for children and adults in large or small groups.

TITLE: **Group Counseling for School Counselors: A Practical Guide**

MEDIA/COST: Book *

GRADES/LENGTH: K-12/293 pages

AUTHORS: Brigman & Earley

PUBLISHER/
  COPYRIGHT: J. Weston Walch, Publisher/1991

NOTES: Lesson plans for group counseling K–12. Topics: "Understanding Yourself and Others," "Friendship," "Self-Concept," "Celebrating Self," "Divorce," "Refusal Skills," "Handling Conflict," "Loss Group," "New-Student Program," and "Personal Growth for Teachers." Each topic has a lesson plan with specific objectives. Letters to parents, parent permission forms, evaluations, and worksheets.

TITLE: **Group Counseling for Secondary Schools**

MEDIA/COST: Book **

GRADES/LENGTH: 7–12/182 pages

AUTHOR: Blum (Editor)

PUBLISHER/
  COPYRIGHT: Charles C. Thomas/1990

NOTES: Detailed plans and activities for group counseling sessions in middle schools and high schools, and practical plans for beginning a group counseling program. Contributing authors actually led the successful groups described.

TITLE: **Group Counseling Strategies and Skills**

MEDIA/COST: Book

GRADES/LENGTH: K–12/314 pages

AUTHORS: Jacobs, Harvil, & Masson

PUBLISHER/
  COPYRIGHT: Brooks/Cole Publishing Co./1988

NOTES: An in-depth look at group process, with an emphasis on strategies and skills for successful group leadership. Covers various kinds of groups and techniques for planning and implementing group programs. Impact of the groups on the leader and members is stressed throughout the book.

TITLE: **Groups: Process and Practice**

MEDIA/COST: Book **

GRADES/LENGTH: K–12/441 pages

AUTHORS: Corey & Corey

PUBLISHER/
  COPYRIGHT: Brooks/Cole Publishing Co./1997

NOTES: Excellent reference book that includes all the information a group leader needs with the exception of activities and evaluation of groups. Well organized and easily read.

12-17 GROUP COUNSELING (CONTINUED)

TITLE:	**Skills for Living**
	Group Counseling Activities for Elementary Students
	Group Counseling Activities for Young Adolescents
MEDIA/COST:	Books **
GRADES/LENGTH:	K–6; 7–12/229 pages
AUTHORS:	Morganett-Smead
PUBLISHER/ COPYRIGHT:	Research Press/1994; 1990

NOTES: *Activities for Elementary Students:* Many activities to use with elementary students in small-group counseling. Units include peacemaking, self-esteem, friendship, divorce, grieving, anger, responsibility, and citizenship. Each unit consists of eight lessons with goals, materials, detailed activities, and evaluation measures. A bibliography of children's books is included.

Activities for Young Adolescents: Practical handbook with detailed plans for groups in middle school and high school. Topics: Divorce; Making and Keeping Friends; Learning Communication Skills; Learning Stress-management Skills; Managing Anger; Surviving and Succeeding in School; and Coping with Grief and Loss. The pre-tests and post-tests for each topic are especially helpful and encourage the counselor to evaluate groups. Sample needs assessments and letters to students, faculty, and parents are also included in this practical manual.

TITLE:	**Successful Small Groups: Ways and Means**
	(Making Choices—Growing Stronger Series)
MEDIA/COST:	Booklet *
GRADES/LENGTH:	2–8/31 pages
AUTHOR:	Falk
PUBLISHER/ COPYRIGHT:	Elizabeth Falk, M.A., LPC/1993

NOTES: Useful information and easy-to-follow format for particular group counseling units. Includes: size, place, time, procedures, referrals, resource material, and group process. One unit entitled, "Getting to Know You" helps children think about themselves in relationship to school, home, and friends. Includes objectives, discussion questions, activities, goals, and handouts for group counseling units.

12-19   INDIVIDUAL COUNSELING

TITLE:	**Bibliocounseling: An Adolescent Literature Update**
	(in *Virginia Counselors Journal, 24,* 78–90)
MEDIA/COST:	Article
GRADES/LENGTH:	7–12/12 pages
AUTHORS:	Brown, Caldwell, Mewborn, Forrester, McPeak, Patch, Shepherd, & Beale
PUBLISHER/ COPYRIGHT:	Virginia Counselor Association (VCA)/Spring 1996

NOTES: Annotated list of books for adolescents in the following categories: (1) Disabilities, (2) Drugs and Alcohol, (3) Eating Disorders, (4) Family Issues, (5) Sexuality, (6) Single Parent Families, and (7) Teenage Pregnancy.

TITLE:	**Suggested Books for Children: Specific Concerns**
	(in *Counseling Children, 4th ed,* 453-468)
MEDIA/COST:	Article in Book (List 12-3)
GRADES/LENGTH:	K–9 (ages noted for each book)/16 pages
AUTHOR:	Hunt, In Thompson & Rudolph
PUBLISHER/ COPYRIGHT:	Brooks/Cole Publishing Co./1996

NOTES: This article includes an *annotated* list of books for children in the following categories: (1) Abandonment, (2) Adoption/Foster Homes, (3) Child Abuse, (4) Children's Worries, (5) Children/AIDS, (6) Death, (7) Divorce, (8) Family, (9) Friendship, (10) Homeless, (11) Latchkey, (12) Relationships with Older Generations, (13) Sex Education, (14) Sexual Abuse, (15) Sex Roles, and (16) Suicide.

12-19 INDIVIDUAL COUNSELING *(CONTINUED)*

TITLE:	**Themes . . . Under One Umbrella, Section VI**
	(in The Literature Teacher's Book of Lists, pp. 211-293)
MEDIA/COST:	Article in Book (List 12-3)
GRADES/LENGTH:	K–12/82 pages
AUTHOR:	Strouf
PUBLISHER/	
COPYRIGHT:	Center for Applied Research in Education/1993

NOTES: Section VI of this book includes lists of books for children and adolescents. Only the title and author are provided in the following categories: (1) Adoption; (2) Disability/Illness, Mental and Physical; (3) Drugs/Alcohol; (4) Ethnic and Multicultural; (5) Heroes including African American, Heroines including African American; (6) Native American Authors, Literature, Relations; (7) Women, Books and Stories, Famous Women, Important Writers, and Women's Issues; and (8) Young Adult Concerns.

TITLE:	**Trust Building With Children Who Hurt: A One-to-One Support Program for Children**
MEDIA/COST:	Book **
GRADES/LENGTH:	1–6/203 pages
AUTHOR:	Arent
PUBLISHER/	
COPYRIGHT:	Center for Applied Research in Education/1992

NOTES: Helps a student reestablish trust in adults after having been neglected, abused, or hurt in some way. This trust is necessary for the student to have empathy for others. One-to-one work begins with teaching the child the concepts of commitment, confidentiality, limits, and dependency. Background, strategies, activities, and stories are given for each concept.

12-20   LEARNING STYLES

TITLE:	**Emotional Intelligence**
MEDIA/COST:	Book *
GRADES/LENGTH:	K–12/432 pages
AUTHOR:	Goleman
PUBLISHER/	
COPYRIGHT:	Bantam Books/1997

NOTES: Stresses importance of emotional growth and how this can have an effect on cognitive growth.

TITLE:	**E. Q. in School Counseling: Promoting Emotional Intelligence**
MEDIA/COST:	Kit *
GRADES/LENGTH:	K–12/3 Presentations
AUTHOR:	Sheldon
PUBLISHER/	
COPYRIGHT:	American School Counselor Association (ASCA)/1996

NOTES: Presentation sheets and overhead masters for presentations to staff, students, and parents. Theory booklet about how emotional intelligence relates to counseling. Everything that is needed for outstanding presentations.

TITLE:	**Learning Styles Counseling**
MEDIA/COST:	Book
GRADES/LENGTH:	K–12/161 pages
AUTHOR:	Griggs
PUBLISHER/	
COPYRIGHT:	ERIC Counseling & Personnel Services Clearinghouse/1991

NOTES: Interesting and relevant information for counselors K–12 who are interested in using knowledge of learning styles in their counseling. Based on a theoretical foundation with validation in a variety of school settings.

12-23   MULTICULTURAL

TITLE:	**Children of Color: Psychological Interventions with Minority Youth**
MEDIA/COST:	Book
GRADES/LENGTH:	K–12
AUTHORS:	Gibbs, Huang, & Associates
PUBLISHER/	
COPYRIGHT:	Jossey-Bass/1989

NOTES: Great resource for understanding students from different cultures. Information about best interventions to use with specific ethnic groups, keeping in mind that each student is unique.

12-23 MULTICULTURAL *(CONTINUED)*

TITLE:	**Counseling the Culturally Different**
MEDIA/COST:	Book
GRADES/LENGTH:	K–12
AUTHORS:	Sue & Sue
PUBLISHER/ COPYRIGHT:	John Wiley & Sons/1990

NOTES: Excellent resource with suggestions for counseling students of many different cultures. Helpful suggestions for cross-cultural counseling.

TITLE:	**Counseling for Racial Understanding**
MEDIA/COST:	Book *
GRADES/LENGTH:	K–12/123 pages
AUTHOR:	Bryant
PUBLISHER/ COPYRIGHT:	American Counseling Association (ACA)/1994

NOTES: Practical guide to reduce the effects of prejudice. Suggestions about how to handle prejudice-related events, help the victims, counsel students who act out feelings of racism, and bring about change in a school.

TITLE:	**Empowering African-American Males to Succeed**
MEDIA/COST:	Audio Tapes/Book/Workbook/ Tapes, *
GRADES/LENGTH:	K–12 (with modifications)
AUTHOR:	Wynn
PUBLISHER/ COPYRIGHT:	Rising Sun Publishing/1992

NOTES: A model of a ten-step strategy to assist in the resolution of issues confronting African American males. Techniques and exercises to develop a consciousness in students to take control over their lives and accept responsibility for their actions. Although there are religious connotations directed to parents, and a reference to African American Churches, the scope and overall content is excellent, practical, and timely. The tapes are not really necessary.

TITLE:	**Many Voices I**
	1. Food for Thought
	2. Hair Scare
	3. Mother Tongue
	4. Positively Native
MEDIA/COST:	Videos/Guides **
GRADES/LENGTH:	3–9/15 minutes
PUBLISHER/ COPYRIGHT:	TV Ontario Video/1991

NOTES: These videos address prejudice and discrimination in a sensitive manner. Recommended that the counselor preview the guide before showing any video to students. Ample opportunity to discuss the material is necessary after showing the video. Excellent videos to show to staff.

Food for Thought is a story about Isa, born in Senegal, West Africa. She worries about how other students will react when she practices her Muslim faith and fasts during Ramadan. When her friend, Ashley, makes light of her fasting, Isa tries to prove that she is not different and goes to gym class, where she faints.

Hair Scare is the story about Amar, a young Sikh boy from India who is harassed at his new school and turned away at the community swimming pool for wearing a turban (putkah). Hoping to avoid further confrontation, he will not remove his turban even to dry his hair. Although one conflict is resolved, another conflict remains unresolved at the end of the video.

Mother Tongue is the story about a young Vietnamese girl who recalls her difficulties when she arrived in her new home. Unable to speak English and taunted by schoolmates, she struggles to adapt to a new language and culture. The use of a camera helps her with this transition.

Positively Native is the story of Martin, a young Iroquois Indian, who makes a video about his Native American life, hoping to dispel some of the stereotypes he faces daily. He is pleased with the response to the finished product, but wonders if he can continue to make changes in people's opinions.

12-23 MULTICULTURAL (CONTINUED)

TITLE:	**Many Voices II**
	5. Quick to Judge
	6. A Sari Tale
	7. To Jew Is Not a Verb
MEDIA/COST:	Videos/Guides **
GRADES/LENGTH:	3–9/15 minutes
PUBLISHER/ COPYRIGHT:	TV Ontario Video/1991

NOTES: These videos address prejudice and discrimination in a sensitive manner. Recommended that the counselor read the guide and preview any video before showing it to students. Ample opportunity to discuss the material is necessary after showing the video. Excellent videos to show to staff.

Quick to Judge is about Neto's hope of winning a poster competition which is shattered when he is accused of stealing. Feeling he has been discriminated against because he is black, Neto destroys his own poster in frustration. His friends help in time for the competition. The teacher's guide presents this issue in a sensitive manner. This video is not appropriate if there is only one African American student in the class.

A Sari Tale is about Geeta, who tries to deny her heritage when her teacher suggests she wear a sari to school for Halloween. When Geeta is faced with doing a presentation on a traditional Hindu celebration, she worries about how her classmates will view her. Video focuses on how to find a solution to Geeta's problem.

To Jew Is Not a Verb is the story of David, a young man who is Jewish, who picks up the term "to jew," for bargaining a price or trading for advantage. After learning about his heritage as a Jewish person from his uncle, he speaks up to his friends about the use of the term and explains that the term is an insult to Jewish people. Teacher's guide presents this issue in a sensitive manner. Not appropriate to show when only one Jewish student is in the class.

TITLE:	**Many Voices III**
	8. What's in a Name
	9. The World at My Door
MEDIA/COST:	Videos/Guides **
GRADES/LENGTH:	3–9/15 minutes
PUBLISHER/ COPYRIGHT:	TV Ontario Video/1991

NOTES: These videos address prejudice and discrimination in a sensitive manner. Recommended that the counselor preview them before showing to students and use the teacher's guide. Ample opportunity to discuss this video after viewing is necessary. Excellent videos to show to staff.

What's in a Name is about Premilla, a young girl from Sri Lanka, who is teased by two boys about her name and also about being an alien. Due to the continual mispronouncing of her name, Premilla changes her name to "Pamela." Her mother is upset about Premilla changing her name. Her mother tells Premilla, "Changing your name will not change you." Premilla (Pamela) must decide how her name will be listed in a concert program. The video ends with Premilla continuing in a dilemma.

The World at My Door is about Elaine, who doesn't think she needs to know about other races and cultures because she lives in an all-white town. Hurtful teasing about her new haircut causes her to wonder whether she is wrong. The topic deals with how parents and community influence our views of others. Although the teacher's guide presents this issue in a sensitive manner, the message may be too complex for elementary students to grasp. The counselor may want to show this video to the staff and parents, and get their reactions before showing it to students.

TITLE:	**Multicultural Counseling Competencies (AMCD)**
MEDIA/COST:	Monograph *
GRADES/LENGTH:	K–12
AUTHORS:	Arredondo, Toporek, Brown, Jones, Locke, Sanchez, & Stadler
PUBLISHER/ COPYRIGHT:	Association for Multicultural Counseling and Development (AMCD)/1995

NOTES: Excellent resource for cross-cultural counseling. Includes three areas: (1) Counselor awareness of own cultural values and biases, (2) Counselor awareness of client's worldview, and (3) Culturally appropriate intervention strategies. Focuses on importance of awareness of attitudes and beliefs, knowledge, and development of skills to achieve competencies and objectives in each of the three areas. Recommended resource for all school counselors.

12-23 MULTICULTURAL *(CONTINUED)*

TITLE: **Multicultural Counseling in Schools: A Practical Handbook**

MEDIA/COST: Book **

GRADES/LENGTH: K–12/254 pages

AUTHORS: Pedersen & Carey (Editors)

PUBLISHER/
 COPYRIGHT: Allyn & Bacon/1993

NOTES: A necessary resource for the school counselor to be informed about diversity, and sensitive to students and their needs.

TITLE: **Multicultural Discovery Activities for Elementary Grades**

MEDIA/COST: Book **

GRADES/LENGTH: K–6/437 pages

AUTHOR: Stull

PUBLISHER/
 COPYRIGHT: Center for Applied Research in Education/1995

NOTES: Many reproducible activities to help students become knowledgeable of and appreciate the contributions made by the major cultural groups within the U.S.: (1) Native American, (2) Asian, (3) Hispanic, (4) African, (5) Near/Middle East, (6) Indian, (7) European, (8) Russian, and (9) Carribean. Organized into sections about literature, games and sports, food, songs, arts and crafts, geography and maps, holidays and celebrations, and famous people.

TITLE: **Multicultural Issues in Counseling: New Approaches to Diversity (2nd ed.)**

MEDIA/COST: Book **

GRADES/LENGTH: K–12/350 pages

AUTHOR: Lee

PUBLISHER/
 COPYRIGHT: American Counseling Association (ACA)/ 1997

NOTES: Specific suggestions for counselors when working with African Americans, Native Americans, Latino/Latina Americans, Asian Americans, and Arab Americans. In addition, a model is provided when counseling African American males and strategies for counseling Korean Americans.

TITLE: **Saving the Native Son: Empowerment Strategies for Young Black Males**

MEDIA/COST: Booklet

GRADES/LENGTH: 3–12/165 pages

AUTHOR: Lee

PUBLISHER/
 COPYRIGHT: ERIC Counseling and Personnel Services Clearinghouse/1996

NOTES: Black males are confronted with a series of obstacles in their attempts to attain academic, career, and personal-social success. Practical interventions to help meet the needs and challenges of helping contemporary African American youth.

TITLE: **Transcultural Counseling: Bilateral and International Perspectives**

MEDIA/COST: Book **

GRADES/LENGTH: K–12/347 pages

AUTHOR: McFadden

PUBLISHER/
 COPYRIGHT: American Counseling Association (ACA)/1993

NOTES: Specific recommendations when counseling Asian Americans, African Americans, Arab Americans, Latino Americans, Native Americans, and Alaskan Natives.

TITLE: **Valuing Diversity and Similarity: Bridging the Gap Through Interpersonal Skills**

MEDIA/COST: Book *

GRADES/LENGTH: K–12/255 pages

AUTHOR: Wittmer

PUBLISHER/
 COPYRIGHT: Educational Media Corporation/ 1992

NOTES: A manual to help facilitate communication among people with different cultural heritages. Activities can be conducted with adults and adapted for students. Includes nonverbal communication. Opportunity to cognitively understand views about culture written from the perspective of African Americans, Asian/Pacific Island Americans, Hispanic Americans, and Native Americans.

12-25   PEER FACILITATION

TITLE: **An In-Depth Look at Peer Helping: Planning, Implementation and Administration**

MEDIA/COST: Book **

GRADES/LENGTH: 6–12/362 pages

AUTHOR: Tindall

PUBLISHER/
  COPYRIGHT: Accelerated Development/1995

NOTES: Overview of peer facilitation and procedures for initiating and maintaining peer programs. Not in-depth but includes selection, program evaluation, team building, and adaptable forms that can be used during each step of training. Attributes of a peer facilitator are listed. Does not include training materials or training exercises.

TITLE: **Children Helping Children: Teaching Students to Become Friendly Helpers (Revised Edition)**

MEDIA/COST: Book

GRADES/LENGTH: 4–8

AUTHORS: Myrick & Bowman

PUBLISHER/
  COPYRIGHT: Educational Media Corporation/ 1991

NOTES: A classic for teaching elementary-age children to help their peers by being good listeners, responding appropriately, making good decisions, and taking responsibility for themselves. Concepts applicable for all students in classroom guidance.

TITLE: **Equip Program: Teaching Youth to Think and Act Responsibly Through a Peer-Helping Approach**

MEDIA/COST: Book *

GRADES/LENGTH: 7–12/392 pages

AUTHOR: Gibbs, et al

PUBLISHER/
  COPYRIGHT: Research Press/1995

NOTES: Outstanding resource to train peer facilitators to help other students resist peer pressure to use alcohol or other drugs, or become involved in at-risk behaviors. Uses a cognitive-behavioral approach.

TITLE: **Peer Power: Becoming an Effective Peer Helper, Books 1 and 2**

MEDIA/COST: Program

GRADES/LENGTH: 7–12/Book 1, 270 pages; Book 2, 111 pages

AUTHOR: Tindall

PUBLISHER/
  COPYRIGHT: Accelerated Development/1985

NOTES: Lesson plans and activities for training peer facilitators. Book 1 includes introduction to the program, attending skill, communication stoppers, assertiveness skills, confrontative skill, problem-solving skill, and putting peer counseling into action. Students rate responses on attending behaviors, paraphrasing, summarizing, genuineness, and confrontation. Practical training program.

TITLE: **Positive Peer Groups**

MEDIA/COST: Book *

GRADES: K–12/86 pages

AUTHOR: Scott

PUBLISHER/
  COPYRIGHT: Human Resource Development Press, Inc./1988

NOTES: Details to start a positive peer group. Shows how to equip youth with the skills to help their friends with problems including drugs, loneliness, and cliques.

TITLE: **Using Peer Mediation to Resolve Conflicts**

(#6, *Scared Scared or Prepared* Series)

MEDIA/COST: Video/Guide/Book ****

GRADES/LENGTH: K–6/35 minutes

AUTHORS: Canter & Garrison

PUBLISHER/
  COPYRIGHT: Lee Canter & Associates, Inc./1995

NOTES: Suggestions to resolve conflicts before the conflicts escalate to violence. Suggestions for conflict mediators, stressing necessary training, the need to be good listeners, and to remain neutral.

12-27   RESPECT

TITLE:	**Character Education in America's Schools**
MEDIA/COST:	Book *
GRADES/LENGTH:	K–12
AUTHORS:	Akin, Dunne, Palomares, & Schilling
PUBLISHER/ COPYRIGHT:	American Counseling Association (ACA)/1997

NOTES: Classroom lesson plans for students to learn and practice trustworthiness, respect, responsibility, justice and fairness, caring, and citizenship.

TITLE:	**Educating for Character: How Schools Can Teach Respect and Responsibility**
MEDIA/COST:	Book
GRADES/LENGTH:	K–12
AUTHOR:	Lickona
PUBLISHER/ COPYRIGHT:	Bantam/1992

NOTES: Numerous school-based strategies to promote respect and responsibility among students and staff. Includes references and research studies.

TITLE:	**Kids on the Block Books and Puppets**
MEDIA/COST:	Books/Puppets/Puppets ****
GRADES/LENGTH:	K–6
AUTHOR:	Aiello
DISTRIBUTOR:	Kids on the Block/21st Century Books

NOTES: Wonderful large puppets, each with a disability. Books provide scripts for children to put on plays with the puppets. Wonderful activity for older children to present to younger children, explaining how it feels to have the particular disability. Three disabilities can be presented in about 45 minutes.

The books help all students understand that students with disabilities are the same as other students except they have a disability. Helpful to use with the puppets, but the puppets are not necessary.

TITLE:	**Next Door Neighbors**
MEDIA/COST:	Dolls/Script
GRADES/LENGTH:	K–5
AUTHOR:	Aiello
DISTRIBUTOR:	Next Door Neighbors

NOTES: Wonderful dolls and scripts about preventing racial and ethnic prejudice and helping neighbors. Also includes scripts on violence prevention, problem solving, self-esteem, being good citizens and good workers, and taking care of the environment. Programs are culturally diverse, and the puppets interact with the audience to encourage children and adults to share their ideas and concerns. Presentations also available.

12-28   SAFETY

TITLE:	**Associations That Can Help for Safety of Children and When There Is Suspected Abuse**

Child Abuse and Neglect Hotline: 1-800-552-7096

National Adolescent Suicide Hotline: 1-800-621-4000

National Center for Missing and Exploited Children
1835 K St., Suite 700
Washington, DC 20006
(202) 634-9821
Toll-free hotline for missing children reports:
1-800-843-5678

Child Find, Inc.
P.O. Box 277
New Paltz, NY 12561
(914) 255-1848

Adam Walsh Child Resource Center
1876 N. University Dr., Suite 306
Ft. Lauderdale, FL 33322
(305) 475-4847

Child Welfare League of America
67 Irving Place
New York, NY 10003
(212) 254-7410

12-28 SAFETY (CONTINUED)

National Center for the Prevention of Child Abuse and Neglect
Department of Pediatrics
University of Colorado Medical Center
1205 Oneida Street
Denver, CO 80220
(303) 321-3963

National Center on Child Abuse and Neglect
U.S. Department of Health and Human Services
P.O. Box 1182
Washington, DC 20013
(202) 245-2860

National Committee for Prevention of Child Abuse
332 South Michigan Ave.
Chicago, IL 60604
(312) 663-3520

National Clearinghouse for Child Abuse and Neglect
Aspen System
1600 Research Blvd.
Rockville, MD 20850
(301) 251-5157

TITLE:	**Confronting Sexual Harassment: Learning Activities for Teens**
MEDIA/COST:	Book *
GRADES/LENGTH:	6–12/192 pages
AUTHORS:	Sabella & Myrick
PUBLISHER/ COPYRIGHT:	Educational Media/1996

NOTES: Treats this controversial subject in a sensitive way. Rationale for students to take more responsibility for a safe and productive school environment. Concepts and skills. Can be integrated into the curricula, taught in eight-session guidance units, or presented to small groups. Reproducible masters, supplemental activities, and assessment.

TITLE:	**Developing a School Safety Plan** (#2, *Scared Scared or Prepared* Series)
MEDIA/COST:	Video/Guide/Book ****
GRADES/LENGTH:	K–6/40 minutes
AUTHORS:	Canter & Garrison
PUBLISHER/ COPYRIGHT:	Lee Canter & Associates, Inc./1995

NOTES: Staff development on how to create a safe and violence-free schoolwide environment. Four sections: (1) Establishing a School Safety Plan, (2) Designing a Schoolwide Discipline Plan, (3) Developing Positive Relationships, (4) Consistency and Enforcement of Policy. Excellent video to raise the awareness level of all staff members. Strategies to help reduce and/or eliminate violence in the school environment. Well-organized handbook with leader's script, key points, discussion questions, group activities, and worksheets.

TITLE:	**Family Violence: How to Recognize and Survive It**
MEDIA/COST:	Book
GRADES/LENGTH:	K–12/64 pages
AUTHOR:	Rench
PUBLISHER/ COPYRIGHT:	Lerner Publications/1992

NOTES: Informative about the abusive environment in which some children live and the coping methods they use to survive. A book for counselors and teachers to read and understand the needs of some children.

TITLE:	**National Runaway Switchboard** (312) 880-9860 (Voice) (800) 621-4000 (Voice) (312) 929-5150 (FAX)

NOTES: Toll-free, 24-hour telephone service for runaways in need of help. Crisis intervention and referral services with complete confidentiality. It will set up conference calls between young people and their parents/guardians at the youth's request. It will deliver a message to the runaway's family, if requested.

12-28 SAFETY *(CONTINUED)*

TITLE: **Runaway Me: A Survivor's Story**

MEDIA/COST: Book *

GRADES/LENGTH: 6–12/384 pages

AUTHOR: Cutler

PUBLISHER/
   COPYRIGHT: Blooming Press/1994

NOTES: A sobering book for teens and parents on how to prevent and cope with runaway crises. Includes questions the young person should be able to answer to be safe and healthy. Also includes guidelines upon return, to discuss root problems to prevent a repeat runaway. Cautions against denial of problems.

TITLE: **Sexual Harassment and Teens: A Program for Positive Change**

MEDIA/COST: Book

GRADES/LENGTH: 7–12/149 pages

AUTHORS: Strauss & Espeland

PUBLISHER/
   COPYRIGHT: Free Spirit Publishing, Inc./1992

NOTES: Proactive, preventive, and ready-to-use program for a partnership between adults and teens to work for change. Addresses the causes and consequences of this pervasive social problem in a cooperative, nonthreatening way. Includes case studies, activities, questionnaires, laws, guidelines, policies, procedures, and resources. Also includes transparencies and many reproducible pages. When this curriculum was tested in the classroom, 61 percent of the males and 68 percent of the females reported that their assumptions about men and women had changed as a result of the course.

TITLE: **STAR: Straight Talk About Risks (Guns and Teens)**

MEDIA/COST: Video/Guide/Curriculum*

GRADES/LENGTH: 1–12/Video, 16 minutes; 6½ hour training of trainers, 259 pages

PUBLISHER/
   COPYRIGHT: Center to Prevent Handgun Violence/1992

NOTES: *Parent notification and permission prior to using with young students. Stresses consequences of those who use guns and those who are left as victims.* Students give some powerful messages about their feelings about guns and dying. Informative, straight forward, and sensitive. Lessons present skills to recognize the dangers of guns and to make decisions to enhance a student's safety. Sections: Grades 1–2, Grades 3–5, Grades 6–8, and Grades 9–12. Activities can be used in a unit or separately. Powerful message; however, it may cause younger more sensitive children unnecessary fear.

TITLE: **Suicide Prevention in the Schools: Guidelines for Middle and High School Settings**

MEDIA/COST: Book *

GRADES/LENGTH: K–12/128 pages

AUTHOR: Capuzzi

PUBLISHER/
   COPYRIGHT: American Counseling Association (ACA)/1994

NOTES: Can help the counselor detect early suicidal preoccupation. Includes counselor and school district prevention programs, information for faculty training, preparation of crisis teams, and individual and group-counseling strategies. Excellent resource for planning and conducting a suicide-prevention program. Also excellent when dealing with the aftermath of a suicide of a student or adult the students know. Practical guide.

TITLE: **The Trauma of Adolescent Suicide**

MEDIA/COST: Booklet *

GRADES/LENGTH: K–12

AUTHOR: Dempsey

PUBLISHER: National Ass'n. of Secondary School Principals (NASSP)

NOTES: Excellent resource for the counselor with information about causes of suicide, myths about suicide, warning signs, prevention, and what to do if the tragedy occurs.

12-30   SELF-ESTEEM

TITLE:	**Esteem Builders' Complete Program** **Esteem Builders for Staff**
MEDIA/COST:	Program/Books *****
GRADES/LENGTH:	K–8
AUTHOR:	Borba
PUBLISHER/ COPYRIGHT:	Jalmar Press/1990

NOTES: Nine components: (1) conflict resolution, (2) positive school climate, (3) social competence, (4) problem-solving skills, (5) character development, (6) resilience, (7) self-acceptance, (8) coping skills, and (9) personal competence and responsibility that are student-centered, in a sequential program. The counselor can start with the trainer starter package.

Includes staff-esteem builders and home-esteem builders for staff development and parent education. Activities build cohesiveness and collegiality among staff.

Manual for parent education contains 40 activities parents can use to build esteem of their children. It includes 15 parent newsletters, handouts, and complete script for a parent inservice.

12-32   SOCIAL DEVELOPMENT

TITLE:	**Skillstreaming the Elementary School Child: A Guide for Teaching Prosocial Skills**
MEDIA/COST:	Book/Forms *
GRADES/LENGTH:	K–6/Book, 254 pages; 28 forms
AUTHORS:	McGinnis & Goldstein
PUBLISHER/ COPYRIGHT:	Research Press/1984

NOTES: Structured learning materials for children who repeatedly deal with daily events like responding to teasing in an immature way. Initially designed for special education students who were entering mainstream classes, but interventions are readily adaptable for all children. Skills include self-control, listening, completing tasks, etc. Particularly effective when teaching social and behavioral skills.

12-33   SPECIAL EDUCATION

TITLE:	**DSM-IV: Diagnostic and Statistical Manual of Mental Disorders (4th ed.)**
MEDIA/COST:	Book
GRADES/LENGTH:	K–12
AUTHOR:	American Psychiatric Association
PUBLISHER:	American Psychiatric Association (APA)

NOTES: Most respected reference for learning about physical and emotional disorders of students.

TITLE:	**The Special Education Teacher's Book of Lists**
MEDIA/COST:	Book **
GRADES/LENGTH:	K–12/363 pages
AUTHOR:	Pierangelo
PUBLISHER/ COPYRIGHT:	Center for Applied Research in Education/1995

NOTES: Excellent resource for school counselor as well as special education teachers because it includes information about symptomatic behavior, procedures for child study teams, special education screening committees, information about the IEP as well as different disabilities, and special education laws.

12-34   SPECIAL POPULATIONS

TITLE:	**At-Risk Youth: Identification, Programs, and Recommendations**
MEDIA/COST:	Book
GRADES/LENGTH:	6–12/158 pages
AUTHOR:	Wells
PUBLISHER/ COPYRIGHT:	Teacher Ideas Press/1990

NOTES: Characteristics of student dropouts and potential dropouts. Complete descriptions of successful programs for students at risk of dropping out of school.

12-34 SPECIAL POPULATIONS *(CONTINUED)*

TITLE:	**A Framework for Understanding and Working With Students and Adults from Poverty**
MEDIA/COST:	Book
GRADES/LENGTH:	K–12
AUTHOR:	Payne
PUBLISHER/ COPYRIGHT:	Sandpiper/1995

NOTES: Practical knowledge about poverty that school employees usually do not know. Four types of poverty: (1) Situational, (2) Generational, (3) Working, and (4) Immigration. Three rules in poverty and how decisions are made. Includes resilience and why students may make a joke of a trying situation. Extremely helpful resource for the counselor who works with a population living in poverty.

TITLE:	**Positive: HIV Affirmative Counseling**
MEDIA/COST:	Book *
GRADES/LENGTH:	7–12/270 pages
AUTHOR:	Kain
PUBLISHER/ COPYRIGHT:	American Counseling Association (ACA)/1996

NOTES: Provides guidelines for respecting and counseling students who have HIV/AIDS. Techniques for helping students throughout the progression of their illness. Special sections focus on the unique concerns of racial and ethnic groups as well as youth.

TITLE:	**Treating the Unmanageable Adolescent: A Guide to Oppositional Defiant and Conduct Disorders**
MEDIA/COST:	Book **
GRADES/LENGTH:	5–12/354 pages
AUTHOR:	Bernstein
PUBLISHER/ COPYRIGHT:	Jason Aronson/1996

NOTES: Practical resource for counselors who work with resistant, arrogant, very difficult at-risk students. Provides helpful suggestions and examples for leading groups to help these students increase their self-control, build their self-esteem, and gain interpersonal skills.

TITLE:	**Youth at Risk: A Prevention Resource for Counselors, Teachers, and Parents**
MEDIA/COST:	Book **
GRADES/LENGTH:	K–12/416 pages
AUTHORS:	Capuzzi & Gross (Editors)
PUBLISHER/ COPYRIGHT:	American Counseling Association (ACA)/1996

NOTES: Prevention to decrease destructive behaviors in children and adolescents. Includes causal factors, identification of behaviors that put youth at risk, and strategies for prevention and intervention programs. Topics: effects of a dysfunctional family, physical and sexual abuse, low self-esteem, depression, stress, eating disorders, pregnancy, AIDS, suicide, gang membership, school dropout, and homelessness. Excellent resource for the counselor.

12-38 SUBSTANCE ABUSE PREVENTION

TITLE:	**About Addiction and Alcoholism** *About Addiction* *About Codependency* *Alcoholic in the Family*
MEDIA/COST:	Booklets * (100–499)
GRADES/LENGTH:	K–12/15 pages
PUBLISHER/ COPYRIGHT:	Channing L. Bete Co./1990

NOTES: *About Addiction:* Information about things to which people can be addicted, other than chemicals, i.e. food, gambling, exercise, etc. Treatment of addictions is included.

About Codependency describes living with an addicted person. Details on how and where the codependent can get help.

Alcoholic in the Family is a resource that can be used with an individual student or special group of children of alcoholics. It must be used with sensitivity and care. Explains the magnitude of the disease of alcoholism, and the impact the disease has on the family.

12-38 SUBSTANCE ABUSE PREVENTION *(CONTINUED)*

TITLE:	**Americans for a Drug-Free America**
MEDIA/COST:	Book
GRADES/LENGTH:	9–12
PUBLISHER/ COPYRIGHT:	American Crisis Publishing, Inc./ 1988

NOTES: Excellent resource with information on prevention, intervention, and education. Specific substance information included.

TITLE:	**Another Chance: Hope and Health for the Alcoholic Family**
MEDIA/COST:	Book *
GRADES/LENGTH:	Adults/324 pages
AUTHOR:	Wegescheider-Cruse
PUBLISHER/ COPYRIGHT:	Science and Behavior Books, Inc./ 1989

NOTES: Dynamics of codependency are explained skillfully with the issues involved. Topics include: (1) Anatomy of Family; (2) The Addiction Spiral; (3) The Family Disease; (4) Family Roles; (5) The Treatment Plan; and (6) Treatment for Codependents. Excellent resource for counselors to gain insight into the addicted family. Author's personal anecdotes and a comprehensive bibliography.

TITLE:	**Children Are People, Inc.**
MEDIA/COST:	Binder *
GRADES/LENGTH:	K–6/100 pages
AUTHORS:	Lerner & Naiditch
PUBLISHER/ COPYRIGHT:	Health Communications/1986

NOTES: Excellent resource. Topics: goal setting, standing up for yourself, friendship selection, alcoholism and the brain, chemical classifications, coping, and more.

TITLE:	**Children of Alcoholics: A Guide for Parents, Educators & Therapists**
MEDIA/COST:	Book *
GRADES/LENGTH:	5–12/198 pages
AUTHOR:	Ackerman
PUBLISHER/ COPYRIGHT:	Simon and Schuster/1987

NOTES: Detailed, easy-to-understand strategies that help children cope with the stresses of living in an alcoholic home. Perspectives of the child of an alcoholic, suggestions for educators, and resource materials for parents. Extensive book list with pamphlets and videos.

TITLE:	**The Complete Drug Reference**
MEDIA/COST:	Book
GRADES/LENGTH:	K–12
PUBLISHER/ COPYRIGHT:	Consumer Reports/1996

NOTES: Descriptions of commonly prescribed drugs, facts, and comparisons. To learn of common reactions to prescribed medications, the counselor may call a local pharmacy or poison control center. A more complete reference is the *Physician's Desk Reference* (PDR) which is available in the public library.

TITLE:	**Conducting Support Groups for Elementary Children**
MEDIA/COST:	Book *
GRADES/LENGTH:	4–12
PUBLISHER/ COPYRIGHT:	Johnson Institute/1991

NOTES: Recommended that counselors who lead a group for children of alcoholics have special training. Outstanding resource for leaders of such groups. Background information, rationale, and logistics for leading groups for children of alcoholics in schools. Two types of support groups: (1) the "Living Skills Group" in which health, wellness, and disease prevention, including chemical dependence, are emphasized; (2) the "Concerned Persons' Group" which is helping children cope with family chemical dependence. Sample parent permission letters, group rules, and how to deal with instances of abuse. Ten lesson plans for both types of groups.

12-38 SUBSTANCE ABUSE PREVENTION *(CONTINUED)*

TITLE:	**Facts, Feelings, Family and Friends**
MEDIA/COST:	Book,*; Set, ****
GRADES/LENGTH:	K–6/150 pages
AUTHOR:	Christensen
PUBLISHER:	Johnson Institute

NOTES: Curriculum for grades K–6 including age-appropriate lessons. Complete booklets for comprehensive approach with all information needed to lead groups. Topics: drug specifics, chemical dependence, and the disease model; how chemical dependence effects family and friends; and how we can help chemically dependent persons. Bibliography for professionals and book list for children are included in each book. Stories, activities, games, and songs, with accurate information. Book teaches kids how to say "No."

TITLE:	**From Peer Pressure to Peer Support**
MEDIA/COST:	Book ***
GRADES/LENGTH:	6–12/323 pages
AUTHOR:	Freeman
PUBLISHER/ COPYRIGHT:	Johnson Institute/1989

NOTES: A classic, practical book in two parts. First part lays the groundwork for alcohol and other drug awareness. Second part deals with alcohol and drug prevention through the group process. Student activities that can be used in groups for conflict resolution, communication, and purposes other than substance abuse.

TITLE:	**Information and Strategies in Alcohol and Other Drug Prevention for Elementary and Middle Schools**
MEDIA/COST:	Binder **
GRADES/LENGTH:	K–8/130 pages
AUTHOR:	Whitlock (Editor)
PUBLISHER/ COPYRIGHT:	Training Center for Alcohol and Other Drug Prevention/1992

NOTES: Information, strategies, and practical tips for establishing programs. Self-esteem, comprehensive drug education and prevention programs, and changing family roles in today's world. Points out how counselors can make a difference.

TITLE:	**It's Elementary: Meeting Needs of High-Risk Youth in the School Setting**
MEDIA/COST:	Booklet *
GRADES/LENGTH:	K–12/28 pages
PUBLISHER/ COPYRIGHT:	National Association for Children of Alcoholics/1989

NOTES: Outstanding booklet to assist school staffs in helping children of alcoholics. Contents: (1) Statistics; (2) Information on what principals, teachers and counselors can do; (3) Rationale for COA groups in the school setting; and (4) Adult children of alcoholics as teachers. Resources for educators and students.

TITLE:	**Learning to Live Drug Free**
MEDIA/COST:	Curriculum Manual
GRADES/LENGTH:	K–6
PUBLISHER/ COPYRIGHT:	U.S. Department of Education/ 1989

NOTES: Supplement to other materials for substance abuse prevention. Materials appropriate for each grade level, information about alcohol and drugs, and information about working with parents and the community.

TITLE:	**On Target: A Road Map to Healthy and Drug-Free Life Styles**
MEDIA/COST:	Activity Book *
GRADES/LENGTH:	K–6
PUBLISHER/ COPYRIGHT:	Target/1991

NOTES: Good reference book for counselors and teachers. Ways to infuse substance abuse prevention education into all curriculum areas and ways to involve parents. Enhances other substance abuse prevention curriculum.

12-38 SUBSTANCE ABUSE PREVENTION (CONTINUED)

TITLE: **Refusal Skills: Preventing Drug Use in Adolescents**

MEDIA/COST: Book *

GRADES/LENGTH: 7–12/176 pages

AUTHORS: Goldstein, Reagles, & Amann

PUBLISHER/
  COPYRIGHT: Research Press/1990

NOTES: Practical, step-by-step approach to teaching 50 important skills: social, relationship, assertiveness, and conflict-management skills to help students avoid peer pressure to use alcohol and other drugs. Especially practical for prevention with younger, at-risk students. Uses "skillstreaming" approach. Excellent resource to use with students and parents.

TITLE: **Substance Abuse in Children and Adolescents: Evaluation and Intervention**

MEDIA/COST: Book

GRADES/LENGTH: K–12

AUTHORS: Schinke, Botvin, & Orlandi

PUBLISHER/
  COPYRIGHT: Sage/1991

NOTES: Evaluations of prevention and intervention programs to stop substance abuse of young people. Information about individual drugs. Information about how to teach skills but does not include actual skills. Excellent resource to use with *Refusal Skills: Preventing Drug Use in Adolescents.*

TITLE: **Too Cool for Drugs**

MEDIA/COST: Book *

GRADES/LENGTH: 1–5/120 pages

AUTHORS: Scott & Hindmarsh

PUBLISHER/
  COPYRIGHT: Human Resource Development Press, Inc./1993

NOTES: Helps parents, teachers, and counselors educate elementary-age children about the harmful effects of tobacco, alcohol, marijuana, and inhalants. Skills and practice scenarios for managing peer pressure to use drugs. Written through the eyes of Nicholas, a cocker spaniel. Nicholas comes across situations for which he gets answers to his questions from a health expert.

TITLE: **Working With Children of Alcoholics**

MEDIA: Book **

GRADES/LENGTH: K–12/253 pages

AUTHOR: Robinson

PUBLISHER/
  COPYRIGHT: Lexington Books/1989

NOTES: This is a step-by-step approach for teachers, counselors, and other professionals. Shows what to look for and what to do for children of alcoholics. Excellent resource section.

TITLE: **Youth and Drugs: Society's Mixed Messages**

MEDIA/COST: Book/Free

GRADES/LENGTH: K–12/174 pages

PUBLISHER: U.S. Department of Health & Human Services

NOTES: Can be used for professional development.

12-40   TRANSITION

TITLE: **Books to Help Children Cope With Separation and Loss: An Annotated Bibliography (4th Ed.)**

MEDIA/COST: Book

GRADES/LENGTH: K–12

AUTHORS: Rudman, Gagne, & Bernstein

PUBLISHER/
  COPYRIGHT: R.R. Bowker/1993

NOTES: Great bibliography of about 60 books dealing with moving. Excellent summary of each book with appropriate ages of students.

TITLE: **Helping Transfer Students: Strategies for Educational and Social Readjustment**

MEDIA/COST: Book

GRADES/LENGTH: K–12

AUTHORS: Jason & Associates

PUBLISHER/
  COPYRIGHT: Jossey Bass

NOTES: Excellent book for the counselor to help students who transfer in or out of the school.

TITLE	LIST	TITLE	LIST
100 Best Colleges for African American	9-2	Behavior Management in the Home	10-9
100 Ways to Enhance Self-Concept	11-17	Being a Friend: What Does It Mean?	8-10
200 Letters for Job Hunters	9-1	Being Friends: You Can Choose!	7-13
90 Minute Resume	9-1	Belief in Self: You Can If You Think You Can	6-18
AAUW Report: How Schools Shortchange	11-8	Bereavement Support Group	12-7
About Addiction and Alcoholism	12-38	Best Foot Forward: Manners	8-14
About Dying	10-6	Best Friends	6-10
ACA Code of Ethics and Standards	12-13	Best Guide to the Top Colleges	9-2
ACES Standards for Counseling Supervisors	12-13	Between You and Me	7-2
ACK-American Careers for Kids	7-1	Beyond Innocence of Childhood	11-5
ACT: American College Test	9-25	Bibliocounseling: Adolescent Literature	12-19
ACT Explore	8-1	Black Is My Color	7-12
Active Parenting	10-4	Black Student's Guide to Colleges	9-2
Active Teaching: Enhancing Discipline	11-7	Black Students in Interracial Schools	9-2
ADD and the College Student	9-2	Books	10-11
After the Tears	10-8	Books About Careers	9-1
Alex Is My Friend	6-6	Books About Interviews	9-1
All Feelings Are O.K.	6-8	Books About Jobs	9-1
All Together: Blended Family	6-9	Books About Safety	8-16
Alone at Home: Kid's Guide	7-16	Books About Safety from Abuse	7-16
Alone Together: Single Parent Activity	10-12	Books for Safety from Rape	9-18
Alphabet Careers	7-1	Books to Help Children Cope	12-40
Alternatives to Violence	8-3	Books: Communication	10-3
Americans for a Drug-Free America	12-38	Bound for Success: Guiding Your Child	10-23
Anger Management & Violence Prevention	12-17	Boy Who Couldn't Stop Washing	7-6
Another Chance: Hope and Health	12-38	Brainstorm: Outreach Project	7-21
AP Tests: Advanced Placement Program	9-25	Break it Up: Teacher's Guide	11-4
Applying Career Development Theory	12-1	Bright Beginnings	6-8
ASCA Membership Services	12-13	Brochures for Problem Solving	9-15
ASCA Student Competencies	12-3	Buford Listens	6-4
ASGW Ethical Guidelines	12-13	Building Blocks of Self-Esteem	7-18
Assertive Discipline: Parent Resource	10-9	Building Resilient Children	10-4
Assertive Discipline: Positive Behavior	11-7	Building Self-Esteem: A Comprehensive Program	11-17
Assns. That Can Help When Suspected Abuse	12-28	Building Self-Esteem With Koala-Roo	6-18
ASVAB Armed Service Vocational Aptitude	9-1	Bully-Proofing Your School	12-4
At-Risk Youth: Identification, Programs	12-34	CAM Report	9-1
Attention Deficit Disorders Intervention	12-10	CAPS: Career Ability Placement Survey	9-1
Attention Deficit Hyperactivity Disorder	10-8	Career Assessment: Where Do You Fit?	9-1
Attention? ADD in School	12-10	Career Choices Curriculum	9-1
Autism & Asperger Syndrome	12-10	Career Education CAREER Motivational	7-1
Bag Bingo	6-20	Career Education: Preparing for the 21st	9-1
Be A Better Listener	6-2	Career Exploration Inventory	9-1
Be Cool: Coping With Bullying	7-3	Career Futures	8-1
Behavior Management in the Classroom	11-7	Career Game	8-1

TITLE	LIST	TITLE	LIST
Group Counseling for School Counselors	12-17	How to Succeed In Middle School	7-23
Group Counseling for Secondary Schools	12-17	How to Talk So Kids Will Listen	10-3
Group Counseling Strategies	12-17	How to Talk to Your Children About AIDS	10-21
Groups: Process and Practice	12-17	How to Write Your College Application	9-2
Growing Smart: What's Working for Girls	11-8	Human Development and Family Life	10-12
Growing Up: Grades 1–6	10-4	Human Race Club	12-12
Gruber's Complete Prep for the New SAT	9-25	Hunter's Guide to College Guides	9-2
Guidance and Counseling Programs	12-3	Hurried Child	10-7
Guidance for Students With Disabilities	12-10	I Blew It! Learning From Failure	8-5
Guidance Units: Study Skills	7-20	I Can Do It: Taking Responsibility	7-15
Guiding Children to Success	10-4	I Can Make Good Choices	6-5
Guiding the Gifted Child	10-7	I Get So Mad!	6-8
Guiding the LD Student	9-2	I Like Being Me: Self-Esteem	8-18
Hal's Pals Dolls	12-10	I Wish I Could Hold Your Hand	7-4
Happy to Be Me	6-18	IDEAS: Interest, Determination	8-1
Harrington O'Shea Decision-Making	9-1	If You Change Your Mind	9-24
Heath Resource Directory	9-2	Images	8-12
Help for Children	12-9	In Depth Look at Peer Helping	12-25
Helping Children Cope	7-4	In Real Life: Sexual Harassment	9-18
Helping Kids Handle Conflict	6-3	Information and Strategies	12-38
Helping Transfer Students	12-40	Inside the SAT & ACT	9-25
Helping Your Pre-Teen Say "NO"	10-27	Inside/Out: A Whole Person's	6-16
Here's What You Need to Know About	10-17	Insider's Guide to the Colleges	9-2
Hi, I'm Adam	7-6	Interactive Fiske Guide to Colleges	9-2
High School Career Course Planner	8-23	Internet Guide for College-Bound	9-2
High-Performing Teacher: Avoiding Burnout	11-12	Invitational Counseling	12-3
Holiday Facts and Fun	11-10	Inviting School Success: Self-Concept	11-17
Home Alone: You're in Charge	7-16	Is It Love . . . Or Is It Gross?	8-16
Home Esteem Builders	10-23	It's Elementary: Meeting Needs of High-Risk	12-38
Homework Without Tears	10-26	It's Not Fair	6-3
Horizons 2000: Career & Life Planning	12-16	It's OK to Learn Differently	7-20
Hostile Hallways: AAUW Survey	11-15	Ivy League Programs at State School Prices	9-2
HOTLINE (Runaways)	12-28	Job Skills for 21st Century	9-1
HOTLINES (Suicide)	12-28	JOB-O	8-1
HOTLINES (Suspected Abuse)	12-28	JOB-O-E Dictionary & Workbook	7-1
How Can I Be Involved in My Child's Education	10-4	Journal of College Admission	9-2
How Can I Fit In?	7-10	Jumpin' Johnny Get Back to Work	7-6
How Can Parents Model Good Listening	10-3	K & W Guide to Colleges for the LD	9-2
How Can We Help Children Learn	10-20	Kelso's Choice	12-4
How Do We Tell the Children?	10-6	Kid Counselor Musicals & Songfest	7-18
How I Learned Not to Be Bullied	6-3	Kid's Guide to a Positive Attitude	6-18
How Important Is Homework?	10-26	Kid's Guide to Getting Along in School	6-20
How Schools Shortchange Girls	12-16	Kid's Guide to Getting Along With Classmates	6-10
How to Help Improve Your Child's Behavior	10-9	Kid's Guide to Getting Along With Family	7-9
How to Help Your Child Succeed	10-26	Kid's Guide to Getting Organized	6-20
How to Help Your Teenager	10-1	Kid's Guide to Good Study Habits	7-20
How to Prepare Your Teen for Work	10-1	Kids on the Block, Books and Puppets	12-27
How to Reach & Teach ADD/ADHD	11-6	Kids Say Don't Smoke	7-21
How to Study	7-20		

TITLE	LIST	TITLE	LIST
Pathfinders: Women in the Workforce	8-1	SAT I Scholastic Assessment Test I	9-25
Peace in the Classroom	11-4	SAT II Subject Test Preparation on CD-ROM	9-25
Peacemaking Skills for Little Kids	6-14	SAT Success	9-25
Peer Power: Becoming an Effective Peer Helper	12-25	Saving the Native Son	12-23
Peers Helping Peers	8-11	Say No and Mean It	7-21
Peervention: Training Peer Facilitators	9-14	Saying Good-Bye (Book)	6-4
Perfectionism: What's Bad About Being	10-7	Saying Good-Bye (Video)	6-4
Peterson's Career & College Quest	9-1	Scholarship Book	9-2
Peterson's Guide	9-2	School Counselors and Censorsorship	12-3
Peterson's Internships	9-1	School Counselor's Letter Book	12-3
PIC: Practical Ideas for Counselors	12-3	School Crisis Survival Guide	12-6
Pioneers in Health & Medicine	7-12	SchoolGirls: Young Women	8-19
Play Therapy	12-3	School-to-Work	9-1
Playground Push-Around	6-3	SCII: Strong-Campbell Interest Inventory	9-1
Playing the Game	6-17	Score Builder for SAT	9-25
Positive Discipline in the Classroom	11-13	SDS: Self-Directed Search	9-1
Positive Peer Groups	12-25	Second Step: Grades 1-3	6-14
Positive: HIV Affirmative Counseling	12-34	Second Step: Grades 4-5	7-14
Power of "No"	7-21	Second Step: Grades 6-8	8-14
Power Parenting, ADD/ADHD	10-8	Second Step: Grades PreK–K	6-14
Praise-Criticism Ratio	11-7	Self-Confidence: Step-by-Step	8-18
Prepare Curriculum: Teaching Prosocial	12-3	Self-Control Patrol	7-17
Preventing Gang Activity	12-4	Self-Controlled Classroom	7-17
Preventing Violence and Intervening Safely	11-4	Self-Esteem Curriculum Module Grades 2–4	6-18
Problem Solving Series	6-13	Self-Esteem Curriculum Module Grades 5–9	8-18
Project Alert Training	8-21	Self-Esteem in the Classroom: Curriculum	11-17
PSAT/NMSQT Preliminary Scholastic	9-25	Sexual Harassment	8-16
Push & Shove	6-3	Sexual Harassment and Teens	12-28
Putting on the Brakes	7-6	Sexual Harassment: Crossing the Line	8-16
Race for Safe Schools: Staff Development	11-15	Sexual Harassment: It's Hurting People	8-16
Raising Children in Troubled Times	10-4	Sexual Harassment: Minimize the Risk	8-16
RAPP! Resource of Activities	7-2	Sexual Harassment: Pay Attention	8-16
Ready, Set, Go! to Kindergarten	10-29	Shortchanging Girls, Shortchanging America	11-8
Ready-to-Use Conflict Resolution Activities	12-4	Siblings' Information Network Newsletter	10-8
Ready-to-Use Social Skills PreK-K	6-19	Siblings Without Rivalry	10-12
Ready-to-Use Social Skills	8-19	SIGI PLUS: System of Interactive Guidance	9-1
Reducing School Violence	12-4	Silence the Violence: Skills	8-3
Refusal Skills: Preventing Drug Use	12-38	Skillful Teacher	11-12
Research on Educational Innovations	11-9	Skills for Living	12-17
Resources Dealing With Bullying	12-4	Skillstreaming in Early Childhood	6-19
Respect Yourself and Others, Too	6-14	Skillstreaming the Elementary Child	12-32
Responsible Kids in School and at Home	11-14	Sleep Book for Tired Parents	10-8
Responsible Rascal	6-5	Social Skills Activities for Special Children	6-19
Rugg's Recommendation on Colleges	9-2	Solution-Focused Counseling in High School	12-3
Runaway Me	12-28	Someone Special Died	6-4
S.A.I.L.: Self-Awareness in Language Arts	12-3	Sooper Puppy Series	6-21
Sacred Art of Dying	12-7	Special Education Teacher's Book of Lists	12-33
Sad Hug, Mad Hug, Happy Hug	6-4	Staff Development: Self-Esteem	11-17
		STAR Midwestern Prevention Program	8-21

TITLE	LIST	TITLE	LIST
When I Grow Up (Professional Women)	7-1	Women in Math & Science (Four Programs)	11-8
When Mom and Dad Separate	6-7	Wonderful Me!	6-18
When Someone Has a Very Serious Illness	6-8	Working It Out: Conflict Resolution	8-3
When to Say Yes! and Make More Friends	8-10	Working It Out: Solving Conflicts	8-3
When Your Mom and Dad Get Divorced	6-7	Working Moms Books	6-1
When Your Parents Get a Divorce	7-7	Working Today and Tomorrow	8-1
When You're Mad, Mad, Mad	8-8	Working Together	7-14
Where in the World Are You Going?	6-23	Working with Children of Alcoholics	12-38
Who Me? Mad? Nah!	7-8	You Can Choose: Decision Making	7-5
Whole Career Sourcebook	9-1	You Can Choose: Saying No	6-5
Why I Won't Do Drugs	7-21	You Can Choose Series	6-18
Windows to Our Children	12-12	You Can Say No: Here's How	8-5
Winning at Parenting Without Beating	10-9	Youth and Drugs: Society's Mixed Messages	12-38
Wizard of No	7-21	Youth at Risk	12-34
Women in Aerospace	9-1		

TOPIC	TITLE	LIST
Career Education	200 Letters for Job Hunters	9-1
Career Education	90 Minute Resume	9-1
Career Education	AAUW Report: How Schools	11-8
Career Education	ACK-American Careers for Kids	7-1
Career Education	ACT Explore	8-1
Career Education	Alphabet Careers	7-1
Career Education	Applying Career Development Theory	12-1
Career Education	ASVAB Armed Services Vocational Aptitude Battery	9-1
Career Education	Books About Careers	9-1
Career Education	Books About Interviews	9-1
Career Education	Books About Jobs	9-1
Career Education	CAM Report	9-1
Career Education	CAPS Career Ability Placement	9-1
Career Education	Career Assessment: Where Do You Fit?	9-1
Career Education	Career Choices Curriculum	9-1
Career Education	Career Educational CAREER Motivational	7-1
Career Education	Career Education: Preparing for 21st Century	9-1
Career Education	Career Exploration Inventory	9-1
Career Education	Career Futures	8-1
Career Education	Career Game	8-1
Career Education	Career Information in Classroom: Workshop	11-1
Career Education	Career Opportunities News	9-1
Career Education	Career Resource Center Materials	12-3
Career Education	Career Search: Internet	12-43
Career Education	Career Skills	8-1
Career Education	Career Tracks 2000	12-1
Career Education	Career World	9-1
Career Education	Careers 2000	12-1
Career Education	Careers Tomorrow	8-1
Career Education	CASE: Career Assessment	8-1
Career Education	Children's Dictionary of Occupational Titles	7-1
Career Education	Children's Occupational Outlook Handbook	7-1
Career Education	CHOICES for Career & College Decisions	9-1
Career Education	CHOICES JR.	7-1
Career Education	CHOICES JR., Planning My Future	8-1
Career Education	Chronicle Occupational Briefs	9-1
Career Education	CIP: Classification of Instructional Programs	9-1
Career Education	COPES: Career Orientation	8-1
Career Education	COPP: Career Orientation & Planning Profile	8-1
Career Education	COPS: Career Occupational Preference Survey	9-1
Career Education	COPS II: Career Occupational Preference Survey	8-1
Career Education	COPS-R: Career Occupational Preference Survey	8-1
Career Education	Counselor & Bias-Free Career Planning	12-1
Career Education	CPP: Career Planning Program 1	8-1

TOPIC	TITLE	LIST
Career Education	Create Your Own Career Center	9-1
Career Education	Creating Portfolios	12-1
Career Education	DAT: Differential Aptitude Test	9-1
Career Education	Developmental Career Counseling	12-1
Career Education	Dictionary of Holland Occupational Codes	9-1
Career Education	DISCOVER	9-1
Career Education	DOT: Dictionary of Occupational Titles	9-1
Career Education	Dream Catchers: Develop Career and Educational Awareness	8-1
Career Education	Early Occupational Awareness Program	6-1
Career Education	Earth Keepers Series	7-12
Career Education	Encyclopedia of Careers	9-1
Career Education	E-WOW (Explore the World of Work)	6-1
Career Education	E-WOW	7-1
Career Education	ExPAN College Search and Occupational Search	9-1
Career Education	Ferguson's Guide to Apprenticeships	9-1
Career Education	Florida Blueprint for Career Preparation	12-1
Career Education	Free Career Materials: A Resource	9-1
Career Education	Free Materials: Geographical	9-1
Career Education	Get a Life (ASCA)	12-1
Career Education	Growing Smart: What's Working for Girls	11-8
Career Education	Harrington O'Shea Decision-Making	9-1
Career Education	High School Career Course Planner	8-23
Career Education	Horizons 2000: Career and Life Planning	12-16
Career Education	How to Help Your Teenager	10-1
Career Education	How to Prepare Your Teen for Work	10-1
Career Education	IDEAS: Interest, Determination	8-1
Career Education	Job Skills for 21st Century	9-1
Career Education	JOB-O	8-1
Career Education	JOB-O-E Dictionary and Workbook	7-1
Career Education	Life Centered Career Education	8-1
Career Education	Major-Minor Finder	9-2
Career Education	Military Career Paths	9-1
Career Education	National Career Development Guidelines	12-1
Career Education	Next Door Neighbors	12-27
Career Education	OOH: Occupational Outlook Handbook	9-1
Career Education	OOH: Occupational Outlook Handbook Quarterly	9-1
Career Education	Opportunities for a Lifetime	8-1
Career Education	OVIS: Ohio Vocational Interest Survey II	8-1
Career Education	Pathfinder: Exploring Career . . . Paths	8-1
Career Education	Pathfinders: Women in the Workforce	8-1
Career Education	Peterson's Career & College Quest	9-1
Career Education	Peterson's Internships	9-1
Career Education	Pioneers in Health & Medicine	7-12
Career Education	School-to-Work	9-1
Career Education	SCII Strong-Campbell Interest Inventory	9-1
Career Education	SDS: Self-Directed Search	9-1
Career Education	Shortchanging Girls, Shortchanging America	11-8

TOPIC	TITLE	LIST
Career Education	SIGI Plus System of Interactive Guidance	9-1
Career Education	Student's Guide to Bias-Free Career Planning	9-1
Career Education	Sure-Hire Resumes	9-1
Career Education	Surviving After High School	9-1
Career Education	Sweaty Palms: Neglected Art of Being Interviewed	9-1
Career Education	Takeoff: African American Role Models 1–6	8-12
Career Education	Takeoff: Hispanic Experience	8-12
Career Education	Teenagers: Preparing for Real World	9-1
Career Education	VIP Jr.: Vocational Implications of Personality	9-1
Career Education	When I Grow Up	7-1
Career Education	When I Grow Up (Professional Women)	7-1
Career Education	Whole Career Sourcebook	9-1
Career Education	Women in Aerospace	9-1
Career Education	Women in Math & Science: Four Programs	11-8
Career Education	Working Moms Books	6-1
Career Education	Working Today and Tomorrow	8-1
College	College Applications/Essays	9-2
College	DISCOVER	9-1
College	100 Best Colleges for African American Students	9-2
College	ACT: American College Test	9-25
College	AP Tests: Advanced Placement Program and Tests	9-25
College	Best Guide to the Top Colleges	9-2
College	Black Student's Guide to Colleges	9-2
College	Black Students in Interracial Schools	9-2
College	Cass & Birnbaum's Guide	9-2
College	CHOICES for Career & College Decisions	9-1
College	College Admissions	9-2
College	College Admissions Data Handbook	9-2
College	College Connector	9-2
College	College Counsel: Parent's College Advisor	10-2
College	College Explorer PLUS	9-2
College	College Freshman Survival Guide	9-26
College	College Search	9-2
College	College Search: Internet	12-43
College	Complete Guide to College Visits	9-2
College	DAT: Differential Aptitude Test	9-1
College	Destination College: PSAT/NMSQT	9-25
College	Essays that Worked	9-2
College	ExPAN Comprehensive	9-2
College	Gruber's Complete Preparation for the New SAT	9-25
College	How to Write Your College Application	9-2
College	Hunter's Guide to the College Guides	9-2
College	Inside the SAT & ACT	9-25
College	Insider's Guide to the Colleges	9-2
College	Interactive Fiske Guide to Colleges	9-2
College	Internet Guide for College-Bound	9-2
College	Ivy League Programs at State School Prices	9-2
College	Journal of College Admission	9-2

TOPIC	TITLE	LIST
College	Looking Beyond the Ivy League	9-2
College	Lovejoy's College Guide	9-2
College	Major-Minor Finder	9-2
College	Making a Difference in College Admission	9-2
College	Multicultural Student's Guide to Colleges	9-2
College	Official Guide to SAT II: Subject Tests	9-25
College	Peterson's Guides	9-2
College	PSAT/NMSQT Preliminary Scholastic Assessment	9-25
College	Rugg's Recommendation on Colleges	9-2
College	SAT I: Scholastic Assessment Test	9-25
College	SAT II: Subject Test Preparation on CD Rom	9-25
College	SAT Success	9-25
College	Score Builder for SAT	9-25
College	Surfing for a College	9-2
College	Taste of College: On-Campus Summer	9-2
College	Test Skills: Test Preparation for the PSAT	9-25
College	TOEFL: Test of English as a Foreign Language	9-25
College	Tooth and Nail: A Novel Approach	9-25
College Financial Aid	College Financial Aid Made Easy	9-2
College Financial Aid	FAFSA Express	12-43
College Financial Aid	Financial Aid	9-2
College Financial Aid	Financial Aid: College Board	9-2
College Financial Aid	Heath Resource Directory	9-2
College Financial Aid	Scholarship Book	9-2
College Financial Aid	Student Guide (Annual)	9-2
College Special Students	ADD and the College Student	9-2
College Special Students	College Guide for Students With LD	9-2
College Special Students	Guiding the LD Student	9-2
College Special Students	K & W Guide to Colleges for the LD Student	9-2
Communication	Be a Better Listener	6-2
Communication	Between You and Me	7-2
Communication	Books: Communication	10-3
Communication	Communicate Junior	6-19
Communication	Communication	6-2
Communication	How Can Parents Model Good Listening	10-3
Communication	How to Talk So Kids Will Listen	10-3
Communication	Parent Involvement: Relationship	10-3
Communication	Parents on Your Side	11-3
Communication	RAPP! Resource of Activities	7-2
Communication	Successful Parenting–Part 2	10-3
Comprehensive	Active Parenting	10-4
Comprehensive	ASCA Student Competencies	12-3
Comprehensive	Building Resilient Children	10-4
Comprehensive	Career Resource Center Materials	12-3
Comprehensive	Challenge of Counseling in Middle Schools	12-3
Comprehensive	Compassionate School: Practical Guide	12-3
Comprehensive	Conners' Rating Scales	12-3
Comprehensive	Counseling and Human Development	12-3

TOPIC	TITLE	LIST
Comprehensive	Counseling Children	12-3
Comprehensive	Counseling Today's Secondary Students	12-3
Comprehensive	Counseling Toward Solutions	12-3
Comprehensive	Counselor in the Classroom	12-3
Comprehensive	Creative Counseling Techniques	12-3
Comprehensive	Developing & Managing Your School Counseling	12-3
Comprehensive	Developmental Guidance and Counseling	12-3
Comprehensive	Developmental School Counseling Programs	12-3
Comprehensive	Elementary School Counseling	12-3
Comprehensive	Facts for Families (Family and Parenting)	10-4
Comprehensive	Growing Up: Grades 1–6	10-4
Comprehensive	Guidance & Counseling Programs	12-3
Comprehensive	Guiding Children to Success	10-4
Comprehensive	How Can I Be Involved in My Child's Education?	10-4
Comprehensive	Invitational Counseling	12-3
Comprehensive	Kindness Is Contagious	12-3
Comprehensive	Leading Parent Groups I, II, and III	10-4
Comprehensive	Literature Teacher's Book of Lists	12-3
Comprehensive	Managing Your School Counseling Program	12-3
Comprehensive	Megaskills	10-4
Comprehensive	Olympic Spirit: Building Resiliency	12-3
Comprehensive	Parent Connection	10-4
Comprehensive	Parent Information and Resource Centers	10-4
Comprehensive	Parenting Insights for Parents of 7–14 Year Olds	10-4
Comprehensive	Parenting Series	10-4
Comprehensive	Parents and Children Together (PACT)	10-4
Comprehensive	Parents and Teachers Take Action	10-4
Comprehensive	Parents Make the Difference: Practical Ideas	10-4
Comprehensive	Partners in Play	12-3
Comprehensive	PIC: Practical Ideas for Counselors	12-3
Comprehensive	Play Therapy	12-3
Comprehensive	Prepare Curriculum: Teaching Prosocial	12-3
Comprehensive	Raising Children in Troubled Times	10-4
Comprehensive	S.A.I.L.: Self-Awareness in Language Arts	12-3
Comprehensive	School Counselors and Censorship	12-3
Comprehensive	School Counselor's Letter Book	12-3
Comprehensive	Solution-Focused Counseling in High School	12-3
Comprehensive	STEP Program	10-4
Comprehensive	Student Aggression: Prevention, Management	12-3
Comprehensive	Substance Abuse Prevention: A Dramatic	12-3
Comprehensive	Successful Parenting—Part Three	10-9
Comprehensive	Survival Guide for Elementary & Middle	12-3
Comprehensive	Survival Guide for the Secondary School Counselor	12-3
Comprehensive	Tales and Tails, Vols. 1, 2, 3	12-3
Comprehensive	Total Quality Counseling	12-3
Conflict Resolution	Alternatives to Violence	8-3
Conflict Resolution	Anger Management and Violence Prevention	12-17
Conflict Resolution	Be Cool: Coping With Bullying	7-3

TOPIC	TITLE	LIST
Conflict Resolution	Between You and Me	7-2
Conflict Resolution	Break it Up: Teacher's Guide	11-4
Conflict Resolution	Bully-Proofing Your School	12-4
Conflict Resolution	Childhood Bullying and Teasing	12-4
Conflict Resolution	Choices, Choices: On the Playground	6-5
Conflict Resolution	Class Meetings	11-13
Conflict Resolution	Conflict Managers	7-3
Conflict Resolution	Conflict Mediation New Generation	12-4
Conflict Resolution	Conflict Resolution Complete Kit	12-4
Conflict Resolution	Conflict Resolution Curriculum	7-3
Conflict Resolution	Conflict Resolution: Elementary Curriculum	12-4
Conflict Resolution	Conflict Resolution: Secondary Curriculum	9-4
Conflict Resolution	Conflict Resolution: Staff Development	11-4
Conflict Resolution	Creative Conflict Resolution: 200 Activities	7-3
Conflict Resolution	Creative Conflict Solving for Kids Grades 4–9	8-3
Conflict Resolution	Creative Conflict Solving for Kids	7-3
Conflict Resolution	Disruptive Child	11-4
Conflict Resolution	Don't Pick On Me!	8-3
Conflict Resolution	Fighting Fair for Families	10-5
Conflict Resolution	Fighting Fair: Grades 4–9	8-3
Conflict Resolution	Gang Intervention Handbook	12-4
Conflict Resolution	Getting Along Program	7-3
Conflict Resolution	Getting Along: Conflict Resolution	8-3
Conflict Resolution	Getting Better at Getting Along	7-3
Conflict Resolution	Helping Kids Handle Conflict	6-3
Conflict Resolution	How I Learned Not to Be Bullied	6-3
Conflict Resolution	It's Not Fair	6-3
Conflict Resolution	Kelso's Choice	12-4
Conflict Resolution	Me and My Parents: Working It Out	8-9
Conflict Resolution	Mediation for Kids: Disputant Settlement	7-3
Conflict Resolution	My Name Is Not Dummy	6-3
Conflict Resolution	Next Door Neighbors	12-27
Conflict Resolution	No More Teasing	6-3
Conflict Resolution	Peace in the Classroom	11-4
Conflict Resolution	Peacemaking Skills for Little Kids	6-14
Conflict Resolution	Playground Push-Around	6-3
Conflict Resolution	Positive Discipline in the Classroom	11-13
Conflict Resolution	Preventing Gang Activity	12-4
Conflict Resolution	Preventing Violence and Intervening Safely	11-4
Conflict Resolution	Push & Shove	6-3
Conflict Resolution	Ready-to-Use Conflict Resolution Activities	12-4
Conflict Resolution	Reducing School Violence	12-4
Conflict Resolution	Resources Dealing With Bullying	12-4
Conflict Resolution	Second Step: Grades 1-3	6-14
Conflict Resolution	Second Step: Grades 4-5	7-14
Conflict Resolution	Second Step: Grades 6-8	8-14
Conflict Resolution	Second Step: Grades PreK-K	6-14
Conflict Resolution	Silence the Violence: Skills	8-3

TOPIC	TITLE	LIST
Conflict Resolution	Student Workshop: Conflict Resolution	8-3
Conflict Resolution	Student Workshop: Solving Conflicts	6-3
Conflict Resolution	"Teacher, They Called Me a _____!"	11-4
Conflict Resolution	Teaching Conflict Resolution	6-3
Conflict Resolution	Teaching Students to be Peacemakers	12-4
Conflict Resolution	Teaching Students to Get Along	11-4
Conflict Resolution	Ten Things to Do Instead of Hitting	6-3
Conflict Resolution	Tough Kid Book	11-4
Conflict Resolution	Valuing Diversity and Similarity	12-23
Conflict Resolution	We Can Work It Out!	6-3
Conflict Resolution	When Anger Turns to Rage	8-8
Conflict Resolution	Working It Out: Conflict Resolution	8-3
Conflict Resolution	Working It Out: Solving Conflicts	8-3
Crises	Childrens Literature on Floods	12-6
Crises	Death in the School Community	12-6
Crises	Disruptive Child	11-4
Crises	Compassionate School: Practical Guide	12-3
Crises	School Crisis Survival Guide	12-6
Death and Grief	About Dying	10-6
Death and Grief	Bereavement Support Group	12-7
Death and Grief	Beyond Innocence of Childhood	11-5
Death and Grief	Buford Listens	6-4
Death and Grief	Compassionate School: Practical Guide	12-3
Death and Grief	Death and Loss: Compassionate	11-5
Death and Grief	Death and the Classroom	11-5
Death and Grief	Death in the School Community	12-6
Death and Grief	Drawing Out Feelings: Facilitator Guide	12-7
Death and Grief	Everett Anderson's Goodbye	6-4
Death and Grief	Fall of Freddie the Leaf	6-4
Death and Grief	Good-Bye Forever	6-4
Death and Grief	Grieving Child	10-6
Death and Grief	Helping Children Cope	7-4
Death and Grief	How Do We Tell the Children?	10-6
Death and Grief	I Wish I Could Hold Your Hand	7-4
Death and Grief	Mourning Handbook	12-7
Death and Grief	Sacred Art of Dying	12-7
Death and Grief	Sad Hug, Mad Hug, Happy Hug	6-4
Death and Grief	Saying Good-Bye (Book)	6-4
Death and Grief	Saying Good-Bye (Video)	6-4
Death and Grief	School Crisis Survival Guide	12-6
Death and Grief	Someone Special Died	6-4
Decision Making	Change My Attitude? Yes!	8-5
Decision Making	Choices, Choices: On the Playground	6-5
Decision Making	Couch Potato Kids	10-7
Decision Making	Deciding: From Dilemmas to Decisions	6-5
Decision Making	Finders, Keepers	7-5
Decision Making	Free the Horses	6-5
Decision Making	Guiding the Gifted Child	10-7

TOPIC	TITLE	LIST
Decision Making	Hurried Child	10-7
Decision Making	I Blew It! Learning From Failure	8-5
Decision Making	I Can Make Good Choices	6-5
Decision Making	Laugh, Learn, and Live	12-8
Decision Making	My Friend Sneezy	6-5
Decision Making	Perfectionism: What's Bad About Being	10-7
Decision Making	Responsible Rascal	6-5
Decision Making	Taking Chances: Teens and Risk	8-5
Decision Making	Taking Part: Introducing Social Skills	6-19
Decision Making	Tonia the Tree	6-5
Decision Making	Too Smart for Trouble	6-5
Decision Making	You Can Choose: Decision Making	7-5
Decision Making	You Can Choose: Saying No	6-5
Decision Making	You Can Say No: Here's How	8-5
Directory	Guiding the LD Student	9-2
Directory	Heath Resource Directory	9-2
Directory	Help for Children	12-9
Directory	Hunter's Guide to the College Guides	9-2
Directory	Network of Educational Opportunities	12-9
Directory	Paperbacks, School Counselor Edition	12-9
Disabilities	ADD & the College Student	9-2
Disabilities	After the Tears	10-8
Disabilities	Alex Is My Friend	6-6
Disabilities	Attention Deficit Disorders Intervention	12-10
Disabilities	Attention Deficit Hyperactivity Disorder	10-8
Disabilities	Attention? ADD in School	12-10
Disabilities	Autism & Asperger Syndrome	12-10
Disabilities	Boy Who Couldn't Stop Washing	7-6
Disabilities	Children and the AIDS Virus	10-8
Disabilities	Children With Tourette's Syndrome	10-8
Disabilities	Chris Has an Ostomy	12-10
Disabilities	Communicate Junior	6-19
Disabilities	Communication	6-2
Disabilities	Complete Drug Reference	12-38
Disabilities	Could Do Better: Why Children Underachieve	11-6
Disabilities	Does AIDS Hurt? Educating Young Children	11-15
Disabilities	Facts for Families (Problem Series)	10-8
Disabilities	Friends for Life	7-6
Disabilities	Friends Who Care	7-6
Disabilities	Guidance for Students With Disabilities	12-10
Disabilities	Guiding the LD Student	9-2
Disabilities	Hal's Pals Dolls	12-10
Disabilities	Hi, I'm Adam	7-6
Disabilities	How to Reach & Teach ADD/ADHD	11-6
Disabilities	Jumpin' Johnny Get Back to Work!	7-6
Disabilities	K & W Guide to Colleges for the LD Student	9-2
Disabilities	Kids on the Block Books and Puppets	12-27
Disabilities	Last One Picked . . . First One Picked On	11-6

TOPIC	TITLE	LIST
Emotions	Human Race Club	12-12
Emotions	I Get So Mad!	6-8
Emotions	Kids on the Block Books and Puppets	12-27
Emotions	Mad, Sad, Glad Game	6-8
Emotions	Moms Don't Get Sick	7-8
Emotions	My Two Homes	7-7
Emotions	Next Door Neighbors	12-27
Emotions	Not So Scary Things	10-11
Emotions	PALS: Playing & Learning	6-8
Emotions	Play Therapy	12-3
Emotions	Stop, Relax, and Think	7-8
Emotions	Uncle Jerry Has AIDS	10-8
Emotions	When Anger Turns to Rage	8-8
Emotions	When Someone Has a Very Serious Illness	6-8
Emotions	When You're Mad, Mad, Mad	8-8
Emotions	Who Me? Mad? Nah	7-8
Emotions	Windows to Our Children	12-12
Ethics	ACA Code of Ethics	12-13
Ethics	ACES Standards for Counseling Supervisors	12-13
Ethics	ASCA Membership Services	12-13
Ethics	ASGW Ethical Guidelines	12-13
Family	All Together: Blended Family	6-9
Family	Alone Together: Single Parent	10-12
Family	Class Meetings—Family Meetings	10-3
Family	Counseling and Human Development	12-3
Family	Every Kids Guide to Understanding Parents	12-14
Family	Family Violence	12-28
Family	Human Development and Family Life	10-12
Family	Kid's Guide to Getting Along With Family	7-9
Family	Me and My Parents: Working It Out	8-9
Family	Me and My Stepfamily	10-12
Family	My Dad's Definitely Not a Drunk	7-21
Family	My Two Homes	7-7
Family	Siblings Without Rivalry	10-12
Family	Strengthening Stepfamilies	10-12
Family	We're a Family	6-9
Friendships	Alex Is My Friend	6-6
Friendships	Being A Friend: What Does It Mean?	8-10
Friendships	Being Friends: You Can Choose!	7-13
Friendships	Best Friends	6-10
Friendships	Drugs, Your Friends & You	8-21
Friendships	Feeling Good About Friends	7-10
Friendships	How Can I Fit In?	7-10
Friendships	Kid's Guide to Getting Along With Classmates	6-10
Friendships	My Friends and Me	6-10
Friendships	When To Say Yes! and Make More Friends	8-10
Gender Equity	AAUW Report: How Schools Shortchange Girls	11-8
Gender Equity	Counselor & Bias-Free Career Planning	12-1

TOPIC	TITLE	LIST
Gender Equity	Gender Bias: In the Classroom	11-8
Gender Equity	Growing Smart: What's Working for Girls	11-8
Gender Equity	Horizons 2000: Career & Life Planning	12-16
Gender Equity	How Schools Shortchange Girls	12-16
Gender Equity	Meeting Guidance Needs of Boys	12-16
Gender Equity	Pathfinders: Women In the Workforce	8-1
Gender Equity	Sexual Harassment and Teens	12-28
Gender Equity	Shortchanging Girls, Shortchanging America	11-8
Gender Equity	Student's Guide to Bias-Free Career Planning	9-1
Gender Equity	Teacher's Guide to Student Bias-Free Career	11-8
Gender Equity	When I Grow Up (Professional Women)	7-1
Gender Equity	Women in Aerospace	9-1
Gender Equity	Women in Math & Science: Four Programs	11-8
Group Counseling	Anger Management and Violence Prevention	12-17
Group Counseling	Complete Group Counseling	12-17
Group Counseling	Counselor and the Group	12-17
Group Counseling	Effective Group Counseling	12-17
Group Counseling	Elements of Group Counseling	12-17
Group Counseling	Energizers & Icebreakers	12-17
Group Counseling	Group Counseling for School Counselors	12-17
Group Counseling	Group Counseling for Secondary Schools	12-17
Group Counseling	Group Counseling Strategies	12-17
Group Counseling	Groups: Process and Practice	12-17
Group Counseling	Peers Helping Peers	8-11
Group Counseling	Skills for Living	12-17
Group Counseling	Successful Small Groups	12-17
Group Counseling	Teaching Helping Skills to Middle School Students	8-11
Group Counseling	Treating the Unmanageable Adolescent	12-34
Individual Counseling	Bibliocounseling: Adolescent Literature	12-19
Individual Counseling	Suggested Books for Children	12-19
Individual Counseling	Themes . . . Under One Umbrella	12-19
Individual Counseling	Trust Building With Children Who Hurt	12-19
Learning Styles	Cooperative Discipline	11-7
Learning Styles	Emotional Intelligence	12-20
Learning Styles	E. Q. in School Counseling	12-20
Learning Styles	It's OK to Learn Differently	7-20
Learning Styles	Learning Styles	11-9
Learning Styles	Learning Styles Counseling	12-20
Learning Styles	Multiple Intelligences in the Classroom	11-9
Learning Styles	Research on Educational Innovations	11-9
Multicultural	100 Best Colleges for African-American	9-2
Multicultural	Black Is My Color	7-12
Multicultural	Black Student's Guide to Colleges	9-2
Multicultural	Children of Color: Psychological Interventions	12-23
Multicultural	Counseling the Culturally Different	12-23
Multicultural	Counseling for Racial Understanding	12-23
Multicultural	Counselor & Bias-Free Career Planning	12-1
Multicultural	DIFFERENT and Wonderful: Raising	10-15

TOPIC	TITLE	LIST
Multicultural	Earth Keepers Series	7-12
Multicultural	Empowering African-American Males	12-23
Multicultural	Everett Anderson's Goodbye	6-4
Multicultural	Fighting Fair: Grades 4-9	8-3
Multicultural	Holiday Facts and Fun	11-10
Multicultural	Horizons 2000: Career & Life Planning	12-16
Multicultural	Images	8-12
Multicultural	Kids on the Block Books and Puppets	12-27
Multicultural	Land of Many Colors	6-12
Multicultural	Many Voices I, II, and III	12-23
Multicultural	Multicultural Counseling Competencies	12-23
Multicultural	Multicultural Counseling in Schools	12-23
Multicultural	Multicultural Discovery Activities	12-23
Multicultural	Multicultural Issues	12-23
Multicultural	Multicultural Student's Guide to Colleges	9-2
Multicultural	Next Door Neighbors	12-27
Multicultural	Open Minds to Equality	8-12
Multicultural	Parents and Schools	10-15
Multicultural	Pioneers in Health & Medicine	7-12
Multicultural	Sacred Art of Dying	12-7
Multicultural	Saving the Native Son	12-23
Multicultural	Student's Guide to Bias-Free Career Planning	9-1
Multicultural	Takeoff: African American Role Models 1-6	8-12
Multicultural	Takeoff: Hispanic Experience	8-12
Multicultural	"Teacher, They Called Me a ___!"	11-4
Multicultural	Transcultural Counseling	12-23
Multicultural	Valuing Diversity and Similarity	12-23
Peer Facilitation	Children Helping Children	12-25
Peer Facilitation	Equip Program: Teaching Youth	12-25
Peer Facilitation	From Peer Pressure to Peer Support	12-38
Peer Facilitation	In Depth Look at Peer Helping	12-25
Peer Facilitation	Peer Power: Becoming an Effective Peer Helper	12-25
Peer Facilitation	Peers Helping Peers	8-11
Peer Facilitation	Peervention: Training Peer Facilitators	9-14
Peer Facilitation	Positive Peer Groups	12-25
Peer Facilitation	Teaching Helping Skills in Middle School	8-11
Peer Facilitation	Using Peer Mediation to Resolve Conflicts	12-25
Problem Solving	Active Teaching: Enhancing Discipline	11-7
Problem Solving	At-Risk Youth: Identification, Programs	12-34
Problem Solving	Being Friends: You Can Choose!	7-13
Problem Solving	Between You and Me	7-2
Problem Solving	Bibliocounseling: Adolescent Literature	12-19
Problem Solving	Brochures for Problem Solving	9-15
Problem Solving	Child's First Book About Play Therapy	10-11
Problem Solving	Choices, Choices: On the Playground	6-5
Problem Solving	Class Meetings	11-13
Problem Solving	Do I Have to Go to School Today?	6-13
Problem Solving	Facts for Families (Treatment Series)	10-17

TOPIC	TITLE	LIST
Respect	Growing Smart: What's Working for Girls	11-8
Respect	Hostile Hallways: AAUW Survey	11-15
Respect	In Real Life: Sexual Harassment	9-18
Respect	Is It Love . . . Or Is It Gross?	8-16
Respect	Kelso's Choice	12-4
Respect	Kids on the Block Books and Puppets	12-27
Respect	Kindness Is Contagious	12-3
Respect	Land of Many Colors	6-12
Respect	Last One Picked . . . First One Picked On	11-6
Respect	Many Voices I, II, and III	12-23
Respect	My Friends and Me	6-10
Respect	Next Door Neighbors	12-27
Respect	No Fair!	6-14
Respect	No More Teasing	6-3
Respect	Not Better—Not Worse	6-14
Respect	Open Minds to Equality	8-12
Respect	Peacemaking Skills for Little Kids	6-14
Respect	Positive Discipline in the Classroom	11-13
Respect	Preventing Violence and Intervening Safely	11-4
Respect	Push & Shove	6-3
Respect	Ready-to-Use Social Skills	8-19
Respect	Respect Yourself and Others, Too	6-14
Respect	Second Step: Grades 1–3	6-14
Respect	Second Step: Grades 4–5	7-14
Respect	Second Step: Grades 6–8	8-14
Respect	Second Step: Grades PreK–K	6-14
Respect	Sexual Harassment	8-16
Respect	Sexual Harassment and Teens	12-28
Respect	Sexual Harassment: Crossing the Line	8-16
Respect	Sexual Harassment: It's Hurting People	8-16
Respect	Sexual Harassment: Minimize the Risk	8-16
Respect	Sexual Harassment: Pay Attention	8-16
Respect	Shortchanging Girls, Shortchanging America	11-8
Respect	Silence the Violence: Skills	8-3
Respect	Skillstreaming in Early Childhood	6-19
Respect	Stick Up for Yourself	7-18
Respect	Student Aggression: Prevention Management	12-3
Respect	Taking Part: Introducing Social Skills	6-19
Respect	Tator Tales	6-14
Respect	"Teacher, They Called Me a ____!"	11-4
Respect	Teaching Students To Get Along	11-4
Respect	Teaching Tolerance	11-13
Respect	Time for Horatio	6-14
Respect	Tough Kid Book	11-4
Respect	What Is Sexual Harassment?	8-16
Respect	What's Respect?	6-14
Respect	Working It Out: Conflict Resolution	8-3
Respect	Working It Out: Solving Conflicts	8-3

TOPIC	TITLE	LIST
Respect	Working Together	7-14
Respect	When Anger Turns to Rage	8-8
Responsibility	How Can We Help Children Learn to Be Responsible?	10-20
Responsibility	I Can Do It: Taking Responsibility	7-15
Responsibility	Responsible Kids In School and At Home	11-14
Responsibility	Teach Responsibility? Yes!	11-14
Responsibility	Trust Me! Learning to Be Responsible	8-15
Safety	Alone at Home: Kid's Guide	7-16
Safety	Alternatives to Violence	8-3
Safety	Associations Help When Suspected Abuse	12-28
Safety	Books About Safety	8-16
Safety	Books About Safety From Abuse	7-16
Safety	Books for Safety From Rape	9-18
Safety	"Caring Connections:" Helping Young People	11-15
Safety	Child Lures	10-21
Safety	Children and the AIDS Virus	10-8
Safety	Compassionate School: Practical Guide	12-3
Safety	Confronting Sexual Harassment: Learning	12-28
Safety	Developing a School Safety Plan	12-28
Safety	Does AIDS Hurt? Educating Young Children	11-15
Safety	Facts for Families (Special Issue Series)	10-21
Safety	Family Violence	12-28
Safety	"Friends" Raping Friends	9-18
Safety	Get Real About Violence	7-16
Safety	Home Alone: You're In Charge	7-16
Safety	Hostile Hallways: AAUW Survey	11-15
Safety	HOTLINE (Runaways)	12-28
Safety	HOTLINES (Suicide)	12-28
Safety	HOTLINES (Suspected Abuse)	12-28
Safety	How to Talk With Your Children About AIDS	10-21
Safety	In Real Life: Sexual Harassment	9-18
Safety	Inside/Out: A Whole Person's	6-16
Safety	Is It Love . . . Or Is It Gross?	8-16
Safety	My Body Belongs to Me	6-16
Safety	National Runaway Switchboard	12-28
Safety	Positive: HIV Affirmative Counseling	12-34
Safety	Preventing Violence & Intervening Safely	11-4
Safety	Race for Safe Schools: Staff Development	11-15
Safety	Runaway Me	12-28
Safety	Sexual Harassment	8-16
Safety	Sexual Harassment and Teens	12-28
Safety	Sexual Harassment: Crossing the Line	8-16
Safety	Sexual Harassment: It's Hurting People	8-16
Safety	Sexual Harassment: Minimize the Risk	8-16
Safety	Sexual Harassment: Pay Attention	8-16
Safety	Silence the Violence: Skills	8-3
Safety	STAR Straight Talk About Guns	12-28
Safety	Strong Families, Competent Kids	10-21

TOPIC	TITLE	LIST
Safety	Suicide Prevention in the Schools	12-28
Safety	Trauma of Adolescent Suicide	12-28
Safety	Victory Over Violence	11-15
Safety	Violence Prevention Brochures	10-21
Safety	What Is Sexual Harassment?	8-16
Safety	Youth at Risk	12-34
Safety	What Young People Should Know AIDS	8-16
Self-Discipline	Classroom Behavior Game	7-17
Self-Discipline	Creative Conflict Solving Grades 4–9	8-3
Self-Discipline	Facing Up	8-14
Self-Discipline	Fighting Fair: Grades 4–9	8-3
Self-Discipline	Getting Along: Conflict Resolution	8-3
Self-Discipline	Go, Go, Goals! How to Get There	8-17
Self-Discipline	Good Behavior Game	7-17
Self-Discipline	Playing the Game	6-17
Self-Discipline	Second Step: Grades 1–3	6-14
Self-Discipline	Second Step: Grades 4–5	7-14
Self-Discipline	Second Step: Grades 6–8	8-14
Self-Discipline	Second Step: Grades PreK–K	6-14
Self-Discipline	Self-Control Patrol	7-17
Self-Discipline	Self-Controlled Classroom	7-17
Self-Discipline	Taking Part: Introducing Social Skills	6-19
Self-Discipline	Teach Responsibility? Yes	11-14
Self-Discipline	Tough Kid Tool Box	7-17
Self-Discipline	Trouble at School	8-17
Self-Discipline	When Anger Turns to Rage	8-8
Self-Discipline	Who Me? Mad? Nah	7-8
Self-Esteem	100 Ways to Enhance Self-Concept	11-17
Self-Esteem	Active Teaching: Enhancing Discipline	11-7
Self-Esteem	Belief in Self: You Can If You Think You Can	6-18
Self-Esteem	Black Is My Color	7-12
Self-Esteem	Black Male & Successful	7-12
Self-Esteem	Bound for Success: Guiding Your Child	10-23
Self-Esteem	Bright Beginnings	6-8
Self-Esteem	Buiding Self-Esteem With Koala-Roo	6-18
Self-Esteem	Building Blocks of Self-Esteem	7-18
Self-Esteem	Building Self-Esteem: A Comprehensive Program	11-17
Self-Esteem	Child's First Book About Play Therapy	10-11
Self-Esteem	DIFFERENT and Wonderful: Raising	10-15
Self-Esteem	DUSO I & II Developing Understanding I & II	6-14
Self-Esteem	Empowering African-American Males	12-23
Self-Esteem	Esteem Builders	12-30
Self-Esteem	Feeling Good About Me	6-18
Self-Esteem	Girls In the Middle	8-18
Self-Esteem	Happy to Be Me	6-18
Self-Esteem	Home Esteem Builders	10-23
Self-Esteem	I Like Being Me: Self-Esteem	8-18
Self-Esteem	Images	8-12

TOPIC	TITLE	LIST
Self-Esteem	Inviting School Success: Self-Concept	11-17
Self-Esteem	Kid Counselor Musicals and Songfest	7-18
Self-Esteem	Kid's Guide to a Positive Attitude	6-18
Self-Esteem	Kylie's Song	6-18
Self-Esteem	MIRRORS: Self-Esteem	10-23
Self-Esteem	My Friends and Me	6-10
Self-Esteem	Next Door Neighbors	12-27
Self-Esteem	No One Quite Like Me	6-18
Self-Esteem	Nobody Is PERFICK	6-18
Self-Esteem	Only One Me: Only One You	8-18
Self-Esteem	Saving the Native Son	12-23
Self-Esteem	Self-Confidence: Step-by Step	8-18
Self-Esteem	Self-Esteem Curriculum Module: Grades 2–4	6-18
Self-Esteem	Self-Esteem Curriculum Module: Grades 5–9	8-18
Self-Esteem	Self-Esteem in the Classroom: Curriculum	11-17
Self-Esteem	Staff Development: Self-Esteem	11-17
Self-Esteem	Stick Up for Yourself!	7-18
Self-Esteem	Successful Parenting, Part 1	10-23
Self-Esteem	Wonderful Me!	6-18
Self-Esteem	You Can Choose Series	6-18
Social Development	"Caring Connections:" Helping Young People	11-15
Social Development	Communicate Junior	6-19
Social Development	Equip Program: Teaching Youth	12-25
Social Development	Getting Along Program	7-3
Social Development	Getting Better at Getting Along	7-3
Social Development	Playing the Game	6-17
Social Development	Prepare Curriculum: Teaching Prosocial Skills	12-3
Social Development	Ready-to-Use Social Skills PreK–K	6-19
Social Development	Ready-to-Use Social Skills	8-19
Social Development	SchoolGirls: Young Women	8-19
Social Development	Skillstreaming in Early Childhood	6-19
Social Development	Skillstreaming the Elementary Child	12-32
Social Development	Social Skills Activities for Special Children	6-19
Social Development	Student Aggression: Prevention, Management	12-3
Social Development	Taking Part: Introducing Social Skills	6-19
Social Development	Tator Tales	6-14
Social Development	"Teacher, They Called Me a ____!"	11-4
Social Development	Unsheltered Lives	7-19
Social Development	Valuing Diversity and Similarity	12-23
Spanish	Comunicacion Entre Nosotros	10-24
Spanish	How to Talk With Your Children About AIDS	10-21
Spanish	Padres eficaces (See STEP Program)	10-4
Spanish	Parents and Schools	10-15
Special Education	DSM-IV Diagnostic and Statistical Manual	12-33
Special Education	Parents' Complete Special Education Guide	10-25
Special Education	Special Education Teacher's Book of Lists	12-33
Special Populations	At-Risk Youth: Identification, Programs	12-34
Special Populations	"Caring Connections": Helping Young People	11-15

TOPIC	TITLE	LIST
Special Populations	Collaborative Discipline for At-Risk Students	11-7
Special Populations	Florida's Challenge: Guide to Educating	11-19
Special Populations	Framework for Understanding Poverty	12-34
Special Populations	Guiding the Gifted Child	10-7
Special Populations	Positive: HIV Affirmative Counseling	12-34
Special Populations	Treating the Unmanageable Adolescent	12-34
Special Populations	Youth at Risk	12-34
Staff Development	Alternatives to Violence	8-3
Staff Development	Life Centered Career Education	8-1
Staff Development	Teaching Children Affected by Substance Abuse	11-21
Stress Management	Stressbusters	6-13
Study Skills	Bag Bingo	6-20
Study Skills	Crossroads: Mentor's Guide	8-20
Study Skills	Ellen Glasgow Mentor Program Components	8-20
Study Skills	Girls in the Middle	8-18
Study Skills	Go, Go, Goals! How to Get There	8-17
Study Skills	Guidance Units: Study Skills	7-20
Study Skills	Homework Without Tears	10-26
Study Skills	How Important Is Homework?	10-26
Study Skills	How to Help Your Child Succeed With Homework	10-26
Study Skills	How to Study	7-20
Study Skills	How to Succeed in Middle School	7-23
Study Skills	It's O.K. to Learn Differently	7-20
Study Skills	Kid's Guide to Getting Along in School	6-20
Study Skills	Kid's Guide to Getting Organized	6-20
Study Skills	Kid's Guide to Good Study Habits	7-20
Study Skills	Mentor Program for At-Risk Youth	8-20
Study Skills	Parents on Board: Building Academic Success	10-26
Study Skills	Study Skills Matinee	7-20
Study Skills	Study Skills Plus Attitude	8-20
Study Skills	Succeed in School	10-26
Study Skills	Successful Parenting, Part Four	10-26
Substance Abuse	About Addiction and Alcohol	12-38
Substance Abuse	Americans for a Drug-Free America	12-38
Substance Abuse	Another Chance: Hope and Health	12-38
Substance Abuse	Brainstorm: Outreach Project	7-21
Substance Abuse	Children Are People, Inc.	12-38
Substance Abuse	Children of Alcoholics	11-21
Substance Abuse	Children of Alcoholics: Guide	12-38
Substance Abuse	Children of Alcoholics: How School Can Help	11-21
Substance Abuse	Common Sense Strategies for Raising . . . Alcohol	10-27
Substance Abuse	Complete Drug Reference	12-38
Substance Abuse	Conducting Support Groups	12-38
Substance Abuse	Counseling the Adolescent Substance Abuser	9-24
Substance Abuse	Downfall: Sports and Drugs	8-21
Substance Abuse	Drug-Free Me	6-21
Substance Abuse	Drug-Proofing Your Children	10-27
Substance Abuse	Drugs, Your Friends and You	8-21

TOPIC	TITLE	LIST
Substance Abuse	Equip Program: Teaching Youth	12-25
Substance Abuse	Facts, Feelings, Family	12-38
Substance Abuse	Florida's Challenge: Guide	11-19
Substance Abuse	From Peer Pressure to Peer Support	12-38
Substance Abuse	Helping Your Pre-Teen Say "NO"	10-27
Substance Abuse	If You Change Your Mind	9-24
Substance Abuse	Information and Strategies	12-38
Substance Abuse	It's Elementary: Meeting Needs of High-Risk	12-38
Substance Abuse	Kids Say Don't Smoke	7-21
Substance Abuse	Learning to Live Drug Free	12-38
Substance Abuse	Let's Talk About Drugs	7-21
Substance Abuse	Making the Grade: Drug Prevention	9-24
Substance Abuse	McGruff's Elementary Drug Prevention	6-21
Substance Abuse	My Dad Loves Me, My Dad Has a Disease	7-21
Substance Abuse	My Dad's Definitely Not a Drunk	7-21
Substance Abuse	My Mom Doesn't Look Like an Alcoholic	10-27
Substance Abuse	Olympic Spirit: Building Resiliency	12-3
Substance Abuse	On Target: Road Map to Healthy	12-38
Substance Abuse	Parenting for Prevention	10-27
Substance Abuse	Power of "No"	7-21
Substance Abuse	Project Alert Training	8-21
Substance Abuse	Refusal Skills: Preventing Drug Use	12-38
Substance Abuse	Say No and Mean It	7-21
Substance Abuse	Sooper Puppy Series	6-21
Substance Abuse	STAR Midwestern Prevention Program	8-21
Substance Abuse	Stop, Think, and Go	7-21
Substance Abuse	Straight at Ya	8-21
Substance Abuse	Student Aggression: Prevention, Management	12-3
Substance Abuse	Substance Abuse in Children	12-38
Substance Abuse	Substance Abuse Prevention Activities	8-21
Substance Abuse	Substance Abuse Prevention: A Drama	12-3
Substance Abuse	Talking About Drugs & Alcohol	11-21
Substance Abuse	Tanya Talks About Chemical Dependence	8-21
Substance Abuse	Teaching Children Affected by Substance	11-21
Substance Abuse	Ten Steps to a Drug Free Future	10-27
Substance Abuse	Too Cool for Drugs	12-38
Substance Abuse	What Every Kid Should Know About Alcohol	7-21
Substance Abuse	What Kids Should Know About Parents	10-27
Substance Abuse	What's "Drunk," Mama?	10-27
Substance Abuse	Why I Won't Do Drugs	7-21
Substance Abuse	Wizard of No	7-21
Substance Abuse	Working with Children of Alcoholics	12-38
Substance Abuse	You Can Choose: Saying No	6-5
Substance Abuse	Youth and Drugs: Society's Mixed Messages	12-38
Substance Abuse	Florida's Challenge: Guide to Educating	11-19
Test-Taking Skills	ACT: American College Test	9-25
Test-Taking Skills	AP Tests: Advanced Placement Program	9-25
Test-Taking Skills	Destination College: PSAT/NMSQT	9-25

TOPIC	TITLE	LIST
Test-Taking Skills	Gruber's Complete Preparation for the New SAT	9-25
Test-Taking Skills	Inside the SAT & ACT	9-25
Test-Taking Skills	Official Guide to SAT II: Subject Tests	9-25
Test-Taking Skills	PSAT/NMSQT Preliminary Scholastic Assessment	9-25
Test-Taking Skills	SAT I Scholastic Assessment Test I	9-25
Test-Taking Skills	SAT II Subject Test Preparation on CD-ROM	9-25
Test-Taking Skills	SAT Success: Peterson's Guides	9-25
Test-Taking Skills	Score Builder for SAT	9-25
Test-Taking Skills	Test Skills: Test Preparation for the PSAT	9-25
Test-Taking Skills	Think Test Bingo	7-22
Test-Taking Skills	TOEFL: Test of English as a Foreign Language	9-25
Test-Taking Skills	Tooth and Nail: A Novel Approach	9-25
Test-Taking Skills	Try Test Bingo	6-22
Transition	Books to Help Children Cope	12-40
Transition	Career Futures	8-1
Transition	CHOICES JR., Planning My Future	8-1
Transition	College Freshman Survival Guide	9-2
Transition	First Day Blues	7-23
Transition	Helping Transfer Students	12-40
Transition	High School Career Course Planner	8-23
Transition	How to Succeed in Middle School	7-23
Transition	Maggie Doesn't Want to Move	6-23
Transition	Moving Gives Me a Stomachache	6-23
Transition	Moving on Video and Workbook	7-23
Transition	Notes from a Traveling Childhood	10-29
Transition	Ready, Set, Go! To Kindergarten	10-29
Transition	Where in the World Are You Going?	6-23

12-43 REPRODUCIBLE LIST OF INTERNET RESOURCES

Alphabetical by Topic

Note: Because of the dynamic, ever-changing nature of the Internet, addresses change and you are sometimes referred to a new location. Search engines may be used when URLs are not available.

TOPIC	SPONSOR	WWW LOCATION (URL)
ACT	ACT	http://www.act.org
ADD	Supp. Group	alt.support.attn-deficit
ADD, Disability	CHADD	http://www.chadd.org
AIDS	Galaxy	http://galaxy.einet.net/galaxy/Community/Health/Diseases/AIDS-and-HIV.html
Al-Anon/Alateen	Al-Anon	http://solar.rtd.utk.edu/~Al-Anon/
Anxiety-Panic Resource	Tapir	http://www.algy.com/anxiety/abw.html
Assessment, Program	Pathways	http://www.ncrel.org/sdrs/areas/issues/envrnmnt/go/go2acc.htm
Behavior	Behavior On-Line	http://www.behavior.net
Career	Career Net	http://www.careers.org/reg/crusa-va.htm
Career	Future Scan	http://www.futurescan.com/
Career Choices	NACE	http://www.jobweb.org/catapult/choice.htm
Career Development	E-Mail Listserv	subscribe to cardevnet-request@world.std.com
Career Development	NCDA	http://www.uncg.edu/~ericcas2/ncda
Career Education	NOICC	http://www.profiles.iastate.edu/ided/ncdc/noice.htm
Career Education	University Manitoba	http://www.umanitoba.ca/counseling/careers.html
Career Explor	B. Hodes Advertis	http://www.careermosaic.com/cm/
Career Occ. Outlook Hdbk	OOH Dept. Labor	http://www.bls.gov/ocohome.htm
Children's Books	Boulden Publishing	http://www.snowcrest.net/jboulden/index.html
Children's Issues	Newsgroup	misc.Kids
Coll. Application	College Application	http://www.CollegeApps.com
College Search	Princeton Review	http://www.review.com/college/
College & Careers	Philadelphia	http://www.philsch.k12.pa.us/Careers.html
College Application	CollegeLink	http://www.collegelink.com
College Fairs	National College Fairs	http://www.nacac.com/faird&l.html
College Info	U.S. Government	http://inet.ed.gov/pubs/Prepare/pt1.html
College Prep., SAT I & II Prep.	College Board	http://www.collegeboard.org/
College Prep., SAT I & II Prep.	Kaplan	http://www.Kaplan.com
College Search	CollegeEdge	http://www.collegeedge.com

TOPIC	SPONSOR	WWW LOCATION (URL)
College Search	M. Conlon	http://www.clas.ufl.edu/CLAS/american-universities.html
College Search Worldwide	EDUFAX	http://www.tiac.net/users/edufax/links.html
College Search, Athletes	EDUFAX	http://www.tiac.net/users/edufax/athlete.html
College, Hispanic	Hispanic Ass'n.	http://www.dcci.com:80/hacu
College, Hist. Black Coll	Hist. Black Coll	http://eric-web.tc.columbia.edu/hbcu/gowebs.html
College/Careers	Virginia VIEW	http://www.nrvcom.com/business/vaview
Comprehensive	ADOL (Adolescence)	http://education.indiana.edu/cas/adol/mental.html
Comprehensive	Counselor Connection	http://www.pris.bc.ca/joliver/index.html
Comprehensive	McCane	http://www.indep.k12.mo.us/WC/wmccane.html
Comprehensive	Peterson's	http://www.petersons.com/
Comprehensive	Psychscapes	http://www.mental-health.com/PsychScapes/
Comprehensive	Russel Sabella	http://www.louisville.edu/~rasabe01/bookmark.htm
Comprehensive, Prevention	TX Prevention Yellow Pgs.	http://www.tyc.state.tx.us/prevention/40001ref.html
Comprehensive, Psychological	Grohol	http://www.behavior.net/grohol/web.html
Counseling	ERIC CASS	http://www.uncg.edu/~ericcas2/
Counseling Ass'n.	E-Mail Listserv	subscribe TCAN to listserv@etsuadmn.etsu.edu
Counselor Ass'n.	AMCD	http://www.wpi.edu/~tbt/AMCD
Counselor Ass'n.	ASGW	http://www.uc.edu/~wilson/asgw/index.html
Counselor Ass'n.	ACA	http://www.counseling.org/
Counselor Ass'n.	ASCA	http://www.edge.net/asca
Counselor Ass'n.	NACAC	http://www.nacac.com/welcome.html
Counselor Netwk.	E-Mail Listserv	subscribe ICN (f. name) (l. name) to listserv@utkvm1.utk.edu
Counselor Supv.	E-Mail Listserv	subscribe CESNET-L (f. name, l. name) to Listserv@univcsvm.csd.scarolina.edu
Counselor Sup.	E-Mail Listserv	subscribe superint (f. Name, l. Name) @vm.temple.edu
Counselors	Mailing Lists	http://plaid.hawk.plattsburgh.edu/cnet/Listservs%20test%20page/listserv.html
Cult-Ex Members	Support Group	alt.support.ex-cult
Depression	Support Group	soc.support.depression.family
Disabilities	Family Village	http://www.familyvillage.wisc.edu/
Disability	SERI	http://www.hood.edu/seri/serihome.htm
Disability, LD	LD Association	http://www.ldanatl.org/
Eating Disorders	EDA	http://members.aol.com/edapinc/home.html
Educ. Association	ASCD	http://www.ascd.org
Educ. Association	NEA	http://www.nea.org/ra
Education	ERIC	http://ericir.syr.edu/

TOPIC	SPONSOR	WWW LOCATION (URL)
Education	U. S. Dep't. of Ed.	http://www.ed.gov/
Elemen. Counseling & Guidance	Judy Swaim	http://fly.hiwaay.net/~swaim/judys.htm
Elemen. Counseling & Guidance	Des Moines Public Schools	http://www.des-moines.k12.ia.us/Other/Counseling/SmootherSailing.html
e-mail	ERIC	ericcas2@hamlet.uncg.edu
Families	AACAP	http://www.aacap.org
Family Partners	OERI	http://www.ed.gov/pubs/ReachFam/index.html
Financial Aid	College Bd. EXPAN	http://www.collegeboard.org
Financial Aid	NASFAA	http://www.finaid.org/
Financial Aid	TX G St. Loan Ten Steps	http://www.tgslc.org:80/adventur/paying.htm
Financial Aid, FAFSA Express	U. S. Dep't. of Ed.	http://www.ed.gov/
Gangs, Guns, & Kids	NES	http://www.bluemarble.net/~nes/hot/htopicgang.html
Gifted & Talented	TAG	http://www.eskimo.com/~user/kids.html
Grief	GriefNet	http://www.rivendell.org/
Group Work Spec.	E-Mail Listserv	Subscribe groupstuff (f. name, l. name) See List 1-70
H. S. Counseling & Guidance	Davea Career Cent	http://daoes.tec.il.us/counselor.html
H. S. Counseling & Guidance	Davis H.S.	http://www.esd105.wednet.edu/DavisHS/counseling/index.html
H. S. Counseling & Guidance	Texas	http://www.tgslc.org/adventur/hscoun.htm
H.S. Counseling & Guidance	Coon Rapids H.S.	http://www.anoka.k12.mn.us.CRHS/guidance.html#group
H.S. Counseling & Guidance	Marblehead H.S.	http://www.marblehead.com/guidance/
H.S. Counseling & Guidance	Millard NE H.S.	http://www.esu3.k12.ne.us/districts/millard/south/guid/msguid.html
H.S. Counseling & Guidance	W. Springfield VA	http://www.wshs.Fairfax.k12.va.us/wshs/careerctr/index.html
Homeless Children	NCH	http://nch.ari.net/edchild.html
Journals Psych	Psychweb	http://www.gasou/edu/psychweb/resource/journals.htm
Kids Help	Kids Help Phone Line	http://kidshelp.sympatico.ca
Kids Power Lesson	Pathways	http://nisus.sfusd.k12.ca.us/schwww/sch569/L2.html
Mental Health	E-Mail Listserv	subscribe computers-in-mental-health to majordomo@netcom.com
Mental Health	Mental Health Net	http://www.cmhc.com
Minority	Grants	http://www.grad.uiuc.edu/minority/Education_Grants.html
Minority/Urban	Nat'l. Parent Info. Net	http://eric-web.tc.columbia.edu/families/
Multicultural	Black Excel	http://cnct.com/home/ijblack/BlackExcel.html
Multicultural	E-Mail Listserv	subscribe transcultural-psychologymailbase@mailbase.ac.uk
Multicultural	Inter-Links	http://www.nova.edu/Inter-Links/diversity.html
Newsgroup K-12	?	http://K12.cnidr.org:90/lists.html
Parent Consultation	NPIN	http://ericps.ed.uiuc.edu/npin/npinhome.html

490

TOPIC	SPONSOR	WWW LOCATION (URL)
Parent Help	Newsgroup	alt.parenting.solutions
Peer Resources	Peer Network	http://www.islandnet.com/~rcarr/peer.html
Psych. Counsel	E-Mail Listserv	subscribe PSYCH-COUNS to mailbase@mailbase.ac.uk
Psych. Journals	Gunther	http://www.gasou.edu/psychweb/resource/journals.htm
Psychologists Assn	APA	http://www.apa.org
Psychopharmacol	Univ. Chicago	http:uhs.bsd.uchicago.edu/~bhsiung/tips/unframed/tips.html
Safe Schools	Natl. Sch. Safety Cr	http://www.bluemarble.net/~nes/hot/htopicsafe.html
SAT I & II	Princeton Review	CDRom-http://www.review.com
SAT I & II	WebWare	http://www.testprep.com/satmenu.html
SAT, TOEFL	ETS	http://www.ets.org
Scholarship	ROTC	http://byte.stthomas.edu/www/afrotc_http/hscouns.html
School Psychology	Stein	http://mail.bcpl.lib.md.us/~sandyste/school_psych.html
Sexual Assault	Bartley	http://www.cs.utk.edu/~bartley/sainfoPage.html
Special Education	E-Mail Listserv	subscribe aus-special-ed(f. Name)(l. Name) lists@uws.edu.au
Study Skills	VA Tech	http://www.ucc.vt.edu/stdysk/stdyhlp.html
Substance Abuse	E-Mail Listserv	subscribe substancd-related-disorders to majordomo@netcom.com
Substance Abuse	VA	gopher://minerva.acc.virginia.edu:70/11/pubs/substance/facts/substance/drug
Suicide Awareness	SAVE	http://www.save.org/
Tests	Buros Institue	http://www.unl.edu/buros/home.html
Tests, Psychological	APA	http://www.apa.org/science/test.html
Va. Ed.	VAPEN	http:.//www.pen.k12.va.us/
Violence	E-Mail Listserv	subscribe caveat-1 to listproc@fhs.mcmaster.ca
Violence & Abuse	Crisis Prev. Inst.	http://www.execpc.com/~cpi/edweb.html

Section 13

POSITION STATEMENTS FOR THE COUNSELOR

(AMERICAN SCHOOL COUNSELOR ASSOCIATION [ASCA])

Position Statements are prepared for school counselors to assist them in articulating the position of the American School Counselor Association (ASCA) on a variety of issues. A position statement represents the association's official view on an issue or topic of prime interest and concern to school counseling professionals.

The statements have been developed and written by a number of people over the years. The statements all have been adopted by ASCA's Delegate Assembly. Longer background statements are available for most of the statements. Single copies may be obtained by sending a self-addressed, stamped envelope to the ASCA office: 801 North Fairfax Street, Suite 310, Alexandria, VA 22314.

13-1 THE SCHOOL COUNSELOR AND ACADEMIC/CAREER TRACKING (ADOPTED 1994)

The school counselor must work in concert with administration, curricular, and instructional leaders to ensure that all students have the opportunity to design academically challenging programs of studies which are not restricted by systematic academic/career tracking.

13-2 THE SCHOOL COUNSELOR AND AIDS (ADOPTED 1988)

The school counselor should focus on AIDS as a disease and not as a moral issue; promote prevention, health, and education; and provide a vital link to the well-being of students, staff, parents, and the community.

13-3   THE SCHOOL COUNSELOR AND ATTENTION DEFICIT DISORDER
(ADOPTED 1994)

The membership of ASCA is committed to facilitating and promoting the continuing development of each student through counseling programs within the schools. We recognize that an important aspect of development involves recognizing students who have been diagnosed with medical, psychological, behavioral, and/or social problems which are very likely to affect their performance at school, home, and in the community. Counselors need to support the rights of ADD students to receive multidisciplinary and multimodal or multifaceted treatment for the ADD symptoms and problems these children often experience.

13-4   THE SCHOOL COUNSELOR AND CENSORSHIP
(ADOPTED 1985)

School counselors have an obligation to support the basic tenets of democracy and to support the fundamental democratic rights guaranteed in the constitution's provision for free speech, free press, and equal protection.

13-5   THE SCHOOL COUNSELOR AND CHILD ABUSE/NEGLECT PREVENTION
(ADOPTED 1981; REVISED 1993)

It is the responsibility of the school counselor to report suspected cases of child abuse/neglect to the proper authorities. Recognizing that the abuse of children is not limited to the home and that corporal punishment by school authorities might well be considered child abuse, ASCA supports any legislation which specifically bans the use of corporal punishment as a disciplinary tool within the schools.

13-6   THE SCHOOL COUNSELOR AND COLLEGE ENTRANCE TEST PREPARATION PROGRAMS
(ADOPTED 1989; REVISED 1993)

It is the position of ASCA that the school counselor assist students and their families in becoming aware of the existence of such preparation programs. It is the responsibility of the students and their families to make any decisions with respect to such programs.

13-7 THE SCHOOL COUNSELOR AND COMPREHENSIVE COUNSELING (ADOPTED 1988; REVISED 1993)

*ASCA endorses, supports, and encourages the incorporation of a systematically planned, comprehensive school counseling program, grades K–12. School counseling programs provide direct services to students, staff, and community to facilitate self-understanding; interpersonal relationships; problem-solving and decision-making skills; and responsibility in educational, career, and avocational development. ASCA formally endorses, supports, and encourages the incorporation of developmental guidance in the role and function of the school counselor. The programs and the counselors are to be reviewed annually. A **counselor/student ratio of 1/100 (ideal) to 1/300 (maximum) is recommended in order to implement a comprehensive developmental school counseling program designed to meet the developmental needs of all students.***

13-8 THE SCHOOL COUNSELOR AND CONFIDENTIALITY (ADOPTED 1974; REVIEWED AND REAFFIRMED 1980; REVISED 1986)

The professional responsibility of school counselors is to fully respect the right to privacy of those with whom they enter counseling relationships. Counselors must keep abreast of and adhere to all laws, policies, and ethical standards pertaining to confidentiality. This confidentiality must not be abridged by the counselor except where there is clear and present danger to the student or other persons. It is the responsibility of the counselor to provide prior notice to the student regarding the possible necessity for consulting with others.

13-9 THE SCHOOL COUNSELOR AND CORPORAL PUNISHMENT IN THE SCHOOLS (ADOPTED 1995)

It is the position of ASCA that corporal punishment be abolished in schools and in other child care and educational institutions.

13-10 THE SCHOOL COUNSELOR AND CREDENTIALING AND LICENSURE (ADOPTED 1990; REVISED 1993)

ASCA strongly endorses and supports the school counselor standards developed by the Council for Accreditation of Counseling and Related Educational Programs (CACREP) and encourages all state education agencies to adopt those professional standards for school counselor credentialing. Further, ASCA supports the credentialing and employment of well qualified counselors who have a background in the schools. It also supports the credentialing and employment of counselors who do not have a background in the schools as long as they have a Master's degree in the helping field with training in all areas specified by the CACREP standards plus a one-year internship in a school under the supervision of a qualified school counselor and a university supervisor.

13-11 THE SCHOOL COUNSELOR AND CROSS/MULTICULTURAL COUNSELING (ADOPTED 1988; REVISED 1993)

School counselors must take action to ensure that students of culturally diverse backgrounds have access to appropriate services and opportunities which promote maximum development.

13-12 THE SCHOOL COUNSELOR AND DISCIPLINE (ADOPTED 1989; REVISED 1993)

The school counselor should urge school districts to develop policies which clearly distinguish the role of the counselor and any professional staff who administer disciplinary action. Such policies should promote the use of the school counselor as a resource person, a person perceived by all as a neutral and resourceful mediator. Such policies should describe the ability and limits of the school counselor being asked to administer any disciplinary action.

13-13 THE SCHOOL COUNSELOR AND DROPOUT PREVENTION/STUDENTS AT RISK (ADOPTED 1989; REVISED 1993)

Counselors should work with other educators to provide early intervention for potential dropouts through a comprehensive, developmental, K–12 counseling program.

13-14 THE SCHOOL COUNSELOR AND THE EDUCATION OF THE HANDICAPPED ACT (ADOPTED 1980; REVISED 1993)

The school counselor might reasonably be expected to perform certain functions in the implementation of Public Law 94-142, the Education of the Handicapped Act, while certain other functions exist that are not primarily those of the school counselor.

13-15 THE SCHOOL COUNSELOR AND EVALUATION (ADOPTED 1978; REAFFIRMED 1984; REVISED 1993)

An annual evaluation of each school counselor should take place. This evaluation must be based on specific facts and comprehensive evaluation criteria recognizing the differences between evaluating counselors and classroom personnel and conforming to local and state regulations.

13-16   THE SCHOOL COUNSELOR AND FAMILY/PARENTING EDUCATION
(ADOPTED 1989)

School counselors need to take an active role in the initiation, promotion, and leadership of providing family/parenting education in the schools.

13-17   THE SCHOOL COUNSELOR AND GENDER EQUITY
(ADOPTED 1983; REVISED 1993)

The members of ASCA are committed to facilitating and promoting the fullest possible development of each individual by reducing barriers of race, gender, ethnicity, age, or handicap and by providing equal opportunity and equal status for both genders. Members in a field committed to human development need to be sensitive to the use of inclusive language and positive modeling of gender equity. ASCA is committed to equal opportunity.

13-18   THE SCHOOL COUNSELOR AND GIFTED STUDENT PROGRAMS
(ADOPTED 1988; REVISED 1993)

School counselors must assist in providing an organized support system within the school counseling program for gifted students that meets their extensive and diverse needs.

13-19   THE SCHOOL COUNSELOR AND GROUP COUNSELING
(ADOPTED 1989; REVISED 1993)

Every school district and every institution of higher learning should include and support the group counseling concept as an integral part of a comprehensive guidance and counseling program.

13-20   THE SCHOOL COUNSELOR AND MILITARY RECRUITMENT
(ADOPTED 1984)

Representatives of all Armed Services should be accorded a reception in schools equal to the reception given the representatives of other career and educational institutions.

13-21   THE SCHOOL COUNSELOR AND THE PARAPROFESSIONAL
(ADOPTED 1974; REVIEWED AND REAFFIRMED 1980; REVISED 1993)

Paraprofessionals in the school counseling program provide for a more effective use of the counselor's time and address the issue of clerical, routine responsibilities of the guidance department.

13-22   THE SCHOOL COUNSELOR AND PEER FACILITATION
(ADOPTED 1978; REVISED 1993)

Peer facilitation programs enhance the effectiveness of the school counseling program by increasing outreach programs and the expansion of guidance services.

13-23   THE SCHOOL COUNSELOR AND THE PROMOTION
OF SAFE SCHOOLS
(ADOPTED 1994)

ASCA believes that students have the right to attend school without the fear or threat of violence, weapons, or gangs.

13-24   THE SCHOOL COUNSELOR AND SEXUAL MINORITY YOUTH
(ADOPTED 1995)

The members of the ASCA are committed to facilitating and promoting the fullest possible development of each individual by reducing the barriers of misinformation, myth, ignorance, hatred, and discrimination which prevent sexual orientation minorities from achieving individual potential, healthy esteem, and equal status. We acknowledge that we are in a field committed to human development and that we need to be sensitive to the use of inclusive language and positive modeling of sexual orientation minority equity. ASCA is committed to equal opportunity regardless of sexual orientation.

13-25   THE SCHOOL COUNSELOR AND STUDENT
ASSISTANCE PROGRAMS
(ADOPTED 1994)

School counselors play a key role in initiating and creating Student Assistance Programs in the schools.

13-26   THE SCHOOL COUNSELOR AND STUDENTS AT RISK
(ADOPTED 1990)

Professional school counselors at all levels make a significant, vital, and indispensable contribution toward the mental wellness of "at-risk" students. Further, school counselors should work as members of a team with other student service professionals including social workers, psychologists, and nurses, in liaison with teachers and parents, to provide comprehensive developmental programs for all students, including those identified as being "at-risk."

13-27   THE PROFESSIONAL SCHOOL COUNSELOR AND THE USE OF NONSCHOOL CREDENTIALED PERSONNEL IN THE COUNSELING PROGRAM
(ADOPTED 1994)

ASCA recognizes that communities across the country are seeking solutions to the highly interrelated problems that are placing youth at risk of school failure. In response to the concerns, school districts employ a diversity of staff to address the needs of students. By using differentiated personnel such as paraprofessionals, peer helpers, volunteers, clerical support staff, and other caring individuals, schools have the ability to maximize their resources. ASCA recognizes and supports cooperation and collaboration to ensure that the complex needs of students are being met in a comprehensive, holistic, and developmental manner. We further believe that it is necessary, within each school setting, to establish the appropriate practices and procedures to achieve the accountability and supervision essential in every school counseling program.

13-28   THE PROFESSIONAL SCHOOL COUNSELOR AND CHARACTER EDUCATION
(ADOPTED 1997)

ASCA endorses and supports character education in the schools. The school counselor needs to take an active role in initiating, facilitating, and promoting character-education programs in the school curriculum.

ACRONYMS AND GLOSSARY

14-1 ACRONYMS USED IN THE PROFESSION

AABT   Ass'n for Advancement of Behavior Therapy

AAC   Ass'n for Assessment in Counseling

AACAP   American Academy of Child and Adolescent Psychiatry

AADA   Ass'n for Adult Development and Aging

AAPC   American Ass'n of Pastoral Counselors

AASA   American Ass'n of School Administrators

ACA   American Counseling Ass'n

ACCA   American College Counseling Ass'n

ACEG   Ass'n for Counselors and Educators in Government

ACES   Ass'n for Counselor Education and Supervision

ACSI   Ass'n of Christian Schools International

ACT   American College Test

ADA   The Americans with Disabilities Act

ADD   Attention Deficit Disorder

ADHD   Attention Deficit Hyperactive Disorder

ADOL   Adolescent Directory On-Line

AE   Age Equivalent

AERA   American Educational Research Ass'n

AGLBIC   Ass'n of Gay, Lesbian, and Bisexual Issues in Counseling

AGS   American Guidance Service

AHEAD   Ass'n for Humanistic Education and Development

AIS   Ass'n of Independent Schools

AISE   Ass'n of Independent Special Education

ALP   Accelerated Learning Program

AMCD   Ass'n for Multicultural Counseling and Development

AMCSUS   Ass'n of Military Colleges and Schools, U.S.

AMHCA   American Mental Health Counselors Ass'n

AMS   American Montessori Society

AOD   Alcohol and Other Drug Use Prevention

AP   Advanced Placement

APA   American Psychological Ass'n

ARC   Ass'n for Retarded Citizens

ARCA   American Rehabilitation Counselors Ass'n

ARSVIC   Ass'n for Religious, Spiritual, and Value Issues in Counseling

ASCA   American School Counselor Ass'n

ASCD   Ass'n for Supervision and Curriculum Development

ASERVIC   Ass'n for Spiritual, Ethical, and Religious Value Issues in Counseling

ASGW   Ass'n for Specialists in Group Work

ASVAB   Armed Services Vocational Aptitude Battery

AUT   Autism

AVA   American Vocational Ass'n

BIE   Business Institute for Educators

CA   Chronological Age

CAC   Computer-Assisted Counseling

CACREP   Council for Accreditation of Counseling and Related Educational Programs

CAT   Children's Apperception Test (A Projective Technique)

CAT-H   Children's Apperception Test (A Projective Technique, Alternative Form)

CCMHC   Certified Clinical Mental Health Counselor

CDTI   Career-Development Training Institute

CEA   Catholic Education Ass'n

CEEB   College Entrance Examination Board

CELT   Comprehensive English Language Test (for Speakers of English as a Second Language)

CEP   Character Education Partnership

CHADD   Children and Adults with ADD

CHDF   Counseling and Human Development Foundation

CIDS   Career Information Delivery System

CIP   Classification of Instructional Programs

CLEP   College-Level Examination Program

CMC   Computer-Managed Counseling

CO   Conscientious Objector of the Military Service

CogAT   Cognitive Abilities Test

CONAP   Concurrent Admissions Program (with the Military and College Admissions)

COPA   Council on Post-Secondary Accreditation

CORD   Center for Occupational Research and Development

CoSN   Consortium for School Networking

CP   Cerebral Palsy

CPAC   Community Parent Advisory Committee

CPS   Child Protective Services

CRCC   Commission on Rehabilitation Counselor Certification

CSE   Committee on Special Education

CSED   Church Schools in the Episcopal Diocese

CSS   College Scholarships Service

CTBS   Comprehensive Test of Basic Skills

DAT   Differential Aptitude Tests

DB   Deaf and Blind

DOT   Dictionary of Occupational Titles

DRP   Degrees of Reading Power (Test)

DSM-IV   Diagnostic and Statistical Manual of Mental Disorders

ED   Emotionally Disturbed

EDI   Electronic Data Interchange

EFC   Expected Family Contribution (Financial Aid)

EH   Emotionally Handicapped

EHA   Education of the Handicapped Act

EMH   Educable Mentally Handicapped

ERIC   Educational Resources Information Center

ESCDA   Elementary School Counseling Demonstration Act

ESE   Exceptional Student Education

ESEA   Elementary and Secondary Education Act

ESL   English as a Second Language

ETS   Educational Testing Service

ExPan   Explorer Plus Guidance and Application Network

FACT   Fair Access Coalition on Testing

FAFSA   Free Application for Federal Student Aid

FAME   Females Achieving Mathematics Equity Program

FAPE   Free Appropriate Public Education

FAQ   Frequently Asked Questions

FECEP   Family and Early Childhood Education Program

FLE   Family Life Education

FOIA   Freedom of Information Act

GATB   General Aptitude Test Battery

GE   Grade Equivalent

GED   General Education Development Tests

GOE   Guide for Occupational Exploration

GPA   Grade Point Average

GT   Gifted and Talented

HI   Hearing Impaired

HIV   Human Immunodeficiency Virus

IAAOC   International Ass'n of Addictions and Offender Counselors

IAMFC   International Ass'n for Marriage and Family Counselors

IDEA   Individuals with Disabilities Education Act

IEL   Institute of Educational Leadership

IEP   Individualized Education Plan

IFSP   Individualized Family Service Plan

IHE   Institutions of Higher Education

IQ   Intelligence Quotient

ISA   Independent Schools Ass'n

ITBS   Iowa Tests of Basic Skills

K-ABC   Kaufman Assessment Battery for Children

LD   Learning Disabled

LDR   Learning Disabilities Resource

LDSC   Learning Disabilities Self-Contained

LEA   Local Education Agency

LMI   Labor Market Information

LPC   Licensed Professional Counselor

LPR   Local Percentile Rank

MA   Mental Age

MAC   Master Addictions Counselor

MAT   Metropolitan Achievement Tests

MECA   Military Educators and Counselors Ass'n

MFT   Marriage and Family Therapy

MMPI   Minnesota Multiphasic Personality Inventory

MMY   Mental Measurement Yearbook

MOD   Moderate Retardation

MR   Mild Retardation

MRT   Metropolitan Readiness Test

MSD   Multidimensional Screening Device

MSEC   Mennonite Secondary Education Council

NAADAC   National Ass'n of Alcoholism and Drug Abuse Counselors

NACAC   National Ass'n for College Admission Counseling

NACCMHC   National Academy of Certified Clinical Mental Health Counselors

NACE   National Ass'n of Colleges and Employers

NAESP   National Ass'n of Elementary School Principals

NAEYC   National Ass'n for Education of Young Children

NAIA   National Ass'n of Intercollegiate Athletics

NAME   National Ass'n for Mediation in Education

NAPE   National Ass'n of Partners in Education

NAPSO   National Alliance of Pupil Service Organizations

NASAP   North American Society of Adlerian Psychology

NASFAA   National Ass'n of Student Financial Aid Administrators

NASPA   National Ass'n of Student Personnel Administrators

NASSP   National Ass'n of Secondary School Principals

NBCC   National Board for Certified Counselors

NCAA   National Collegiate Athletic Ass'n

NCAS   National Coalition of Advocates for Students

NCATE   National Council for the Accreditation of Teacher Education

NCC   National Certified Counselor

NCCC   National Certified Career Counselor

NCDA   National Career Development Ass'n

NCE   Noncategorical-Early Childhood Program

NCE   National Counselor Exam

NCGC   National Certified Gerontological Counselor

NCRVE   National Center for Research in Vocational Education

NCSC   National Certified School Counselor

NECA   National Employment Counseling Ass'n

NMHA   National Mental Health Ass'n

NMSA   National Middle School Ass'n

NMSQT   National Merit Scholarship Qualifying Test

NOICC   National Occupational Information Coordinating Committee

NOSAPP   National Organization of Substance Abuse Programs and Partners

NPHA   National Peer Helpers Ass'n

NPIN   National Parent Information Network

NPR   National Percentile Rank

NSBA   National School Boards Ass'n

NSHDS   National Society for Hebrew Day Schools

NSSB   National Skill Standards Board

NTE   National Teacher Examinations

NYCN   National Youth Center Network

OAP   Occupational Aptitude Patterns

OCD   Obsessive-Compulsive Disorder

OERI   Office of Educational Research and Improvement

OLSAT   Otis-Lennon School Abilities Test

OOH   Occupational Outlook Handbook

OT   Occupational Therapy

OTA   Office of Technological Assessment

PAR   Psychological Assessment Resources

PD   Physical Disabilities

PDD   Pervasive Developmental Disorder

PDK   Phi Delta Kappa

PDSC   Physically Disabled Self-Contained Program

PE   Physical Education

PET   Parent Effectiveness Training

PI   Physically Impaired

PIAT   Peabody Individual Achievement Test

PIE   Policy Information Exchange (Health and Mental Health Issues)

PINS   Person in Need of Supervision

PMH   Autistic or Profoundly Mentally Handicapped

POS   Program of Studies

PPT   Pupil Personnel Team

PPVT–R   Peabody Picture Vocabulary Test–Revised

PR   Percentile Rank

PS   Partially Sighted

PSAT   Preliminary Scholastic Assessment Test

PSEN   Pupils with Special Educational Needs

PT   Physical Therapy

REG   Regulation

RIC   Rank in Class

SAC   Superintendent's Advisory Council

SACC   School-Age Child Care

SACS   Southern Ass'n of Colleges and Schools

SAD   Separation Anxiety Disorder

SAI   School Abilities Index

SAR   Student Aid Report

SAT   Scholastic Assessment Test

SAVE   Suicide Awareness/Voices of Education

SCA   Student Council Ass'n

SD   Severe Disabilities

SEA   State Education Agency

SEOG   Supplementary Educational Opportunity Grants

S/L   Speech and Language Impaired Program

SLD   Specific Learning Disabilities

SLEP   Secondary Level English Proficiency Test

SOICC   State Occupational Information Coordinating Committee

SOL   Standards of Learning

SOMCA   System of Multi-Cultural Assessment

SOQ   Standards of Quality

SR&R   Student Responsibilities and Rights

SSN   Social Security Number

STEP   Sequential Tests of Educational Progress

STEP   Systematic Training for Effective Parenting

STWOA   School-To-Work Opportunities Act

SULA   Step Up Language Arts

SUM   Step Up Mathematics

TAC   Teacher Advisory Council

TAP   Teacher Assistance Program

TAT   Thematic Apperception Test

TESA   Teacher Expectation and Student Achievement

TIEE   The Institute for Education & Employment

TIP   Tests in Print

TMH   Trainable Mentally Handicapped

TOEFL   Test of English as a Foreign Language

TOWL   Test of Written Language

TPAD   Technical Preparation Associate Degree

TS   Tourette Syndrome

TSA   Total School Approach

TSE   Test of Spoken English

TTT   Time-To-Teach

TWE   Test of Written English

VI   Visually Impaired

WAIS-R   Wechsler Adult Intelligence Scale–Revised

WISC-R   Wechsler Intelligence Scale of Children–Revised

WISC-III   Wechsler Intelligence Scale for Children–III

WPPSI-R   Wechsler Preschool and Primary Scale of Intelligence–Revised

WRAT-R   Wide Range Achievement Test–Revised

YES   Youth Engaged in Service

14-2 GLOSSARY OF TERMS

ACADEMIC COUNSELING AND GUIDANCE   Assisting students to achieve school success and develop skills to successfully engage in life-long learning.

ACTIVE LISTENING   Attentive, involved listening demonstrated by the listener's reflection, clarification, or summarization of the speaker's statements. Listener puts him- or herself in the place of the speaker and does not change the subject.

AFFECTIVE   Refers to feelings, emotions, or beliefs.

ANECDOTAL RECORD   Record of observations of behavior. Usually an objective, narrative description of the behavior.

ASSERTIVENESS   Expression of self and personal rights without violating the rights of others. Appropriately direct, open, and honest communication.

ATTENTION DEFICIT HYPERACTIVE DISORDER (ADHD)   A psychiatric classification to describe individuals who exhibit poor attention, distractibility, impulsivity, and hyperactivity. A complete physical examination and comprehensive psychological assessment are necessary for accurate diagnosis.

BULLYING   Physical, verbal, social, or emotional harassment that occurs over a period of time. Teasing and intimidation are forms of bullying. Victimization and bullying are interpersonal violence and include verbal or physical threats, physical assaults, harassment, and theft of property. Bullying is intentional and addresses an imbalance of power.

BURNOUT   A state of fatigue or frustration brought on by a devotion to a cause, a way of life, or a relationship that failed to produce the expected reward. Burnout is a problem of good intentions, when people try to reach unrealistic goals and end up depleting their energy and losing touch with themselves and others.

CAREER   A chosen pursuit, sometimes a life work. Usually there are many jobs at different levels of expertise within a career. Workers can advance and increase their knowledge, skills, and earning power within a career. Many jobs or positions exist within a career.

CAREER COUNSELING AND GUIDANCE   Assisting students to become aware of life/career choices and participate in career development activities to prepare for the world of work. A sequential process by which elementary and secondary students learn the relationship of school to work.

CAREER EDUCATION   Totality of experiences through which a student becomes knowledgeable about and makes preparation for working in a career. Helps students recognize their particular interests, abilities, aptitudes, and strengths, as well as gain information about various careers and requirements for entrance as well as success in those careers.

CAREER GUIDANCE   A program to help students acquire information about work; the education required for different careers; specifics about postsecondary education; and career opportunities including technical school, jobs, and apprenticeships.

CERTIFICATION   Minimum standards usually required by the state to be hired as a school counselor. Certification by professional associations is voluntary. Certification of counselor education programs is also voluntary.

CHANGE AGENTS   Educators who are influential in developing themselves, their colleagues, their school, their community, and their profession toward taking action to enhance opportunities for a better life for all people.

CHILD STUDY TEAM   A group of professionals from the same school who meet on a regular basis to discuss children's problems and offer suggestions or a direction for resolution.

CLARIFICATION   Usually a request for the speaker to be more specific, to explain more fully, provide examples, or to make certain that the listener understands.

COLLABORATOR   One who works on a team or is an associate or colleague. The counselor is a collaborator with other educators and members of the community as an advocate for students.

COMPREHENSIVE DEVELOPMENTAL GUIDANCE PROGRAM   A sequential program from kindergarten through grade 12, based on the developmental stages of growth of children. Developmental guidance is preventative in its focus and developmental in its content and process. Developmental guidance is for all students, and its purpose is to maximally facilitate personal development.

CONFIDENTIALITY   An ethical duty to the student and parent not to reveal to people—other than the parent—information that was disclosed during a private counselor–student interaction. The legal rights of minors to provide consent to enter counseling or release information about counseling generally resides in the custodial parent or guardian as a matter of common law and state statutes.

CONFIDENTIALITY OF RECORDS   Parents may inspect records of their child upon request and access must be granted. School district procedures should be written and available and must be followed.

CONFLICT MEDIATION   A process in which trained negotiators listen to the disputants who are involved in a conflict and present their different perspectives. The mediators enforce previously agreed-upon ground rules, actively listen to the definitions of the problem, attempt to find common desires, brainstorm solutions, and problem solve, concluding with one agreed-upon solution.

CONSULTATION   Collaboration of the school counselor with teachers and parents to plan appropriate services for a student. Consultations may focus on the needs of an individual student or groups of students. Staff development activities for teachers or parent education groups focus on specific issues and topics to help students.

COORDINATION   Organization and administration of a wide range of services and activities. The school counselor assumes primary responsibility for the coordination of the schoolwide counseling and guidance program in which teachers, student helpers, parent volunteers, and administrators conduct programs.

COUNSELING   A helping relationship, a problem-solving process, a reeducation, and a method for changing behavior. A method for helping students cope with developmental problems and a preventive process.

COUNSELING PROGRAM   Comprehensive services, tasks, and functions delivered by a professional school counselor in an elementary, middle/junior high, or high school setting. The school counseling program exists to improve the learning environment by involving students, staff, parents, community, and others who influence the learning and development of students. Through individual and group contacts over a period of time, the counselor helps students develop adequate and realistic concepts of themselves; become aware of educational, occupational, and avocational opportunities; and integrate their understanding of self and opportunities in making informed decisions.

CULTURAL GROUPS   Groups that may be identified according to historical and geographic origins as well as to racial heritage.

CULTURE   Patterns of learned perception, behavior, attitudes, and beliefs shared by a group of individuals. Culture provides individuals with a set of cultural expectations, largely unconscious, for use in a social context.

DISCIPLINE   Actions by a teacher or counselor to encourage students to apply themselves to learn, not fool around or be disruptive, preventing others from learning. The next step is to motivate students to use self-discipline and intrinsic motivation.

DIVERSITY   Individual differences of people including age, gender, language, physical ability or disability, religion, sexual orientation, social class, and additional characteristics by which someone may define themself.

DUAL RELATIONSHIP   Two roles that conflict with each other; for instance, when a counselor has duties to discipline or evaluate the same students the counselor is to counsel. Confidentiality is a problem when the counselor must function in two differing roles.

ECLECTICISM   Use of more than one theory. Technical eclecticism is selecting specific interventions based on particular theories to help students with identified problems.

ETHICAL   The principle of right or professional conduct.

ETHNIC GROUPS   People who share a unique social and cultural heritage passed on from one generation to the next. They share customs and traditions.

EVALUATION   Judgments or informed decisions about the worth of a program, procedures, or anything being judged.

EXCEPTIONAL STUDENTS   Students whose school performance shows significant discrepancy between ability and achievement, and who, as a result, require special instruction, assistance, or equipment. These are students who have special needs, including children who are gifted.

GENDER EQUITY   Students, male and female, provided with equal opportunities and treated with the same respect. There should be no obstacles in the school which inhibit students from developing their full potential. Counselors must be aware of the conscious and often unconscious ways in which gender bias limits the development of human potential; how gender stereotyping limits both women and men.

GROUP COUNSELING   Usually from three to fifteen students who meet with the counselor and focus on satisfactorily solving or working on a similar problem—personal, educational, social, or vocational. Generally oriented toward the resolution of specific and short-term issues. Has preventative and educational purposes as well as remedial goals. Members develop interpersonal skills, and the group provides support and challenge for self-exploration and development.

GUIDANCE   Information or prevention presented in groups of twelve or more students. Often presented by the counselor and teacher together with classroom groups. Topics deal with college information, developmental concerns, safety, study skills, substance abuse, communication, problem-solving, or other topics identified by the teacher or counselor. Guidance is meant to be provided to the overall school population.

GUIDANCE CURRICULUM   Learning goals and instructional procedures designed to assist all students in achieving academic, career, and personal/social development. These goals and procedures are written into the school curriculum. School counselors provide resources and materials and present some of the activities with teachers in the classroom.

INCLUSION   Exceptional students are placed in regular classes with other students.

INDIVIDUAL COUNSELING   Assistance to a student on a variety of educational and personal concerns. Concerns are explored and plans of action developed to solve the problem.

INDIVIDUAL EDUCATIONAL PLAN   A written educational program that outlines an exceptional child's current levels of performance, related services, educational goals, and modifications. This plan is developed by a team including the child's parent(s), teacher(s), and supportive staff.

LEARNING DISABLED   A permanent disorder that effects the way a student with average or better-than-average academic ability internalizes, retains, or communicates information.

LEARNING STYLES   Ways in which students get information, retain it, think about it, and solve problems. Students differ in the ways in which they learn best.

LICENSURE   See CERTIFICATION.

MAINSTREAMING   See INCLUSION.

MARKETABLE SKILL   A specific area of expertise that employers need and are willing to pay for. A job that requires a marketable skill pays more than the minimum wage.

MEDIATION   See CONFLICT MEDIATION.

MULTICULTURAL COUNSELING   Preparation and practice that integrates multicultural and culture-specific awareness, knowledge, and skills into counseling interactions.

PARAPHRASE   To restate generally, without using the precise words.

PARENTING EDUCATION   Specialized instruction on the practices of child rearing. Instruction and strategies are provided by trained group leaders who offer guidance, resources, and consultation. Family/parenting education programs positively influence the attitudes of parents and cause behavioral changes in their children.

PEER FACILITATORS Students who are selected and trained in communication and helping skills provide assistance to other students who may be reluctant to speak with a parent, teacher, or counselor about their problems. Peer facilitators provide help, resources, and referral sources to these students.

PERSONAL/SOCIAL COUNSELING AND GUIDANCE Assisting students to develop an understanding of self and others and define personal goals and a plan of action with awareness of consequences and consideration of others. This includes decision making and problem solving. The counselor respects the dignity, integrity, and self-worth of all counselees and helps them become self-respecting human beings, accepting responsibility for their own actions.

PERSPECTIVE, POINT OF VIEW A way of viewing interactions, problems, and solutions. Student facilitators are taught how to see situations from different perspectives. See ROLE PLAY.

PREVENTION The goal of prevention is the reduction or elimination of problems by providing information and solutions before such problems occur.

PRIVILEGED COMMUNICATION A legal right accorded the clients of certain specified professionals through statutory law specifying that judges may not compel disclosure of professional–client oral or written communications in a court of law. School counselors and their students in some states have full or partial privileged communication; in other states they do not.

PROFILE A standard form that some colleges require for financial aid. Some questions relate to a particular college.

REFERRAL School counselors help students and their families receive assistance from other programs and services in the school system and from agencies outside the school. Counselors work closely with teachers, administrators, the school psychologist, and school social worker when referring families for help.

RELAXATION EXERCISES Simple relaxation activities such as slower speech, counting to ten, or breathing slowly to reduce tension and stress.

ROLE PLAY A scenario in which one student (the actor) takes the perspective of another student (the observer). The actor behaves or reacts to help the observer learn how his or her behavior is perceived by others. The actor learns empathy and sensitivity for the observer by experiencing the situation from the observer's perspective. Both the actor and the observer learn about each other's feelings. Other student-observers learn and understand the problem from the viewpoint of both the actor and the observer. Also teaches a student a new behavior by practicing it; sometimes referred to as behavioral rehearsal.

SCHOOL COUNSELING Counseling that involves alert, reflective, and cognitive contemplation on the part of students. Short-term and situation-oriented. Counseling is conducted to facilitate normal growth and development when learning is interrupted by social, emotional, or academic concerns.

SELF-CONCEPT The way one sees himself or herself.

SELF-ESTEEM/SELF-CONFIDENCE A positive sense of self-worth and competence; a view of self as a responsible and successful person.

STEREOTYPES Rigid preconceptions about *all* members of a particular group: ethnic, racial, religious, sexual, or other group.

STUDENT ASSESSMENT Use of results of standardized tests, inventories, observations, interviews, or other procedures to gather information about students' abilities, behaviors, and achievements to enable appropriate decisions about educational placement and instruction.

STUDENTS AT RISK Students who are in danger of a negative future event.

SUBSTANCE ABUSE The continued use of any substance despite adverse consequences to health; family or parenting relationships; or legal, financial, social, educational, or vocational dimensions of one's life.

SUPERVISION Activities to enhance professional development. Encourages greater self-awareness and professional identity. Consists of (1) assessment of the individual's strengths and areas for improvement, (2) time to practice new skills, and (3) additional feedback or periodic statements of progress.

TECHNIQUES OR PROCEDURES Planned methods to logically achieve stated goals.

THEORY A conceptual framework or guide that integrates highly diffuse data into a meaningful whole; clarifying events and leading to predictions about related events.

VALUES Principles that are experientially determined and are esteemed, prized, or deemed worthwhile and desirable by a person or a culture. Educational values are values that are expected by all students in the school.

VIOLENCE Behavior that intentionally harms or injures a person. Includes aggressive acts toward a person or another person's property.

VIOLENCE PREVENTION The goal of reducing or eliminating violence by providing information and solutions before the violence occurs. Providing ways to settle conflicts by communicating feelings peacefully and not resorting to physical aggressive acts. See CONFLICT MEDIATION.

DISTRIBUTORS AND PUBLISHERS OF COUNSELING MATERIALS

15-1 DISTRIBUTORS AND PUBLISHERS OF COUNSELING MATERIALS

AAUW Sales Office
1-800-225-9998 Ext. 346

Accelerated Development
(317) 284-7511

ACCESS ERIC
1-800-LET-ERIC

Active Parenting
1-800-825-0060

Addison-Wesley
1-800-447-2226

Al-Anon Family Groups
(212) 302-7240

Aladdin Books (Macmillan Publishing Co.)
1-800-428-5531

Allyn & Bacon
1-800-278-3525

AMACOM (American Management Association)
1-800-225-3215

American Academy of Child & Adolescent Psychiatry (ACAP)
(202) 966-3891

American College Testing (ACT) Educational Services Division
1-800-498-6068

American Counseling Association (ACA)
1-800-422-2648

American Crisis Publishing, Inc.
(512) 266-2485

American Day Treatment Centers
(703) 691-2900
(401) 224-2382

American Guidance Services (AGS)
1-800-328-2560

American Management Association
1-800-225-3215

American Psychological Association (APA)
1-800-374-2721

American Psychiatric Association
1-800-368-5777

American School Counselor Association (ASCA)
1-800-401-2404

American Vocational Association (AVA)
1-800-826-9972

Anti-Defamation League of B'nai Brith
1-800-343-5540

Arco
(Macmillan General Reference)
1-800-428-5331

Armed Service Vocational Aptitude Battery (ASVAB)
1-800-323-0513

Association of American Colleges
(202) 387-3760

Association for Multicultural Counseling and Development (AMCD) (ACA)
1-800-422-2648

Association for Supervision and Curriculum Development (ASCD)
(703) 549-9110
1-800-933-2723

Atschul Group Corp.
1-800-323-9084

Bantam Books
1-800-223-6834

Barron's Educational Series, Inc.
1-800-645-3476

Baywood Publishing Co. Inc.
1-800-638-7819

Beckham House Publishers, Inc.
1-800-444-2524

Behavior Products
(714) 826-5711

Behavioral Products
Dayton, OH 45419

Black Moss Press (Firefly Books, Ltd.)
Ontario, Canada
1-800-387-5085

Blooming Press Co.
1-800-775-1500

Boulden Publishing
1-800-238-8433

Brooks/Cole Publishing Company
1-800-354-9706

Bureau for At-Risk Youth
1-800-99-YOUTH

Bureau of Career Development
Florida Department of Education
Tallahassee, FL 32301

The Buros Institute of Mental Measurements
The University of Nebraska Press
1-800-755-1105
(402) 472-3584

Cambridge University Press
1-800-872-7423
(212) 924-3900

CAPS Publications
University of Michigan
(313) 764-9492

Career Communications, Inc.
1-800-669-7795

Career, Education, & Training
    Associates, Inc.
Columbus, OH 43220

Career World
Weekly Reader Corp.
Delran, NJ 08370

Careerware - Computer Programs
ISM Information Systems Mgt.
1-800-267-1544

"Caring Connections"
(SFM Direct Marketing, Inc.)
Ellisville, MO 63021

Carol Publishing Group
Secaucus, NJ 07094

The Center for Applied Psychology,
    Inc.
(Childswork/Childsplay)
1-800-962-1141

Center for Applied Research in
    Education
1-800-288-4745

Center for Cognitive Therapy
(714) 964-7312

Center for Gestalt Development, Inc.
(914) 691 7192

Center for Occupational Research
    and Development (CORD)
(817) 772-8756

Center on Education and Training for
    Employment
Vocational Instructional Materials
    Laboratory
1-800-848-4815

Center on Families, Communities,
    Schools, and Children's Learning
The Johns Hopkins University
Baltimore, MD 21218

Center to Prevent Handgun Violence
(202) 289-7319

CFKR Career Materials, Inc.
1-800-525-JOBO

Channing L. Bete Co., Inc.
1-800-628-7733

Charles C. Thomas Publishers
1-800-258-8980

CHEF - Comprehensive Health
    Education Foundation
1-800-323-2433

Chesterfield Communities In Schools
(804) 560-5706

Child Obsessive Compulsive
    Information Center
1-800-789-2647
(608) 836-8070

Childswork/Childsplay
(Center for Applied Psychology, Inc.)
1-800-962-1141

Chronicle Guidance Publications,
    Inc.
1-800-622-7284

Chronicle of Higher Education
1-800-728-2803

Clarion Books (Houghton Mifflin)
1-800-225-3362

The College Board (Computer)
1-800-223-9726

The College Board Publications
1-800-323-7155
(212) 713-8000

College Bound Communications,
    Inc.
(201) 634-5743

College Counsel
1-800-248-5299

The College Counselor
(202) 333-0175

CollegeEdge
1-800-394-0404

College Entrance Examination Board
    (CEEB)
New York, NY 10019

CollegeLink
1-800-394-0404

Committee For Children
1-800-634-4449

Commonwealth of Virginia
    Department of Education
1-804-225-2928

Community Board Program, Inc.
(415) 552-1250

Community Education Services
Children's Television Workshop
New York, NY 10133-0044

Community Intervention, Inc.
1-800-328-0417

Community Mediation Center
Harrisonburg, VA
(703) 434-0059

Comprehensive Health Education
    Foundation
1-800-323-2433

Consulting Psychologists Press
1-800-462-6420

Consumer Reports Books
1-800-221-7945

Council for Exceptional Children
1-800-232-7323

Counseling Center
University of Illinois
Champaign, IL 61820

Devonshire Administrative Center
Fairfax County Public Schools
(703) 876-5225

Doulos Productions
1-800-354-9982
(704) 294-2918

Drug Planning and Outreach Staff
(202) 260-3954

Drug Strategies
Washington DC 20037

Dynamic Training and Seminars
1-800-262-4387

Educational and Industrial Testing
    Service
(619) 222-1666

Educational Media Corp.
1-800-966-3382
(612) 781-0088

Educational Testing Service (ETS)
(609) 734-5667

Elizabeth Falk, M.A., L.P.C.
(512) 855-6786

ERIC/Counseling and Personnel
    Services (ERIC/CAPS)
The University of Michigan
(313) 764-9492

Eye On Education, Inc.
(914) 833-0551

Faber/Mazlish Workshops LLC
1-800-944-8584
(914) 967-8130

Fairfax Network
Fairfax County Public Schools
1-800-233-3277

Fearon Teacher Aids
1-800-876-5507

Foreign Service Youth Foundation
Washington, DC 20016

Free Spirit Publishing, Inc.
1-800-735-7323

Garrett Park Press
(301) 946-2553

Gestalt Journal Press
1-800-247-6553

Glencoe Publishing (McGraw Hill)
1-800-334-7344

Good Year Books (Addison-Wesley)
1-800-447-2226

Grace Contrino Abrams
Peace Education Foundation, Inc.
(305) 576-5075

Greenwillow Books
(William Morrow & Co. Inc.)
1-800-843-9389

Griefwork of Cincinnati, Inc.
(513) 922-1202

Growing Up
(317) 423-2624

GSI Publications
(315) 446-4849

GTE Corp./National PTA
(312) 670-6782

Guidance Associates
1-800-431-1242

Guidance/Career Development
Services
Alexandria City Public Schools
(703) 824-6823

Guilford Publications, Inc.
1-800-365-7006

Harcourt Brace & Co.
1-800-544-6678

Harper Collins
1-800-331-3761

Harper & Row
1-800-638-3030

Harvard Common Press
1-800-462-6420

Hawthorne Educational Services, Inc.
(314) 874-1710

Health Communications, Inc.
1-800-851-9100

Heath Resource Center
1-800-544-3284

Henry Holt & Co., Inc.
(801) 972-2221

Holt, Rinehart, & Winston
1-800-225-5425
1-800-479-9799

Hope Press
(818) 303-0644

Houghton Mifflin Company
1-800-225-3362

Human Resource Development Press
1-800-822-2801

Hunter's Guide to the College Guides
Naples, FL 33941

Impact Publishers
1-800-2-IMPACT
(805) 543-5911

Impact Publications
(703) 361-7300

Innerchoice Publishing Company
(619) 698-2437

The Institute for Education &
    Employment (TIEE)
(610) 969-7100

Instructional Media Institute (IMI)
1-800-635-6231

Instructional Technology, Inc.
(313) 565-7053

Interaction Book Company
(612) 831-9500

Interpretive Scoring Systems
Minneapolis, MN 55135

Jalmar Press
1-800-662-9662

James Stanfield Publishing Co.
Santa Barbara, CA 93101

Jason Aronson
Northvale, NJ 07647

Jesana Limited
1-800-443-4728

J. G. Ferguson Publishing Co.
(312) 580-5480

JIST Works, Inc.
1-800-648- 5478
(317) 264-3720

JIST Workbooks
1-800-537-0909

J. Mart Printing
1-800-487-4060

John Wiley and Sons, Inc.
1-800-225-5945

Johnson Institute
1-800-231-5165

Jossey-Bass
(415) 433-1740

Journal of Cognitive Psychotherapy
Kent State University
Kent, OH 44242

Journal of Reality Therapy
Northeastern University
Boston, MA 02115

J. Weston Walsh, Publishers
1-800-341-6084

Karol Video
1-800-884-0555

Kids Are Worth It
1-800-729-1588

Kids on the Block
1-800-368-KIDS
(301) 290-9095

KIDSRIGHTS
1-800-892-KIDS

Laurel Oaks Hospital
1-800-225-4930
(407) 352-7000

Learning Co.
1-800-852-2255

Learning Seed
1-800-634-4941

Learning Tree Publishing, Inc.
(303) 740-7777

Lee Canter & Associates
1-800-262-4346

Lerner Publications
1-800-328-4929

Lexington Books
1-800-328-0417

Lingui Systems, Inc.
1-800-PRO-IDEA

Live Wire Video Publishers
(415) 564-9500

Living Skills Press
Sebastopol, CA 95473

Love Publishing Co.
(303) 757-2579

MAC Publishing Co.
(303) 331-1048

Macmillan Publishing Co. Inc.
1-800-428-5531

Magination Press Book
(Brunner/Mazel, Inc.)
1-800-825-3089

MAR*CO Products, Inc.
1-800-448-2197
(215) 956-0313

Marsh Media
1-800-821-3303

McDonald's Corp. and CBS
Media Tech.
Chicago, IL 60610

McGrath Systems
Santa Barbara, CA 93101

Melius and Peterson Publishing Co.
(605) 226-0488

Meridian Education Corp.
1-800-727-5507

M.G.G. Enterprises
Wayne, MI 48184

Modern Sponsored Marketing
Services
1-800-237-4599

Monarch Press
1-800-413-3300

MTI Film & Video
1-800-621-2131

Mustang Publishing
1-800-462-6420

NAL-Dutton (Penguin USA)
1-800-331-4624

National Association for Children of
Alcoholics
(301) 468-0987

National Association for College
Admission Counseling (NACAC)
(703) 836-2222

National Association. for Education
of Young Children
(202) 328-2601

National Association of Elementary
School Principals
(703) 684-3345

National Association of Secondary
School Principals
(703) 860-0200

National Cancer Institute
1-800-4-CANCER

National Career Development
Association (NCDA)
(703) 823-9800

National Center for Research in
Vocational Education (NCRVE)
University of California
1-800-637-7652

National Center for Violence
Prevention
1-800-962-6662

National Clearinghouse for Alcohol
and Drug Information
1-800-729-6686

National Council for Self-Esteem
San Jose, CA 95120

National Crime Prevention Council
(202) 466-6272

National Crisis Prevention Institute,
Inc.
1-800-558-8976

National Easter Seal Society
1-800-221-6827

National Education Association
(NEA)
(202) 822-7700

National Institute on Drug Abuse
(301) 443-6480

National Institute of Mental Health
(NIMH)
(301) 443-4513

National PTA
(312) 670-6782

Network Publications
(408) 438-4080

Newmarket Press
(212) 832-3575

Next Door Neighbors
1-800-225-5220
(410) 756-4227

National Occupational Information
Coordinating Committee (NOICC)
1-800-654-4502
(202) 653-5665

Noonday (Farrar, Straus, & Geroux,
Inc.)
1-800-788-6262

North American Society of Adlerian
Psychology
(312) 629-8801

North York Career Centre
Ontario, Canada
(416) 395-4881

Octameron Associates
(703) 836-5480

Ohio Psychology Publications
Columbus OH 43215

Ohio State University Press
1-800-437-4439

Opportunities For Learning, Inc.
1-800-243-7116

Orchard House, Inc.
1-800-423-1303

Oryx Press
1-800-279-6799

Overseas Briefing Center
U.S. Department of State
(202) 783-3238

PALS
1-800-996-3660

Paperbacks for Educators
1-800-227-2591
1-800-288-4745

The Parent Institute
1-800-756-5525

Parenting Insights
1-800-790-7889

Parenting Press, Inc.
1-800-992-6657

Parker Publishing Co.
1-800-288-4745

Paulist Press
(201) 825-7300

PBS Video
(703) 739-5380

Peace Education Foundation, Inc.
1-800-749-8838
(305) 576-5075

Peguis Publishers
Canada
1-800-667-9673

Penguin Books USA, Inc.
1-800-766-1156

Peterson's Guides
1-800-338-3282

Phi Delta Kappa
1-800-766-1156

Positive Communications, Inc. (PCI)
(914) 855-9600

Prentice Hall
1-800-288-4745

Priam Publications, Inc.
(517) 351-2557

PRIDE
1-800-241-7949

Princeton Review
1-800-566-7737
(617) 272-7027, Ext. 212

Producers Communication Services,
Inc.
(314) 968-7220

Project Alert
1-800-ALERT-10

Psychological/Assessment Resources
(PAR), Inc.
1-800-331-TEST

Psychological Corporation
(Harcourt Brace & Co.)
(210) 299-2700

Public Health Department
1-800-729-6686

Rainbow Educational Video
1-800-331-4047

Ready Reference Press
1-800-424-5627

Research for Better Teaching, Inc.
(508) 369-8191

Research Press Co., Inc.
1-800-519-2707

Rhinestone Press
(503) 672-3826

Richards & Taylor Productions
1-800-544-2219

Rick Trow Productions
New Hope, PA 18938

Rising Sun Publishing
1-800-524-2813

Rocky River Publishers
(304) 876-2711

R. R. Bowker
1-800-521-8110

Ruggs' Recommendations
(805) 462-9019

Sage Science Press (Sage Publications,
Inc.)
(805) 499-0721

Sandpiper Paperbacks (Houghton
Mifflin)
1-800-225-3362

Scholastic, Inc.
1-800-526-0275

Science and Behavior Books, Inc.
1-800-937-8000

Scott Foresman (Harper Collins)
1-800-331-3761

Sex Information and Education
Council of the U. S. (SIECUS)
(212) 673-3850

Siblings Information Network
Newsletter
University of Connecticut
(203) 344-7500

SIGI PLUS
Educational Testing Service
(609) 222-1666

Simon and Schuster
1-800-328-0417

Social Studies School Services
1-800-421-4246

Sopris West, Inc.
(303) 651-2829

South Carolina ETV
1-800-277-0829

Southeast Regional Center For
Drug-Free Schools and Communities
(502) 852-0052

Southern Poverty Law Center
Montgomery, AL 36104

St. Martin's Press, Inc.
1-800-221-7945

State Farm Insurance Companies
Public Relations Department
Bloomington, IL 61710-0001

Stop Violence Coalition of Kansas
City
Merriam, KS 66204

Sulzberger and Graham
1-800-366-7086

Sunburst Communications, Inc.
1-800-431-1934

Talent Assessment, Inc.
1-800-634-1472

The Talman Company
1-800-537-8894

Target
1-800-366-6667

Teacher Ideas Press
1-800-237-6124

Ten Speed Press
1-800-841-BOOK

Thinking Publications
(Childswork/Childsplay)
1-800-225-4769

Timberline Press, Inc.
(503) 345-1771

Times Books (Random House)
1-800-726-0600

Tom Snyder Productions
1-800-342-0236

Training Center for Alcohol and
Other Drug Prevention
Virginia Commonwealth University
(804) 367-1309

TS Media
1-800-876-6334

TV Ontario Video
1-800-331-9566

Twenty-First Century Books
1-800-421-0021
(301) 698-0210

United Learning
1-800-424-0362

United Ostomy Association, Inc.
(213) 413-5510

U. S. Department of Defense
Government Publications
University of Louisville
Louisville, KY 40292

U.S. Department of Education
National Library of Education
1-800-424-1616

U.S. Department of Health & Human
Services.
Center for Mental Health Services
(CMHS)
1-800-789-2647

U. S. Department of Labor
Office of Public Affairs
(202) 219-7316

University of Illinois
Counseling Center
Champaign, IL 61820

Vermont Department of Education
Montpelier, VT 05620-2501

VGM Career Horizons (NTC
   Publishing Group)
1-800-323-4900

Virginia Counselors Association
   (VCA)
(804) 846-2404

Virginia Extension Service
(703) 324-4386

Virginia Health Council, Inc.
(804) 379-0573

Virginia VIEW
Virginia Tech
Blacksburg, VA 24061

Vocational Biographies
1-800-255-0752

Wadsworth Publishing Co.
1-800-354-9706

Walker & Co.
1-800-289-2553

Wellington House Printers
1-800-257-8481

Western Public Radio
1-800-5-LISTEN

Whitman
1-800-255-7675

Wintergreen Orchard House
1-800-321-9479
(504) 866-8658

Woodbine House
1-800-843-7323

Wooden Publishing House
(802) 985-8458

Woodland Press
(612) 926-2665

WORKLINK Program
Educational Testing Service
(202) 659-0616

Workman Publishing Company
1-800-722-7202

World Future Society
(301) 656-8274

Index

519

NOTES

NOTES

NOTES

NOTES

NOTES

NOTES

NOTES

NOTES

NOTES

NOTES

NOTES

NOTES

Notes